“2011 计划”司法文明协同创新中心资助

"十二五"国家重点图书出版规划

法学译丛·证据科学译丛 / 丛书主编 张保生 王进喜

艾伦教授论证据法（上）

Professor Allen on Evidence (Volume I)

[美] 罗纳德·J·艾伦 (Ronald J. Allen) 著

张保生 王进喜 汪诸豪 等 译

中国人民大学出版社

·北京·

序言：艾伦教授阐释的证据理念

张保生

自2002年1月在美国西北大学法学院他那间面朝蓝色密歇根湖的办公室第一次见到艾伦教授，一晃已过去12年。这期间，艾伦教授拖着条打了钢钉的病腿19次来中国讲学或出席学术会议，像一位虔诚的布道者，执著地传播着他的证据理念。他获得2014年中国政府“友谊奖”，是当之无愧的。

艾伦教授1992年至今一直是西北大学法学院威格莫尔教席（John Henry Wigmore Professor of Law）唯一的特座教授。威格莫尔教授是西北大学法学院第一任院长、世界级著名证据法学家，以他命名的教席是一把镶着金边的扶手椅，摆在艾伦教授办公室里，象征着一种学术荣誉。

艾伦教授2004年第一次到中国参加学术会议，2006年受聘为中国政法大学兼职教授、证据科学研究院外国专家咨询委员会主席、诉讼法学研究院客座研究员，2007年入选教育部“长江学者讲座教授”，2011年任我们共同创建的国际证据科学协会主席。他和我已联合培养了6名中国法学博士、1名博士后。他已3次来中国政法大学讲授“美国证据法”36学时本科生课程。2012年，他被聘为最高人民法院常务副院长沈德咏大法官为首席专家的国家社科基金重大项目“诉讼证据规定研究”唯一的外国顾问。

本书收录的艾伦教授15篇文章，绝大部分是他在中国政法大学的讲座稿或参会论文，并以中、英文在《证据科学》杂志首发过，不仅有很高的学术价值，而且对中国读者很有针对性。按原计划，我们本想以中、英文对照方式出版此书，以将其作为专业英语教材，但突如其来的获奖消息以及颁奖仪式日期的临近打乱了原来那个排版费时的计划。现在这部书提前与读者见面，也是对艾伦教授获奖的一份祝贺。

在上述15篇文章中，艾伦教授所阐释的证据理念主要包括：

一、证据法是法治的基石

这个观点最初是艾伦教授2005年在《刑事诉讼的法理和政治基础》的演讲中阐述的。他说：“在一定意义上，证据法在任何诉讼制度中都是最重要、最基础的方面；确切地说，它是法治的基石。”（In one sense，the law of evidence is the most important, and most fundamental, aspect of any system of litigation; indeed, it is the bedrock of the rule of law.）“这个理念乍一看似乎令人不解。实际上，证据法对于任何一个创设了权利或义务的制度都是基础性的。权利和义务取决于准确的事实认定；如果没有准确的裁判，权利和义务根本就没有意义。”这个理念表明了证据法在法律体系中的重要地位，也就是说，证据制度是法治国家的基本法律制度。换句话说，证据制度不健全，法治的基础就不牢固。

证据法是法治基石的理念，可以追溯到边沁“证据是正义之基”（Evidence is the basis of justice）的思想。[①] 李学灯先生也阐述过大致相同的思想：“惟在法治社会之定分止争，首以证据为正义之基础，既需寻求事实，又需顾及法律上其他政策。认定事实，每为适用法律之前提。因而产生各种证据法则，遂为认事用法之所本。”[②]

在收入本书的另一篇文章《证据法的理论基础和意义》中，艾伦教授从争端解决过程中事实与权利和义务的实际关系角度，进一步展开了论证。他说：“权利和义务固然都很重要，但启蒙运动更根本的理念是认识论上的革命，即认为有一个客观上可知的外在于我们思想的世界；然而，对洛克、贝克莱、休谟乃至康德认识论著作中关于这种主张的引用，却非常之少且相去甚远。这就颠倒了事实与权利/义务之间的实际关系。事实先于权利和义务而存在，并且是权利和义务之决定性因素。没有准确的事实认定，权利和义务就会失去意义。”他举例说：如果一位同学正在用电脑做课堂笔记，但我却要求你归还“我的”电脑，我坚持说你所用的电脑事实上是属于我的。你会怎么做？你会找一个裁判者，向他提供你购买、得到或被赠与这部争议电脑的证据。如果成功，那位裁判者将赋予你那些权利，并强迫我履行相应义务。这里的关键在于，那些权利和义务取决于什么事实将被认定。把法治与真实世界的情况联系起来的努力，锚定了可知事物中的权利和义务，并使其摆脱了反复无常和任性的支配。这就把法律制度系在事实准确性的基石上了。

我们可以看出艾伦教授的论证思路：（1）事实先于权利和义务而存在，并且是权利和义务之决定性因素。（2）权利和义务取决于准确的事实认定，否则，它们便没有意义。（3）证据法规制事实认定，因而是法治的基石。

① ［英］边沁：《司法证据原理》（Bentham, *Rationale of Judicial Evidence*, 1827），第三编第一章。转引自［美］特伦斯·安德森、［美］戴维·舒姆、［英］威廉·特文宁：《证据分析》（第2版），张保生、朱婷、张月波等译，中国人民大学出版社2012年版，第1页。

② 李学灯：《证据法比较研究》，五南图书出版公司1992年版，序部分。

上述观点在本书收入的几乎每一篇文章中都反复提到过。艾伦在《证据与推论/概率与似真性》中还指出："正义比事实更重要"的观点是不正确的，因为正义也要依赖于事实，包括宪法权利和人权。显然，只有准确认定事实，才能使权利、义务和正义得到实现，有效地解决争端。因此，准确认定事实是各国证据法的共同价值追求。如何才能准确认定事实？这是相关性规则肩负的使命。

二、相关性是证据的根本属性

相关性是证据与待证事实之间的一种逻辑联系。相关性规则旨在促进准确的事实认定。艾伦教授在《相关性和可采性》一文中强调："……证据法中的第一个实质性领域，这就是相关性。相关性是起点。"该文从两个方面阐述了相关性。

首先，他区分了相关性和实质性的概念。他认为，相关性定义包含了证据与事实主张、事实主张与审判之间的两种关系。《美国联邦证据规则》规则401对相关性的定义是："'相关证据'是指使任何事实的存在具有任何趋向性的证据，即对于诉讼裁判的结果来说，若有此证据将比缺乏此证据时更有可能或更无可能。"该定义涉及两个问题：第一，一个证据如果有助于证明或反驳某个事实主张，它就是相关的。也就是说，相关性指的是证据与事实主张之间的关系。第二，该事实主张如果与诉讼有实际关系，它就具有"实质性"(materiality)。也就是说，实质性指的是事实主张与审判之间的关系。他举例说，假设某人被控违反了反托拉斯法，并假定政府要求他母亲就他有棕色头发作证。这位母亲的证据与他有棕色头发的主张是相关的（相关性是证据与主张之间的关系），但这一关于他有棕色头发的主张与该审判并没有关系（实质性是主张与审判之间的关系）。因此，在判断某证据是否具有相关性时，法官必须考虑两个问题③：其一，提出某个证据，与证明案件中的某个"要素性事实"是否相关？这个问题又称为"实质性"问题，是指运用证据将要证明的问题属于依法需要证明的要素性事实。其二，提出的证据，对该实质性问题是否具有证明作用，即提出该证据是否有助于确立实质性问题。相关证据必须使一个要素性事实更有可能或更不可能，换言之，一个证据必须使一个要素性事实"更可能或更不可能"，它才是相关的。

③ ［美］罗纳德·J·艾伦等：《证据法：文本、问题和案例》，张保生、王进喜、赵滢译，满运龙校，高等教育出版社2006年版，第149～158页。

其次，他解释了“任何趋向性”之最小相关性检验标准，并强调《美国联邦证据规则》规则 401 是一个鼓励采纳证据的规则。按照这个最低检验标准，如果提供一个证据，与不提供或不知道该证据相比，将使要素性事实的存在更可能或更不可能，法官就将认定其具有相关性。为相关性设置如此低的标准，旨在鼓励事实认定者（法官、陪审团成员）能够自由地获得信息流，旨在抑制法官对陪审团成员拦截证据。因此，相关性不是充分性。相关性的门槛并不高，只要所提供的证据与待证事实有任何逻辑联系，有助于事实认定者对于事实发生的可能性作出判断就够了。相比之下，“充分性是指该证据足以允许一项裁决”。有时候，我们容易将相关性和充分性相混淆。比如，有人可能说：某个证据是不相关的，因为它并未证明该案件。其实，这个人说的不是相关性，而是充分性。因此，提供相关的证据来证明或反驳一种事实主张，与提供充分的证据来证明或反驳某个人有罪或有责，是两个性质不同的问题。如在人民诉詹森案中，辩方提出一个证据：“狱警在牢门打开前就带着防护手套”。这个证据性事实与什么要素性事实相关呢？与“狱警们先动手打人”、“詹森作了自卫性还击”这两个要素性事实相关。这两个要素性事实于辩护方的“正当防卫”之辩，属于依法需要证明的“实质性”问题。狱警们收餐盘时本不该戴防护手套，但他们却佩戴了，这就意味着他们想挑起战斗。这个证据对于证明警察先动手并不是非常充足的。然而，相关性并不在于该证据证实狱警们先动手是真是假，而只要有助于证明狱警们是否先动手就够了。艾伦教授说：“相关性是证据在审判中被提供时加以判断的，而充分性是在所有证据被采纳后加以判断的……对一个可接受的裁决来说，相关性本身是必要但非充分的。”

三、事实认定是一个经验推论过程

在《相关性和可采性》一文中，艾伦教授解释了事实认定的经验推论性质。他认为，准确性以相关性为逻辑基础，相关性的检验标准是逻辑和一般经验。也就是说，什么证据具有相关性，不是由法律来规定的，而要借助逻辑、常识或一般经验来判断。相关证据有助于事实认定者评估要素性事实存在的可能性，而这种可能性是以人的日常生活经验或概括为根据的。“相关性的核心问题是，一个证据性事实能否与事实认定者先前的知识和经验联系起来，从而允许该事实认定者理性地处理并理解该证据。如果一个正常人在处理该证据之后考虑该案要素性事实时受到了这个证据的影响，该证据就是相关的，否则，就是不相关的。”

判断一个证据是否具有相关性，需要三个连续性推论：一是从证据性事实

（证据提出者主张的事实）得出推断性事实（事实认定者推断的事实），二是由此推出要素性事实（事实认定者经推论确信且对于该争端的法律解决至关重要的事实），三是由此推出其与实体法规定的要件。④

四、证据法具有普适性

正因为事实认定是一个经验推论过程，这个过程不是由法律所决定的，而是要依靠逻辑、常识或一般经验来判断，而人类的常识、逻辑和经验具有共同性，所以，艾伦在《刑事诉讼的法理和政治基础》中阐述了一个重要观点，即“证据法具有普适性”（evidence law is universal），并将其视为与刑事诉讼法的不同之处。因为，就证据法而言，“它涉及人们如何认识外界环境的问题。逻辑、认识论以及感知材料在中国和美国并没有什么差别。两种文化间的惟一相异之处，是不得不认真对待当事人愿意接受的采纳全部相关证据之一般原则的例外……然而重要之点在于，我认为，证据法所处理的知识和理性，在很大程度上包含着普适性而非地方性的内容。”

他认为，与证据法具有普适性相比，刑事诉讼法具有地方性。世界上有许多引进别国刑事诉讼程序而悲惨失败的例子，原因就是忽视了社会文化和历史方面的差别，更重要的原因在于刑事诉讼程序体现了不同的制度安排和设想，其中一种程序中的一套含义完全不同于另一种程序。他强调，研究美国“刑事诉讼法”，不能仅仅考察成文法律和案例，还要深入了解美国的历史、文化、经济以及其他影响因素。

五、证据法兼有限制和激励功能

证据法具有促进事实真相的发现即“求真”和维护社会普遍价值即“求善”的双重功能。然而，对于这两种功能，人们过去常常从证据规则的限制作用来理解。在《相关性和可采性》一文中，艾伦教授从五个方面论述了证据法的激励作用，即“证据法……为基本行为和诉讼行为创造了关键性激励因素”：一是可以激励人们以对社会有益的方式行事或“行善”，如修复危险情况或者提供医疗援助；二是鼓励提出特定的诉求，例如，为了鼓励被害人提出强奸指控，而排除强奸被害人先前性行为的证据；三是通过排除和解或辩诉交易的证据，鼓励争端和平解决，鼓励私人和解而不是鼓励正式诉讼；四是特免权规则

④ 参见［美］罗纳德·J·艾伦等：《证据法：文本、问题和案例》，张保生、王进喜、赵滢译，满运龙校，高等教育出版社2006年版，第149～158页。

保护并鼓励诸如婚姻、律师与委托人、心理诊疗师与患者等重要的社会关系，例如，允许配偶作证互相反对可能会破坏婚姻；五是规制专家、科技证据的使用。很明显，证据法的意义远远超出了审判本身。

在《排除规则的困难》一文中，艾伦教授分析了“美国排除规则”的一个传统却错误的观点，即用排除证据作为一种惩罚去强制人们遵守某些法律标准。然而，这种努力失败了。他认为，“主要行为”和“诉讼行为”之间存在密切关系。许多排除规则都对主要行为具有激励作用，甚至可以说，所有证据规则都包含激励作用，如提供医疗协助的规则和特免权规则，显然旨在影响主要行为。甚至品性证据规则，由于其不纠缠于一个人的过去，也可以激励人们改进和悔过。其他如最佳证据规则，可以激励合同被签署并按最佳证据规则来保存，文件被创建并按业务档案例外规则来保存，等等。这种行为减少了长期交易成本包括诉讼成本。

在《司法证明的性质》一文中，艾伦教授指出：特免权规则确实阻碍陪审团了解相关信息，大部分特免权规则旨在为某些其他价值而牺牲对真相的探寻。然而，律师—委托人特免权，最好被理解为促进而不是限制了信息的提供，因为该特免权旨在鼓励委托人对律师的充分信息披露。

六、证据排除规则外延很宽

我国一些证据法学教材存在着以合法性代替可采性的问题，误将合法性作为证据的三个基本属性之一。2010 年“两院三部”《关于办理死刑案件审查判断证据若干问题的规定》和《关于办理刑事案件排除非法证据若干问题的规定》颁布后，非法证据排除规则更是铺天盖地成为研究的热点，仿佛“非法证据排除规则＝证据排除规则”。

艾伦教授在《排除规则的困难》的演讲中，厘清了美国证据排除规则的几个关键问题：一是证据排除规则要远远大于非法证据排除规则，像相关性、偏见性、传闻、品性、倾向等，都是构成证据排除的理由；二是很难按照目的不同来区分证据排除规则，因为几乎所有排除规则都包含激励功能；三是证据排除规则的实施，由于规则本身的复杂性和执法官员行为的调整而变得很困难；四是证据排除并非实施证据规则和程序规则的唯一可取方法。上述观点对证据法研究具有重要启示。2010 年以来，我国证据排除规则研究主要关注非法证据排除规则，而对品性证据规则、传闻证据规则、不得用以证明过错和责任的证据规则、特免权规则等缺乏应有的关注。这种对证据排除规则的狭义化理解，对证据法研究是非常不利的。艾伦教授这篇文章，希望我们的研究力量能够更多地关注证据排除规则的整体，而不仅仅是非法证据排除规则。

本来，证据法的基本精神是鼓励采纳证据，就事实认定的准确性而言，显然证据越多越好。也许正是在这个意义上，边沁说“排除证据，就是排除正义”⑤，因为，如果把证据都排除了，就很难“拼出”事实真相了。所以，证据法要求减少对证据的“特异性”排除，不要动辄排除证据。艾伦这篇文章介绍了证据排除规则在美国所遭遇的困难，也回应了我国司法实践中成功排除非法证据案例罕见的现状。他从一个新角度提醒我们，证据排除之所以出现困难，也许在于这种方式本身，即排除证据不是实施证据规则的唯一可取方法。他提出一个尖锐的问题：“什么是最佳规制形式：排除还是惩罚?”如果证据排除不是唯一可取的方法，那么，惩罚可能具有替代作用。确实，因为某个警察或检察官非法取证，就把他获取的证据排除掉，这似乎成本太高，也许不排除这些证据反而是对于非法取证的人实施制裁的一个更好的办法?然而，对个人实施制裁，又会导致对官员的过度威慑，可能导致警察过于谨慎甚至懈怠，在犯罪行为发生时不采取应有的行为。

七、最佳解释推论是司法证明性质研究的前沿

1. 在《司法证明的性质》一文中，艾伦教授指出：“一般性的概率论，以及具体的相对频率论，能够作为一种有力的思想工具，在理解司法证明的某些方面发挥作用，但其并不能为理解司法证明提供一个稳固的基础。”

2. 关于经验推论的似真性。艾伦在《证据与推论/概率与似真性》一文中从以下方面讨论了司法证明的性质：首先，不能把证据局限于审判中提出的证言、展示件等。审判中出示的东西本身没有意义，必须经过智慧的观察者运用其关于这个世界的经验和知识来进行评价，它们才产生意义。因此，证据中包括着语言含义、逻辑规则、常识和经验等。司法证明的核心问题是复杂性。其次，我们不得不忍受错误。法律制度的关键问题是“驾驭和驯化复杂性”，为此就要以概率方式思考问题。比如，在民事案件中，说服责任是超过50%的概率；在刑事案件中，“确信无疑”是认定犯罪的高概率。对这些事情以概率方式进行思考，是很自然的事情，但它有严重的困难。证据概率论需求太多信息；在能够计算概率之前，人们必须已知结果。概率解释的主要错误在于，把

⑤ ［英］边沁：《司法证据原理》(Bentham, *Rationale of Judicial Evidence*, 1827)，第三编第一章。转引自［美］特伦斯·安德森、［美］戴维·舒姆、［英］威廉·特文宁：《证据分析》(第2版)，张保生、朱婷、张月波等译，中国人民大学出版社2012年版，第1页。

证据模型化为赋予证据的假设概率。司法证明不是概率性的，而是包含着解释或最佳解释推论。我们该如何理解确信无疑呢？如果没有似真犯罪案情，此人就是无罪的；如果有似真犯罪案情，且没有似真无罪案情，此人就是无罪的。如果有似真犯罪案情和似真无罪案情，此人就是无罪的。这就是对最佳解释之推论的主要解释，它表明了合取悖论的解释方式。比起概率来，似真性和最佳解释推论更能决定证明力。总之，似真性决定概率，而非相反。

3. 最佳解释推论正在取代概率论研究。

许多法学家都试图从概率论角度来解释司法证明，但艾伦教授认为，概率论虽然具有解释力且被人们熟知，但从根本上看，对司法证明更好的解释是：其涉及的是最佳解释推论，而不是就支离的命题作出盖然性判断。证据法应该考虑到司法证明是解释性的而不是盖然性的。

在《司法证明的性质》一文中，艾伦教授说："关于司法证明更好的一种解释，也是我认为正确的解释，是在哲学著作中已经阐述过的最佳解释推论（inference to the best explanation）。在审判中，会产生潜在的解释，并在解释性基础上就其中一个解释展开推论。第一阶段……主要由当事人（包括刑事案件中的政府）完成，当事人必须就事件提出对抗性的说法，如果该说法是真实的，将能够解释庭上提交的证据。对其起诉或者辩护负有证明负担的当事人提出关于事件的说法，该说法包括构成其具体起诉或辩护的形式要素；另一方当事人提供的关于事件的说法，而该说法未包括一个或多个形式要素。此外，如果法律允许，当事人可以就事件提供其他说法来解释证据。最后，事实认定者并不受限于当事人明确提出的可能解释，而是可以建构其自己的解释，要么在评议过程中就此告知其他陪审员，要么自己得出其能接受的结论。"

在司法证明中，实体法和当事人主张的不同事件观点（争议事实）之间的对照，是决定事实认定者在对解释进行评价的两个因素：首先，实体法要求对证据进行充分、详尽的解释，以表明原告有权获得救济。其次，如果当事人没有达成一致意见，为了在形成对比的各种解释中作出选择，需要关注适当的细节。在刑事案件中，检控方必须提出关于合理故事的证据。如果辩护方未提出合理的无罪案件，则会被认定有罪。如果辩护方提出了合理的无罪案件，则会被宣告无罪。"提出合理案件"并不必然意味要站在证人席上或者作证，证据可以以各种方式提交，包括通过被告人之外的其他证人、交叉询问，等等。

在《第四届证据理论与科学国际研讨会闭幕词》中，艾伦教授强调，审判裁决的相对似真模型，是人们实际推理方式的经验描述。通过询问事件各种可能情况的解释而进行推理，然后再判定哪种解释最似真。在审判中，多半是由当事人提供各种解释，然后设法提供证据来支持他们的故事。这种解释被用来填补审判中留下的漏洞，即人们不能通过概率推理来使其变得完全清楚的事情。在人的加工处理过程中，似然性判断的制作涉及所有认知工具，包括归纳推理、演绎推理、概率论、一致性、相容性、符合、效益，等等。最佳叙事解释可能包含着错误因素。如果事件解释的一个要素或成分是错误的，该解释就是错误的。相对似真论的知识背景是在哲学和科学领域均具有革命性的一种方法，即所谓对最佳解释的推论。这并不意味，它是法律制度的最佳解释，但可以肯定的是，对其进行研究具有重要意义，这正是在美国证据法研究中发生的事情。

八、推定规则间接体现证据政策

在《民事诉讼推定再思考》一文中，艾伦教授认为，“推定”一词仅仅是一个标签，它被适用于与审判的适当模式和行为有关的广袤而又十分不同的裁决领域。那种认为“推定”仅适用于证据性裁决的观点是错误的，它是造成围绕推定的所有混乱和争论产生的原因，也是在推定性质问题上不遗余力地论述却徒劳无功的原因。与其在“推定”一词的诸多用法上作无谓的调和，不如专注于分析在这个标签使用中潜在的一些证据问题。推定可能被用于实现 4 种不同的结果，包括：被用以构建裁决规则，分配说服责任，给陪审团作关于事实之间关系的指示，分配举证责任。然而，这些结果中没有一个称得上是通过推定的运用或由于有了推定而实现的。各种证据问题的解决，其实都是根据所涉特定政策考虑而解决的，而不是根据推定是什么，以及系在结果上的“推定”标签是什么。因此，更好的解决方案是完全弃用推定，通过直接适用明确的证据规则，并通过对于目前正由推定的间接使用而实现的潜在政策的考察，来避免含混不清的目的。该文虽以民事推定为题，但讨论的却是推定的基本法理问题，其启发意义在于，应摆脱推定这一混乱的名词，去发现其背后的证据规则问题。

九、说服责任或证明标准的盖然性

在艾伦的字典中，证明标准常常是用说服责任来表述的。举证责任是提出证据的则，说服责任则是提出充分证据以说服陪审团作出事实认定的责任。在《证据法、诉讼法和实体法的关系》一文中，艾伦指出：在刑事诉讼中，国家作为“原告”不仅承担着提出证据的举证责任，还承担着提供充分证据的说服责任。说服责任的要求是，必须对于指控犯罪的每一要件事实的证明都达到让事实认定者确信无疑的程度。“说服责任则是指陪审团为了对特定争点作出认定而必须具有的确定性程度……在民事案件中，陪审团必须通过优势证据认定原告的诉求是真实的。优势证据意味着可能性高于 50%，或‘可能的几率高于不可能的几率’。在刑事案件中，说服责任意味着在有罪问题上要‘确信无疑’。”[⑥] 证明标准既是证明主体对案件事实的证明所应达到的标准，又是事实认定者作出裁决时被这些证明说服的程度。在民事诉讼中，说服责任是相对的。如果原告有超过 50%的说服责任，并使陪审团能够确信原告对事实的陈述是真实的，那么，被告将会败诉。反之，如果被告没能履行说服责任，那么，陪审团就会相信原告对事实的陈述有超过 50%的可能是真实的。

在《证明标准与法律分析的局限性》一文中，他指出，虽然“举证责任和说服责任，共同构成一般意义上的‘证明标准’”，或者“尽管习惯上仍保留着举证责任和说服责任的区分，但麦克诺顿（McNaughton）教授很久前就论证了举证责任是说服责任的一种功能。[⑦] 衡量举证责任是否满足的标准是：在证据出示后是否还遗留下可裁判的事实问题——换句话说，是否需要后续诉讼程序来解决事实不清的问题。这取决于双方的证据状况，但关键还是取决于说服责任的履行是否充分……因此，‘证明标准’这一关键概念性问题，就可被归纳为说服责任的含义和适用问题。”

在《证明责任》一文中，艾伦教授进一步指出，“弄清举证责任和说服责任之间的关系是很重要的”，举证责任的满足是证明存在着争议，而说服责任的满足则是该争议或分歧的解决。“如果理性人能够一致认为原告或被告已满足了相关的说服责任，那么，就没有理由再审理该争议事实。”因此，举证责任是说服责任的一项功能。他用三种可能的情况来说明这个问题：

第一种情况，一方提供的证据不是很有说服力，对事实真实性的支持概率为 10%～35%，这表明其未能履行举证责任，陪审团不能断定提供证据的当事人应当胜诉，那就没有理由对该问题继续审理，否则，将是浪费时间和金钱。第二种情况，举证责任得到了满足，一方提供的证据产生了一个陪审团争点，显示了一个 40%～60%的合理说服力范围，陪审团成员对证据的含义意见不一致，那么该争点将被送交陪审团继续审理。第三种情况，陪审团对证据的含义不存在合理的分歧，提供的证据表明相关事实真实性的概率为 65%～

⑥ 参见［美］罗纳德·J·艾伦等：《证据法：文本、问题和案例》，张保生、王进喜、赵滢译，满运龙校，高等教育出版社 2006 年版，第 253～254、807 页。

⑦ 约翰·T·麦克诺顿（John T. McNaughton）：《举证责任：说服责任的一项功能》，载《哈佛法学评论》，第 68 卷，1995 年，第 1382 页。

90%，举证责任不但得到满足，而且陪审团在何方应该胜诉的问题上不会不一致，但应当继续审理以便给对方提供相反证据的机会。在对方当事人进行反驳证明之前，负有最初举证责任的当事人不能胜诉；在对方当事人反驳证明之后，一方或双方当事人可以再次要求法官检验该证据的充分性。如果负有举证责任的当事人提供了充分的“反驳”证据，那就又回到了第二种情况，对方当事人可对新提供的证据再次进行反驳证明，继续进行审理，直到双方当事人都没有新提供的证据为止；如果其间提供的新证据符合第一种情况，法官就会对争点作出有利于对方当事人的裁定；如果提供的新证据符合第二种情况，法官就应当将该争点提交陪审团继续审理；如果提供的新证据符合第三种情况，法官就应当对该争点作出有利于最初承担举证责任的当事人的裁定。因此，举证责任是说服责任的一个功能。

艾伦教授在《证明责任》一文中，将优势证据标准和中国一些学者所主张的高度盖然性证明标准作了比较。他认为，高度盖然性标准继承了大陆法传统，设立了高于75%的标准。证明标准的提高将导致更多有利于被告的错判和更少有利于原告的错判，提高证明责任导致了有利于被告的错误数量的增加。刑事案件确信无疑的证明要求，也可通过这个方法得到解释：如果将其从0.95降低到0.7，就会将更多有罪者定罪，但同样也会将更多无辜者定罪。

十、准确性与成本及其他证据政策具有竞争关系

在《证据法的未来》一文中，艾伦教授讨论了证据法的准确性与其他价值追求即价值政策之间的关系。他指出：“证据法并非只关心求真；它是一个同时追求许多不同利益的法律制度之不可分割的部分，这些利益常常具有竞争性……法律制度的设计者面临大量政策选择。一些是与事实准确性的追求一致，但很多又与其相反。”准确性价值的实现是需要成本的，“而且有时成本过高。一个法律制度过于专注事实的准确性，也许会破坏该法律制度正试图维护的社会环境。一个只值一美元的争端，却要花费一千美元的诉讼才得到一个事实准确的结论，那大概就不该对簿公堂了。这种诉讼可能只会减少整体社会福利，并阻碍纠纷的私人和解”。考虑所有这些因素都意味着成本，成本下降将导致消费的增加，人们有任何争端都要到法院来打官司；花费的成本太高，人们便将寻求非诉讼争端解决方式，如妥协和谈判。事实准确性不仅与成本有竞争关系，还与政府可合理追求的其他政策有竞争关系，包括特免权规则、事后补救措施规则等等。

目 录

证据法的理论基础和意义*

张保生 张月波 译**

"证据"和"证据法"是两个截然不同的概念。"证据"一般是指，在裁决过程中能以理性方式影响最终判决结果的那些"输入"信息。理性方式是这里引入的第三个概念。在美国，"证据"还有一个专业性法律意义，特指在审判中提出的证言和展示件，但这是一个存在争议的定义。在美国，事实认定者（陪审团在判断事实的过程中）可能会将他们对证人的观察（"言行举止"）考虑进来，从"证据"这个术语的实用意义上说，这显然就是"证据"。但问题在于，进一步讲，如果不使用大量预先设定的概念、观察和决策工具（例如逻辑、溯因推理***、实用工具等）知识库，就不能对观察到的现象进行法律层面的加工和思考。因此，一个有用的证据概念不应局限于"审判输入"，还应该包括对证人证言和展示件的观察。在此，"理性"意味着，把所有输入和认知能力应用于事实发现，使其对过去某个时刻的事情能够达到最佳发现效果，然后得出与事情原委一致的权利和义务裁判。

相比之下，"证据法"是指证据性程序的组织方式，但证据性程序的组织方式显然取决于"证据"和"理性"之性质。于是，证据法领域便延伸至，我们称为"证据"的过去事件的痕迹，这种过去事件的痕迹在人类决策过程中被

* 本文系艾伦教授2010年6月在中国政法大学所做的讲座。本译文原载于《证据科学》，第18卷，2010年第4期。

** 张保生，中国政法大学证据科学教育部重点实验室教授；张月波，中国政法大学硕士研究生。

*** 译注：abduction，又译为"不明推论式"，是指大前提完全正确，但小前提仍有问题的三段论推理。参见《现代英语综合大词典》。早期皮尔斯（1868年）分别描绘了这三种推理的三段论形式：

演绎：规则——来自这个袋子的所有豆子是白色的。
情形——这些豆子来自这个袋子。
结果——这些豆子是白色的。

归纳：情形——这些豆子来自这个袋子。
结果——这些豆子是白色的。
规则——来自这个袋子的所有豆子是白色的。

假设：规则——来自这个袋子的所有豆子是白色的。
结果——这些豆子是白色的。
情形——这些豆子来自这个袋子。

加工和依赖的方式，以及根据正式证据程序之法律规则进行的规制。所以，证据法取决于且必须处理至少三件事情：人类社会普适真理，政府性质有关方面及其法律制度，以及对事实真相之追求有帮助或阻碍作用的具体政策。我将逐一讨论这些问题。

普适真理：尽管人类文化大都是由社会决定的，但认知能力并非如此。能力是如何发展和运用的可能有所不同，但感知、加工和记忆的潜在认知能力，以及与所观察到的事情有关的能力，是人类自身条件的组成部分。显然，它们在社会中的不同个体之间是不同的，但它们为有能力的所有成年人所普遍拥有。人类用来帮助自己理解周围环境的许多工具也是共同的。数学和逻辑不因地点不同而改变，如效用函数和成本曲线等决策工具。我将把这些认识论上的能力和常规工具一起统称为“理性工具”。这些理性工具使人们能够理解和掌控周围环境。它们包括诸如简单的演绎推理，概括能力，溯因推理（对一系列数据点之解释的探究），对因果关系、必要条件和充分条件的理解，以及很多其他事项。这些问题就是认识论或知识论研究的内容，而证据法实际上就是法律认识论。我需要指出的是，在一些关于证据法之基础的讨论中，对概率论和认识论作出了区分。从某种意义上说，这可能是有益的区分，但在我看来，概率论仅仅是促进认识论目标追求的理性工具之一。

文化和社会的影响确实在各个层面对基本理性工具发挥着作用。两个来自不同文化背景的个体，也许经历着相同的感性事件，但基于其各自熟悉的可疑事件类型及其背景知识，他们会有完全不同的理解。同样，启动逻辑过程的假设可能是不同的，而且成本收益和相对权重的设置也可能不同。

坦率地说，尽管很多人认为除了认识能力之外还存在普遍的人性，但我对此却不那么确信。对于普世正义感和普世人权有很多宽泛的探讨，但 20 世纪是一个使那些把“人性”看作仁慈的或关心陌生人福利的人蒙羞之世纪。那么，或许经济学家在某种意义上是正确的，即人们都追求（或应当被设想为追求）自身利益，而不论那些利益被设想成什么。显然，人们确实都在追求他们自己及其家人在财物和医疗上的私利。在人类繁荣的可能性框架内享有宁静生活，肯定是一个普遍愿望，但却很难把这视为依赖于人类通性。不仅 20 世纪对这种观点来说是个羞辱，大部分有文字记载的历史也是如此。而刚刚开始的 21 世纪则表明与千年历史并没有什么大的变化。

正如我下面将详细说明的，证据法的主要任务之一是处理和领悟这套精细考虑因素，并据其创造一个服务于共同体利益的争端解决机制。

政府的随意性及其法律制度：尽管人性有很多共同之处，但人类组织自身生活方式的变量却几乎是无穷的。法律制度是政府的关键成分，它们反映了争端解决的深层政治理论。基于美国的政治史，我们的国父们断定，政治权力应当被分散于政府三个分支，每一分支需要另一个或另两个分支才能发挥作用。这旨在抵消西方观察家们几乎公认的所有权力都具有对内集权和对外扩张的趋势。简而言之，这就是为何我们有独立法院传统，我们将其视为制约其他政府分支的潜在刹车器。

当然，政府能以无数种其他方式加以建构。无论选择何种政府形式，更重要的是，无论以何种假设作为其基础，显然都将影响其法律制度的性质，进而将影响争端解决和证据规制的方式。

虽说如此，争端解决有一个共性，它是人们可能想不到的方面。在西方有一种误解认为，启蒙运动之基本政治理念以及支持现代西方政府的最强有力的政治纲领，都与权利和义务有某种联系。在西方法律学术中对霍布斯、洛克和卢梭的观点有大量引用，并且都强调了这一点。权利和义务固然都很重要，但启蒙运动更根本的理念是认识论上的革命，即认为有一个客观上可知的外在于我们思想的世界；然而，对洛克、贝克莱、休谟乃至康德认识论著作中关于这种主张的引用，却非常之少且相去甚远。这就颠倒了事实与权利/义务之间的实际关系。事实先于权利和义务而存在，并且是权利和义务之决定性因素。没有准确的事实认定，权利和义务就会失去意义。思考一下你所穿衣服的所有权这个简单例子。你对那些衣服的所有权，允许你“有权”占有、消费和处置那些财产，但假定我要求你归还“我的”衣服，即我坚持说你所穿的衣服事实上是属于我的。你将会怎么做？你会找一个裁判者，向他提供你购买、制作、得到或被赠与这件争议之衣服的证据。如果这种努力获得成功，那位裁判者将切实赋予你那些权利，并强迫我履行相应义务。这里的关键点在于，那些权利和义务取决于什么事实将被认定，并从中得出什么结论。这一点的意义不能被过分夸大。把法治与真实世界的实际情况相联系的努力，锚定了可知事物中的权利和义务，并使其摆脱了反复无常和任性的支配。这就是相关性和实质性的理念对于法律制度构建具有根本重要性的原因。它们把法律制度系在事实准确性的基石上了。

这一点确实具有普适性。在缺乏事物实际相关状况之知识的情况下，不仅权利或义务无法追求，政策选择也无从做起。因此，即使在治理方式不确定的情况下，我们也发现证据法具有普适性。当然，人们可能思考事实被最准确或最充分认定的方式，何种政策可以抵消事实准确性的意义，在这些问题上存在合理的分歧。

政策问题的意义：法律制度的设计者面临众多的政策选择。某些政策是与事实准确性追求一致的，但很多又与其相悖。请注意我用“政策问题”这个短语来对应社会所追求的各种利益。因而它包括某些可能称为“价值论”的问题。然而，政府追求的所有政策并非都是道德的；很多政策是相当实际和功利的。的确，政府追求的大多数政策可能都是实际和功利的。在道德和功利性政策之间作出区分确实是合理的，但它们是政府所追求的更大利益范畴的组成部分，并且在思考证据法时可被有效地结合在一起。另一种可以做但我没有做的区分，是政策问题来源之间的区分。某些政策来源只是所有政府都会面临的标准问题，包括在美国被我们误导性地称为警察权力之一般运用的问题，即规制影响健康、安全和福利的州权力运用问题。相比之下，在任何特定国家无论采用什么宪法形式，其他政策来源都是由宪法明确规定的。有些评论家将宪法性问题从其他政策问题中挑选出来，这也是合理的。然而，这种区分无助于理解证据法，因此我不再费力做这种区分。证据法确实在做源于宪法赋予的某些事情，但从最高层面之一般原则来说，这与把证据法塑造为追求未被载入宪法文本的利益是一回事。

现在我转入证据法中必须安排的一些政策问题。

对事实准确性的追求。人们可能合理地假定，基于先天认识论能力的自然推理过程会合理运行得很好，因此在追求事实准确性时通常应当予以遵从。然而，这也许会重导人们犯错误的情况。在这种情况下，证据规则可以努力纠正这种系统性错误。这解释了《联邦证据规则》规则 403 授权排除那些可能引起误导或不公正偏见的证据的原因。这也构成了其他规则的基础，比如对品性和倾向证据的限制，以及关于证人只能根据亲身知识作证的要求。而在何种情况下个人会犯系统性错误，很可能主要取决于文化。

准确性价值。事实准确性肯定是我们想得到的最重要结果，但它绝非我们想得到的唯一结果。它是有代价的，而且这个代价有时候会过高。一个过于追求事实准确性的法律制度，可能会毁灭该法律制度致力于培育的最佳社会环境。一个只值一美元的争端，如果需要花费一千美元对簿公堂来得到一个事实准确的结论，那大概就不应当通过诉讼来解决了。这样的诉讼很可能会减损社会整体福利，而且阻碍争端的私了。当然，很难说这种成本的界限在哪里，确切地说这取决于本土观念。我会在第二讲中更多讨论这个问题。

激励价值。事实准确性不仅与成本有竞争关系，与政府可以合理追求的一些其他政策也有竞争关系。这类政策的清单很长，而且同样取决于文化因素。豁免权法可以培育和保护很多社会关系（配偶关系、法律关系、医疗关系、宗

教关系、政府关系，等等)。一场事故后诉讼不应当阻碍风险减少（事后补救规则)。与诉讼相比，人们可能更偏爱争端的调解解决，所以调解过程中的陈述要排除在证据之外。鼓励调解也是不降低诉讼费用的一个原因。诉讼之公共补贴越多，诉讼就可能越多，私了谈判就会越少。还有其他可以追求的政策。在美国，考虑到规制警察调查行为的需要，我们设置了很多排除规则。证据规则还可以鼓励或妨碍提起特定种类的诉讼。同样是在美国，在过去一段时期内我们认为强奸被害人报案的积极性受到了重挫，为了纠正这种情况，我们创造了减少滥用这类个人信息的证据规则，以免其在庭审中可能被曝光。

总体公正考量也会对证据法产生影响，尽管这个变量之精确效果常常难以从更公开的实用目的来衡量。有人认为，对不公正偏见证据的限制不仅反映了对准确性的关注，也反映了对羞辱的关注，就像强奸相关性规则一样。对先前行为和倾向证据的限制，也部分反映了个人不应当受制于过去行为的信念。传闻证据规则在一定程度上反映了与反对你的证人对质权的价值。

错误风险。一种不犯错误的法律制度是不可能的。至关重要的是认识到可能会犯两种类型的错误：一是对原告的错判（包括判无辜者有罪)，我们称之为Ⅰ型错误或积极错误；二是对被告的错判（包括判有罪者无罪)，我们称之为Ⅱ型错误或消极错误。资源配置和其他决定将影响这两种错误类型的关系。

常人可能会质疑这两种错误类型的重要意义，但法律制度的建构必须兼顾这两种错误类型。在美国，我们试图平衡对原被告所造成的错误并减少错误总量，以构建民事诉讼。相比之下，刑事司法程序旨在减少错误定罪的可能性，这是以容忍在无罪裁决上犯更多错误为代价的。这个问题虽然很复杂，但这些观点在很大程度上解释了民事案件的优势证据标准和刑事案件的确信无疑证明标准。在民事案件中，无论哪种错误都会造成同样的资源分配不当。如果原告错赢一项五百美元的裁决，一位公民（被告）就必定错失五百美元。如果被告错赢一项他/她不欠五百美元的裁决，一位公民（原告）就会被错夺他/她有权拥有的五百美元。从分析的角度看，这两种情况是一样的。相比之下，在刑事案件中，在美国，我们认为错误定罪比错误无罪裁决更有害，因此，通过要求确信无疑的证明而使定罪更难。我们坚持这么做，即使可能（但绝非一定）导致错误无罪裁决的数量增多乃至错误总量增多。我明天将会更多谈到这个问题，并对这些简单理念在实践中的实现情况提出一些质疑。

各种政策问题。还有许多其他相关问题必须由法律制度设计师来加以回答。最重要的是为法律戏剧中的各种角色分配责任。这些问题包括：审判是应当像在欧洲流行的那样分段进行，还是应当像在美国那样一气呵成？审判法官

应当拥有多大的自由裁量权，而当事人应当在多大程度上控制审判过程？审判法官和上诉法官之间是什么关系？在上诉法院，是应当重新审判，还是限于复审法律错误？小额民事案件和大宗商事案件的区别对待具有正当性吗？刑事案件又该如何对待？

上述事项的讨论表明了证据法之基础和意义的广度。我现在要做四点分析，其中三点对于理解任何法律机体的基础和意义均至关重要，第四点则对清晰思考证据法非常重要。它们包括：

1. 书本上的法律和行动中的法律之间的区别。

2. 一方面是诉讼（程序）法与证据法的关系，另一方面是它们与实体法的关系，特别是它们与实体法的相互联系而非区别。

3. 经济学或如我们在美国所说的：天下没有免费的午餐。如果你在这里为了一个目的用了一美元（或一元人民币），你就不能再为另一目的把它花到别处。

4. 审判是理想方式还是非正当方式。法律制度旨在鼓励审判还是鼓励调解？它应当被设计成旨在何为？

我将逐个讨论这些变量及其意义。

1. 书本上的法律；行动中的法律。宪法被制定出来，立法获得了通过，行政官员发布命令和指示，法院作出裁定，人们便认为我们余下之人多少就是服从了。不幸的（或许幸运的）是，生活并非如此简单。当宪法或法律在任何多党决策过程中被表决通过时，对于法律语言的含义都会有多重理解。某些立法者可能会为法律的通过投赞成票，尽管他们认为其中还有不尽如人意（乃至走得太远）的地方；别的立法者可能恰恰出于同一理由而投票反对这部法律。对于某个特定条款的确切含义或作用也可能存在严重分歧。一个人可能认为该法律语言有某种隐含意思，别的人可能认为它有不同的隐含意思。抽象的成文法语言经常不能解决那些措辞的含义问题。法律语言常常故意留下模糊之处，因为立法者对其确切含义不能达成一致，或者因为对预见一个特定问题会出现的所有可能情形总是感到无能为力，这进一步加剧了这种困难。

在美国，存在着权力分立增加的复杂性。制定法律是立法机关的工作，包括大多数州的证据法，但使法律生效是法院的工作。法官们对立法机关所采用的语言之含义可能有不同的理解，他们的制度性关注也会有所不同。因此，法院的法律适用也许与立法机关或立法者个人意图中法律的理想化含义有所不同。

证据法具有的一种潜在独特结构加剧了这种不确定性。证据法的外观，在为规则运行提供必要和充分条件的意义上很像规则。但证据法的重要组成部分只是简单分配了责任和自由裁量权，这完全是因为相关问题对于像是条约的规则来说太复杂了。证据法之大概最重要的方面——相关性——正具有这种属性。对于任何特定审判中出示的大多数证据之相关性来说，陈述一种先验的必要性和充分条件是不可能的。那些决定因素将必然与每一审判的唯一性有关，而且事先逐字逐句地清楚阐释它们是不可能的（我们何以能够辨别一位当下未知的证人将对一个当下未知的话题撒谎?）。因此，证据法将责任赋予某人——当事人或法官——来决定提供什么证据，并根据相当一般性指导原则提供证据。在美国，相关证据被定义为可以增加或减少某个关键事实之真实性概率的证据，但实际上并没有具体说明何时可以符合这种条件。

最后一个可能导致书本上的法律与行动中的法律不同的因素是，证据法的某些领域必须设法安置完全相反的原则或动力。这可能导致该法律的某个部分作出一个约定，而另一个部分又推翻了那个约定。这种情况在美国证据法中的两个重要例子，就是传闻证据规则和反对品性和倾向证据的规则。传闻证据规则约定了排除传闻证据，但数世纪以来传闻证据规则的例外却一直有增无减。在民事案件中，对传闻证据排除的约定鲜有履行，甚至在刑事案件中传闻证据也常被采纳。同样，证据法约定了品性和倾向证据的排除，却又为其采纳开辟了坦途。

2. 实体法和诉讼（程序）法之间的关系。实体法有时候被认为与证据性（和程序性）法律有很大区别，但这是误导，事实上二者具有复杂的和相互作用的关系。在美国，由于保护宪法权利具有重大意义，这一点已变得特别清楚，并成为利益法学研究的主题，但该观点也适用于一般证据事项。美国最高法院的裁决延伸并强化了个人权利，这被视为对警察和检察官强加了极大限制，然而，法律制度却没有受到这些裁定的很大干扰。这些制度充满了活力和无限的适应性，因而能够并且确实以无法预见和令人惊奇的适应性回应了社会变化。因此，对动态过程的“改革”，常常不能通过只有愿望而没有预期结果的离散性措施（discrete measures）来强制施行。这种动态现象的一个重要方面是，合法的实质性变化可以实际上冲淡来自法院或法律改革者的任何程序性革新。

这一点在美国的一个例子，涉及限制不合理搜查和扣押的宪法第 4 条修正案。假设，警察想要拦截汽车对犯罪行为进行突击检查；但法院裁定，宪法第 4 条修正案要求，警察在拦截车辆之前必须有其从事犯罪行为的合理根据。立法机关要使这个法院命令实际失效，只需把刑法扩展到包含更严格的驾驶要求。立法机关本质上可使立法接近于驾驶时不可能不违反刑事法规（如越过中心线，与前车车距过近，未及早或过早打开转向灯，等等）。如果立法机关通过了这种法律，警察实际上就能拦截任何车辆，办法是跟随一辆汽车直到司机违反其中一个规制驾驶的法条。这种拦截是凭所谓“合理根据”，但这种立法将极大地扩张合理根据的潜在来源，因此只要警察任何时候想拦截车辆，每个人都会受到拦截，无论法院为禁止该过程作出何种努力。同样，如果政府没有合理根据就不能截获特定信息，它就会经常转由要求个人保留政府想得到的信息记录，并把这些记录泄露给政府。

这一点普遍存在于证据法和程序法中。最明显的例子是实质性，其由实体法直接决定却有更深的目的。通过改变诉因要件，立法机关可使根据那些诉因的求偿变得更容易或更可能。关于合同条款含义的口头证言是否被允许——在美国被我们称作“口头证据规则”——显然冲击了证据制度。同样明显的是，正如侵权法中的“不证自明”的作用一样，要求特定合同必须以书面形式订立的反欺诈法通常也支配着证据原则。

正如实体法能够影响证据程序一样，证据法也能影响实体法。这样的例子很多。排除规则通常增加诉讼成本，采纳规则通常减少诉讼成本。随着特免权的扩张，在大多数情况下诉讼成本加大了，并导致执法权加大。传闻证据的简化采纳使证明更加容易（尽管同时大概减少了可靠性），等等。证据开示规则能够极大地影响当事人形成并寻找证据的动机。像强奸相关性规则等个别规则，能够影响案件可被证明之难易程度。证明责任的分配可以鼓励或阻碍特定诉因的形成，等等。同样，我们明天将花费大部分时间来更深入地探讨这类问题。

实体法和证据法之间还有另一种相互作用，对此我们应当引起注意。在美国，但在中国也许不是这样，由于在美国所有事情都可能陷入诉讼，因而证据是律师做任何事情之基础。遗嘱、刑事事务（判决部分取决于什么有记录）、反托拉斯、商务工作等所有事情。证据与每个其他法律领域都有关，所有法律交易中最糟糕的场景就是陷入诉讼。在诉讼中，一个关键变量是什么能被证明。因此，每位律师，不管其从事的事务离法庭多么遥远，他都必须将法庭纳入考量因素，这意味着在诉讼之前就要重视证据规则，以便诉讼一旦发生，必要的事实便能得到证明。例如，档案材料须妥善保存并符合可采性之形式要求。

3. 经济因素。在美国我们有种说法：“天下没有免费的午餐”，意思是说，如果有人“邀请”你吃午饭，他很可能想与你谈些事情或可能图个回报。无论人们对此怎么看，“天下没有免费的午餐”对政府来说是字字珠玑。政府受其经济状况制约，而经济是有限的。在理论上，在政府能做的众多有价值的事情中，它们只能选择其中某些事情去做。如果资源被用于一个目的，就剩不下什么资源去做其他事情，而总体上，需要做的不同“事情”太多了，不能都给它们拨款。同样，私人资源也是有限的，尽管其被消耗的方式几乎是无限的。

在思考诉讼制度时，有限的资源限制是至关重要的考虑因素。对于资源在整个政府利益范围内的分配，包括法律制度的运行，都需要艰难的抉择。我再举一个戏剧性的例子。对刑事司法的投入，显然与在其他社会福利领域的投入有竞争性。如果政府奉养更多的法官、警察，或者为穷人请律师提供资金，那么，用于经济发展或医学研究等其他事业的资源就会减少。警察每天都面临这类问题。面对犯罪增加，他们必须不断决定如何分配其有限资源。警察应当在城市这个地区还是应当在那个地区巡逻？他们是应当集中打击经济犯罪、暴力犯罪，还是集中打击欺诈犯罪？在刑事司法程序中的投入，很可能与在同一程序中不同部分的投入有竞争关系。如果政府奉养更多的法官，大概就只能奉养更少的警察。

经济因素的影响进一步延伸且具有戏剧性。例如，考虑一下目前在中国对你们很重要的一个问题——聘请律师的权利。如果辩护律师的积极参与增加了审判所花的总量时间，显然就会有更少的审判，因为可用于审理案件的总量时间是有限的。总之，随着案件平均成本的增加，能够审理的案件总量就会减少。这又意味着，有效的律师咨询要么将减少定罪数量，要么将促使政府改用其他执法手段。

类似情况也存在于民事案件中，但有细微差别。尽管问题很复杂，但民事诉讼的理想数量可能与刑事诉讼的理想数量有所不同。如果民事案件诉讼费用下降，人们就能预测诉讼数量将会增加。从某种意义上说这是一种公共利益；诚然，无论在你们国家还是我们国家，难以接近、成本、诉讼程序的拖延，通常都被认为是需矫正的问题。然而，它们也有积极作用，特别是通过它们鼓励了争端私了。的确让一些人震惊的是，在美国，甚至大多数刑事案件，是通过被告和政府之间本质上是私人谈判的方式即辩诉交易来解决的。

这就引出我的第四个论点。

4. 理想模式的审判与社会崩溃化身的审判。正如我所要指出的，证据法的意义远远超出了审判本身。不过，从实际情况和公众心态来看，证据法和审判有着紧密联系。并且，西方的审判常常被理想化了并享有荣耀。其部分原因是陪审团在我们的政治理论和自我概念中所扮演的角色；还有部分原因是法治的荣耀（让我补充说，这是当之无愧的），审判将公开的辩护证明具体化了。我不知道，中国在多大程度上也是如此。证据法的制定着眼于其在审判中的运用，这一点虽然显而易见，然而从后果论意义上说，人们如何看待审判，可以影响人们思考什么是理想的证据规则。

无论一个人拥有什么样的审判观，都会对审判观和证据法之间的关系持有一定的看法。在美国，如果人们接受了理想化、被媒体美化的审判观，就可能想要把证据规则之目的塑造成进一步为法治和人权作公开辩护。那就应当给予刑事被告和民事诉讼中的"弱者"更大的回旋余地。被告人的最终陈述权应当得到保护，等等。

即便法治应当享有荣耀（我认为确实如此），但审判是否应当享有荣耀却并不如此清楚。对所有审判戏剧来说，审判反映了法治中的衰弱。审判发生于对错误行为的控诉——民事的或刑事的——并且当事人无法对解决争端达成一致。因此，审判从某种意义上说是病态的。审判会耗费资源，而这些资源原本能以更具建设性的方式来更好地利用（虽然以正确的或其他方式获得事实也是繁荣昌盛的重要条件）。从更高概念层次上讲，在关于争端本身性质之本体论问题上可能还存在合理的分歧。争端主要是个人之间的吗？抑或它们还有社会性的方面？

我在此提出这些问题，并非要回答它们，而是要进一步说明，在"证据法的理论基础和意义"这个带有一定欺骗性的直白标题下，潜藏着许多深奥的问题。

我现在对上面讲到的各种考虑因素做一个总结。我认为，"证据法的理论基础和意义"提出了如下五组问题和思考：

1. 从其最直接的表现形式看，证据是关于争端解决的研究，其焦点是戏剧中各种角色之间的相互作用与规制：审判法官、陪审团成员/外行评价者、律师、当事人和证人（包括外行证人和专家证人）。证据规则构造了这些个人之间的关系，但这些规则本身是对一组复杂因素相对粗糙的提炼，而那组复杂因素包含着证据真正的"基础和意义"。证据规则是那些潜在理念的反映。

2. 人们构建审判的方式，以及因此而塑造、促进审判的证据规则，是人们信念的一种功能，这种信念关涉人类思想和哲学的基本问题之一——知道某件事情到底意味着什么？审判是一种认识论意义上的事件，在审判中，知识之主张被预设、考量、否定和接受。哲学起源于关于思维和求知意味着什么的系统思考，这至今仍是哲学的主题。例如，现代相对主义哲学就是由基本怀疑论所驱动的，启示之渴望则反映在那些具有宗教取向的哲学家身上。但这不是唯一传统。在现代科学中有令人惊奇的成功范例；为了清晰思考法律过程，必须把人们的思想置于这种思潮之中或靠近这种思潮的某个位置。你是否认为历史事实真相是可知的，这将在很大程度上决定你对特定证据规则的看法。在事实之"历史性"重构与"社会性"重构之间，二者是否存在着区别？的确，谈论"知道"过去，是否合乎逻辑？如果非也，审判应当发挥什么作用、追求什么价值？事实认定应当在多大程度上指望随机遴选的外行事实认定者，又应当在多大程度上依赖法官的"专业知识"？两种途径各有什么风险？证据规则应当在多大程度上对诉讼当事人一方有利？诸如此类的问题。

3. 还有另一个根本性问题：审判的目的是什么。典型回答是与事实认定有关的某些东西，正如我试图讲清楚的，这种典型回答具有重要意义。但是，审判像科学一样吗？它们有何不同？这种与科学的类比其实有些空洞。尽管更多的信息尚未收集到，法律裁决却不能推迟。还有，所做的判决是实际上发生了什么，而非潜在的普适法律可能是什么。最有效的解释是，大概没有像在科学中那样的知识体系可适用于典型案件。相反，事实认定者为了作出裁决，不得不输入必要的背景知识。如果经过再三思考，审判并不那么像科学（至少某些科学类型），那么它们像历史学吗？历史学关注事实，但一般而言，那被视为一种更伟大的谅解手段。在审判中，谅解在很大程度上是不相关的（作为说服事项的情况除外）。

4. 但审判可服务的所有其他目的是什么？什么是关于审判的经济学方面？不仅是当事人，律师、法官、法院书记员以及所有法院工作人员都在审判中注入了经济利益。什么是审判的象征性目的？什么是审判的政治目的？等等。一系列非常复杂的问题集，都在告诉我们审判的性质。根据所有这些因素，证据规则的目的可能是什么？问题再次提出来了，对这些问题的答案如何影响审判方式的建构？审判应当在多大程度上看起来像自由市场？它们应当在多大程度上由政府进行规制？哪种模式很可能促进有效求真，为什么？除效率和寻求真相外，还有什么其他价值是或应当是利害攸关的？

5. 证据法不仅构造事实认定，它还创造了各种各样的动机。准确事实认定的意义如何与其他社会价值竞争？

证据和证据法并不像人们通常所想的那样，在众多因素中只投身于正义和公正社会的追求，但正如我试图表明的那样，它们对这种追求都扮演着至关重要的角色。具有某种讽刺意味的是，尽管作为我们制度之基石、基础的证据非常重要，但在西方，证据的意义仍然受到忽视。证据的意义确实非常重要。在中国，你们正体验着市民社会的不同组织形式，不能忽视证据问题。没有准确的事实认定，就没有理性的证据法，所有其他追求即使不是不可能，也会造成极度的困难。

The Theoretical Foundations and Implications of Evidence

Ronald J. Allen *

"Evidence" and "evidence law" are two quite distinct concepts. "Evidence" generally refers to those inputs to decision making that influence its outcome in what, to introduce a third concept, is normally referred to as a rational manner. In the United States, "evidence" also has a technical legal meaning to refer to the testimony and exhibits introduced at trial, but this is problematic. In the United States, fact finders may take into account their observations of witnesses ("demeanor"), which obviously is "evidence" in any useful sense of the term, and more deeply no observation may be processed and deliberated upon without the use of a vast storehouse of preexisting concepts, observations, and decision makings tools (such as logic, abduction, utilities, and so on) . A useful concept of evidence must thus expand considerably far beyond the mere "trial inputs" —the observations of witness testimony and exhibits. What "rational" means here is putting all of the inputs and cognitive capabilities to the use of discovering as best can be done the way the world was at some prior time, and then to let rights and obligations be determined consistently with the preexisting state of affairs.

"Evidence law", by contrast, refers to the manner in which the evidentiary process is organized, but obviously the organization of the evidentiary process is contingent on both "evidence" and the nature of "rationality." The domain of evidence law, then, extends to the traces of the past that we colloquially refer to as "evidence," the manner in which such traces of the past are processed and relied upon in human decision making, and the regulation by law

* John Henry Wigmore Professor of Law, Northwestern University, President, Board of Foreign Advisors, Evidence Law and Forensic Sciences Institute, Fellow, Procedural Law Research Center, CUPL.

of the formal evidentiary process. Evidence law is thus contingent upon, and must accommodate, at least three things: Universal truths of the human condition, contingent aspects of the nature of government and its legal system, and highly specific policies to be pursued in addition or opposition to the pursuit of truth. I will say a word about each of these in turn.

Universal Truths: Although much of human culture is socially determined, cognitive capacities are not. How capacities are developed and employed may differ, but the underlying epistemological capacities to perceive, process, remember, and relate what was observed are part of the human condition. Obviously, they differ over individuals within societies, but they are universally present in all competent adults. Many of the tools that humans employ to assist in understanding their environment likewise are universal. Mathematics and logic do not vary from place to place, nor do decision tools such as utility functions and cost curves. Together, I will refer to these epistemological capacities and formal tools as the "tools of rationality." These tools of rationality are what permit humans to understand and control their environment. They include such things as simple deductive reasoning, the capacity to generalize, abductive reasoning (the search for the explanation of a series of data points), an understanding of cause and effect and of necessary and sufficient conditions, and many other things as well. These issues comprise the study of epistemology—the study of knowledge—and the law of evidence is in fact the law's epistemology. I should note that in some discussions of the foundations of the law of evidence a distinction is made between probability theory and epistemology. That may be a useful distinction for some purposes, but in my opinion probability theory is just one of the tools of rationality that facilitate pursuing epistemic tasks.

There surely are cultural and social influences operating on the basic tools of rationality, and at all levels. Two individuals from different cultures may experience the same perceptual event but understand it completely differently based on their respective familiarity with the type of event in question and their background knowledge. Similarly, the assumptions that begin logical processes may differ, and both the sets of costs and benefits and their relative weights may vary, as well.

I am less sure that there is a universal human nature beyond the epistemological capacities, frankly, although many think that there is. There is much lose talk about a universal sense of justice and universal human rights, but the twentieth century is a reproach to any who would see "human nature" as beneficent or concerned about the welfare of strangers. Perhaps, then, the economists are correct in a sense that people pursue, or should be conceived of as pursuing, their own self-interest, however those interests are conceived. Obviously, people do pursue their own financial and medical self-interest and those of their families. There certainly is a widespread desire for the conditions of a peaceful life with the possibility of human flourishing, but it is hard to see this as resting upon universals of the human condition. Not only is the twentieth century a reproach to such a view, so, too, is most of recorded history. And the twenty-first century is off to a start that suggests not much has changed from the millennium.

As I will elaborate below, one of the primary tasks of the law of evidence is to process and digest this elaborate set of considerations and create in their light a system of dispute resolution that serves the interests of the community.

Contingencies of Government and its Legal System: Although there is much that is common to humanity, the ways in which humans organize themselves varies almost infinitely. Legal systems are critical components of government, and they reflect the resolution of issues of deep political theory. One need look no further than China and the United States to see this clearly. Because of the political history of the United States, our founders concluded that political power should be diffused over the three branches of government, with each needing one or both of the others in order to be effective. This was designed to counteract what western observers almost universally believe is the centripetal force of all power centers and their tendency to aggrandizement. In brief, this is why we have a tradition of independent courts that we conceive of as being a potential brake on other branches of government.

And of course there are innumerable additional ways in which governments can be constructed. Whatever form of government is chosen, and more importantly whatever assumptions form its foundation, will obviously impact the nature of the legal system, which in turn will impact the way in which disputes are resolved and evidence is administered.

Having said all that, there is one universal aspect of dispute resolution, and it is not what one might think. There is a misconception in the West that the fundamental political insight of the Enlightenment, and the strongest plank supporting modern western governments, has something to do with rights and obligations. Citations to Hobbes, Locke, and Rousseau are found in abundance in legal scholarship and underscore this point. While rights and obligations are important, the more fundamental insight of the Enlightenment was the epistemological revolution that there is a world external to our mind that may be known objectively through evidence; however, citations to the epistemological work of Locke, Berkeley, Hume, or even Kant for this proposition, are few and far between. This reverses the actual relationship of facts and rights/obligations. Facts are prior to and determinative of rights and obligations. Without accurate fact finding, rights and obligations are meaningless. Consider the simple case of ownership of the clothes you are wearing. Your ownership of those clothes allows you the "right" to possess, consume, and dispose of those assets, but suppose I demand that you return "my" clothes. That is, I insist that the clothes that you are wearing actually belong to me. What will you do? You will search for a decision-maker to whom you will present evidence that you bought, made, found, or were given the clothes in question, and, if successful in this effort, the decision-maker will indeed grant you those rights and impose upon me reciprocal obligations. The critical point is that those rights and obligations are dependent upon what facts are found and are derivative of them. The significance of this point cannot be overstated. Tying the rule of law to true states of the real world anchors rights and obligations in things that can be known and are independent of whim and caprice. This is why the ideas of relevance and materiality are so fundamentally important to the construction of a legal system. They tie the legal system to the bedrock of factual accuracy.

This point is truly universal. Neither rights or obligations, on the one hand, or policy choices on the other, can be pursued in the absence of knowledge of the actual, relevant states of affairs. Thus, even within the contingencies of ways of governing, we find a universal aspect of the law of evidence. Of course, how one might think that facts are most accurately or efficiently found, and what policies may offset the significance of factual accuracy, are matters of reasonable disagreement.

The Significance of Policy Issues: An enormous number of policy choices face the designer of a legal system. Some are consistent with the pursuit of factual accuracy, but many are in opposition to it. Note that I use the phrase "policy issues" to accompany all interests that society may pursue. It thus encompasses what some might call "value theory." However, not all the policies governments pursue are moral; many are quite practical and utilitarian. Indeed, maybe most policies governments pursue are practical and utilitarian. It is surely acceptable to make the distinction between moral and utilitarian policies, but they are parts of the larger category of interests governments pursue and can effectively be lumped together when thinking about the law of evidence. Another distinction that could be made, but that I do not make, is between the sources of policy issues. The source of some are just the standard questions that all governments face everywhere, that involve the ordinary exercise of what we call , misleadingly, in the United States, the police power—the power of the State to regulate issues affecting health, safety, and welfare. By contrast, the source of others are explicit constitutional provisions, whatever the form a constitution may take in any particular country. Some commentators sort out constitutional questions from other kinds of policy questions, which again is coherent. However, the distinction is not helpful to understanding the law of evidence, and thus I do not bother with making it. Evidence law does some things because of constitutional commitments, but at the highest level of generality that is no different than fashioning evidence law to pursue an interest that is not embedded in a constitutional document.

I now turn to many of the policy issues that must be accommodated by the law of evidence.

Pursuit of Factual Accuracy. One might reasonably suppose that natural reasoning processes based on innate epistemological capacities work reasonably well, and thus typically should be deferred to in the pursuit of factual accuracy. However, there may be recurring situations that lead people to error. In such a case, rules of evidence may attempt to correct for that systematic error. This explains FRE 403's authorization to exclude evidence when it may be misleading or unfairly prejudicial. It also underlies other rules, such as limitations on character and propensity evidence, and the requirement that witnesses testify from firsthand knowledge. The circumstances under which individuals systematically make errors probably is heavily dependent on culture.

The Value of Accuracy. Factual accuracy is surely the most significant desideratum, but it is by no means the only one. It has a cost, and the cost can sometimes be too high. A legal system overly preoccupied with factual accuracy may undermine the very social conditions that the legal system is trying to foster. A dispute worth only a dollar that would take a thousand dollars to litigate to a factually accurate conclusion perhaps should not be litigated. Such litigation may very well reduce overall social welfare and discourage private settlement of disputes. Where the limit is reached is difficult to say, of course, and surely depends on local views. I will say much more about this in my second lecture.

The Value of Incentives. Factual accuracy competes not just with cost but with other policies that a government reasonably may pursue. The list of such policies is long, and again culturally contingent. The law of privileges may foster and protect numerous relationships (spouses, legal, medical, spiritual, governmental, etc.). Litigation of an accident should not discourage reduction of risk (the subsequent repair rule). Perhaps settlement of disputes is preferred to their litigation, which leads to the exclusion of statements made during settlement talks. The encouragement of settlement is also a reason not to price litigation too low. The more the public subsidizes litigation, presumably the more of it there will be, and the less of private negotiation. There are still other policies that can be pursued. In the United States, we rest a vast body of exclusionary rules on the perceived need to regulate police investigative activities. Rules of evidence also can encourage or discourage certain kinds of law suits from being brought. Again in the United States, we went through a period in which we thought rape victims were being overly discouraged from reporting crimes against them, and one response was to create rules of evidence that reduced the abuse at trial that such individuals may have been exposed to.

General Considerations of Fairness may also influence the law of evidence, although the precise effect of this variable is often hard to sort out from more overtly utilitarian motivations. Some think that the limit on unfairly prejudicial evidence reflects not just the concern about accuracy but the concern about humiliation, as is also the case with rape relevancy rules. The limits on prior behavior and propensity evidence reflect in part a belief that an individual should not be trapped in the past. The hearsay rule to some extent reflects the values of the right to confront witnesses against you.

The Risk of Error. A mistake free legal system is not possible. It is critically important to recognize that two types of errors can be made—a wrongful verdict for a plaintiff (including a conviction of an innocent person), which we call a Type I or false positive error, and a wrongful verdict for a defendant (including an acquittal of a guilty person), which we call a Type II or false negative error—and resource allocation and other decisions will affect the relationship between these two types of errors.

Reasonable people can disagree as to the significance of these two types of errors, but both must be taken into account in the construction of the legal system. In the United States, we structure civil litigation to attempt to both equalize the errors made on behalf of plaintiffs and defendants and to reduce the total number of errors. The criminal justice process, by contrast, is designed to reduce the possibility of wrongful conviction at the admitted expense of making more mistakes of wrongful acquittals. Although the matter is complicated, these perspectives explain in large measure the preponderance standard in civil cases and the standard of proof beyond reasonable doubt in criminal cases. In civil cases, an error either way results in identical misallocation of resources. If the plaintiff wrongly wins a $500 verdict, a citizen (the defendant) wrongly must part with $500. If the defendant wrongly wins a verdict that he or she does not owe $500, a citizen (the plaintiff) wrongly will be deprived of $500 that rightfully he or she should possess. These two cases are identical analytically. In criminal cases, by contrast, in the United States we view a wrongful conviction as a more serious harm than a wrongful acquittal, and thus make convictions hard to obtain by requiring proof beyond reasonable doubt. We do so even though it is possible (but by no means certain) that a side effect will be increased numbers of false acquittals and an overall increase in the total number of errors. Again, I will say much more about this tomorrow, and I will cast some doubt upon how well these simple ideas work out in practice.

Miscellaneous Policy Questions. There are many other contingent questions that must be answered by the architect of a legal system. Most importantly are those allocating responsibility over the various actors in the legal drama. These involve such questions as whether trials should be episodic events as is somewhat more prevalent in Europe or single shot events as in the United States, how much discretion should the trial judge have and how much should the parties control the process, what is the relationship between trial judges and appellate judges. Should there be trial de novo in the appellate court or is it limited to review of legal errors? Are small civil cases different from large commercial cases in ways that justify different treatment? What about criminal cases?

The matters discussed above indicate the breath of the foundations and implications of the law of evidence, and I now wish to make four analytical points, three of which are critical to understanding the foundations and implications of any body of law, and the fourth of which is critical to thinking clearly about the law of evidence. They involve:

1. The distinction between the law on the books and the law in action;

2. The relationship between procedural and evidentiary law, on the one hand, and substantive on the other law, and in particular how procedural and evidentiary law are in fact quite interrelated with rather than distinct from substantive law;

3. Economics, or as we say in the United States, there is no free lunch. If you use a dollar (or yuan) here for one purpose you cannot use it there for a different purpose.

4. Whether trials the ideal or instead are perverse. Is the legal system designed to encourage trials or settlement? What should it be designed for?

I will discuss in turn each of these variables and their significance.

1. <u>The law on the books; the law in action</u>. Constitutions are enacted, legislation is passed, executives issue orders and directives, courts decide, and one would think that the rest of us more or less obey. Unfortunately (or perhaps fortunately), life is not so simple. When constitutions or laws are

adopted in any multi-party decision making process, there will be multiple understandings of what the legal language connotes. Some legislators may vote for the passage of a law even though they do not believe it goes far enough in its coverage (or even though it goes too far); others may vote against it for just the same reasons. There also may be serious disagreements as to precisely what a particular provision is supposed to mean or do. One person may think the legal language has one implication, and someone else may think it has a different implication. Statutory language in the abstract often will not resolve the meaning of those phrases. Compounding the difficulty even further, legal language is often deliberately left vague because of the inability to come to agreement as to precisely what it should say or because of the omnipresent inability to anticipate all possible scenarios in which a particular problem might arise.

In the United States, there is the added complexity of separation of powers. It is the legislature's job to enact law, including in most states the law of evidence, but it is the courts' job to put that law into effect. The judges may have different understandings of the implication of the language adopted by the legislature, and their institutional concerns will differ as well. Thus, the application of the law by the courts may differ from the idealized meaning of the law intended by a legislature or an individual legislator.

The law of evidence has one potentially unique structural aspect that exacerbates the problem of indefiniteness. Aspects of the law of evidence are rule-like in the sense of providing necessary and sufficient conditions for the operation of a rule, but important parts of the law of evidence simply allocate responsibility and discretion precisely because the relevant issue is too complicated for rule-like treatment. Perhaps the single most important aspect of the law of evidence—relevancy—has precisely this attribute. It is impossible to state *a priori* the necessary and sufficient conditions for the relevance of most evidence presented at any particular trial. Those determinations will necessarily be contingent on the unique characteristics of each trial, and it is literally impossible to articulate them in advance (how could we identify when a presently unknown witness will lie about a presently unknown topic?). Thus, the law of evidence vests responsibility in someone—party or judge—to determine what evidence to offer, and does so under quite general guidelines. In the United

States, relevant evidence is defined as evidence that may increase or decrease the probability of some material fact being true, but virtually no effort is made to specify when the condition may be met.

One last factor that may result in the law on the books being different from the law in action is that some areas of evidence law must try to accommodate quite opposed principles or impulses. This can result in part of the law making a promise and another part subverting that promise. Two important examples of this from American evidence law are the hearsay rule and the rule against character and propensity evidence. The hearsay rule promises to exclude hearsay, but there has been a unidirectional growth of the exceptions to the hearsay rule for centuries. In civil cases, the promise of the exclusion of hearsay is rarely redeemed, and even in criminal cases hearsay is routinely admitted. Similarly, the law of evidence promises the exclusion of character and propensity evidence but then creates broad avenues of admission.

2. The Relationship Between Substantive Law and Procedural Law. Substantive law is sometimes conceived of as quite distinct from evidentiary (and procedural) law, but this is misleading, for the two are in a complex and interactive relationship. This has become particularly clear, and is the subject of interesting legal research, in the United States due to the significance of the point for the protection of constitutional rights, but the point applies to general evidentiary matters as well. The decisions of the United States Supreme Court extending and enforcing individual rights have been viewed as imposing considerable constraints on the police and prosecutors, yet the legal system has not been greatly disturbed by these rulings. These systems are dynamic and infinitely adaptable and thus can and do respond to changes in unpredictable and astonishingly varied ways. Thus, "reform" to a dynamic process often cannot be imposed unproblematically through discrete measures that will have only the desired and no unintended consequences. One important aspect of this dynamic phenomenon is that legitimate substantive changes can blunt virtually any procedural innovation that emerges from courts or law reformers.

An example of this point in the United States involves the fourth amendment limit on unreasonable searches and seizures. Suppose the police want to stop cars to do cursory inspections for criminality, but courts rule that the fourth amendment requires that the police have probable cause that a crime has been committed before a car can be stopped. All the legislature need do to make this judicial command a practical nullity is to expand the criminal law to include more rigorous driving requirements. The legislature can essentially make it next to impossible to drive without violating a criminal statute (such as crossing the center line, driving too closely to the car ahead of you, not putting your turning light indicator on early enough or too early, etc.) . If the legislature passes such laws, the police will be able to stop virtually any car by following it until the driver violates one of statutes regulating driving. The stop will be on "probable cause" but the legislation will have expanded dramatically the potential sources of probable cause, thus subjecting everyone to being stopped by the police whenever the police decide to do so, notwithstanding the attempt by the courts to forbid just that process. Similarly, if the government cannot seize certain information without probable cause, it can often instead require that individuals keep records of the information it wants and divulge those records to the government.

This point generalizes across evidentiary and procedural law. The most obvious example is materiality, which is directly determined by the substantive law, but the point goes deeper than that. By changing the elements of causes of actions, legislatures can make recovery under those causes of actions easier or more difficult. Whether oral testimony concerning the meaning of contractual provisions is allowed—what we call the "parol evidence rule" in the United States—obviously impacts the evidentiary regime. Equally obviously, the statute of frauds that requires certain contracts to be in writing dominates normally evidentiary principles, as does *res ipsa loquitur* in tort law.

Just as substantive law can affect the evidentiary process, evidence law can affect substantive law. The examples are legion. Rules of exclusion typically increase and rules of admission typically decrease the costs of litigation. As privileges expand, the cost of litigating and thus enforcing rights goes up in most instances. The ready admission of hearsay makes proof easier (although at the same time perhaps less reliable), and so on. Discovery rules can dramatically affect parties' incentives to create and search for evidence. Individual rules like the rape relevancy rules can affect the ease with which cases may be proven. Allocation of burdens of proof can encourage or discourage the bringing of certain causes of action, and so on. Again, we will spend most of tomorrow talking in greater depth about such matters.

There is one other interaction between substantive and evidence law that should be noted. In the United States, but perhaps not in China, evidence underlies everything the lawyer does, since in the United States everything can collapse into litigation. Wills, criminal matters (sentencing based in part on what's in record), anti-trust, commercial work, everything. Evidence bears upon every other legal field, and the worst case scenario of every legal transaction is the collapse into litigation. In litigation, a crucial variable will be what can be proven. Thus every attorney, no matter how remote from the courtroom, must take the courtroom into account, which means taking the rules of evidence into account prior to litigation so that if litigation ensues the necessary facts can be proven. Good records must be kept and be in an admissible format, for example.

3. Economics. We have a saying in the United States that "There is no such thing as a free lunch," which means that, if someone "invites" you to lunch, he probably wants to talk to you about something or may expect a favor in return. Whatever one thinks about this in general, it is literally true for government that "there is no such thing as a free lunch." Governments are constrained by their economies, and economies are finite. Of the many valuable things that, in theory, governments could do, they are able to choose to do only some of them. If resources are used for one purpose, there are simply fewer resources left to do other things, and there are in total too many different "things" to do to fund them all. Similarly, private resources are finite, whereas the ways in which they can be consumed are almost infinite.

In thinking about the litigation system, the finite limitation of resources is critically important. Difficult choices need to be made about the allocation of resources across the whole range of governmental interests, including the operation of the legal system. Again, let me give a dramatic example. Investments in the criminal justice process obviously compete with investments in other social goods. If government provides more judges, police, or funds counsel for poor people, less resources will be available for economic development or medical research, or whatever. The police face an aspect of this problem daily. Faced with a surplus of crime, they must constantly decide how to allocate their limited resources. Should the police patrol this part of the city or that part? Should they concentrate on economic crimes, crimes of violence, or fraud? Investments within the criminal justice process likewise compete with other investments in different parts of that same process. If government provides more judges, perhaps it can provide fewer police.

The implications of economics extend further and are dramatic. Consider for example an issue of importance to you in China right now—the right to counsel. If the active involvement of defense counsel increases the total time a trial takes, obviously there can be fewer trials, as the total time available to try cases is finite. In general, as the average cost of a case increases, the total number of cases that can be tried decreases. That in turn means that effective counsel will either reduce the number of convictions that occur or will cause the government to substitute other means of enforcement.

Analogous but subtly different issues exist with respect to civil cases. The optimal amount of civil litigation may differ from the optimal amount of criminal litigation, although the matter is complicated. If the costs of litigating civil cases go down, one would predict that the amount of litigation would increase. There is a sense in which this is a public good; indeed, both in your country and mine the inaccessibility, cost, and delay of the litigation process are often identified as problems to be rectified. Yet, they have positive effects as well, in particular through their encouragement of private resolution of disputes. Indeed what to some seems shocking, in the United States even most criminal cases are resolved through what is essentially private negotiation between an accused and the government that results in a plea agreement.

Which leads me to my fourth point.

4. Trials as the Ideal v. Trials as the Embodiment of Social Breakdown. As I have tried to indicate, the implications of the law of evidence go far beyond trial itself. Nonetheless, there is a close association between the law of evidence and trials both in fact and in the public mind. And trials in the west are often idealized and glorified. In part this is because of the role of juries in both our political theory and our self-conception; in part it is because of the glorifi-

cation (well deserved, let me add) of the rule of law, with trials embodying its public vindication. To what extent this is true in China, I do not know. It is obvious, though, that evidence law is written with an eye toward its use at trial, and consequently how one conceives of a trial may affect what one thinks are the optimal rules of evidence.

The relationship between one's conception of trials and the law of evidence holds no matter what one's conception of trials happens to be. If one accepts the idealized, media glossed view of trials in the United States, one would want to fashion rules of evidence that further the purposes of the public vindication of the rule of law and human rights. Great latitude should then be given to criminal defendants and to the "underdog" in civil litigation. Rights of allocution should be protected, and so on.

But it is not so clear that trials should be glorified in this way, even if (as I believe is true) the rule of law should be. For all their drama, trials reflect a break down in the rule of law. They occur because there have been accusations of wrong doing—civil or criminal—and the parties have not been able to come to an agreement to resolve their dispute. Trials thus are in a sense pathological. They may consume resources that could be better spent in more productive ways (although again getting the facts right one way or the other is critically important to the conditions of flourishing). At a still higher conceptual level, there can be reasonable disagreements about the ontology—the nature—of disputes themselves. Are disputes primarily between individuals? Or do they have a social aspect?

I raise these questions here not to answer them but to further illuminate the depth and profundity of the questions that lurk under the deceptively straight forward label "the theoretical foundations and implications of evidence."

I will now try to sum up the various considerations alluded to above. In my opinion, "the theoretical foundations and implications of evidence" pose the following five sets of issues and questions:

1. In its most straight forward manifestation evidence is the study of dispute resolution, with the focus being the interaction and regulation of the various actors in the drama: trial judge, jurors/lay assessors, attorneys, par-

ties, and witnesses (both lay and expert) . The rules of evidence structure the relationships between these individuals, but the rules are themselves relatively rough distillations of a complex set of factors, and that set of factors contains the real "foundations and implications" of evidence. The rules of evidence are reflective of those underlying ideas.

2. How one constructs trials, and thus the rules of evidence one fashions to facilitate trials, is a function of one's beliefs concerning one of the fundamental questions of human thought and philosophy—what does it mean to know something? A trial is an epistemological event at which claims of knowledge are advanced, considered, rejected, accepted. Philosophy began with systemic thought on what it means to think and to know, and it remains the dominant question today. Modern relativist philosophies are driven by a fundamental skepticism, for example, as is the desire for revelation reflected in those philosophers with a religious orientation. But this is not the only tradition. There is the spectacularly successful example of modern science; and in order to think clearly about the legal process, one must locate one's thoughts somewhere in or near this spectrum. Whether you think truth of historical facts is obtainable will determine in large measure your view of particular evidence rules. Is there a difference between an "historical" reconstruction of facts, and a "social" one? Indeed, is it even coherent to talk about "knowing" the past? If not, what role should trials play, what values pursued? To what extent should fact finding be located in randomly selected fact finders, and to what extent should the "expertise" of the judges be relied upon? What are the risks of either approach. To what extent should rules of evidence favor one class of litigants over another? And so on.

3. There is another fundamental question: what the purpose of trials is. The typical response has something to do with fact finding, and as I have tried to make clear that typical respond has enormous significance. But, are trials like science? How do they differ? The analogy to science is somewhat tenuous. Legal decision making cannot defer judgment until more information is collected. Also, the judgment to be made is what actually happened rather than what the underlying universal laws might be. Most tellingly, perhaps, there is no organized body of knowledge that is applicable to the typical case, as there

is in science. To the contrary, the fact finder has to import the necessary background knowledge for decision. If on reflection trials do not seem a lot like science (at least some types of science), are they like history? The focus of history is on facts, but as a means, generally, of greater understanding. At trials, understanding is largely irrelevant (except as a matter of persuasion) .

4. But what about all the other purposes that trials may serve? What about the economic aspects of trials? Not only the parties but the lawyers, the judges, the court reporters, and all the court personnel have vested economic interests in trials. What about the symbolic purposes of trials? The political purposes? And so on. There is an extraordinarily complex set of issues that inform the nature of trials. In light of all this, what might be the purposes of the rules of evidence? And again, how do the answers to these questions affect how trials should be constructed? To what extent should trials look like free markets; to what extent should they be regulated by the government? Which model is likely to foster efficient truth-seeking, and why? What other values than efficiency and truth seeking are or should be at stake?

5. Evidence law does not just structure fact finding; it also create incentives of various kinds. How does the significance of accurate fact finding compete with that of other social values?

Evidence and evidence law are not normally thought of as among the many factors that enter into the pursuit of a just and fair society, but as I have tried to show they are critical to such a pursuit. In the West, this neglect of the significance of evidence rests, somewhat ironically, on just how important evidence is to the bedrock foundation of our institutions. It is so important that it is just taken for granted. You in China who are experimenting with different forms of civil organization cannot be so blase about the matter. Without accurate fact finding, and thus without a rational law of evidence, all other pursuits are made exceedingly difficult if not impossible.

刑事诉讼的法理和政治基础*

张保生　李哲　艾静　译**

今天，我非常荣幸受邀来给大家做演讲。我要感谢诉讼法学研究中心的樊崇义主任，也要感谢我的学生、中国政法大学副校长张保生教授安排我来中国访问。张保生教授曾到美国西北大学在我的指导下系统学习了美国法律，特别是诉讼法和证据法。我们很珍惜他在芝加哥和我们一起度过的美好时光，并盼望他能再回来，同时欢迎中国继续派其他教授来西北大学和我们一起从事研究工作。我尤其为他取得的学术成就感到自豪，并感谢他在翻译我的证据法著作方面付出的努力。

我愿继续为中美两国人民搭建合作交流的桥梁。中国和西方在21世纪将会有更加密切的合作和交流。这两种伟大的文明将共同决定未来百年发展的很多事情。中国在经济方面，到本世纪中期将与欧盟和美国比翼齐飞。中国的大学也正在成为世界级的教学和学术中心，更多的创新和改革将在中国发生。身在美国的我们对这些发展感到非常震惊，也非常高兴，尽管这些对我们构成了挑战。我们之所以为此感到高兴，是因为我们坚信，在法治环境下的这种竞争不但会使你们和我们达到双赢，也将是全人类的福祉。最重要的是，我们共同的合作将成为世界和平与发展的关键，它将为世界法治奠定基础，并把法治已经带给你们和我们的福祉播向世界。

我刚才提到“法治”。我们认为，法治是美国在各个领域取得发展的关键。法治的核心内容是：(1) 法律标准以一种清晰易懂的语言预先制定；(2) 司法裁判独立（独立于立法权和行政权）；(3) 任何人，包括政府，均受法律约束。把法律看作是对选择权和行为的束缚这样一种传统观点是错误的；法律明确了行为的合法限制而得以彰显，因而使人们在那些限制中合作共事。这反过来又建设性地解放了个人，使其释放出创造力；法治保护了人们消费、使用和处置自己先前通过自觉生产所提供的生产物的权利。我目前对中国法律的研究仅处于起步阶段，所以，对你们所面对的问题我不敢妄称为专家。不过，我也理解

* 根据艾伦教授2005年在中国政法大学的演讲稿翻译，发表时略有删节。本译文原载于《证据科学》，第15卷，2007年第1、2期合刊。

** 李哲、艾静，中国政法大学硕士研究生。

你们目前对法治的重要性所给予的高度重视，你们感到也许需要一些改变，并且正在通过对法律制度某些方面的反思而努力取得更大的成就。毫无疑问，法治原则对于司法程序是至关重要的；实际上，它应当成为其规定性特征。同样清楚的是，如果不进一步深化和强化法治，司法程序方面的任何改革都没有意义。

然而，在这里我并不想告诉你们什么需要改革，应当进行何种改革。我并不完全了解你们的法律制度或改革需要。我只想和大家讨论一些别的问题，我想讨论刑事程序的基础问题。尽管讨论将集中于刑事程序，但我要说的许多东西也与民事诉讼有关，因而更一般地涉及法治的基础问题。我将讨论一些决定应当采用何种刑事程序的因素，它应当如何被贯彻，等等。我想和大家谈谈，在美国这些因素的复杂性以及它们的含义。然而，我首先还是想简要讨论一下证据法。在一定意义上，证据法在任何诉讼制度中都是最重要、最基础的方面；确切地说，它是法治的基石。

证据法对于一种诉讼制度来说是基础性的并构成法治的基石，这个理念乍一看似乎令人不解。实际上，证据法对于任何一个创设了权利或义务的制度都是基础性的。权利和义务取决于准确的事实认定；如果没有准确的裁判，权利和义务根本就没有意义。我将通过一个简单的例子来论证这一观点。

在座各位都会主张对某物的所有权，比如大家穿的衣服。我对自己系的这条领带拥有所有权，那意味着，我有权按照自认为适当的方式占有、使用和处置这条领带。这是私人财产所有“权”的标准含义。然而，假设某人要争夺我对这条领带的所有权，这会有什么情况发生呢？在所有文明国度，该争端将提交给没有利害关系的裁判者——法官，在美国也许是一个陪审团——来解决，他们将决定，是我还是别人有权占有、使用和处置这条领带。这个决定将根据提供给裁判者的证据而作出。因此，当我对这条领带宣示所有权时，我实际上是在宣示，如果我的所有权受到质疑，我将能够向裁判者提供这样的证据，后者将据此断定这条领带属于我，我实际上拥有占有、消费和处置它的权利。

正如我们在这个例子中所看到的，权利和义务取决于事实。事实是先于权利和义务而存在的，因而更具有基础性。没有准确的事实认定，权利和义务就会变得毫无意义。当然，正是证据法决定了事实得以确定的方式。因此，确切地说，权利和义务取决于证据法。

由于证据法的这种基础性质，在美国，我们没有把证据法区分为刑事诉讼的和民事诉讼的证据法典。我们有一部适用于任何司法事实认定的证据法。显然，刑事和民事案件可能遇到不同的问题，因此，某些证据规则的适用性更侧重于刑事法律或民事法律领域。但总体上，我们的证据法是统一的。统一的目的是促进准确的事实认定，因而相关性被赋予了一种广义。只要证据是相关的，当事方就可予以提供，除非受到排除规则的限制。排除规则旨在促进某种价值，这些价值所具有的重要意义足以证明排除相关性证据是正当的。配偶交流特免权和律师—委托人特免权就是这方面的例子。还有一些其他的例子，如事后补救措施，旨在鼓励个人采取减少损害风险的行为。总的来说，我们的证据法旨在让负有证明义务的当事人决定使用什么证据，以促进民事和刑事案件的自由证明制度。

如果大家感兴趣的话，我可以在提问和回应阶段继续详细讨论有关美国证据法的问题。下面概括一下我对证据法的观点，正如我开始讨论时所谈到的，它与刑事诉讼法的不同之处在于，证据法具有普适性（universal）。它涉及人们如何认识外界环境的问题。逻辑、认识论以及感知材料在中国和美国并没有什么差别。两种文化间的唯一相异之处，是不得不认真对待当事人愿意接受的采纳全部相关证据之一般原则的例外。这些决定可能容易通过地方性特色而得知。然而重要之点在于，我认为，证据法所处理的知识和理性，在很大程度上包含着普适性而非地方性的内容。

在美国，证据法不仅与刑事程序有一定联系，证据法还同样适用于刑事和民事案件。联邦宪法蕴含了几个仅仅适用于刑事案件的排除规则，这是通行于刑事或民事法律领域的证据规则具有特殊性的主要例子。它们非常著名，你们可能听说过的“米兰达规则”就是一个例子，宪法第 4 条修正案关于非法搜查和扣押的证据排除规则也是一个例子。我听说你们正在考虑从其他国家吸收借鉴某些诸如此类的规则和程序，也许你们应当考虑这样做。然而，应当记住，这些根植于其他国家法律制度和文化的诉讼程序，也许与你们自己国家的程序有很大差别。

关于这一点，即刑事诉讼法具有地方性，而证据法具有普适性，也许尚未得到足够的强调。其他国家的人们通过刑法所追求的目的，在某些方面（尽管肯定不是所有方面）也许不同于你们国家所追求的目的。不同民族的历史和文化是不同的。因此，我既赞赏你们知难而进评价自己的制度，同时也提醒大家注意，为了清楚和准确地看到自己正在做的事情和为什么这样做，必须首先认真考察你们自己的做法，然后再通过考察其他国家的制度环境来审视来自别国的经验。有许多引进别国刑事诉讼程序而悲惨失败的例子，原因是忽视了社会文化和历史方面的差别，更重要的原因在于刑事诉讼程序体现了不同的制度安排和设想，其中一种程序中的一套含义完全不同于另一种程序的。[①]

我进一步解释一下这个问题。“刑事诉讼法”不能仅仅从成文法、法典或者美国法院的判决来理解。虽然这些确实是构成刑事诉讼的重要方面，但却不是全部。比如，如果某人考察了美国各种刑法典，就会看到美国检察官无处不在的极大的自由裁量权：检察官可以决定什么样的案件追诉，什么样的不予追诉；什么事情予以指控，什么不予指控；谁被调查和指控，谁被完全按照法律来起诉，谁可以进行辩诉交易。[②] 同样，如果仔细考察支配着美国刑事审前程序模式的重大宪法性刑事诉讼案件，就会发现，无论是州还是联邦立法机关都无权通过定义犯罪的立法权而使长久以来形成的判例失效。我可以不断扩展这些实例，目的是强调，研究美国“刑事诉讼法”，不能仅仅考察成文法律和案例，它还要求深入了解美国的历史、文化、经济以及其他影响因素。

再谈谈“政府”问题。美国关于“政府”作用的观念是，政府的存在是为了创造和维系个人能够按自己的道德要求据以生存发展的条件。政府是服务于民的，而非民众服务于政府。当然，这是所谓“自由民主”的本质，其基本构想来自欧洲启蒙哲学家。美国的经验进一步丰富了这个体系，并强化了对中央集权政府的不信任。在美国历史形成过程中，政府不仅被视为社会遇到问题的解决办法，它还被看作是问题本身的一部分，因而要在很多方面、以许多不同的方式使其受到约束、限制和制约。[③] 这不仅反映了我们从欧洲祖先那里移植过来的政府三权（立法权、执法权和司法权）分立的思想，而且我们还通过将宪法规定之最终解释权和成文法解释权赋予法官以及确立法官终身制，赋予司法权至高无上的权威，而丰富了三权分立的思想。当然，这就是我们的法院所拥有的著名的“司法审查权”[④]。

我们并不满足于宪法在形式上通过分权对政府行使权力施加的结构性限制，我们的民众坚持一系列的个人权利来对抗政府权力，并以“权利法案”（美国宪法前 10 条修正案）的专门条款为基础，使公民享有“正当法律程序”

① 一个很好的例子是，欧洲各国在引进对抗制程序的某些方面所做的努力。德国在 19 世纪，意大利在 20 世纪。

② 例如，参见 United States v. Cox，342 F. 2d 167，cert denied sub nom. Cox v. Hauberg，381 U. S. 935（1965）。

③ 这一点很复杂。相较于（1781 年制定的）《邦联条款》，《美国宪法》在一定程度上是为了建立一个更强大的中央政府。然而，最重要的问题是要制约中央政府的集权趋势。除了本文中介绍的几种方法外，原计划中的核心在于设立一种联邦体系，其中各州在许多方面依然保持自治权，而宪法赋予联邦的仅为维持中央政府有效运行的有限权力。

④ Marbury v. Madison，5 U. S.（1 Cranch）137（1803）.

和“平等法律保护”[5] 的权利。所有这些法律条文都发挥着很大的作用；特别重要的是，这些规定使定罪非常艰难。个人有权受到从大范围人口中挑选出来的、由非政府雇员组成的大陪审团对其被起诉进行审查（尽管某些州没有使用大陪审团）[6]，由外行组成的不同的陪审团只有在“确信无疑”的基础上才能认定其是否有罪[7]；任何个人都享有不受强迫自证其罪的权利[8]；政府不得无理搜查和扣押[9]；被告有权传唤有利于己方的证人并对控方证人进行交叉盘问[10]；以及在犯罪所发生的州或地区被告人从其被正式起诉起在相当短的时间内被公开审判的权利；[11] 等等。避免双重危境的权利，也从根本上限制了政府对一个人的特定犯罪只能定罪一次。

对个人的保护甚至更加完善。刑法必须易于理解，否则就会被法院以违宪性模糊而拒绝适用。美国法吸收了普通法的“从宽原则”[12]。这是一项解释原则，即当某一刑法规定可以有两种不同的解释时，法院将采用对个人被告有利的解释。这并未穷尽对被告人所有的保护。[13]

然而，这些个人权利并不是从人们能够想象到的权利体系中随便挑选出来的，应该说这些权利是与宪法相统一的，因为它们是构成政府和民众关系的一元化观点的有机组成部分。这种观点的核心是，政府必须是有限的，政府权力的集权化趋向应当受到抵制，刑事定罪的道路上必须有艰难险阻，并且在很大程度上要得到民众的同意（通过大陪审团和小陪审团成员的作用）。

我所描述的政府概念兼有善恶两个方面，在这里我无意对其加以赞美或批评，而只是对其进行解释。只有在这种背景下，人们才能理解美国宪法中诸如聘请辩护律师等阐述个人权利的分散规定。人们不能孤立地看待一个程序要求并大谈其一致性，而必须在一定的语境中把握它，在其与基本概念的关系中或

⑤ 美国宪法第5、14条修正案（U. S. Const. amend. V，XIV，§ 1.）。

⑥ 美国宪法第5条修正案（U. S. Const. amend. V.）。

⑦ 美国宪法第6条修正案和关于温希普案由［U. S. Const. amend. VI and In re Winship，397 U. S. 358 (1970)］。

⑧ 美国宪法第5条修正案（U. S. Const. amend. V.）。

⑨ 美国宪法第4条修正案（U. S. Const. amend. IV.）

⑩ 美国宪法第6条修正案（U. S. Const. amend. VI）。

⑪ 美国宪法第6条修正案（U. S. Const. amend. VI）。

⑫ 例如，参见圣扎迦利·普赖斯：《作为结构原则的从宽原则》，载《福特汉姆法律评论》，第72卷，2004年，第885页（阐释了该原则正在逐渐受到冷落）。

⑬ 例如，美国宪法第5条修正案的避免双重危险的保护，美国宪法第8条修正案禁止过量保释金、过量罚金以及“残酷和不同寻常”的惩罚。Brady v. Maryland，373 U. S. 83 (1963)，要求该州检控方披露有利于被告的证据。

者与那些旨在实施或表达的概念体系的关系中审视它。

让我来概括一下，当人们谈论“刑事程序改革”的时候，这个论题实际上属于法理学或政治学问题。法治的基本概念、政府机关的角色及其与民众的关系，是《美国权利法案》的题中应有之义，而不是从中派生出来的东西。

在刑事程序的形成过程中，还需要考虑诸如社会、文化和政治等因素及其影响。在美国，比如我们经常提到“隐私权”，这个措辞是很模糊的，但它至少涉及三个不同的意思：（1）在个人隐私领域的排他权，包括政府在内，这是“隐私权”的本质；（2）为自己和家庭作出选择的权利，比如目前在美国争议很大的堕胎权，更好的表达是“自治”；（3）受到包括政府在内的他人以一定方式的善待权，这确实涉及“尊严”利益。这些个人利益中的每一项都与作为其镜像的公共利益充满张力。在决定刑法及其执行的范围时，社会必须在这些相互影响和冲突的利益之间作出选择。

我的第一个观点可以概括为，刑事程序不能与其周围因素隔绝开来而被孤立地加以看待，而实际上，它正是源于那些关于政府性质、政府与民众的适当关系等具有深远意义的观点，以及关于个人利益的性质等深刻的哲学观点。人们不能抽象地看待“刑事程序”还有第二个原因。这不仅是由于刑事司法制度的各个组成部分构成了一个动态过程，而且同样重要的是，事物并非总是它们表面上看起来的那个样子。在我的《刑事诉讼概论》[14] 一书中，我和合著者提出了一个学习美国刑事诉讼法的方案，即为了理解美国刑事司法制度的实际运作，不仅要了解“法律”的规范命令，还要深入研究上面简略论及的法理和政治问题，至少有下面四个方面：

1. 书本上的法律与实践中的法律之间的差别；

2. 程序法与实体法之间紧密的相互关系，特别是事实上程序法是实体法的载体，而非我们习惯上所认为的相反的情况；

3. 一般的历史，特别是种族关系和种族歧视问题；

4. 经济因素，美国有一句谚语，“世上没有免费的午餐”，就是说，如果你把一美元（或一元人民币）用于这一目的，那就不能再用于其他目的。

下面逐一讨论这些因素及其意义。

1. 书本上的法律与实践中的法律。宪法是制定的，立法是通过的，执法是发布命令或指令，法院是作出决定，人们还可以思考我们多多少少所服从的其他东西。不幸或有幸的是，生活并非如此简单。在宪法或法律的制定过程中

⑭ 罗纳德·J·艾伦等：《刑事诉讼概论》，2版，2005年。

（比如很普通的对宪法的投票或者一个立法机关投票表决通过某个法律），对于法律语言的言外之意总有多种理解。某个立法者可能投票赞成一个法案中的某一段内容，尽管他们并不认为整个法案有多大价值（甚至认为根本没有什么价值）；而其他人可能基于同样的理由而投反对票。也许还存在对于某些规定究竟所指什么或所干什么的理解严重不一致的情况。一个人可能认为法律语言是这种含义，而另一个人却理解为不同的含义。例如，在美国，对于宪法第 14 条修正案的正当程序条款与权利法案、美国宪法前 10 条修正案之间的关系，就存在尖锐的分歧。[15] 抽象的成文法或宪法语言往往无法解决这些短语的含义。

困难还不止于此，法律语言常常故意留下含糊之处，因为对于它究竟应当如何精确表述不能达成一致意见，或者由于对具体问题可能出现的所有情形一般不能预见。来自美国宪法的一个例子是，第 8 条修正案的神圣但却是模棱两可的语言：不可强加残酷的或非同寻常的惩罚。虽然完美无缺，但究竟什么使一种惩罚变得残酷和非同寻常？这段话在 1791 年被通过的时候，其语言所具有的含义，如何适用于其从未预见到的新的发展？对这种问题可能不存在现成的答案。

即使法律规定的语言十分清楚，立法者也可能不执行自己制定的法律，就像美国总统和各州州长们所做的那样。因此，他们的解释，可能对于一个法律规定的执行来说是至关重要的。撇开语义这个语言学问题，还有更深层的问题。执法者也许不能完全分享立法机关所持的关于贤明政策的同样观点，因此，执法者也许或多或少地热衷于各种法律的执行。即使执法者知道某项法律的含义，并且热心于贯彻执行，实际上也没有一种法律能够不折不扣地执行。这样做既缺乏足够资源，且实现任务的必要方法常常会违反其他规范。一个简单的例子是，我们两个国家尽管在根治犯罪方面投入了巨大资源，但犯罪还是在不断发生。如果不采用干涉隐私权或侵犯其他权利的方法，某些犯罪就不可能被根除。这些方法，可能被看作是比容忍某种程度的犯罪更邪恶的东西。总之，执法者必须在法律规定的含义、优先权和执行的方法之间作出选择。

书本上的法律与实践中的法律之间的第二个不同是，由于实践中的法律是从书本中翻译过来的，这使它变得比从政府最高层到大街上的警察之间的组织链条还要复杂。这里，对程序法的影响就更加明显了。在一个中间层次上，我已经提到过检察官在决定追诉什么案件的问题上具有很大的自由裁量权。任何立法都无法改变这一点，因为任何一项这样的立法，都没有足够的财力来对所

⑮ 《美国宪法》第 1～10 条修正案。

有潜在犯罪行为进行调查。这是一种未来判断。在这一点上，警察的情况和检察官的是一样的。在任何一个复杂社会，犯罪无处无时不在，虽然大都是一些低级的犯罪，但依然属于犯罪。人们走在芝加哥或者北京的大街上，会看到从乱丢垃圾到走路不遵守交通规则，再到交通事故，以及盗窃甚至袭击和斗殴等数不清的各种犯罪行为。[16] 警察和检察官一样拥有对何种犯罪予以调查的自由裁量权，无论是我们或者我们的法律理论喜欢还是不喜欢这一点。[17] 同样重要的是，警察所做的大部分事情并非都是法律的实际执行，也包括复杂情况的管理，比如疏导交通或者控制拥挤，等等。

这种自由裁量权在程序规则中有一些暗示。我举一个明显的例子。假设人们对调查活动施加限制，像美国宪法第 4 条修正案规定的免受无理搜查和扣押的权利。进一步假设，这种限制是通过排除规则而强制实行的，即禁止使用违反程序规则所获得的证据，该排除规则的原理当然根植于美国法律。

现在假设，警察和检察官把诸如卖淫等许多社会问题看作是管理的问题来加以解决，而不是当做犯罪来解决。在地方官员的眼里，“解决”这些问题的一种方式也许是侵扰那些涉及卖淫的人，使其知难而退，而不是追求将其定罪，这样就鼓励那些人“转移到”其他地区或城市去了。这种侵扰可能会造成大街上的人身威胁或暴力，也可能涉及逮捕等。重要的是，除非警察或检察官关注定罪问题，否则排除规则对于他们就没有影响。书本上的法律看起来至高无上，但实践中的法律却并非如此。

2. 实体法与程序法的关系。美国最高法院对个人权利加以拓展和强化的判例，被认为在很大程度上限制了警察和检察官的权利，但我们的法律制度还没有受到这些裁决的严重干扰。正如刚才谈到的一个原因是，只有当一个人真想起诉的时候，其起诉事项才会遇到程序性屏障。这就是制度动态性一般观点的实例，因此可以用各种无法预知的方式对变化作出不同的回应。如果认为对动态过程的“改革”可以毫无疑问地通过各种孤立的措施而得到渴望和预想的结果，那就大错特错了。恰恰相反，像刑事司法程序这样的人类制度是有机的，是不断适应环境而变革的，而且具有惊人的多样性。目前，最重要但却未得到正确评价的例子是，正统立法机关的变革，实际上可能挫伤来自法院和法律改革家的任何程序性改革。

⑯ 一些州将“乱穿马路”之类的交通违章定义为“违章”或“违例”，而非“重罪”或“轻罪”。但这些行为仍属于犯罪。

⑰ 参见罗纳德·J·艾伦：《警察和实体性规则制定：促进和谐与便利的原则》，载《警察和实体性规则制定：一个简短的反驳》。

这里我将宪法第 4 条修正案对无理搜查和扣押的限制作为例子。假设警察针对犯罪行为想要拦截一辆汽车进行快速检查，可是宪法第 4 条修正案所要求的法院规则是，警察对犯罪已经实施要有可能的根据才能对车辆进行拦截。所有立法机关要使该司法命令在实践中失效，就需要把刑事法律扩展到包括更严格的驾驶限制。立法机关可以使不违反刑事法律的驾驶在本质上达到不可能的地步（比如，越过中心线、车距太近、太迟或太早拨动转向指示灯等）。如果立法机关通过了这样的法律，那么警察实际上就可以按照这个法律拦截任何车辆，只要能抓住驾驶员违反了交通规则中的任何一项规定。这种拦截将根据“可成立理由”（probable cause），但立法将戏剧性地扩展可成立理由的渊源，因此，警察无论何时决定这样做，就都可以使任何人受到拦截，尽管法院试图禁止这种做法。同样，如果政府没有可成立的理由而不能查获一定信息的话，可能常用的替代性做法，就是要求个人保存其想要的记录并向政府披露。

总的来说，随着刑事法律的扩张，个人权利的实际保障逐渐被削弱了，而且这几乎成为在政府行政部门掌控中的专门事项。为了理解美国刑事审前程序如何实际运作，这是一定要考虑的因素。

3. 历史和种族平等的追求问题。历史对于理解任何现行制度所具有的意义都是显而易见的，我不占用时间来阐述什么是历史，该如何理解历史。普遍和显而易见的观点是，历史在一定程度上决定了现在的制度安排，美国的许多刑事诉讼法都是国家为消除种族主义影响而建立起来的。

4. 经济因素。美国商人的格言是：“世上没有免费的午餐。”就是说，如果另一个商人“邀请”你吃午饭，那他大概要和你谈某些事情，也许期望某种回报。不管人们怎么去想商界的事情，对政府来说，“世上没有免费的午餐”确实是一个真理。政府受到经济上的限制，反过来经济因素也是有限的。从理论上说，政府能够做许多有价值的事情，但实际上它们只能有选择性地来做其中一部分。如果资源都被用于某一目的的话，那就剩不下什么资源来做其他的事情了，但是却有许多不同的“事情”需要资金支持。

在考虑刑事司法制度的时候，资源有限性的限制是一个非常重要的考虑因素。当代社会的一个教训就是：没有哪一个社会能够根除犯罪。只不过更多的犯罪采取了不断变化的形式。关于这一点，一个最好但却有讽刺意味的例子是，随着资源被倾注于根治犯罪，其他形式的犯罪却雨后春笋般生长出来，比如渎职和贪污。而且，政府用来打击犯罪的手段也是受限的。民众对于侵犯性的犯罪调查手段的容忍也随文化不同而不同。还有，当代历史也一再清楚地表明，所有文化和社会都受到有效的限制，政府一旦超越这些限制就会招致人民的反对和抗议。因此，在政府关心的所有领域配置资源，包括犯罪调查和起诉，将是艰难的选择。犯罪及其调查需要被视为一个流畅和动态过程的组成部分，而非能够被完美控制的孤立实体。

我来提供一些例子。投资刑事司法过程显然与在其他社会物资领域的投资具有竞争关系。如果政府提供更多的法官、警察或者为穷人提供援助律师，那么用于经济发展或者医药研究等其他领域的资源就会减少。就像我之前谈到的，警察每天都会遇到这方面的问题。以有限的资源处理这么多的犯罪，结果就是有些犯罪得不到处理，因此他们必须不断决定如何配置有限的资源。警察是应该在城市的这个区域巡逻，还是在那个区域巡逻？他们是应该更关注经济犯罪、暴力犯罪，还是欺诈行为？在刑事司法领域的投资与在其他领域不同部分的投资的竞争关系是一样的。如果政府提供了更多的法官，那大概就只能提供更少的警察。

经济因素的影响甚至更远。最后再以聘请辩护律师的权利为例。伴随被告辩护律师对刑事审判程序的影响力的加大，每个案件的成本也不断增加。随着中等成本案件的增加，能够被审判的案件总数便减少了。如果辩护律师的积极介入增加了审判所花费的时间，显然审判的数量就可能减少，因为用于审理案件的总时间是有限的。

除了资源分配的最直接的问题之外，也许是更为深层的经济学观点是与刑事司法制度结构有关的，即关于错误的微观经济学。一个完全没有错误的刑事审判制度是不存在的。最重要的是承认可能犯两种不同类型的错误——使无辜的人被错误定罪和使有罪的人被错误地宣判无罪，而且，资源的配置将影响着这两类错误之间的关系。

理性人可能对这两种错误类型的意义存在分歧。在美国，我们建构刑事审判程序的目的，是以承认许多被错误宣判无罪的代价来使错误定罪的可能性最小化。在美国，我们认为，十个有罪的人被无罪释放比一个无辜的人被定罪要好得多。尽管事情很复杂，但这种观点却在很大程度上解释了为什么刑事案件适用“确信无疑”的高证明标准[18]，这也解释了被告人的辩护律师为何在美国被认为非常重要的另一个原因。高标准的证明和法律代理人虽然会使对有罪之人定罪变得更加困难，但却可以使无辜的人得到保护。[19]

以经济学的视角来观察刑事程序，强调自由和安全交替换位的困难，这也

⑱ 参见罗纳德·J·艾伦：《对说服责任和贝叶斯定理裁决规则的澄清：对凯教授的回应》。

⑲ 然而，有另一种相关经济学观点非常关注制裁的威慑作用。例如，参见理查德·A·波斯纳：《刑法的经济学理论》；加里·S·贝克：《犯罪和惩罚：一种经济学研究进路》。

许是贯穿我今天演讲的中心。现在该是做一个概括的时候了。我想说的是，今天我在这里演讲的目的不是赞扬或者批评你们或我们国家的制度，而是揭示一些在考虑这些重要问题时需要注意的重要因素，无论关注的问题是你们的体制改革还是理解我们的制度。在结束这个演讲的时候，我还想重申，在考虑我们两国的刑事司法制度的时候，我们该牢记它们是有机的整体，其中一部分的变化也许会对其他部分产生不知不觉的影响。例如，如果未提供辩护律师和进行有效辩护的话，审判的成本将会降低，但是这样却可能增加错误定罪方面的成本，反之亦然。因此，在思考你们期望的刑事审判程序类型的时候，也应该考虑我所讲到的这些重要问题。

最后，我想重申诉讼法典和证据法在一个关键方面的区别。诉讼法是本土化的，属于地方性知识；像实体法一样，它反映了时间、空间的特殊性。证据法是普适的；它是人类理性的产物，是人类精神实现认识和改造周围环境的目的的方式。确实存在某些限制民事或刑事审判的政策，这些政策通过我们称之为“证据规则”的东西可以得到促进。通常，这些排除规则以相反的方式对真相之有效证实的全部目的发挥着作用。我不知道是否应该向你们提供关于变化的意见，但是我愿意留给你们这样一种思想。在构建你们的证据法时，我推荐你们从普适性起步，然后再去解决从真相之有效证实原则出发的方法问题。如果你们这样做，我认为你们不久就会看到，证据法的大部分内容在人类所有的诉讼程序中都是相同的，只有极其微小的例外。

The Jurisprudential and Political Foundation of Criminal Procedure

Ronald J. Allen

I am honored and pleased to be asked to address you today. I would like to thank Dr. Fan of the Procedural Law Research Center. I would also like to thank my student, and now Vice President of China University of Political Science and Law, Prof. Baosheng Zhang, for arranging my trip to China. Prof. Baosheng Zhang studied various aspects of American law, in particular procedure and evidence law at Northwestern University with me. We were very glad to have had him with us in Chicago, and hope that he will return and that other professors from China will continue to study with us at Northwestern University. I am especially proud of his accomplishments, and grateful for his effort in translating my book on Evidence into Chinese.

I am also pleased to be here to continue to build bridges between the people of China and the United States. The twenty-first century will be characterized by ever increasing cooperation and interaction between China and the West. These two great civilizations will together determine much of the course of the next hundred years. Already China's economy is on target to match that of both the European Union and the United States by the middle of the century. Your universities are emerging world-class centers of teaching and learning. More and more innovation comes from Chinese inventors and entrepreneurs. We in the United States are impressed by these developments, and welcome them, even though they constitute a challenge to us. We welcome them because we firmly believe that competition within the rule of law will make both you and us better, and lead to advances that will benefit all mankind. Most importantly, it will be critical to world peace and prosperity for you and us to work together cooperatively, to lay the foundation for an international rule of law that will bring to the world the benefits the rule of law has brought to you and to us.

I just mentioned "the rule of law." We believe that the rule of law has been critical to the development of the United States in virtually every respect. The central ingredients of the rule of law are 1) legal standards are articulated in advance in clear and understandable language; 2) independent (of the legislature and executive authorities) adjudicate disputes; and 3) everyone, including the government, is bound by the law. The conventional view of law as constraining choice and behavior is false; law liberates by making the legitimate limits of action clear, thus allowing people to work together cooperatively within those limits. This in turn liberates individuals to unleash their creative abilities in productive ways, and the protection provided by the rule of law to the right to consume, use, or dispose of what is produced provides much of the incentive to produce it in the first place. I am only now beginning my studies of Chinese law, and so I do not purport to be an expert on the issues that you face. Nonetheless, it is my understanding that you, too, place great emphasis on the importance of the rule of law, feel the need for some change perhaps, and are now rethinking certain aspects of your legal institutions in an effort to further the great strides your country has made. There is no question that the rule of law is critical to the legal process; indeed, it should be its defining characteristic. Equally clear is that there is no point to "reforming" any aspect of the legal process except to further, deepen, and strengthen the rule of law.

I am not here, however, to instruct you as to what needs to be reformed, or what reforms you should adopt. I do not yet know enough about your legal system or your needs to do so. Rather, I wish to discuss something else. I wish to discuss the foundations of the criminal process. Although I will concentrate on the criminal process, much of what I have to say is relevant to civil litigation as well, and thus more generally is relevant to the foundations of the rule of law. I will discuss the factors that determine what criminal process should be adopted, how it should be implemented, and so on. And I will tell you a little bit about the complexity of those factors and their implications for us in the United States. I want to begin, however, by first discussing briefly the law of evidence. In one sense, the law of evidence is the most important, and most fundamental, aspect of any system of litigation; indeed, it is the bedrock of the rule of law.

The idea that the law of evidence is fundamental to a system of litigation and is the bedrock of the rule of law may at first glance seem strange. In fact, the law of evidence is fundamental to any system that creates rights or enforces obligations. Rights and obligations are dependent upon accurate fact finding; without accurate adjudication, rights and obligations are essentially meaningless. I will demonstrate this point through a simple example.

Each of you here today would assert ownership of something—the clothes you are wearing for example. I own this necktie that I am wearing, which means that I have the right to possess, consume, and dispose of this necktie as I see fit. This is the standard meaning of the "right" of ownership of personal property. Suppose, however, that somebody contests my ownership of this necktie. What will happen? In all civilized countries, the dispute will be presented to a disinterested decision maker—maybe a judge, in the U. S. maybe a jury—who will decide whether I or someone else has the right to possess, consume and dispose of this necktie. That decision will be made on the basis of the evidence presented to the decision maker. Thus, when I claim ownership over this tie, what I am really claiming is that, if my ownership is contested, I will be able to present to a decision maker evidence from which he or she will conclude that in fact the tie is mine to possess, consume, and dispose of.

What we see in this example is that rights and obligations are dependent on facts. Facts are anterior to rights and obligations, and in that sense are more fundamental. Without accurate fact finding, rights and obligations become meaningless. And of course, it is the law of evidence that determines how facts are established. Thus, it is literally true that rights and obligations are dependent upon the law of evidence.

Because of the fundamental nature of the law of evidence, in the United States we do not have separate evidence codes for the criminal and civil processes. We have one law of evidence that is applicable to any juridical fact finding. Obviously, criminal and civil cases can present different problems, and thus there are some rules whose applicability is confined more or less to either the civil or criminal law. In general, though, our approach to evidence law is uniform. The objective is to facilitate accurate fact finding, and thus a broad definition of relevancy is provided. So long as evidence is relevant, it may be offered by the parties unless it fits within a limited set of exclusionary rules whose purpose is to advance some value deemed important enough to justify the cost of excluding relevant evidence. The marital and attorney client privileges are examples. There are others, such as the exclusion of subsequent remedial measures, which is designed to encourage individuals to take action to reduce risks of harm. In general, though, our law of evidence is designed to facilitate a system of free proof in both civil and criminal cases, with the parties having the obligation to decide what evidence to employ.

I can discuss with you during the question and answer session the details of our law of evidence if you are interested. Let me just conclude my discussion of evidence law by saying that unlike the law of criminal procedure, which I am about to begin discussing, evidence law is universal. It deals with how the human mind comes to know its environment. Logic, epistemology, sense data, are not different in China and the United States. The only relevant differences between the two cultures would have to do with exceptions to the general principle of admitting all the relevant evidence the parties wish to admit. Those decisions could easily be informed by local conditions. Still, the important point is that the law of evidence deals with the nature of knowledge and rationality, which I believe to involve universal not local matters for the most part.

There is a connection between the law of evidence in the United States and the criminal process beyond the mere fact that the law of evidence applies to both civil and criminal cases alike. There are a few exclusionary rules uniquely applicable to criminal cases that have been found to be implicit in our Federal Constitution, and they are the primary example of rules of evidence that are specific to the domain of either the civil or the criminal law. They are quite famous, and you may have heard of them. The *Miranda* rule is an example. The Fourth Amendment exclusionary rule for an unlawful search seizure is another example. I understand that you may be considering adopting rules and procedures such as these and perhaps others from other countries, and perhaps you should consider doing so. However, always you must keep in mind that procedures in other countries are embedded in legal systems and cultures that may differ from your own.

This point—that criminal procedure is local，whereas evidence law is universal—cannot be emphasized strongly enough. The objectives pursued by the people in other countries through the criminal law may differ in some respects (although certainly not all respects) from your own. The histories and cultures of the respective nations will differ，and so on. Thus，I want both to commend you for pursuing this difficult process of appraising your own institutions but warn you that you must look carefully first at yourselves so that you see clearly and precisely what it is you are doing and why，and second you must scrutinize suggestions from other countries to see their institutions in context. There are many examples of efforts to import parts of one country's criminal process into another that have failed miserably because of the neglect of the cultural and historical aspects of society，and more importantly because of the differing institutional arrangements and assumptions that meant that an approach to criminal procedure would have one set of implications in one setting but quite a different set of implications in another. ①

I would press this point even further. "Criminal procedure" cannot be understood simply by looking at the statutes，codes，and in the case of the United States，the decisions of the courts. Such things are an important aspect of what constitutes criminal procedure，to be sure，but they do not occupy the field. If，for example，one looks at the various criminal codes in the United States，nowhere is there a reference to the great discretionary power of the prosecutor in the United States to choose what cases to pursue and what cases not to pursue，what charges to file and what charges to drop，whom to investigate and charge，whom to prosecute to the fullest extent of the law and whom to plea bargain with. ②Similarly，one can closely examine the great constitutional criminal procedure cases that dominate the formalities of the American criminal pre-trial process and never learn that in almost every case state or

① A good example is the effort of various European countries to import aspects of adversarial procedure. Germany in the 19th Century，Italy in the 20th.

② *See*，*e. g.*，United States v. Cox，342 F. 2d 167，*cert denied sub nom.* Cox v. Hauberg，381 U. S. 935 (1965).

federal legislatures have the ability to nullify the most far reaching procedural decision through the legislative power to define crime. I could extend this list considerably, all to make the point that to study "criminal procedure" in the United States requires much more than simply consulting the statutes and the cases; it requires engaging with history, culture, politics, economics, and many other variables.

The American conception of the purpose of government is that government exists to create and sustain the conditions under which individuals can flourish according to their own moral dictates. Governments exist to serve the people, rather than the people to serve the government. This, of course, is the essence of what is referred to as "liberal democracy," the basic contours of which emerged from the European Enlightenment philosophers. The American experience added to this a systematic and widespread distrust of centralized government. Government, in the formative period of American history, was not viewed just as the solution to the problems society faced; it was viewed as part of the problem, and had to be cabined, limited, constrained in many, many different ways. ③ This is reflected not only in the separation of powers in the three branches of government (the legislature, executive and judicial branches), which we imported from our European forbears; we added to it judicial supremacy vested in judges with life time tenure that gives the final say over the meaning of Constitutional provisions and statutory interpretation to the judges. This, of course, is the famous "right of judicial review" possessed by our courts. ④

Not content with the structural inhibitions to the exercise of governmental authority formally created in the Constitution through the separation of powers, our founding generation insisted on a series of individual rights against the government, found in the specific provisions of the Bill of Rights (the first ten

③ There are complexities here. The U. S. Constitution was to some extent an effort to create a stronger central government than existed under the Articles of Confederation. Still, the overriding concern was constraining the centralizing tendencies of national governments. In addition to the ways in which this was done mentioned in the text, central to the original plan was a federal system in which the states maintained their sovereignty in many respects, and only those powers necessary for an effective national government were given to it in the Constitution.

④ Marbury v. Madison, 5 U. S. (1 Cranch) 137 (1803) .

amendments to the Constitution), and general admonitions that citizens have the right to "due process of law" and the "equal protection of the law."[⑤] Collectively these provisions do many things; of particular importance for this Seminar, they make it difficult to obtain convictions. An individual has a right to a grand jury indictment returned by a group of non-government employees selected from the population at large (although some states do not use grand juries)[⑥], a different jury of laymen must find guilt beyond reasonable doubt[⑦], the individual has a right not to be compelled to incriminate himself[⑧], the government may not engage in unreasonable searches and seizures[⑨], the defendant has the right to subpoena witnesses in his own behalf and to cross-examine the government's witnesses[⑩], and to do so at a public trial held within a relatively short period of time from the date of the formal accusation against the defendant in the state and district where the crime occurred.[⑪] The right to be free from double jeopardy limits the government, essentially, to a single effort to convict a person for a particular crime.

The protections of an individual go even further. Criminal laws must be readily comprehensible, or else they will be struck down by the courts as unconstitutionally vague. American law has embraced the common law "rule of lenity."[⑫] This is an interpretive canon to the effect that, if a criminal statute is susceptible of two differing interpretations, the courts will adopt the interpretation most favorable to the individual defendant. Even this does not exhaust the individual protections that surround a criminal defendant.[⑬]

⑤ U. S. Const. amend. V, XIV, § 1.

⑥ U. S. Const. amend. V.

⑦ U. S. Const. amend. VI and In re Winship, 397 U. S. 358 (1970).

⑧ U. S. Const.. amend. V.

⑨ U. S. Const. amend. IV.

⑩ U. S. Const. amend. VI.

⑪ *Id.*.

⑫ *See, e. g.*, Zachary Price, *The Rule of Lenity as a Rule of Structure*, 72 Fordham L. Rev. 885 (2004) (arguing that this rule is increasingly out of favor).

⑬ For example, U. S. Const. amend. V protects against double jeopardy and U. S. Const. amend. VIII prohibits excessive bail, excessive fines and punishments which are "cruel and unusual." Brady v. Maryland, 373 U. S. 83 (1963), requires that the State disclose evidence favorable to the defendant.

These individual rights were not selected randomly over the total of set of rights that can be imagined, however. Rather, they were incorporated into the Constitution because they in turn were the parts that composed a unified view of the relationship between the government and the citizen. That view has as its core that governments must be limited, that the centralizing tendency of all governmental power must be resisted, and that the path to a criminal conviction must be difficult, arduous, and in large measure require the consent of the people (through their role as grand and petit jurors) .

The conception of government I am describing has both its virtues and its drawbacks, and I am here today to neither praise nor criticize it; rather, I am here to explain it. It is only with this background that one can understand the discrete provisions dealing with individual rights in the U. S. Constitution, such as the right to counsel. One cannot view a procedural requirement in an isolated fashion and say much coherent about it. One must take it in context, and view it in relationship to the fundamental concept or concepts it is designed to implement or express.

Let me generalize this point. When one talks about "reform of the criminal process," the topic is in fact these underlying jurisprudential and political issues. Basic conceptions of the rule of law, the role of governmental institutions, and their relationship to the citizenry are implemented in not derived from such things as are found in the American Bill of Rights.

There are additional variables that need to be considered in fashioning the criminal process that have social, cultural, and political dimensions and implications. For example, in the United States, we often refer to the "right to privacy." This phrase is ambiguous, however, and refers to at least three different ideas: 1) The right to exclude others, including the government, from one's private sphere, which is the essence of "privacy"; 2) The right to make choices about and for oneself and one's family, such as the much contested right to an abortion in the United States, which is better thought of as "autonomy"; and 3) The right to treated in a certain way by others, including the government, which really refers to a "dignitary" interest. Each of these individual interests is in tension with communal interests that are their mirror images. In deciding the scope of the penal law and its enforcement, a society must make choices over these interacting and conflicting interests.

My first general point, then, is that criminal procedure cannot be viewed in isolation from its surroundings, and that in fact what it is derives from perspectives on profound questions concerning the nature of government, the appropriate relationship between government and the citizen, as well as from views about such deep philosophical questions as the nature of individuality. There is a second reason why one cannot look at a "criminal procedure" in the abstract. Not only are the components parts of a criminal justice system integral to a dynamic process, but also, and just as importantly, things are not always what they appear to be. In my book, Comprehensive Criminal Procedure,[14] my co-authors and I have developed a framework for studying criminal procedure in the United States. To understand the actual operation of the criminal justice system in the United States, one must address, in addition to the formal commands of the "law" and the deep jurisprudential and political issues briefly commented on above, at least the following four variables:

1. The distinction between the law on the books and the law in action;

2. The intimate interrelationship between procedural law and substantive law, and in particular how procedural law is in fact a hostage of substantive law, rather than the other way around as is conventionally believed;

3. History in general, and in particular race relations and racial discrimination;

4. Economics, or as we say in the United States, "There is no free lunch" if you use a dollar (or yuan) here for one purpose you cannot use it there for a different purpose.

I will discuss in turn each of these variables and their significance.

1. The law on the books; the law in action. Constitutions are enacted, legislation is passed, executives issue orders and directives, and courts decide, and one would think that the rest of us more or less obey. Unfortunately (or perhaps fortunately), life is not so simple. When constitutions or laws are adopted in any multi-party decision making process (such as a popular vote on a constitution or a vote in a legislature to adopt a law), there will be multiple

⑭ Ronald J. Allen, et al., *Comprehensive Criminal Procedure* (2nd, 2005).

understandings of what the legal language connotes. Some legislator may vote for the passage of a bill even though they do not believe it goes far enough in its coverage (or even though it goes too far); others may vote against it for just the same reasons. There also may be serious disagreements as to precisely what a particular provision is supposed to mean or do. One person may think the legal language has one implication, and someone else may think it has a different implication. In the United States, for example, there was once sharp disagreement about the relationship between the due process clause of the fourteenth amendment and the Bill of Rights, the first ten amendments to the U. S. Constitution. [15] Statutory or constitutional language in the abstract often will not resolve the meaning of those phrases.

Compounding the difficulty even further, legal language is often deliberately left vague because of the inability to come to agreement as to precisely what it should say or because of the omnipresent inability to anticipate all possible scenarios in which a particular problem might arise. An example from the United States Constitution is the regal but ambiguous language of the eighth amendment that neither cruel nor unusual punishments may be imposed. That is all very well and good, but what exactly makes a punishment cruel and unusual? How does whatever the phrase may have been meant in 1791 when the language was adopted apply to new developments that were never anticipated? No formulaic answers to such questions can exist.

Even if the language of a legal provision were perfectly clear, legislators do not execute their own laws. Executives do, such as the President and the Governors of the States in our system. Thus, their interpretations can be critical to the implementation of a legal provision. Beyond just the linguistic problem of meaning lies an even deeper problem. The executive may not share precisely the same view of wise policy as held by the legislature, and thus the executive may be more or less enthusiastic about the execution of various laws. Even if the executive knew what each of the laws meant and was quite enthusiastic about its enforcement, virtually no law can be enforced perfectly. There are inadequate resources to do so, and the methods necessary to ac-

[15] U. S. Const. amend. I-X.

complish the task would often violate other norms. A simple example here is that crime in both our countries continues to be committed notwithstanding vast resources invested in its eradication. Some crimes could not be eradicated without using measures that would be so intrusive into privacy or violative of other rights that the methods would be viewed as worse than the toleration of some level of criminality. In any event, executives must make choices about the meaning of legal provisions, and priorities in and methods of enforcement.

How the law on the books gets translated into the law in action becomes even more complex as one descends the organizational chain from the highest levels of government down toward the policeman on the street. And here the impact on procedural law becomes even more evident. At an intermediate level, I have already mentioned the great discretion that prosecutors have in deciding what cases to pursue. No legislation could change this because no such legislation would ever carry with it a large enough appropriation of funds to permit all potential criminal acts to be investigated. What is true of the prosecutors is doubly true of the police. In any complex society, crime swirls around us at all times, much of it low level crime to be sure, but crime nonetheless. Walk down the streets of Beijing or Chicago, and you will see untold numbers of crimes being committed from littering to jaywalking to vehicular offenses to theft to assault and battery. [16]The police, like the prosecutors, thus have discretion as to what crimes are investigated, whether we or our legal theories like it or not. [17]Equally importantly, much of what a policeman does is not really law enforcement at all, but the management of complex situations, such as traffic flow or crowd control and the like.

This discretion has implications for procedural rules. I will give one stark example. Suppose one imposes limits on investigation, such as the right to be free from unreasonable searches and seizures contained in the fourth amendment to the U. S. Constitution. Suppose further that this is to be enforced

[16] Some states label such things as "jaywalking" traffic violations as "violations" or "offenses" rather than "felonies" or "misdemeanors." They remain criminal, however.

[17] *See* Ronald J. Allen, *The Police and Substantive Rulemaking: Reconciling Principle and Expediency*, 125 Pa. L. Rev. 62 (1976), *The Police and Substantive Rulemaking; A Brief Rejoinder*, 125 Pa. L. Rev. 1172 (1977).

through exclusionary rules that suppress evidence obtained in violation of the procedural rule, elements which of course can be found in the U. S. law.

Now suppose that the police and prosecutors view some social issue, such as prostitution, as a problem to be managed rather than involving crime to be solved. One way to "solve" the problem in the eyes of the local officials may be to make it go away by harassing those involved in it, with no intent to obtain convictions, thus encouraging those involved to "move on" to some other city or part of the country. The harassment might involve real on the street physical threats or violence, it might even involve a series of arrests, and so on. The point is that unless the police or prosecutors care about convictions, exclusionary rules will have no effect on their behavior. The law on the books appears quite regal; the law in action will be quite different.

2. The Relationship Between Substantive Law and Procedural Law. The decisions of the United States Supreme Court extending and enforcing individual rights have been viewed as imposing considerable constraints on the police and prosecutors, yet the legal system has not been greatly disturbed by these rulings. One reason, as just discussed, is that procedural barriers to prosecution matter only if anyone really is interested in prosecution. This is an example of the general point that these systems are dynamic and thus can and do respond to changes in various unpredictable ways. It is simply false to think that "reform" to a dynamic process can be imposed unproblematically through discrete measures that will have only the desired and no unintended consequences. Quite the contrary, human institutions like the criminal justice process are organic and infinitely adaptable, and in an astounding variety of ways. By far the most important but underappreciated example is that legitimate legislative changes can blunt virtually any procedural innovation that emerges from courts or law reformers.

Here I will use the fourth amendment limit on unreasonable searches and seizures as the example. Suppose the police want to stop cars to do cursory inspections for criminality, but courts rule that the fourth amendment requires that the police have probable cause that a crime has been committed before a car can be stopped. All the legislature need do to make this judicial command a practical nullity is to expand the criminal law to include more rigorous driving requirements. The legislature can essentially make it next to impossible to drive without violating a criminal statute (such as crossing the center line, driving too closely to the car ahead of you, not putting your turning light indicator on early enough or too early, etc.) . If the legislature passes such laws, the police will be able to stop virtually any car by following it until the driver violates one of statutes regulating driving. The stop will be on "probable cause" but the legislation will have expanded dramatically the potential sources of probable cause, thus subjecting everyone to being stopped by the police whenever the police decide to do so, notwithstanding the attempt by the courts to forbid just that process. Similarly, if the government cannot seize certain information without probable cause, it can often instead require that individuals keep records of the information it wants and divulge those records to the government.

The general point is that as the criminal law expands, the actual constraining force of individual rights becomes attenuated, and this is a matter almost exclusively within the control of the political branches of government. This must be taken into account in order to understand how the pre-trial criminal process really works in the United States requires.

3. History and the Pursuit of Racial Equality. The significance of history to understanding any ongoing system is obvious, and I will not take time here to develop the point beyond noting that to understand what is, one must often understand what was. In addition to the general and obvious point that history determines to some extent present arrangements, much of the law of criminal procedure in the United States has developed as part of the national effort to eliminate the effects of racism.

4. Economics. Businessmen have a saying in the United States that "There is no such thing as a free lunch." They mean by this that, if another businessman "invites" you to lunch, he probably wants to talk to you about something or may expect a favor in return. Whatever one thinks about the business world, it is literally true for government that "there is no such thing as a free lunch." Governments are constrained by their economies, and economies in turn are finite. Of the many valuable things that, in theory, governments could do, they are able to choose to do only some of them. If resources are used for one purpose, there are simply fewer resources left to do other things, and there

are in total too many different "things" to do to fund them all.

In thinking about the criminal justice system, the finite limitations of resources is critically important. One lesson of modern times is clear: No society can eradicate crime. There is simply too much crime in ever changing forms. Perhaps the best example of this is that, ironically, as resources are poured into the effort to eradicate crimes, other forms of crime spring up as a result, such as graft and corruption. Moreover, there is a limit to the methods that government can employ to combat crime. The toleration of the citizenry for aggressive investigation of crime may differ over cultures, but again modern history makes it clear that all cultures and societies have their effective limit beyond which government cannot go without sparking resistance and protest from the population. Consequently, difficult choices need to be made about the allocation of resources across the whole range of governmental interests, including the investigation and prosecution of crime. Crime and its investigation need to be conceived of as parts of a fluid and dynamic process rather than as discrete entities that can be perfectly managed.

I will give a few examples. Investments in the criminal justice process obviously compete with investments in other social goods. If government provides more judges, police, or funds counsel for poor people, less resources will be available for economic development or medical research, or whatever. As I suggested earlier, the police face an aspect of this problem daily. Faced with too much crime to be dealt with by their limits resources, they must constantly decide how to allocate their limited resources. Should the police patrol this part of the city or that part? Should they concentrate on economic crimes, crimes of violence, or fraud? Investments within the criminal justice process likewise compete with other investments in different parts of that same process. If government provides more judges, perhaps it can provide fewer police.

The implications of economics extends further. Consider for one last time the example of the right to counsel. As the ability of counsel for the accused to effect the criminal justice process increases, the more costly each case becomes to try. As the median cost of a case increases, the total number of cases that can be tried decreases. If the active involvement of defense counsel increases the total time a trial takes, obviously there can be fewer trials, as the total time available to try cases is finite.

In addition to the straight forward questions of allocation of resources, there is a second, perhaps more fundamental, economic perspective that is relevant to the structure of the criminal justice system, and that is the micro-economics of errors. A mistake free criminal justice system is not possible. It is critically important to recognize that two types of errors can be made-a wrongful conviction of an innocent person and a wrongful acquittal of a guilty person-and resource allocation decisions will affect the relationship between these two types of errors.

Reasonable people can disagree as to the significance of these two types of errors. In the United States, we structure the criminal justice process to minimize the possibility of wrongful conviction at the admitted expense of making many more mistakes of wrongful acquittals. In the United States, we say that it is better that ten guilty people go free than that one innocent person be convicted. Although the matter is complicated, this perspective explains in large measure the high standard of proof of beyond reasonable doubt in criminal cases[18] and is another reason why counsel for the accused is viewed as so important in the United States. High standards of proof and legal representation will tend to protect innocent people even though they make convicting guilty people more difficult. [19]

Viewing the criminal process through the economic lens highlights the difficult trade off between freedom and security that is perhaps the central thread running through my remarks today, and thus is perhaps a fitting place to conclude. Let me just say one last time that my purpose here today has been to neither praise nor criticize my system or yours, but instead to uncover some of the significant variables that must inform thinking about these important issues, whether the concern is reforming your system or understanding ours. I also want to reiterate in closing that, in thinking about the criminal justice processes of both our countries, it is critical to bear in mind that they form or-

---

⑱ *See* Ronald J. Allen, *Clarifying the Burden of Persuasion and Bayesian Decision Rules: A Response to Professor Kaye*, 4 Int. J. of Evidence & Proof 246 (2000).

⑲ There is yet another relevant economic perspective, which focuses on the deterrent effect of sanctions. *See*, *e. g.* Richard A. Posner, *An Economic Theory of the Criminal Law*, 85 Colum. L. Rev. 1193 (1985), Gary S. Becker, *Crime and Punishment: An Economic Approach*, 76 J. Pol. Econ. 169 (168).

ganic wholes, and that changes in one part may have unintended effects in other parts. If, for example, counsel and an effective ability to contest the charges are not provided, costs will be reduced of conducting trials, but another form of cost in terms of wrongful convictions will increase, and vice versa. Thus, to think about the type of criminal justice process you want to have, you have to also think about these larger issues that I have identified.

Last, I want to reiterate that procedural codes and evidence law differ in one critical respect. Procedural law is indigenous and local; like substantive law, it reflects that particularities of time and place. Evidence law is universal; it is derivative of the nature of rationality and how the human mind comes to know and deal with its surroundings. There are, to be sure, policies that are limited to either the civil or criminal arenas that can be furthered through what we could call "evidence rules." Normally, these are exclusionary rules that work in opposition to the overall objective of the efficient establishment of the truth. I am hesitant to offer you suggestions for change, but I would leave you with this one thought. In constructing your law of evidence, I would recommend that you begin with the universal and then deal with ways in which you wish to depart from the principle of the efficient establishment of the truth. If you do so, I think you will soon see that the law of evidence for the most part will be the same in all proceedings, with only a few minor exceptions.

证据法、诉讼法和实体法的关系*

张保生　张月波　汪诸豪　译**

我昨天给大家概述了证据法的许多基础性问题，这些问题是构建一部理性证据法所需考虑和安置的问题。今天，我将通过对证据法、诉讼法与实体法之间关系的考察，对昨天简要触及的一些问题做深入讲解。

首先，我们需要一些定义。证据法是直接决定审判或听审中证据的可采性或不可采性的法律体系。诉讼法是规制案件审判或上诉之正式准备工作的法律体系。两者结合，证据法和诉讼法一起直接影响诉讼行为。实体法是确定权利和义务并直接影响主要行为的法律体系。“主要行为”是指人们和机构在诉讼语境之外的行为，换言之，就是人们的日常行为。

这些定义反映了三个领域的不同作用范围。证据在很大程度上是由认识论关系推动的；程序是由效率关注推动的；实体法所反映的则是政府为创造繁荣社会必须不断努力安置的一系列复杂的人类利益。然而，这三个概念之间的区别不应被夸大或过分强调。这些定义仅具有指引作用，而非纯分析性的陈述。人们可以在诉讼法中找到影响证据的规定，证据法中的某些规定也具有程序性质。对这些术语的所谓“正确”含义进行争论，或给某些条款扣上“实际上”是证据法、程序法或实体法的帽子，都是浪费精力。诚然，重要之点在于三大规则领域确实存在：规制主要行为的规则；为诉讼做准备及呈现案件的规则；以及审判中运用证据的规则。

一些法律制度把证据法视为诉讼法的一部分。从某种意义上说，这又是一个不值得争论的问题。人们可以用无数方式来组织事情，问题并不在于某种组织方式是否“正确”，而在于它是否有用。例如，人们可以将“程序”归类为实体法的一个分支，因为程序显然影响行为。不过，把证据归为程序的一部分会掩盖证据法的独特性，即其认识论上的视域。这反过来指明了证据区别于程序的另一个重要方面，在这个意义上，程序法和实体法更为相似。人类的推理

* 本文系艾伦教授2010年6月在中国政法大学所做的讲座。本译文原载于《证据科学》，第18卷，2010年第6期。

** 汪诸豪，中国政法大学证据科学研究院讲师，美国宾夕法尼亚大学法学院LLM，美国印第安纳大学法学院JD。

和认知能力是普遍的；它们在任何地方都大致相同。证据法正是建立在这种普适性基础上，而程序法和实体法则更多具有地方性和偶然性。

虽然思考证据、程序和实体之间的区别是有益的，但在许多情况下它们的效用是类似的。除了追求事实真相，还有各种政策促动证据法。虽然证据法的主要动因确实是追求事实真相的确定，不过许多证据规则明显是由其他问题促动的。同样，诉讼法虽然不像证据法具有明显的认识论视域，但很多程序机制却直接涉及证据问题，如证据开示规则或撤销指控动议。与此相似，证据和程序都能为主要行为而不仅是诉讼行为创造激励因素，在这方面，它们又与实体法交叉重叠。

请注意，我们现在有两组不同的范畴。第一组由三种法律组成：证据法、诉讼法和实体法。第二组是两种行为：主要行为和诉讼行为。现在我将花点时间来探讨第二组范畴。正如昨天所讨论的，主要行为和诉讼行为的区别是很清楚的，尽管它们也有一些重叠。主要行为是指公民活生生的生存行为，实体法提供了规范那些行为的规则。诉讼行为是指通过正式法律手段解决争端的活动。

法学界按照其内在逻辑，习惯于把主要行为和诉讼行为分开，将其视为不同的领域。主要行为涉及社会上认为正确或错误的事情，为效率经济行为创造条件，对社会交际和制度等进行规制。实体法之各种形式的正当理由，几乎与其调整的主要行为一样纷繁复杂，但总的来说都是处理社会认同的道德上正确和经济上有效的行为。促进这种行为一般是社会组织尤其是法律的典型目的。相比之下，诉讼行为涉及当事人寻求争端解决的努力，产生于因不适当的主要行为而导致的诉求，或矫正那些因所称违反实体法而发生的社会性破坏。

主要行为和诉讼行为之间区别的最具批判性的含义，对大多数法律评论者而言，大概是诉讼所花费的资源是社会净损失，或像我们在美国所说的“为洒掉的牛奶而哭泣——覆水难收”。这种理念是，诉讼本身不增加社会价值，即它不产出有用的货物、物质或知识资本，因此，花费在诉讼行为上的资源等于白白扔钱。这就是为什么大多数诉讼法典或证据法典都以这样的语句开篇，如《联邦民事诉讼规则》规则 1，大意是，民事诉讼规则“应当解释为并有助于确保每一诉讼和程序得到公正、迅速和便宜的裁判。”这在《联邦证据规则》规则 2 中也得到了回应，其规定：“解释本证据规则应确保公正执法，消除不合理的费用和拖延，促进证据法的成长和发展，以实现查明事实真相和公正处理诉讼为目的。”这些都是对证据法和诉讼法崇高志向的著名表达，然而它们完全是误导。让我再重复一遍：它们完全是误导性的。

首先，让我简单解释一下这些著名表述背后潜在的原理。为此，我需要先介绍一些简单的微观经济学概念。实体法所做的一件重要事情，就是试图确保人们能够承受自己行为的真实成本。这是一个简单的表达，但它具有深刻意义。主要行为几乎总是并非仅仅产出具有社会价值的货物，它通常还附带着成本。例如，当一个工厂生产汽车或电脑时，它还生产了环境废物。另一个例子是，驾驶汽车使交通更便利而成为一种社会福利，但它同时也产生了废物并可能引起车祸。实体法最重要的方面之一，就是努力使成本与行为相匹配，因为这对我们所讨论的创造行为产品的最佳激励是至关重要的。设想一个诸如生产汽车或电脑等有用东西的工厂。如果该工厂能把废物排放到河里或其邻居的土地上，它就能以低于实际成本的成本生产汽车或计算机——该工厂将部分成本转嫁给它的邻居或那些依靠河流谋求福利的人们了，因而是这些人补贴了汽车或电脑的生产。这反过来意味着，工厂的产品将不按其真实成本定价——部分成本被该工厂的那些足够倒霉的邻居承担了。在这种情况下，大多数经济学家会预测，汽车和电脑产品的生产将过剩。降低一项产品的成本将刺激它的生产，而提高成本则会产生相反的效果。一般而言，以实际成本进行生产，人们能够接近社会货物的理想化生产。因此，实体法的重要目的之一，就是要使人们精确承受自己行为的真实成本。

这个概念适用于社会中的所有事情。工厂应当承担其行为的真实成本。当你们开始认真对待曾经为政府政策所容忍的环境破坏时，中国今天也面临着同样的问题。你驾驶汽车时，也应当承担自己行为的真实成本。你开车时，不仅得到了利益，也给他人强加了风险。同样，其他人也把风险强加给你。有很好的理由相信，让每个人承担其行为的真实成本，相比于把我们的行为与成本隔绝开或把那些成本转嫁给他人来说，将使我们每个人更可能对主要行为作出最佳选择。在我闯了红灯并撞了另一辆车时，我应当承担那些成本，就像一个生产汽车的工厂应承担其产品的全部成本一样。

这种从微观经济学角度对社会行为规则的考察，是极其有力的且好评如潮。进一步说，在我看来，这对社会组织的确是一条最重要的指导方针。这并不是说，没有其他也很重要并可能与微观经济学路径相冲突的指导方针了。显然在治理活动中还有其他的考虑因素，但在我看来，没有什么比试图建构法律以便所有社会角色都承担其行为真实成本更重要的指导方针了。

现在我们从微观经济学视角考虑一下主要行为与诉讼行为的关系。这样做将使我们弄清楚，是什么激发了像我从《联邦民事诉讼规则》和《联邦证据规则》中引用的那些雄心勃勃的语句。诉讼费用增加了潜在主要行为的成本。请再思考一下我们举的汽车厂的例子。除了支付工资、购买原材料和机器并处理废物，该工厂将不得不承担法律诉讼的费用。这些费用提高了生产产品的成本，但却并没有提供任何价值。汽车并没有比提高成本前造得更好，污染也没有减少，等等。正是在这个意义上，大多数法律评论者将诉讼费用视为社会净损失。它们没有提供任何回报。这样，目的就是要使诉讼成本趋近于零，换言之，确保以资源零消耗来服从法律。那就是目的，那就是我上面引用的规则中潜藏的东西。

问题在于，这个目的是不可能实现的。不可能存在执法成本为零的法律制度。请记住，政府能够补助诉讼也不是这一问题的答案。问题并不只是谁为某些事情买单，而是有没有任何人来买单。当政府补贴诉讼时，该补贴就成为诸如此类潜在行为的一种激励因素，无论这种行为是否对社会有益。因此，问题是：面对诉讼或任何争端解决形式所含的不可避免的交易成本，一种法律制度应当如何构建？

这就是事情的复杂之处。要看清其有多么复杂，我需要再添加一些复杂性。迄今为止，我们一直在讨论“成本”，仿佛这个术语仅适用于纯粹经济上的开支，但它还有第二个方面。可能存在并非直接货币化或大概无法完全货币化的社会成本。我们能够称这些为社会成本。我至此讨论的一直是所谓无成本的法律制度理想。请思考这个理念。对今天在座的听众来说，拥有一个能够简直免费解决法律争端的法律制度，这乍听起来不是很有吸引力吗？请记住，我们不是在谈论隐蔽的政府补贴，因为那些是真正的成本；我们是在想象一个凭借司法制度使争端真正免费得到终局性解决的理想世界，并且假定，这个假设的制度还不会犯错误。实际上，这只是向你们表明，对法律制度进行分析的经济学方法的微妙性，不犯错误的假定蕴含在无成本决策的假定之中，因为错误本身就是成本。

现在思考一下所有问题将被免费而准确的决策过程所解决的情况。这听起来棒极了，是吧？这听起来像是你们和我们的政府几个世纪以来一直努力奋斗所争取的东西。这听起来像是你们法学院课程一直在讲的内容，也是自启蒙运动以来所有社会理论家和政治理论家所渴求的东西。这样一种模式不像什么呢？

让我给这个问题一个答案，但我将通过另一个问题来回答。如果明天一个免费而准确的争端解决制度像变魔术一样开始运行，你预测将发生什么？让我问你一个相关的问题。当受欢迎的商品或东西降价时，你会观察到发生什么情况？当你痴迷的品牌店打折，你喜欢的衣服或垂涎的珠宝减价时，你会做什么？让我来替你回答吧，你会买得更多。这是一段时间以来，我一直致力于解决的核心问题。价格影响消费。随着任何喜欢的商品降价，消费就会上升。如果明天争端解决的价格降低，你们和我都会预言消费将会上升。如果价格降为零，消费将会相应地急剧上升。

“那又会怎么样?”你们现在可能会这样问。这样发展下去会出什么问题?我难道不是已经承认减少诉讼费用将使某些问题得到改善吗？回答是，一个无须花钱的法律制度非常可能刺激其产品生产过剩，并且实际上产生社会损害。让我来告诉你们我这么说的意思。因为法律争端并不是无成本的，个人和机构必须对争端解决方式作出决策——是使用正式的法律程序还是其他手段。假定你拥有一套住宅或租用一间公寓，你将会与不定量的个人打交道，有人或许将损害你的权利，或者你将损害他们的权利。在你的土地上生长的植物果实或许会落在他们的土地上。他们或许会把汽车停在你泊车必经的通道上。你怎样处理这类事情呢？你与侵犯你权利的人进行谈判来处理。然而，如果诉讼费用为零，你可能就直接起诉他们，而不是去与他们谈判了。因此，如果把诉讼费用降到零，可能会戏剧性地影响到人们在社会中的交际方式，而你们当中一些人可能认为那些改变是令人不快的。人们不再通过交谈和谈判来解决日常生活中的问题，而是通过政府来获得官方解决。一点都看不出来，相比现在的情况，生活在这样一个世界真是一种实质进步。

再明确一下我这里介绍的复杂情况，我的观点是，争端解决的方式是相互竞争的，而且对某种问题的解决来说，某些方式可能比其他方式更可取。如果人们可以过于轻易地求助于政府来解决特定争端，这可能是一种社会损耗。因此，诉讼成本并不必然是净损失。它们可为以其他方式解决争端提供激励因素，而不是通过正式诉讼或政府介入，从而对社会公益作出贡献。

我现在想要概括一下前几分钟所阐述的观点。与法学家们的传统观点相反，诉讼过程不可以脱离其对主要行为的影响来进行分析。主要行为和诉讼行为之间不是彼此密封的，它们不能被抽象地分割开来加以分析。它们之间的相互影响必须予以考虑。主要行为显然影响诉讼行为，但诉讼行为也同样影响主要行为，并且是以一种比传统上认为的更微妙的方式影响主要行为。

这是一个强有力的观点，但也有颇多的麻烦，因为它意味着社会组织的问题比人们通常认为的要复杂得多。例如，也许有一些类型的诉讼，可以由低成本或零费用达到行为最佳化（包括主要行为和诉讼行为）。然而，也许有其他类型的诉讼是通过极高费用来达到最佳的，换言之，这类案件是不宜提起诉讼的。家事纠纷也许是这种类型的例子。其他类型的案件可能介于两者之间，其行为是通过强加某些费用来实现最佳化的。现在，当我说社会组织的问题比看起来更复杂时，你可以精确地明白我的意思了。法律制度的任务包括，在面对这种复杂性时设法决定如何回应，哪些案件的起诉应当鼓励，哪些不应当鼓励。

正如我今天所讲的，在美国，我们正在为解决这些确切问题而奋斗，因而在某种程度上强调了证据法、诉讼法和实体法之间的关系。[①] 我们联邦诉讼规则和证据规则的制定，在某种程度上弥补了它们所取代制度中的被认为扭曲了的方面。先前制度被认为是由于过高地提高了成本而对原告不利。对这个问题的解决就是简化对起诉的要求，并允许案件进行被认为是低成本的证据开示，伴之以低成本的审判。证据开示成本之所以低，是因为假定当事人双方分享了案件知识，所以证据开示不需要实质性投入。另外，当事人双方将具有使证据开示成本保持在其必要最小值中的动机。你马上可以看到，这些概念如何体现在我们今天所讨论的内容中。在一个信息对称和交易成本低的世界，联邦规则最可能在不曲解潜在实体法的前提下实现促进争端准确和高效解决的目标，联邦规则所取代的诉讼领域的一些价值并未得到切实保护。如果原来关于诉讼的假设是正确的，程序上的争论就没有意义了。然而，不必要的诉讼成本使潜在实体权利降低了价值，那可能会曲解实体法。我们在这里看到的是证据与程序的互动。民事案件的优势证据证明标准作为一般标准优化了社会价值，但这种优化的前提是，提起诉讼的案件没有偏离或曲解人们拥有的潜在争端样式。

相比之下，如果法律程序对提起诉讼的案件造成了曲解，优势证据标准就不可能是最优标准了。在联邦规则通过之前，诉讼成本大概整体上不利于原告。如果原告和被告的状态不是随机的（例如，更多的行人而不是汽车司机在事故中应当得到赔偿，这样就会有更多的行人起诉汽车司机而不是相反），那么，程序制度的作用加上标准化证据规则的适用，就可能破坏实体法。在汽车的例子中，有过错的司机如果由于原告诉讼成本高而逃避责任的太多，汽车司机将不能充分内在消化他们行为的成本。联邦规则的通过，由于去除了某些有利于被告的程序障碍而达到准确裁判，可能已部分矫正了这

① 以下3页内容借用并改写自罗纳德·J·艾伦和艾伦·E·盖伊：《作为通布利案和伊克巴尔案的特例的康利案：证据法、程序法的交叉及其规则性质的考察》，载《宾夕法尼亚州法学评论》，第115卷，2010年，第1页。

种情况。

我们今天在美国所面对的问题是，关于知识和成本的假设在某些案件中并不正确。知识并未对称分布，证据开示的成本也许在很大程度上与诉求的价值相关，也呈现了不对称分布。在这些类型的案件中适用原来对规则的理解，将不能促进准确和高效裁判的潜在目的，并将由错误和正确结果的配置不当而破坏这些规则原有的成就。这反过来又将破坏实体法。

如果原告和被告的地位已经从“前规则”情境所信奉的东西中颠倒过来，那就证明对起诉进行更严格的审查是正当的，这意味着在那一点上强加了更高成本。起初，程序制度有利于被告，因而补贴了社会性浪费活动；现在，在一些类型的案件中有利于原告，就产生了相反效果。在这种情形下，被告不是被法律而是被诉讼成本阻止了诉讼活动，这增加了对实际上不道德诉讼的恐惧值，给被告施加了和解的压力以及超出合法行为的负担。潜在被告将采取很可能是社会性浪费的避免诉讼策略，他们将用和解来逃避诉讼费用，而不是按是非曲直来承担风险责任。这增加了那些本身不具有可诉性行为的成本，但这可能看起来无异于在有高度把握的起诉中出现的情况。

我们正开始看到证据法、诉讼法与实体法的关系是多么复杂。这部分是因为引起诉讼行为的证据和程序是复杂的领域，但影响主要行为的实体法也是如此。最重要的是，其复杂性源于优化它们的需要。我将就这种复杂性再给出一个例子，并给出一个传统法律思维犯下严重错误的例子。正如我前面所提到的，我们把证明责任规则设想为，旨在通过促进诉讼行为与主要行为的最佳关系来促进实体法，并进一步促进各种社会利益。例如，在民事案件中，原告和被告在法律面前是无差别的。假定，他们的诉讼标的为 1 000 美元。法律并不知道谁应得到那笔钱。因此，在民事案件中，为了反映他们在法律面前的平等，为了减少我们犯错误的总量，我们运用优势证据标准，这有助于适当构建他们的诉讼动机。在刑事案件中，我们认为给无辜的人定罪比宣告一个有罪的人无罪更为糟糕，所以，为了保护无辜的人不被定罪，我们采用确信无疑的说服责任，使得给任何人定罪都很困难。这有时候是指布莱克斯通比率，即主张宣告十个有罪的人无罪比给一个无辜的人定罪要好。我将在明天“司法证明的性质”一讲中更多谈到这些事项，但我想通过这样的论证来结束今天的课程，即部分是由于忽视了证据法、诉讼法和实体法之间的关系，关于说服责任的传统观念深深地陷入了问题。我将集中讨论刑事案件，因为那里的影响是最具戏剧性的。然而，我想强调的是，我的这种分析观点也适用于民事案件。

虽然布莱克斯通比率所含说服责任的方式，是刑事案件中说服责任的传统正当理由，但根据最近的分析，它具有特别重要的意义。[②] 首先考虑一下关注审判中错误率所引发的难题。在美国，有数据表明，在强奸谋杀案审判的死刑定罪中，重罪审判的错误率大约在3.5%～5.0%之间。假定这些数字反映了重罪审判的一般错误率。我们并不完全清楚为什么这是一个备受关注的比率，或者从整个制度的角度人们可以从中得出什么。如果错误率对于生成准确的定罪或宣告无罪是不必要的，它也许会被认为过高了，根据传统的确信无疑证明目标的观点，这似乎是不可能的。例如，如果错判无罪和错判有罪之间的适当比率是10∶1，一个3.5%～5.0%的错判有罪比率将要求35%～50%错判无罪比例，也就是说仅剩下45%～61.5%的案件是正确裁判的。这与在审判中实现生成准确结果的重要目标大相径庭。进一步说，错误率也许太低而不能获得错判无罪与错判有罪的正确比率。也许其他所有案件都是错判无罪，留下了1∶19（在5%错判有罪比率上）的布莱克斯通比率。如果是这样，我们大概就需要更多的错判有罪，同时获得一些准确的结果，来降低该比率以达到10∶1的适当水平。

如果这看起来像一个古怪的分析式，大概是因为考察这个问题的整个方式误入歧途了。我确信如此，并将对此作出简短的解释。然而，在这样做之前，要注意到对刑事司法制度中错误率的评价同样至关重要的另一个基准数据的缺乏，那就是未破犯罪案件率。未破犯罪属于很可能从多方面加大社会成本的错误，包括丧失威慑力和失去行动能力、不能满足被害人的报应感、缺乏终局性、增加不安全感和财产损失。正如我今天所一直讨论的，审判、辩护和整个刑事司法制度只是更大社会架构下的组成部分。而且，在不知其怎样适应更大图景的情况下，关于审判错误的基准数据何以能被孤立地加以评价，这是完全不清楚的。例如，一些最新著作认为错判死刑的错误率大约是2%。[③] 尽管错误率之裸经验性主张可能是准确的，但是，对错判死刑数与全部死刑判决进行比较的重要意义仍不十分清楚。例如，为什么不对错判死刑数与谋杀罪总数进

② 以下几页内容借用并改写自罗纳德·J·艾伦和劳瑞·劳丹：《致命的困境》，载《得克萨斯技术与法学评论》，第41卷，2008年，第45页。

③ 参见塞缪尔·R·克罗斯 & 芭芭拉·O·布赖恩：《错误定罪的频度和预测变量：为什么我们知之甚少及关于死刑案件的新数据》[《密歇根大学法学院公共法律研究报告》，第14～15卷（No. 93）和《密歇根大学法律Coll. 法学研究报告》No. 50—14，2007年]，见 http://ssrn.com/abstract=996629。另参见塞缪尔·R·克罗斯等：《美国的免罪：1989到2003年》，载《刑事与犯罪学杂志》，第95卷，2007年，第523、532页。

行比较？为什么不将它们与同期发生的他杀死刑判决总数相比较？而且，这个数字的政策含义也是不清楚的。如果人们关心错判死刑的错误率，人们就可以像通过减少错判有罪的比率那样，尽可能多地增加死刑执行率来改变这种情况，因为死刑案件错误率可通过对犯罪事实确凿的定罪谋杀犯的大量处决来戏剧性地降低。

另一个令人伤脑筋的问题现在出现了：何为错误？一定的错误率为过高的言下之意是：存在着其他将比现状产生更大功用的选择。但这里指的到底是什么？如果死刑具有任何重要的威慑力，废除死刑将不会使错误被处死的损失最小化；很可能实质上会增加无辜者的死亡。即使死刑没有威慑力，监狱里的犯人仍然会不断地被杀死（徒刑显然是死刑的一种替代），因此，废除死刑转变的也许仅仅是谁将被处死的问题。的确，如果在死刑案件中可能发生的误判是废除这个程序的充足理由，接下来的逻辑是，监狱也应当立即被关闭。因为再度恢复死刑与已执行死刑相比，会使更多“无辜的”人被杀死在监狱里，更不用说错误处决了。④

还有更为棘手的问题。监狱不仅是一个危险的生存场所，而且被监禁的生活几乎肯定减少了一个人离开监狱后的预期寿命。离开监狱的人就业前景堪忧⑤，而且监狱搅乱了他们的社会关系。⑥ 最重要的是，释放后的居民经常带

④ 参见克里斯多夫·J·穆莫拉：《美国司法统计局关于2001—2004年州监狱医学死因偏差率》，2007年，第1页，见 http：//www.ojp.usdoj.gov/bjs/ pub/pdf/mcdsp04.pdf。据司法部统计，在2001到2004年间，在州监狱有12 129人死亡，大约10％是他杀或自杀。同上。司法部将这种特殊研究导入地方监狱和州监狱的自杀和他杀问题。参见克里斯多夫·J·穆莫拉：《美国司法统计局州监狱和地方监狱的自杀和他杀》（2005年），见 http：//www.ojp.usdoj.gov/bjs/pub/pdf/shsplj.pdf。在2002年，监狱自杀率是十万分之十六，他杀率是十万分之四。同上。有趣的是，监狱死亡率微高于所有人群（非洲裔美国人除外）中非监禁个人的可比死亡率。参见国家生命统计系统、疾病控制与防疫中心：《在以种族和性别划分的10岁组总死亡人数中的死亡人数百分比：美国2003年》，2003年，第1～83页，见 http：//www.cdc.gov/nchs/data/dvs/ lcwk2 _ 2003.pdf（死因一览表）。这是因为年轻黑人男性的主要死因是谋杀，一种可怕的讽刺性比率则在监狱下降了。参见同上。

⑤ 参见伊娃·S·尼尔森：《体面、尊严和赏罚：重建人类惩罚理念的宪法性论述》，载《哥伦比亚大学戴维斯分校法律评论》，第41卷，2007年，第111、134页（发现被假释的人只挣到没进过监狱的同样境况的人的一半工资）。滥用药物、文盲和无家可归，是在被释放狱犯中普遍存在的现象，而且被释放一年后有70％～80％的人仍然没有找到工作。同上，第135页。

⑥ 参见达瑞尔·K·布朗：《刑法的成本效益分析》，载《加利福尼亚法律评论》，第92卷，2004年，第323、346～349页。先前定罪使其法律权利受到限制，从选举限制到限制性教育援助，在获取政府援助和政府为低收入者建造的住房方面都降低了资格。参见黛比·A·穆卡梅尔和保罗·N·塞缪尔：《对有刑事犯罪记录的人的公民权利的法定限制》，载《福特海姆市法律杂志》，第30卷，2003年，第1501页。

着关押期间感染的疾病而往往过早失去生命。[⑦] 那些年所有被缩短的生命，都是刑事司法制度不公正地强加的错误，它们肯定比对无辜的人执行刑罚失去的工时更珍贵。

所有这些奇特后果从何而来？一个可能的来源是，它们是忽视证据法、诉讼法和实体法之间关系的结果。布莱克斯通比率对说服责任的分析方法仅专注于审判中发生了什么，看似头头是道，但实际上存在深刻的问题。布莱克斯通比率所做的仅仅是，在 100 起具有代表性的刑事审判中，确保不超过 9 起的错判有罪。但需注意的是，如果每 100 起审判中有 9 起错判有罪，至少就要求有 90 起错判无罪来抵消其影响，最多留下了 100 起案件中仅有 1 起正确裁决的可能性。也就是说，实际上每一个无辜的被告人都被定罪，而且，实际上每一个有罪的被告人都被宣告无罪了。

举一种不那么极端的情境。假定，在连续 100 起审判中有 50 起被判有罪，其中有 5 起误判。10∶1 的布莱克斯通比率将明确要求有 50 起错判无罪。因此，每一起无罪判决都将是误判，这意味着 50 个有罪重罪犯将逃脱惩罚，45 个有罪重罪犯将被判有罪。在这种情境下，一个无辜被告人被定罪的风险是 100%，是一个重罪犯被定罪风险的两倍。这种情境显然与前一种情境一样是不正当的。然而，这是符合布莱克斯通比率的。

如果我们细想更为合理的情境，布莱克斯通比率的问题并不在于该比率导致的不可接受的结果，而是它根本没有导出结果。假设，作为一个一般规则，在审判中 75%的被告人被判有罪，而这其中有 5%是误判有罪。在这种情况下，在每 100 起审判中粗算将有 4 个无辜被告人被定罪。布莱克斯通比率要求这个比例以抵掉 40%的错判无罪。但在这种情境下，仅有 25 个无罪开释，即

⑦ 参见国家通信委员会（Nat'l Comm'n on Corr）：《卫生健康：被释放不久的居民卫生保健和健康状况：给国会的报告》17（2002），见 http：//www.ncchc.org/stbr/Volume1/Chapter 3.pdf。其估计，狱犯带有艾滋病病毒和患有艾滋病的比率是正常人口的 5 倍，而且 17%的艾滋病患者经历过监狱生活。同上。大约 8% 的监狱人口患有性病，包括梅毒、衣原体或淋病。同上。这三种疾病在一般人口中的比率低于 1%。参见国家疾病控制委员会：《2003 年美国疾病控制、值得报告的性病发展趋势》，2003 年，第 1～3 页，见 http：//www.cdc.gov/std/stats03/2003SurveillanceSummary.pdf（每 100 000 人中报告的衣原体病 304 例，每 100 000 人报告的淋病 116 例，每 100 000 人报告的梅毒 2.5 例）。在监狱服刑的人至少有 1/3 患有丙型肝炎。国家通信委员会（Nat'l Comm'n on Corr），《卫生健康》，同上，第 7 页。在城市和县监狱，感染肺结核的人口是全国平均水平的 17 倍。同上。但健康危害已超越了监狱围墙。参见詹森·施尼特克尔 & 安德里亚·约翰：《永久的耻辱：监禁对健康的长期影响》，载《健康与社会行为杂志》，第 48 卷，2007 年，第 115、125～127 页。在美国监狱里，监狱强奸是一种流行病。参见《人权观察：无法逃脱：美国监狱中的男性强奸》（2001 年），见 http：//www.hrw.org/reports/2001/prison/ report.html。

使我们难以置信地假设每一个无罪开释的被告人都是有罪的。简而言之，考虑到美国庭审的运行方式，要求 10∶1 的错判无罪与错判有罪的比率，这个貌似有理的假设在美国法院基本上是不能实现的。这一点可以由一个一般公式的简单证明来概括：

$$BR_{max} = [1/F\ (CF)] \times [\ (1/CR)\ -1]$$

在该公式中，BRmax 是布莱克斯通比率在任何刑事司法制度中的上限，由已知定罪率（CR）和错判有罪的已知部分[F（CF)]组成。由这个法则可以看到，任何司法制度——这可能包括实际上大多数司法制度，都具有 5%的错误定罪率，而≥67%的定罪率大概不能达到 10∶1 的比率。

解决错误的传统方法的一个衍生品，是错误定罪率（可以理解为无辜人被定罪的比率）必须尽可能最小化。一般理念是，通过分析无辜者被定罪的频度，我们就能判断一个司法制度是否公正。

像布莱克斯通法则一样，这个错误定罪率最小化的论点并未受到非常仔细的检验。要探究其原因，我们通过考察两个假设的审判制度，看看为什么是这样。假定，在司法辖区 A，每 100 起审判中有 75 起被判有罪，错误定罪率为 5%。相比之下，在司法辖区 B，每 100 起审判中有 25 起被判有罪，但错误定罪率是令人惊恐的 10%。很清楚，如果我们关注的是错误定罪率的最小化，相比于 B 我们应该更喜欢 A。但麻烦的问题是，A 是每 100 起审判中有 3.75 个无辜者被错误定罪，而 B 是每 100 起审判中只有 2.5 个无辜者被错误定罪。假设两个辖区有大致相等的审判数量，理智健全的人似乎不会希望生活在一个错误定罪风险高出 50%的法律制度中。他们将选择错误定罪风险较低的司法辖区，即使该辖区被证明有更高的错误定罪率。我们另外再提出第三个司法辖区 C，该司法辖区每 100 起审判中有 25 起被判有罪（和 B 区一样），错误定罪率 20%，但仅有我们在 A 区和 B 区审判数量的 20%。尽管 C 辖区错误定罪率显然过高了，但相比于 A 区和 B 区，一个无辜公民反而更不可能在 C 辖区被定罪。更抽象地说，一般观点是，错误定罪率没有考虑整体定罪率或审判频度，这两个因素恰恰都可能极大地影响究竟有多少无辜者将被错误定罪。

由此我们发现，证据法、诉讼法与实体法之间的关系是极其复杂的。在很大程度上，当代法律学术界由于将这些领域中的每一个都看作彼此封闭隔绝的而被误导了，这导致了我已证成的那些问题。人们未能正确地分析这三个领域之间的关系，还有另一个原因。[⑧] 当今大多数法律论述，都把法律规则分析为

⑧ 以下两页借用并改写自艾伦和盖伊注①文章。

一系列可以直接适用于其领域的必要和充分的条件，以致可以得出推演性结论。[⑨] 这就是常常在带孩子时以及主要讨论“法治”时所使用的游戏规则概念。位于该概念中心的概括和适用概括的过程，可能已在人们头脑中根深蒂固了，因为对于那些以有限智力资源与几乎无限的威胁进行较量的生物来说，它显然具有生存意义。如果某人的孩子在河边玩耍时不幸被鳄鱼吃了，除非这个人吸取某些关于鳄鱼与河流的一般教训，否则他的基因可能会很快消亡。然而，还有一些其他种类的规则和其他种类的推理。另一种规则的概念是一套可废止的条件。[⑩] 如果这条河是人们蛋白质的唯一来源，禁止孩子去河边同样会导致其基因消亡，因此，生存取决于某种并不依赖从关于孩子、河流和鳄鱼的规则所做的直接推演。[⑪]

规则的简单概念是单调逻辑的一个实例，而可废止的论证是非单调逻辑的实例。虽然尚未正式提出这样的术语，但许多现代超越规则的法学争论，都超越了这些不同逻辑形式的善恶问题，比如规则幅度的上下波动、规则与潜在目的、规则与标准，等等。在当今法学争论中，也许人们很少关注到这些争论背后的驱动力是具有复杂性的。单调逻辑在运用其假说更准确地捕捉有关事实与理由的总体时效果更好，因此它们在诸如游戏等简化环境中的效果更好。非单调逻辑在环境变得更复杂时，比如模拟自然推理的过程，效果更好。因此，超越规则以及无论什么替代品的争论，在很大程度上是关于相关领域之复杂性和人们对各种错误容忍度的隐性讨论。

举个关于这种差别的简单例子。考虑一下这个“规则”：“晚上请用水管清洗该船。”水管中的水压对这条规则很重要。人们可用以下形式进一步细化该规则：“把水龙头旋转两整圈，打开水流，然后清洗它”；或者，人们可以说“将水管开到水压足以冲洗掉船边赃物但又不要强到损坏涂层的程度”。重要之点是，来自水管的精确水压和完成该任务所需要的水压，并不取决于怎样拧水管，而是取决于一些其他变量，如温度、该系统中的水压、该区域的用水情况、附在船边赃物的性质，等等。这里适用的规则——清洗船只——目的十分明确，然而，如何实现那个目的却非常复杂，并取决于一系列连续变量的优

⑨ 关于这些规则，参见吉唐·戈特利布：《选择的逻辑》（1968 年）；约瑟夫·拉兹：《实践理性和规范》（1999 年）；弗雷德·绍尔：《游戏规则》（1992 年）；拉里·亚历山大和艾米丽·舍温：《规则之规则》（2001 年）；路易斯·卡普洛：《规则与标准》，载《杜克法律杂志》，第 42 卷，第 557 页；弗雷德·绍尔和拉里·亚历山大：《法律的有限领域面对道德的万能王国》，载《威廉和玛利亚法律评论》（第 48 卷，第 5 期，2007 年）。

⑩ 例如参见亨利·普拉肯和乔瓦尼·萨托编著：《法律论证的逻辑方法》（1997 年）。

⑪ 参见道格拉斯·N·沃尔顿：《溯因推理》（2004 年）。

化。当系统变化时，其调控者也必须保持正常运行。体力大致也是如此。例如，生物体的体内平衡，是通过许多相互作用系统的动态均衡来实现的，几乎肯定不能还原为可计算的运算法则。[12]

我今天所考察的在某种意义上最深刻的法学观点是，包括主要行为和诉讼行为的社会组织涉及一个复杂动态系统。它的各部分具有个别的复杂性，它们以令人困惑的复杂方式相互作用。法律分析者不必被传统证据、诉讼和实体的分类而蒙蔽，也不必假定这些事情可以通过静态的规则概念而得到理解或规制。社会组织和法律分析者的任务是使这个复杂有机动态系统最优化。证据法、诉讼法和实体法为实现该任务提供了工具，但它们必须在彼此的相互关系中才能得到理解，而且必须把它们作为社会最佳复杂系统的组成部分来进行分析。

⑫ 认知本身可以用比计算性术语更好的动力学术语得到描述。例如，参见蒂姆·温·格尔德：《如果不去计算，认识可能是什么?》，载《哲学杂志》，第92卷，1995年，第345页。

The Relationships among Evidence Law, Procedural Law, and Substantive Law

Ronald J. Allen

Yesterday, I gave you an overview of many issues that are foundational to the law of evidence and that must be thought about and accommodated in the structuring of a rational law of evidence. Today I want to go a little bit deeper into some of the issues that I touched upon briefly yesterday. I intend to do this by examining the relationship between evidence law, procedural law, and substantive law.

First, we need some definitions. Evidence law is that body of law that directly determines the admissibility or inadmissibility of evidence at a trial or hearing. Procedural law is that body of law that governs the formal preparation of a case for trial or for appeal. Together, evidence and procedure law directly affect litigation behavior. Substantive law is that body of law that determines rights and obligations and that directly affects primary behavior. "Primary behavior" refers to the actions of people and institutions outside of the context of litigation—everyday actions of people, in other words.

These definitions reflect the differing domains of the three fields. Evidence is largely motivated by epistemological concerns; procedure is motivated by efficiency concerns; and substantive law reflects the complex set of human interests that government must constantly try to accommodate in order to create the conditions of a flourishing society. However, the distinctions between these three concepts should not be overdrawn or overemphasized. These definitions are useful guides and not analytically pure statements. One can find within procedural law certain provisions that affect evidence, and within evidence law certain provisions which are procedural in nature. It is a waste of energy to engage in extended dispute about the "true" meaning of these terms or whether something "really" is evidence or procedure or substantive law. Rather, the important point is that three large domains of regulation exist: the regulation of primary behavior; the regulation of preparing and presenting cases for litigation; and the regulation of the evidentiary process at trial.

Some systems of law view the law of evidence as a part of the law of procedure. In one sense, this is another argument not worth having. One can organize things in an infinite number of ways, and again the question is not whether one organization is "true" in some sense but whether it is useful. One can categorize "procedure" as a branch of substantive law, for example, because procedure obviously affects behavior. Nonetheless, lumping evidence in as a part of procedure obscures what it is unique about the law of evidence—and that is precisely its epistemological focus. That in turn points out another important manner in which evidence differs from procedure, and in which procedure and substantive law are much more similar. Reason and cognition are universals of the human species; they are largely the same everywhere. Evidence law builds on that universal foundation, whereas procedural and substantive law are much more localized and contingent.

Although it is helpful to think of evidence, procedure and substance as distinct, in many instances their effects are analogous. There are various policies in addition to the pursuit of truth that motivate evidence law. While it is true that the primary motivation is truth determination, nonetheless many rules of evidence are explicitly motivated by other issues as well. Similarly, the law of procedure is not oblivious to the epistemological concerns of the law of evidence, and many procedural devices are directly involved with evidentiary concerns, such as discovery rules or motions to dismiss. Similarly, both evidence and procedure can create incentives for primary behavior, not just litigation behavior, and in that respect they overlap with substantive law as well.

Note that we now have two distinct sets of categories. The first is comprised of three kinds of law: evidence, procedure, substance. The second is two types of behavior: primary and litigation. I now want to spend a few moments on this second set. As I discussed yesterday, the distinction between primary and litigation behavior is clear, although again there may be some overlap. Primary behavior refers to the actions of citizens in living their lives, and the substantive law provides the rules that govern those actions. Litigation behavior refers to the activity of resolving disputes through formal legal means.

It is conventional in legal scholarship to view primary and litigation behavior as separate and distinct areas with internal logics of their own. Primary behavior deals with what a society thinks is right and wrong, with creating the conditions for efficient economic behavior, regulating social interactions and institutions, and so on. The various forms of justification for substantive law are almost as varied and as complex as the behavior they regulate, but in general have to do with what a society believes to be morally correct and economically efficient behavior. Facilitating such behavior is the typical objective of social organization generally, and the law specifically. Litigation behavior, by contrast, involves parties attempting to get resolutions of disputes that have arisen over claims about inappropriate primary behavior or to rectify social disruptions that have occurred through alleged violations of substantive law.

Perhaps the most critical implication of the distinction between primary and litigation behavior is that resources spent on litigation appear to most legal commentators as dead weight social losses, or as we say in the United States, "crying over spilt milk." The idea is that litigation itself adds nothing of value to society. It does not produce useful goods, material or intellectual capital, and thus resources spent on litigation behavior is equivalent to throwing good money away. That is why almost most procedural and evidentiary codes begin with phrases such as that found in Rule 1 of the Federal Rules of Civil Procedure to the effect that the rules of civil procedure "should be construed and administered to secure the just, speedy, and inexpensive determination of every action and proceeding." This is echoed in Rule 2 of the Federal Rules Evidence, which states: "These rules shall be construed to secure fairness in administration, elimination of unjustifiable expense and delay, promotion of growth and development of the law of evidence to the end that the truth may be ascertained and proceedings justly determined." These are noble expressions of high aspirations for the law of evidence and procedure and they are radically misleading. Let me repeat that: They are radically misleading.

First, let me briefly explain the rationale underlying these noble expressions. To do so requires that I introduce some simple micro-economic concepts. One of the things that the substantive law does is to try to ensure that people will bear the true cost of their behavior. This is a simple expression but it has profound implications. Primary behavior almost invariably does not simply produce socially valuable goods; it usually does so with costs attached. When a factory produces cars or computers, it also produces environmental waste, for example. Another example: driving a car can be a social good by making transportation more efficient, but it, too, produces waste products and can cause injury. One of the most important aspects of the substantive law is the effort to align costs with behavior because this is critically important to creating the optimal incentives for the production of the behavior in question. Imagine a factory that produces something useful, such as cars or computers. If the factory can just dump its waste product in the river or on its neighbor's property, it can produce cars or computers at a cost lower than its actual cost—the factory has externalized some of its costs to its neighbors or those who live on the river or rely on it for their welfare. These people thus subsidize the production of the cars and computers. That in turn means the product of the factory will not be priced at its true cost—some of the cost is being borne by those unlucky enough to be the neighbors of the factory. In that case, most economists would predict that there will over production of cars and computers. Lowering the cost of the production of an item encourages it production, as raising the cost has the opposite effect. Generally speaking, one can approximate optimal production of social goods by having them produced at their actual cost. Thus, one of the important objectives of the substantive law is precisely to make people bear the true cost of their behavior.

This concept applies to everything in society. Factories should bear the true cost of their behavior. You are facing this question in China today as you begin to come to grips with the devastation of the environment that previously had been tolerated by some of your government's policies. When you drive a car, you, too, should bear the true cost of your behavior. You not only get benefits but impose risks on others when you drive. And other people impose risks on you, too. There is good reason to believe that making everyone bear the true cost of their behavior will lead to each of us making choices that will more likely optimize primary behavior than if we are insulated from the costs of our action or if we can externalize those costs to others. When I run a red light and hit another car, I should bear those costs, just as a factory that produces cars should bear all the costs of their production.

This micro-economic way of looking at the regulation of social behavior is extremely powerful and contains much to commend it. Indeed, I would go further and say that in my opinion it is the single most important guideline for social organization. This is not to say that they are not other guidelines that are also important and on occasion may be in conflict with the micro-economic approach. Obviously there are other considerations in governing, but none more important in my opinion than the guideline of attempting to structure the law so that all social actors bear the true cost of their activity.

Now consider the relationship between primary behavior and litigation behavior from the micro-economic perspective. Doing so makes clear what motivates aspirational statements like those I quoted from the Federal Rules of Civil Procedure and the Federal Rules of Evidence. Litigation costs increase the cost of the underlying primary behavior. Consider again our car factory. In addition to having to pay wages, purchase raw material and machinery, and dispose of waste products, the factory will have to bear the litigation costs of law suits. These raise the cost of producing goods, but without providing any value. The cars are not better built than they otherwise would be; pollution is not decreased, and so on. It is in this sense that most legal commentators view litigation expenses as dead weight social losses. They provide nothing in return. Thus, the objective is to get the costs of litigation to zero—to assure, in other words, compliance with the law with zero expenditure of resources. That is the objective, and that is what underlies the provisions in our rules quoted above.

The problem is that this objective is impossible to achieve. It is not possible to have a legal system where the cost of enforcement is zero. And remember that it is not an answer to this point that the government can subsidize litigation. The question is not just who is paying for something, but whether or not anyone is paying for something. When the government subsidizes litigation, that subsidy acts as an incentive for whatever the underlying behavior is, whether socially useful or not. Thus, the question is: how should a legal system be structured in the face of the unavoidable transaction costs that litigation, or any form of dispute resolution, involves?

This is where things get complicated. To see how complicated, I need to add one more complication. So far I have been talking about "costs" as though the term applied only to pure economic expenditures, but it has a second aspect to it as well. There can be social costs that are not directly monetizable, or perhaps not monetizable at all. We can call these social costs. Implicit in what I have been discussing so far is the ideal of a costless legal system. Think about this idea. Just sitting here today in the audience, doesn't it sound initially attractive to have a system in which legal disputes could be resolved literally free of charge? And remember that we are not talking about hidden governmental subsidies, for those are real costs; we are imagining a world of truly free dispositive resolution of disputes by the judicial system. And assume that this hypothetical system also made no errors. Actually, just to show you the subtlety of the economic approach to analyzing the legal system, the assumption of no errors is implicit in a costless decision making assumption, because mistakes would be costs.

So, now think of all the problems that would be solved by a free and accurate decision making process. It sounds wonderful, doesn't it? It sounds like what both your and my governments have been striving for throughout the centuries. It sounds like what your faculty lecture about incessantly and what all social and political theorists have aspired to since the Enlightenment. What is not to like about such a model?

Let me suggest an answer to that question, but I will do it through another question. What would you predict would happen if by magic a free and accurate dispute resolution system were put into effect tomorrow? Let me ask you a related question. What do you observe happening whenever the price of desired good or item goes down? What do you do when your favorite store holds a sale and reduces the price of the clothes that you like or the jewelry that you covet? Let me answer for you. You buy more of it. This, of course, is the central theme that I have been developing for some time now. Price affects consumption. As prices go down on any desired good, consumption goes up. If the price of dispute resolution went down tomorrow, you and I would both predict that consumption would go up. If the price went to zero, consumption would commensurately go up dramatically.

"So what?", you might very well be asking right now. What would be wrong with such a development? And have I not already admitted that reducing the cost of litigation would ameliorate some problems? The answer is that a costless legal regime could very well stimulate the overproduction of its product, and actually produce social harm. Let me tell you what I mean by that. Because legal disputes are not costless, individuals and institutions must make decisions as to how to dispute—whether to use the formal legal process or some other means. Suppose you own a home or rent an apartment. You will come into contact with untold numbers of individuals who perhaps will violate your rights or you will violate theirs. Perhaps vegetation from your land will fall onto theirs. Perhaps they will park their car in such as a way as to impede your access to your parking place. How do you handle such matters now? You do so by negotiating with the alleged violator of your rights. If the costs of litigation were zero, however, you could simply sue them rather than negotiate with them. Reducing the costs of litigation to zero thus could dramatically affect the manner in which people interrelate in society and some of you may think that those changes would be undesirable. Rather than having to talk to and negotiate with people to solve everyday problems of life, you could get an official resolution by government. It is not at all clear that living in such a world would be a substantial improvement over the alternatives.

To be clear about the complication that I have introduced here, my point is that forms of dispute resolution compete with each other, and some may be preferable for some sorts of problems than other ways such disputes could be resolved. It might be a social loss if people could too easily turn to the government to resolve certain kinds of disputes. Thus, the costs of litigation are not necessarily dead weight losses. They may contribute to social goods by providing incentives for the resolution of disputes in other ways than through formal litigation or the involvement of government.

I now want to generalize the point I have been developing the last few minutes. Contrary to the conventional view of legal scholarship, the litigation process cannot be analyzed separately from its effects on primary behavior. Primary and litigation behavior are not hermetically sealed off from each other, and they cannot be analyzed separately in the abstract. Their interactive effects must be taken into account. Primary behavior obviously affects litigation behavior, but so too does litigation behavior affect primary behavior and in more subtle ways than conventionally is believed.

This is a powerful insight but is also deeply troubling, for it means that the problem of social organization is much more complicated than it is typically believed to be. For example, there may be some types of litigation where behavior (both primary and litigation) are optimized by a low or zero cost litigation process. However, there may be other types of litigation that are optimized by infinitely high costs—in other words, cases that should not be brought. Perhaps family disputes are an example of this latter category. Other cases may be somewhere in between in that behavior is optimized by the impositions of some costs. But now you see precisely what I mean when I say that the problem of social organization is more complicated than it appears. The task for the legal system includes trying to determine how to respond in the face of such complexity—which cases should be encouraged to be brought, and which should not.

As I speak to you here tonight, in the United States we are struggling with these exact issues, and in a way that highlights the relationship between evidence, procedure, and substantive law. ① Our Federal rules of procedure and evidence were enacted in part to offset what was believed to be distorting aspects of the systems that they replaced. The previous systems were believed to disadvantage plaintiffs by raising their costs much too high. The solution to this was to simplify pleading requirements and allow cases to get on to what was believed to be low cost discovery, followed by low cost trials. Discovery costs would be low because the assumption was that knowledge of the typical cases was shared by both parties and thus a substantial investment in discovery would not be required. In addition, both parties would have the incentive to

① The next three pages are borrowed and paraphrased from Ronal d J. Allen & Alan E. Guy, *Conley* as a Special Case of *Twombly And Iqbal*: *Exploring the Intersection of Evidence and Procedure and the Nature of Rules*, 2010, 115 Penn St. L. Rev. 1

keep costs of discovery to their necessary minimum. You can immediately see how these conceptions map onto things we have been discussing tonight. In a world of symmetrical information and low transaction costs, the Federal rules most likely accomplished the goal of facilitating the accurate and efficient resolution of disputes without distorting the underlying substantive law, values that the procedural regime the Federal rules replaced did not adequately secure.

If the original assumptions about litigation are true, procedural wrangling serves no purpose. However, unnecessary litigation costs make the underlying substantive right less valuable, and that can distort substantive law. Here we see the interaction of evidence and procedure. The standard of proof in civil cases of a preponderance of the evidence as a general matter optimizes social value, but it can only do so if the cases brought to trial are not a skewed or distorted sample of the underlying disputes that people have.

If, by contrast, the legal procedure creates distortions in the cases that are brought to trial, the preponderance standard is not likely optimal. Prior to the Federal rules being adopted, perhaps procedural costs systematically disfavored plaintiffs. If the status of plaintiff and defendant are not random (e. g. more pedestrians than car drivers deserve to recover for accidents and thus more pedestrians sue car drivers than vice versa), then the effect of the procedural regime, coupled with applying the standard evidentiary rules, could be to undermine the substantive law. In the car example, car drivers would not adequately internalize the costs of their behavior if too many at-fault drivers escape liability because of litigation costs of plaintiffs. The adoption of the Federal Rules might have rectified this in part by clearing away some procedural impediments to accurate adjudication that favored defendants.

The problem we face today in the United States is that the assumptions about knowledge and cost are not true in some set of cases. Knowledge is not symmetrically distributed, and discovery costs may be large relative to the value of claims and also asymmetrically distributed. Applying the original understanding of the rules in that subset of cases will not further the underlying purpose of accurate and efficient adjudication, and will undermine the original achievements of the Rules by misallocating errors and correct outcomes. That in turn will undermine the substantive law.

If the positions of plaintiff and defendant have been inverted from what was believed to be the pre-Rules situation, that justifies more intense scrutiny of the complaints, which means imposing higher costs at that point. Originally, the procedural regime favored defendants and thus subsidized socially wasteful activity; now in some set of cases it favors plaintiffs with the opposite effect. In such cases, defendants will be deterred from productive activities not by the law but by litigation costs that increase the *in terrorum* value of even meritless suits that puts pressure on a defendant to settle and burdens otherwise lawful conduct. Potential defendants will engage in litigation avoidance tactics that are likely to be socially wasteful, and they will settle to avoid litigation costs rather than risk liability on the merits. This increases the cost of conduct which is not itself actionable, but which might appear indistinguishable from that which is if a complaint is drawn with a high degree of generality.

We are beginning to see how complex the relationships are among evidence, procedure, and substantive law. This is in part because both evidence and procedure that produce litigation behavior on the one hand are complicated regimes, but so too is substantive law that affects primary behavior. Most importantly, the complexities come from the need to optimize them both. I will give you one more example of this complexity, and one more example of where conventional legal thinking has made a serious mistake. We conceive of burden of proof rules, as I alluded to above, as being designed to further the substantive law by facilitating the optimal relationship between litigation and primary behavior and as furthering various social interests. In civil cases, for example, the plaintiff and defendant are indistinguishable before the law. Assume they are suing over $1, 000 (7000 Yuan) . The law does not know who should get the money. Thus, in civil cases we employ the preponderance standard in other to reflect their equality before the law, to reduce the total number of errors that we make, and to help structure their incentives appropriately. In criminal cases, we think it is worse to convict an innocent person than it is to acquit a guilty person, and so we employ a burden of persuasion of beyond reasonable doubt in order to protect against convicting innocent people by making it difficult to convict anyone; this is sometimes referred to as the Blackstone ratio that asserts that it is better to acquit ten guilty people than convict one innocent person. I will have more to say about these matters in tomorrow's lecture on The Nature of Juridical Proof, but I just want to end tonight's lecture by demonstrating how the conventional beliefs about these burdens of persuasion are deeply problematic in part because of their neglect of the relationships among evidence, procedure, and substantive law. I will focus on criminal cases because that is where the effect is most dramatic. I want to emphasize, however, that the analytical points that I am making apply to civil cases as well.

Although the approach to burdens of persuasion embodied in the Blackstone ratio is the conventional justification for the burden of persuasion in criminal cases, it has highly peculiar implications upon closer analysis. ② Consider first the difficulties engendered by focusing on the error rate at trial. In the United States, there is data indicating that the error rate of felony trials is somewhere between 3.5% and 5.0% in convictions of capital rape-murders at trial. Assume these figures reflect the error rates of felony trials generally. It is completely unclear why that is a rate of much concern or what one should make of it with regard to the system as a whole. It may be considered too high if the error rate were not necessary to generate accurate convictions and acquittals, which seems impossible under conventional views of the purpose of proof beyond reasonable doubt. For example, if the proper ratio between false acquittals and false convictions is 10 to 1, a rate of false convictions of 3.5%~5.0% would require 35%~50% wrongful acquittals, leaving only between 45%~61.5% of the cases to be correctly decided. That hardly seems to accomplish the important goal of generating accurate outcomes at trial. Moreover, the error rate may be too low to get the right ratio of false acquittals to false convictions. Maybe all the other cases are false acquittals, leaving a Blackstone ratio of 1 to 19 (at the 5% false conviction rate). If so, perhaps we need more false convictions to lower the ratio to the proper level of 10 to 1, and at the same

② The next few pages are borrowed and paraphrased from Ronald J. Allen & Larry Laudan, *Deadly Dilemmas*, 41 Texas Tech. L. Rev. 45 (2008).

time get some accurate outcomes.

If this seems like a peculiar form of analysis, perhaps that is because this entire way of examining the problem is misguided. I believe that it is and will shortly explain why. Before doing so, however, note the absence of another datum equally critical to an appraisal of the error rate of the criminal justice system—the rate of unsolved crimes. Unsolved crimes are mistakes that very likely impose large social costs in a multitude of ways, including loss of deterrence and incapacitation, failure to satisfy victims' retributive feelings, lack of closure, increased sense of insecurity, and property loss. As I have been discussing tonight, trials, pleas, and the entire criminal justice system are just instrumental parts of the larger social fabric. Again, how a datum about trial errors standing alone can be appraised without knowing how it fits into that larger picture is completely unclear. For example, some recent work suggests the error rate of wrongful death sentences is about 2%.③ Although, the bare empirical assertion of the error rate may be accurate, the significance of comparing wrongful death sentences to total death sentences is unclear. Why not, for example, compare wrongful death sentences to the total number of murder convictions? Why not compare them to the total number of death-eligible homicides that have occurred over the same time period? Again, the policy implications of this number are completely opaque. If one is concerned about the error rate of wrongful capital convictions, one can change that just as much by increasing the execution rate as by reducing the wrongful conviction rate—for the error rate in capital cases could be drastically lowered by executing many of the convicted murderers for whom there is essentially no doubt about their factual guilt.

There is another the vexing question that now arises: what is a mistake? Implicit in arguments that a certain rate of error is too high is the idea that there is an

③ *See* Samuel R. Gross & Barbara O'Brien, *Frequency and Predictors of False Conviction: Why We Know So Little and New Data on Capital Cases* 14-15 (Univ. of Mich. Law Sch. Pub. Law Research Paper No. 93 and Mich. Univ. Coll. of Law Legal Studies Research Paper No. 50-14, 2007), *available at* http://ssrn.com/abstract=996629; *see also* Samuel R. Gross et al., *Exonerations in the United States: 1989 to 2003*, 95 J. Crim. L. & Criminology 523, 532 (2007).

alternative that would produce greater utility than the status quo. But what exactly would that be here? If capital punishment has any significant deterrent effect, eliminating capital punishment would not minimize the wrongful loss of lives; it would likely substantially increase innocent deaths. Even if there is no deterrent effect, people are killed with regularity in prisons (penal sentences being the obvious alternative to capital punishment), and thus, eliminating capital punishment may merely shift who is being killed. Indeed, if possible error in capital punishment cases were a sufficient reason to eliminate the process, it follows that prisons should also be closed immediately. More "innocent" people have been killed in prison since the reinstitution of the death penalty than have been executed, let alone wrongfully executed. ④

The problem is even more intractable. Prison is not only a risky place to live, but being incarcerated almost surely reduces one's life expectancy upon leaving prison. People exiting prison have reduced job prospects, ⑤ and prison disrupts their social relationships. ⑥ Most significantly, released inmates often carry diseases contracted while incarcerated and die at a younger age than oth-

④ *See* Christopher J. Mumola, *Bureau of Justice Statistics*, *U. S. Dep't of Justice*, *Medical Causes of Death in State Prisons*, *2001—2004*, at 1 (2007), *available at* http: //www. ojp. usdoj. gov/ bjs/ pub/pdf/mcdsp04. pdf. According to the Department of Justice, there were 12, 129 deaths in state prisons between 2001 and 2004, with nearly 10% attributable to either homicide or suicide. *Id.* The Department of Justice conducted this special study into the problems of suicide and homicide in local jails and states prisons. *See* Christopher J. Mumola, *Bureau of Justice Statistics*, *U. S. Dep't of Justice*, *Suicide and Homicide in State Prisons and Local Jails* 1 (2005), http: //www. ojp. usdoj. gov/bjs/pub/pdf/ shsplj. pdf. In 2002, the suicide rate in jails was 16 per 100, 000 prisoners and the homicide rate was 4 per 100, 000. *Id.* Interestingly, death rates in prison are slightly higher than comparable death rates for non-incarcerated individuals for all groups except African-Americans. *See* Nat'l Vital Statistics Sys. , *Ctrs. for Disease Control & Prevention*, *Deaths*, *Percentage of Total Death in 10 Year Age Groups by Race and Sex*: *United States 2003*, at 1—83 (2003), http: //www. cdc. gov/nchs/data/dvs/ lcwk2 _ 2003. pdf (listing causes of death) . This is because the primary cause of death of young black men is murder, the rate of which, in a gruesome irony, goes down in prison. *See id.*.

⑤ *See* Eva S. Nilsen, *Decency*, *Dignity*, *and Desert*: *Restoring Ideals of Human Punishment to Constitutional Discourse*, 41 U. C. Davis L. Rev. 111, 134 (2007) (finding that paroled individuals earn only half as much as similarly situated people who have not been in jail) . Substance abuse, illiteracy, and homelessness are widespread among released prisoners, and 70%—80% remained jobless a year after their release. *Id.* , at 135.

⑥ *See* Darryl K. Brown, *Cost-Benefit Analysis in the Criminal Law*, 92 Cal. L. Rev. 323, 346-49 (2004) . Former convicts face limits on their legal rights, ranging from voting limitations, to limited educational assistance, to reduced eligibility for public assistance and public housing. *See* Debbie A. Mukamel & Paul N. Samuels, *Statutory Limitations on Civil Rights of People with Criminal Records*, 30 Fordham Urb. L. J. 1501, 1501 (2003) .

erwise would have been the case. [7]All of those years of shortened lives are mistakes the criminal justice system unjustly imposes, and they surely outweigh the man-hours lost through the executions of innocent persons.

Where do all these peculiar implications come from? One possible source is that they are a product of the neglect of the relationships among evidence, procedure, and substantive law. The Blackstone ratio approaches to burdens of persuasion focuses exclusively on what happens at trial, and it does so in a way that is superficially attractive but in fact is deeply problematic. All the Blackstone ratio does is to guarantee that, in a representative run of 100 criminal trials, there would be no more than nine false convictions. But note that if there are 9 false convictions in every 100 cases, at least ninety false acquittals would be required to offset them, leaving at best the possibility that one verdict out of 100 was correct. Virtually every innocent defendant is convicted and virtually every guilty defendant is acquitted.

Take a less extreme scenario. Suppose there are fifty convictions in a sequence of 100 trials, five of which are false. The Blackstone ratio of 10：1 would clearly require fifty false acquittals. Therefore, *every* acquittal would have to be false, meaning fifty guilty felons would go free and forty-five guilty felons would be convicted. The risk that an innocent defendant runs of being convicted under this scenario is 100%, twice the risk that a felon runs of being

⑦ *See Nat'l Comm'n on Corr. Health Care*, *The Health Status of Soon-to-be-Released Inmates*: *A Report to Congress 17* (2002), *available at* http://www.ncchc.org/stbr/Volume1/Chapter 3. pdf. Prisoners are estimated to have HIV/AIDS at five times the rate of the general population, and 17% of the population with AIDS has passed through the prison system. *Id.* Approximately 8% of the prison population had another sexually transmitted disease—syphilis, chlamydia, or gonorrhea. *Id.* The rate of these three diseases in the population at large is less than 1%. *See Ctr. for Disease Control*, *Trends in Reportable Sexually Transmitted Diseases in the United States*, *2003*, at 1-3 (2003), *available at* http://www.cdc.gov/std/stats03/2003SurveillanceSummary.pdf (reporting 304 cases of chlamydia per 100, 000 people, 116 cases of gonorrhea per 100, 000 people, and 2.5 cases of syphilis per 100, 000 people). At least a third of the population with hepatitis C has served time in a prison. Nat'l Comm'n on Corr. Health Care, *supra*, 7. In city and county jails, the population contracted tuberculosis at seventeen times the national average. *Id.* But the health effects go beyond the walls of the prison. *See* Jason Schnittker & Andrea John, *Enduring Stigma*: *The Long-Term Effects of Incarceration on Health*, 48 J. Health & Soc. Behav. 115, 125-27 (2007). Prison rape is an epidemic in American prisons. *See* Human Rights Watch, *No Escape*: *Male Rape in U.S. Prisons* (*2001*), *available at* http://www.hrw.org/reports/2001/prison/ report.html.

convicted. This scenario is clearly as perverse as the previous one. Yet this, too, is Blackstone compliant.

If we contemplate more reasonable scenarios, the problem with the Blackstone ratio is not that the ratio leads to unacceptable results, but that it produces*no* results at all. Suppose that, as a general rule, 75% of defendants on trial are convicted and that some 5% of those convictions are false. In this case, roughly four innocent defendants will be convicted in every 100 trials. The Blackstone ratio requires this to be balanced against roughly forty false acquittals. But under this scenario, there are only 25 acquittals to be had, even if we implausibly suppose that every acquitted defendant is guilty. In short, requiring a 10 to one ratio of wrongful acquittals to wrongful convictions cannot in principle be satisfied in American courts, given plausible assumptions about how American trials work. This point can be generalized by a simple proof that produces the general formula:

$$BR_{max} = [1/F\ (CF)] \times [\ (1/CR)\ -1]$$

In this formula, BR_{max} is the Blackstone ratio's upper limit in any system of criminal justice with a given rate of conviction (CR) and a given fraction of false convictions [F (CF)]. It follows from this rule that any system with a 5% false conviction rate, which probably includes most of the judicial systems in the world, and a conviction rate ≥67% cannot possibly achieve a 10 to 1 ratio.

A derivative of the conventional approaches to errors is that the false conviction rate (understood as the proportion of the convicted who are innocent) must be minimized as much as possible. The general idea is that we can judge whether a justice system is indeed just by analyzing how frequently the innocent figure among the convicted.

Like the Blackstone rule, this thesis of minimizing the rate of false convictions has not been examined very carefully. To see why not, begin by considering two hypothetical regimes of trial. Suppose that in jurisdiction*A*, there are 75 convictions in every 100 trials, and that the false conviction rate is 5%. By contrast, in jurisdiction *B*, there are 25 convictions per 100 trials, and the false conviction rate is an alarming 10%. Clearly, if our concern were with minimizing the false conviction rate, we should prefer *A* to *B*. The trouble is *that A* is falsely convicting 3. 75 innocent persons in every 100 trials while *B* is falsely convicting only 2. 5 innocents in every 100 trials. Supposing that both jurisdictions have roughly the same number of trials, it seems that few sane people would wish to live under a legal system in which their risk of false conviction is 50% higher. They would opt instead for the jurisdiction with the lower false conviction risk, even if that turned out to be the place with a higher false conviction rate. For good measure, throw in a third jurisdiction, *C*, with a false conviction rate of 20% and 25 convictions per 100 trials—like *B*—but with only 20% as many trials as we find in *A* and *B*. Despite the apparently exorbitant false conviction rate in *C*, an innocent citizen is less likely to be convicted in *C* than in either *A* or *B*. Put more abstractly, the general point is that the false conviction rate fails to account for either the overall conviction rate or the frequency of trials, both of which may dramatically affect how many innocent people will be falsely convicted.

We thus see that the relationships among evidence, procedure, and substantive law are extraordinarily complicated. In large measure, contemporary legal scholarship has been misdirected by viewing each of these areas as sealed off from the others, leading to the kinds of problems I have identified. There is another cause of the failure to analyze correctly the relationship between these three areas. ⑧ Most contemporary legal discourse analyzes legal rules as a set of necessary and sufficient conditions which may be applied straightforwardly to their domain so as to allow deductions to be drawn. ⑨ This is the concept of rule at play in games, often in raising children, and predominantly in discussions of "rule of law." The process of generalizing and applying the generalization at the heart of the concept is probably hardwired in human brains as it obviously has survival benefits for creatures with limited intellectual resources encountering a nearly infinite set of threats. If one's child wanders to the river

⑧ The next two pages are borrowed and paraphrase from Allen & Guy, supra n. 1.

⑨ On rules, see Gidon Gottlieb, *The Logic of Choice* (1968); Joseph Raz, *Practical Reason and Norms* (1999); Fred Schauer, *Playing By the Rules* (1992); Larry Alexander & Emily Sherwin, *The Rule of Rules* (2001), Louis Kaplow, *Rules Versus Standards*, 42 Duke Law Journal 557, Fred Schauer & Larry Alexander, *Law's Limited Domain Confronts Morality's Universal Empire*, William and Mary Law Review (Volume 48, Issue 5, 2007).

and gets eaten by a crocodile, one's DNA is likely to die out quickly unless one internalizes some general lessons about crocodiles and rivers. There are, however, other kinds of rules and other kinds of reasoning. Another concept of a rule is a set of defeasible conditions. ⑩ If the river is one's only source of protein, denying one's children access to it will just as surely lead to one's DNA dying out, and thus survival depends on something other than the straight forward deduction from the rule about children, rivers, and crocodiles. ⑪

The simple concept of a rule is an example of monotonic logic, and defeasible argumentation is an example of nonmonotonic logic. Although not normally put in such terms, many of the modern jurisprudential arguments over rules are arguments over the virtues and vices of these different forms of logic, such as the over- and under-breadth of rules, rules v. their underlying purposes, rules v. standards, and so on. Perhaps even less noticed in the current jurisprudential debates is that the driving force behind these arguments is complexity. Monotonic logics work better as their assumptions more accurately capture the relevant universe of reasons and facts, and thus they work better in simplified environments such as games. Nonmonotonic logics work better as the environment becomes more complex, such as in the efforts to model natural reasoning processes. Thus, much of the debate over rules and whatever the alternative might be is largely an implicit discussion about the complexity of the relevant domain and one's tolerance for mistakes of different kinds.

Here is a simple example of the difference. Consider the "rule": "At the end of the day hose down the boat to clean it." The water pressure from the hose will matter to such a rule. One could further elaborate the rule in such a form as "turn the spigot two full revolutions to start the water flow and then hose it down," or one could say "turn the spigot until the water pressure from the hose is adequate to loosen the material on the side of the boat but not so strong as to adversely affect the paint job." The point is that both the precise water pressure from a hose and the pressure needed to do the job will depend

⑩ *See*, *e.g.*, *Logical Models of Legal Argumentation* (Henry Prakken & Giovanni Sarto eds., 1997).

⑪ *See* Douglas N. Walton, *Abductive Reasoning* (2004).

on other variables than turning the spigot, such as temperature, water pressure in the system, water usage in the area, the nature of the stuff stuck to the side of the board, and so on. There is a rule here to be applied—clean the boat—the objective of which is quite clear, yet how to accomplish that objective is quite complicated and depends on the optimizing of a large number of continuous variables. As the system changes, so, too, must its regulators to keep it functioning normally. Many physical forces are like this. For example, homeostasis in organisms is achieved through dynamic equilibria of many interacting systems that almost surely could not be reduced to a computable algorithm. [12]

In one sense the deepest jurisprudential point that I have been examining tonight is that social organization, which includes both primary and litigation behavior, involves a complex, dynamic system. Its parts are individually complicated, and they interact in a bewilderingly complex fashion. The legal analyst must not be blinded by the conventional categories of evidence, produce and substance, nor assume that these matters can be understood or regulated through a conception of rules as static devices. The task of social organization, and of the legal analyst, is to optimize a complex organic dynamic. Evidence, procedure, and substantive law provide tools to be brought to that task, but they must be understood in relationship to each other and they must be analyzed as parts of a complex system of social optimization.

⑫ Cognition itself may be better described in dynamical than computational terms. *See*, *e. g.*, Tim Van Gelder, *What Might Cognition Be*, *if Not Computational*?, 92 J. of Phil. 345 (1995).

司法证明的性质*

王进喜　杜国栋　梁　良　译**

大部分证据学研究直接针对的是理论规则，如相关性、传闻、品性证据、专家证言，等等。这些规则相当重要，我在中国的演讲已经涉及了其中的大多数。但这之外，还有一系列问题，具体而言，这些问题针对的是证据法的概念基础，或更普遍的法律规则。在我的第一次讲座中，在讨论证据、程序及实体法的关系时，我已经涉及其中的某些问题。今天我想讨论另外一个基本问题，实际上，这可能是证据法最基本的问题，即司法证明的性质是什么？

这似乎是一个很奇怪的问题，因为从两点来看答案是如此明显。第一，似乎显而易见的是，司法证明并无异于其他学科中的证明，最明显的是历史学和科学（因为它们与法学最为相似）。第二，正如在法学中一样，在历史学和科学中，证明显而易见是盖然性的。决策总是在不确定的情况下作出的，人们对某个法律命题的证据的力度进行分级，就像人们在生活中对任何其他命题依据这样或那样的概率度量进行分级一样。你们可能非常熟悉司法证明的传统观点，即要通过对说服负担所要求的形式上的必需要素的证明来确定责任，通常情况下在民事案件中要达到优势证据，在刑事案件中要达到排除合理怀疑。在通常的概率计算中，这些证明负担被理解为一种概率度量，范围为 0.00 到 1.00，优势证据的概率要超过 0.50，而排除合理怀疑的证明的概率非常高（0.90 或者可能是 0.95）。①

这些传统的观点——司法证明与历史学和科学非常相似，以及证据本质上是盖然性的——在某些方面极具误导性，而在其他方面直接就是错误的。今晚我会探讨这些问题，在某种程度上是指明道路，即在中国，必须开展证据领域的基础研究。研究证据法的理论是重要的，但也要研究这些理论所立足的基本概念。

* 本文系艾伦教授 2010 年 6 月在中国政法大学所做的讲座。

** 王进喜，中国政法大学证据科学教育部重点实验室教授；杜国栋，中国政法大学博士研究生；梁良：北京市西城区人民法院法官。本文原载于《证据科学》，第 19 卷，2011 年第 6 期。

① 下面几页的内容源自我的若干文章，其中最重要的一篇是罗纳德 · J · 艾伦：《事实性歧义与一种证据理论》，载《西北大学法律评论》，第 88 期，1994 年，第 604 页。

首先，我们来探讨一下司法证明与其他学科的证明之间的关系。我之所以选择历史学和科学，是因为对大多数观察家来说它们好像与法学关系密切。历史学研究不仅仅包括认定历史真相，正如 19 世纪德国历史学家奥利波德·冯·兰德所主张的那样。相反，“历史学家们几乎总是将他们自己的观点裹挟进他们的描述当中，要么是明示地进行（提出自己的历史哲学），要么是悄然地进行（通过旨在达致连贯的叙述而达致连贯性）”②。正如卡尔·亨普尔所指出的那样，历史学解释旨在说明有关事件并不是“偶然事件”，从某些以前或者当时的条件来看，这是意料之中的。③ 这里所说的意料并不是预言或者占卜，而是根据一般规律的假定所进行的理性的、科学的预测。

在今天，对于亨普尔的观点是有争议的，但是它在某种程度上强调了历史学与司法证明之间的差别。争议的问题是，是否存在能为人们所知的一般性历史规律，或者人们是否能够对来自过去的支离破碎的证据作出解释。法律所关切的与此不同，这既不同于历史学研究中的科学观念，也显著不同于解释性的描述。在审判中，人们实际上总是致力于重建某一事件，恰像亨普尔所反对的古代德国史学思想那样讲述事情。其目的既不是发现一般的因果规律，也不是要清楚地表达某一事件的历史解释。相反，一般性的因果规律被作为证据所援用，证明发生的某些事件，而它们本身可能也是证据问题。对该事件的历史解释或者任何其他解释，与其说是重建活动的结果，不如说是重构活动的“仆人”。一个显而易见的例子是，动机总是具有可采性，但实际上从未被要求作为诉因的一个要素。

如果司法证明并不与历史学类似，那么它是否与专门从事获取事实真相的典型学科——科学相类似呢？与法学不同，在科学中，数据几乎是没有问题的。已实际发生的事件通常是对事件发生原因的解释活动的毫无争议的出发点。如果数据是含糊不清的，通常会反复试验直到取得令人满意的证实，从而排除观测的不充分，仅仅留下理论上的不充分，并对此进行解释。在法学中，恰恰相反。原始数据（“灯当时是红的”—“不，当时是绿的”）的不一致是常态，且重现通常不可能。争议的焦点在于实际究竟发生了什么。为什么会发生某件事情（无论发生了什么）可能在证据上存在争议。我的意思是，当事人会向事实认定者提出不同的甚至相互冲突的概括，但在提出这些概括时，是以一

② 詹姆斯·T·克龙彭伯格：《客观与历史主义：美国历史写作的一个世纪》，载《美国历史评论》，第 94 期，1989 年，第 1011～1029 页。

③ 卡尔·G·亨普尔：《普通法在历史中的作用》，载《哲学评论》，第 39 期，1942 年，第 35 页。

种导向某个事实结论的推论结构的形式进行的，而不是以关于普遍法则、原则或者理论的推论结构的形式进行的。

科学与法学之间，至少还有一个显著的差别。不管发现的过程如何，科学知识是按照假说—演绎的方式组织的。一般原则被视为假说，据此组织越来越具体的原则。不仅是在组织知识，也是在组织研究。研究活动通过消除异常（经验上或者理论上）以及偶尔修改或者替代该领域的概念结构，进一步系统化既存知识的演绎结构。虽然某些科学哲学家认为这些活动非常不同，但是它们各自的从业人员有许多共同点。他们共享组织良好的实体和方法论知识，虽然他们可能对这一知识的解释力的观点不一致。不过，就充分界定的问题仍然会存在分歧，只不过这些分歧掩盖在了一致之下。即使那些攻击某个领域的概念基础的人，通常也与那些在该领域工作的人共享方法论和数学原则，能够就被视为证据的事项达成一致，并能够以易于了解的方式表达其分歧的范围。

然而，对科学研究活动的这种描述方法并不能描述法律程序中的事实探究，虽然其原因违反直觉。科学探究具有高度复杂性，而就日常生活进行判决相当简单，但二者的差异不在于此，而是恰恰相反。科学在很大程度上是通过对现象进行简单化而进步的，特别是通过控制尽可能多的变量，科学知识的层次结构促进了这种现象的简单化。相反，对日常事件的判断几乎从来没有、也不能被视为可控实验的结果。太多的变量持续不断地、必然地发挥作用。并且，审判中的事实判断甚至更难驯服，因为审判过程的复杂性背后是现实生活的波谲云诡、气象万千。

让我们看一个简单的例子。假设一名证人作证。事实认定者必须判断什么构成了证言，但请思考这是多么困难的事呀。第一，这些都是常见的可信性问题，但是都非常复杂。举止不仅仅是举止，而是一套复杂的变量。证人出汗或者肌肉抽搐了吗？如果这样，是出于无辜地紧张、撒谎的压力、身体问题，或者仅仅是在令人遗憾的童年当中形成的不雅习惯？身体语言是在暗示诚实还是逃避；作证时的慵散是证明了其在撒谎还是在轻松地讲述坦率的故事？证人是在直视询问者的眼睛吗？如果这样，这说明其品性值得称赞还是表明这是善于交际的万灵油推销员的一种自信？声音变调表明的是正直人的端正品性还是紧张，紧张的声音表明的是捏造还是在关心案件的结果？等等。

相关变量远不止可信性的问题，举止仅是其中之一。当证人在阐明某命题时，事实认定者必须确定该命题要主张什么，以及事实认定者相信其主张的是什么。这一工作也涉及数量巨大的变量。此外，在证人首次陈述其命题之前，事实认定者基于其观察也拥有某些知识，例如从律师处获得的知识。还有更多的例子。法学如果要作为一门科学，就要求将很多这样的变量置于一种演绎结构中，并说明其充要条件。在实际生活中是没有办法来创造这样的结构的，其太复杂。

虽然科学知识和外行知识的结构在组织和获取上有差别，但是二者都隐含了这样的问题，即不能说明知识的充要条件。稍微有点违反直觉的是，外行知识更能反映上述问题，因为其具有复杂性，并且因而缺少消除商定含混之处的有组织活动。在外行的世界，芸芸众生并不屈尊于以一种有组织的方式、类似于科学家工作的方式来解决得到清晰表达的问题。这主要不是因为问题琐碎，而是因为含糊不清的范围太大。无论如何，我认为确实可以这么说，我们就以下事物缺乏共识，包括：日常事务（某些人知道或认为其知道别人所不知道的事）的知识和按照什么顺序方面研究（与在审判中真伪不辨相比，一些人会对品酒时的莫辨楮叶更耿耿于怀，其他人不这样）。当然，法律争议之外，在有组织地消除日常的含糊不清方面（这可能是我们为什么要投入资源的原因），与当前相比，投入更多的资源会取得什么样的回报，我们并不一目了然。尽管如此，关键的问题是，与可想象到的最复杂的科学相比，关于外行世界的日常知识其实更为复杂。

因此，看起来在某些重要方面，法律的事实认定任务与明显的类似物——历史学和科学——是不同的，并且在一定程度上是独一无二的。在今天讲座的最后，我会讨论这种独特性的含义，以及法律是如何处理这一棘手的复杂性的。在此之前，我将要讨论第二个常见的观点，该观点也极具误导性并在某些方面是错误的，该观点为，司法证明是盖然性的。

我上次在中国政法大学做讲座时，简要地探讨了一些证明悖论的问题，这些悖论表明司法证据并不是盖然性的。我现在回顾一下其中的某些问题。[④]两个独立事件发生的概率是它们各自概率的乘积。如果抛掷硬币，正面朝上的概率是1/2，一次两个硬币正面朝上的概率（或者抛掷两枚硬币得到正面的概率）是1/2 ×1/2，或者1/4。用通常的概率方法来表述司法证明，存在着严重的问题。在民事案件中，每个要素都必须认定到相关证明标准要求的水平。该标准通常是优势证据，常常被界定为“比不可能更可能”或者是“50％＋”。但是，只有当原告诉因中的所有要素都是真实的时候，原告才能赢得民事审判。我们都同意这种观点，即被告非故意地造成了原告的伤害，或者有意这样

④　以下几页内容源自于罗纳德·J·艾伦：《民事审判的概念重构》，载《波士顿大学法律评论》，第66期，1986年，第401页。

做但没有造成伤害，而原告却因故意侵权获得了赔偿，此时便是错误的。然而，这种理解与联合规则（the conjunction rule）是不一致的。

假设事实认定者认定故意的概率是0.6，而因果关系的概率也是0.6。假定这些要素是独立的，它们同时发生的概率是0.36。因此，“它们当中至少一个不是真实”时的概率——这会导致对于被告的裁决——即1－0.36，或者是0.64。因此，我们适用说服负担的方式和希望审判作出裁决的方式之间存在分歧。如果这些数字是对该案件所属的案件类别的精确评估（也就是说，从长远来看，在大约2/3的这些案件中，取得赔偿的必要要素中至少一个是不真实的），那么系统将不利于被告人，也就是会发生更多的倾向于原告方而不是被告方的错误。

联合原则的一个引申是，它在纠纷的审判中注入了一个确凿无疑的不平等待遇，也就是诉因要素数量的功能。比较两个诉因。假设第一个诉因含有两个要素，而第二个有三个要素。为研究不平等待遇，假定两个诉因里面的每一个要素发生的概率都证明到了0.75，这一概率超过了优势证据的要求。但是要注意联合原则的后果。在第一个案件当中，两个要素均真实发生的概率（我们还是假设这都是独立发生的）是0.75×0.75，即0.56。在这种情况下，尽管存在这种联合效应，但是对原告的判决显然还是合理的。现在，思考第二个案件的结果，其中所有的三个要素都真实发生的概率是0.75×0.75×0.75，即0.42。这样，我们的例子证明错误偏爱原告而不偏爱被告。此外，通过比较两个案件的结果，我们还发现了另一个问题。被告作为一个类别，在第二个案件中比第一个案件中的情况更糟糕，即使每一个独立的要素在两个案件当中都是通过优势证据来认定的。

概括来说，如果两个要素，只要概率略微低于1－0.5×0.5，即0.75时，对原告作出的裁决是：被告不应承担责任。当涉及三个要素时，只要概率略低于1－（0.5 x 0.5 x 0.5），即0.875时，对原告作出的裁决是：被告不应承担责任。此外，当要求各个要素的概率乘积超过0.5时，不平等的影响不可能被消除。这样做的后果仅仅是将不平等待遇从被告转移至了原告。由于每一个额外要素通常都会降低联合发生的概率，为达到一定的水平，要素越多，证实的每一要素（平均而言）的概率则必须更高，不论它是0.5还是其他。因此，按照适用于这种情况的传统概率论，随着新的独立要素的增加，原告的任务会变得更加困难。因此，原告会因诉因中要素数量的偶然性而受到区别对待，而被告会因诉因中要素数量的不同而受到区别对待。如果传统的概率论适用于纠纷的审判，这样或那样的不平等会必然存在。

此外，传统概率论的联合原则和传统的审判观点的互动还产生了另一件怪事。比较两个案件，每一个都包含两个要素。假定第一个案件当中，每一个要素的概率都被证明为0.6，结果是裁决有利于原告。假设在第二个案件中，第一个要素的概率被证明为0.9，第二个要素的概率被证明为0.5，由于0.5的概率没有满足证据优势标准，第二个案件的结果是有利于被告。然而，如果两个要素是独立的，在第一个案件当中，概率是1－（0.6×0.6），即0.64，则至少有一个要素不真实；在第二个案件中，概率是1－（0.9×0.5），即0.55的概率，则至少有一个要素是不真实的。换句话说，第一个案件的概率高于第二个案件，被告不承担责任，但是根据传统的审判观点，判决会在第一个案件当中支持原告而在第二个案件中支持被告。

因此，我们看到用传统的概率来分析司法证明会产生悖论。另外还有一些概念上的困难。每个人的头脑中都存在为他们自己在日常生活中使用的概率观念。实际上，每个人拥有两个这种概念——作为相对几率的概率和作为一种确信的概率。实际上，还有两个其他的概率观念——作为倾向的概率和逻辑概率——但是这二者对司法证明都没有意义。因此，我们应该专注于相对频率和确信概率。但两者都没有为司法证明提供一个令人满意的基础。

对说服负担这一概念通常的解释（尽管是含蓄的）是，这是一种相对频率方法。当事实认定者确定一些要素的概率是0.6时，这意味着在一些类似的案件当中，10次当中有6次该要素是真实的。但问题是事实认定者几乎从未拥有允许作出这一决定的数据。审判通常不涉及类似于抛掷硬币的事件，它们涉及的是独一无二的事件，因此没有相对频率来测量。没有相对频率用以测量，对证明规则进行相对频率的解释便也没有了意义。

如果没有任何相对频率的数据，对司法证明适用相对频率概念的唯一途径是，民事案件的原告表明有关时刻万物的所有可能状况及其含义，如未能做到这一点将视为有利于被告。然而，有关时刻万物有着大量的存在可能（如果不是无限的话）。无限的一半仍然是无限，只有拥有超人能力的最不知疲倦的原告才能够进行这样的证明（并且没有人类的事实认定者能够活到足够长来听审它）。可能在一些异乎寻常的案件中，原告可能可以构筑一个运算法则来说明，所有有利于被告的案件，包括那些为审判证据支持的案件和那些没有举出直接证据的案件，其概率的总计说明没有责任的概率不足0.5，但是我认为仅仅说明这种逻辑可能性，足以排除它作为审判过程的一般解释。

传统概率理论的拥护者可能会在这一点上提出异议，即我上述的分析没有什么意义，他们认为在审判中事实认定者的任务是将庭上的证据与适当的参考类别相配，并因此判决案件。[5] 可是困难在于，没有预定的参考类别来与庭审证据进行比较。例如，假设有人在良好的观察条件下驱车经过仓库，并对一名乘客说："那儿有一个仓库。"假设特工观察到了一个真实的仓库，并且也认为它是充斥了数以百计的假仓库（虽然它们从正面看起来像是仓库，但仅仅是仓库的假门面而不是真正的仓库）的小镇上为数不多的真仓库中的一个。即使特工的结论是真实的，并且根据其真实性（看到了一个真实的仓库）得出了结论，并且它是经过可靠的过程形成的（在良好条件下的感知），这一结论也不能被称作知识，因为尽管这是真实的，但是只是偶然发生的。特工并不知道他看到了一个真实的仓库。特工会形成同样的信念，即使他观察到的仅是城里的许多假仓库之一。要具备拥有知识的资格，报告人需要能够辨识相关的反事实条件状况。由于在这些情况下，特工的能力不够敏感，就城镇的仓库而言，他是一名不可靠的报告者。

现在假定，虚假仓库镇位于仓库县，在那里真正的仓库数量远远多于伪仓库数。假设神奇的是，加上特工是在仓库县这一事实后，在那个镇中看起来不可靠的特工现在看起来是可靠的。但是，现在进一步假设，在虚假仓库州（仓库郡所在之地），伪仓库的数量远远多于真实的仓库数量。局势扭转，特工在该州当中现在又变成了一个不可靠的报告者。或者反方向思考：假设观察发生在真实仓库大街，在那里所有的仓库都是真实的。他在那条大街上是可靠的报告者，等等。

问题的关键在于：所考虑的事件（对仓库的观察）是无数个参考类别中的一个，而该参考类别的限制条件可以以不计其数的方式加以改变，就特定的参考类别而言，某些限制条件导致形成了认为特工是可靠的推论，而在某些限制条件下导致形成了认为特工不可靠的推论。而且——就仅仅构成事件本身的参考类别的外部而言——在自然的世界中，没有什么能够具有使其成为正确的类别的特免权或者使自己作为正确的类别脱颖而出；相反，我们对它们所产生的各种推论的兴趣，使得某些类别更具相关性或者更不具相关性。为了说明这一点的重要性，特别是其对司法目的的重要性，假定对特工（例如，作为法庭上的证人）的能力进行经验检验以确定仓库的准确性。对于进行该检验来说，"合适的"基线（基本比率）是什么？该基线是"真实仓库大街"的真实仓库的比率，还是虚假仓库镇的真实仓库的比率，抑或是仓库郡的真实仓库的比

[5] 以下几页内容源自于罗纳德·J·艾伦和迈克尔·帕尔多：《存有疑问的证据数学模型之价值》，载《法学研究杂志》第36期，2007年，第107页。

率，或者虚假仓库州（或者美利坚仓库合众国）的真实仓库的比率？这个问题不存在先验的正确答案，其取决于有关的利益。

一般性的概率论以及具体的相对频率论，能够作为一种有力的思想工具，在理解司法证明的某些方面发挥作用，但其并不能为理解司法证明提供一个稳固的基础。

作为相对频率概率的竞争对手，主观概率也不能为理解司法证明提供一个稳固的基础。或许下次我来中国的时候我会针对主观概率论及贝叶斯定律做一场讲座。但在这次讲座中，我将与大家重新回顾我上次在中国时与大家所讨论的问题，即，案件审判中错误的实际分布取决于进入审判的案件的基线，以及对案件概率进行评价的准确性（从原告应该胜诉等概率角度出发）。我将通过下图来阐述该问题，希望大家再度思考。

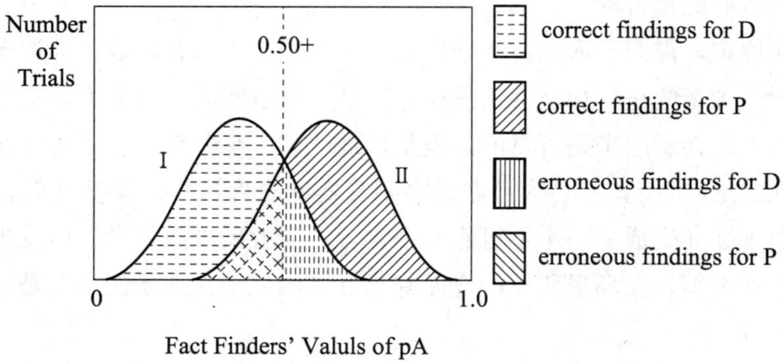

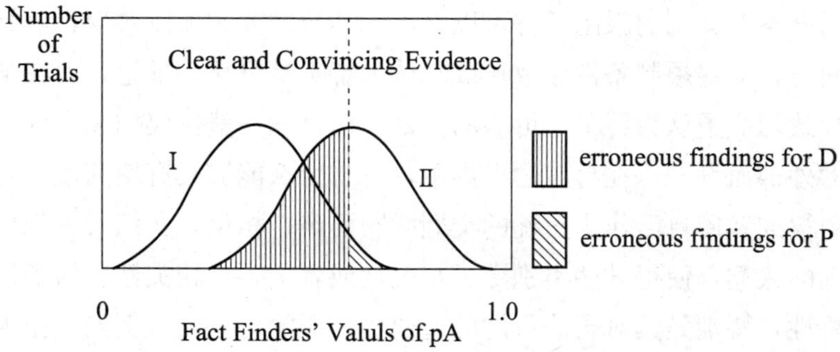

这些图是事实认定者作出的假想决策。正如我们在 12 月份所讨论的，错判的实际分布取决于所审判的两类案件的规模——这两类案件是：原告应该胜诉的案件，被告应胜诉的案件——以及事实认定者对概率的评估。在 12 月份的讲座中我主要讨论了子集的规模问题。我当时指出，这些子集的规模可能不同于我在上图中所述情形。确实，它们可以反映任何分布。现在我将主要讨论第二个变量——事实认定者对概率的评估。事实认定者的主观信念状态可能与对相关概率客观评价存在各种关系。比如，二者之间可能存在相反的关系；当关于有罪的主观信念上升时，有罪的客观概率就会下降，等等。显然，这也并不能作为司法证明的性质的稳固基础。

关于司法证明更好的一种解释，也是我认为正确的解释，是在哲学著作中已经阐述过的最佳解释推论（inference to the best explanation）。[6] 在审判中，会产生潜在的解释，并在解释性基础上就其中一个解释展开推论。第一个阶段的工作相当简单，主要由当事人（包括刑事案件中的政府）完成，当事人必须就事件提出对抗性的说法，如果该说法是真实的，将能够解释庭上提交的证据。对其起诉或者辩护负有证明负担的当事人提出关于事件的说法，该说法包括构成其具体起诉或辩护的形式要素；另一方当事人提供的关于事件的说法，而该说法未包括一个或多个形式要素。此外，如果法律允许，当事人可以就事件提供其他说法来解释证据。最后，事实认定者并不受限于当事人明确提出的可能解释，而是可以建构其自己的解释，要么在评议过程中就此告知其他陪审员，要么自己得出其能接受的结论。

在第二个阶段，问题变得更加复杂和充满争议。在民事案件中说服负担适用优势证据标准，证明取决于关于证据的最佳解释是否支持原告或被告。事实认定者根据当事人提出的以及其自身或者其他陪审员可能构建的关于事件的解释的相对合理性作出裁决。一般情况下，事实认定者推论认为最具合理性的解释是实际的解释，并根据这一接受的说法作出有利于实体法所支持的当事人的认定。经验证据已经证实，决策者（事实认定者）根据诸如连贯性、完整性和唯一性等标准，通过就事件建构能够说明审判中提出的证据的叙述式说法，来形成事实结论。这一过程是在解释性基础上进行的，即建构叙述以解释证据，并通过运用与科学哲学所援用的标准相类似的标准在各个选项中进行抉择。这些叙述就是一种“不证自明”的解释。即被接受的事件说法对证据作出解释，证据则提供理由，证成将该说法接受为正确说法的正当性。正如在科学中那样，这些说明是获得真实信念的工具，关注于解释的作用有助于说明推论的过程。

该过程在审判中的运行取决于法律体系及事实认定者的推论兴趣。为了对特定的若干证据进行解释，可以构建几个截然不同的叙述（或理论），所有这

⑥ 下文源自于迈克尔·帕尔东和罗纳德·J·艾伦：《司法证明和最佳解释》，载《法律与哲学》，第27期，2008年，第223页。

些叙述都具有同等的合理性。确实，这些叙述的数量不可胜数——事故是发生在正午，还是 12：01，抑或是二者之间不计其数的时间点的一个（正如 Zeno 所教导我们注意的）？等等。一般而言，解释的细致程度必须取决于相关背景。“事故发生在 12：00：01”或许过于繁细；“事故发生在 6 月 16 日中午”则可能已足够；“事故发生在过去的某个时间”则可能不够详尽。再来看一个人胃疼的例子。在妻子看来，丈夫吃了某些辛辣的东西这一事实足以作出解释，因为（根据妻子的推论兴趣）说明了适当的对照；至于该辛辣的食物是否是含有墨西哥胡椒粉的辣味奶酪汉堡（或其他辛辣的东西）则并不重要，因为这些食物都可能导致胃疼。对于其他情形或具有其他推论兴趣的人而言，如正在为他进行诊断的医生，则更为详细，各种各样的细节则更为合适。

在司法证明的背景中，两个因素决定了事实认定者在对解释进行评价时所关注的推论兴趣以及合适的详尽程度。这两个因素是：实体法和当事人主张的不同事件观点（争议事实）之间的对照。首先，实体法要求对证据进行充分详尽的解释，以表明原告有权获得救济（例如，“被告做了某些坏事”这样的解释通常是不够详尽的）。但是，有时候实体法允许当事人提供相当宽泛的解释。例如，事实自证（res ipsa loquitur）原则甚至允许在原告提出“我遭受的伤害是被告所做的什么事情造成的”这样的解释的情况下，只要这样的理论能够就证据提供最佳解释，就可获得赔偿。其次，如果当事人没有达成一致意见，为了在形成对比的各种解释中作出选择，需要关注适当的细节。如果被告主张说汽车事故发生时其正在州外的某个地方度假，则应该关注的合适的对照主张应该是他在州内（并驾驶着导致事故发生的汽车）还是州外，而不是其当时是否正在驾驶汽车，或者在后排座位，或者在宇宙的任何其他位置。我们接着看这个假想案件，假设该案件的争点是事故发生在中午还是什么其他时间。如果被告试图根据如下理由进行辩护，即虽然事故发生在正午，但证据并未准确表明事故发生在 12：00 还是 12：01，被告显然会败诉，因为实体法对此并不关心。最佳解释推论过程通过表明其如何聚合与区分如此众多的解释，解决了对解释过多的忧虑问题。

另一个可能的忧虑是潜在的说明过少。可能存在这样的情况，即任何一方当事人都未对证据提供特别合理的解释，要么是因为任何一方都未就关键证据作出解释，要么是因为证据不足，可以进行各种各样的解释，其中没有一个是比其他更好（或者更可能）一点的解释。在第一个场景中——各方就相同的或不同的关键证据所作出的解释均存在问题——关键点在于过程的对比性。裁决将要（并且应该）支持较好的（或可得的最好）的解释，无论该解释是一方当事人的还是事实认定者建构的。如果提出的解释实际上都是不好的（或都是好的）的，包括建构的额外的解释，裁决将要（并且应该）对负有说服负担的当事人不利。如果就潜在解释进行区分的证据太少，裁决也会对负有说服负担的当事人不利；该当事人未履行其提出证据的负担，以使理性的事实认定者可以就潜在的、形成对比的解释作出选择。通过以解释性方式理解证明责任，民事审判的结构因此缓和了对潜在解释过少的忧虑。

在刑事案件中，也有类似的过程。检控方必须提出关于合理故事的证据。如果辩护方未提出合理的无罪案件，则会被认定有罪。如果辩护方提出了合理的无罪案件，则会被宣告无罪。“提出合理案件”并不必然意味要站在证人席上或者作证；证据可以以各种方式提交，包括通过被告人之外的其他证人、交叉询问，等等。

让我总结一下今天所讨论的问题。人们会自然地从盖然性角度思考问题，而且毫无疑问的是，概率论对科学及日常生活来说都是有力的工具。这并不令人吃惊，许多法学理论工作者都试图从概率论角度来解释司法证明，从这个角度进行思考也相当自然。我今天试图说明的是，虽然概率论具有解释力且被人们所熟知，但从根本上看，对司法证明更好的解释是：其涉及的是最佳解释推论，而不是就支离的命题作出盖然性判断。这个结论除了有助于我们的理解外，还具有某些引申。最为重要的是，证据法应该考虑到司法证明是解释性的而不是盖然性的。

至少在美国证明了这一点。例如，存在各种优先于技术规制性或者排除性证据规则的完整性规则。这些完整性规则的作用是通过采纳与具体证言相关的材料，以通常的故事形式为事实认定者提供数据。其中的一个例子就是《联邦证据规则》规则 106：“当一方当事人提出书面材料或者录制性陈述，或者其中的一部分时，对方当事人可以要求同时提出从公平角度出发应当与此同时提出的该书面材料或者录制性陈述的任何其他部分，或者任何其他书面材料或者录制性陈述。”还有一些例子，包括司法辖区的“有关事实规则”（res gestae rule），该规则实际上允许在审判中提出与争讼问题有关的所有背景情况，以使相关事件更加丰满，无论背景材料在技术上是否可采。另一个例子就是对共谋者进行共同审判的标准做法，以便“向陪审员呈现一个更为全面的规则”。与之类似，正如我之前提到的，动机从不是一项要素，但是在民事和刑事案件中实际上总是具有可采性。如果民间说法正确的话，如果没有关于动机的证据，在刑事案件中获得有罪判决就近乎不可能。动机弥补了缺失，并将抽象的形式结构转化为具有人性的事件。《联邦证据规则》规则 612 就是另外一个例子。如果为了作证，证人通过书面材料唤醒其记忆，则该书面材料具有可采性，而无须考虑排除规则。同样，这也是为了让事实认定者看到整个图景，即我所说的“故事”。相对于要素模式来说，开局陈述与终局辩论也与故事模式更一致。开局陈述告诉事实认定者要讲什么故事，终局辩论实际上是在说明这个故事与对方的故事相比，更为合理。

证据规则的某些方面看上去与故事模式并不一致，但是这种不一致不过是徒有其表。排除规则就是一个例子。通过使证据同陪审团隔离，整个图景就不可能呈现。但是，一般性的排除规则少之又少。除了其目的与我的观点无关的宪法性排除规则以外，只有两种这样的排除规则：相关性证据规则和传闻证据规则。相关性排除规则确实使陪审员不能获得某些信息，但这些信息是任何人都不会合理地作为依据的信息，或这些证据的偏见价值远远大于其证明价值。这些都是相当宽松的可采性规则，因此，与司法证明的解释模式是一致，或至少是不相抵触的。

传闻证据规则与故事模式也是一致的。在理论上是一个问题，但在实践中却是这种故事模式的同盟。最重要的传闻形式，即自认和先前陈述，在很大程度上从传闻证据的范围内被排除了，或者根据例外被采纳了。此外，还有大量的明确的例外——《联邦证据规则》中有 27 个例外，以及两个其他例外。所有这些根据前文所说的“相关之事”原则上都是可采的。该原则是一条一网打尽的可采性规则，适用于许多根据明示的传闻例外或者其他不具有可采性的陈述例外。任何就可采性有着三十多个明示的例外及两项其他例外的规则，都会造成实际上无法使大量的相关信息同事实认定者隔离，因此，这些规则与故事模式也是一致的。

特免权规则确实使得陪审团了解不到相关信息，但是这种与我的基本理论的不一致之处也并不突出。大部分特免权规则旨在为某些其他价值而牺牲了对真相的探寻，因此，这无异于比较证明规则的传统观点和相当的具体案件建议。此外，律师—委托人特免权，作为一项重要的特免权，最好被理解为为促进而不是限制信息的提供，因为该特免权旨在鼓励委托人对律师的充分信息披露。

一方面，我即将结束关于司法证明性质的此次探索，另一方面，我希望这只是开始了中国对这个问题的探索。我衷心希望本次讲座能够促使大家——我们的中国学生们就此问题展开研究。

The Nature of Juridical Proof

Ronald J. Allen

Much of evidence scholarship deals with straight forward doctrinal rules, such as relevancy, hearsay, character evidence, expert testimony and the like. These rules are extremely important, and I have lectured on many of them in China. There is another set of questions, though, questions that deal with the conceptual foundations of the law of evidence specifically, or the rule of law more generally. In my first lecture, I touched on some of these issues in discussing the relationship between evidence, procedure, and substantive law. Today I wish to talk with you about another fundamental question, in fact perhaps the most fundamental question pertaining to evidence law, and that question is: What is the nature of juridical proof?

This may seem like a curious question to be asking, because the answer seems so obvious in two different ways. First, it may seem obvious that juridical proof is no different from proof in other disciplines, most notably (because most analogous to the law) history and science. Second, in both history and science, as in the law, obviously proof is probabilistic. Decision is always decision under uncertainty, and one grades the strength of evidence for a legal proposition as one does for any other proposition in life through a probabilistic measure of one sort or another. It will sound quite familiar to you that the conventional view of juridical proof is that liability is determined by proof of the formally necessary elements to the requisite burden of persuasion, typically a preponderance of the evidence in civil cases and proof beyond reasonable doubt in criminal cases. Those burdens of proof in turn are understood to be probability measures in the conventional probability calculus that ranges from 0.00 to 1.00, with preponderance being more than a .50 probability and proof beyond reasonable doubt being some very high probability (.90 or .95 perhaps).[①]

Both these conventional beliefs—that juridical proof is just like history and science and that evidence is essentially probabilistic—are highly misleading in certain respects and simply wrong in others. I will examine these matters tonight, in part to point the way that fundamental research in the field of evidence must develop in China. Research into the doctrines of evidence law is important, but so too is research in the fundamental concepts upon which the doctrines rest.

Let me begin with the relationship between juridical proof and proof in other disciplines. I choose history and science because these seem to most observers as close analogues to the law. Historical research involves not just finding the facts as they really are, as the nineteenth century German historian Leopold von Ranke might have argued. To the contrary, "historians have almost always smuggled themselves into their accounts either explicitly by presenting philosophies of history or implicitly by providing coherence through narratives calculated to provide coherence."[②] As Carl Hempel put it, historical explanation aims at showing that the event in question was not "a matter of chance," but was to be expected in view of certain antecedent or simultaneous conditions.[③] The expectation referred to is not prophecy or divination, but rational scientific anticipation which rests on the assumption of general laws.

Hempel's view is controversial today, but in a way that highlights the differences between historical and juridical proof. The controversy is whether there are general historical laws that can be known or instead whether the best one can hope for is interpretations of scattered pieces of evidence from the past. The law has a different concern that markedly distinguishes it from both the scientific conception of historical research and the interpretive version. At trial, the effort virtually always is to reconstruct a particular event, to tell things as they were in a fashion quite consistent with the ancient Germanic con-

① The next few pages are from my articles, the most important one is Ronald J. Allen, *Factual Ambiguity and a Theory of Evidence*, 88 Nw. U. L. Rev. 604 (1994).

② James T. Kloppenberg, *Objective and Historicism: A Century of American Historical Writing*, 94 Am. Hist. Rev. 1011, 1029 (1989).

③ Carl G. Hempel, *The Function of General Law in History*, 39 J. Phil. 35 (1942).

ception of historiography that Hempel rejects. The purpose is neither to uncover general causal laws nor to articulate historical interpretations of an event. Instead, general causal laws may be invoked intermediately as evidence that some event occurred, and themselves may be the subject of evidence. Historical interpretations, or any other kind for that matter, are the handmaidens of reconstruction rather than its result. An obvious example is that motive is always admissible but virtually never required as an element in a cause of action.

If juridical proof is not like history, is it like science, that paradigmatic discipline that specializes in getting the facts right? In science, unlike the law, the data are virtually never problematic. What actually happened is typically the uncontroversial starting point for attempting to explain why it happened. If the data are ambiguous, experiments generally will be repeated until replication is satisfactorily achieved, thus ruling out observational insufficiencies and leaving only theoretical insufficiencies as the explanation. In the law, exactly the opposite obtains. Inconsistent primary data ("the light was red" — "no, it was green") are the norm, and replication is generally impossible. Controversy virtually always settles on what happened. Why something happened (whatever did happen) may be evidentially controversial, by which I mean parties may advance varying and conflicting generalizations for the benefit of the fact finder, but they will be advanced in an inferential structure leading to a conclusion about a fact or series of facts rather than about a universal law, a principle, or a theory.

There is at least one other significant difference between science and law. Regardless of the process of discovery, scientific knowledge is organized in a hypothetico-deductive fashion. General principles are taken as assumptions under which are organized principles of increasing specificity. This organizes not only knowledge but also research. Research focuses on systematizing further the deductive structure of preexisting knowledge through the elimination of anomalies (empirically or theoretically) and on occasion on the modification or replacement of the conceptual structure of the field. While some philosophers of science see these activities as quite distinct, their respective practitioners have much in common. Both share a well-organized body of substantive and methodological knowledge, although they may disagree about the explanatory power of that knowledge. Still, the disagreement typically exists over well-defined issues and is swamped by the scope of agreement. Even those assaulting the conceptual foundations of a field typically share with those doing work within a field methodological and mathematical principles, agree on what counts as evidence, and are able to express their scope of disagreement comprehensibly.

This description of the activity of scientific research does not describe factual inquiry in the legal process, although for a counterintuitive reason. The difference is not that scientific inquiry is highly complicated and lay judgments about ordinary life quite simple, but the exact opposite. Scientific progress in large measure proceeds through the simplification of phenomena, in particular through controlling as many variables as possible, which the hierarchical structure of scientific knowledge facilitates. Judgments about ordinary events, by contrast, virtually never are and cannot be recast as the results of controlled experiments. Too many variables are constantly and necessarily in play. And factual judgments at trial are even more resistant to domestication because the complicating features of the trial process are draped over the bubbling cauldron of real life.

Consider a simple example. Suppose a witness testifies. The fact finder must decide what to make of the testimony, but consider how difficult that is. First, there are all the normal credibility issues, but these are enormously complicated. Demeanor is not just demeanor; it is instead a complex set of variables. Is the witness sweating or twitching, and if so is it through innocent nerves, the pressure of lying, a medical problem, or simply a distasteful habit picked up during a regrettable childhood? Does body language suggest truthfulness or evasion; is slouching evidence of lying or comfort in telling a straight forward story? Does the witness look the examiner straight in the eye, and if so is it evidence of commendable character or the confidence of an accomplished snake oil salesman? Does the voice inflection suggest the rectitude of the righteous person or is it strained, and does a strained voice indicate fabrication or concern over the outcome of the case? And so on.

The list of relevant variables goes far beyond credibility issues, of which demeanor is only one. When a witness articulates a proposition, the fact finder must determine what the proposition is designed to assert and what the fact finder believes it asserts. That task, too, involves an immense number of variables. In addition, the fact finder will possess some knowledge based on its observations leading up to the first articulated proposition by a witness, acquired from the lawyers for example. And there are many more examples. For the law to proceed as a science would require that many of these variables be in a deductive structure with their necessary and sufficient conditions spelled out. No such structure could be created; it would be too complex.

Although the structures of scientific and lay knowledge differ both in organization and acquisition, implicit in them both is the inability to state the necessary and sufficient conditions for knowledge. Lay knowledge is, somewhat counter-intuitively, an *a fortiori* case because of its complexity and the resultant lack of organized attempts to eliminate agreed-upon ambiguity. In the lay world, hordes of laymen do not descend in an organized fashion on well-articulated problems to resolve them in a fashion analogous to the work of scientists. This is not primarily because the problems are trivial but instead because the scope of ambiguity is far too wide. I think it fair to say, at any rate, that we lack consensus over the extent of our knowledge of conventional affairs (some people know, or believe they know, matters that elude others) or in what order aspects of it should be studied (some people regret ambiguity about wine more than ambiguity about truthfulness at trial; others do not) . And of course, it is not obvious, outside of legal disputes, what the payoff might be for investing greater resources than we presently do in an organized effort to eliminate conventional ambiguity, which is probably why we invest the resources that we do. Nonetheless, the critical point is that conventional knowledge of the lay world is more complicated than the most complicated science imaginable.

Thus, it appears that in certain crucial respects, the law's fact finding task differs from the obvious analogues of history and science, and to some extent is unique. At the end of the lecture tonight, I will address the implications of this uniqueness and how the law handles this intractable complexity. Before doing so, I wish to address the second of the conventional beliefs that is also highly misleading and wrong in certain respects, and that is the juridical proof is probabilistic.

When I last lectured here, I briefly discussed some of the proof paradoxes that suggest that juridical evidence is not probabilistic. Let me review some of those issues now. ④The probability of two independent events occurring is the product of their separate probabilities. If the probability of getting a head is 1/2 on the flip of a coin, the probability of getting two in a row—or of getting two heads from two identical coins—is 1/2 x 1/2, or 1/4. This is a serious problem for an account of juridical proof in conventional probability terms. In civil cases, each element must be found to the level required by the relevant standard of proof. That standard is normally a preponderance of the evidence, which is usually defined as "more probable than not" or as "50%+." Nonetheless, a plaintiff deserves to win a civil trial only if all of the elements of the cause of action are true. We would all agree that an error was made if a plaintiff recovered for an intentional tort where the defendant caused the injury but did not intend it, or intended it but did not cause it. This understanding, however, is not consistent with the conjunction rule.

Suppose a fact finder found the probability of intentionality to be .6 and that of causation to be .6 as well. Assuming that these elements are independent, the probability of their conjunction is .36. Thus, the probability of at least one of them not being true—which should result in a defendant's verdict—is 1 - .36, or .64. There is thus a divergence between how we apply burdens of persuasion and how we wish trials to come out. If these numbers were to be at all accurate assessments of the class of cases into which this individual case fell—that is to say that over the long run in about two-thirds of such cases at least one of the necessary elements of recovery is not true—then the system will be biased against defendants, and more errors favoring plaintiffs than defendants will be made.

One implication of the conjunction principle is that it injects a certain inequality of treatment into the trial of disputes that is a function of the number of

④ The next few pages borrows from Ronald J. Allen, *A Reconceptualization of Civil Trials*, 66 B. U. L. Rev. 401 (1986).

elements of a cause of action. Compare two causes of action. Assume that the first has two elements and that the second has three. To see the inequality of treatment, assume that in both causes of action each element is established to a probability of .75, which more than satisfies the requirement of a preponderance of the evidence. But note the consequences of the conjunction principle. In the first case, the probability of both elements being true, again assuming independence, is .75 x .75, or .56. In that case, a verdict for the plaintiff is obviously justifiable notwithstanding the effect of conjunction. Now consider the result in the second case where the probability that all three elements are true is .75 x .75 x .75, or .42. Here we have an example where errors will favor plaintiffs over defendants. In addition, we have another problem that emerges from comparing the results in the two cases. Defendants as a class are considerably worse off in the second case than in the first even if each individual element is found in both cases by a preponderance of the evidence.

To generalize, a verdict may be returned for a plaintiff if there are two issues whenever there is a slightly lower probability than 1 — (.5 x .5), or .75, that a defendant should not be liable. When there are three issues, a verdict for a plaintiff may be returned whenever there is a slightly lower probability than 1 — (.5 x .5 x .5), or .875, that a defendant should not be liable. Moreover, inequality cannot be eliminated by requiring the product of the individual elements too exceed .5. The effect of doing that merely shifts the differential treatment from defendants to plaintiffs. Since each additional element will generally lower the probability of the conjunction, the more elements there are, the higher is the probability to which, on average, each will have to be established in order to reach a specified level, regardless of whether it is .5 or something else. Thus, according to conventional probability theory as it would apply in this modified situation, plaintiffs' tasks will become more difficult as each new independent element is added. As a result, plaintiffs will be treated differentially based upon the fortuity of the number of elements in a cause of action, whereas under our present rules defendants are treated differentially based on the number of elements. If conventional probability theory is applicable to the trial of disputes, one or the other disparity must exist.

There is yet another curiosity emanating from the interaction of the conjunction principle of conventional probability and the conventional view of trials. Compare two cases, each containing two elements. Assume that in the first case each element is established to a probability of .6, thus resulting in a verdict for the plaintiff. Assume that in the second case one element is established to a probability of .9 and the second element is established to a probability of .5. Since a probability of .5 would not meet the preponderance of the evidence standard, the second case would result in a verdict for the defendant. However, if the two elements are independent, there is a 1 — (.6 x .6) or .64, probability that at least one of the elements is not true in the first case, and a 1 — (.9 x .5), or .55, probability that at least one element is not true in the second case. In other words, the probability is higher in the first case than in the second that the defendant is not factually liable, yet under the conventional view of trials a verdict will be returned for a plaintiff in the first case and the defendant in the second.

Thus we see that there are paradoxes that arise from modeling juridical proof as involving conventional probability. There are additional conceptual difficulties. Everyone carries around in their head a concept of probability that they employ in everyday life. In fact, everyone carries around two such concepts—probability as a relative frequency and probability as a state of belief. In fact, there are two other conceptualizations of probability—probability as a propensity and logical probability—but neither is of any significance for juridical proof, and thus we can concentrate on relative frequency and states of belief. Neither of these provides a satisfactory foundation for juridical proof.

The normal, although implicit, interpretation given to the concept of a burden of persuasion is that it is a relative frequency measure. When the fact finder determines the probability of some element to be .6, this means that the element will be true six out of 10 times in the set of similar cases. The problem is that the fact finder virtually never has the data that would permit such a determination. Trials do not typically involve matters analogous to flipping coins. They involve unique events, and thus there is no relative frequency to measure. Without a relative frequency to measure, a relative frequency interpretation of the proof rules makes no sense.

Without any relative frequency data, the only way to apply a relative frequency concept to juridical proof is for the plaintiff in a civil case to demonstrate all the possibly true states of the universe at the time in question as well as their implications, and the failure to do so would count in every instance in the defendant's favor. However, there are a large if not infinite number of ways the universe might have been at the time in question. One half of infinity remains infinity, and only the most tireless plaintiff with superhuman powers would be able to make such a showing (and no human fact finder would ever live long enough to hear it) . Perhaps in some unusual case a plaintiff could construct an algorithm demonstrating that the sum of the probabilities of all the cases favoring the defendant, those supported by trial evidence plus those for which no direct evidence has been adduced, amounts to less than a . 5 probability of no liability, but I suggest that the mere articulation of this logical possibility adequately disposes of it as a general explanation of the trial process.

An objection might be interposed at this point by a defender of conventional probability theory that the previous analysis misses the point and that the fact finder's task at trial is to fit the evidence at trial into the appropriate reference class and judge the case accordingly. ⑤The difficulty is that there is no predetermined reference class by which to compare the trial evidence. For example, suppose someone drives past a barn under good observation conditions and utters to a passenger: "there's a barn." Assume that the agent observed a real barn, but also assume that it is one of the few real barns in a town filled with hundreds of barn facades, which, although they look like barns from the front, are just fake barn fronts and not real barns. Even though the agent's conclusion was true and its truth (seeing a real barn) caused the conclusion, and it was formed by a reliable process (perception under good conditions), the conclusion does not qualify as knowledge because while true it is only accidentally so. The agent does not know he saw a real barn. The agent would have formed the same belief even if he had observed one of the hundreds of fake barns in the town. To qualify as knowledge, the reporter would need to be able

⑤ The next few pages are from Ronald J. Allen & Michael Pardo, *The Problematic Value of Mathematical Models of Evidence*, 36 Journal Legal of Studies 107 (January, 2007) .

to distinguish between relevant counterfactual situations. Because the agent's capacities are not sensitive enough under these circumstances, he is an unreliable reporter of barns in this town.

Now suppose that Fake Barn Town sits within Barn County in which real barns vastly outnumber the barn facades. As if by magic, the agent, who looked unreliable in the Town, now appears reliable when we attend to the fact that he in Barn County. But now suppose further that in Fake Barn State (in which the county is located) barn facades vastly outnumber real ones. The switch flips and the agent is now an unreliable reporter in the state. And so on. Or going in the reverse direction: suppose that the observation took place on Real Barn Street, in which all the barns are real. He is a reliable reporter on that street. And so forth.

Here is the critical point. The event under consideration (the observation of the barn) is a member of an infinite number of reference classes, the boundary conditions of which can be gerrymandered in countless ways, some of which lead to the inference that the agent is reliable and some that he is unreliable, given that particular class. And—outside of the reference class consisting only the event itself—nothing in the natural world privileges or picks out one of the classes as the right one; rather, our interests in the various inferences they generate pick out certain classes as more or less relevant. To see the significance of this point, and in particular its significance for juridical purposes, suppose an empirical test were being run as to the ability of our agent (a witness at trial, for example) to identify barns accurately. What is the "proper" baseline (base rate) for running such a test? Is it the proportion of true barns on Real Barn Street, Fake Barn Town, Barn County, or Fake Barn State (or maybe the United Barn States of America)? There is no *a priori* correct answer; it depends on the interests at stake.

Probability theory generally, and relative frequencies specifically can be powerful tools of thought, and they are useful in understanding some aspects of juridical proof, but they do not provide a secure foundation for understanding juridical proof.

Neither does the main competitor to probability as a relative frequency, which is subjective probability. Perhaps the next time I come to China I will do a lecture that focuses explicitly on subjective probability and Bayes' Theorem. For now, let me simply remind you what we discussed the last time I was in China, and that is that the actual distributions of errors at trial depend on the baseline of cases that go to trial and the accuracy of the appraisals of probability of those cases (in terms of the probability that the plaintiff should win and so on) . I illustrated this point with the following graphs that I want you to consider again.

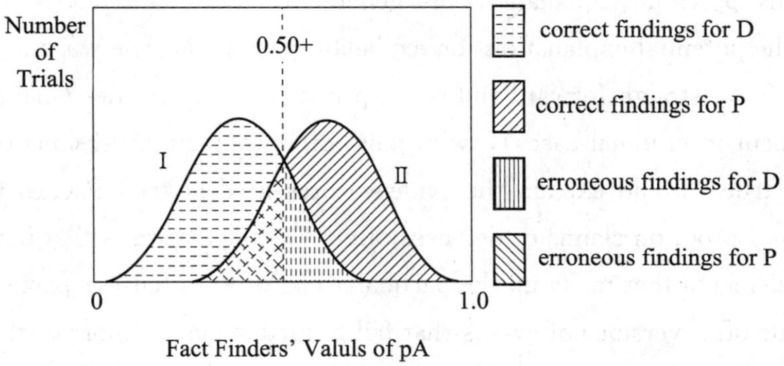

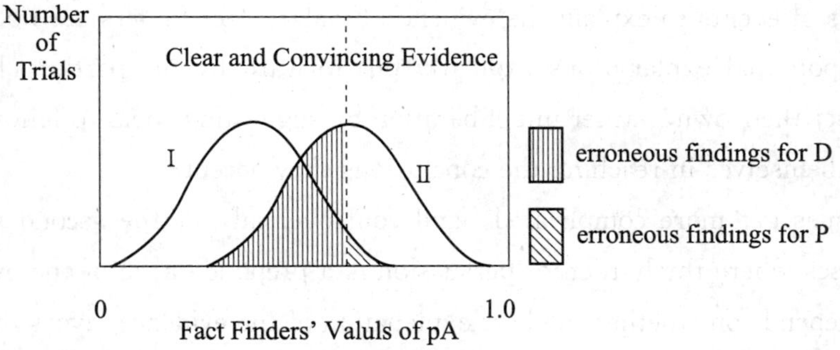

These are graphs of hypothetical decisions made by fact finders. As we discussed in December, the actual distributions of errors depend upon the size of the two sets of cases that go go trial—those two cases being one in which plaintiffs deserve to win and one in which defendants deserve to win—and the fact finder's assessments of probability. In December, I focused on the issue of the size of the subsets. I pointed out that the size of these subsets can vary from the way that I have drawn them in the graphs. Indeed, they could reflect any distribution whatsoever. Now I want to focus on the second variable—that fact finder's assessment of probability. The subjective belief state of the fact finder can be in any relationship at all to an objective appraisal of the relevant probability. For example, there might be an inverse relationship; as the subjective belief state of guilt goes up, the objective probability of guilt goes down, and so on. Plainly, this, too, cannot be a secure foundation for the nature of juridical proof.

A better, and I think correct, explanation of juridical proof is what is known in the philosophical literature as inference to the best explanation. [⑥]At litigation, potential explanations are generated, and an inference is made to one of the potential explanations on explanatory grounds. The work at the first stage is fairly straightforward and is left primarily to the parties (including the government in criminal cases), who must offer competing versions of events that, if true, would explain the evidence presented at trial. Parties with the burdens of proof on claims or defenses offer versions of events that include the formal elements that make up the particular claims or defenses; parties on the other side offer versions of events that fail to include one or more of the formal elements. In addition, parties may, when the law allows, offer alternative versions of events to explain the evidence. Finally, fact-finders are not limited to the potential explanations explicitly put forward by the parties, but may construct their own, either in deliberation by suggesting them to fellow jurors or for themselves in reaching the conclusions they accept.

Issues get more complicated, and controversial, at the second stage. In civil cases where the burden of persuasion is a preponderance of the evidence, proof depends on whether the best explanation of the evidence favors the plaintiff or the defendant. Fact finders decide based on the relative plausibility of the versions of events put forth by the parties, and possibly additional ones constructed by themselves or fellow jurors. As a general matter, fact finders infer the most plausible explanation as the actual explanation and find for the party that the substantive law supports based on this accepted version. Empirical evidence has confirmed that decision makers (fact finders) formulate factual conclusions by constructing narrative versions of events to ac-

⑥ What follows is from Michael Pardon & Ronald J. Allen, *Juridical Proof and the Best Explanation*, 27 Law & Philosophy 223 (2008).

count for the evidence presented at trial based on criteria such as coherence, completeness, and uniqueness. This process proceeds on explanatory grounds—narratives are constructed to explain the evidence and choose among alternatives by applying similar criteria to those invoked in the philosophy of science. These narratives function as "self-evidencing" explanations: the accepted version of events explains the evidence and the evidence provides reasons justifying acceptance of that version as the correct one. As in science, these explanations thus function as a tool for acquiring true beliefs, and a focus on the role of explanation helps to illuminate the inferential process.

How this process proceeds at trial depends on the inferential interests of the legal system and the fact-finders. Several distinct narratives (or theories) can be constructed to explain a given body of evidence, all of which are equally plausible. Indeed, their number is infinite—did the accident occur at noon or 12: 01 or at one of the infinite slices of time in between (which Zeno taught us to notice)?, and so on. In general, how fine-grained the explanation must be will depend on the context. "The accident occurred at 12: 00: 01" may be too detailed; "The accident occurred in the afternoon on June 16" may be good enough; and "An accident occurred sometime in the past" may be not detailed enough. Consider a man with heartburn. From the wife's perspective, the fact that he ate something spicy may be a good enough explanation because it identifies an appropriate contrast (based on the wife's inferential interests); it does not matter whether the spicy food was a chili cheeseburger with jalapenos (or something else spicy) because any such food would have caused the heartburn. For other contexts or for others with different inferential interests, such as his doctor making a diagnosis, more details and different details will be appropriate.

In the context of juridical proof, two factors set the inferential interests and the appropriate level of detail at which fact finders should focus in evaluating explanations. These factors are the substantive law and the points of contrast between the versions of events offered by the parties (the disputed facts). First, the substantive law will require a sufficiently detailed explanation of the evidence to show the plaintiff is entitled to relief. (E. g. , explanations such as "the defendant did something bad" typically will not be detailed enough.)

Sometimes, however, the substantive law allows parties to provide quite broad explanations. For example, the doctrine of res ipsa loquitur allows plaintiffs to recover even by offering explanations such as "My injuries were caused by *something* done by the defendant" when such a theory provides the best explanation of the evidence. And second, where the parties choose to disagree focuses attention on the appropriate details for choosing among contrasting explanations. If the defendant contends that he was on vacation somewhere out of state during the car accident, then the appropriate contrast on which to focus is whether he was in state (and driving the car that caused the accident) or out of state, and not on whether he was driving or in the back seat or the trunk or any other place in the universe. Consider further the hypothetical focusing on whether an accident occurred at noon or some other time. If a defendant tries to defend on the ground that, although the accident occurred around noon, the evidence does not show precisely whether it was at 12: 00 or 12: 01, the defendant will obviously lose because the substantive law is indifferent to the matter. The IBE process thus accommodates the concern of too many explanations by showing how to aggregate and differentiate among them.

A complementary possible concern is having too few potential explanations. There may be cases where neither party offers a particularly plausible explanation of the evidence, either because neither side can explain key pieces of evidence or because there is such a paucity of evidence that it can be explained in multifarious ways none of which are any better (or more likely) explanations than any other. In the first scenario—where each side has problems explaining the same or different critical items of evidence—the key point is the comparative aspect of the process. A verdict will (and should) be rendered for the*better* (or best available) explanation, whether it is one of the parties' or another one that is constructed by the fact-finder. If the proffered explanations truly are equally bad (or good), including additionally constructed ones, judgment will (and should) go against the party with the burden of persuasion. If there is too little evidence from which to differentiate among potential explanations, again judgment goes against the party with the burden of persuasion; they have failed to meet their burden of producing evidence from which a reasonable fact-finder could differentiate among the potential, contrasting explanations. Through burdens of proof understood in an explanatory manner, the structure of civil trials thus assuages concerns associated with too few potential explanations.

In criminal cases, a similar process is at play. The prosecution must present evidence of a plausible story. If the defendant does not present a plausible case of innocence, there is a conviction. If the defendant does present a plausible case of innocence, there is an acquittal. "Presenting a plausible case" does not necessarily mean taking the stand or testifying; evidence is presented in a multitude of ways, including through other witnesses than the defendant, cross-examination, and the like.

Let me close by summing up the journey we have taken tonight. People think naturally in probabilistic terms, and there is no question that probability theory is a powerful tool not only of science but of everyday life. Not surprisingly, many legal theorists have attempted to explain juridical proof in probabilistic terms, and it is quite natural to think in those terms. What I have attempted to show tonight is that, notwithstanding both the power and the familiarity of probability theory, a better explanation of juridical proof at the foundation level is that it involves inference to the best explanation rather than probability judgments about discrete propositions. In addition to simply adding to our understanding, this conclusion has certain implications. Most importantly, the law of evidence plausibly should take into account that juridical proof is explanatory rather than probabilistic.

And, as it turns out, it does, at least in the United States. There are, for example, various rules of completeness that override technical regulatory or exclusionary rules of evidence. The effect of these completeness rules is to provide data to fact finders in conventional story form by admitting surrounding material relevant to specific testimony. An example is Federal Rule of Evidence 106: "When a writing or recorded statement or part thereof is introduced by a party, an adverse party may require the introduction at that time of any other part or any other writing or recorded statement which ought in fairness to be considered contemporaneously with it." Other examples are the res gestae rule found in many jurisdictions which permits virtually any background matter to the litigated question to be produced at trial in order to flesh out the relevant events—regardless of the technical admissibility of the background material—and the standard practice of trying conspirators jointly "to give the jury a fuller picture of the scheme." Analogously, as I mentioned before motive is never an element but is virtually always admissible in both civil and criminal cases; and if the folk lore is correct, convictions in criminal cases are next to impossible to obtain without evidence of motive. Motive fills in the gaps and converts formal structures into human events. Federal Rule of Evidence 612 is yet another example. If a witness relies on a writing to refresh memory for purpose of testifying, that writing is admissible regardless of exclusionary rules. The point, again, is to allow the fact finder to see the entire picture, the "story" in my lexicon. Opening statements and closing arguments are also more consistent with the story model than the elements model. The opening statement informs the fact finder of the story to be told, and the closing argument is essentially a demonstration that one story is more plausible than its competitors.

Some aspects of the rules of evidence appear inconsistent with the story model, but the inconsistency is more apparent than real. Exclusionary rules are one example. By keeping evidence from the jury, the full picture will not emerge. There are remarkably few general exclusionary rules, however. Apart from the constitutional exclusionary rules whose purposes bear no relationship to my argument, there are only two: relevancy and hearsay. Relevancy exclusions do keep information from juries, but only that information upon which no person could reasonably rely, or whose prejudicial value substantially outweighs its probative value. These are quite liberal rules of admission, and thus quite consistent with, or at least not adverse to, the explanatory model of juridical proof.

Hearsay is consistent with the story model as well. Hearsay is a theoretical problem, but a practical ally. The most important forms of hearsay, admissions and prior statements, are largely excluded from the definition of hearsay, or admitted under exceptions. In addition, there are numerous explicit exceptions—twenty-seven in the Federal Rules of Evidence, and two residual exceptions. All of this is qualified by the res gestae principle previously mentioned, which acts as a catch-all rule of admission for many statements not otherwise admissible under an explicit hearsay exception or the residual exceptions. Any rule which has thirty or so explicit exceptions and two residual grounds for admission makes keeping much information from the fact finder practically impossible, and thus is quite consistent with the story model.

Privilege rules do keep information from the jury, but even here the inconsistency with my basic thesis is not striking. Most privilege rules are designed to sacrifice truth-seeking to other values, and thus they are indifferent to the comparison of the conventional view of the proof rules and the equally well specified cases proposal. Moreover, an important privilege—the attorney-client privilege—is best understood as promoting rather than retarding the production of information by encouraging full disclosure by the client to the attorney.

In one sense, this brings to a close my exploration of the nature of juridical proof, but in another sense I hope it is just the beginning of the exploration of that question in China. It is my fondest hope that this lecture will stimulate research into such questions from you, my Chinese students.

相关性和可采性*

张保生　强　卉　译**

今天我很高兴来到这里，并且很荣幸能与你们一起探讨改善中国法律制度的有关问题。这一周，我将就证据法问题作5次讲座。今天第一讲我有两个目标：讲座的前半部分，我将与大家一起回顾一年半前我在这里讲过的一些内容；讲座的后半部分，我将与你们讨论证据的相关性和可采性。随后4天中，我将讲授第二讲“民事和刑事案件的举证责任和证明标准”；第三讲“推定的理论阐释”；第四讲“传闻证据规则的理论阐释”；以及第五讲“证据、推论/概率与似真性”。

首先，我要提醒你们注意证据领域及其知识基础的重要性。从本质上讲，证据是从对抗式审判角度进行的对争端解决方式的研究，焦点在于戏剧性场景中各色人等之间的互动和规则：审判法官、陪审团成员（或外行评判者）、律师、当事人和证人（包括外行和专家）。当然，证据规则构造了这些个人之间的关系，因此，必须对这些规则予以极大的关注。然而，这些规则本身是一系列复杂因素的升华，并且这一系列因素才是证据的真正主题。在此，我想强调的最重要之处是，当你们学习证据规则时，你们不是仅仅孤立地学习证据规则，而是在运用证据规则研究这些规则所反映的非常复杂的问题。

例如，人们构建审判的方式，就是人们关于知识性质之信念和关于社会中适当的政治与社会关系之观点的方程。“知道”某些东西意味着什么？对事实的“历史”重构和“社会”重构之间有无区别？确实，人们可能连贯一致地谈论“知晓”过去的事情吗？如果不是这样，审判应当发挥什么作用，应当寻求什么价值？

在何种程度上，应当由随机挑选的事实认定者来进行事实认定？在何种程度上应当依赖法官的“专家意见”？两种方式各有什么风险？法官也许是更具有一致性的事实认定者，但从长远来看，他们还可能较少地考虑民众的观点。在何种程度上，证据规则如《美国联邦证据规则》规则412～415中的品性证

* 2010年6月在中国政法大学所做的演讲。本译文原载《证据科学》，第18卷，2010年第3期。

** 强卉，中国政法大学博士研究生。

据或强奸相关性规则，应当对当事人一方而不是对另一方有利？

在能够构建证据规则之前，人们不得不首先解决诸如此类的问题。因为人们对证据规则的建构依赖于对这些问题的解答。所以同样地，当你们学习证据规则时，你们实际上是在学习所给出的这些类似问题的答案。

当一个人开始思考证据规则时，立刻就会看到一个基本的、先验的问题：审判的目的是什么？典型的回答总是与事实认定有关。但审判和科学一样吗？它们的区别何在？将其比作科学有点牵强。法律裁决不可能等到收集了更多的信息才作出判决，而且，所作出的判决是实际发生了什么，而不是潜在普适的法律可能是什么。也许最有说服力的是，这里不像在科学领域那样存在着适用于典型情况的知识框架，相反，事实认定者不得不为裁决引入必要的背景知识。如果经过再三思考，审判与科学（至少某些科学门类）似乎并非相像，那么审判是否与历史学相像呢？历史学关注事实，但一般来说，其是一种增进理解的手段。在审判中，理解在很大程度上是不相关的（作为说服事项除外）。法律上的事实认定与科学或历史学中的事实认定并不一样，看起来有其独特之处。

我要明确一点，我在这里所作的是质疑对审判的传统理解，也是质疑关于事实认定之性质和意义的更宽泛的传统理解。让我们更深入地来看这个问题。事实认定是审判的主要目的，还是诸多共存的目的之一？审判的经济方面如何？这里不要忽略：不仅双方当事人与审判有一定的经济利益，而且，律师、法官、法庭书记员和所有法院工作人员都与审判中的经济利益相连。

审判的象征性目的是什么？政治目的？诸如此类。存在着一系列揭示审判性质的非常复杂的问题。反过来说，这一点对于理解审判方式的演进是必要的。换个不同的问题：根据你的审判目的观，证据规则的目的可能是什么？

当人们开始思考与审判有关的一系列复杂问题时，一些不同寻常的含义就会浮现出来。例如，我们通常认为，审判应当是政府工作的组成部分，每个人都应当获得其服务。但是，我这里只给你举一个有困难的例子，就是审判中暗含的经济因素：司法是有代价的，有时候这个代价可能被认为过高。举例来说，如果一个争端的标的是五十多元，而该争端的审判要花费一百元，那么该审判显然就没有什么社会利益。在这种情况下，除非有某种超越经济利益之外的其他目的，也许就不应当诉诸审判。人们也可以说审判具有象征性或者政治性目的等类似的话。

我说的这些是需要思考的问题，而不是关于孰是孰非的结论。为了理解证据规则，这些是你们需要思考的例子。要理解证据规则，你们需要思考证据规则在审判过程中通常所发挥的作用。而且，你们必须确定：对你们来说，什么是审判的基本结构？对于存在多种不同解决方式的法律争端来说，你们想要达到什么目的？在接下来的5天里，我们将考察来自英美法传统的证据法，审判在我们的文化中有点像中间商的性质，在很大程度上由当事人控制。

审判也可选择其他方式，可以由各种政府角色来主导，如法官、侦查人员等。随着我的讲座对这些问题的深入探究，你们应该通过这些讲座思考下述问题：审判应当在多大程度上看起来像是自由市场？它们应当在多大程度上由政府进行规制？哪种模式更能有效地寻求真相，为什么？除了效率和求真的价值外，还有哪些价值面临风险？在考虑这些问题时请记住，因为有法官坐在那里适用证据（和程序）规则，审判并不真的像自由市场。限制那种有点像中间商的审判，其意义何在？

证据领域包括对以下问题的研究：

（1）各种参与者的作用：法官、陪审团成员、律师和公诉人、当事人、证人；（2）通过正式规则和非正式惯例（礼仪、审判策略）对上述参与者的规制；（3）推理的性质和意义，尤其是关于经验世界。

但这些规则不仅建构事实认定，它们还创造了各类激励因素：

（1）所谓“相关性”规则，可以激励人们以对社会有益的方式行事，如修复危险情况或者提供医疗援助。

假设一个人在一座桥上因为某种危险情况受伤。这座桥的所有者在该事故发生后对其进行修复的事实，应当被采纳用以证明其曾存在危险情况吗？从一个方面看，该证据确实倾向于证明该桥在事故发生时存在危险情况。然而，允许这个证据被用于反对那个桥主，就会挫伤桥主消除危险情况的积极性。这里存在一个两难困境，因为在减少社会性危险情况的问题上，我们不得不在提倡理性思考与设置激励措施之间进行取舍。

（2）相关性规则还鼓励提起特定诉求，例如，强奸案相关性规则以及那些被控性犯罪的被告人先前的不良行为。

我给你们举个这方面的例子。在美国，我们遇到过一个难题，在强奸案中，妇女先前性行为背景的证据可因该事实能确定其同意之概率而被采纳。然而，结果是，许多妇女因为不想在审判中受到羞辱而不提起刑事指控。

为了鼓励被害人提起强奸指控，我们采用了一条证据规则以排除妇女先前性行为背景的证据。

所以在这里我们再次看到了可悲的取舍：毫无疑问该证据是相关的，但它同时会产生有害的副作用。因此，需要通过制定这条证据规则对该证据加以限制。

（3）相关性规则能够通过排除和解/辩诉交易的证据，鼓励争端的和解。

前面我给你们举了一个关于争端标的还不及审判成本的例子。无论你们怎么看待这种情况，无论你们同意还是不同意这种解决方式，关于任何法律制度结构的一个非常重要的问题是：一个法律制度中私人谈判与正式的争端解决相比应占多大比例？在美国，我们认为私人谈判与和解是非常好的事情。

如果你与邻居有一个争端，在大多数情况下，与他谈判要好于将他诉至法院。因此，对证据规则来说一个非常重要的问题是，要在多大程度上鼓励私人和解而不是鼓励正式诉讼。

（4）特免权规则保护并鼓励婚姻、律师与委托人、心理诊疗师与患者等关系。有一些社会视为重要的特定关系，如果允许从那些关系中获得证据就可能摧毁这些关系。

例如，允许配偶作证互相反对可能会破坏婚姻，但如果不允许丈夫或妻子作证，就可能在审判中得到错误的结果。于是，证据规则再次面临提倡理性与保护特定关系的社会利益之间的可悲取舍。

（5）证据规则还决定着专家、科学技术证据的使用。我下次来中国时会讲这个问题，因为它也是一个非常重要的领域，而且随着时间的推移越来越重要。

正如我刚才所说的，很明显，证据法的意义远远超出了审判本身。我在第二讲中将详细阐述证据法如何为基本行为和诉讼行为创造了关键性激励因素。

但证据的意义又以另一种方式延伸至审判以外。由于任何事情都可能卷入诉讼，证据法能够成为任何事情的基础。

遗嘱、刑法、反托拉斯法、商业活动，任何由法律规制的事情都可能产生争端，进而受到证据法的规制。证据对所有的法律领域都有影响，所有合法交易中的最糟糕的情况就是卷入诉讼。在诉讼中，一个关键变量是什么能够得到证明。因此，每位律师或公诉人，不管距法庭多远，都必须把法庭考虑在内，也就是说，都要考虑到证据规则。

人们可以将证据作为一个技术领域而加以思考，但事实上，这个技术领域对于所有律师、法律制度的所有方面都是绝对关键的。

避免争端的最好办法就是拥有确凿证据——不能相矛盾且能表明你的法律主张正确的证据。我从技术角度揭示的证据的意义，正是律师需要做的事情，也是任何参与可能的商业交易的人需要做的事情。他们需要了解，如果某些事情出了问题，什么是不得不被证明的事情。这就是我说证据法为基本行为和诉讼行为创造关键性激励因素的原因。重要的是，理解我所说的基本行为和诉讼行为这两个术语。基本行为是公民在法庭外社会中的行为，是在其可能根本没有想到诉讼或争端时从事的行为。诉讼行为是直接影响诉讼的行为。但二者能够联系起来，并且都受到证据规则的影响。

我所谈到的这些问题都是潜在于人类思想和哲学中的一些基本问题，其中一个问题是：知道某件事情，意味着什么？审判是一种认识活动，其中，知识的主张被提出、考虑、拒绝或接受。哲学始于对思维和认知之含义的系统思考，这依然是今天的主流问题之一。现代相对论哲学是由一种基本怀疑论推动的，例如，那些带有宗教倾向的哲学中反映出的寻求启示的愿望。但这并不是唯一的传统。现代科学有取得辉煌成就的例子。为了清晰地思考法律过程，人们必须将其思想置于这个范围之中。比如，你是否认为历史事实的真相可以获得，将在很大程度上决定着你对特定证据规则的看法，例如，思考一下《美国联邦证据规则》规则 401、702，也许还有规则 801。

最重要的是，证据法是法治的关键所在。事实在某种重要意义上比权利更为根本，权利和义务取决于事实。再考虑一下个人财产所有权这种最基本的权利。如果我主张你的财产是我的，你会做什么？你将向官方事实认定者提供证据，以说服其相信，在过去的某个时间点上事物处于这样一种状态：你有权占有、消费或处置某些个人财产。

没有准确的事实认定，权利和义务就变得毫无意义。因此，你们的政府和在座的学者决定重点进行证据法律的改革是绝对正确的。正是证据规则及其实践决定了一个法律制度中准确认定事实的适当方式。

在座的各位将是当代中国法律制度改革的领头羊，而在这个过程中最为重要的就是为审判中的事实准确裁决提供条件。

这一点也是至关重要的。每次来中国，我都乐于有机会探讨这个问题。我认为，你们今天的社会正为法治的重要性所迷倒，你们正处在法治建设进程中。尽管如此，我想强调的重要一点是：没有准确的事实认定的法治是毫无意义的。说得更清楚一点儿，你们在几个月前正式实施了新的《物权法》。所有权包括占有、消费和处置有形物或无形物的权利。我们今天的翻译认为他拥有这个非常漂亮的文件包，我说这是我的，那他会做什么？他将找一位事实认定者，并向那个人提供其证明在某个时间点他得到它、制作它、捡到它或购买它的证据。如果这位事实认定者（一名法官或者陪审团成员）未准确认定那些事实，我就带着这个文件包回家了。所以，对这个文件包的占有、消费和处置的权利，完全取决于准确的事实认定。

有了以上铺垫，我接下来要讲证据法中的第一个实质性领域，这就是相关性。相关性是起点。要理解相关性概念，就必须讲清楚相关性、证明力和偏见影响，这是我今晚的讲座所要达到的目的。

《美国联邦证据规则》规则 401 定义了相关性，但它实际上涉及了两个不同的概念。相关性的逻辑含义，要求一个主张的清晰表达和支持该主张的证据。如果一个证据有助于证明或反驳所表达的主张，它就是相关的。然而，还有第二个问题：该主张和审判之间的联系是什么？这由诉因的要件来决定。这种关系被称为“实质性”（materiality）。一个主张如果在审判前就与诉讼有实际关系，它就是“实质性的”。

让我给你们举一个愚蠢的例子，只是为了说明相关性和实质性之间多么不同。假设某人被控违反了反托拉斯法，并假定政府要求他母亲就他有棕色头发作证。这位母亲的证据与他有棕色头发的主张是相关的，但这一关于他有棕色头发的主张与该审判并没有关系。这个例子有助于我们区分两种不同的逻辑现象。相关性是证据与主张之间的关系，实质性是主张与审判之间的关系。

当我稍后讲到附条件的相关性时，对这两个概念的理解就会变得重要了，因为这两个概念之间的关系有助于理解附条件的相关性。

按照我刚讲到的内容，我们需要界定几个概念：

（1）诉因：案件的整体，例如，1）过失；2）合同；3）刑事指控。

（2）要件（EE）：构成一项诉因的正式定义。

（3）辩护：正式辩明无罪或免除罪责问题，如自我辩护，或合同履行不能。

（4）证据性事实（EF）：向事实认定者真正地提供的东西，可以是：1）证言证据：证人所说的东西；2）实物证据：作为争议组成部分的文件或物体；3）示意证据：图表、照片等有助于推理的证据；4）其他观察资料，比如行为举止。

（5）推断性事实（IF）：事实认定者从所提供的证据性事实推断出的主张。

（6）要素性事实（FOC）：于诉讼具有实质性的事实。

如何把所有这些概念整合在一起？请参考我的《证据法：文本、问题和案例》一书第 142 页至第 143 页上的图表。

证据性事实(EF)——→	推断性事实(IF)——→	要素性事实(FOC)——→	要件(EE)
休斯顿作证说，他的胫骨在搏斗后受了伤	休斯顿的胫骨在搏斗后确实受了伤	詹森的搏斗造成了该伤	詹森对休斯顿使用了武力和暴力

证据性	推断性	推断性	推断性	要素性	要素性	
事实 ⟶	事实 1⟶	事实 2⟶	事实 3⟶	事实 1⟶	事实 2⟶	要件
（EF）	（IF1）	（IF2）	（IF3）	（FOC1）	（FOC2）	（EE）
巴特勒作证说，狱警们佩戴着防护手套	狱警们佩戴了防护手套	狱警们准备进行接触	狱警们企图打人	狱警们先动手打人	詹森作了自卫性还击	詹森使用武力并不违法

如果人们可以得出这些推论，而不仅仅是证据性事实（EF）与要素性事实（FOC）是“相关的”这样简单的结论，那么《美国联邦证据规则》规则403的定义就得到了满足。

请注意，《美国联邦证据规则》规则401相关性定义中的“任何趋向性”，是个很低的标准。如果任何正常人在评估要素性事实（FOC）的概率时可能受到影响，那么，该证据就达到了相关性标准。这是一个鼓励采纳证据的规则。在我们的法律制度中，该规则旨在限制审判法官的权力，增加给陪审团的信息流。在你们的法律制度中，则通过明确规定法官只有在证据完全不具推论价值的情况下才能将其排除，来削弱法官的权力从而增加当事人的权力。

以下是其全部运作过程。首先，有一个证据性事实，如证言，暗含着一个推断性事实，即其本身与诉讼的一个要素性事实相关。请考虑一个不像上面举的母亲为儿子头发颜色作证那么愚蠢的例子。假定有一场车祸，问题是谁闯了红灯。原告传唤的证人作证说，当被告驶过路口时是红灯。现在这个证言并不意味着或确定对于当时是红灯排除了全部怀疑。一位事实认定者要得出那个结论，仍须通过一个完整的长长的推论列表。有时候，在证言或证据（证据性事实）与该证据所隐含的东西（即能够从该证据性事实推断出来的东西）之间存在着一种混淆。仅仅证人说当时是红灯的事实，并不同于（不等同于）当时确实是红灯。证人可能看错了、记错了当时的情况，或者证人也许在撒谎。从关于当时是红灯的证言推断出当时确实是红灯，需要大量的推论，涉及可信性等问题的推论。如果事实认定者得出结论，即当时是红灯这一事实可以推断出来，那么就有助于确立一个关于过失的要素性事实。

关于这个问题有两点非常重要。如上所说，在美国，我们用“任何趋向性”标准去检验证据性事实（EF）和推断性事实（IF）之间的关系。如果关于证据性事实（EF）的证言对于任何常人论证该推断性事实（IF）的真实性具有任何趋向性，我们就说它是相关的，即使有人不同意该证据性事实（EF）

有助于证明该推断性事实（IF）。为相关性设置如此低的标准，是为了鼓励事实认定者（无论是法官还是陪审团成员）能够自由地获得信息流。更具体地说，这旨在抑制法官对陪审团成员拦截证据。

其次，如何判定“任何趋向性”？在我为期 5 天的讲座中，这一部分最为重要。请思考下面这个从我的《证据法：文本、问题和案例》一书第 144 页而来的图表：

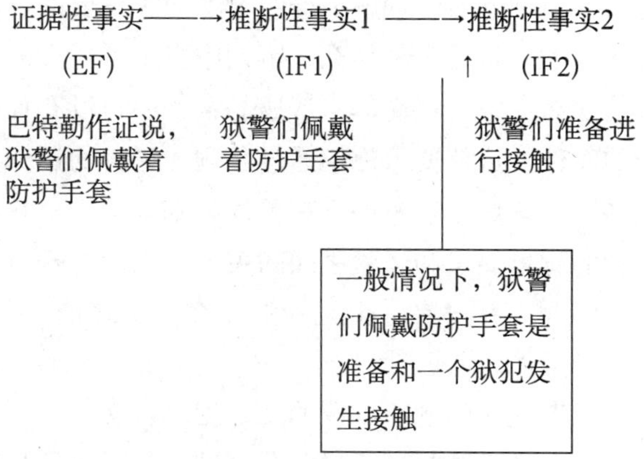

请重点看方框里的话：“一般情况下，狱警们佩戴防护手套是准备和一个狱犯发生接触。”事实认定者如果相信，狱警通常佩戴防护手套是准备与狱犯进行接触这一点是真的，那么，推断性事实 1（IF1）就意味着推断性事实 2（IF2），也就是说，推断性事实 1（IF1）与推断性事实 2（IF2）是相关的。

请注意关于证据性事实（EF）的同一动力，我们省略了一个方框里的话，即证人通常都讲真话。我们把这些方框中的内容称为“中间性主张”。它们位于中间，因而对证据性事实（EF）和第一个“推断性事实”（IF1），或两个“推断性事实”，或一个“推断性事实”（IF）和一个要素性事实（FOC）来说，是“中间性的”。

如何对“任何趋向性”作出评价是绝对关键性的问题。正如我前面说到的，这是我这 5 天讲座中最重要的部分。我现在来解释一下这个运作过程。请考虑一个例子：证人作证说，信号灯是红的。你想要由此推断信号灯确实是红灯，是什么允许你这样推断？教室里的每个人都认为这个推论是正确的，但为什么正确？这个问题是理解相关性的关键。当你听到证据时，你就把那个证据与你自己的知识和经验联系起来了，正是你听到的作为证据的东西与你拥有的独立的知识和经验之间的关系，允许你从该证据得出推论。

换句话说，相关性问题就变弱为一个人能否相信必要的中间性主张，从而允许一个正常人在不确定的时候作出该推论。法官必须断定这一点，但问题不是法官对其相信与否，而是事实认定者相信与否。相关性的核心问题是，一个证据性事实能否与事实认定者先前的知识和经验联系起来，从而允许该事实认定者理性地处理并理解该证据。如果一个正常人在处理该证据之后考虑该案要素性事实时受到了这个证据的影响，该证据就是相关的，否则，就是不相关的。

我刚才讨论的这些理念对于理解证据绝对是至关重要的，所以我想再回顾一下。相关性的问题不仅是证言是什么、审判中发生了什么的问题，还包括在审判开始前你相信什么主张。在简单、普通的案件中，没有什么问题。但审判中有很多更复杂的案件，这就要求你们通过我刚才讨论的逻辑关系进行思考。

还有一点更关键。请重新思考一下相关性的基本结构，它包含着审判中的证据与事实认定者的背景知识和经验之间的关系。人们立刻就能发现，对于某件事情是否相关的问题，并没有一个先验的（在事实之前）、绝对的答案，答案取决于特定审判的条件。

让我们进一步思考这个问题。以我的《证据法：文本、问题和案例》一书第一章“审讯笔录”中谁先挑起战斗的问题为例：是狱犯还是狱警？该案被告想要提供这样一个证据性事实（EF），即狱警们在去关押狱犯的牢房前就已经佩戴了防护手套。被告想提供该证据性事实（EF）来暗示，狱警们打算挑起打人事端。这个推理是，企图挑起一场斗殴的动机增加了狱警们先动手开打的概率。如果狱警们先动手开打，那么，该被告就仅仅是实施了正当防卫，而没有犯罪。

现在这个证据具有相关性吗？你们可以将这个案例与我之前举的那个关于棕色头发的愚蠢例子作一个比较，然后回答这个问题：佩戴防护手套与先动手开打之间有什么联系？这取决于你认为狱警在监狱中的行为方式应当如何。也许只有在打算挑起战斗而要保护自己的情况下，狱警们在去牢房之前才佩戴防护手套。如果相信这一点是合理的，那么这个证据就是相关的；如果相信这一点是不合理的，就意味着该证据是不相关的。相关性取决于狱警们为何佩戴防护手套这个中间性主张。

现在假定法官说：“我对狱警们在监狱里佩戴防护手套将做什么一无所知。”这意味着该证据将不被采纳吗？并非如此，而这一点也非常重要。如果一位法官那样说了，你们现在就能够提供证据——一个证据性事实——关于狱警们在企图动手打架时才佩戴防护手套的主张的证据。你们可以提供关于狱警们使用防护手套和打架的证据，这些证据一起暗示了狱警们先动手打架。现在，考虑一下这种情况的含义。它表明，相关性是动态的而非静态的，也就是说，诉讼是一个互动过程。这再一次说明，没有一个关于特定证据性事实（EF）是否与一个推论性事实（IF）相关的先验规则，它完全取决于具体案件中事实认定者的知识范畴和当事人提供的证据。决定一个证据性事实（EF）与一个推论性事实（IF）是否相关的中间性主张，来自于当事人和他们的律师。当遇到某个证据性事实（EF）与某个推论性事实（IF）是否相关的问题时，当事人或律师必须清楚地表达其属于事实认定者知识范围内的中间性主张，以使其合理地相信该证据性事实（EF）与该推论性事实（IF）是相关的。即使一位法官最初说该证据不具有相关性，也不一定意味着该证据不能被采纳。相反，希望该证据被采纳的当事方必须提供进一步的证据，以支持使法官感到允许一个正常人得出该推论为必要的中间性主张。

这种分析产生了一个最重要、最深入的关于证据的分析性观点。人们把证据视为那些在法庭上呈现的东西。但是，被呈现在法庭上的东西自己不会说话，也不会说出该证据也许拥有什么含义。证据必须由某个理解其含义的人进行评说。法庭上被呈现的东西，只有在参考庭审参与人内在经验和知识的情况下，才能为人们所理解。这意味着——这正是深入分析得出的观点——所谓“相关证据”，包括审判中的证据与事实认定者内在知识和经验之间的一种相互作用。这就是为什么我说相关性的核心问题是：一个证据性事实（EF）是否“备份”（backs up）进入了事实认定者先前的知识和经验，从而允许事实认定者理性地处理和理解该证据并为其所影响。若是这样，该证据就是相关的；若不是这样，它不一定意味着该证据是不相关的，但你必须提供进一步的证据来证明，那个中间性主张本身在作出推论有疑义的情况下是可以被依赖的。

至此，我们已经引出了关于证据最重要和最困难的课题之一，那就是附条件的相关性。我不知道中国是否有与附条件的相关性相同或相似的概念。无论有没有，在审判中进行理性分析时这个概念是极其有用的。相关性的概念性难题集中于中间性前提（intermediate premises），正如我之前所讲的，它们本身可能成为支持或削弱那些前提的证据主题。出现的第一个问题是：那些中间性主张的证据何时才不得不被提出？我们给当事人一些选择的自由，允许证据在当事人证明其相关性之后被有条件地采纳。这实际上解决了一个有趣的概念性难题。从形式上说，如果一个诉因有两个以上的要素，在一个要素未得到证明的情况下，对另一个要素的证明是不相关的。以一个只包括要约和承诺的简单合同为例。假设有人只提供证据对要约作证，但如果没有关于承诺的证言，该要约就没有任何相关性。同样，没有要约存在的证言，关于承诺的证言也没有相关性。“附条件的相关性”允许我们等待和查看所有必要的联系是否已经具备。诸如要约和承诺等诉因要素的真实性，也就是使证据相关的中间性主张的真实性。例如，你也许会认为狱警们佩戴防护手套的行为没有相关性，但在之后的审判中如果能够提出关于在监狱中狱警的行为以及他们为何佩戴防护手套的证据，那将使该证据具有相关性。

我想以最后三个分析性观点来结束今晚的讲座。第一是论述直接证据与间接证据的区别。虽然有定义，但并不十分有用。直接证据是如果相信了就能证实要件的证据。间接证据是在证实一个要件之前需要得出其他推论的证据。目击证人的证言是直接证据，DNA 是间接证据。关于直接证据和间接证据的区别就是推论链条长短之间区别的观点，推论链条越短发生错误的概率越低是这种观点的体现，但这是错误的。有的“直接证据”有很长且不可靠的推论链条，比如，一位证人其可信性受到多方面的抨击；而某些“间接证据”有短且有力的推论链条，比如 DNA 证据。美国当代证据法已开始不再关注和应用这种区分方式。

第二个需要强调的观点是：相关性不是充分性。充分性是指该证据足以允许一项裁决。相关性仅仅检验证据与要素性事实（FOC）和推断性事实（IF）之间的逻辑关系，那是由“任何趋向性”标准来决定的。有时候你们将发现自己倾向于说证据是不相关的，因为它并未证明该案件。无论何时你发现自己有这种倾向，那很可能说明你混淆了相关性和充分性的关系。请思考一下我最后举的那个狱警佩戴防护手套就意味着他们想挑起战斗的例子。你可能认为狱警们也许出于其他理由而佩戴防护手套，佩戴防护手套对于证明他们先动手打架并不是足够强有力的证据。然而，相关性的问题并非在于证据是否证实狱警们先动手打架是绝对真实的，而只是有助于证明狱警们是否先动手打架。

相关性是证据在审判中被提供时加以判断的，而充分性是在所有证据被采纳后加以判断的。这就是为什么单个证据本身很微弱，但证据片段的集合仍能强有力地证明一个案件的。对一个可接受的裁决来说，相关性本身是必要但非充分的。

我对相关性的概念性问题作个总结。相关性取决于中间性前提，那些中间性前提本身又可能成为支持或削弱那些前提的证据主题。因此，如果不看到所有的证据，一个人是永远不可能知道某些证据片段是否相关的。再回想一下前面讨论的合同诉讼。如果没有关于承诺的证据，一个要约的证据是没有相关性的，反之亦然。附条件的相关性消除了这种无限的回归。证据能以“得到”后来的证据对其相关性的证明为前提而被采纳。这能够在一方当事人举证结束时得到检验，或者通过指令裁决、简易判决或撤销指控等动议，在诉讼结束阶段得到检验。

今晚我将提醒你们的最后一点是，在美国对可采性有两个限制。第一个是不公正的偏见，这种观念指证据既能证明一个事实为真，但又会将其他能够使事实认定者产生偏见的事实展示出来。

最好的例子也许是一个人先前的刑事定罪不良记录。一个人先前的记录可能与他现在被指控的其他行为是相关的，但是，一旦事实认定者得知了该人的记录，事实认定者在这种考虑之下，也许就不会在乎它是否将造成此案的错误。在美国，如果不公正的偏见在实质上超过了证据的证明价值，我们就允许排除该证据。

最后，另一个对可采性的限制，可能就是我在今晚讲座开始时讲到的创造激励措施之类的政策。人民和社会，可能对于遵循什么政策、哪项政策重要到让审判中对真相的追求为之妥协具有正当理由，是有不同看法的。

谢谢大家！

Relevancy and Admissibility

Ronald J. Allen

I am very pleased to be here today, and I am much honored to be working with many of you in this room to improve the Chinese legal system. This week, I will deliver five lectures on the law of evidence. In this first lecture, I have two objectives. During the first half of the lecture, I will review some of the topics that we covered when I was last with you a year and a half ago, and in the second half of the lecture, I discuss relevancy and the admissibility of the evidence. In the following four days, I will lecture on 2) Burden and Standard of Proof in Civil and Criminal Cases; 3) A Theoretical Account of Presumptions; 4) A Theoretical Account of the Hearsay Rule, and 5) Evidence and Inference/Probability and Plausibility.

So, let us begin. First, I want to remind you of the significance of the field of evidence and its intellectual foundations. In essence, evidence is the study of dispute resolution from the perspective of adversarial trials. The focus is on the interaction and regulation of the various people in the drama: trial judge, jurors (or lay assessors), attorneys, parties, and witnesses (both lay and expert) . The rules of evidence structure the relationships between these individuals, of course, and thus great attention must be paid to those rules. However, the rules are themselves distillations of a complex set of factors, and that set of factors is the real subject matter of evidence. The single most important point that I want to emphasize here is that, when you study the rules of evidence, you are not just studying the rules of evidence alone. Rather, you are using the rules of evidence to study the very complex issues that the rules reflect.

For example, how one constructs trials is a function of both one's beliefs concerning the nature of knowledge and one's views about the appropriate political and social relationships in society. What does it mean to "know" something, and is there a difference between an "historical" reconstruction of facts, and a "social" one? Indeed, is it even coherent to talk about "knowing" the past? If not, what role should trials play, and what values should be pursued?

To what extent should fact finding be located in randomly selected fact finders, and to what extent should the "expertise" of judges be relied upon? What are the risks of either approach? Judges may be more consistent fact finders, but they also may be less reflective, over the long run, of the views of the citizenry. To what extent should rules of evidence favor one class of litigants over another, as Federal Rules of Evidence (FRE) 412—415, the character evidence/rape relevancy rules, do?

These are examples of the questions that have to be addressed before you can construct the rules of evidence. The rules of evidence you construct depend upon the answers to these questions. So again, when you study the rules of evidence, you really study the answers that have been given to the questions like this.

When one begins to think about the rules of evidence, one sees immediately that there is fundamental, *a priori*, question: what the purpose of trials is? The typical response has something to do with fact finding. But, are trials like science? How do they differ? The analogy to science is somewhat tenuous. Legal decision making cannot defer judgment until more information is collected. Also, the judgment to be made is what actually happened rather than what the underlying universal laws might be. Most tellingly, perhaps, there is no organized body of knowledge that is applicable to the typical case, as there is in science. To the contrary, the fact finder has to import the necessary background knowledge for decision. If on reflection trials do not seem a lot like science (at least some types of science), are they like history? The focus of history is on facts, but as a means, generally, of greater understanding. At trials, understanding is largely irrelevant (except as a matter of persuasion). Legal fact finding begins to look somewhat unique, and not exactly like either science or history.

Let me be clear that what I am doing here is to question the conventional understanding of what a trial is, and also to question the broader conventional understanding of the nature and significance of fact finding. Press the matter more deeply. Is fact finding the primary purpose of trials, or one that co- exists with many others? What about the economic aspects of trials? Here do not neglect that not only the parties but the lawyers, the judges, the court repor-ters, and all the court personnel have vested economic interests in trials.

What about the symbolic purposes of trials? The political purposes? And so on. There is an extraordinarily complex set of issues that inform the nature of trials. That point, in turn, is necessary to understand the manner in which trials have developed. Now ask a different question: In light of your view of the purpose of trials, what might be the purposes of the rules of evidence?

When one begins to think about the complex set of issues pertinent to trials, some unconventional implications emerge. For example, we normally think that the trial should be part of an official governmental process that everybody should have access to. But, I have just given you an example of a difficulty here, and that is the economic implications of trials. Justice comes at a price and sometimes that price can be thought to be too high. For example, if a dispute is over 50 yuan, but it takes one hundred yuan to have a trial of that dispute, it is not obviously a social good to have that trial. Unless there is some other purpose in addition to the economic one in a case like this, perhaps there should not be at the trial. One can say a similar thing about the symbolic or political purposes of the trial as well.

I am presenting these as questions to be thought about and not as conclusions about what is right what is wrong. These are examples of what you need to think about in order to understand the rules of evidence. To understand the rules of evidence, you need to think about the role rules of evidence in the context of trials generally. Moreover, you must determine what for you is the basic structure of trials; what do you wish to accomplish, for there are many different ways to resolve legal disputes. The law of evidence that we will examine in these next five days comes from the Anglo-American tradition, and trials in our cultural are somewhat entrepreneurial, and largely controlled by the parties.

Alternatives exist. Trials could be much more dominated by government actors of various kinds-judges, investigators, etc.. You, the students, must reflect as these lectures proceed on these matters. To what extent should trials look like free markets; to what extent should they be regulated by the government? Which model is likely to foster efficient truth-seeking, and why? What other values than efficiency and truth-seeking are at stake? As you think about this set of ideas, remember that trials are not truly like free markets, for the judge sits there applying the rules of evidence (and procedure) . What is the implication of this constraint on otherwise entrepreneurial trials?

The field of evidence involves the study of:

a. Role of various actors: judge, jury, attorneys, parties, witnesses.

b. Regulation of these actors through formal rules and informal conventions (decorum, trial strategy) .

c. The nature and implications of reasoning, in particular about an empirical world.

But the rules do not just structure fact finding; they also create incentives of various kinds:

a. What are called "Relevance" rules can give people incentives to act in socially beneficial ways, such as to fix dangerous conditions or offer medical aid.

Suppose for example a person is injured because of a dangerous condition on a bridge. Should the fact that the owner of the bridge fixes it after the accident be admissible to show there was dangerous condition? On the one hand, the evidence does tend to show that there was dangerous condition. However, allowing that evidence to be used against the owner of the bridge creates a disincentive for the owner to correct the dangerous condition. There is a tragic dilemma here because we have to trade off advancing rationality with creating incentives to reduce socially dangerous conditions.

b. Relevance rules can also encourage bringing certain claims, such as the rape relevancy rules and prior bad acts of those accused of sexual misconduct.

Let me give you an example of this. We had a problem in US that in a rape case the women's prior sexual background was admitted evidence because the fact goes to the probability of consent. However, the result was that many women did not press criminal charges because they did not want to be humiliated at the trial.

We adopted a rule of evidence in order to exclude women's prior sexual background to encourage them to bring forth claims of rape.

So here again we just see the tragic trade off; there is no question that the evidence is relevant but at the same time it has perverse secondary consequences that are controlled by creating the rule of evidence.

c. Relevance rules can encourage the settlement of disputes by excluding evidence of settlement/plea negotiations.

Earlier in this lecture, I gave you an example where perhaps a trial of dispute is not worth the cost of the trial. Whatever you think about example, whether you agree or disagree about it, nevertheless a very important question about the structure of any legal system is how much private negotiation a system should have as compared to formal dispute resolution. In the United States, we think private negotiation and settlement is a very a good thing.

If you have a dispute with your neighbor, it is better to negotiate with your neighbor rather than sue the neighbor in most cases. Consequently, a very important question for the rules of evidence is how much you want to encourage private settlement and discourage formal litigation.

d. Privilege rules protect and encourage relationships—marriage, lawyer/client, therapist/patient, etc.. There are certain relationships that society views as important and allowing evidence from those relationships can destroy the relationships.

For example, allowing spouses to testify against each other may destroy the marriage, but if you do not allow the evidence from the husband or wife, you may get the wrong result at trial. Once again, there is a tragic trade-off between advancing rationality and protecting the social good of the relationship.

e. Rules of evidence also determine the use of expert, scientific, technical evidence. The next time I came to China, I will lecture about this because it is also a very important area and one that will become increasingly important over time.

As is obvious from what I have just said, the significance of the law of evidence goes far beyond trials themselves. I will elaborate in Lecture Two how evidence law creates critical incentives for both primary and litigation behavior.

But the significance of evidence stretches beyond trials in another fashion as well. Evidence law underlies everything, since everything can collapse into litigation.

Wills, criminal law, antitrust, commercial work—everything regulated by the law can generate a dispute that, in turn, is regulated by the law of evidence. Evidence bears upon every other legal field, and the worst case scenario of every legal transaction is its collapse into litigation. In litigation, a crucial variable will be what can be proven. Thus every attorney, no matter how remote from the courtroom, must take the courtroom into account, which means taking the rules of evidence into account.

One can think of evidence as a technical field, but in fact that technical field is absolutely critical for every lawyer and for all aspects of the legal system.

The best way to avoid a dispute is to have unimpeachable evidence—evidence that cannot be contradicted that shows that your legal claims are correct. This is what I mean by the significance of evidence in a technical sense, what the lawyer needs to do, what anybody involved with a possible commercial transaction needs to do. They need to know what has to be proved if something goes wrong. That is why I say that evidence law creates critical incentives for both primary and litigation behavior. It is important to understand what I mean by these two terms primary and litigation behavior. Litigation behavior is that behavior that directly affects litigation. Primary behavior is the behavior of the citizen out there in society when the citizen might not be even thinking about the litigation or disputes. But the two can be connected and the rules of evidence affect both.

Underlying all of what I have discussed so far is one of the fundamental questions of human thought and philosophy—what does it mean to know something? A trial is an epistemological event at which claims of knowledge are advanced, considered, rejected, or accepted. Philosophy began with systemic thought on what it means to think and to know, and it remains one of the dominant questions today. Modern relativist philosophies are driven by a fundamental skepticism, for example, as is the desire for revelation reflected in those philosophies with a religious orientation. But this is not the only tradition. There is the spectacularly successful example of modern science, and in order to think clearly about the legal process, one must locate one's thoughts somewhere on this spectrum. Whether, for example, you think truth of historical facts is obtainable will determine in large measure your view of particular evidence rules. Consider FRE 401, for example, and FRE 702. Or FRE 801, perhaps.

Most importantly of all, the law of evidence is the key to the rule of law. Facts in one important sense are more fundamental than rights. Rights and obligations depend upon facts. Consider again the most basic right of ownership of personal property. If I claim that your property is mine, what will you do? You will present evidence to an official fact finder to convince that person that the universe was in such a state at some point in the past that you have the right to possess, consume, or dispose of some personal property.

Without accurate fact finding, rights and obligations are meaningless. Thus, your government and the faculty here with us today are absolutely correct in their decision to focus reform on the law of evidence. It is the evidentiary rules and practices that determine how well a legal system finds facts accurately.

Those of you in this room will be the leaders of the evolution of Chinese legal system into the modern age and the single most important part of that process will be providing for the conditions of factually accurate verdicts at trial.

This too is absolutely and critically important. Each time I come to China, I am grateful to have the opportunity to talk about this. Your society today I think is fascinated by the significance of the rule of law, and you are making progress on establishing it. Still, the important point I wish to emphasize is that the rule of law is meaningless without actuate fact finding. Let me be clear about this. You have a new property law that was adopted a few months ago. Property involves the rights to possess, consume and dispose of tangible or intangible things. Our translator tonight thinks that he owns this very nice briefcase. I say it is mine. What is the translator going to do? He is going to find a fact finder and present evidence to that person to show at some point of time he was given it, he made it, he found it or he bought it. If the fact finder, a judge or juror, does not find those facts accurately, I walk home with this briefcase. So the rights to possess, consume, and dispose of this briefcase depend entirely on accurate fact finding.

With that background, let me turn to the first substantive area of the law of evidence that I will address, which is relevancy. Relevancy is the starting point. To understand the concept of relevancy, one must address relevance, probative value, and prejudicial effect, which I will do in my remarks tonight.

FRE 401 defines relevance, but it actually involves two different concepts. The logical meaning of relevance requires the articulation of a proposition and evidence to support it. Evidence is relevant if it tends to prove or disprove the proposition articulated. However, there is a second question: what is the connection between the proposition and the trial? That is determined by the essential elements of the cause of action. That relationship is referred to as "materiality" . A proposition is "material" if it matters to the litigation before the court.

Let me give you a silly example just to make a point of how relevance and materiality differ. Suppose somebody is accused of violating the antitrust law, and suppose the government calls his mother to testify that he has brown hair. The mother's evidence is relevant to the proposition that he has brown hair, but the proposition that he has brown hair does not have matter to the trial. This helps us to distinguish that are two different logical phenomena. Relevancy is the relationship between evidence and propositions. Materiality is the relationship between the propositions and the trial.

This will become important later today when we address conditional relevancy because the relationship between these two helps to make sense of conditional relevancy.

In light of what I have just said, we need definitions:

A. Cause of action-the case in its entirety. Examples are:

1. Negligence.

2. Contract.

3. Criminal charge.

B. Essential Elements (EE): the formal definition that constitutes a cause of action.

C. Defenses: a formal exculpatory or exonerating issue, such as self-defense, or in contract impossibility.

D. Evidentiary fact (EF): literally what is presented to the fact finder, which can be

1. Testimonial evidence：what witnesses say.

2. Real evidence：documents or objects that are part of the underlying dispute.

3. Demonstrative evidence：aids to reasoning，such as charts，pictures，and so on.

4. Other observations，such as demeanor.

E. Inferred fact（IF）：a proposition inferred by a fact finder from the evidentiary facts presented.

F. FOC-a Fact of Consequence：this is a fact that is material to the litigation.

How do all these concepts fit together? Consider the following charts on pp. 142，143 of my book.

Diagram 3—3

EF →	IF →	FOC →	EE
Huston testifies that he had a gash on his shin after the struggle	Huston did have a gash on his shin after the struggle	Johnson's struggling caused the gash	Johnson used force and violence against Huston

Diagram 3—4

EF →	IF1 →	IF2 →	IF3 →	FOC1 →	FOC1 →	EE
Butler testifies that guards were wearing gloves	Guards were wearing gloves	Guards prepared to have contact	Guards intend to fight	Guards start fight first	Johnson fights in self-defense	Johnson's use of force not unlawful

If one may draw these inferences，that the EF is "relevant" to a FOC，and thus the definition of FRE 403 is satisfied.

Note the very low standard in the definition of relevancy in FRE 401 of "any tendency". If any reasonable person could be influenced in his or her assessment of the probability of a FOC，then the evidence meets the standard of relevancy. This is a rule greatly favoring the admissibility of evidence. In our system, it is designed to limit the power of trial judges and increase the flow of information to juries. In your system, it would increase the power of parties at the expense of judges by making clear that judges should not keep evidence out unless it is quite clear that it has no inferential value.

Here is how this all works. First, there is an evidential fact like testimony, which implies an inferred fact that itself pertains to a fact of consequence for the litigation. Consider an example that is not silly like my example above of the mother testifying to the color of her child's hair. Suppose there is a car crash and the question is who ran the red light. The witness is called by the plaintiff to testify that the light was red when the defendant went into the intersection. Now this testimony does not mean or establish beyond all doubt that the light was red. A fact finder still has to draw a whole long list of inferences to get to that conclusion. There is sometimes a confusion between testimony or evidence (evidential fact) and what that evidence implies, what you can infer from the evidential fact. The mere fact that the witness says the light was red is not the same (not equal) to the light actually being red. The witness may make a mistake, misremember what is going, or maybe the witness is lying. To infer from the testimony about the light being red to the light actually being red requires a vast number of inferences to be drawn about credibility, and so forth. If the fact finder concludes that the fact the light was red may be inferred, that tends to establish one fact of consequence about negligence.

Now I have two very important things to say about this. As I noted above, in the United States we test the relationship between EF and IF by the standard of "any tendency" . If the testimony about an EF has any tendency for any reasonable person to demonstrate the truth of the IF, we say it is relevant even if people can disagree about whether the EF tends to prove the IF. The reason for this very low standard of relevance is to encourage the free flow information to the fact finder whoever it is (judge or juror) . More particularly, this is designed to inhibit judges from keeping evidence from jurors.

Second, how is the determination of "any tendency" made? This is the single most important part of my five days of lectures here. Consider the chart below, which is from p. 144 of my evidence book:

Focus on the box that says: "Guards typically wear gloves to prepare to

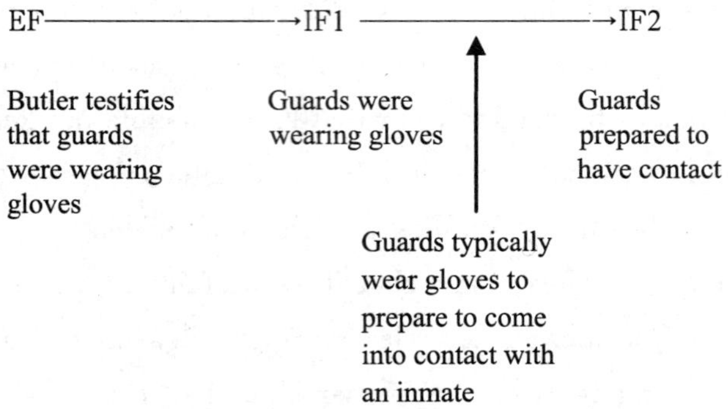

come into contact with an inmate. ” If a fact finder believes that it is true that guards typically wear groves to prepare to come into contact with inmates, then IF1 implies IF2, which means IF1 is relevant to IF2.

Note the same dynamic with regard to the EF we have just left that box out, which would say: witnesses normally tell the truth. We call the contents of these boxes “intermediate propositions. They are in between, and thus “intermediate” to the EF and the first IF or between two IF’s or between an IF and a FOC” .

The absolutely critical question is how is the estimation of “any tendency” is made. As I said above, this is single most important part of my five days of lectures here. I am now going to explain how this process works. Consider as an example that the witness testifies that the light was red, from which you want to infer that actually the light was red. What allows you to do that? Everyone in the room thinks that inference is correct, but why is it? That very question is the key to the relevance relationship. When you hear evidence, you relate that evidence to your own knowledge and experience, and it is the relationship between what you hear as evidence and your independent knowledge and experience that allow you to draw inferences from the evidence.

In other words, the issue of relevancy reduces to whether a person could believe a necessary intermediate proposition that permits a reasonable person to draw the inference in question. The judge must determine this, but the question is not whether the judge believes it. Rather, the question is whether the fact finder could believe it. The central question of relevancy is whether an evidentiary fact relates to the fact finder’s prior knowledge and experience in order to permit the fact finder rationally to process and understand the evidence. and having processed the evidence, if a reasonable person could be influenced by it with regard to a fact of consequence in the case, the evidence is relevant; if not, it is not relevant.

The ideas I have just discussed are absolutely critical to understanding evidence, and so I want to go over them again. The question of relevance is not just what the testimony is, what incurred at trial; it is also what propositions you believe before the trial began. In simple, conventional cases, there is no problem. But many cases at trial are more complicated and require you to think through the logical relationships I have discussed.

There is one more critical point. Reconsider the basic structure of relevancy that involves the relationship between evidence at trial and a fact finder's background knowledge and experience. One can immediately see that there is no absolute *a priori* (before the fact), absolute answer to the question whether something is relevant. The answer depends on the conditions of the particular trial.

Let us consider this further. Take as an example from the transcript in the first chapter of my evidence book the question of who started the fight, the prisoner or the guards? The defendant wants to produce the EF that the guards wore gloves before they went to the cell where the prisoner was kept. The defendant wants to produce this EF to imply that the guards intended to start a fight. The reasoning is that the intent to start a fight increases the probability that the guards did start the fight. If the guards started that fight, then the defendant simply engaged in self-defense and did not commit a crime.

Now does this evidence have relevance? You can compare this example with the silly example about the Brown hair I gave you earlier. The question to ask is: What is the connection between putting on gloves and starting the fight? That depends on what you believe about guards' conduct in prisons. Maybe guards put on their gloves before going to jail cells only when they want to protect themselves because they intend to start a fight. If it is reasonable to believe this, then the evidence is relevant; if it is not reasonable to believe this, that means the evidence is not relevant. Relevancy depends on this intermediate proposition about why guards put on gloves.

Now suppose the judge says, "I have no knowledge about what guards will do with gloves in the jail" . Does that mean the evidence will never come in? No—and this, too is critically important. If a judge says that, you can now present evidence—an EF—about the proposition that guards put on gloves when they intend to start a fight. You can produce evidence about the guards' use of gloves and fights that together imply that the guards started the fight. Now, consider the implications of this. It shows that relevancy is dynamic rather than static, which means in turn that litigation is interactive. Again, there are no *a priori* rules about whether a particular EF is relevant to an IF—it all depends on what a fact finder knows and the evidence the parties produce. The intermediate propositions that determine whether an EF is relevant to an IF come from the parties and their lawyers. When the question is whether some EF is relevant to some IF, the parties or lawyers must articulate the intermediate proposition that is within a fact finder's knowledge that makes it reasonable to believe the EF has relevance to the IF. Even if a judge initially says that evidence is irrelevant , it does not necessarily mean that the evidence can not be admitted. Rather, the party wishing to admit the evidence must produce further evidence to support the intermediate proposition that the judge feels is necessary to allow a reasonable person to draw the inference.

This analysis leads to one of the most important, and analytically deepest, points about evidence. You think of evidence as those things presented at trial. But what is presented at trail never speaks itself, and does not say what implications the evidence may have. The evidence must be appraised by somebody to be understood. What is presented at trial can only be understood by reference to the underlying experience and knowledge of somebody who takes part in the trial. That means—and this is the deep analytical point—that what is called "relevant evidence" involves an interaction between the evidence at the trial with the underlying knowledge and experience of the fact finder. This is why I say that the central question of relevancy is whether an EF "backs up" into the fact finder's prior knowledge and experience in order to permit the fact finder rationally to process and understand the evidence and to be influenced by it. If so, the evidence is relevant; if not, it doesn't necessary mean the evidence is irrelevant, but you have to produce further evidence to show that the intermediate proposition itself may be relied upon in drawing the inference in question.

What we have covered so far leads to one of the most important and most difficult topics of evidence, which is conditional relevance. I don't know if you in China have the same or similar concept of conditional relevance. Whether you do or not, the concept is extremely useful when analyzing rationality at trial. The conceptual problem of relevancy focuses on the intermediate premises that, as I have just discussed, themselves can become the subject of evidence that either supports or undermines those premises. The first question that arises is when does evidence of those intermediate propositions have to be produced? We give the parties some latitude and permit the evidence to be conditionally admitted subject to the party demonstrating its relevance later. This actually solves an interesting conceptual problem. Formally speaking, if a cause of action has two or more elements, proof of one is not relevant in the absence of proof of the other ones. Take as an example a simple contract involving offer and acceptance. Suppose somebody produces evidence to testify to the offer, but the offer doesn't have any relevancy if there is no testimony about acceptance. Similarly, testimony of acceptance has no relevancy without testimony of the existence of the offer. "Conditional relevance" permits us to wait and see if all of the necessary connections are made. What is true of the elements of the cause of action, such as offers and acceptance, is also true of the intermediate propositions that make evidence relevant. For example, you might think that there is no relevance to the guards wearing gloves, but I can later in the trial put evidence in about the behavior of guards in prisons and why they wear gloves that will make the evidence relevant.

I want to end tonight's lecture with three final analytical points, the first dealing with the distinction between circumstantial and direct evidence. There is a definition, but it is not terribly helpful. Direct evidence is evidence, which, if believed, establishes an essential element; circumstantial evidence is evidence that requires other inferences to drawn before it establishes an essential element. Eyewitness testimony is direct evidence; DNA is circumstantial evidence. The idea is to distinguish between longer and shorter inferential chains. The shorter the inferential chain, the lower the probability of error, was the idea. But, this is false. Some "direct evidence" has long and unreliable inferential chains, such as a witness whose credibility is attacked in various ways, and some "circumstantial evidence" has a short and powerful inferential chain, such as DNA. The modern evidence law in the US is beginning to let go off and not utilize this distinction.

The second point that needs to be emphasized is that relevancy is not sufficiency. Sufficiency means that the evidence is adequate to permit a verdict. Relevancy simply tests the logical relationship between evidence and FOC and IF. That is decided by the "any tendency" standard. You will sometimes find yourself inclined to say evidence is not relevant because it does not prove the case. Whenever you find yourself with that inclination, it likely means you are confusing the relationship between relevancy and sufficiency. Consider one last time my example that the guards putting on gloves means they want to start a fight. You might think the guards might put on gloves for other reasons and that putting on gloves is not strong enough evidence to prove they started the fight. However, the question of relevancy is not whether evidence establishes that it is absolutely true that the guards started the fight but instead whether it tends to prove they started the fight.

Relevancy is judged at the time the evidence is offered at trial, and sufficiency is judged after all the evidence is admitted. This is why a collection of pieces of evidence, each of which itself is weak, can still make a strong case. Relevance alone is necessary but not sufficient for an acceptable verdict.

Let me summarize the conceptual problem of relevancy. Relevancy depends on intermediate premises that themselves can become the subject of evidence that either supports or undermines those premises. Therefore, one can never know if some piece of evidence is relevant until one has seen all the evidence. Consider the discussion above of contract litigation. Evidence of an offer is not relevant unless there is evidence of acceptance, but evidence of acceptance is not relevant unless there is evidence of an offer. Conditional relevance eliminates this infinite regress. Evidence can be admitted "subject to" later evidence demonstrating its relevance. This can be tested at the end of a party's presentation of evidence or at the end of the case through motions for directed verdicts, summary judgment, or dismissal.

The last point I will make tonight is to remind you that in the United States there are two limits on admissibility. First, unfair prejudice is the idea that evidence can both show a fact to be true but also show other facts that can bias the fact finder.

Maybe the best example is the person's bad prior record of criminal convictions. That a person has a prior record probably is relevant to other acts he is now charged with, but, once the fact finder learns the person's record, the fact finder may no longer care whether it makes a mistake in the case under consideration. In the United States, we allow evidence to be excluded if its unfair prejudice substantially outweighs its probative value.

Finally, another constraint on admissibility can be policies of the sort I discussed at the beginning of tonight's lecture that create incentives. And once again people, and societies, can disagree about what policies to pursue, and which are important enough to justify compromising the pursuit of truth at trial.

Thank you very much for your attention.

证明责任*

蒋雨佳　强卉　张姝丽　译**　张保生　校

非常荣幸来到这里。我受邀的演讲题目是证明责任。我要讲四部分内容。首先，我将解释一下证明责任的传统理论。我还将指出，传统理论如何扩展到并解释法律过程中的其他方面，尤其是排除动议。排除动议是在全部证据举证结束之前终止一个案件的程序机制；简易判决和指令裁决都是排除动议的例子。在第二部分，我将进而分析指出，证明责任的传统理论何以对事实的司法认知实践也具有启示，并理清在推定问题上的全部混乱。第三部分，我将把这次讲座提升到一个更高的理论水平，阐述传统证明责任理论的致命缺陷。在本部分，我将介绍一些目前美国学术界研究的新理念。坦白地讲，我担心讲座的这部分内容晦涩难懂，因为它对传统的证明责任理论提出了挑战，但这也是中国学者需要开发的一个研究领域。第四部分，我将对第三部分揭示的证明责任的理论难题提出一些尝试性的解决方案。美国证据法学界目前对本讲座第四部分的议题有大量的研究。

一、证明责任的传统理论

在讨论关于证明责任的传统理解之前，必须了解三个重要的起始性观点。第一，像所有构建证明过程的规则一样，证明责任规则也来源于并践行着某种争端解决理论。在美国，主流的争端解决理论是对抗性程序。与第一点相关的第二点是，不同的争端解决理论，如对抗制或大陆法系（有时被称为纠问式）的审判制度，本身来源于民事案件私人个体之间争端解决中以及刑事案件公诉中政府之适当角色的潜在概念。

在英美法传统中，政府在私人争端解决中的作用是辅助性的。政府只为私人争端的公正解决提供一个公平而无偏私的论坛，这基本上就是政府有义务甚或有权去做的全部事情。从特定意义上看，这一争端解决概念也影响着刑事案件。政府提起公诉，但政府方被视为类似于私人当事人，即在法院上与另一方

* 本文是艾伦教授2012年7月30日在中国政法大学、吉林大学、武汉大学司法文明协同创新中心主办、中国政法大学证据科学研究院承办的漠河“证据法学前沿高级研讨班”上的演讲。

** 蒋雨佳，美国西北大学法学院JD；张姝丽，中国政法大学博士研究生。

私人当事人处于平等地位的一方私人当事人。换言之，法院是中立的，而不是一个在具体诉讼中为促进政府特定政策而构建的政府机构的组成部分。的确，众所周知，美国法院正是通过诸如证据排除规则等方式阻挡了政府的政策目标。

第三，在更深的概念层次上，司法和其他政府部门均旨在促进反映在诸如美国宪法等立国文献和传统中的政治理念。在这里，须注意中国和美国的一个重要区别。在美国，委托人与代理人理论是政府治理的核心政治问题：政府是人民的代理人，而主要问题是委托人——人民——如何能够控制其代理人——政府。出于对中央政府过度集权的焦虑而设法将其控制和限制，这个理论本身便很好地解释了联邦制和“三权分立”这两个典型的美国政治结构特征。而在中国，由于中国共产党一党执政理论，核心的政治问题是如何高效地实现政府的政策目标。这些不同显然影响了在此基础上建立的两国的法律制度。可以预见到，中国政府为了更有效地实现其政治目标会倾向于对争端解决程序施加较多的力量和控制。与之相对，美国政府的力量更为有限，并且美国法院大体上是一个中立场所。

这两个区别——不同类型的法律制度和政府理论——并不必然陷入截然对立，但会呈现出不同的差别。举个例子，即使在拥有许多共同特征的代议制民主体制中，关于政府在争端解决中的角色的观点也不尽相同。例如，在许多西欧国家，争端并不像在美国那样被视为“私事”，政府在诉讼的所有阶段均发挥着更为积极的作用。与美国的情况相比，这些国家的政府经常更积极地参与案件调查，法院对审判过程也施以更多的控制。这反映了公民之间的争端具有公共性的观点，因此，争端解决是集体关注的事项。①与此相比，在美国，私人争端在很大程度上并不被视为值得社会关注的事情，政府也较少扮演积极的角色。当事人承担了案件调查和案件庭审准备的责任，并在很大程度上控制着庭审证据的出示。同样，上诉法院往往只根据当事方提供的论据而作出裁定，因此，产生了虽然案件事实实质上相同但由于提出的法律论据不同而出现不同裁定的可能性。这里的关键之点是理解，法院的职责是基于当事人提出的材料正确裁定案件，而非竭尽全力“正确”裁定案件。

还有另外两个变量影响着法律制度的结构。第一个涉及法律认识论。这是

① 关于这个问题及相关事项的讨论，参见［美］米尔建·R·达马斯卡：《司法和国家权力机关的面孔：比较视野中的法律程序》，1986年；［美］米尔建·R·达马斯卡：《定罪的证据壁垒和刑事诉讼的两种模式》，载《宾夕法尼亚大学法律评论》，第121卷，1973年，第506页。

指关于不同争端解决形式使准确裁决何以有效的信念。在美国，一般认为，对抗制调查和证据出示比法院主导的审判过程更可能产生与事实真相一致的裁决。当事人比任何他人更了解自己的案件，并有充足的动机在争端解决中投入最佳的资源。无论是从对案件的了解还是从最佳的动机来说，政府部门都不能与当事人同日而语。而那些对纠问制独有钟情的人则强调，由没有利害关系的法院所主导的审判，将减少证据的滥用和操控。他们认为，这可以增加裁决与事实真相一致的机会。②

然而，查明事实真相并不是唯一的社会福祉，并且，关于特定社会福祉与其他社会福祉（如隐私权）之间如何相互作用，还存在着不同的意见。在美国，主流观点认为，在民事诉讼中，当事人在庭审开始前应不受限制地获取一切与争端相关的信息。获取这种信息的程序被称为证据开示，强有力的证据开示制度已成为美国法律制度的典型特征之一。其理念是，审判应当真正成为一种认识论成果，不应当充斥着意外和路障。正如我们将要看到的，证明责任理论，在很大程度上就植根于这一假定。在采取和未采取证据开示的法律制度中，证明责任有一系列不同的机制——这对于你们理解这个问题来说是一个关键点。在不同的法律语境下，一个一方可以“强迫”对方提供证据的制度，与一个没有该种机制的制度相比，证明责任的运作并不必然相似。

要说的最后一个重要的变量是陪审团或者非专业陪审员对法律制度结构的影响。在美国，陪审团曾经受到崇拜，然而也被视为法律专业领域的外来入侵者而须加以规范和控制，其中一种方法，就是证明责任的各种运用，这一点我将在后面详细阐述。

总之，当我们着手分析证明责任时，须牢记以下5点：

（1）证明责任是诉讼理论的组成部分；

（2）诉讼理论本身又是政府理论的组成部分；

（3）政府理论千差万别；

（4）争端解决涉及事实认定，在以何种最有效和高效的方式获得真相以及当查明真相与其他社会福祉相互竞争时如何进行价值排序等问题上，学术界存在着分歧；

② 相关的讨论，参见约翰·H·朗本：《德国民事诉讼中的优势》，载《芝加哥大学法律评论》，第52卷，1985年，第823页；罗纳德·J·艾伦、斯提凡·库贝克、库尔特·莱彻伯格和D·托比·罗森：《德国民事诉讼中的优势：比较研究中对更多细节和更少概论的呼吁》，载《西北大学法律评论》，第82卷，1988年，第705页。

(5) 陪审团成员等外行事实认定者的存在，也可以影响诉讼程序的构建方式。

在开始阐述证明责任理论之前，就先说了这么一堆复杂的问题，让人疑惑到底是否有这样一种理论存在。这种怀疑是错误的。确实存在一套健全的证明责任理论，但同时，该理论的含义又受到上述各种因素的影响。下面，我们转入一般证明责任理论。

实际上，有三种责任可强加给诉讼当事人，它们一起构建了诉讼。当事人可被要求提出争点，就争点提出证据，并承担对该争点的说服责任。这三种要求依次为提出诉讼主张的责任（burden of pleading）、举证责任和说服责任。

提出诉讼主张的责任尽管常被人们忽视，却极为重要。提出诉讼主张是使当事人和法院知悉诉讼主题的一种手段，这是诉讼中至关重要的第一步。法院需要某些理由认为，确实存在一个提起诉讼的争端。在真正的“纠问”制下，政府方对案件可以自行调查并裁定诉讼事项。这种做法通常效率低下。与依赖政府方调查不同的一种方法，是要求起诉方必须通知被诉一方和法院，究竟为何提起诉讼。这是通过向法院递交陈述诉因并宣布与另一方就某事争诉之动机的诉状来完成的。除了提供所追求之诉讼的通知外，诉状还展现了诉因的基本参数。对抗制通常要求递交回应性的诉辩状，在某些司法辖区，如果被告认为，除了原告提出的争点外，尚有其他诉讼争点，就必须提出这些具体争点，例如，积极抗辩通常必须由被告来提出主张。③

如上所述，提出诉讼主张的责任如此直白和显然易见，所以常被忽视，然而它却解决了一个严肃的认识论问题，该问题是，世界纷繁复杂，诉讼可能涉其任何方面。在这个错综复杂的现实中，当事人知道哪些方面卷入了诉争，提出诉讼主张的责任作为第一步，就是为了解决当事人之间的争端，而使这些错综复杂的现实能为常人所理解并使其一目了然。简而言之，起诉方需要解释他为什么要起诉，而被告方则需要解释为什么此诉毫无根据。这些诉、辩状一起构成了需要裁定的问题。

当双方都提交了他们的诉、辩状并进行了其可选择的证据开示后，他们就做好了庭审准备，而庭审需要构建：谁先进行，一方传唤证人之后接着发生什么，等等。这些都是首先通过分配举证责任的规则来规制的。诉讼中的每一个

③ 一般参见 E·克利里：《假定与辩护：关于法律不成熟的一篇随笔》，载《斯坦福法律评论》，第 12 卷，1959 年，第 5 页。

争点，无论是案件的一个要件还是积极抗辩，都伴随着举证责任，这要求一方或另一方提供与这一特定争点相关的证据（因此被称为“举证责任”）。如果负有举证责任的一方未能就此特定争点提供充分证据，该当事方便将承担不利后果。因此，举证责任向案件双方发出了如下通知：在没有证据或证据不足的情况下，争点将如何被裁定；如果当事人不希望得到一种缺乏证据所带来的不利后果，他们就必须提供与争点相关的证据。

举证责任与提出诉讼主张的责任常常并行不悖，但这并不是说二者不可被加以分析。要求一方提出诉讼争点，而另一方对该争点承担举证责任（或对该事项承担说服责任），有时候这样做是很明智的。在美国，提出诉讼主张和举证的责任，其功能集合在一起的范例涉及刑事被告。在某些争点上，刑事被告必须提出一定的“抗辩”（我给抗辩加上引号，是因为要件与抗辩的划分是任意的，一个是另一个的镜像——如下文所列举的，人们只要简单地在要件前面加上“非”，就可轻而易举地将一个要件转变为积极抗辩），譬如正当防卫或精神失常。这是因为，刑事案件中一般并不涉及这些抗辩，只有被告知道他们在特定案件中是否应当进行抗辩。一旦被告通知政府方，该案件涉及上述某种“抗辩”，政府方通常就对那些争点承担证明责任。④

然而，人们何以知道负有举证责任的一方已提供了足够证据？当举证责任所含的要求得到满足时，此责任即告完成。在民事案件中，举证责任的主要目的，在于确保案件争点在进一步的诉讼中得到证成。这里，使用和不使用陪审团的制度有一个重要区别：当何方应获胜可能仍存在合理分歧时，问题就需要由陪审团而非法官来解决。如果不存在合理分歧，就没有理由再花费任何费用，法官就应当作出对适当的一方有利的裁决（或以其他方式处置案件，如驳回诉讼）。因此，举证责任的另一个含义是，如果无法满足其要求，将导致对方在特定争点上“获胜”。即使在没有陪审团的制度中，这一点也同样重要。一旦事实认定者听审了足够证据而认为在某一争点上可能没有合理的争端，便不应有更多的资源被浪费在进一步的诉讼上。

人们如何判断在某一问题上可能没有合理的争端？要决定在哪一方应当获胜的问题上是否可能存有合理的争端，法官必须参照指导其判案的裁决规则以及既有的证据，来检验当事人提供的证据。这种裁决规则通常被称为“说服责任”。说服责任告诉裁决者如何按照证据的含义来裁决案件。例如，一个可能

④ 我说“通常”，是因为在美国有51个不同司法辖区（每个州和联邦政府），而它们对这些问题采用不同的方法。

的裁决规则是，仅当证据证实原告的案子达到一种确定性（100%真实）时，原告才应当胜诉。这个规则要求，须由原告证实的事实之真实性如果存在任何可疑的话，就要作出对被告有利的裁决。

确定性裁决规则有一种天然吸引力——不应当要求人们（被告人）赔偿，除非他们已做了某些错事。尽管有这种天然吸引力，它并不是民事诉讼中普遍确立的规则，因为它将置原告于一种极其不利的地位。要把任何事实证明到确定的程度，如果不是不可能（我要说，实际上是不可能的），也是困难的。要求原告这样做，以牺牲应得到保护的原告为代价，将导致被告胜诉的错误裁决不成比例地增加。相反的裁决规则——要求被告对于他们不应当承担责任的证明达到一种确定性——将产生相反的效果。最重要的是因为争诉双方在法律面前应当平等，这两种裁决规则所造成的结果均非最佳。法院没有哪一方应当胜诉的理念，并且，一个有利于原告的错误裁决和一个有利于被告的错误裁决，并没有什么差别，二者都剥夺了一个私人当事人的权利（我在下文详述这一点）。

要求一方或另一方把自己的案子证明到确定性程度，而不是采取将原告或被告置于极为不同地位这两种极端做法之一，在民事诉讼中始终如一的实践是采用优势证据的说服责任，其目的是最大限度地减少错案总量且同等对待双方当事人。原告必须将其必要的事实主张证明到优势证据的程度，被告必须以相同标准证实积极抗辩。这通常被界定为“真实性大于50%几率”。因此，任务是决定证据是有利于诉因中关于事实要素之原告案情，还是有利于积极抗辩中被告之案情。相比之下，在刑事案件中，双方当事人在法律面前并不存在关键意义上的平等。在美国，我们认为，一个错误定罪要比一个错误的无罪裁决更糟糕。因此，为了减少将无辜者错误定罪的危险，我们强加了确信无疑的说服责任。无论是否同意这个原则，人们都能立即看到说服责任如何可被用于实现政策选择。我说“可被用于”，正如我将在本讲座第三部分再次阐明的，是因为事情要比其表现出来的那样要复杂得多。

在详细阐述这些复杂内容之前，弄清举证责任和说服责任之间的关系是很重要的。如果已提出的充足证据表明，存在着需要进一步诉讼的相关事实问题，并且理性人对该事项可能产生分歧，那么，举证责任就应被视为得到满足。该分歧将结束于裁决规则——说服责任——是否得到满足。如果理性人能够一致认为原告或被告已满足了相关的说服责任，那么，就没有理由再审理该争议事实或者将已发生的司法程序继续进行下去。因此，正如麦克诺顿教授在一篇重要论文中所阐述的，举证责任是说服责任的一项功能。[5] 检验一项举证责任是否已完成的方法，是根据证据来确定，是否仍然存在哪一方应当获胜的合理分歧。如果可能存在这种分歧，进一步的诉讼也许就是正当的。如果不存在合理分歧，法官将尽可能快地处理该案件。

举证责任和说服责任的关系还需要进一步考察。让我们先假定，事实认定者（法官、陪审团成员、外行评判者）和我们其余的人一样，通过粗略的估计来确定事实为真的概率，而优势证据意味着相关事实为真的可能性大于50%。我在第三部分会指出这种假设是大有问题的，但为了方便理解证明责任的运作，我们暂且接受这种假设。

根据该假设，裁决是基于概率判断，证明过程可以通过图解形式来突出举证责任和说服责任的关系。假定，负有举证责任的一方提出某个证据，那个证据将表明，相关事实有一定的可能性为真。然而，该证据就其所产生的概率程度来说很可能并不十分确切。通过考察那个证据，理性人可能对该证据证实某个必要事实的概率产生分歧。这是否意味着，每当就任何争点出示证据时，由于总会存在对证据影响力的合理分歧，案件就必须继续进行下去？答案显然是否定的。只有在哪一方应当胜诉仍存在合理分歧而又要求履行说服责任的情况下，该案件才应当继续审理下去。请考虑下图所列出的 3 种可能性：

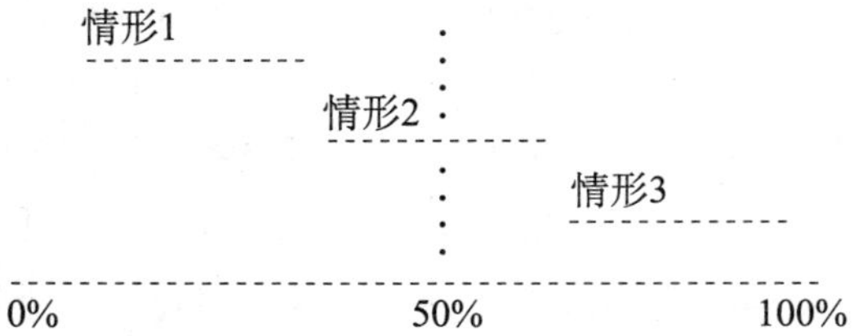

上图按证据的影响力以图形展现了 3 种相关的可能性。第一，所提出的证据也许并不十分具有说服力。理性人经过考察可能会得出这样的结论，它确有一些说服力，但并不非常充分。这种可能性如上图情况（1）所示。它表明，根据所提供的证据，事实为真的概率为 10%～35%。为了清楚和检验大家的理解，我可以将那个线段画在 0～50%之间的任何一个地方，只要它不超过50%。在这种情况下，由于没有理性人会断定提出证据的一方应当胜诉，举证责任便没有得到满足。重要之点在于，举证责任是通过参考相关的说服责任来检验的，或如麦克诺顿教授所说的那样，举证责任是说服责任的一种功能。

[5] 约翰·T·麦克诺顿：《证据提出的责任：说服责任的一个功能》，载《哈佛法律评论》，第 68 卷，1955 年，第 1382 页。

现在来看情况（2），证据表明了一个40%～60%的合理的说服力。这里再考察一下大家的理解，我可以将该线段画在与50%有交叉的任何地方。在这种情况下，由于理性人仍可能对证据的影响力存有分歧，将该争点的证明在进一步的诉讼程序中进行下去便是正当的。情况（3）与情况（1）相似，理性人对证据的影响力都不存在合理的分歧。证据显示，相关事实为真的可能性大约在65%～90%，这里，该线段可以画到50%右边的任何地方。

情况（3）与情况（1）有一个差别。我们一直是假定，承担举证责任的一方已提供了证据。在情况（1）中，举证责任并未得到满足，因此没有理由继续进行审理。在情况（2）中，举证责任已得到满足，案件将继续进行审理。在情况（3）中，举证责任不仅得到满足，而且超额了。没有理性人会对哪一方应获胜产生分歧，尽管这个结论只是基于一方提供的证据。因此，在情况（3）中，对方在审判中应得到出示相反证据的机会，以便证明对相关事实仍存有合理的争端。在情况（1）中，没有理由让对方继续举证，因为负有举证责任方的证据本身表明相关事实不能被证实。再让对方提出更多证实其结论的信息将是浪费时间和金钱。然而，在情况（3）中，对方的证据尚未听审，而其很可能掌握着将影响对相关事实乃至全部证据（包括对方的）之分析方式的信息。因此，在情况（3）中，将给对方回应的机会。

审判中的证明过程可按以上三种分析可能性的不断重复加以分析。假定承担举证责任的当事方提出了足够的证据，那么类似情况（2）的情况就会产生。在这种情况下，对方将有回应的权利。对方的证据很可能将减少相关事实为真的概率，因而使图中的概率范围向左移动。在大部分司法辖区，原先负有举证责任的当事方有权在对方回应之后再提供反驳证据，即回应对方所提供的证据，对方通常也可以反过来提供新证据予以回应（即我刚才说的不断重复）。此过程将持续到双方都没有新证据提供为止。此时，证据从整体上看将是前述三种分析可能性图形中的一种情况。如果证据符合情况（1），那么，法官将对争点作出有利于对方的裁定。如果证据符合情况（2），那么，如果有陪审团，此问题应由陪审团来裁决；如果没有陪审团，法官就必须对事实和案件作出裁决。如果证据符合情况（3），法官就应当对该争点作出对于原先负有举证责任一方有利的裁决。

现在我将阐述传统的证明责任理论如何解释并应用于诸如指令裁决和简易判决等排除动议。在美国以及任何有外行事实认定者的制度中，要求法官以对哪一方有利的方式作出裁决，这取决于此要求在何时提出。一种可能性是，一方可以在任何证据出示之前就提出简易判决动议。如果法官可根据诉状和任何诉讼支持文件判定该案中没有需通过司法途径解决的争点，此种动议将被准许。然而，这样一个裁定等于说，存在情况（1）或者情况(3）的情况——或者承担举证责任的当事方未能满足它，或者对方未能表明仍有足够存疑的事实需要在审判中加以证明。如果情况（2）存在，那么（任何一方提出的）简易判决动议将被驳回，该诉讼将继续进行。不过，这里重要之点是注意，法官的裁决将取决于一方当事人是否满足了其举证责任，以及对方是否有能力以足够证据回应一方的证明，来证明诉讼程序继续进行是正当的。尽管简易判决通常并不作为与举证责任和说服责任密切相关的问题放在一起讨论，但这些概念显然是紧密相连的。[6]

如果一个案件进入取证阶段，一方在主诉（讼）末尾可以提出指令裁决动议的方式要求法官检验证据的强度。这里的分析与简易判决动议的分析非常相似，实际上只有一个重要区别，如果你能理解我所阐述的理论，那就完全理解了证明责任复杂成分的分析。在负有举证责任的当事方提供证据后，如果情况（1）存在，法院就应当作出对对方有利的指令裁决；如果情况（2）存在，审判显然应当继续进行。如果情况（3）存在，因为对方尚未提供证据，审判也要继续进行。只要反对一项排除动议的当事方仍有可能影响案件分析的证据要提供，排除动议就不应当被准许。指令裁决的分析通常并不从举证责任和说服责任的角度来进行，但这些理念的相似之处又是很明显的。排除动议是使证据影响力受到检验的一种手段，而证据的影响力又是举证责任特别是说服责任的一个功能。因此，不止是举证责任是说服责任的一个功能，排除动议也是如此。

在一个有完善的证据开示的制度中，由哪一方来承担举证责任并不重要。在有证据开示的制度中，每一方都可以接触基本上所有相关证据并能在审判中出示，从而导致关于是非曲直的裁决。因此，在这样一个制度中，没有什么正当理由制定分配举证责任的复杂规则，而一般来说唯一复杂的是，人们要在裁决中找到所列特定争点作为抗辩而非要件的位置。[7] 原告负有提出诉讼主张并提出关于要件证据的责任，而被告负有提出关于抗辩证据的责任，但要注意，

⑥ 美国最高法院已在 Anderson v. Liberty Lobby，Inc.，106 S. Ct. 2505 (1986) 和 Celotex Corporation v. Catrett，106 S. Ct. 2548 (1986) 等案件中注意到这种关系。关于这个问题的一个杰出讨论，参见迈克尔·S·帕尔多：《诉辩、证明和判决：民事诉讼的统一理论》，载《波士顿大学法律评论》，第51卷，2010年，第1451页。

⑦ 在强有力的证据开示制度建立之前，举证责任的分配可能在很大程度上影响案件的结果，明确阐述的复杂的考量规则指导这种分配。参见小弗莱明·詹姆斯：《证明责任》，载《弗吉尼亚法律评论》，第47卷，1961年，第51页。

“要件”和“抗辩”的标签又是任意的，只要给要件加上“否定”性描述，人们就将要件转换为抗辩，反之亦然。举例来说，人们可以说，原告负有证明合同案件中损害存在的责任，人们也可以说，作为抗辩，被告负有证明合同案件中不存在损害的责任。举证责任的分配只在一种情况下会有重大区别，即关于诉讼中的某一争点不存在非常有力的证据，如果没人能获得有力的证据，无论谁负有举证责任，都将败诉。

相比之下，在一个没有证据开示的制度中，举证责任可能就很重要了。首先，它可以作为证据开示机制，强迫一方或另一方提供证据，否则，便要承担败诉后果。这意味着，在确定谁承担举证责任的问题上应谨慎为之。如有可能，它应施加于能更好地获得证据的一方。如果它被分配给没有机会获得证据的对方，又没有健全的证据开示制度，那么，该当事方将不能满足举证责任而败诉。这是我前面提到在不同法律制度中举证责任运作不同的一个范例，这里关键的区别在于，双方当事人是否可获得充分的证据。

现在我们关注一下说服责任，尽管本讲座的第三部分将专门讨论这个问题。说服责任指导着对不确定性的裁决方式。正如我在前面谈到的，传统的说服责任理论在于其是错误的分配规则。优势证据规则合并了关于诉讼参与者的一个潜在假设：被告作为和原告一样的等级，一般应受到同等对待。民事原告和被告的等价性是值得强调的至关重要的观点。想象有一个原告为 1 万元而起诉被告。如果原告错赢了该诉讼，被告就被错误地剥夺了 1 万元。然而，如果原告错输了诉讼，原告就被错误地剥夺了 1 万元。在这两种错误中，都是一个私人当事人被错误地剥夺了同样数目的金钱。在对这个特定的争端提出任何证据之前，可以合理地假定，很可能是被告拒绝偿还应付款项，这与原告试图获得本不属于他的某些东西是一样的。

优势证据标准概括了这个基本观点，根据特定假设，人们可以看到它是如何发挥作用的。假定，在所有进入审判的案件中，应获胜的原告和应获胜的被告一样多，现在比较一下那些原告事实上应赢和那些被告事实上应赢的案件。在大多数原告应赢的案件中，证据将支持那样的结论，因此创设了一个大于 0.5 的概率评估，这一评估将产生一个原告胜诉的裁决。只有在那些概率评估是或小于 0.5 的案件中才会产生有利于被告的错误裁决。反之，被告应赢的案件亦然。假定在大多数那些案件中证据显示被告应赢，由此创设了一个是或小于 0.5 的概率评估。只有在那些概率评估大于 0.5 的案件中才存在有利于原告的错误裁决。如果人们假定，这两种情况的概率评估是在其相对范围内正态分布的，那么，所犯的有利于原告的错误数量与有利于被告的错误数量大约一样，而优势证据标准就完成了它的任务。

下图以几何形式展现了这种概率。[8] 横轴为事实认定者（法官、陪审团成员或外行评判者）赋予案件的概率，竖轴是被赋予特定概率的案件数量。图Ⅰ是被告应赢（其意味着，如果我们知道所有事实之确定性，被告将赢）的案件集，图Ⅱ是原告应赢的案件集。

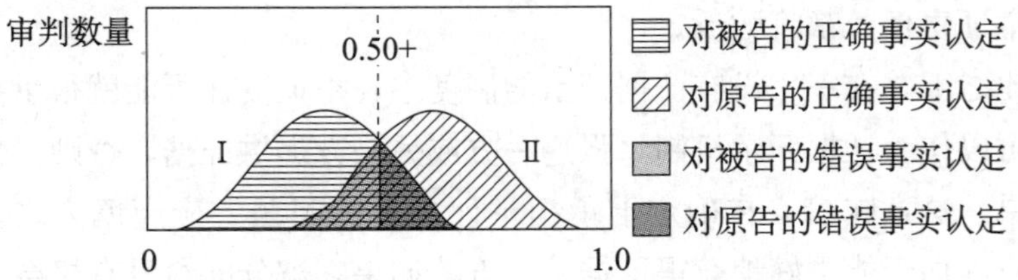

事实认定者得出正确结论的概率值

在图Ⅰ中，错误由0.5右边的所有那些案件代表，即图中的重阴影部分。这个区域表示被告应获胜但却不能提供足够的证据，因而事实认定者将认定一个倾向于原告的高于0.5的概率。在那种情况下，通过应用优势证据标准，事实认定者将会作出一个原告胜诉的错误裁决。同样，在图Ⅱ中，错误由0.5左边的区域代表，还是图中的重阴影部分。错误的数量由图中的区域代表——区域越大，错误越多；区域越小，错误越少。只要重阴影部分在两个图中的面积几乎同样大，那么，优势证据标准就将在原告和被告之间有均等的错误，从而达到了平等对待原、被告的伴侣目标。然而，请注意，只有在两个图中的相关区域差不多均等大时才会如此，而这本身是一个实证问题。如果两个图的轮廓与我们所表达的明显不同，或者，如果原告应赢的案件数目大于或小于被告应赢的案件数目，那么，图中的阴影部分的面积将改变，而在原、被告之间可被分配的错误便不平等了。这个问题我将在第三部分论述。我用上述图的绘制方式，体现了与民事案件相关的一些假设，但在刑事案件中不一定适用，这是我要在下文中论述的。

这些图还展现了，为改变错误的分配，在民事诉讼中替代性说服责任有时是如何被依赖的。许多司法辖区要求民事诉讼中关于诈骗或具有刑事性质的指控，要由清楚且令人信服的证据来加以证明。该理论认为，由于这种指控的严重性，错误应当对被指控的人有利。这也解释了为什么刑事诉讼要求更高的说服责任。如上文作出同样的假设，将说服责任从优势证据提高到“清楚且令人

⑧　这些图表来自理查德·贝尔：《决策论和正当程序：对最高法院证明责任立法的批评》，载《刑法与犯罪学杂志》，第78卷，1987年，第557页。

信服的证据”的效果，可在下图中体现出来：

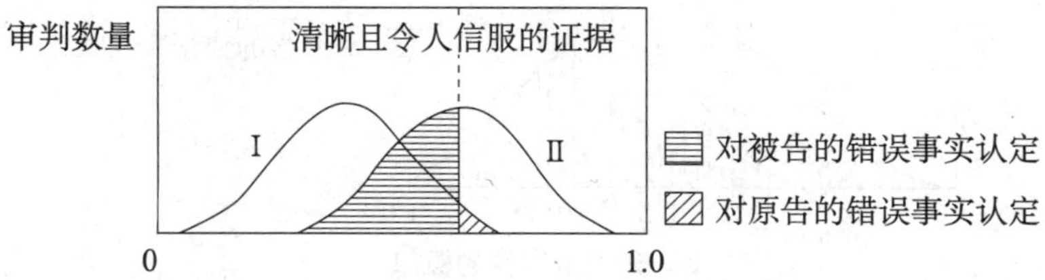

事实认定者得出正确结论的概率值

阴影区域仍代表错误，提高证明责任的效果是显而易见的：有利于被告的错误增加了，而有利于原告的错误减少了。这恰恰是提高说服责任旨在达到的效果。不过，应牢记这些图标在现实中的模样是一个实证而非纯分析的问题。如果在这个问题上能获得可靠数据，根据那些信息，修改说服责任就可能是正当的。比如，我们可能在审查数据后判定，在诈骗案指控中出现了太多对被告有利的错误，这种错误的几率可能因降低说服责任而受到影响。

我们还能看到改变证明标准的影响，将优势证据标准和中国一些学者所主张的高度盖然性证明标准比较一下，尽管就我所知，中国法院在民事案件中执行何种证明标准的问题上仍有分歧。此外，我知道，伴随着对客观真实说越来越多的批评，中国学者已或多或少理解了审判中的裁决是不确定性裁决（或如这些学者所说，法院应追求“法律真实”而非“客观真实”），但他们尚未就仅采取优势证据标准还是少数学者所主张的高度盖然性标准达成一致。⑨ 你们比我更了解中国法律的现状，因此我将这个问题留给你们去解决。然而，我想利用这个机会巩固一下我们对说服责任的理解。

就我所知，高度盖然性标准继承自大陆法传统，其设立了高于75%的标准。⑩ 下图说明了这一较高说服责任在民事案件中的潜在影响。正如前面所强调的清楚且令人信服的标准那样，证明标准的提高将导致更多有利于被告的错判和更少有利于原告的错判：事实上，这个图与上文论证的清楚且令人信服的证据图基本相同。阴影部分代表错案，提高证明责任导致了有利于被告的错误数量的增加。

刑事案件确信无疑的证明要求，也可通过这个方法得到解释：

⑨ 关于中国现今施行的一种高度盖然性标准，或大陆法系国家的一种较高证明标准的论述，参见牟军：《民事证明标准论纲——以刑事证明标准为对应的一种解析》，载《法商研究》，2002（4）；易延友：《证据法的体系与精神——以英美法为特别参照》，北京大学出版社2010年版。

⑩ 参见［德］汉斯·普维庭著，吴越译：《现代证明责任问题》，法律出版社2000年版。

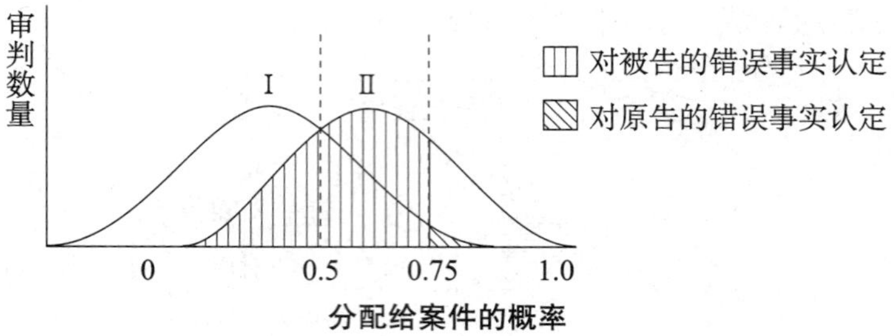

这样一个方案的曲线图Ⅰ，将是刑事案件中所有无辜者受审的集合。曲线下的阴影区域仍代表错误，如我对这些曲线所描绘的那样，宁可错判无罪而不错判有罪的政策得到了满足。你也可以看到降低说服责任的影响。如果将其降低到0.7，就会将更多有罪者定罪，但同样也会将更多无辜者定罪。总之，这些曲线图，有趣且有力地展示了说服责任应该如何对错误分配发挥作用。然而，请注意，它们仅仅是基于优势证据标准假设的分析性图——它们仅代表如果优势证据标准实际达到其将原告置于与被告平等地位之目标时的应然情况，它们在何种程度上反映现实将是下文第三部分的主题。

二、证明责任理论向推定和司法认知的延伸

尽管没有让我讲解推定和司法认知，我还是想分别对它们讲几句。[11] 尽管推定和司法认知在传统上被看作是单独的证据类别，但实际上，它们和证明责任有密切关联。一个关于证明责任的讲座如果没有对这些证据概念之间的分析性相似点加以认知，将是不完整的。我先讲一下司法认知。

（一）司法认知

之前我们已经看到，能施加于当事人的有三种责任，这三种责任共同构成了证明过程，它们是提出诉讼主张的责任、举证责任和说服责任。司法认知乍看起来似乎和证明责任无关，但它允许法官在缺乏证据时推断事实为真。一个范例是《美国联邦证据规则》规则201（b）允许司法认知的事实：“（1）审判法院辖区内周知的事实；或者（2）通过借助其准确性不容合理置疑的来源而能准确和易于确定的事实。”如果一个事实在一个司法辖区内基本上是无可争辩的，那么，允许就该事实进行诉讼，简直就是对资源（如法官的时间和当事人的金钱资源）的浪费，显然可以将其花费在其他更好的地方。问题在于，确

⑪ 有关详细的讨论，参见罗纳德·J·艾伦：《刑事案件中陪审团裁决的构建：一种证据手段的统一宪法方法》，载《哈佛法律评论》，第94卷，1980年，第321页。

定何时某些事情为“周知”，或者“不容合理质疑”。对此问题的一般回答是，明确表达一些启人疑窦的请求和基本上是对该规则语言重申的循环解释。[12]

如果从证明责任角度看司法认知，这种不能具体界定司法认知的问题便迎刃而解了。司法认知和举证责任一样，取决于说服责任。[13] 如果它是常识——被共同体中每一个有感知能力的人知道——事实的可能性超出相关的说服责任，或者，事实的不可能性超出了说服责任（司法认知在两个方向都起作用），那么，在审判中就该事实或非事实花费时间就变得毫无意义了。争辩今天我们是否在中国漠河，是毫无意义的。如果某人非要就该问题提起诉讼，他们显然能够提出令人满意的证据来解决它，但这样做的效果只是时间和金钱的浪费。因此，司法认知大体上是诸如指令裁决和简易判决等绝对动议的变体，它也允许在花费更多资源变得无意义时使诉讼程序发生短路，但何时花费更多资源会变得无意义，取决于说服责任。

这个观点阐明了司法认知最怪的特征，当事人经常提供那些他们声称允许法官采取司法认知的信息。《美国联邦证据规则》规则 201（e）又是一个例子，其允许法院听审关于司法认知适当性的“信息”，这确实赋予了当事人对该事项进行听审的权利。“信息”一词显然只是“证据”的一种委婉说法，因此，这个规则规定，法官可以为了判定是否存在一个争点而听审证据。虽然这听起来像指令裁决或简易判决的措词，实际上它也确实如此，唯一的不同的是，由于借口是“证据”未被提交，审判程序的正式形式并未应用。因此，从头到尾，司法认知都提供了一种简化和减少审判成本的方法，但它完全取决于说服责任。

关于司法认知可以说得更多，或许值得单独为其举办一次讲座。这里我只简单地说，你们应当能够看到，我所提出的中心点延伸到了“司法认知”一词用于各种法律制度的其他方式。例如，在出现不重要的证明失效的情况下，它有时被用于保存明显正确的裁决。这么做的要点是，重审的费用，甚或每个人都知道是明显不正确的裁决的记录，应当避免，而司法认知允许通过严格的证据规则来改善进一步的实质正义。更深刻的是，审判结果能够并仅应当以当庭

⑫ 例如，艾奥瓦州最高法院，关于 *Tresnak*，297 N. W. 2d 109（Iowa，1980）案的评论，对于“每个人都知晓的事实”可采用司法认知，在 Meredith v. Fair，298 F. 2d 696（5th Cir.，1962）案中，法院欣然接受了“每个人都知晓的显见事实”的标准。这些仅是对相同一般观点的重述，并没有对适当标准作进一步详述。

⑬ 更完整的讨论，参见罗纳德·J·艾伦：《法典化分析的阐释价值——以法典中的组织原则而非其应用为参照》，载《西北大学法律评论》，第 79 卷，1984—1985 年，第 1080、1091～1094 页。

出示的“证据”为根据的理念，存在着内在的松散性⑭，而司法认知改善了这种松散性。⑮

（二）推定⑯

人们告诉我，数年前中国证据法学者对推定问题研究的兴趣很浓，但这种兴趣现在消退了。我希望这是因为中国证据学者已开始意识到就“推定”一词的含义进行争论毫无意义。在西方法律制度中，所有围绕这一术语的全部复杂性和困难都只是概念混乱的副产品。一旦人们承认，没有“推定”这种事情，所有关于推定的困难就消失了。“推定”一词仅仅是一个标签，它被应用于一系列关于适当审判模式之广泛不同的裁决机制，以及事实被证实以解决法律争端的不同方式。在每个“推定”一词的用法中，无论做了什么，都是由普通证据概念和政策决定的，其中最重要的是证明责任，这正是我将这部分内容纳入本讲座的原因。所有围绕推定的困惑和争论——我的意思是说，所有——都是因为没能认识到“推定”一词仅仅是一个标签，它被应用于一系列证据性裁

⑭ 罗纳德·J·艾伦：《事实的模糊性和证据理论》，载《西北大学法律评论》，第88卷，1994年，第604页。

⑮ 罗纳德·J·艾伦：《法典化分析的阐释价值——以法典中的组织原则而非其应用为参照》，载《西北大学法律评论》，第79卷，1984—1985年，第1080、1091～1094页。这个观点同样解释了《美国联邦证据规则》中大概最奇怪的规则——规则201（g）规定：“在刑事案件中，法院将指示陪审团，它可以，但并不要求，将任何司法认知的事实接受为确定性的。”中国读者一开始就应当注意到，在美国，所有这些都是受宪法保护的陪审制度的功能之一。在任何情况下，告诉陪审团，它“可以”接受司法认知的事实，这是自相矛盾的。司法认知是用来解决争议的。该不一致可用法官在刑事案件中享有的权力小于在民事案件中享有的权力来解释，这反映在刑事案件中没有指令裁决这一误导性的观点中［它是误导性的，因为它是错误的，参见 United States v. Bailey，444 U. S. 394（1980）案：拒绝就被告承担却未能满足举证责任的问题对陪审团作出指示这一行为本身，就具有对被告抗辩指令裁决的同样效力］。对一个事实的司法认知，就是对它的一个指令裁决，因为该争点不归陪审团决定了，但这与陪审团成员在刑事案件中的角色的传统观点是冲突的。规则201（g）通过声称允许不具有约束力的司法认知，回应了对司法认知的正统理解和刑事案件的正统路径之间的明显冲突。这种回应显得十分不连贯，更好的方法也许是有意识地限制陪审团在刑事案件中之事实认定者的作用。规则201（g）在美国刑事审判制度这一特殊语境中有另一个优点：在公诉方对某个事实的主诉存在缺失而法官认为无可争议时，它允许法院拒绝指令一个对被告有利的裁决。更为重要的是，通过允许陪审团得到关于“司法认知”事实的指示，规则201（g）授权了一种对于可能有利于一方当事人的证据进行评论的形式。如果法官认为，一个事实几乎确定是真的，法官可以告诉陪审团，它“可以”接受这一事实为真，如果它选择这样做的话。这就允许法官去评论那些明显的、众所周知的或者无可非议的事情，尽管在特定点上没有提出证据。当完全理解了其含义之后，虽然它也许会引起政治上的争议，但关于这样一个规则并没有什么特别的神秘可言。规则201（g）唯一奇特的方面，是它在法条中的位置及特别措辞。它应当作为一条直接授权法院对证据进行评论的规则，而不是作为一条关于司法认知的规则。

⑯ 关于详细的论述，参见罗纳德·J·艾伦：《民事诉讼中的推定再思考》，载《艾奥瓦法律评论》，第66卷，1980—1981年，第843页.

决，而这些裁决之作出均基于诉讼建构之各种理由。

为了表明推定一词缺乏独立意义，我需要提出一个初步观点。除了能加诸当事人的三个责任外，还有两个被用于构建审判证明过程的分析手段。一个手段是去影响某项实质性主张的证据分量，该手段由于陪审团的存在而在美国显得非常重要，但在中国的重要性应当是有限的。为了鼓励陪审团达到法官认为适当的结果，法官经常就适当的推论对陪审团作出指示，也会对证据作出评价。同样，中国也许有相似的情况，立法机关常常通过法令宣布一个特殊类型的证据（如X光片图像）是某些关键事实（如肺病存在）的证据。[17] 第二，裁决规则有时也被用来构建对于裁决者如何裁决案件作出指示。例如，在美国，一个失踪7年而杳无音信的人，将在法律上被宣告死亡。

总之，司法证明构建于以下5种方式：

- 案件裁决规则的创设；
- 提出诉讼主张的责任的分配；
- 举证责任的分配；
- 说服责任的分配；
- 对于推断关键事实之证据分量的影响。

这些方式中的每一种都基于各种政策理由。施加责任，是为了促进审判或信息发现。裁决规则的创制，是为了促进结果符合政策选择，而赋予证据不同分量，是为了促进得出实际上准确的推论。创立裁决规则、分配责任，等等，所有这些事情都是由立法机关和法院完成的。对推定的困惑源于同时使用“推定”一词来指称这些手段中任何一种的施行。所有这些事情都可以使用“推定”一词来描述，但也可以直接描述。而且，上面列的只是使用“推定”一词来表达的事情。例如，“无罪推定”仅仅是将刑事案件的说服责任设置在确信无疑的程度。适当邮寄的信件被收到的推定，仅仅赋予了邮寄证据的分量。失踪7年的人已死亡的推定，仅仅是将失踪7年等同于死亡的一个裁决。除非被告作正当防卫之辩，否则，一个行为不属于正当防卫的推定，是一个答辩责任规则，等等。我再重复一遍，“推定”一词的每一次单独使用，都将符合这些分类中的一种，而这些分类的存在与使不使用“推定”一词无关。不存在着关于推定的独立含义。

所有关于什么是推定的困惑，以及对于界定这一术语所付出的无用分析努力，都是由于法律制度试图将这一词语应用于这些完全不同的类型，并在整个

[17] 例如，参见 Usery v. Turner Elkhorn Mining Co.，428 U.S. 1 (1976)。

诉讼程序的不同时点使用。然而，使用“转移举证责任的推定”这一词语，也没有什么意义。我们只需说，如果 X 为真，在审判中关于 Y 的举证责任由对方承担。通常，这正是法律制度的做法。人们无须说“如果一个人失踪 7 年被推定为死亡”，人们只需说“一个人如果失踪 7 年便可在法律上宣告为死亡”。这样一些规则也是法律制度中的普遍做法。

由“推定”一词引发的完全不必要的困惑，源于将其用于所有这些不同的事情，进而引起了超越该词含义的歧义。学者和法官们争论推定是否转移举证责任或说服责任，他们争论推定是否能增加证据的分量，等等。这些都是完全无用和多余的争论。人们一旦看到“推定”一词本身被应用于构建证明的各种方式，并且它的使用并没有增加法院和立法机关构建诉讼的权力，所有的困惑就都将烟消云散。使用“推定”一词所做的每一件事情，其实都可以直接去做，而根本无须使用该词。“推定”一词仅仅是一个标签，而被应用于描述上述列举的事项，如分配责任或创建裁决规则。

现在注意一下“推定”一词的这 5 种用法，其中有 4 种是与说服责任密切相关的。[⑱] 三种直接分配责任的规则显然属于此列，运用推定来增加证据分量的规则同样如此。显然，如果存在着没有推定的帮助裁决者就不能在考虑说服责任的情况下得出正确结果的担忧，推定和说服责任确实密切相关。甚至第五种用途——建构裁决规则——也与说服责任相关，它实际上使一个争点上的说服责任决定另一个争点的解决。举个例子，如果人们提供优势证据证明一个人已失踪 7 年，那么，这将解决该死亡的事实性问题。

总之，没有一个据称是通过使用推定获得的结果，实际上是由于推定而获得的。反而，各种证据难题都是根据特别的政策考量而得到解决的，而不是根据推定是什么，“推定”标签是在得到结果后才附加上去的。在这些政策中最重要的是处理说服责任分配的政策。这些事项涉及的内容甚广，也许以后要单独举办一个关于推定的讲座。

三、天堂的缺陷和美好的新世界：传统理论的局限性和证据程序所依赖的概率解释

我讲座中这部分的标题几乎和讲座内容一样长！到目前为止，我所介绍的

⑱ 另一个重要的初始性观点是说服责任的相互性：说国家负有确信无疑地证明一个要件的责任，就是说被告承担着揭示该争点存在合理怀疑的责任。同样的道理也适用于优势证据标准：说一方必须证明一个事实比不可能更可能是真实的，就是说另一方必须揭示它很可能并非虚假。

是一个具有重要解释力且经过整合的一般证明责任理论。在本讲座的前面部分，我回顾了分析家们花费数十年才形成的理论解释，在许多方面它取得了重要成就。然而，研究在不断地更新着人们的知识，我为你们展示的传统解释中存在的重大问题也越来越清晰。本讲座的这个部分将涉及这些问题，在最后一部分将讨论关于这些问题的可能解决方法。问题有两种：首先，该理论自身存在内在局限性和矛盾。其次，该理论关于证据的概率解释及其处理的假设，作为现实的一种描述几乎必然是不适当的，并且无助于指导理性的行为。本节及下一节将介绍一些新的资料，也许更难于理解。在讲座进行中大家可以随意提问。

传统解释的内在问题和矛盾

首先，回顾一下之前的两个图，它们以几何学形状呈现了传统理论解释和证成说服责任的方式。回想在民事案件中，目的是使错误总量最小化，以及当事人在法律面前受到平等对待。正如这些图所描绘的，政策目标得到保障。然而，绝对关键的一点是，这些图的形状是经验性的，而非逻辑上必然的。我绘制这些图是为了阐明说服责任的传统理论。在现实世界，这些图可能与我所描绘的相当不同，它们的实际形状将取决于两个经验变量：第一，案件两个子集（应胜诉的原告和应胜诉的被告）谁去打官司的相对比率和事实认定者（无论事实认定者是法官还是陪审团成员）对诉讼案件的概率评估。就像我所描绘的那样，没有合理的理由认为子集将大小均等，或概率评估将呈正态分布。第二，成本和风险规避等重要问题明显地能够影响谁去打官司。因此，在现实世界，说服责任和政策目标之间没有必然联系，这种联系是偶然的和经验性的。这是一个令人深思的结论，因为它使追求政策目标更加困难。

例如，在民事案件中，被告也许不愿意冒险，而原告可能勇于冒险。在那种情况下，相对于应胜诉的原告来说，更少的应胜诉的被告愿意去打官司，因为，应胜诉的被告将更愿意和解而不愿冒审判风险。如果这是真的，图可能好像是这样的：

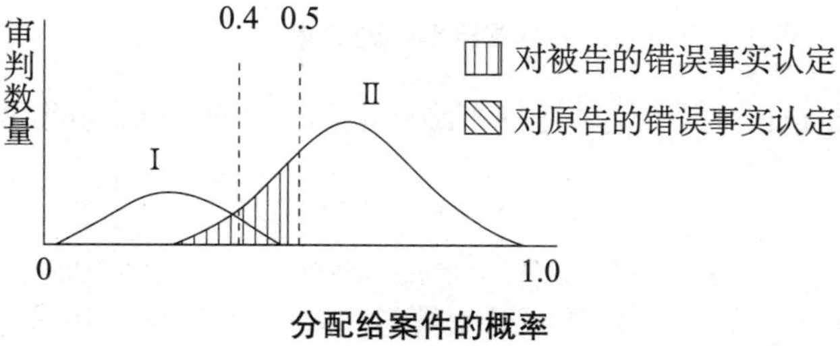

当然，上图仍然是不一定符合实际情况的。由于被告更厌恶风险，情况还可能是，那些决定去法院的被告可能比那些铤而走险去打官司的原告有更好的诉讼结果。因此，尽管支持各方的案件总量相对变化，应获胜案件的数量却可能保持不变。然而，这个额外变量不是削弱而是支持了我这里的观点，即证明标准的影响问题纯粹是经验性的，而非逻辑必然的。

你们是否从经验角度认为，上图反映了你们审判制度的现实，你们法律制度的重要影响力似乎跳跃了阶段，即说服责任被设置得过高了。如果它被降低到 0.4，人们就会看到，错判总数会更少，并且原告和被告将大致受到平等对待。那么，为什么不降低说服责任？或许应当降低，但存在着额外的考虑。人们根据说服责任选择是否去打官司。如果说服责任被降低，原告和被告对于什么情况下要打官司可能作出不同的选择，这反过来将影响错误的分配和正确的裁决。由于受到初始责任分配的影响，改变责任分配的效果不可能获得逻辑上必然的预测。这个观点强调了我们目前所考察的问题的经验性质。法律制度是由一套相互联系的部分组成的，如果其中一部分发生变化，它很可能将要影响该制度的其他部分。⑲

同样的观点在刑事案件中也是正确的：说服责任的效果不可能由逻辑必然性来决定，改变说服责任的效果也不可能由逻辑上的必然性来决定。它们都是经验性问题。例如，思考下面的图，与第二部分中的图相比，它可能是对刑事案件更逼真的描述。无辜的被告去打官司的情况可能更少，因为当局清除无辜的人。如果该图描述的是现实，我们可能会认为，将刑事案件的证明标准降低到 0.7 是最佳的，但该标准影响人们是否铤而走险去打官司的决定。如果该标准降低，检察官就会就假如标准更高时不会起诉的案件提起诉讼。据此可以预测提起诉讼的不同组合情况，导致错误与正确裁决的不同组合情况。

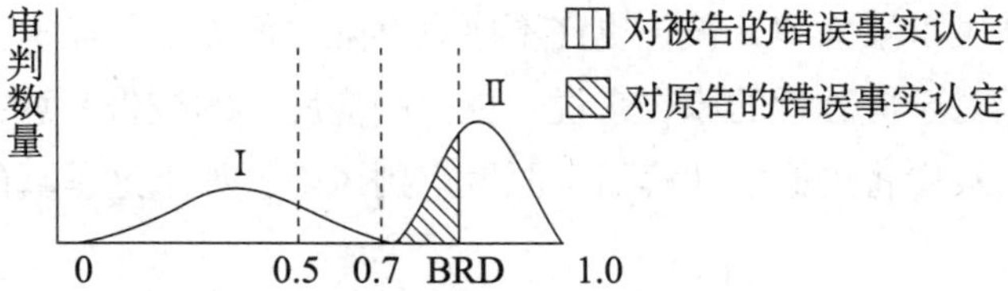

虽然说服责任的实际效果是一个经验的而非逻辑分析的问题，但这并不意

⑲ 罗纳德·J·艾伦与艾伦·E·盖伊：《作为通布利和伊克巴尔案特例的康利案：关于证据、程序和规则性质相互作用的考察》，载《宾夕法尼亚州法律评论》，第 115 卷，2010 年，第 1 页。

味着说服责任不受制于通过法律的智能操作。你们很可能认为，自己对于诉讼制度如何运作或如何改进，均有良好的理解力。你们可能认为，特定类型的案件和其他案件有所不同，且理应得到特殊对待。这些图又一次帮助我们看清了事实究竟如何。再考虑一下上面民事案件的图示。在美国，我们有理由相信，它准确地表示了一系列特定侵权案件——在那些案件中，原告无法感知影响到自己的事件，比如，他在外科手术中处于被麻醉的状态。因为原告缺乏直接感知正在发生的事情的能力，即使他应当在起诉其外科医生侵权的案件中胜诉，他仍面临着很大错误风险。在美国和英国侵权法中，对应这种可能性的是“res ipsa loquitur”（事实自证）原则（“事情本身就说明了问题”）。该拉丁文的含义是指，在特定侵权案件中，原告的说服责任将被减轻。理由是要重建该图中所清晰展示的错误之适当关系。

证明责任传统理论的第一个主要限制条件是：认为证明责任的效果可以通过逻辑分析来预测的观点是错误的。第二个是质疑该理论的性质。如我所说，民事案件中的说服责任应该是平等对待双方当事人，并减少错误总量。在刑事案件中，该政策是通过难以给任何人定罪的方式来保护无辜的人，这可能是通过偏移有利于无罪释放罪人的错误来实现的（给一个无辜的人定罪要比释放一个有罪的人邪恶 10 倍）。请注意这种思考方式的特异之处。审判中会形成 4 种裁决，所有裁决都涉及社会效益或成本：两种正确的裁决类型和两种错误的裁决类型。无视正确的裁决会导致不寻常的结果，例如，只要受审案件的基础比率包括大致相同数量的应获胜的原、被告，在每一单个案件中所犯的错误就符合错误均等化政策。在刑事案件中，10 个错误释放与一个错误定罪的比率，是由 99%的案件被错判达成的。

与忽视正确裁决相关的是，传统理论无视审判裁决只是法律制度输出结果的一部分。在民事案件和刑事案件中，当事人谈判协商结果，而那些案件中的结果显然是法律制度之整体社会福利效益的一部分。一个合理的政策将使该制度中的错误优化为一个整体，而非仅为其中一部分。这又导致一个更为复杂的涉及诉讼和基础行为相互作用的裁决难题。审判中完全随机的结果或相对较高的成本可能是社会上最理想的，因为它们鼓励当事人和解。我并未断言这是真的，坦白地说，我对此有怀疑，但这个观点强调了证明责任的分析有多么复杂。[20]

[20] 劳瑞·劳丹、罗纳德·J·艾伦：《致命的困境Ⅱ：保释和犯罪》，载《芝加哥—肯特法律评论》，第 85 卷，2010 年，第 23 页。

我们还没有完成将这些事情变得更复杂的工作，因为还有第三个问题，与前两个问题一样棘手。[21] 在民事案件中，证明责任的传统理论要求事实认定者，仅当每个相关要素都被优势证据证实时，才能作出有利于原告的认定。事实认定者将比较每一要素的概率与其否定性概率，仅当该要素为真的概率超过其为假的概率时，才作出对原告有利的裁定。因为一个要素的概率只有要么为真要么为假这两种可能性，传统理论便陷入了一种要求，即原告对每一要素的证明都要超过 0.5 的概率。加上另外两个因素，这个概念的逻辑困难便显现出来了：其一，如果诉因要素之一并未出现，例如，在侵权案中，如果被告无过失，或者未造成伤害，则原告胜诉的裁决将是错误的。其二，既然事实认定过程中错误是无法避免的，而错误的分配是可塑的，那么问题就在于如何分配这些错误，传统的答案是在原、被告之间平等分配。

现在考虑一下传统说服责任理论的困难。如果诉因的两个独立要素之一——如侵权诉讼中违反义务和因果关系——的概率均为 0.6，它们同真的概率是 0.6×0.6＝0.36。这意味着，被告并未过失伤害原告的概率为 1.0－0.36＝0.64。换言之，支持原告胜诉、被告败诉的比例将大约是二分之一。事实上，从表面价值判断，传统理论将产生怪异的结果。假定，在案例 1，另一个侵权案例中，违反义务被证明到 0.9，因果关系被证明到 0.4，并假定不存在其他要素。裁决将支持被告胜诉，因为其中一个要素——因果关系——并未被优势证据证明。比较一下案例 2，该案中这两个要素均证明到 0.6。在案例 2 中，裁决将支持原告胜诉。现在比较一下这两个案件。在这两个案件中，被告过失伤害原告的概率是相同的（0.9×0.4＝0.6×0.6＝0.36），然而，在一个案件中裁决原告胜诉，在另一个案件中裁决被告胜诉。这里又是一个怪异的结果。假定，在案例 1 中，因果关系被证明到 0.5。案例 1 仍然会导致裁决被告胜诉的结果，因为 0.5 低于优势证据标准，但此时被告过失伤害原告的概率为 0.9×0.5＝0.45。在案例 1 中，将有一个被告胜诉的裁决，即使被告过失伤害原告的概率（0.45）超过案例 2 中被告过失伤害原告的概率（0.36）（请记住，这里将有一个原告胜诉的裁决）。

在许多情况下，诉因的要素并非随机或有条件独立。除非它们完全是从属性的，否则，以上所描述的现象将依然存在，但会因从属性程度而减少。如果它们完全是从属性的，那么意味着每个要素都是所有其他要素的重述。这是一

[21] 以下几段主要参考了罗纳德·J·艾伦：《司法证明的性质》，载《卡多佐法律评论》，第 13 卷，1991 年，第 373、374～375 页。

种怪异的可能性，我们无须花时间进一步探讨。

证明责任的传统解释被第四种困难损害：它取决于一种证据概率解释。在一个特定层面，概率解释是有力的，但在更深的层面，它显然又是不适当的。其有力之处在于，它似乎抓住并解释了对世界的判断，而且与人们所用的语言一致（“明天下雨的机遇有多大?”“你认为他做那事的可能性有多大?”），把审判过程看作根据新证据来更新一个先前概率的过程，表面上看很吸引人。然而，这个表面魅力具有误导性：除了作为信念主观程度的概率之外，概率的概念化在审判中发挥不了什么作用。逻辑概率和倾向解释显然无法运行。相对频度表面上看很吸引人，但实际上从未有任何相关频度的数据。的确，请考虑一下，要求其以优势证据即被设想为大于 0.5 的相对频度来证实自己的案子，这对当事人而言可能意味着什么：原告将不得不采取解释事情可能如此的每一种可能的方式，并表明超过一半的这些可能能证明被告有责任。当然，那是一种不可能的标准。或者考虑一个刑事案件。这个国家不得不证明世界上不可能存在符合清白标准的国家吗？被告人能仅带着当地电话簿来辩护，以表明世界上存在有人已实施了该行为的很多其他的可能性吗？没有一种法律制度如此运作，因为这将自我毁灭。

在我看来，司法证明的概率解释肯定是错误的，你们应当注意，原告的说服责任标准是否太高或太低完全是不清楚的。合取悖论表明，该标准太低了。在一个多要素案件中，即使每个要素都被证明到大于 0.5，至少一个要素为假的概率仍将很高。这就是不确定的概念，而且它有利于原告。然而，模糊性对被告有利。如果原告不得不证明争端当天事情究竟如何的所有可能，以及超过一半的这些可能能证明被告有责任，这是将司法证明理解为包含相对频度的一种方式，那么，原告的标准几乎是不可能满足的。这，在最低限度上是一组怪异因素。

上面讨论的证据之概率解释的一些困难，是将说服责任应用于个别要素所造成的。一个替代选择是，将说服责任概念化为适用于作为整体的案件，但这将使说服责任自身遭到弱化。第一，随着要素数量的增加，原告的任务变得更加艰巨。他无须表明每一要素都高于 0.5 的可能性，却不得不表明合取超过了那个门槛。但即使一个案件中有三个要素，每一要素将必须被证明到大约 0.8 的概率，也将是一个令人畏缩的任务。第二，每一要素的证明程度，将由存在多少其他要素以及它们的依赖关系来决定，但那将导致古怪的结果，即不同诉因的同一要素将不得不被证明到不同的概率程度。例如，侵权法上的“意图”

与合同法上的“意图”将必须被不同地加以证明。[22]

总之，除了个别数据保存良好的有限案件（或许一些医疗事故案件）之外，审判中的事实认定似乎不能概念化为包含相对频度。这就把信念度或者贝叶斯主观概率遗留为唯一可能运作的概率概念化，但审判的条件与贝叶斯方法是冲突的。事实认定者，不论是法官还是外行评判者，均被告知不要根据新证据更新先前信念。他们通常甚至直到案件结束时才知道争点是什么，而且不管怎样，事实认定者的主观信念状态都是不相关的。人们期望事实认定者认定事实，却不表达他们特殊的心理状态。[23] 贝叶斯理论为事实认定带来了进一步的困难，最重要的是计算复杂性。仅有少数变量，贝叶斯定理的计算性要求将很快超越甚至最强大的计算机能力，更不用说人类了。[24] 更糟糕的是，审判中的证据通常是高度相互依赖的，因此，单个证据片段之间的依赖性必须为已知，并在计算过程中被考虑在内。[25] 这些相互依赖性简直不能为人所知，因为每一

[22] 罗纳德·J·艾伦：《民事审判的概念重建》，载《波士顿大学法律评论》，第66卷，1986年，第401、407页。其他处理方式以及类似问题包含在罗纳德·J·艾伦：《司法证明的性质》，载《卡多佐法律评论》，第13卷，1991年，第373页；罗纳德·J·艾伦：《合理性、算法和司法证明：一个初探》，载《证据与证明》，1997年第1期，第254页。

[23] 罗纳德·J·艾伦：《合理性、算法和司法证明：一个初探》，载《证据与证明》，1997年第1期，第254页；罗纳德·J·艾伦、莎拉·A·杰尔：《民事案件的说服责任：算法与解释》，载《密歇根州法律评论》。例如，参见苏珊·哈克的《法律概率论：一个认识论异议的手稿》(7-8)（可上美国社会科学研究网SSRN下载），批评《麦考密克论证据》第2卷§339（第483页）中的特定陈述时，认为超越合理怀疑的指示“表明我们真正关注什么，陪审团的心理状态”，他们主张，这与优势证据指示不同，因为它“将注意力转移至证据”。在证据和人们的心理之间确实存在一种关系，但同样确实的是它并非“陪审团的”，因为陪审团并没有这种心理。如果它有，除了少数贝叶斯论者之外的每个人都会说，正如哈克所清晰重建的指示那样，为了准确认定事实而对证据所进行的理性思考更受关注。在这个问题上，很难说证据“分散了注意力”。这是至关重要的，即使其本身并不充分。

[24] 诉讼实际上多么复杂，是经常被忽视的。考虑一下我几年前所举的例子（参见罗纳德·J·艾伦：《事实的模糊性和证据理论》，载《西北大学法律评论》，第88卷，1994年，第604、626～626页）：假设一位证人开始作证，因此一个事实认定者必须裁定证言说明了什么。相关变量是什么？首先，存在着全部一般可信性问题，但考虑一下它们有多复杂。行为不仅仅是行为，而是一组复杂变量。证人正在出汗或抽搐吗？如果是这样，是无辜地紧张、搪塞的压力、医学问题，或仅仅是在可悲的童年养成的不良习惯？肢体语言显示出诚实或逃避：在讲述一个直截了当的故事时，有说谎或坦然的无力证据吗？证人直视着询问者的眼睛吗？如果是，这是值得赞赏的品性证据，还是娴熟的蛇油推销员的自信？声调变化表明正直、诚实还是紧张？紧张的声调显示了作伪证或者对案件结果的担忧吗？如此等等。列举的这些相关变量远远超出了可信性问题，行为仅仅是其中之一。当一个证人表达一种主张时，事实认定者必须判定该主张旨在主张什么，以及事实认定者认为它主张什么。这个任务也包含巨大变量。此外，在证人最初明确表达的主张之前，事实认定者必须拥有某些基于其观察的知识。还有许许多多的例子。为了法律像一种科学那样运行，就要求这些变量以其必要且充分的条件清楚地处于一种推理结构之中。这种结构是不能被创设的，它太复杂了。

[25] 克雷德·R·卡伦：《关于大错觉的注释：证据法中贝叶斯定理运用的一些限制》，载《印第安纳法律期刊》，第57卷，1982年，第1页。

个审判都是独一无二的。

四、解决办法：最佳解释推论[26]

司法证明的性质从根本上说不是概率性的，而是解释性的，并且是最佳解释推论的一个例证。审判证明的一般结构将基于解释之解释推论过程的两个经典阶段——生成和接受——实例化了。在第一阶段，潜在解释得以生成；在第二阶段，以解释性理由对潜在解释作出推论。在审判中，当事人（包括刑事案件中的政府方）提供竞争性事件版本，如果属实，就将解释审判中所出示的证据。对主张或抗辩负有证明责任的当事人，提供包括正式要件在内的以构成特定主张或抗辩的事件版本；对抗方提供未包括一个或更多正式要件的事件版本。另外，在法律允许的情况下[27]，当事人可以提供解释该证据的事件替代版本。最后，事实认定者并不受限于当事人明确作出的潜在解释，却可以建构他们自己的解释，或者用于与多个事实认定者审议案件，或者作为他们得出结论的根据。

在民事案件的裁决阶段，说服责任是一种优势证据，证明取决于证据的最佳解释支持原告还是被告。[28] 事实认定者作出裁决，是根据当事人提出的事件版本的相对似真性，可能还有他们自己建构的额外事件。事实认定者从最似真的解释中推断真实的解释，并根据这个可接受的版本认定实体法所支持的一方胜诉。在美国，经验证据已证实，事实认定者通过建构叙述性事件版本来解释审判中基于诸如一致、完整和独一无二等标准所出示的证据，从而得出事实结论。[29] 这个过程基于解释性理由进行——事实认定者建构叙事以解释证据，并通过将相似标准应用于那些在科学中被援引对象的方式，在多项选择中作出选择。这些结果不应让人惊奇，因为它们只是几乎每个人理解整个世界之方式的一个例证。司法事实认定者，不论是法官还是陪审团成员，除了以与他在别处运用证据基本上相同的方式来运用审判中的证据之外，没有选择。

---

[26] 该节内容多出自罗纳德·J·艾伦、迈克尔·帕尔多：《司法证明和最佳解释》，载《法学与哲学》，第27卷，2008年，第223页。

[27] 有时候，当事人也许被阻止提供相互矛盾的说明。See McCormick v. Kopmann，161 N. E. 2d 720（Ill. App. Ct.，1959）.

[28] 参见罗纳德·J·艾伦：《事实的模糊性和证据理论》，载《西北大学法律评论》，第88卷，1994年，第604页；罗纳德·J·艾伦：《司法证明的性质》，载《卡多佐法律评论》，第13卷，1991年，第373页。

[29] 参见南希·彭宁顿、里德·黑斯蒂：《陪审团成员裁决的认知理论：故事模型》，载《卡多佐法律评论》，第13卷，1991年，第519页.

这个过程在审判中究竟如何进行，取决于法律制度和事实认定者的推论兴趣，例如，解释应细致到何种程度必将取决于语境。如果诉讼涉及一项意外事故，“该意外事故发生于 12 点 01 分”的解释也许就太详细了；“该意外事故发生在 6 月 16 日下午”可能就足够了；而“一个意外事故发生在过去的某个时间”也许又太不详细了。再来考虑一个胃痛病人的情况：在他妻子看来，他吃了某些辛辣食物的事实也许是一个足够好的解释，因为它鉴别了一个适当的比对（根据其妻子的推论偏好）；而该辛辣食物是不是黑丝墨西哥辣椒味（或其他辣味）的奶酪汉堡，那就无所谓了，因为任何这种食物都会导致胃痛。在其他语境下，或对于其他有不同推论偏好的人来说，如对他的诊断医生而言，更详细和不同的细节将是适当的。

在司法证明语境中，两个因素决定了利益攸关的推论偏好，以及事实认定者在评价解释时应当关注适当细节的程度。这些因素是实体法和当事人所提供的不同事件版本之间的反差点（争端事实）。首先，实体法将要求对证据进行足够详细的解释，以表明原告有权申冤，而像“被告做了某些坏事”之类的解释，是不够详细的。然而，实体法有时允许当事人提供相当宽泛的解释。回到上文用过的例子，事实自证原则甚至允许原告通过提供诸如“我的伤害是由被告做的某些事情造成的”这样的解释来获得补偿，特别是当这样一种理论提供了该证据的最佳解释时。其次，当事人选择不同意将注意力集中于适当细节，以便在对比解释中作出选择。如果被告主张，在所称交通事故发生期间，他在国外某个地方度假，那么，所关注的适当对比是，他在国内（以及他是否驾驶了造成事故的汽车）还是出国了，而不是他是否在驾驶车辆、待在车后座还是行李厢中，或是宇宙的其他地方。进一步考虑的假设，集中在一个事故是否发生在正午或其他时间。如果一个被告试图抗辩的理由是，虽然事故发生在正午前后，但证据并未精确显示是在 12：00 还是 12：01，那么，该被告显然将会败诉，因为实体法并不关心这个问题。因此，最佳解释推论以如何整合与区别它们的方式，协调了过多解释的担忧。

一个额外的合理忧虑是，潜在的解释太少。可能有一些案件，当事人双方均未就证据提出特别似真的解释，或者因为双方都不能解释证据的关键部分，或者因为缺乏某种证据，使得能以多种方式进行解释，但其中，没有一种解释比其他解释更好（或更可能）。在第一种情形——每一方在解释证据之相同或不同的关键部分时都存在困难——下，关键点是该过程的可比方面。一个裁决将（且应当）因为有更佳（或最适当）的解释而作出，不论事实认定者所建构的是当事人一方还是另一方。如果所提供的解释确实同样糟（或者好），包括额外建构的解释，判决将（且应当）不支持说服责任的承担方。在第二种情形——证据太少而不能从中区别潜在的解释——下，结果也应当是作出对说服责任承担方不利的判决。因为他们未能履行提出证据的责任，理性的事实认定者从这些证据中不能区别潜在的、对比性的解释。因此，民事审判的结构便通过证明责任缓和了与潜在解释太少有关的忧虑。

在刑事案件中，事实认定者不是从潜在解释中推断出最佳解释，而是推断（且应当推断）出被告人无辜，每当存在着与无辜相一致的证据之充分似真的解释（且应当在没有与无辜相一致的似真解释，假定存在与有罪相一致的似真解释时，作出有罪裁决）。[30] 当存在与无辜相一致的证据之似真解释时，存在这样一种伴随可能性，即该解释是正确的（真实的解释），因此，被告人是无辜的，由此而产生应当制止事实认定者有罪推断的合理怀疑。

类似的考虑也适用于清楚且令人信服的证据标准。事实认定者不是从可用的潜在解释中推断出最佳解释，而是应当在有比支持另一方的解释更似真的充分解释时（不仅是在说服责任承担方提出了更佳解释时），推断出一个有利于说服责任承担方的结论。解释得多么充分、更似真才符合标准？该解释必须足够似真，即它比那些支持另一方的解释更清楚且令人信服地似真。这不是循环，它只是表达了常识判断，一些解释有时不只是好于而是非常好于其他解释。

显然，一项必须满足“确信无疑”或者清楚且令人信服的标准的解释，究竟该多么“充分似真”，是存在模糊性的，但这种模糊性是证明标准本身所固有的。因而缺乏精确性可成为对证明标准的批评，但它并不是对基于解释的计算的批评。即使一方当事人的全部证据的强度可以被量化，对一种概率方法来说模糊性依然存在。[31] 58％的可能性是清楚且令人信服的吗？还是 65％或72％？85％是确信无疑吗？90％呢？95％呢？[32]

在结束这个讲座时，我将简要解释一下，最佳解释推论（IBE）如果并未

[30] 如果控辩双方都提出对证据难以置信的解释，事实认定者应当宣告无罪。该意见十分相似于罗纳德·J·艾伦在《合理性、算法和司法证明：一个初探》（载《证据与证明》，1997 年第 1 期，254、273 页）中提出的观点。约瑟夫森教授提出了一个合理怀疑标准的定义，即是否存在代表无辜之“真实可能性”的解释。参见约翰·R·约瑟夫森：《最佳解释推论的证明动力学》，载《卡多佐法律评论》第 22 卷，2001 年，第 1621、1642 页（“一种真实可能性并不假定对任何已知自然法的违反，也不假定任何行为完全是独特或前所未有的，或任何极其不可能的巧合的链条”）。

[31] 模糊性的一个例子，参见美国第七巡回法院联邦民事陪审团指令 35（http：//www. ca7. uscourts. gov）（将“清楚且令人信服”的标准释义为“非常有可能属实”）。

[32] 参见 United States v. Fatico，458 F. Supp. 388，410（E. D. N. Y.，1978）（提供了一个地区法官对于他们有关各种说服标准之概率的考察——法官们意见相异）；理查德·西蒙、L. 摩诃：《证明责任的量化：以合议庭、陪审团和教室为视角》，载《法律与社会》，第 5 卷，1971 年，第 319 页。

完全解决上面提到的关于证据概率解释的各种困难，那该如何改良的问题。与概率计算不同，IBE并不要求在证据形式方面的不可能。IBE并非不切实际地假设相对频度数据的存在，而是解释自然人推理者如何处理在其环境中自然发现的各种证据。同样，相对似真性裁决规则同时适应它们的环境和它们在所有时间的应用。主观概率论的不可计算性要求被消除了。同样，在并非精确的消除中，合取悖论被认为是无关紧要的，因为它们被分散在当事人的案件中。最后，裁决规则指导双方当事人介绍他们最似真的案情，这完全合理地假定了，它将在审判中产生可靠和合理有效的结果。当事人最了解自己的案子，知道什么将证实事实，也清楚任何诉讼对他们具有多大价值。

你们已经很耐心地听我讲了几个小时，对此非常感谢。我也期待你们提问，并与你们一起讨论这些问题。虽然这个讲座很长，但至少在下列主题上还有要多说几句的地方，而且我很乐意以后有机会讲述这些主题：

（1）证明责任传统分析的替代者来自经济学家，他们还分析了说服责任。我没有把太多时间花在这些问题上。由于他们思想的褊狭（他们像是完全没意识到他们所谈论问题的相关文献或基础理论），他们的大部分观点有缺陷，极不现实，实际上没有什么益处。[33] 不过，经济学分析总的说来还是很有力的，而且值得关注。

（2）关于推定和司法认知可能还有更多值得探讨的问题。

（3）一般来说，关于概率论尤其是贝叶斯定理还有很多可以探讨的东西。

谢谢大家。

㉝ 最近的例子是，路易斯·卡普洛：《证明责任》，载《耶鲁法律期刊》，第121卷，2012年，第738页。

Burdens of Proof

Ronald J. Allen*

It is a great pleasure to be here. I was asked to lecture on Burdens of Proof. I will do so in four parts. First, I will explain the conventional theory of burdens of proof. I will also show how the conventional theory extends to and explains other important aspects of the legal process, in particular preclusive motions. Preclusive motions are mechanisms to terminate a case prior to a full presentation of all the evidence; examples are summary judgment and directed verdicts. In Part II, I will extend the analysis to show how the conventional theory of burdens of proof also enlightens the practice of judicial notice of facts and clears up all the confusion over presumptions. Third, I will take this lecture to a higher theoretical level and begin to explain critical flaws in the conventional theory of burdens of persuasion. In this third part of the lecture, I will introduce some new ideas that are the focus of ongoing research in the United States. To be frank, I am concerned that this part of the lecture will appear to be complicated and somewhat difficult to follow, precisely because it will challenge the conventional theory of burdens of proof, but this is also the area where Chinese research needs to develop. Fourth, I will propose tentative resolutions to the theoretical difficulties of burdens of proof uncovered in the third part of the lecture. Evidence research in the United States is focusing heavily on the issues I will discuss in Part IV of the lecture.

I. The Conventional Theory of Burdens of Proof

There are three important preliminary points that must be understood before I turn to the conventional understanding of burdens of proof. First, burden of proof rules, like all rules that structure the process of proof, are de-

* I am indebted to Jiang Yujia, a second year law student at Northwestern University, for her research assistance.

rived from and implement a theory of dispute resolution. The dominant theory of dispute resolution in the United States is the adversarial process. The second and related point is that theories of dispute resolution, such as the adversarial system or continental (sometimes called the inquisitorial) system, are themselves derived from underlying conceptions of the appropriate role of government in the resolution of disputes between private individuals in civil cases and in the prosecution of criminal cases.

In the Anglo-American tradition, the role of the government in private dispute resolution has generally been largely facilitative. The government simply provides a fair and disinterested forum for the impartial resolution of private disputes, and that is essentially all the government has an obligation, or even a right, to do. In an extraordinary way, this conception of dispute resolution affects criminal cases as well. The government prosecutes cases, but the government is conceived of as analogous to a private party that stands on equal footing with the other private party, the defendant, before the courts. The courts are neutral, in other words, and are not part of the organs of government structured to further the government's specific policy interests in the particular trial; indeed, as is well known, the courts in the United States are famous for obstructing the policy objectives of the government through such things as exclusionary rules.

Third, and at a deeper conceptual level, the judiciary and the other branches of government are all designed to further the political aspirations reflected in the founding documents and traditions of the country, such as the United States Constitution. Here must be noted a critical distinction between China and the United States. The central political problem of governing in the United States is a principal-agent problem: The Government is the agent of the people, and the primary problem is how the principal—the people—can control its agent—the Government. This concern about controlling and limiting the central government out of fear of its tendency to concentrate power in itself is what explains the two defining features of the political structure of the United States, federalism and separation of powers. In China, with its theory of unitary political power located in the Communist Party, the central political problem is the efficient implementation of the policy objectives of Government. These differences plainly affect the legal systems that are constructed in their reflection. One would predict that the Chinese government will tend to exercise more power and control in the dispute resolution process in order to efficiently implement its policy goals. In contrast, in the United States the government has more limited power and the courts are primarily a disinterested forum.

These two distinctions—between types of legal systems and theories of government—do not necessarily involve stark contrasts but come in many different shades. For example, the conception of the role of the government in the resolution of disputes is not uniform even in representative democracies that otherwise share many traits. In many Western European countries, for example, disputes are not "private" matters to the extent that they are in the United States, and the government plays a much more active role in virtually all phases of litigation. The government often is more actively involved in investigation, and the trial process is controlled more by the court than is true in the United States. This reflects the view that disputes between citizens have a public feature, and thus that the resolution of disputes is a matter of collective concern. [①]In the United States, by contrast, private disputes are not understood to be matters of social concern for the most part, and the government plays a much less active role. The parties are responsible for investigating and preparing the case for trial, and in large measure controlling the presentation of evidence at trial. Similarly, appellate courts often purport to decide cases based only on the arguments presented to them by the parties, thus generating the possibility that cases with virtually identical facts will be decided differently due to the legal arguments advanced. The critical point to understand is that the obligation of the court extends to deciding the case correctly based on what the parties have put forth rather than to decide it "correctly" for all purposes.

The structure of legal systems is also affected by two additional variables. The first involves legal epistemology, which refers to beliefs concerning how effective different forms of dispute resolution are in producing accurate verdicts. In the United States, it is generally although not universally believed

① For a discussion of this and related matters, see Mirjan r. Damaska, *The Faces of Justice and State Authority: A Comparative Approach to the Legal Process* (1986), and Mirjan R. Damaska, *Evidentiary Barriers to Conviction and Two Models of Criminal Procedure*, 121 U. Pa. L. Rev. 506 (1973).

that adversarial investigation and presentation of evidence is more likely to yield a verdict consistent with the truth than is a process more dominated by a tribunal. The parties know their case better than anyone else and have the proper incentive to invest the optimal resources in dispute resolution. A government bureaucracy normally would be a poor substitute for the more thorough knowledge and more finely calibrated incentives of the parties. Those who favor more inquisitorial systems emphasize that control by a disinterested tribunal will lead to less abuse and manipulation of the evidence, which they believe may increase the chance that verdicts is consistent with the truth will emerge. ②

The pursuit of truth is not the only social good, however, and there are disagreements about how that particular social good interacts with others, such as privacy. In the United States, the general view is that in civil cases the parties should have essentially unfettered access to all the pertinent information concerning a dispute before the trial begins. The process of obtaining that information is called discovery, and its robustness is one of the defining features of the American legal system. The idea is that trial should truly be an epistemological event and not full of either surprises or road blocks. The theory of burdens of proof, as we shall see, is heavily dependent on such assumptions. Burdens of proof have one set of implications in a system that employs discovery mechanisms and another in a system that does not—this, by the way, is a critical point for you to understand. It is not necessarily true that burdens of proof will operate similarly in different legal contexts, especially in a system where a party can "compel" production of evidence as compared to a system where no such mechanism exists.

The last important preliminary point to mention is the affect that juries or lay assessors have on the structure of a legal system. In the United States, juries are at once revered and treated as alien intruders into the otherwise professional world of the law who must be regulated and controlled. One means of do-

② For a discussion, see John H. Langbein, *The German Advantage in Civil Procedure*, 52 U. Chi. L. Rev. 823 (1985); Ronald J. Allen, Stefan Koeck, Kurt Reichenberg, and D. Toby Rosen, *The German Advantage in Civil Procedure: A Plea for More Details and Fewer Generalities in Comparative Scholarship*, 82 Nw. U. L. Rev. 705 (1988).

ing so is through various uses of burdens of proof, as I shall elaborate later in this lecture.

To sum up, as we proceed to analyze burdens of proof, we must keep in mind these five points:

1. Burdens of proof are part of a theory of litigation

2. Theories of litigation are themselves part of a theory of government

3. Theories of government vary dramatically

4. Dispute resolution involves fact finding, and there are disagreements about the most efficient and effective way to get to the truth, and relatedly the value of truth when it compete with other social goods

5. The presence of lay fact finders such as jurors may affect how the litigation process is otherwise structured.

Before even getting to the theory of burdens of proof, I fear that I have made it sound as though such a thing does not even exist because of all these complexities I have mentioned, but that is false. There is a robust theory of burdens of proof, but at the same time the implications of that theory are affected by the various matters that I have discussed. I now turn to the general theory of burdens of proof.

There are in fact three burdens that can be imposed upon a party to litigation, and together they structure litigation. A party can be required to plead an issue, to produce evidence on an issue, and to bear the burden of persuasion with regard to that issue. These three requirements in order are the burden of pleading, the burden of production, and the burden of persuasion.

The burden of pleading is often overlooked but it is critically important. A means of putting both parties and the courts on notice as to subject of litigation is a critical first step in litigation. The courts need some reason to think there is a dispute to be litigated. In a truly "inquisitorial" system, the government could do its own investigation and decide what will be litigated, but that often involves massive inefficiencies. An alternative to relying on governmental investigation is to require that a party who wants to litigate must give notice to the party being sued and the court what the litigation is about. This is done by filing pleadings that state a cause of action and announce an intent to litigate a matter with another party. In addition to providing notice that litigation is to be pursued, the pleading also presents the basic parameters of the cause of action. The adversary is then typically required to file a responsive pleading, and in some jurisdictions must raise specific issues if that party wishes those issues to be litigated in addition to the issues raised by the plaintiff. For example, affirmative defenses often must be pleaded by the defendant. ③

As I mentioned above, the burden of pleading is often neglected because it seems to be straight forward and unnoteworthy, but it solves a serious epistemological problem. That problem is that the world is complex and litigation can involve any aspect of it. The parties know what aspects of that unruly reality is in question, and the burden of pleading is the first step in taking that impossibly complex reality and domesticating and simplifying it for purposes of resolving the dispute between the parties. In essence, the party suing needs to explain why he is suing, and the party being sued needs to explain why the suit is baseless. Together, these pleadings structure the problem to be decided.

After the parties have pleaded their cases and engaged in whatever discovery options are available to them, they are ready to proceed at trial, but the trial needs to be structured: Who goes first, what happens after one party produces a witness, and so on. This is done in the first instance through rules governing the allocation of burdens of production. Each issue to be litigated, whether it is an element or an affirmative defense, has a burden of production associated with it that requires one party or the other to produce evidence relevant to the particular issue (hence the name "burden of production") . If the party with a burden of production fails to produce sufficient evidence on a particular issue, that party will lose on that issue. Thus, the burden of production informs the parties how issues will be decided if no or inadequate evidence is produced; and if the parties wish an outcome different from what would result if no evidence is produced, they must produce evidence on the relevant issues.

The burden of production often parallels the burden of pleading, but there is no analytical requirement that this be so. Sometimes it can be sensible to require one party to plead an issue and the other party to bear a burden of pro-

③ See generally E. Cleary, *Presuming and Pleading: An Essay on Juristic Immaturity*, 12 Stan. L. Rev. 5 (1959) .

duction (or a burden of persuasion for that matter) on the issue. A good example in the United States that brings together the functions of burdens of pleading and production involves criminal defendants. On some issues, criminal defendants must plead certain "defenses" (I put "defenses" in quotes because what is an element and what is a defense is arbitrary; the one is a mirror image of the other—one can simply turn an element into a defense by adding "not" before it, asis illustrated below) such as self-defense or insanity. This is because these issues are normally not involved in criminal cases, and only the defendant knows if they should be in any particular case. Once the defendant puts the government on notice that the case involves one of these "defenses", the government often bears the burden of proof on those issues. ④

How, though, is one to know when a party with a burden of production has produced sufficient evidence? A burden of production is satisfied when the underlying purpose of the requirement is met. In civil cases, the primary purpose of a burden of production is to ensure that there are issues in the case that justify further litigation. Here there is an important difference between systems with and without juries. Issues need to be resolved by juries rather than judges when there could be reasonable disagreement about which party should prevail. If there could be no reasonable disagreement, there is no reason to go to any further expense, and the judge should render a verdict for the appropriate party (or otherwise dispose of the case, by dismissal for example) . Thus, another implication of a burden of production is that the failure to satisfy its requirements will result in the adversary "winning" on that particular issue. Even in systems without juries, though, this is an important point. Once a fact finder has heard enough to know that there can be no reasonable dispute about an issue, no further resources should be wasted on litigating it further.

How can one tell if there can be no reasonable dispute about an issue? To decide if there could be reasonable disagreement about which party should prevail, the judge must test the evidence produced by a party by reference to a rule of decision that tells the judge how to decide a case, given the evi-

④ I say "often" because in the United States there are 51 different criminal jurisdictions (each state and the federal government) and they pursue different approaches to such questions.

dence. This decision rule typically is referred to as a "burden of persuasion." A burden of persuasion informs the decision maker how to decide a case in light of the implications of the evidence. For example, one possible rule of decision is that a plaintiff should prevail only if the evidence establishes the plaintiff's case to a certainty (100% true). This rule would require a verdict for the defendant if there is any doubt about the truth of the facts that must be established by the plaintiff.

A decision rule of certainty has an intuitive appeal to it—people (defendants) should not be required to pay unless they have done something wrong. Notwithstanding this intuitive appeal, it is not the rule generally found in civil litigation because it would put plaintiffs at a serious disadvantage. It is difficult if not impossible (and I would say impossible, actually) to prove any fact to certainty. Requiring plaintiffs to do so would result in a disproportionate number of wrongful verdicts for defendants at the expense of deserving plaintiffs. The opposite rule—requiring defendants to show to a certainty that they should not be held liable—would have the opposite effect. Neither result is optimal, most importantly because these two parties should be equal before the law. The court has no idea who deserves to win the case, and a wrongful verdict for plaintiff is indistinguishable from a wrongful verdict for the defendant; in both cases a private party is deprived of their rights (I elaborate on this point below).

Rather than adopt either of the two extremes that would treat plaintiffs and defendants radically differently by requiring one or the other party to prove their case to certainty, the virtually uniform practice in civil litigation is to adopt a burden of persuasion of a preponderance of the evidence that is designed to minimize the total number of errors and treat the parties in an equivalent fashion. Plaintiffs must prove each of their necessary factual claims to a preponderance of the evidence, and defendants must establish affirmative defenses by the same standard. This is usually defined as meaning "more than a 50 percent chance of being true". Thus, the task is to determine whether the evidence favors the plaintiff's story with respect to the factual elements of a cause of action and to determine whether the evidence favors the defendant's story with respect to affirmative defenses. In criminal cases, by contrast, the parties are not equal before the law in a critical sense. In the United States, we think a wrongful conviction is much worse than a wrongful acquittal. Consequently, we impose the burden of persuasion of beyond reasonable doubt in order to skew errors against convicting innocent people. Whether you agree with this principle or not, you can immediately see how burdens of persuasion might be used to implement policy choices. I say "might be used" because, as I will develop in Part III of this lecture, the matter is, once again, more complicated than it appears.

Before I elaborate on those complications, it is important to see how burdens of persuasion relate to burdens of production. A burden of production should be deemed satisfied if enough evidence has been produced to indicate that there is a need for further litigation of the relevant factual question, and that occurs when reasonable people could disagree about the matter. The disagreement would be over whether or not the rule of decision—the burden of persuasion—has been satisfied. If no reasonable person could disagree that a plaintiff or defendant has satisfied the relevant burden of persuasion, then there is no reason to try the fact in question or to prolong any judicial proceedings that have already occurred. Thus, as Professor McNaughton developed in an important article, the burden of production is a function of the burden of persuasion. ⑤ The test to determine if a burden of production has been met is whether, in light of the evidence, there could be reasonable disagreement over which party should win. If there could be such disagreement, further litigation may be justifiable. If not, the judge will dispose of the case as expeditiously as possible.

The relationship between burdens of production and burdens of persuasion deserves a closer look. Let us assume for the moment that fact finders (judges, jurors, lay assessors) evaluate evidence in conventional probabilistic terms, as do the rest of us, by making rough estimates of the probability of facts being true, and that a preponderance of the evidence means more than a 50 percent chance of the relevant fact being true. As I show in Part III, this assumption is

⑤ John T. McNaughton, *Burden of Production of Evidence: A Function of a Burden of Persuasion*, 68 Harv. L. Rev. 1382 (1955).

deeply problematic，but we will make it now because it facilitates understanding the operation of burdens of proof.

Under the assumption that decisions are based on probability judgments，the evidentiary process can be diagramed in such a way as to highlight the relationship between burdens of production and burdens of persuasion. Assume that the party with a burden of production produces some evidence. That evidence will indicate that there is a certain chance that the relevant facts are true. However，the evidence is likely to be not perfectly clear as to what probability it generates. Looking at that evidence，reasonable people could disagree about the probability to which the evidence establishes some necessary fact. Does that mean that every time evidence is produced on any issue the case must proceed further because there always will be reasonable disagreement about its implications? The answer is an emphatic No. The case should proceed further only when there can be reasonable disagreement about which party should win，and that requires referring to the burden of persuasion. Consider the three possibilities charted below：

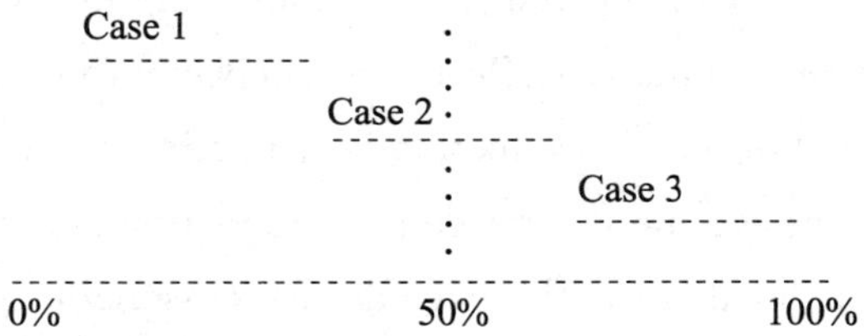

This chart presents in graphic form the three relevant possibilities in terms of the implications of the evidence. First，the evidence produced may not be very convincing. A reasonable person looking at it may conclude that it has some persuasive force，but not very much. That possibility is represented by (1) above. It indicates that，given the evidence，the probability of the fact being true that the evidence is being relied upon to establish ranges from about 10 to 35 percent. To be clear，and to test your understanding，I could have drawn that line segment anywhere between 0 and 50 percent，just so long as it did not exceed 50 percent. In this case，the burden of production has not been satisfied because no reasonable person could conclude that the party producing the evidence should win. The critical point，though，is that a burden of production is tested by reference to the associated burden of persuasion，or as Prof. Mc-

Naughton said, the burden of production is a function of the burden of persuasion.

Now consider case (2) . The evidence indicates a range of reasonable persuasiveness from about 40 to 60 percent, and here again to test your understanding I could have drawn the line segment in any fashion so long as it intersected the 50 percent line. Since reasonable people could disagree about the implications of the evidence in this case, the issue justifies further proceedings. Case (3) is similar to case (1) in that again no reasonable disagreement could exist as to the implications of the evidence. The evidence indicates somewhere between a 65 and 90 percent chance of the relevant fact being true and here the line could be drawn anywhere to the right of 50 percent.

Case (3) is different from case (1) in one respect. We have been assuming that the party with the burden of production has produced evidence. In case (1), the burden has not been met, and thus there is no reason to proceed further. In case (2), the burden of production has been met, and the case will proceed. In case (3), the burden has not only been met, but exceeded. No reasonable person could disagree about who should win. This conclusion, though, is based solely on the evidence produced by one party. Thus, in case (3), the opponent at trial must be given a chance to produce contrary evidence in order to demonstrate that there is a reasonable dispute about the relevant fact. In case (1), there is no reason to have the adversary proceed because the party's evidence itself indicates that the relevant fact cannot be established. Having the adversary produce still more information substantiating that conclusion would be a waste of time and money. In case (3), however, the adversary has not yet been heard from and may be in possession of information that would affect the analysis of how likely the relevant fact is, given all the evidence (including the adversary's) . Accordingly, in case (3), the adversary will be given a chance to respond.

The process of proof at trial can be analyzed as repeated iterations of these three analytical possibilities. Assume that the party with the burden of production produces sufficient evidence so that something akin to case (2) is generated. At that point, the adversary will have the right to respond. The adversary's evidence will likely decrease the probability of the relevant fact being true, thus shifting the probability range on the chart to the left. In most jurisdictions, after the adversary has responded the party with the initial burden of production is entitled to produce rebutting evidence, which is evidence that responds to the evidence produced by the adversary, and typically the adversary may respond in turn to that new offer of evidence (these are the repeated iterations I just referred to) . This process continues until neither party has anything new to offer, at which point the evidence taken as a whole will be in one of the three analytical possibilities diagrammed in the chart. If the evidence fits into case (1), the judge should decide the issue in favor of the adversary; if the evidence fits into case (2), the issue should go to the jury if there is one and if there is not the judge must decide the facts and thus the case; if the evidence fits into case (3), the judge should decide the issue in favor of the party who initially bore the burden of production.

I will now show how the conventional theory of burdens of proof extends to and explains preclusive motions, such as directed verdicts and summary judgment. In the United States, and in any system with lay fact finders, the manner in which the judge is asked to decide the case in favor of one party or another depends upon the time at which the judge is asked to do so. One possibility is that, before any evidence is produced, a party can move for summary judgment. The motion will be granted if the judge can determine from the pleadings and any supporting documentation that there are no issues in need of judicial resolution in the case. Such a decision, however, is equivalent to saying that either case (1) or case (3) is present—either the party with the burden of production will not be able to meet it or the adversary will not be able to show that there is a fact sufficiently in doubt to justify a trial. If case (2) is present, the motion for summary judgment (by either party) will be denied, and the litigation will proceed. The important point to note, though, is that the judge's decision will depend upon whether a party has satisfied its burden of production and the adversary's ability to respond to a party's proof with sufficient evidence to justify proceeding further. Although summary judgments are not conventionally discussed as being intimately related to burdens of produc tion and burdens of persuasion, the concepts are obviously closely related. [6]

If a case goes to the evidence taking phase, the judge may be asked to test the strength of the evidence by a motion for directed verdict at the end of the party's case. The analysis here is quite similar to the analysis of summary judgment motions; in fact there is only one significant difference, and if you follow what I am about to say, then you fully understand this complex component of burden of proof analysis. After the party with the burden of production produces its evidence, if case (1) is present the court should direct a verdict for the adversary; if case (2) is present, the trial obviously should proceed. It will also proceed if case (3) is present because the adversary has not yet been heard from. So long as the party resisting a preclusive motion has evidence to offer that might affect the analysis of the case, preclusive motions should not be granted. Again, the analysis of directed verdicts is not typically approached from the perspective of burdens of production and persuasion, but the similarity of the ideas is obvious. The preclusive motions are the means by which the implications of the evidence are tested; and the implications of the evidence are a function of the burdens of proof, in particular the burden of persuasion. Thus, not only are burdens of production a function of burdens of persuasion, but preclusive motions are as well.

Which party bears what burdens of production is not important in a system with adequate discovery. In a system with discovery, each side has access to essentially all the relevant evidence and can produce it at trial, leading to a decision on the merits. There is, accordingly, no justification for complex rules allocating burdens of production in such a system, and typically the only complexity that one finds resides in the decision to list certain issues as defenses rather than elements. [7] The plaintiff bears the burden of pleading and producing

[6] The Supreme Court of the United States has noticed this relationship in Anderson v. Liberty Lobby, Inc., 106 S. Ct. 2505 (1986) and Celotex Corporation v. Catrett, 106 S. Ct. 2548 (1986). For an excellent discussion of this complex area, *see* Michael S. Pardo, *Pleadings, Proof, and Judgment: A Unified Theory of Civil Litigation*, 51 B. C. L. Rev. 1451 (2010).

[7] Prior to the creation of robust discovery systems, allocations of burdens of production could significantly affect the outcome of cases, and complex sets of considerations were articulated to guide such allocations. *See, e. g.*, Fleming James Jr., *Burden of Proof*, 47 Va. L. Rev. 51 (1961). In modern American jurisdictions, these considerations are now largely an irrelevancy.

evidence on elements, and the defendant on defenses, but note the labels "element" and "defense" are quite arbitrary. One turns an element into a defense by putting "not" in the description, and the reverse is true. For example, one can say that the plaintiff has burden of proving damages in a contract case, or one can say the defendant has the burden to prove, as a defense, that there were no damages. The only situation in which the allocation of a burden of production should make a significant difference is if there simply is not very good evidence concerning the issue being litigated. If no one has access to good evidence, whoever has the burden of production will lose.

By contrast, in a system without discovery, the burden of production can be critically important. First, it can act as a discovery mechanism, forcing one party or the other to produce evidence or lose the case. That means that care should be given in determining who bears the burden of production. It should be placed, if possible, on the party with better access to the evidence. If it is placed on the opposite party, the party without access to evidence, and if there are no robust discovery provisions in place, then the party will be unable to meet his burdens of production and will lose the case. This is a perfect example of what I noted previously that burdens of proof will operate differently in different systems, where here the critical difference is whether both parties have adequate access to the evidence.

I turn my attention now to burdens of persuasion, although note that I will be returning to them in Part III of this lecture. Burdens of persuasion instruct how to decide in the fact of uncertainty, and the conventional theory of burdens of persuasion is that they are error allocation rules, as I have noted above. The preponderance rule incorporates an underlying assumption concerning the participants in litigation: That plaintiffs as a class and defendants as a class generally ought to be treated in equivalent ways. The equivalence of civil plaintiffs and defendants is a critically important point deserving of emphasis. Imagine a plaintiff is suing a defendant for 100 000 Yuan. If the plaintiff wrongfully wins the suit, the defendant is wrongfully deprived of 100 000 Yuan. However, if the plaintiff wrongfully loses the suit, the plaintiff is wrongfully deprived of 100 000 Yuan. In either case of a mistake, a private party is wrongfully deprived of exactly the same amount of money. Before any evidence about this particular dispute is produced, it is reasonable to assume that it is just as likely that the defendant is refusing to pay what is owed as that the plaintiff is attempting to obtain something that he does not have a right to.

The preponderance of the evidence standard generalizes this basic point of view, and under certain assumptions one can see how it functions. Assume that in the set of all cases going to trial there are approximately as many deserving plaintiffs as deserving defendants. Now compare the set of cases where plaintiffs in fact deserve to win to the set of cases where defendants in fact deserve to win. In most of the cases where plaintiffs deserve to win the evidence will support that conclusion, thus creating a probability assessment of more than 0. 5, which will result in a verdict for the plaintiff. Only in those cases in which the probability assessment is 0. 5 or less will wrongful verdicts for defendants be entered. The reverse is true with respect to the set of cases where defendants deserve to win. Presumably the evidence in most of those cases will demonstrate that the defendant deserves to win, thus creating a probability assessment of 0. 5 or less. Only in those cases in which the probability assessment is more than 0. 5 will there be wrongful verdicts in favor of plaintiffs. If one assumes that the probability assessments for these two sets are in a normal distribution over their relative ranges, then the number of errors made for plaintiffs will approximate the number of errors made for defendants, and the preponderance of the evidence standard will have done its job.

The following graph demonstrates this possibility geometrically. ⑧The horizontal axis is the probability that fact finders (judge, juror, or lay assessor) assign to cases, and the vertical axis is the number of cases assigned a particular probability. Graph I is the set of cases in which defendants deserve to win (which means if we knew all the facts to certainty, the defendant would win); graph II is the set of cases in which plaintiffs deserve to win.

Errors are represented in graph I by all those cases to the right of the 0. 5 level, which is the area heavily shaded in the graph. This area representing de-

⑧ These graphs are from Richard Bell, *Decision Theory and Due Process: A Critique of the Supreme Court's Lawmaking for Burdens of Proof*, 78 J. Crim. L. & Criminology 557 (1987).

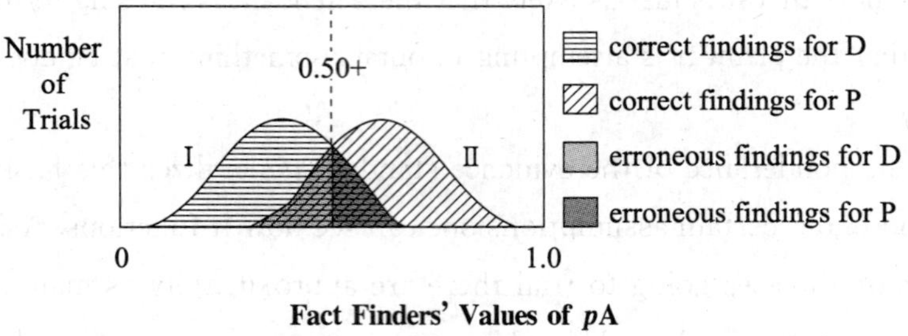

serving cases for the defendant where the defendant was not able to present adequate evidence, and thus the fact finder will find a more than 0. 5 probability for the plaintiff. Applying the preponderance standard, the fact finder will mistakenly render a verdict in favor of the plaintiff in that situation. Similarly, in graph II, errors are represented by the area to the left of the 0. 5 level, which again is the heavily shaded area. The number of errors is represented by the area under the graph—the larger the area the more errors and the smaller the area the fewer errors. So long as the heavily shaded areas under the two graphs are of approximately equal size, then the preponderance standard will have equalized errors among plaintiffs and defendants, and achieved the companion goal of treating the parties equally. Note, however, that this will be so only when the relevant areas under the two graphs are roughly equal in size, which is an empirical question. If the contours of the two graphs differ markedly from what we have presented, or if the number of cases in which plaintiffs deserve to win is substantially larger or smaller than the number of cases in which defendants deserve to win, then the size of those areas under the graphs would change, with the result being that errors may not be allocated equally over plaintiffs and defendants, a point to which I will return in Part III. The manner in which we have drawn these graphs reflects assumptions that are pertinent to civil cases, but are dubious in criminal cases, a matter we will also return to below.

These graphs also demonstrate how alternative burdens of persuasion are occasionally relied upon in civil cases in order to alter the allocation of errors. Many jurisdictions require allegations in civil cases of fraud or of activity that would be criminal to be proven by clear and convincing evidence. The theory is that, because of the seriousness of such allegations, errors should favor the person against whom such allegations are made, which also explains the higher burdens of persuasion in criminal cases. Making the same assumptions as we did above, the effect of raising the burden of persuasion from preponderance to "clear and convincing evidence" can be seen in the following graph:

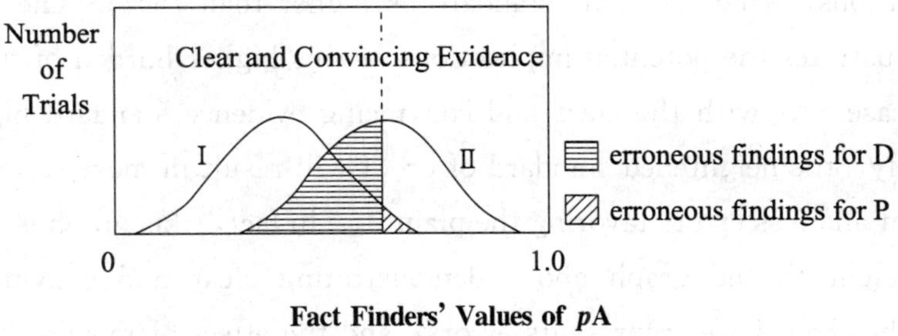

The shaded area again represents errors, and the effect of raising the burden of proof is obvious. Errors favoring defendants are increased and errors favoring plaintiffs are decreased, which is precisely the effect that the higher burdens of persuasion is designed to accomplish. Again, though, bear in mind that what these graphs look like in reality is an empirical, not an analytical question. Should reliable data ever be obtained on that issue, it might be justifiable to modify the burden of persuasion in light of that information. For example, we might decide after reviewing the data that too many errors favoring defendants are made where there is an allegation of fraud. The rate of such errors can be affected by lowering the burden of persuasion.

We can also see the implications of changing the standard of proof by comparing the preponderance standard with the high degree of probability standard that some scholars assert is used in China, although as I understand the matter, there are disagreements about what standard of proof Chinese courts implement in civil cases. Again, as I understand it, following serious criticism of the "objective truth" standard, scholars in China have more or less come to understand that decision at trial is decision under uncertainty [or as these scholars seem to say, that the court will pursue "truth in law" instead of "objective truth"], but they have not agreed on whether this can be done by a mere preponderance of evidence or, as a minority of scholars assert, a high degree of probability.⑨ You know the state of Chinese law better than I do, and so I will leave that to you. However, I want to use this occasion to solidify our understanding of burdens of persuasion.

So far as I can tell, the high degree of probability is inherited from civil law traditions, which sets the standard as higher than 75%.⑩ The following graph illustrates the potential implications of this higher burden of persuasion in civil cases. As with the clear and convincing evidence standard highlighted previously, the heightened standard of proof will result in more errors for the defendant and less errors favoring the plaintiff: in fact, this graph is essentially equivalent to the graph above demonstrating clear and convincing evidence. The shaded area represents errors, and the effect of raising the burden of proof results in an increased number of errors for defendants:

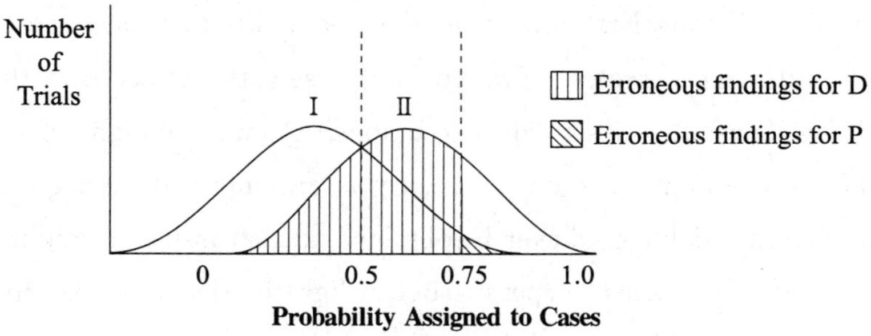

The requirement of proof beyond reasonable doubt in criminal cases can also be explicated by this approach:

Graph I of such a scheme would be the set of all innocent people who go to trial in criminal cases. Again, the shaded areas under the curves represent errors, and as I have drawn these graphs the policy of preferring erroneous acquittals over erroneous convictions is satisfied. You can also see the effect of lowering the burden of persuasion. If you lowered it to 0.7, you would convict more guilty persons, but you would also convict many more innocent peo-

⑨ For the argument that China nowadays implement a high degree of probability standard, or a standard similar to heightened standard of proof in civil law countries, *see* Mo Jun, *Outlining Standard of Proof in Civil Cases- An Analysis as Compared to Standard of Proof in Criminal Cases*, 4 Studies in Law and Business 35 (2002); Yi Yanyou, The System and Spirit of Evidence Law- With Special References to Anglo-American Law 318—322 (Peking University Press, 2010).

⑩ *See* Hans Pruetting, Gegenwarts probleme der Beweislast108 (Wu Yue trans., Law Press 2000) (1981).

ple. These graphs, in short, are interesting and powerful representations of how burdens of persuasion are supposed to function with regard to error allocation. However, note that they are only analytical graphs drawn based on the assumptions of the preponderance standard—they simply represent how the world would look if the preponderance rule actually achieves its goal of putting the plaintiff on an equal footing with the defendant. How well they reflect reality will be the topic of Section III, below.

II. The Extension of the Theory of Burdens of Proof to Presumptions and Judicial Notice

Although I was not asked to lecture on either judicial notice or presumptions, I want to say a few words about each. [11] Although both presumptions and judicial notice are conventionally viewed as separate evidentiary categories, in fact they are intimately tied to burdens of proof, and a lecture on burdens of proof would be incomplete without recognizing the analytical similarity between these evidentiary concepts. I will start with judicial notice.

JUDICIAL NOTICE

We have previously seen that there are three burdens that can be imposed upon a party and together these three burdens structure the process of proof. To remind you, those are the burdens of pleading, production, and persuasion. Judicial notice at first glance seems to have nothing to do with burdens of proof but instead permits judges to conclude that facts are true in the absence of evidence. A perfect example is from Federal Rule of Evidence 201 (b) that allows notice of facts "(1) generally known within the territorial jurisdiction of the trial court or (2) capable of accurate and ready determination by resort to sources whose accuracy cannot reasonably be questioned" . If a fact is essentially incontestable within a jurisdiction, permitting litigation over that fact is simply a waste of resources (such as the judge's time and the parties' financial resources) that could obviously be spent better elsewhere. The problem has been to specify when something is "generally known" or "cannot reasonably be questioned", and the general response has been to articulate a number of question begging and circular explanations that basically reiterate the general

[11] For detailed discussions, *see* Ronald J. Allen, *Structuring Jury Decisionmaking in Criminal Cases: A Unified Constitutional Approach to Evidentiary Devices*, 94 Harv. L. Rev. 321 (1980) .

language of the rule. ⑫

This inability to specify further when judicial notice should be taken evaporates when the issue is viewed through the lens of burdens of proof. Judicial notice, like burdens of production, depends on burdens of persuasion. ⑬ If it is common knowledge—known to every sentient person in the community—that the probability of a fact exceeds the relevant burden of persuasion, or if its negative does (judicial notice works in both directions), then it is pointless to spend time at trial on that fact or its negation. It is pointless to contest that we are in Mohe, China, today. If someone is forced to litigate that question, they could obviously bring in satisfactory evidence to resolve it, and the only effect of the exercise would be a waste of time and money. Judicial notice, then, is largely a variant of peremptory motions such as directed verdicts and summary judgments. It, too, allows the litigation process to be short-circuited when it is pointless to spend further resources, but when it is pointless to spend further resources depends on the burden of persuasion.

This perspective clarifies the oddest feature of judicial notice, which is that the parties often provide information to the judge which the parties claim permits the judge to take judicial notice. Again, an example from FRE 201 (e) which allows the court to hear "information" concerning the propriety of taking notice, and indeed gives the parties a right to be heard on the matter. The word information is obviously just a euphemism for "evidence," and thus such rules provide for judges to hear evidence in order to determine if there is an issue in dispute. Again, though, that sounds like directed verdict or summary judgment language, and indeed it is. The only difference is that, because of the pretense that "evidence" is not being offered, the formalities of the trial process do not apply. Thus, from beginning to end, judicial notice provides a means of simplifying and reducing the cost of trial, but it is entirely dependent upon the burden of persuasion.

⑫ For example, the Iowa Supreme Court commented in *In re Tresnak*, 297 N. W. 2d 109 (Iowa, 1980), that judicial notice may be taken of "matters which everyone knows". The Court in *Meredith v. Fair*, 298 F. 2d 696 (5th Cir., 1962) embraced the standard of a "plain fact known to everyone". These are simple restatements of the same general point and provide no further elaboration of the proper standard.

⑬ For a more complete discussion, *see* Ronald J. Allen, *The Explanatory Value of Analyzing Codifications by Reference to Organizing Principles Other Than Those Employed in the Codification*, 79 Nw. U. L. Rev. 1080, 1091—1094 (1984—1985).

Much more could be said about judicial notice, and it is probably deserving of a lecture of its own. I will just say briefly here that you should be able to see the extension of the central point I have been making to other ways in which the term "judicial notice" has been employed in various legal systems. For example, it is sometimes applied to preserve obviously correct verdicts where there has been a trivial lapse of proof. The point of doing so is that the expense of retrials, or even worse the entry of what everyone knows to be an obviously incorrect verdict, should be avoided, and judicial notice permits the rigors of the evidence rules to be ameliorated to further substantial justice. More deeply, there is a deep incoherence in the idea that the outcomes at trial can be based on, and only on, the "evidence" presented at trial,⑭ and again judicial notice domesticates that deep incoherence. ⑮

⑭ Ronald J. Allen, *Factual Ambiguity and a Theory of Evidence*, 88 Nw. U. L. Rev. 604 (1994).

⑮ Ronald J. Allen, *The Explanatory Value of Analyzing Codifications by Reference to Organizing Principles Other Than Those Employed in the Codification*, 79 Nw. U. L. Rev. 1080, 1091—1094 (1984—1985). This perspective also explains what on its face is perhaps the most curious rule in the Federal Rules—FRE 201 (g)'s provision that "In a criminal case, the court shall instruct the jury that it may, but is not required to, accept as conclusive any fact judicially noticed." It should be noted at the outset by Chinese readers that all of this is a function of a jury system that is constitutionally protected in the United States. In any event, it is contradictory to tell the jury that it "may" accept a fact that has been judicially noticed. Judicial notice is supposed to dispose of issues. The incongruity is explained by the recognition that judges are allowed less authority over the facts in criminal cases than in civil cases, which is reflected in the misleading shibboleth that there are no directed verdicts in criminal cases. [It is misleading because it is false. *See* United States v. Bailey, 444 U.S. 394 (1980): refusing to instruct a jury on a defense for which the defendant bears but has not met the burden of production is in effect a directed verdict against the defendant on that defense]. To notice a fact is to direct a verdict on it, since the issue is removed from the jury, and that conflicts with the conventional view of the role of jurors in criminal cases. FRE 201 (g) responds to the apparent conflict of the normal understanding of notice and the normal approach in criminal cases by purporting to allow non-binding notice. The response may appear to be quite incoherent, but that may be preferable to consciously limiting the jury's fact finding role in criminal cases. FRE 201 (g) has other advantages in the context of the peculiar system of criminal trials in the United States. It permits a court to refuse to direct a verdict for the defendant where there has been a lapse in the prosecution's case concerning a fact that the judge thinks is indisputable. More importantly, by allowing the jury to be instructed on "noticed" facts, FRE 201 (g) authorizes a form of comment on the evidence that can benefit either party. If the judge believes a fact is almost certainly true, the judge may tell the jury that it "may" accept it as true if it chooses to do so. This allows the judge to comment on the obvious, the generally known, or the indisputable even though evidence on the particular point has not been adduced. There is nothing particularly mysterious about such a rule when fully understood, even though it may be politically controversial. The only truly curious aspect of FRE 201 (g) is its placement and its consequent peculiar wording. Instead of being placed in a rule on judicial notice, it should be in a rule that directly authorizes the court to comment on the evidence.

PRESUMPTIONS[16]

I have been told that a few years ago there was considerable interest in presumptions among Chinese evidence scholars, but that the interest has waned. I hope this is because Chinese evidence scholars have come to realize that the dispute over the meaning of the term "presumption" is pointless, and that all the complexity and difficulties that surround the term in western legal systems are simply the by-products of conceptual confusion. All the difficulties about presumptions are eliminated once one recognizes that there is no such thing as a "presumption". The word "presumption" is simply a label that has been applied to a widely differing set of decisions concerning the proper mode of trial and the manner in which facts are to be established to resolve legal disputes. In every single case of the use of the term "presumption", whatever is done is determined by normal evidentiary concepts and policies, most importantly the burden of proof, which is why I have included this section in this lecture. All the confusion and controversy surrounding presumptions —and I mean that literally, all of it—has been caused by the failure to recognize that the word "presumption" is simply a label applied to a range of evidentiary decisions that are made for the various reasons that inform the structuring of litigation.

In order to show the lack of independent significance to the term "presumption", I need to make a preliminary point. In addition to the three burdens that can be placed upon a party, there are two other analytical devices that are used to structure the proof process at trial. One is of great importance in the United States because of its jury system, but should be of limited importance in China, and that is to affect the weight that is given to evidence of some material proposition. Judges often instruct juries on appropriate inferences, and similarly comment on the evidence, in order to encourage juries to reach the results that the judge thinks is proper. Similarly, and here there may be a counterpart in China, legislatures often pass statutes that say a particular type of evidence (illuminations on radiographs for example) are evidence of

⑯ For a detailed discussion, *see* Ronald J. Allen, *Presumptions in Civil Actions Reconsidered*, 66 Iowa L. Rev. 843 (1980—1981).

some material fact (presence of lung disease, for example).[17] Second, decision rules are occasionally constructed instructing decision makers how to decide cases. For example, in the United States a person who has been missing and unheard from for seven years will be declared legally dead.

In sum, juridical proof is structured in the following fives ways:

- Creation of a rule to decide cases
- Allocation of burdens of pleasing
- Allocation of burdens of production
- Allocation of burdens of persuasion
- Affecting the weight that evidence has for the inference of a material fact

Each of these is done for various reasons of policy. Burdens are imposed to facilitate trial, and perhaps the discovery of information. Decision rules are created in order to encourage outcomes consistent with policy choices, and weight is given to evidence in order to encourage factually accurate inferences being drawn. All of these things are done directly by legislatures and courts. Decision rules are created, burdens are assigned, and so on. The confusion over presumptions stems from simultaneously using the word "presumption" to refer to the implementation of one of these devices. All of these things can be done directly or they can be done with the use of the term "presumption." Moreover, the list above captures the only things that are done through the use of "presumptions." The "presumption of innocence," for example, simply sets the burden of persuasion at criminal cases at beyond a reasonable doubt. The presumption that a letter that is properly mailed is received simply gives weight to the evidence of mailing. The presumption that a person not heard from for seven years is dead is simply a decision ruling equating the absence for seven years with death. The presumption that an act was not in self-defense unless the defendant pleads self-defense is a burden of pleading rule. And so on. Let me repeat. Every single use of the word presumption will fit into one of these categories, and these categories exist regardless of the use of the word "presumption." There is no independent meaning of presumption.

All the confusion over what is a presumption, and the futile analytical ef-

[17] For an example, *see* Usery v. Turner Elkhorn Mining Co., 428 U.S. 1 (1976).

forts to define the terms, are a result of legal systems using the term to apply to these quite different categories, and to do so at varying times throughout the litigation process. But literally no point is served by referring to a "presumption that shifts the burden of production." All one needs to say is that, if X is true, a burden of production on Y rest on the opponent at trial, and often that is exactly what a legal system will do. One need not say that "a person is presumed dead if unheard from for seven years." All one needs to say is that "a person may be declared legally dead if unheard from for seven years," and again such rules are common place in legal systems.

The completely unnecessary confusion over "presumptions" stems from using the term to do all of these different things, which then gives rise to ambiguity over the meaning of the term. Scholars and judges debate whether a presumption shifts the burden of production or the burden of persuasion; they debate whether a presumption can add weight to evidence, and so on. These are completely futile and unnecessary debates. Once one sees that the term "presumption" is applied to all the various ways proof is structured, and that its use adds nothing to the power of a court or legislature to structure litigation, all the confusion dissipates. Everything done using the term "presumption" can be done directly, without using the term at all. The term "presumption" is simply a label applied to the decision to do one of the things in the list above, such as to allocate burdens or create rules of decision.

Now, note that of these five uses of the term "presumption," four of them are intimately connected with burdens of persuasion. ⑱ The three direct allocations of burden rules obviously are, but so, too, is the use of a presumption to give weight to evidence. That would only be done, obviously, if there is a concern that decision makers will not get to the correct outcome, given the burden of persuasion, without the nudge from the presumption. Even the fifth use—constructing rules of decision—is related to burdens of persua-

⑱ Another important preliminary point is that the burden of persuasion is reciprocal. To say that the state bears the burden to prove an element beyond reasonable doubt is to say that the defendant bears the burden to show a reasonable doubt on the issue. The same is true of the preponderance standard. To say that one party must show that a fact is more likely than not to be true is to say that the other party must show that it is just as likely as not to be false.

sion. It essentially makes the burden of persuasion on one issue dispositive of another. For example, if one proves by a preponderance of the evidence that a person has been unheard from for seven years, then that disposes of the factual question of death.

In sum, none of the results purportedly achieved through the use of presumptions are in fact achieved because of presumptions. Instead, various evidentiary problems are resolved on the basis of the particular policy considerations involved rather than on the basis of what a presumption is, and the label "presumption" is then attached to the result. The most important of those policies has to do with the allocation of burdens of persuasion. There again is much more that could be said about these matters, and perhaps presumptions are deserving of a separate lecture at some later time.

III. Problems in Paradise and a Brave New World: The Limits of the Conventional Theory and the Probabilistic Account of the Evidentiary Process that it Depends Upon

The title to this section of my lecture is almost as long as the lecture itself! What I have presented so far is an integrated general theory of burdens of proof that has significant explanatory power. It took analysts decades to generate the theoretical account that I have reviewed in the previous sections of this lecture, and in many respects it is a significant achievement. Research, however, continues to advance knowledge, and it has become increasingly clear that the conventional account that I have lain out for you has significant problems. I am going to address those problems in this section of the lecture, and in the final section I will discuss some possible solutions to those problems. The problems are of two sorts. First, there are internal limitations or contradictions in the theory itself. Second, the theory assumes a probabilistic account of evidence and its processing that is almost surely inapt as a description of reality and unhelpful as prescription for rational behavior. This and the next section will be presenting new materials and may be more difficult to follow. Feel free to ask questions as we proceed.

INTERNAL PROBLEMS AND CONTRADICTIONS IN THE CONVENTIONAL ACCOUNT

First, reconsider the two graphs reproduced earlier that geometrically represent how the conventional theory explains and justifies burdens of persuasion. Recall that in civil cases, the objectives are to minimize the total number of errors and to treat the parties equally before the law. As those graphs are drawn, the policy objectives are secured. However, and this is the absolutely critical point, the shape of those graphs is an empirical, not an analytical, matter. I drew those graphs in order to explicate the conventional theory of burdens of persuasion. In the real world, those graphs could be quite different from what I have drawn. Their actual shape would depend upon two empirical variables: first, the relative size of the two subsets of cases (deserving plaintiffs and deserving defendants) who go to trial and the probability assessments given to the cases that go to trial by the fact finder (regardless whether the fact finder is a judge or juror) . There is no good reason to think that the subsets would be of equal size or that the probability assessments would take the form of normal distributions, as I have drawn them. There are significant questions of costs and risk avoidance that plainly could affect who goes to litigation. Thus, in the real world, there is no necessary connection between burdens of persuasion and policy objectives. The connection is contingent and empirical. That is a sobering conclusion, for it makes pursuing policy objectives much more difficult.

For example, defendants may be risk averse in civil cases and plaintiffs may be risk takers. In that case, fewer deserving defendants would go to trial relative to deserving plaintiffs, because deserving defendants would tend to settle rather than risk trial. If that were true, the graphs would like something like this:

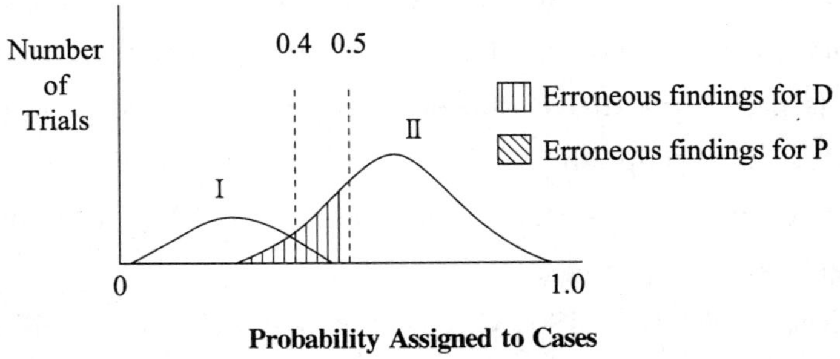

Of course, the above graph again does not necessarily capture real life. As the defendants are more risk averse, it is also possible that those who decided to go to the court might have better cases than those plaintiffs who simply take the risk and sue. Thus, though the total number of cases for each side changed relatively, the number of deserving cases might stay the same. However, this additional variable does not weaken, but rather support my point here that the question of the implications of standard of proof is purely empirical, not analytical.

If you believed that empirically, the graph above captured the reality of your trial system, an important implication for your legal system seems to leap off the page, and that is that the burden of persuasion has been set too high. If it were lowered to 0.4, one can see that fewer total errors would be made and plaintiffs and defendants would be treated roughly equally. Why not lower the burden of persuasion, then? Perhaps one should, but there is an additional consideration. People select to go to trial in light of the burden of persuasion. If the burden of persuasion were lowered, plaintiffs and defendants might make different choices about what cases to litigate. That in turn would affect the distribution of errors and correct decisions. As with the effects of the initial allocation of burdens, the effect of changing them cannot be predicted analytically. This point emphasizes the empirical nature of the question we are presently examining, and it also highlights its complexity and organic nature. The legal system is a set of interconnected parts; if one part is changed, it is quite likely going to affect some other part of the system. [19]

The same points are true in criminal cases: The effect of burdens of persuasion can not be determined analytically and neither can the effect of a change in the burden of persuasion be determined analytically. They are both empirical questions. For example, consider the graph below, which is probably a more realistic portrayal of criminal cases than the graph in Section II. Fewer innocent defendants probably go to trial because the authorities weed out the innocent. If the graph below depicts reality, we might think that it would be optimal to lower the standard of proof in criminal cases to 0.7, but again what the stand-

⑲ Ronald J. Allen & Alan E. Guy, *Conley as a Special Case of Twombly and Iqbal: Exploring the Intersection of Evidence, Procedure, and the Nature of Rules*, 115 Penn. St. L. Rev. 1 (2010).

ard is affects the decisions that people make about whether to risk trial. If the standard is lowered, prosecutors will have the incentive to bring cases that they would not bring if the standard is higher. One again would predict that a different mix of cases would go to trial, resulting in a different mix of errors and correct decisions.

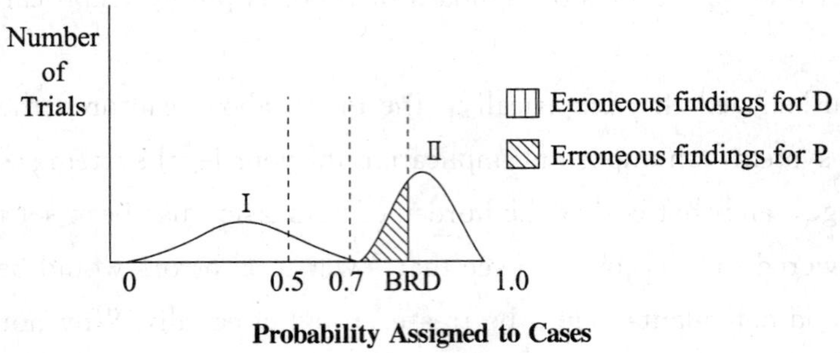

Although the actual effect of burdens of persuasion is an empirical rather than analytical question, this does not mean that burdens of persuasion are not subject to intelligent manipulation through law. You may very well think that you have a good idea how the litigation system is working, and perhaps how it could be improved. You might think that certain classes of cases are different from others and deserve special treatment. And again these graphs help us to see precisely when that is the case. Reconsider the graph of civil cases immediately above. In the United States, we have reason to think that it accurately represents a certain set of torts cases—those in which the plaintiff is unable to perceive the events affecting him, such as during surgery when he is anesthetized. Because the plaintiff lacks the ability to perceive first-hand what is happening, he faces a greater risk of error, even when he should win a tort case against his surgeon. The tort law in the United States and England responded to this possibility through the doctrine of resipsa loquitur ("the thing speaks for itself") . All the fancy Latin phrase means is that, in a certain subset of torts cases, the plaintiff's burden of persuasion will be reduced. The reason is to reestablish the proper relationship of errors, which the graph demonstrates clearly.

The first major qualification of the conventional theory of burdens of proof is that it is a mistake to think their effects can be predicted analytically. The second questions the very nature of the enterprise. As I have noted, burdens of persuasion in civil cases are supposed to treat the parties equally and to reduce the total number of errors. In criminal cases, the policy is to protect innocent people by making it hard to convict anyone, and this supposedly is done through skewing errors in favor of acquitting the guilty (the mantra being that it is ten times worse to convict an innocent person than acquit a guilty person). Note something quite peculiar about this way of thinking about things. Four decisions can be made at trial, and all have social benefits or costs: two types of correct decisions and two types of errors. Neglecting correct decisions can lead to remarkable results. For example, the error equalization policy is satisfied by making errors in every single case, so long as the base rates of cases that go to trial include roughly the same number of deserving plaintiffs and defendants. In criminal cases, the ratio of 10 incorrect acquittals to one incorrect conviction is satisfied by 99 out of every 100 cases being wrongly decided.

Related to the neglect of correct decisions, the conventional theory neglects that trial decisions are only one part of the output of the legal system. Parties negotiate outcomes in both civil and criminal cases, and the outcomes in those cases are obviously part of the total social welfare effects of a legal system. A rational policy would optimize errors in the system as a whole, rather than in just one part of it. That leads again to a much more complex decision problem involving the interaction of litigation and primary behavior. Quite random outcomes at trial or relatively high costs could be socially optimal because they encourage party settlement. I am not asserting this to be true, and frankly I doubt that it is, but the point emphasizes how complex the analysis of burdens of proof is. [20]

And we are not done with making these matters even more complicated, because there is a third problem that is as troublesome as the first two. [21]The conventional theory of burdens of proof in civil cases requires the fact finder to find for the plaintiff only if each of the relevant elements is established by a

⑳ Larry Laudan & Ronald J. Allen, *Deadly Dilemmas II: Bail and Crime*, 85 Chi.-Kent L. Rev. 23 (2010).

㉑ The next few paragraphs are heavily indebted to Ronald J. Allen, *The Nature of Juridical Proof*, 13 Cardozo L. Rev. 373, 374—375 (1991).

preponderance of the evidence. The fact finder compares the probability of each of the elements to the probability of its negation and decides for the plaintiff only if the probability of the element being true exceeds the probability of its being false. Because the probability of an element being either true or false exhausts the possibilities, the conventional approach collapses into a requirement that the plaintiff prove each element by more than a 0.5 probability. With the addition of two factors, the logical difficulties of this conception become evident. First, if one of the elements of a cause of action did not occur—for example, in a torts case if the defendant either was not negligent or did not cause the harm—a verdict for the plaintiff would be in error. Second, since errors in fact finding are inevitable but their distribution malleable, the question arises how to distribute them, and the conventional answer is to distribute them equally over the sets of plaintiffs and defendants.

Consider now the difficulties with the conventional theory of burdens of persuasion. If the probability of each of two independent elements of a cause of action, such as breach of duty and causation in tort litigation, is 0.6, the probability of their both being true is $0.6 \times 0.6 = 0.36$. That means that the probability of the defendant not having negligently harmed the plaintiff is $1.0 - 0.36 = 0.64$. Errors, in other words, will favor plaintiffs over defendants at a ratio of approximately 1/2. In fact, taken at face value the conventional theory produces bizarre results. Assume that in Case 1, another torts case, breach of duty is proven to 0.9 and causation to 0.4, and assume there are no other elements. The verdict would be for the defendant, since one of the elements—causation—is not proven by a preponderance of the evidence. Compare that to Case 2 in which both elements are proven to 0.6. In Case 2, the verdict would be for the plaintiff. Now compare the two cases. The probability of the defendant having negligently harmed the plaintiff is the same in both cases ($0.9 \times 0.4 = 0.6 \times 0.6 = 0.36$), yet in one case there would be a verdict for the plaintiff and in the other for the defendant. Here is another bizarre outcome. Assume that in Case 1, causation is proven to 0.5. Case 1 would still result in a verdict for the defendant, since 0.5 is less than a preponderance of the evidence, but now the probability of the defendant having negligently harmed the plaintiff is $0.9 \times 0.5 = 0.45$. There would be a verdict for the defendant in Case 1 even though the probability that the defendant negligently harmed the plaintiff (0. 45) exceeds the probability in Case 2 of the defendant having negligently harmed the plaintiff (0. 36) (where, remember, there would be a verdict for the plaintiff) .

In many instances, elements of a cause of action will not be stochastically or conditionally independent. Unless they are completely dependent, the phenomenon described above will still occur but be lessened by the extent of the dependency. And if they are completely dependent, that means each is a restatement of all the others, a bizarre possibility that we need not take time exploring further.

The conventional account of burdens of proof is vitiated by a fourth difficulty. It depends upon a probabilistic account of evidence. Again, at a certain level, the probabilistic account is powerful, but at a deeper level it is obviously inadequate. It is powerful in that it seems to capture and explain judgments about the world, and is consistent with the language people employ ("What is the chance of rain tomorrow?" "What do you think the likelihood is that he did it?"), and it is superficially attractive to think of the trial process as updating a prior probability in light of new evidence. The superficial attractiveness is misleading, however. None of the conceptualizations of probability except probability as subjective degrees of belief can function at trial. Logical probability and propensity interpretations obviously do not work. Relative frequency is superficially appealing, but there is virtually never any relative frequency data. Indeed, consider what it might mean for a party to be required to establish his case by preponderance of the evidence where this is conceived of as a relative frequency greater than 0. 5. The plaintiff would have to account for every possible way the world might have been and show that half plus one of those ways favor liability. That, of course, is an impossible standard. Or consider a criminal case. Does the State have to show that there is no possible state of the world consistent with innocence? Can the defendant defend simply by bringing in the local phone book to show that there are many other possibilities out that in the world who theoretically could have committed the act? No legal system operates this way because it would be self-destructive.

Confirming, in my opinion, that probabilistic explanations of juridical proof are false，you should note that it is entirely unclear whether the standard burden of persuasion for a plaintiff is too high or too low. The conjunction paradox suggests it is too low. Even if each element in a multi-element case is proved to greater than 0.5，the probability that at least one is false will be high. This is the concept of uncertainty，and it favors the plaintiff. However，ambiguity favors the defendant. If the plaintiff has to show all the ways the world might have been on the day in question，and that half of them plus one favor liability，which is one way to understand juridical proof as involving relative frequencies，then the plaintiff's standard is almost impossible to meet. This，at a minimum is a strange set of factors.

Some of the difficulties with a probabilistic account of evidence discussed above are caused by applying burdens of persuasion to individual elements. An alternative would be to conceptualize the burden of persuasion as applying to the case as a whole，but this suffers from debilitating problems of its own. First，as the elements increase in number，the plaintiff's task becomes increasingly arduous. Rather than show each element is more than 0.5 likely，he would have to show the conjunction exceeds that threshold; but with even three elements in a case，each element would have to be proved to about a 0.8 probability，which would be a daunting task. In addition，the level of proof of each element would be determined by how many other elements there are，and their dependencies，but that leads to the curious result that elements common to various causes of action would have to be proved to different levels of probability. "Intent" in tort would have to be proved differently than "intent" in contracts，for example. ㉒

In sum，fact finding at trial can not plausibly be conceptualized as involving relative frequencies except in a few limited cases where good data exists (some instances of medical malpractice perhaps). That leaves degrees of belief，or Bayesian subjective probability as the only remaining conceptualization of probability that might work，but the conditions of trial are directly inconsis-

㉒ Ronald J. Allen，*A Reconceptualization of Civil Trials*，66 B. U. L. Rev. 401，407 (1986). Other treatments of this and similar issues include Ronald J. Allen，*The Nature of Juridical Proof*，13 Cardozo L. Rev. 373 (1991)；Ronald J. Allen，*Rationality*，*Algorithms and Juridical Proof*：*A Preliminary Inquiry*，1 Int. J. of Evidence & Proof 254 (1997).

tent with Bayesian approaches. Fact finders, whether judge or lay assessor, are told not to update prior beliefs in the light of new evidence. They often do not even know what the issues are until the end of the case, and in any event the subjective belief state of fact finders is irrelevant. Fact finders are supposed to find facts and not express their idiosyncratic states of mind. ㉓There are further difficulties with a Bayesian approach to fact finding, the most important being computational complexity. With only a small number of variables, the computational demands of Bayes' Theorem soon outstrips the capacity of even the most powerful computers, let alone humans. ㉔Even worse, the evidence at trial is normally highly interdependent, and thus the dependencies between in-

㉓ Ronald J. Allen, *Rationality, Algorithms and Juridical Proof: A Preliminary Inquiry*, 1 Int'L J. Evidence & Proof 254 (1997); Ronald J. Allen & Sarah A. Jehl, *Burdens of Persuasion in Civil Cases: Algorithms v. Explanations*, 2003 Mich. St. L. Rev. 893 (2003). *See, e.g.*, Susan Haack, *Legal Probabilism: An Epistemological Dissent* at ms. 7-8 (available on SSRN), taking to task the peculiar statement in 2 McCormick on Evidence § 339, at 483 (Kenneth S. Broun, ed., 6th ed., 2006) that the beyond reasonable doubt instruction "points to what we are really concerned with, the state of the jury's mind," which they assert is unlike the preponderance of the evidence instruction because it "divert [s] attention to the evidence." There surely is a relationship between the evidence and someone's mind, but it is equally surely not the "jury's" as it does not have one. If it did, everyone other than a few dedicated Bayesians would say, as the instructions Haack reproduces make clear, that the concern is with a rational consideration of the evidence in an effort to find the facts accurately. The evidence is hardly a "diversion" in such a matter. It is critically important, even if not sufficient itself.

㉔ Just how complicated litigation actually is often gets overlooked. Consider an example I gave some years ago, Ronald J. Allen, *Factual Ambiguity and a Theory of Evidence*, 88 Nw. U. L. Rev. 604 (1994), at 626-626: Suppose a witness begins testifying, and thus a fact finder must decide what to make of the testimony. What are some of the relevant variables? First, there are all the normal credibility issues, but consider how complicated they are. Demeanor is not just demeanor; it is instead a complex set of variables. Is the witness sweating or twitching, and if so is it through innocent nerves, the pressure of prevarication, a medical problem, or simply a distasteful habit picked up during a regrettable childhood? Does body language suggest truthfulness or evasion; is slouching evidence of lying or comfort in telling a straight forward story? Does the witness look the examiner straight in the eye, and if so is it evidence of commendable character or the confidence of an accomplished snake oil salesman? Does the voice inflection suggest the rectitude of the righteous or is it strained, and does a strained voice indicate fabrication or concern over the outcome of the case? And so on. The list of relevant variables goes far beyond credibility issues, of which demeanor is only one. When a witness articulates a proposition, the fact finder must determine what the proposition is designed to assert and what the fact finder believes it asserts. That task, too, involves an immense number of variables. In addition, the fact finder will possess some knowledge based on its observations leading up to the first articulated proposition by a witness, acquired from the lawyers for example. And there are many more examples. For the law to proceed as a science would require that many of these variables be in a deductive structure with their necessary and sufficient conditions spelled out. No such structure could be created; it would be too complex.

dividual pieces of evidence must be known and taken into account in the computations.[25] These interdependencies are literally never known because each trial is unique.

IV. Solution: Inference to the best explanation.[26]

The nature of juridical proof is not fundamentally probabilistic, but instead explanatory, and is an example of inference to the best explanation. The general structure of proof at trial instantiates the classic two-stage explanation—based inferential process of explanation generation and acceptance. At the first stage, potential explanations are generated; at the second, an inference is made to one of the potential explanations on explanatory grounds. At trial, the parties (including the government in criminal cases) offer competing versions of events that, if true, would explain the evidence presented at trial. Parties with the burden of proof on claims or defenses offer versions of events that include the formal elements that make up the particular claims or defenses; opposing parties offer versions of events that fail to include one or more of the formal elements. In addition, parties may, when the law allows,[27] offer alternative versions of events to explain the evidence. Finally, fact finders are not limited to the potential explanations explicitly put forward by the parties, but may construct their own, either in deliberation in cases with multiple fact finders or as the foundation for the conclusions they reach.

At the decision stage in civil cases where the burden of persuasion is a preponderance of the evidence, proof depends on whether the best explanation of the evidence favors the plaintiff or the defendant.[28] Fact finders decide based on the relative plausibility of the versions of events put forth by the parties, and possibly additional ones constructed by themselves. Fact finders infer the most plausible explanation as the actual explanation and find for the party that the

[25] Craig R. Callen, *Notes on a Grand Illusion: Some Limits on the Use of Bayesian Theory in Evidence Law*, 57 Ind. L. J. 1 (1982).

[26] This section borrows heavily from Ronald J. Allen & Michael Pardo, *Juridical Proof and the Best Explanation*, 27 Law & Philosophy 223 (2008).

[27] Parties may sometimes be precluded from offering contradictory accounts. *See* McCormick v. Kopmann, 161 N. E. 2d 720 (Ill. App. Ct., 1959).

[28] *See* Ronald J. Allen, *Factual Ambiguity and Theory of Evidence*, 88 Nw. U. L. Rev. 604 (1994); Ronald J. Allen, *The Nature of Juridical Proof*, 13 Cardozo L. Rev. 373 (1991).

substantive law supports based on this accepted version. In the United States, empirical evidence has confirmed that fact finders formulate factual conclusions by constructing narrative versions of events to account for the evidence presented at trial based on criteria such as coherence, completeness, and uniqueness. [29]This process proceeds on explanatory grounds—fact finders construct narratives to explain the evidence and choose among alternatives by applying similar criteria to those invoked in science. These results should not be a surprise, because they are simply an instantiation of how virtually everyone reasons about the world at large. Juridical fact finders, whether judge or juror, has no choice but to engage the evidence at trial in fundamentally the same manner he engages evidence elsewhere.

Precisely how this process proceeds at trial depends on the inferential interests of the legal system and the fact finders. For example, how fine grained the explanation must be will depend on the context. If the litigation involves an accident, the explanation that "The accident occurred at 12: 00: 01" may be too detailed; "The accident occurred in the afternoon on June 16" may be good enough; and "An accident occurred sometime in the past" may be not detailed enough. Consider the case of a man with heart burn. From his wife's perspective, the fact that he ate something spicy may be a good enough explanation because it identifies an appropriate contrast (based on the wife's inferential interests); it does not matter whether the spicy food was a chili cheeseburger with jalapenos (or something else spicy) because any such food would have caused the heartburn. For other contexts or for others with different inferential interests, such as his doctor making a diagnosis, more details and different details will be appropriate.

In the context of juridical proof, two factors determine the inferential interests at stake and the appropriate level of detail at which fact finders should focus in evaluating explanations. These factors are the substantive law and the points of contrast between the versions of events offered by the parties (the disputed facts) . First, the substantive law will require a sufficiently detailed

[29] *See* Nancy Pennington & Reid Hastie, *A Cognitive Theory of Juror Decision Making: The Story Model*, 13 Cardozo Law Review 519 (1991) .

explanation of the evidence to show the plaintiff is entitled to relief, explanations such as "the defendant did something bad" will not be detailed enough. Sometimes, however, the substantive law allows parties to provide quite broad explanations. To return to the example used previously, the doctrine of resipsa loquitur allows plaintiffs to recover even by offering explanations such as "My injuries were caused by something done by the defendant" when such a theory provides the best explanation of the evidence. And second, where the parties choose to disagree focuses attention on the appropriate details for choosing among contrasting explanations. If the defendant contends that he was on vacation somewhere out of state during an alleged car accident, then the appropriate contrast on which to focus is whether he was in state (and driving the car that caused the accident) or out of state, and not on whether he was driving or in the back seat or the trunk or any other place in the universe. Consider further the hypothetical focusing on whether an accident occurred at noon or some other time. If a defendant tries to defend on the ground that, although the accident occurred around noon, the evidence does not show precisely whether it was at 12: 00 or 12: 01, the defendant will obviously lose because the substantive law is indifferent to the matter. Inference to the best explanation thus accommodates the concern of too many explanations by showing how to aggregate and differentiate among them.

A complementary possible concern is having too few potential explanations. There may be cases where neither party offers a particularly plausible explanation of the evidence, either because neither side can explain key pieces of evidence or because there is such a paucity of evidence that it can be explained in multifarious ways none of which are any better (or more likely) explanations than any other. In the first scenario—where each side has problems explaining the same or different critical items of evidence—the key point is the comparative aspect of the process. A verdict will (and should) be rendered for the better (or best available) explanation, whether one of the parties' or another constructed by the fact finder. If the proffered explanations truly are equally bad (or good), including additionally constructed ones, judgment will (and should) go against the party with the burden of persuasion. In the second scenario—too little evidence from which to differentiate among potential explanations—the result should also be judgment against the party with the burden of persuasion; they have failed to meet their burdens of producing evidence from which a reasonable fact finder could differentiate among the potential, contrasting explanations. Through burdens of proof, the structure of civil trials thus assuages concerns associated with too few potential explanations.

In criminal cases, rather than inferring the best explanation from the potential ones, fact finders infer (and should infer) the defendant's innocence whenever there is a sufficiently plausible explanation of the evidence consistent with innocence (and ought to convict when there is no plausible explanation consistent with innocence, assuming there is a plausible explanation consistent with guilt) [30]. When there is a plausible explanation of the evidence consistent with innocence, then there is a concomitant likelihood that this explanation is correct (the actual explanation) and thus that the defendant is innocent, which in turn creates a reasonable doubt that should prevent the fact finder from inferring guilt.

Similar considerations apply to the clear-and-convincing-evidence standard. Rather than inferring the best explanation from the available potential ones, fact finders should infer a conclusion for the party with the burden of persuasion when there is an explanation that is sufficiently more plausible than those that favor the other side (not just when the party with the burden has offered a better one) . How sufficiently more plausible must the explanation be to meet the standard? The explanation must be plausible enough that it is clearly and convincingly more plausible than those favoring the other side. This is not circular; it simple expresses the common sense judgment that some explanations are on occasion considerably better, not just better, than others.

Obviously, there is vagueness in how "sufficiently plausible" an explana-

[30] If both the prosecution and the defense offer implausible explanations of the evidence, the fact finder ought to acquit. Suggesting something quite similar to Ronald J. Allen, *Rationality, Algorithms and Juridical Proof: A Preliminary Inquiry*, 1 Int. J. of Evidence & Proof 254, 273 (1997), Professor Josephson has proposed a definition of the reasonable-doubt standard that turns on whether there is an explanation that represents a "real possibility" of innocence. *See* John R. Josephson, *On the Proof Dynamics of Inference to the Best Explanation*, 22 Cardozo L. Rev. 1621, 1642 (2001) ("A real possibility does not suppose the violation of any known law of nature, nor does it suppose any behavior that is completely unique or unprecedented, nor any extremely improbable chain of coincidences") .

tion must be in order to satisfy either the beyond-a-reasonable-doubt or the clear-convincing-evidence standard, but this vagueness inheres in the standards themselves. Lack of precision may thus be a critique of the standards, but it is not a critique of an explanation-based account. Even if the strength of a party's total evidence could be quantified, the vagueness remains for a probability approach as well. [31]Is 58% likelihood clear and convincing? Is 65%? Is 72%? Is 85% beyond a reasonable doubt? Is 90%? Is 95%?[32]

I will end this lecture by briefly explaining how inference to the best explanation (IBE) ameliorates if it does not entirely resolve the various difficulties noted above regarding probabilistic accounts of evidence. Unlike probabilistic accounts, IBE does not require the impossible in terms of the form of evidence. Rather than unrealistically assuming the existence of relative frequency data, IBE explains how natural human reasoners deal with the kinds of evidence naturally found in their environment. Similarly, a decision rule of relative plausibility that both fits their environment and which they use all the time is employed. The impossible computational demands of subjective theories of probability are eliminated. Similarly, the conjunction paradoxes, while not precisely eliminated, are rendered inconsequential because they are distributed over both parties' cases. Last, the decision rules instruct the parties to present their most plausible case, which it is entirely reasonable to assume will lead to reliable and reasonably efficient outcomes at trial. The parties know their case best, what will establish the facts, and how much any litigation is worth to them.

You have listened patiently to me for many hours, and I thank you for that. I also look forward to your questions and to discussing these issues with you. Although this lecture has been long, there is much more to say on at least the following topics, and I'd be happy to lecture of these topics at some later

[31] For an example of the vagueness, see Federal Civil Jury Instructions of the Seventh Circuit 35 (available at www. ca7. uscourts. gov) (defining the "clear and convincing" standard as "highly probable that it is true") .

[32] *See* United States v. Fatico, 458 F. Supp. 388, 410 (E. D. N. Y. , 1978) (providing a survey of district judges on the probability they associated with various standards of persuasion—judges differed); *see also* R. J. Simon. & L. Mahan. , *Quantifying Burdens of Proof: A View from the Bench, the Jury, and the Classroom*, 5 L&Soc'y Rev. 319 (1971) .

date:

1. Alternative to the conventional analysis of burdens of proof has come from economists who have also analyzed of burdens of persuasion. I have not spent much time on those efforts here because they are for the most part quite flawed due to their insularity (they seem unaware of the pertinent literature or the foundations of the problem they purportedly address) and so unrealistic to be of virtually no interest. [33] Still, economic analysis in general is powerful and worthy of attention.

2. Considerably more could be said about presumptions and judicial notice.

3. And much more could be said about probability theory in general and Bayes' Theorem in particular.

Thank you.

---

[33] The most recent example is Louis Kaplow, *Burden of Proof*, 121 Yale L. J. 738 (2012).

民事诉讼推定再思考*

张家骥 译** 张保生 校

梅森·拉德介绍他最近的论文说："尽管广泛的评论一直致力于推定这个主题，但在它们的运用应当如何得到规制的问题上仍未达成一致。"[①] 在这一点上，拉德院长无疑是正确的。[②] 在民事诉讼推定[③]的性质及适当规则的问题上，争论一直僵持不下，而由这些争论所引发的混淆也未曾展现出缓和的迹象。詹姆斯·布拉德利·塞耶在将近一百年前就说过："在我们的案例中，无数主张都是以推定名义出现的，而且在种类上是那样不同且无可比性，在构思和表述上是那样地随意，完全缺乏缜密思考，根本无法运用，更谈不上什么说服力。"最近，一个威望甚高的法院发表评论说：在诉讼审判中，如何运用推定并发挥其适当的作用，一直是困扰法官和律师的源头所在。这是教材编撰者、法学教师和法学文章作者们热衷写作的主题，却很少有人能够说清楚。

不幸的是，法院对推定性质详细阐述的效果，并不比评论家们的更好。在对推定的法律进行评论时，博学的汉德说："若是连法官们都对此感到迷惑，就没人能说清楚它到底是什么意思了。"

拉德院长的文章，考察了长久以来围绕推定的性质和作用而产生的争论，文中彰显了求实精神。他缜密的思维和清晰的表达使得该文成为拉德全部著作中的代表之作。他首先对争论的基本问题、主要人物的各种不同观点进行了细致分析，其清晰而朴实的论证风格可谓独树一帜。在此基础上，他转入对于规制推定适用的各种规则的思考，并为这些规则的采用提出了一个他认为最适合其用意且令人信服的学说。简而言之，拉德院长这篇文章所取得的学术成就，对一位学者来说已达到了巅峰，它必将被证明是对推定学说的一个重要贡献。

然而，鉴于他这篇文章仅是学术研究的一个内在组成部分，拉德的努力无

* 原文载《艾奥瓦法律评论》，第 66 卷，1981 年第 4 期。本译文原载《证据科学》，第 19 卷，2011 年第 4 期。

** 张家骥，中国人民大学法学院博士研究生。

① 拉德：《民事诉讼中的推定》，载《亚利桑那州法学杂志》（1977 Ariz. St. L. J. 275，275）。

② 例如，参见摩根：《推定》，载《华盛顿法学评论》，第 12 卷，1937 年，第 255 页。

③ 例如，参见塞耶：《普通法证据初论》，第 312～352 页，1898 年。

法终结关于推定的争论。或许是为相当现实的观点所驱动，法院和立法机关将不会简单地放弃对推定的适用，而学术界试图通过对推定的性质及适当作用加以区分并清晰阐述的方式，来调和在推定问题上的分歧。不幸的是，这些努力在很大程度上都是误导性的，因为如果脱离了其他证据手段和以其他名义运行的程序，推定根本就无法独立存在。

"推定"一词仅仅是一个标签，它被适用于与审判的适当模式和行为有关的广袤而又十分不同的裁决领域，在这些裁决过程中，事实是出于解决法律争端之目的而被证实的。这些裁决是，至少应当是，依赖规范性证据概念和政策而实现的。进一步说，那种认为"推定"仅仅适用于一系列证据性裁决的观点是错误的，这种错误是造成围绕推定的所有混乱和争论产生的原因，也是在推定的性质问题上不遗余力地详细论述而徒劳无功的原因。与其在"推定"一词诸多用法的调和上作无谓的努力，不如专注于分析这个标签在使用中潜在的一些证据问题。

然而，这种主张需要确证。确证可由以下论证来支持，即每一个涉及证据问题的解决，都能够而且常常是以无关任何推定概念的作用的相同方式实现的。而且，那种证明方式还表明，不依赖推定而解决所涉及的任何问题，都将降低因其不良后果的概率增加而产生的混淆风险。

一、推定的用处

推定可被用于实现 4 种不同的结果：它们可被用以构建裁决规则，以避免在审判中产生事实僵局；分配说服责任；为陪审团作出关于事实之间关系的指示；分配举证责任。然而，就像我们将看到的，这些结果中没有一个称得上是通过推定的运用或是由于有了推定而实现的，代之出现或至少应当出现的情况是，各种证据问题的解决都是根据所涉特定政策考虑，而不是根据推定是什么，以及之后系在结果上的"推定"标签是什么。此外，我们还会发现，如果不承认推定在普通证据问题的解决中只是个标签，其结果便是给推定的特性化带来了极大的混淆和模糊。

1. 对裁决规则的建构

一个案件的结果也许偶尔取决于这样一个问题，该问题没有令人满意的证据。一个例子是，在有死于同一起事故的当事人，却没有关于谁先死亡的证据的情况下，生者对死者名下财产的享有权（survivorship）问题。财产的分配也许取决于哪一个继承人幸存，因此，在没有生者对死者名下财产的享有权的证据时，一个僵局也许可以通过对财产分配的推论来解决。而且，依据规范性说服责任，可能导致不公平的结果。为了避免可能的僵局和不公平，各种各样的推定被创设出来，用于回答生者对死者名下财产的享有权问题。

确实，这种推定的创设，解决了生者对死者财产的享有权问题，但这种解决并不是由于推定中具有某些独一无二的特性而实现的，相反，问题得到解决，是由于裁决规则已被建立起来。比如，一种决定死亡顺序的解决办法将是“创设推定”，即两个当事人中一个幸存，即进行财产分配。然而，这相当于构建了一个规则，即在缺乏生者对死者财产的享有权证据的情况下，当事人财产的分配将与死亡一方当事人无关。无疑，推定的性质将有助于实现这一目标。相反，挂上“推定”的标签，只是用于裁决规则的构建，后者的创设理由完全与推定性质中隐含的概念无关，人们完全可以创建一个功能相同的规则，不用“推定”这个词也无妨。

不能正视一些相关的证据性问题，并由此而产生混淆，在失踪 7 年后为死亡的推定以及有关死亡时间的伴随推定中也有所体现。当某人失踪或者杳无音讯达 7 年之久时，死亡推定即宣告成立。一个裁决规则再次以推定为幌子而建立起来：在连续 7 年失踪之后，法律制度将视该人仿佛已经死亡。这个规则背后的政策是，让受失踪者影响的人们的事务处于这种悬而未决的状态是不公平的，尤其是在失踪者很有可能确已死亡的情况下。然而，精确确定失踪人何时死亡，也许是重要的，比如，继承人的权利可能受日期影响。因此，第二个推定通常又被创设出来，即该人死于第七年的最后一天。

不幸的是，当一方提出反驳时，这一前一后两种推定的使用就会出现问题，它给该推定事实的反对方提供了证明陪审团裁决正当性的充分证据。假设在一个司法辖区，依照这样一个规则，对一个失踪 7 年之人的财产分配提起异议诉讼。进一步假设，如果该人死于第七年的最后一天将会有一种财产分配方法；但如果此人并非死在这一天，财产将会以另一种不同的方式分配。最后假设，死亡时间推定的反对方设法提出充足的证据，证明该死者并非死于第七年的最后一天以寻求一项陪审团裁决，但该陪审团却并不相信该证据。

这种案件结果会引发另一种僵局。由于遭到“反驳”，死亡时间推定便从这种情况中被剔除了，但又没有令人信服的证据来确定死亡时间。因此，可能的结果会是原告败诉，因为他无法满足说服责任。然而，让诸如此类案件中的争端产生这样的结果几乎是没有意义的，这种结果能否避免取决于提起诉讼一方的偶然性。而且，只有在该案件运行过程中存在可反驳推定的情况下，偶然性才能发挥控制作用。

相比之下，如果裁决规则没有把它考虑为推定，从而产生扭曲，困难之解决办法就变得清晰了。规则的建立就是要避免一种僵局。如果相同的僵局被略加修改的形式取代，其目的就很难达成。因此，解决办法是建立一个安置另一种僵局可能性的略微不同的规则。比如，一种解决办法将是规定，死者的财产将在第七年的最后一天被分配，除非实际死亡日期以优势证据在审判中得到确定。根据这项规则，财产将遵循管辖权的裁决规则而被分配，而不是根据谁提起诉讼的偶然性。这将有利于更好地适应管辖权政策。

性质略微不同的不必要的歧义，也可能归因于没有意识到 7 年失踪推定只是为解决证明的特定问题而构建的一个简单裁决规则。比如，如果失踪者的配偶 5 年后再婚，会发生什么？是否犯重婚罪？既然未到 7 年之限，那么失踪者就被假定还活着，从而使第二次婚姻的效力受到质疑。然而，也有一种对第二次婚姻效力的推定适用于再婚。这样就出现了两种被视为冲突的推定，法院在对“冲突的推定”进行漫长讨论之后，通常会遵循冲突解决办法。通常情况下，给出的答案是，婚姻效力的推定“胜过”失踪者仍活着的推定。

如果法院简单而直接地去做那些本该通过运用推定而间接完成的事情，那么冲突性推定的修辞学就没有必要了。要求达到 7 年时间的失踪才宣告法律上的死亡，肯定存在其所追寻的利益。婚姻制度也追寻其他同样重要的利益。一种假设可能会在案件中引起利益如何交叉的问题：很可能，基于对家庭单元的社会关注，便证明失踪 5 年后再婚是正当的；也可能并非如此。无论如何，这个问题被解决了。把该问题视为一种冲突性推定的情况，并未促进问题的解决。真正的问题在于，是否应该制定一项允许在配偶失踪 5 年后再婚的规则。过于关注“冲突性推定”的标签，只是转移了对该问题本身的关注。

那么，很明显，当推定被用于创立裁决规则时，实际过程是一个规则被创立了，然后将“推定”的标签系在这个规则上。当然，以那种方式使用“推定”这个词没有什么必然错误，只要我们牢记在做什么就是了。然而，一直以来的问题是，一旦我们使用了这个标签，它往往就会变得根深蒂固，以至于对争端的解决产生负面影响。因此，我们应该摒弃这个标签的使用。

2. 说服责任的分配

在民事审判中，与案由相关的各种事实问题的真伪即对事实认定者的说服责任，通常是由原告承担的，但在一些特殊问题上，立法机关和法院有时候也会把说服事实认定者的责任置于被告方。立法权和司法权以此在当事人之间分配说服责任的方式，已得到确立，该权力的行使回应了各种政策考虑。

当一个问题的说服责任被直接设置给被告时，通常是指一项积极抗辩。比如，（美国）《联邦民事诉讼规则》规则 8（c）列举了一些积极抗辩，必须由被告人进行辩护和证明。不过，说服责任有时候根据推定进行分配，将说服责任转移给该推定的反对者。例如，在生父确认程序中若丈夫否认其合法性，就有了一个关于孩子出生于婚姻关系存续期间的合法性推定，这要求被告就孩子为非婚生而说服事实认定者。

然而，就对被告来说存在着一个关于“分配或转移说服责任的合法性推定”而言，这和说存在一个要求被告证明该事实的“非婚生子女积极抗辩”，其实是在作一个作用相同的陈述。确实，提及作为转移或分配责任的推定，其唯一理由是强调，为原告在民事案件中承担说服责任的惯常规则创设了一个例外。因此，一个“分配说服责任的推定”在应用于积极抗辩时，仅仅是一个可选择的标签。正如创设裁决规则的推定一样，在推定概念中并无促进说服责任分配之说。相反，转移说服责任的推定仅仅是积极抗辩，其创设基于相同的政策考虑，都是为了告知裁决分配说服责任。实际上，积极抗辩是以其惯用标签来判断，还是以推定来判断，似乎纯属偶然。

然而，需要进一步考察的是，有一个转移推定责任的变种。“推定”这个标签有时候被应用于一组可被称为附条件的强制性责任（conditional imperative）的证据关系。当且仅当附条件的需要成立时，说服责任转移到先证实某些其他事实的当事方。

积极抗辩和附条件的强制性责任的区别从一个简单例子就可以看出来。假设，一个继承人起诉强迫分配一个失踪且杳无音信 7 年以上者的财产。如果选择这样做，一个司法管辖权就能把立遗嘱人仍然活着的证明责任一边倒地强加于财产保管人一方。若如此，结果将会引发一场积极抗辩。因此，当继承人起诉财产保管人时，该保管人就能够通过证明立遗嘱人仍然在世而胜诉。另一种方法是，一个司法管辖权可以要求权利请求人证明立遗嘱人死亡，但也可以对立遗嘱人失踪和杳无音信超过 7 年提供证明，而财产保管人必须证明立遗嘱人仍然活着。因此，证明相关事实的责任通常落在原告一方，但如果 7 年失踪被证实，证明立遗嘱人仍然活着的责任就转移到被告一方。在后一种情况下，附条件的强制性责任便成立了——根据对基础事实的证明，该保管人必须证明第二个事实，否则，将败诉。

通常，这种附条件的强制性责任被认为是由推定创设的。这类推定不同于一般积极抗辩之处，在于其关键方面——陪审团经常被指示可以作出选择。在这种情况下，法官指示陪审团，说服责任在原告一方，除非陪审团被说服立遗嘱人确系失踪并杳无音信达到 7 年。如果陪审团确实被说服，则证明立遗嘱人仍活着的说服责任便转移给财产保管人。

关于附条件的强制性责任的陪审团指示的存在，并未给推定带来什么值得一提的东西，却可能因为那个误导性词汇的使用而产生的混淆。本来，所有附条件的强制性责任实际上就是一种裁决，不过是一个关于说服责任应当如何分配的普通证据问题的裁决。这个具备了基本合理性的裁决的得出，并非因为适用了推定，而是出于政策原因，“推定”这个标签仅仅是依附在政策之上罢了。

然而，更重要的是，当谈及附条件的强制性责任时，“推定”一词的使用再一次证明该标签的使用可能会引发不良后果。也许因为这类推定一般都被视为规制陪审团裁决的手段，陪审团常常要负责决定基础事实——此处的失踪 7 年与否——的真假。然而，当这个过程被视为推定但未产生扭曲影响时，事情就变得十分清楚了：陪审团不应当为了达到分配附条件事实之说服责任的目的，而决定基础事实是否存在。这种决定事关初步事实之性质，因此，它应该由法官作出。

请考虑一下司法管辖权为何给某些其他事实的存在附加了说服责任的条件。理由是，分配说服责任的决定会受到争议事实真伪的影响。例如，假定一个司法管辖权始终根据对概率的预先评估来分配说服责任，那就可以得出结论说，由于立遗嘱人正常地活着，任何宣称有权分配的人都不该去证明它。然而，一旦立遗嘱人被证明已失踪或杳无音信达到 7 年，先前的概率也许就变了，立遗嘱人更有可能死了。因此，对案件子集问题的一般裁决规则的适用就产出这样的结果，即保管人现在应当就立遗嘱人还活着承担说服事实认定者的责任。

那么，7 年失踪是一个根据证据规则而得出的事实。在这个问题上，要确定两个人是否因特免权规则而结婚，是根据口头证据规则提供证明，还是就这一点使举证责任得到满足，其实并没有什么区别。因此，从便利性、一致性和专业化角度考虑，应当把这些事实的认定分配给法官，由法官对于立遗嘱人是否已杳无音信或失踪 7 年作出初步决定，然后再相应地分配说服责任。

从表面看来，在经常漠视审判法官的适当作用基本上是某歧义的功能，该歧义产生于错误地把这些证据问题的解决视为推定的性质和相伴而生的认为陪审团应当决定基础事实的错误所具有的功能。这种理解上的失误已引发了许多其他重大误解，其中一个重大误解再次涉及冲突性推定，要经受严格审查。

在当下语境中，麦考密克院长举了一个关于“冲突性推定”的范例：

一位寡妇声称她是丈夫的遗孀，主张自己享有丈夫的财产权，并证明了她和丈夫的结婚日期。对抗方则证明，她和这位丈夫结婚前三四年，这个所谓的寡妇就嫁过另一个男人。该寡妇的证明给她带来了婚姻有效推定的利益。对抗方的证明，则引起一个关于身份存续期间或一旦证明存在条件的一般推定，以及一个婚姻关系存续期间的具体推定。

如果第一段婚姻的存续驳倒了第二段婚姻的有效性，反之亦然，那么麦考密克院长所描述的推定便不能同时合法存在，因为，在一个特定时间点上，只有一方对一个问题承担说服责任。因此，推定被认为是有冲突的，并且问题就在于如何解决冲突。麦考密克院长提供的答案是：应该保留“分量更重的”推定——在我们的假设中，第二段婚姻具备有效性——或者作为选择，去创建一个在后续婚姻中较早的婚姻已终止的新推定，因而要求该主张的反对方去作相反的证明。麦考密克院长的解决办法是有效的，但是，他们这样做与推定中固有的一些概念毫无关系。实际上，他们进一步论证了这个术语的破产。

首先，提议的两种解决方法实际上是一个。如果第二次婚姻的有效性“残存”的推定，将要求对方去证明第一次婚姻从未终止，那么，这恰恰是第二种解决方案的思路。然而，更重要的是，所谓“新的”或“残存的”推定，仅仅是对事实的混淆，麦考密克院长所做的，是为了该证据问题的公正、权威和充分性提出解决办法。婚姻存续的推定反映着一种信念，即一种关系的创设暗示了它的存续。相比之下，婚姻有效性的推定，反映了我们赋予这种制度以重要性。正是因为它如此重要，就不难理解为什么攻击一个婚姻的有效性，就要求须用较高的说服责任标准来证明它的无效性，没有更多的关于另一次三四年前的婚姻的证据，肯定会被认为没有达到证明后一段婚姻无效所必须达到的证明标准。

然而，假设第一段婚姻发生在第二段婚姻之前三四周（或小时），那么，第二段婚姻有效性的“分量更重”的推定还依旧存在吗？如果从表面价值来判断麦考密克院长的解决方案，答案是肯定的。然而，答案应当是否定的，因为第一段婚姻的时间离得越近，第二段婚姻有效性的可能性就相应降低。在某个时间点上，这种可能性如果非常低的话，就可以证明得出第二段婚姻无效的结论。总之，在转移说服责任的推定中实际上每出现一个所谓冲突，都会陷入证据充分性的难题。

在这种情况下，冲突性推定的问题进一步说明，除了制造模糊和歧义之外，依赖推定去做那些可以直接去做的事情，是不会产生任何效果的。还可以举出另外一些（有关）不必要混淆和歧义的例子来佐证这个结论，但主要之点已得到充分证明。法院和立法机关分配说服责任的权力，以及法院根据充分证据作出决定的权力，已经得到良好的确立。对推定的依赖，并未以任何方式增强那种权力。然而，由于它会产生混淆的风险，所以没有任何理由继续以这种方式来使用这个误导性的术语。

3. 就事实之间的关系给陪审团的指示

就一项事实的证明来说，陪审团常常得到的指示是，另一个事实的推定的出现，使第一个事实的证明成为第二个事实的证据；或者，他们得到的指示是，该推定本身“是”陪审团在评议时考虑的证据，或与证据具有“同样的分量”。通常，这些指示是在被证实的事实暗示了第二个事实时作出的，但在被证实的事实与第二个事实具有极为薄弱的逻辑关系时也会作出这样的指示。据说，后一种情况下的指示是合理的，因为立法机关和法院如果非常倾向于运用推定，就有权给被证实的事实附加“额外权重”。然而，推定之玄学只能使实际上发生了什么事变得晦涩。关于处理具有逻辑关联的事实的推定之证据分量的指示，仅仅是对证据的一种不增加任何信息的评论。相比之下，尽力提供已证明的事实，比证明它们之间的逻辑合理性有更大的意义，这才是对第二个事实履行说服责任的方法。

首先考虑这样一个指示：一旦事实 A 被证明，就有一个事实 B 的推定，并且陪审团将会考虑事实 A 或推定本身作为事实 B 之证据的分量。进一步假定，陪审团或立法机关得出结论认为，事实 B 通常可由事实 A 推论而出。显然，该指示的要义是，鼓励陪审团在事实 A 被证实的基础上认定事实 B。这种鼓励来自法官以结论性方式（作出的）给陪审团的关于事实的指示，包含着法官或立法机关对事实间关系的看法。当法官担心陪审团不能鉴别事实间的关系时，法官就会如此给予推定性指示，从而增加陪审团以法官认为是错误结果为错误结果的可能性。结果是，该指示旨在把陪审团置于一种睿智的决策者地位，从而增加了陪审团得出法官或立法机关认为是正确结论的可能性。

这样一个指示的效果是，通过增强事实 A 的作用，修正陪审团在推论过程中出现的行为方式。这种效果与对证据强度的司法评论是无法区分的。给出这种推定性指示的理由，与司法评论的理由相同，本来就是预期的结果。所以，这种推定就是对证据进行司法评论的一种形式而已。

然而，这种推定性指示和传统的对证据的司法评论之间存在着的一项差别，进一步证明了，我们轻率依赖推定所产生的有害影响。明确的司法评论试图告知陪审团与其决定可能相关的因素以及它们为什么可以相关，而推定性指示仅仅告知陪审团在事实 A 得到证明的基础上，会产生事实 B 的推定。而很少或没有作出努力去告知陪审团，该指示意味着什么，或者，为什么一个特定结果是适当的。因此，一项推定性指示可能易于促成非理性的裁决过程，尽管它也许还可以在潜在推论有效的程度上增加更准确结果的概率。

一个非理性推论过程，是由给陪审团的推定性指示促成的，其向陪审团推荐了“把推定考虑为证据”这样不可思议的精神壮举。正如摩根教授所质疑的：“人们怎么能将推定与证据相提并论或混为一谈呢？究竟是出于什么心理？”当然，答案是，陪审团不会“把推定考虑为”证据，因为它不是证据，它仅仅是一个被用于感知事实之间关系的标签。因此，这种指示的目的是，或应该是，鼓励陪审团“权衡推定中潜在的事实以及可以伴随那些事实而来的推论”。然而，陪审团仅仅从现实的角度被告知什么是应该做的，仅仅被告知应该把推定考虑为证据这样一个不可能的任务。那显然，由于陪审团无法理性地评价这种指示，由此而来的裁决过程的非理性也许易于被这种指示强化。

即使潜在的推论是有效的，关于一项将推定考虑为证据的陪审团指示也是相当麻烦的，因为它会削弱陪审团的作用。陪审团可能作出一个决定，并非基于对事实的独立思考并从中得出的合理推论，而是遵从该指示中的立法或司法裁判的表达，即所得出的推定是某个其他事实的证明。当有人可能会为结果更精确的潜在可能性而喝彩时，我却怀疑存在这样的共识，不应该以这种削弱陪审团在审判过程中的作用的方式来获得准确性。

具有讽刺意味的是，这类推定性指示最可能成为一种手段，在很大程度上避免了立法机关对司法评论施加的限制。鉴于许多法院给陪审团事实指导的能力十分有限，必定“常常……（正）试图以‘推定’冒充法院认为很可能从已知事实得出结论”。靠这么做，法官可以声称服从许多州已经通行的对司法评论的限制，同时可以向陪审团提供一些指导。当然，讽刺在于，避免对证据进行明确评论的意愿，显然会造成评论信息的匮乏，从而导致非理性的陪审团裁决。

因此，这再次表明，对推定概念不必要的依赖产生了有害的后果。人们可能愿意，也可能不愿意允许对证据进行评论。不过，是否允许评论都与任何称为推定之事的性质无关。对推定概念的依赖仅仅使真正的问题变模糊了，那就是，在任何情况下对证据的司法评论都是被允许的。

当一个推定被作为证据权衡时，便放弃了对事实之间实际关系的默认信赖，它常常给予事实 A 超出其逻辑意义的“额外分量”。在这些情况下，事实 A 与 B 本来没有什么逻辑相关性，但给出的指示仍然是，对事实 A 的证明引发出一个可被考虑为事实 B 的证据的推定。审视这种指示的一种方式是，将其看作对证据的不准确的评论。然而，不准确评论的效果是暗中转移了说服责任，举个例子就可以很好地阐明这一点。

请考虑一个过失审判，其中存在一个共同过失问题，必须由原告以优势证据加以反驳。假定，根据举出的证据，一个睿智、理性的陪审团将得出结论说，原告很可能有共同过失。该裁决有利于被告，因为原告未能履行说服责任。然而，假定审判法官对陪审团作出指示说，原告受到伤害的证明导致了一个对原告方合理注意的推定，并应由陪审团在审议时考虑为证据。进一步假定，作为该指示的结果，同一陪审团这次得出结论说，原告共同过失的几率只有40%。该裁决现在有利于原告。为逃避这个裁决，被告将不得不举出原告有过失的更强的证据。

假定，被告预料到审判法官对上述推定作出了指示，从而举出了更强有力的证据，证据现在足够、充分，以至于陪审团得出原告很可能有共同过失的结论，因而作出了有利于被告的认定。如果睿智的陪审团在没有该指示的情况下评价这些更强的证据，肯定会得出共同过失几率大于50%的结论。那么，就像理性、睿智的事实认定者作出的判断那样，由于有了该指示，被告就需要证明比仅仅证实原告有共同过失更多的东西，这要求被告作出更充分的证明，以达到更高却虚无缥缈的标准。

这样一种指示的作用是创设一个积极抗辩。尽管陪审团形式上将应用一般规则，把证明没有共同过失的责任赋予原告方，但实际情况却是，该指示降低了原告方对没有共同过失的证明责任，随之而来的是，提高了被告证明此问题的责任。一旦被告不得不适应一个高于一般规则所允许的证明标准，便创设了一个积极抗辩。

因此，对于可考虑为证据的推定作出指示的效果，不是在对该证据作评论，就是在操控说服责任。在这两种情况下，对推定概念的依赖都无法使该过程变得更顺利，反而模糊了眼下的问题。靠推定对证据作出司法评论，使我们避开了直面评论之适当作用的问题。同时，我们给陪审团的裁决过程注入了非理性的成分。由于完全无法知道这些指示会被陪审团翻译成多高的说服责任，所以，依靠这种转移说服责任的推定，我们可能已为该裁决过程注入了更大的非理性成分。此外，不同的陪审团无疑会以不同的方式看待该指示及其暗中强加的责任。所以，该指示可能对陪审团的某些特别裁决造成额外的负面影响。

4. 对举证责任的分配

推定的最后一个用途是分配举证责任。尽管与诉讼案件相关的大多数问题的举证责任通常都由原告承担，就像他们通常还承担着说服责任一样，但有时候，由于推定的存在，举证责任会转移给被告。然而，推定“标签”背后是关于各方当事人适当证据性关系的一个极普通的决定，其作出原因与任何归结为推定的概念完全无关。

首先，分配举证责任的司法权和立法权已很健全。因此，如果一种管辖权希望将举证责任置于一方当事人，大可直接去做。而用“推定”一词来做这件事，一点也不会影响这种权力的范围。而且，对于转移举证责任之推定创设的两种正当理由——鼓励举证和促进审判——的考察，不仅将证明根本没有独立起作用的推定概念，而且在这种依赖推定的语境下还制造了不必要的混乱和论战。

将举证责任置于一方当事人，的确可以鼓励举证，但把这个分配过程称作推定并没有太大的激励作用。把举证责任置于一方当事人，确实给不能举证提供了一种制裁——驳回诉讼或指令裁决，但这种制裁是举证责任的应有功能，而非推定的独立属性。而且，很难想象如今在一个案件中，可能的驳回诉讼制裁会比证据开示的解决方案产生更多的证据。因此，为了产生证据而依赖推定来转移举证责任，不仅会使本可直接完成的工作间接化，而且也不再服务于其原本目的。

使用推定的第二个正当理由，转移举证责任——促进审判，其境况并不比第一个更好。有些固有的（推定）问题未必与审判相关，我们通常不理会它们也可处理得很好。描述那个转移过程的一种方式是说，我们将“假定”该问题没有异议，除非被告人就该问题提出“反驳”该推定的证据。这只是举证责任被分配给一方当事人的另一种说法，“推定”一词的用途只是这个语境中的一个便利的“标签”。但不幸的是，这个标签的使用再次引起了混乱，应当避免这种事情发生。这种混乱最重要的例证是，论战已经发展为关于这种推定何以能被反驳的争论。

“对推定进行反驳”，在这个语境中仅仅意味着满足举证责任。不过，显然是由于未能把推定视为子虚乌有，因其他理由而达成一个决定之标签适用的情况除外，一些法院才得出结论说：转移举证责任的推定可以被反驳，而那是陪审团应当作出的决定。因此，已经开发出来的判定这些推定是否受到反驳的方案，只能被形容为怪异。例如，一些法院认为，如果一个推定的对抗方提出了陪审团认为充足的证据，从而证明对一个相反事实的认定具有正当性，即使陪审团未被说服，该推定也是可反驳的。另一些法院则认为，对抗方必须提出充分证据来证明，一个没有被陪审团明确表示怀疑的陪审团裁决是正当的。还有其他一些观点，这里不赘述。

如果这些法院根据该错误假定无法运行某些称为推定在起作用的事情，它们肯定会意识到，这个无比复杂且显然不可行的方案是完全没必要的。不管举证责任分配的理由是什么，对审判法官来说，举证责任是否得到满足，是一个决定运用司法裁判权希望法官运用的何种标准的问题。如果认识到这个简单事实，围绕转移举证责任推定这个方面的争论就会像它应当的那样简单地消失。

二、通向更加理性的途径

在其所有各种表现形式中，推定只是一个在各方当事人证据性关系上用于进行选择的标签，除了与一些政策理由相关之外，“推定”一词没有任何独立的含义。不仅如此，使用这个标签所产生的明显负面作用是，没有提供或至少没有提供更多的补偿效益。相应地，对于“推定难题”，唯一明智的解决办法是停止使用这个术语，而直面我们裁判制度的解决办法所可能带来的各种证据问题。

伴随弃用推定的一个可以想象的结果是，由于摆脱了推定的法律所强加的各种限制，法院将开始为其面临的各种证据问题提供更多不同的解决方案。在某种意义上，这个提议与先前的一个建议非常相似，即每一推定的效果应当根据其产生原因而定。那个建议很快就被称为“一项几乎不可能的任务，一个比疾病更可怕的诅咒，一个更理性但却不如一个简单规则所提供的解决办法更受欢迎”。同样，麦考密克院长也得出结论说：“试图根据审判便利性、实验概率性和一方当事人事实证明路径的优越性等不同来源而进行分类，或者从外部政策考虑，而区别处理（推定）问题，似乎都是不切实际的。”

这些批评无论理由多么充分，都是误导性的。提供大批规制证明责任配置的规则，并对证据进行司法评论，来取代推定法律的一致性，很可能是不切实际的。不过，其不切实际的原因与推定无关，相反，正因为可能导致出现一套过于复杂的规制司法评论和证明责任实践的规则，它才不切实际。

奇怪的是，人们所写的文章中很少抱怨评论和证明责任规则过于复杂，甚至那些了解推定和证明责任分析之间关系的人们，也只把这种抱怨限于推定的法律。然而，这种明显不一致的原因是容易理解的。对任何诉讼问题来说，要决定证明责任归于哪一方，或是否允许评论，只需要简单地查一下成文法和先例就行了。相比之下，在涉及推定的成文法或意见中，根本无从确定该术语的确切含义，除非，在极其罕见的情况下，立法机关或法院煞费苦心地提供一个适当的定义。避免这种含糊不清的一种方法，是在裁判权中建立一个统一的推定规则。也正是出于避免含糊不清的愿望，才产生了对有关单一推定规则的需求。更好的解决方案是完全弃用推定，并通过直接适用明确的证据规则，通过对于目前正因推定的间接使用而实现的潜在政策的考察，来实现这样的目的。

最后还有一个需要注意的问题。这篇文章的中心论点是，根本就没有推定这样一种东西，然而，证据法领域中的权威人士们，却对于我试图证明并不存在的某种东西的"性质"问题进行了长期而激烈的争论。该争论中最著名的阵营包括以塞耶和威格莫尔为代表的一方，以及以摩根为代表的另一方。塞耶和威格莫尔主张，推定应当转移举证责任；而摩根则认为，推定应当转移说服责任。然而，对这场争论更仔细的考察，仅仅证实了这样的结论，即推定没有独立的含义。

威格莫尔和塞耶以一个简单的理由将"推定"限制于转移举证责任，即这个术语的其他使用都涉及法院和立法机关已经拥有的权力的实施，为此已提供了一个标签。两个人都认为，说服责任能够出于政策理由来分配；并且都信奉对证据进行评论的司法权力。因此，"推定"所服务的唯一目的，就是为关于"影响举证责任的法律裁定"提供一种便利方法。

摩根似乎也很早就认识到，法院在推定这个标题下所做的事情，是可以直接完成的。事实上，他对推定的最早想法表明："推定应根据证明其产生和存在的正当性理由而进行分类"。他还认为，他的"建议只是呼唤与实际上普遍应用于分配说服责任的推理的同类者，虽然其结果是用机械公式表达出来的"。

然而，他的建议对法院并未产生太大影响。围绕推定的模糊与混乱仍在持续，而摩根显然变得坚信，在一个赋予"推定"一致含义的简单规则被提出之前，这种混乱将继续下去。而且，那个含义不能是威格莫尔和塞耶提出的那种，因为那会对大多数推定产生不适当的影响。因此，摩根断定，一般规则应当是，推定转移说服责任。然而，即使他信奉那个规则，他也认识到什么将会击败它。总之，塞耶、威格莫尔和摩根之间的公开争论，并非针对推定性质上的差别，而是对法律制度理性行使其责任的能力持有不同意见。

我还怀疑，拉德院长注重实效的方法是出于与埃德蒙·摩根相似的忧虑，即担心在推定问题上是否能得到明白无误的证明。尽管法律制度在坚持使用推定的问题上一如既往地表现出毫不妥协，但也证明仍然不能以一种明智的方式使用它们。因此，我认为，那些希望看到为推定构建一个单一规则的学者们所偏爱的解决办法，是不能令人满意的。相反，我们必须努力把培训律师和法官的工作做得更好，以消除他们对“推定”概念的无知。实际上我认为，这种失败对于那些在法律制度中从事日常事务的人们来说倒还不那么要紧，要紧的是，对于身处法学院的我们来说，允许推定概念残存在我们的以后要成为律师和法官的学生们的头脑中。我们必须更好地培养他们，我相信这也是拉德院长满腔热情支持的一个目标。

Presumptions in Civil Actions Reconsidered*

Ronald J. Allen

Mason Ladd introduced his last article by nothing that "[d] espite the extensive commentary that has been devoted to the subject of presumptions, there is still no agreement on how their use should be governed…"① On that score, Dean Ladd was unmistakably correct. ② The long-standing controversy over the nature and proper rule of presumptions in civil actions③ continues undiminished, and the confusion generated by the controversy similarly shows no signs of abating. Nearly a hundred years ago, James Bradley Thayer remarked that "the numberless propositions figuring in our cases under the name of presumptions, are quite too heterogeneous and noncomparable in kind, and quite too loosely conceived of and expressed, to be used or reasoned about without much circumspection." More recently, a respected court has commented that the proper function and use of a presumption in the trial of lawsuits continues to be the source of much confusion on the part of bench and bar alike. It is a subject on which text writers, teachers of law, and authors of legal articles have written much and clarified little.

And, unfortunately, the efforts of the courts to elaborate on the nature of presumptions have fared no better than those of the commentators. Commenting of the law of presumptions, Learned Hand said that "[j] udges have mixed it up until nobody can tell what on earth it means."

Dean Ladd's article examined the long-standing controversy surrounding

* Printed From the Iowa Law Review, May, 1981, vol. 66/No. 4. Copy right by the University of (Iowa Law Review).

① Ladd, *Presumptions in Civil Actions*, 1977 Ariz. St. L. J. 275, 275.

② See, e. g., Morgan, *Presumptions*, 12 Wash. L. Rev. 255, 255 (1937).

③ See, e. g., J. Thayer, *A Preliminary Treatise on Evidence at the Common Law* 312-52 (1898).

the nature and role of presumptions, and his article is vintage Ladd, evidencing the pragmatism, carefulness of thought, and clarity of expression that he brought to all his work. He first meticulously analyzed the basis of the controversy, demonstrating in his clear and unadorned style precisely where and how the various protagonists differed. From there, he moved to a consideration of the various rules that have been propounded to regulate the use of presumptions, and he provided a typically convincing rationale for the adoption of the rule that he concluded was best suited to its purpose. Dean Ladd's last article was, in short, a fitting capstone to his marvelously productive years as a scholar, and it will certainly prove to be a valuable addition to the extensive scholarship concerning presumptions.

For reasons that are intrinsic to the body of scholarship of which his article is a part, however, Ladd's efforts will not bring the controversy over presumptions to an end. Perhaps motivated by the quite realistic view that courts and legislatures simply will not forego the use of presumptions, that scholarship has attempted to harmonize the disparate treatment presumptions have received by trying to isolate and articulate the nature and appropriate role of presumptions. Unfortunately, these efforts are for the most part misdirected, because presumptions do not exist independently of other evidentiary devices and procedures that go by other names.

The word "presumption" is simply a label that has been applied to a widely disparate set of decisions concerning the proper mode of trial and the manner in which facts are to be established for the purpose of resolving legal disputes. These decisions are, or at least should be, reached by relying on normal evidentiary concepts and policies. Moreover, it is the failure to recognize that the world "presumption" is simply a label applied to a range of evidentiary decisions that has caused essentially all the confusion and controversy surrounding presumptions, as well as doomed to failure the extensive efforts to elaborate on the nature of presumptions. Rather than engaging in the futile task of attempting to reconcile the many usages of the word "presumption," efforts would be better spent by analyzing the evidentiary problems that underlie the use of the label.

Such a proposition needs corroboration, however. That corroboration can be supplied by demonstrating that each involves the resolution of evidentiary problems that can be, and often are, resolved in functionally the same manner without reference to any concept of a presumption. Moreover, that demonstration will also show that resolving whatever issue involved without relying on presumptions will reduce the risk of confusion with its attendant increased probability of an undesirable outcome.

1. USES OF PRESUMPTIONS

Presumptions have been used to accomplish four distinct ends. They have been used to construct rules of decision to avoid factual impasse at trial; to allocate burdens of persuasion; to instruct the jury on the relationship between facts; and to allocate burdens of production. As will be shown, however, none of the results purportedly achieved through the use of presumptions are in fact achieved because of presumptions. What occurs instead, or at least what should occur, is that various evidentiary problems are resolved on the basis of the particular policy considerations involved rather than on the basis of what a presumption is, and the label "presumption" is then attached to the result. Moreover, as will also be shown, the confusion and ambiguity that characterize presumptions are largely results of the failure to recognize that presumptions are merely labels that are applied to the resolution of standard evidentiary problems.

1. Constructing Rules of Decision

The outcome of a case may occasionally depends upon an issue for which there is no satisfactory evidence. An example is the determination of survivorship in cases in which the parties died in the same accident and there is no evidence as to who died first. Distribution of the property among the heirs may depend upon who survived, and thus without evidence of survivorship an impasse may develop that could interfere with the distribution. Moreover, relying on the normal rules of burden of persuasion may yield unjust results. In order to avoid a possible impasse and unfairness, various presumptions have been created to supply an answer to the question of survivorship.

Creating such presumptions does, to be sure, resolve the problems of survivorship, but the resolution is not accomplished because of something unique in the nature of a presumption. Rather, the problem is resolved because a rule of decision has been constructed. For example, one solution to the problem of determining the order of death would be to "create the presumption" that each party survived the other and to distribute the property accordingly. This is equivalent, however, to constructing the rule that, in the absence of evidence of survivorship, the property of the parties shall be distributed without reference to the death of the other party. There is nothing peculiar to the nature of presumptions that would facilitate accomplishing that objective. Rather, the label "presumption" would simply have been applied to the construction of a rule of decision that was created for reasons entirely independent of any concept implicit in the nature of presumptions, and a functionally identical rule could be constructed without using the word "presumption."

The failure to confront directly the relevant evidentiary problem, and the resulting confusion generated by that failure, can also be seen in the presumption of death after seven years absence and the concomitant presumption as to time of death. When a person has been absent and unheard from for seven years, a presumption of death is said to arise. Again, a rule of decision has been constructed under the guise of a presumption: After seven years of unbroken absence and silence, the legal system will proceed as if the person were dead. The policy behind the rule is that it is unfair to require that the affairs of other persons affected by those of the missing person be held in abeyance indeterminately, especially when there is a good chance that the missing person is in fact dead. It may be of importance, however, to determine precisely when the missing person died. For example, the rights of heirs might be affected by the date. Accordingly, a second presumption is usually created that the person died on the last day of the seventh year.

Unfortunately, the use of these two presumptions in tandem raises problems when one rebuts, it is produce sufficient evidence to the contrary of the presumed fact to justify a jury verdict. Assume that an action in a jurisdiction with such a rule is brought to contest the distribution of the property of a person who has been missing for seven years. Assume further that if the person died on the last day of the seventh year the property would be distributed in one manner; but if he died on some other day, the property would be distributed differently. Finally, assume that the opponent of the presumption of time of death manages to produce sufficient evidence to justify a jury verdict that the decedent did not die on the last day of seventh year， but that the jury does not believe the evidence.

The result in such a case would be another impasse. The presumption of time of death， having been "rebutted，" is out of the case， but there is no convincing evidence establishing the date of death. Thus， the probable outcome will be that the plaintiff will lose， because he will not be able to satisfy his burden of persuasion. However， it hardly makes sense to let the outcome of disputes in cases such as these hinge on the fortuity of who filed suit if such a result can be avoided. Moreover， fortuity will control only of one assumes that there is a rebuttable presumption at work in the case.

If， by contrast， the rule of decision is viewed without the distortion caused by referring to it as a presumption， the resolution of the difficulty becomes clear. The rule has been constructed to avoid an impasse. It hardly serves its purpose if it can be supplanted by a slightly modified form of the same impasse. Accordingly， the resolution is to construct a slightly different rule that accommodates the possibility of another impasse. For example， one resolution would be to provide that the property will be distributed as though the decedent died on the last day of the seventh year， unless the actual date of death is established at trial by a preponderance of the evidence. Under this rule， the property will be distributed according to the rules of decision of the jurisdiction rather than according to the fortuity of who filed suit， which should better serve the policies of the jurisdiction.

Unnecessary ambiguity of a slightly different nature can also arise from the failure to perceive that the presumption of death from seven years absence is simply a rule of decision constructed to resolve certain problems of proof. What happens， for example， if the spouse of the absent person remarries after five years? Has bigamy occurred? Since seven years have not passed， the missing person is presumed to be alive， thus casting doubt on the validity of the second marriage. However， there is also a presumption of the validity of the second marriages that is applicable to the remarriage. Thus， these two presumptions are seen to be in conflict， and the resolution of conflict by the courts normally follows after a lengthy discussion of "conflicting presumptions." Typically, the answer given is that the presumption of the validity of the marriage "outweighs" that of the absent person being alive.

The rhetoric of conflicting presumptions would not be necessary if the courts would simply do directly what is now done indirectly through the use of presumptions. There are certain interests served by requiring seven years to pass before declaring a person legally dead. There are other equally important interests served by the institution of marriage. The issue posed by cases such as the one hypothesized is how those interests intersect. It may very well be that the societal concern for the family unit justifies remarriage after five years absence; it may also be that is does not. However that issue is resolved, the resolution is not facilitated by viewing the issue as being a case of conflicting presumptions. The real issue is whether a rule should be created that allows remarriage after a spouse has been absent for five years. Focusing on the label "conflicting presumptions" will merely divert attention from that issue.

It is clear, then, that when presumptions are used to create rules of decision, the actual process is that a rule is constructed and the label "presumption" is then attached to it. There is nothing necessarily wrong with using the word "presumption" in that fashion, of course, so long as we keep well in mind what is being done. The problem has been, however, that upon using the label it tends to assume a life of its own that on occasion has a detrimental impact on the resolution of disputes. Accordingly, we should forego the use of the label.

2. Allocating Burdens of Persuasion

In a civil trial, the responsibility for persuading the fact finder as to the truth or falsity of the various factual issues relevant to the cause of action normally rests upon the plaintiff, but occasionally the legislature or courts place upon the defendant the burden of persuading the fact finder on a particular issue. Both the legislative and the judicial power to allocate burdens of persuasion between the parties in this fashion is well established, and the power is exercised in response to various considerations of policy.

When the burden of persuasion of an issue is placed directly on a defendant, it is normally referred to as an affirmative defense. For example, rule 8 (c) of the Federal Rules of Civil Procedure lists a number of affirmative defenses that must be pled and proven by defendants. Occasionally, though, burdens of persuasion are said to be allocated by presumptions that shift the burden of persuasion to the opponent of the presumption. In paternity suits in which the husband denies legitimacy, for example, there is said to be a presumption of legitimacy of a child born during wedlock that requires the defendant to persuade the fact finder of the child's illegitimacy,

To say, however, that there is a "presumption of legitimacy that allocates or shifts the burden" to the defendant and that there is an "affirmative defense of illegitimacy" that requires the defendant to prove the fact is to make functionally identical statements. Indeed, the only reason for referring to a presumption as shifting or allocating the burden is to emphasize that an exception has been created to the normal rule that plaintiffs bear the burden of persuasion in civil cases. Accordingly, a "presumption that allocates the burden of persuasion" is simply an alternative label applied to an affirmative defense. As with presumptions that create rules of decision, there is nothing in the concept of a presumption that facilitates the allocation of a burden of persuasion. Rather, presumptions that shift the burden of persuasion are simply affirmative defenses that are created for the same reasons of policy that generally inform the decision to allocate burdens of persuasion. Indeed, whether an affirmative defense goes by its usual label or that of a presumption seems entirely fortuitous.

There is one variant of burden shifting presumptions that requires closer examination, however. The label "presumption" is occasionally applied to a set of evidentiary relationships that may profitably be referred to as conditional imperative. When a conditional imperative is in operation, the burden of persuasion shifts if, but only if, the party first establishes some other fact.

The distinction between a conditional imperative and an affirmative defense can be easily demonstrated by a simple example. Assume that an heir sues to compel distribution of the estate of a person who has been missing and unheard from for over seven years. A jurisdiction could, if it chose to do so, place the burden of proving the testator alive on the conservator of the estate in all cases. Were that done here, the result would be to create an affirmative defense. Thus, when an heir sues a conservator, the conservator could prevail by proving the testator to be alive. Alternatively, a jurisdiction could require claimants to prove the death of the testator, but also provide that if the testator is proven to be missing and unheard from for more than seven years, the conservator must then prove the testator is alive. Thus, the burden of proving the relevant fact normally would rest upon the plaintiff; but if seven years absence were established, the burden of proving the testator alive would shift to the defendant. In the latter case, a conditional imperative would be created—upon proof of a basic fact, the conservator must prove a second fact or lose.

Often this conditional imperative is said to be created by a presumption. This class of presumptions differs from a normal affirmative defense in one crucial aspect—the jury is often instructed in the alternative. In such cases, the judge instructs the jury that the burden of persuasion lies on the plaintiff unless the jury is persuaded that the testator has been missing and unheard from for seven years. If the jury is so persuaded, then the burden of persuasion to show the testator is alive shifts to the conservator.

The existence of jury instructions on conditional imperatives is less attributable to something known as a presumption than it is to the confusion generated by the use of that misleading word. In the first place, all a conditional imperative amounts to is, once again, a decision concerning the common evidentiary problem of how a burden of persuasion should be allocated. That decision is made not because a presumption is applicable; rather, the decision is made, at least if it is done rationally, for reasons of policy and the label "presumption" is merely attached to it.

More importantly, however, the use of word "presumption" when referring to a conditional imperative demonstrates once again how the application of that label can have deleterious results. Probably because presumptions of this type are generally viewed as devices to regulate jury decision making, the jury is often responsible for determining the truth or falsity of the basic fact—here, absence for seven years. However, when this process is viewed without the distorting effect that results from thinking of it as involving a presumption, it becomes quite clear that the jury should not determine the existence of the basic fact for purposes of allocating the burden of persuasion of the conditional fact. That determination is of the nature of a preliminary fact, and thus it should be made by the judge.

Consider why a jurisdiction would condition the burden of persuasion of a fact on the existence of some other fact. The reason is that the decision to allocate burdens of persuasion is influenced by the truth or falsity of the fact in question. Assume，for example，that a jurisdiction allocates burdens of persuasion consistently with its a priori appraisal of probability. It may then conclude that since testators are normally alive，anyone alleging one is not should prove it. However，once the testator has been proven to have been missing or unheard from for seven years，the *a priori* probability may change，making it more likely that the testator is dead. Accordingly，an application of the general rule of decision to the subset of cases produces the result that the conservator should now bear the burden of persuading the fact finder that the testator is alive.

Seven years absence，then，is a fact upon which a rule of evidence depends. In that regard，it is quite similar to determining whether two people are married for purposes of the rules on privilege，whether an offer of proof is within the parol evidence rule，or，for that matter，whether a burden of production has been satisfied. Accordingly，for the same reasons of expediency，consistency，and expertise ，allocate the finding of these facts to the judge，so too should the judge make a preliminary determination whether or not the testator has been unheard from and missing for seven years and then allocate the burden of persuasion accordingly.

The frequent failure to appreciate the proper role of the trial judge seems to be primarily a function of the ambiguity generated by erroneously viewing the resolution of these evidentiary problems as a function from the nature of presumptions an the concomitant error，juries should decide the basic facts. This failure of perception has generated a number of other significant misunderstandings. One of these，once again involving conflicting presumptions，bears closer scrutiny.

Dean McCormick provided an excellent example of "conflicting presumptions" in the present context：

> W，asserting that she is the widow of H，claims her share of his

property, and proves that on a certain day she and H were married. The adversary then proves that three or four years before her marriage to H, the alleged widow married another man. W's proof gives her the benefit of the presumption of the validity of a marriage. The adversary's proof gives rise to a general presumption of the continuance of a status or condition once proved to exist, and a specific presumption of the continuance of a marriage relationship.

If the continuation of the first marriage disposes of the validity of the second, and vice versa, then the presumptions described by Dean McCormick cannot logically exist simultaneously, since only one party can bear a burden of persuasion on an issue at a given point in time. Thus, the presumptions are said to conflict, and the issue is viewed as how to resolve the conflict. The answer Dean McCormick supplied is that the "weightier" presumption should survive—the validity of the second marriage in our hypothetical—or, alternatively, to create a new presumption that in successive marriages the earlier ones were terminated, thus requiring the opponent of that proposition to prove the contrary. Dean McCormick's solutions would work, but they would do so for reasons having nothing to do with some concept inherent in presumption. In fact, they demonstrate further the bankruptcy of the term.

First, the two suggested solutions are in reality one. If the presumption of the validity of the second marriage "survives", that would require the opponent to prove that the first marriage was never terminated, which is precisely what the second proposed solution does. More importantly, however, the talk of "new" or "surviving" presumptions merely obfuscates the fact that what Dean McCormick has done is to suggest a solution to a fairly standard sufficiency of the evidence problem. The presumption of the continuation of a marriage reflects a belief that the creation of a relationship implies that it continues. The presumption of the validity of a marriage, by contrast, reflects the importance we attach to that institution. Because of that importance, it is certainly comprehensible to require someone attacking the validity of a marriage to prove its invalidity by a high standard of persuasion, and proof of another marriage three or four years earlier, without more, can certainly be viewed as being inadequate to achieve the level of proof necessary to prove the later marriage invalid.

Suppose, however, that the first marriage had occurred three or four weeks (or hours) before the second marriage. Would the "weightier" presumption of the validity of the second marriage still survive? If Dean McCormick's solution were taken at face value, the answer would be in the affirmative. However, the response should be in the negative because as the time of the marriage gets closer, the likelihood of the validity of the second diminishes accordingly. At some point, that likelihood will be sufficiently low to justify concluding that the second marriage is invalid. The "conflict in presumptions", in short, collapses into a sufficiency of the evidence problem, as does practically every other purported conflict in presumptions that shift burdens of persuasion.

The problem of conflicting presumptions in this context further illustrates that no purpose but the generation of ambiguity is served by reliance on presumptions to do that which can be done directly. There are yet other examples of unnecessary confusion and ambiguity that could be presented to corroborate that conclusion, but the point has been adequately made. The power of the courts and legislatures to allocate burdens of persuasion and of courts to make determinations of sufficiency of the evidence is quite well established. Relying on presumptions does not add to that power in any way. Since it generates a risk of confusion, however, there is no reason to continue to use the misleading term in this fashion.

3. Instructing Juries on the Relationship Between Facts.

Juries are often instructed that, upon proof of one fact, a presumption of another fact arises that makes proof of the first fact evidence of the second. Alternatively, they are instructed that the presumption itself "is" or "has weight as" evidence that the jury is to consider in its deliberation. Normally, these instructions are given when the proven fact implies the second fact, but they are also given when the proven fact's logical relationship to the second fact is tenuous at best. An instruction in the latter case is justified, it is said, because legislatures and courts are entitled to give "additional weight" to proven facts by presumptions if they are so inclined. Again, however, the metaphysics of presumptions merely obscures what is in fact occurring. Instructions on the evidentiary weight of presumptions that deal with facts that are logically related are simply uninformative comments on the evidence. By contrast, providing proven facts with an effect greater than that justified by their logical significance is a method of manipulating the burden of persuasion of the second fact.

Consider first an instruction that once fact A is proven, there is a presumption of fact B and the jury is to weigh fact A, or the presumption itself, as evidence of fact B. Assume further that the judiciary or the legislature has concluded that fact B normally is inferable from fact A. The point of such an instruction, obviously, is to encourage the jury to find fact B once fact A is established. The encouragement comes from the judge indicating to the jury in a conclusory fashion the facts judge's or the legislature's perception of the relationship between the facts. The judges would so instruct, presumable, when the judge feared that the jury might not appreciate the relationship between the facts, thus increasing the likelihood that the jury would reach what the judge believed to be an erroneous result. Consequently, the instruction would be designed to put the jury in the position of an informed decisionmaker, thus increasing the likelihood of the jury arriving at a result the judge or legislature deems correct.

The effect of such an instruction is to modify the manner in which the jury's inferential process occurs by enhancing the role of fact A. That effect is indistinguishable from the effect of a judicial comment on the strength of the evidence. The reason for giving this type of presumptive instruction is identical to that of judicial comment, as is the anticipated outcome. Thus, presumptions of this sort are nothing but a form of judicial comment on the evidence.

There is, however, one difference between this type of presumptive instruction and traditional judicial comment on the evidence that further demonstrates the deleterious effect of our ill-advised reliance on presumptions. While explicit judicial comment attempts to inform the jury of the factors that may be relevant to its decision, and why they may be relevant, presumptive instructions do little more than inform the jury that upon proof of fact A a presumption arises of fact B. Little or no effort is made to inform the jury what the instruction means or why a particular result might be appropriate. Consequently, a presumptive instruction may tend to promote an irrational decision-making process, even though it may also enhance the probability of a more accurate result to the extent the underlying inference is valid.

An irrational inferential process is promoted by a presumptive instruction that recommends to the jury that it engage in the impossible mental feat of "weighing the presumption as evidence." As Professor Morgan has asked, "How can one weigh a presumption against, or with, or as, evidence? Just what will be the mental process?" The answer is, of course, that the jury can not "weigh the presumption" as evidence, for it is not evidence. It is merely a label that has been applied to perceived relationship between facts. Thus, the aim of the instruction is, or ought to be, to encourage the jury to "weigh the facts underlying the presumption and the inferences that may follow from those facts." The jury, however, is rarely informed in realistic terms of what it should do; it is only informed that it should weigh the presumption as evidence, which is an impossible task. Obviously, then, the irrationality of the resultant decision-making process may tend to be enhanced by an instruction of this sort since the jury has no basis for rationally evaluating the instruction.

What is particularly troublesome about a jury instruction to weigh a presumption as evidence, even if the underlying inference is valid, is that it may diminish the role of the jury, The jury may reach a decision not on the basis of its independent consideration of the facts and the inferences from the facts that is concludes are reasonable, but rather by deference to the legislative or judicial judgment expressed in the instruction that a presumption has arisen which is proof of some other fact. While one may applaud the potential for improved accuracy in results, I suspect there would be general agreement that accuracy should not be obtained at the expense of diminishing the role of juries in the trial process in this manner.

Ironically, presumptive instructions of this sort most likely arose in large measure as a means to avoid the restrictions on judicial comment imposed by the legislative branch. In view of the very limited ability possessed by many courts to give the jury guidance on the facts, it must "often… [be] tempting to cast in terms of a 'presumption' a conclusion which a court thinks probable from given facts. " By doing so, a judge can purport to obey the restrictions on judicial comments that have developed in many states and at the same time perhaps provide some guidance to the jury. The irony, of course, is that the desire to avoid explicit comment on the evidence has apparently resulted in a less informative brand of comment that also leads to irrational jury decision-making.

Thus, once again it is apparent that the unnecessary reliance on the concept of presumptions has deleterious consequences. It may or may not be desirable to allow comment on the evidence. Whether comment is allowed has nothing to do with the nature of anything called a presumption, however. Reliance on the concept of presumptions merely obscures the real issue, which is under what circumstances judicial comment on the evidence is to be allowed.

Occasionally a presumption that is to be weighed as evidence foregoes even implicit reliance on the actual relationship between the facts, and it used to give "additional weight" to fact A beyond its logical significance. Normally in these cases fact A has little logical relevance to B, but the instruction is till given that proof of fact A gives rise to a presumption that is to be weighed as evidence of fact B. One way of viewing such an instruction is that it is an inaccurate comment on the evidence. The effect of an inaccurate comment, however, is to implicitly shift the burden of persuasion, a point which can best be clarified by an example.

Consider a negligence trial in which there is an issue of contributory negligence that must be disproved by the plaintiff by a preponderance of the evidence. Assume that on the basis of the evidence adduced, a well-informed, rational jury would conclude that it is just as likely as not that the plaintiff was contributorily negligent. The verdict would be for the defendant, since the plaintiff would have failed to meet the burden of persuasion. Assume, however, that the trial judge instructs the jury that proof of plaintiff's injuries gives rise to a presumption of due care on the part of the plaintiff that is evidence to be weighed by the jury in its deliberations. Assume further that as a result of that instruction, the same jury would now conclude that there is only a forty percent chance that the plaintiff was contributorily negligent. The verdict now would be for the plaintiff. In order to escape the verdict, the defendant would have to adduce stronger evidence of the plaintiff's negligence.

Assume that the defendant, in anticipation of the instruction, adduced stronger evidence, that the trial judge instructed on the presumption, and that the evidence was now so strong that the jury nonetheless would conclude that it is just as likely as not that the plaintiff was contributorily negligent, thus finding for the defendant. If the well-informed jury had evaluated the much stronger evidence without the instruction having been given, it surely would have concluded that there was a much higher chance of contributory negligence than fifty percent. As a result of the instruction, then, the defendant had to do more than merely establish that contributory negligence was as likely as not, as judged by what a rational, well-informed fact finder would conclude. The defendant was required to make a showing sufficient to reach some higher, unarticulated standard.

The functional effect of such an instruction is to create an affirmative defense. Although the jury formally will be applying the normal rule that the burden of proving lack of contributory negligence is on the plaintiff, the reality is that the instruction has lowered the plaintiff's burden of proving lack of contributory negligence, and concomitantly has raised the defendant's burden of establishing the issue. And whenever a defendant has to meet a higher standard of proof than the normal rule allows, an affirmative defense has been created.

Thus, the effect of instructing on a presumption that is to be weighed as evidence is either to make a comment on the evidence or to manipulate a burden of persuasion. In neither case does reliance on the concept of a presumption facilitate the process, but it does obfuscate the issues at hand. By relying on presumptions to make judicial comment on the evidence, we have avoided facing the question of the proper role of comment. At the same time we have injected an irrational component into the jury decision-making process. We have probably injected an even greater irrational component into the decision-making process by relying on a presumption of this kind to shift burdens of persuasion, since there is no way of knowing just how high a burden of persuasion these instructions will be translated into by juries. Moreover, various juries will undoubtedly view the instruction, and the burden it implicitly imposes, in differing ways. Thus, the instruction probably has the additional undesirable effect of contributing to ad hoc decision-making by juries.

4. Allocating Burdens of Production.

The final use to which presumptions have been put is to allocate burdens of producing evidence. Although plaintiffs normally bear the burden of production of most issues relevant to a litigated case, just as they also normally bear the burden of persuasion, occasionally a presumption is said to exist that shifts a burden of production to a defendant. However, underlying the label of presumption is a quite common decision concerning the proper evidentiary relationship of the parties that is made for reasons entirely independent of any concept attributable to presumptions.

In the first place, the judicial and legislative power to allocate burdens of production is well established. Thus, if a jurisdiction wishes to place a burden of production on a party, it may do so directly. Doing so by use of the word "presumption" in no way affects the scope of the power. Furthermore, an examination of the two justifications normally given for the creation of a presumption that shifts a burden of production—to encourage the production of evidence and to expedite trials—not only will demonstrate that there is no independent concept at play, but also that reliance on presumptions in this context produces unnecessary confusion and controversy.

Placing a burden of production on a party may in fact encourage the production of evidence, but no greater encouragement comes from referring to the process of allocation as a presumption. Placing a burden of production on a party does provide a sanction for failing to produce evidence—dismissal or a directed verdict—but the sanction is a function of the meaning of burdens of production rather than an independent attribute of presumptions. Moreover, it is difficult to imagine a case today in which the sanction of possible dismissal would generate more evidence than discovery schemes. Thus, reliance on a presumption to shift a burden of production in order to generate evidence is not only doing indirectly what can be done directly, but also no longer serves the stated purpose.

The second justification for using presumptions that shift burdens of production—to expedite trials—fares no better than the first. There are some issues that are so inherently unlikely to be relevant at trial that we normally can proceed without reference to them. One way to describe that process is to say that we will "presume" the issue is not to be contested unless the defendant "rebuts" the presumption by producing evidence on the issue. This is simply another way of saying that a burden of production has been allocated to a party, and the use of the word "presumption" is nothing more than a handy label in this context. Unfortunately, however, again there has been confusion caused by the use of the label that can and should be avoided. The most important example of the confusion is the controversy that has developed concerning how presumptions of this kind can be rebutted.

"Rebutting the presumption" in this context merely means satisfying the burden of production. Nevertheless, apparently because of the failure to see presumptions as involving nothing but the application of a label to a decision reached for other reasons, a number of courts have concluded that presumptions shifting the burden of production can be rebutted and that the jury should make that determination. As a result, a scheme for determining whether these presumptions have been rebutted has developed that can only be described as bizarre. For example, some courts have held that a presumption is rebutted if the opponent of the presumption produces sufficient evidence believed by the jury that would justify a finding to the contrary even though the jury is not convinced by it. Others have held that an opponent must produce sufficient evidence to justify a jury verdict that is not positively disbelieved by the jury. And there are still other views that need not be recited here.

Were these courts not operating under the mistaken assumption that something called a presumption was at play, they surely would have realized that none of this incredibly intricate and obviously unworkable scheme is necessary. Whether a burden of production is satisfied, regardless of the reasons for the allocation of that burden, is a question for the trial judge to decide employing whatever standard the jurisdiction wishes the judge to employ. Were this simple fact to be realized, this aspect of the controversy surrounding presumptions that shift burdens of production would simply disappear, as indeed it should.

2. TOWARD A MORE RATIONAL APPROACH

In all of its various manifestations, a presumption is simply a label applied

as has actually been applied in allocating the burden of persuasion generally, even though its results have there been expressed in mechanical formulae."

His proposal did not have a significant effect on the courts, however. The ambiguity and confusion surrounding presumptions continued unabated, and Morgan quite obviously became convinced that the confusion would continue until a simple rule was propounded that gave the word "presumption" a consistent meaning. Moreover, that meaning could not be the one suggested by Wigmore and Thayer, for that would give to most presumptions an inadequate effect. Accordingly, Morgan concluded that the general rule should be that presumptions shift burdens of persuasion. Yet even as he embraced that rule, he recognized what an admission of defeat it entailed. In short, the well-publicized debate between Thayer, Wigmore, and Morgan does not rest on a difference over the nature of presumptions; instead, it rests on a disagreement over the legal system's ability to exercise its responsibilities rationally.

I also suspect that Dean Ladd's pragmatic approach was motivated by concerns similar to Edmund Morgan's, concerns that were and still are unmistakably justified. Still, although the legal system has proven to be remarkably intransigent in its insistence upon using presumptions, it has also proven to be incapable of using them in a sensible fashion. Thus, I do not think the solutions preferred by those scholars who desire to see a single rule for presumptions constructed are satisfactory. Instead, we must strive to do a better job of educating lawyers and judges on the emptiness of the concept of "presumptions." In fact, the failure, it seems to me, lies less with those who conduct the day-to-day affairs of the legal system and more with those of us in the law schools who have permitted the concept of presumptions to survive in the minds of our students who then become lawyers and judges. We must do a better job of educating them, which is a goal that I am sure Dean Ladd would have enthusiastically endorsed.

证明标准与法律分析的局限性*

周蔚　张洪铭　译**　张保生　校

一般来说，在审判中，当事人可能被强加三种责任：提出诉（辩）状的责任、提供证据的责任以及说服责任。提出诉（辩）状的责任，明确了哪些事实或法律问题将被包括在一个诉讼案件中。这些责任可按立法者的意愿分配，虽然它们通常被分配给提出改变现状请求的当事人。不过，出于这样或那样的政策性考虑，该一般规则也有例外，如刑事被告人提出一项不在犯罪现场的具体辩解，即使“不在犯罪现场”的辩解并无实质内容而仅为一般性否认。提出诉（辩）状的责任，其意义在于，它们创造了审判的支架；不过，它们并未造成概念上的挑战，因而可以暂不考虑。①

其余两种证明责任——举证责任和说服责任，共同构成一般意义上的“证明标准”。不同国家给这两个概念起了不同的名字，如证据性责任和证明标准，但不论其称谓如何，其基本概念是清楚的。当事人可被要求提出证据，否则，就会输在某一争点上或者败诉。一旦证据性基础夯实，就要达成一项针对不确定性的裁决，而说服责任具体规定了所运用的裁决规则。这些都是普遍性分析要求，是由诉讼的概念属性所规定的。② 如果是由利益无涉的第三方来裁定事实，就必须提供证据，而裁决实际上总具有不确定性。

尽管习惯上仍保留着举证责任和说服责任的区分，但麦克诺顿（McNaughton）教授很久前就论证了举证责任是说服责任的一种功能。③ 衡量举证

* 在此感激我的朋友，合作作者，为本文作出贡献的拉里·劳登和迈克尔·帕多，感谢他们对本文草稿的评论。

** 周蔚，中山大学博士研究生；张洪铭，中国政法大学博士研究生。

① 联邦诉讼实践中的通布利案革命，通过直接使得起诉的充分性依赖于对允许案件继续进行下去的成本/收益分析，实际上带来了起诉负担，根据本文的中心论点，这种分析的一部分即是对成功概率的价值分析。罗纳德·J·艾伦、艾伦·E·盖伊：《作为通布利案和伊克巴尔案的特例的康利案：证据法、程序法的交叉及其规则性质的考察》，载《宾夕法尼亚州立法律评论》，第115卷，2010年，第1页。

② 一些大陆法系理论家试图以通过“内心确信”标准避免错误为由而否认这一点，但这是不可能的，除非欧洲任命的法官是“全能的上帝”，我对此存疑。因此，像乔迪·费雷尔·贝尔特伦（Jordi Ferrer Beltrán）这样的明智的学者认识到这一口号的缺陷，确实是一个积极的发展。参见《法律证明和法律真相：重新审视边沁》，第18页。

③ 约翰·T·麦克诺顿（John T. McNaughton）：《举证责任：说服责任的一项功能》，载《哈佛法学评论》，第68卷，1995年，第1382页。

责任是否满足的标准是：在证据出示后是否还遗留了可裁判的事实问题，换句话说，是否需要后续诉讼程序来解决事实不清的问题。这取决于双方的证据状况，但关键还是取决于说服责任的履行是否充分。如果负有举证责任的一方当事人提出了某一争议事实的证据，履行了说服责任，而理性人仍不能作出对其有利的认定，那么，在那个争议事实上再花更多资源就没有意义了，于是就应当进入判决（然而这是在每一特殊程序语境中完成的）。因此，“证明标准”这一关键概念性问题，就可被归纳为说服责任的含义和适用问题。

本文想要审查这些概念性问题。首先，我将论证，说服责任的法律意义和解释功能，就其范围来说，已远远超出对举证责任含义的简单确定。在本文第一部分，我将假定，从概率测度来把握说服责任的传统理解是准确的。在上述假设的帮助下，我将证明，说服责任是理解诉讼过程的关键概念工具之一。其次，我将介绍当前关于说服责任实质内容的争论，以及与说服责任和错误之间关系有关的争论。这种分析主要包括对说服责任之概率测度假说的考察。确实，我将试图论证，关于说服责任的传统理解以及最近对其缺陷进行回应的努力，作为相关现象的经验描述是不充分的。进一步说，这种不充分性表明，该分析工具并非受调查对象的启发而被误用了。

最后我要介绍，实际上如同所有话题一样，法学界许多关于说服责任的学说，并非要追求论述充分或对知识发现作出贡献，而是要代之以规范性。我在此所作的努力则与之背道而驰。我将努力揭示关于说服责任之知识增长难题的某些有趣方面，并且，我将不对这些事项发表主观评论。诚然，就有关事项之事实的更清晰的理解，也许屈从于更多强迫性规范分析，但我的目的是予以理解，而不是对调查事项发表主观评论。也许具有讽刺性的是，如果人们想要获得对法律现象更深入的理解，这种分析就必须采用法律分析的不同工具。当然，这更深层次的理解是否为一种愿望，这完全是主观的，而我的论证将是：如果这是一种愿望，那么，肯定会有某种结果。

一、说服责任的意义

正如我们已经看到的，说服责任决定举证责任的含义。它也是理解诸如积极抗辩、推定、推论、司法评论和司法认知等离散的陪审团控制手段的关键，以及理解诸如指令裁决、简易判决和（法官）据法判决等更宏观的控制手段的关键。在每一种情况下，说服责任都被直接或间接地强加给一方当事人，或者以修正型适用于一方当事人。由于很快就会清晰起来的原因，对说服责任的直接操作和间接操作做一个分类将是有用的。我从前者谈起。

大量的情况是说服责任的直接分配。实体法通过对要件和抗辩的规定来确定谁负有说服责任，要件和抗辩之间的唯一区别就是谁承担说服责任。在英美法领域，这种分配经常明确地出现在成文法或普通法规则中。关于该过程，没有什么概念上的困难，尽管谁应当承担什么责任可能存在合理的争议。例如，共同过失（被害人本身的过失——由被告提出）是应当成为过失案由的因素，还是应当成为抗辩案由的因素？是应当由刑事被告来证明其患有精神病，还是必须由政府方确信无疑地证明其精神正常？之前可能存在对一方有利的道德和实践上的双重考量，但裁决一旦作出，其执行就是直截了当的。如果原告或州对一个争点承担说服责任，它就被贴上要件标签；如果被告人承担说服责任，它就被贴上抗辩标签（有时，一项“积极抗辩”将共同过失与直接否定等诸如此类的事情区分开了）。另外，法律可能将举证责任和说服责任进行混合与搭配。要求被告人承担某一争点的举证责任，而由原告承担该说服责任，这并非不合逻辑。当然，在一致的情况下，这样做要实现什么并不清楚，这又像是举证责任乃说服责任的一种功能。因此，均势只在文字上有所区别，这种情况实际上非常少见。④

通过推定的运用，说服责任的分配以及由此而创设的抗辩，虽然在某种程度上有些模糊但仍直接发生了。这是以法律语言“基于 X 的证明，Y 的推定出现，除非其必被一方或另一方所反驳”的效果来实现的。“推定”一词无处不在，却毫无意义；这一切实际上是说服责任的直接分配。“推定”一词还有其他用法，但在每一种情况下，这种语言所附带的现象，仅仅是使原本简单的关系变得模糊复杂了。总的来说，推定有四个不同的功能，其中三个是直接分配或影响说服责任。它们被用于澄清法律规则——这些是所谓不可反驳的推定，如上所述，直接分配说服责任，以及分配我们所看到的包含说服责任的举证责任。⑤ 下面，我将讨论“推定”的这三种用法，然后将转入推定的第四种用法——提供用来推论并对证据进行评价。该术语的这种用法包括说服责任的间接操作，将在此情景下进行讨论。

出于各种各样的理由，法律对其他一些可能会有争议的事实规定了直接解决办法。例如，一个人超速驾驶或者驾驶时体内酒精含量超标的证明，或者一

④ 事物在实践中的运行方式也许与理论有别。一些研究表明，优势证据往往被理解为比 0.5 的概率要高很多。不幸的是，这些研究并没有展示出任何对口头描述而言的操作性结果。例如，参见丽塔·西蒙、L. 马汉：《证明责任的定量：从法官席、陪审团和课堂的视角》，载《法律和社会评论》，第 5 卷，第 319 页（1971 年）；D. 卡格西罗、W. C. 斯坦顿：《证明责任标准的法律与量化的界定》，载《法律以及人类行为》，第 9 卷，1985 年，第 159 页，提及关于事实认定者解释责任的经验研究。

⑤ 罗纳德·J·艾伦：《反思民事案件中的推定》，载《艾奥瓦法律评论》，第 66 卷，1981 年，第 843 页。

个人违反安全法规的证据，曾经一度被认为创设了一项关于过失的不可反驳的推定。然而，所有这些都意味着，那些基础条件——超速、醉酒驾驶、违背安全法规——的证明，满足了案由要件，从而也满足了说服责任在其不发挥作用的情况下要满足的东西。在其他情况下，类似证明被认为创设了可反驳的推定，例如，关于已交邮信件被收件人收到的推定。这一结论可被反驳，或通过出示优势证据来证明相反情况，或通过证明理性人凭借优势证据能够得出相反的结论——而这是说服责任分配和举证责任分配的关键区别。虽然，在每一种情况下，主要特征通常是说服责任的一种或另一种直接操作的类型。

正如迈克尔·帕顿（Michael Pardon）最近所论证的，这个确切的相同点适用于各种宏观控制手段，如指令裁决、简易判决、忽视陪审团裁决的判决、重新审判令。⑥ 这些手段只适用于没有陪审团问题，或陪审团达成一项站不住脚的评议结果，因而案件将取决于说服责任的情况。重新审判令赋予了审判法官一些更大的自主权，来处理二阶证明问题*——法官对于唯一站得住脚的结果或者一项站不住脚的结果，究竟有多么确信？如果非常确信，那就作出指令裁决、简易判决、忽视陪审团裁决的判决。如果比合理确信稍低一些，一项重新审判令允许第二轮陪审团审查。然而，这里重要之处在于，这个完整的分析是由说服责任直接驱动的。

关于说服责任，还有一些间接操作。很多证据手段以及证据的采纳或排除，都能影响相对说服责任，即使明确的说服责任也许并未受到影响。⑦ 证据评论，对推论的陪审团指示（关于证据评论的），相关证据的排除或误导性证据的采纳，都改变了相对说服责任。⑧ 上面提到的第四种推定形式也是一样。它常常通过“推定”语言创设了变相的评论/推论的陪审团指示。一种典型的陪审团指示是：“基于 X 的证明，Y 的推定得出，那是 Y 的证据。”除了鼓励事实认定者基于对推定之基础事实的认定来认定事实之外，“一个推定是某个事实的证据”没有什么可能性含义。显然，这是对证据的一种评论。

⑥ 迈克尔·S·帕多：《提出诉（辩）状、证明以及判决：民事诉讼的统一理论》，载《波士顿大学法律评论》，第 51 卷，2010 年，第 1451 页。

* 译注：“二阶证明问题”（second order proof problems）是指，法官对证据证明事实之概率的确信程度。例如：某一证据证明某一事实发生的概率是 70%，这是“一阶”的证明问题，而法官对上述概率的确信程度可能为 30%、50%或者 70%，该确信程度的高低即是一个二阶证明问题。

⑦ 这个现象在罗纳德·J·艾伦的《刑事案件中陪审团判决作出的结构化：一种统一的宪法性分析》[《哈佛法学评论》，第 94 卷，1980 年，第 321、331 页] 一文中首次被证成。拉里·劳丹在《现在到了将“确信无疑标准”废掉的最后时刻?》一文第 11 页提到这一点。

⑧ 参见罗纳德·J·艾伦，前引⑧，第 332～339 页。下述一些问题很多也来源于此。

这些关于说服责任的各种证据性操作的影响，可以通过两起案件的比较来说明。这两起案件的唯一区别是，其中一起包含这些操作中的一种，而另一起不包含。假定两起案件有基本上相同的事实——涉及知晓持有赃物罪，而唯一的知晓证据是持有最近偷的物品。进一步假定，法官认为，持有最近的赃物与对该物品属性的知晓有非常高的对应性，但法官还认为，这种知晓并不为组成陪审团的普通人所广泛拥有。最后假定，在一起案件中，法官对该证据作出司法评论，或者对持有和知晓之间的关系作出了推论性指示，而在另一起案件中，法官对此不置可否。

在没有司法评论的案件中，陪审团可能令人信服地作出有罪裁决，但无罪开释的机会比第二起案件中要高。在后一起案件中，法官对“持有最近被偷物品”的含义进行解释。法官的评论通过强化控方证据的效果，增加了定罪的机会。为了使第二起案件中被告人获得无罪开释的机会与前一案件中的被告人相同，被告人就必须比在前面第一起案件中提供更多具有说服力的反驳性证据。尽管控辩双方的正式关系是相同的——陪审团在每一案件中都适用合理怀疑标准——司法评论却通过改变陪审团作出其裁决的事实矩阵而修正了相对说服责任。这表明，如同积极抗辩和举证责任的配置一样，司法评论的效果在于通过修正一方当事人对某一争点承担的相对说服责任，来改变当事人的相对地位。相关证据的排除以及不相关、误导性证据的采纳，也有着完全相同的后果。正如在审判中，受证据裁决逆向影响的一方当事人，必须更加努力地去履行自己的说服责任。⑨

对这种分析的一种反对意见应当予以注意并予以解决。该反对意见认为，说服责任归属于一方当事人而非另一方，因此，谈论转移相对说服责任看起来好像没有任何意义。这种传统观点是错误的。说服责任是相互的。说原告承担着对案件的证明达到优势证据标准的责任，等于说被告不得不证明原告并未以优势证据表明自己的案子该赢，或者被告要提出否定意见，即其至少有一半机会来主张自己案件的真实性。甚至在刑事案件中，据说被告对要件事实不承担说服责任，这种说法是错误的，他们实际上承担着说服责任。公诉人必须确信无疑地证明一个犯罪要件，而被告人则必须证明存在合理怀疑，这两个陈述说的是一回事。

总之，将说服责任概念化为常规概率方法具有巨大的解释力。它使“推

⑨ 相关证据的采纳和不相关证据的排除也是如此，但要假设这些活动促使裁决者去作出理想化的正确裁决。

定”这一术语的含义得到明确[10]；它允许一套关于证据和程序手段的统一分析[11]；在美国，它甚至允许对确信无疑之宪法要求的复杂性给出命令。[12] 然而，逐渐清楚的是，将说服责任模型化为一种常规概率法，在准确性及实用性上还存在局限性。这反过来又对法律分析家们无所不用的法律分析工具提出了质疑，或者是对他们正在研究的现象概念的充分性提出了质疑。我下面转入这些问题。

二、法律分析的局限

对说服责任进行概率分析具有明显吸引力，此分析与同样具有吸引力的新证据引入可对概率更新的证据过程概念化相一致。两者结合在一起，看似解释了审判的证据过程以及审判的最后决策规则的适用，然而，此理论进路上的努力在经验上和分析上的不足也变得明显起来。比如，只有当说服责任中包含了相对概率，说服责任才能在证据过程的概念化中充当应有的角色(但我们对概率之外关于潜在错误的影响如何表达?)。而对概率理论仅有的解释是，司法证明中所具有的任何可能的解释能力来自于主观信念的状态。事实上，审判中从来没有与频率有关的知识，但DNA技术是一个有趣的例外，并且不存在使用这样的研究趋向或者概率逻辑理论的应用。[13] 此主观性理论从描述性的角度来看，对于美国显然为假，没有事实发现者被要求从自身的主观信念状态或个人的功能处寻求信息，而是被指示尽可能地合理思考从而发现案件事实。此外，审判的结构与主观概率理论的使用的要求非常不一致，事实发现者并未被指示需对新的证据进行信念更新，并且对于任何事件的信念更新在计算上都是难以跟踪的。[14] 不论主观概率理论作为规范性理论的吸引力为何，或者其他使用此理论的运用（例如，试探法）如何，此理论在经验上都是不充分的描述方法。

概率分析方法还存在更多的问题。拉里·劳丹对确信无疑证明的意义进行了多方面攻击，指出在概率论的背景下，确信无疑被理解为高的概率。[15] 他的

⑩ 同前引⑤。

⑪ 同前引⑥。

⑫ 同前引⑤。

⑬ 对于概率论的讨论，参见唐纳德·吉利斯：《概率的哲学理论》(2000年)。

⑭ 罗纳德·J·艾伦：《理性、规则体系与司法证明：初步探究》，载《证据与证明国际杂志》，1997年（特别专题），第254页。

⑮ 拉里·劳丹：《真理、错误与刑法》(剑桥大学出版社，2006年版)。

部分攻击使用了我与他合著文章中所确立的说服责任证成的共识，但此攻击（不仅在刑事案件中）一般不令人完全信服。⑯ 此证成对错误进行分配使之符合各种社会政策，在民事案件中，普遍的社会政策是公平地对待当事人各方，并减少错误的总量。在刑事案件中，社会政策是制定对任何人难以定罪的说服责任，从而保护无辜的人，这些社会政策希望通过排除错误来有利于无罪裁决（因为我们信仰的法律准则是：对无辜人定罪的糟糕程度十倍于错误判有罪的人无罪）。

尽管这样的口号和思考方式或许已经存在数个世纪，但其具有明显不可弥补的缺陷。第一，在审判中我们可以作出四种决策，并且每个决策都具有社会价值或社会成本。除了这些错误决策，正确的决策可以作出，而忽视这些正确决策是不恰当的。比如，在民事案件中，错误可在每个单独案件中出现，错误均等政策从而被满足，只要所有案件的基础概率即法院应支持的原告与被告数量大致相同。类似地，在刑事案件中，10 个错误的无罪裁决与 1 个错误的有罪裁决之比，满足被错判案件中百分之九十九的情形。进一步说明，如果未知进入审判关于法院应支持的原告与被告数量的基础概率以及事实发现者所做评价和真实事态间的关系⑰，可以非常确定的是：无法预计说服责任对正确或错误判决的影响。比如，如果参与审判的每个人都是有罪的*，那么就不可能存在无罪判决，且不论此证明标准为何。对证明责任的常规分析同样假定在静态系统之上，然而事实上此系统是动态的，此动态性的一个方面是，当事人各方决定哪些案件应当进一步进入诉讼程序，并且当事人各方可以根据规则的变动调整自身的决策。因此，简单地假定降低刑事案件中的证明标准将导致更多错误的有罪裁决，或任意其他证明责任与结论间所主张的因果关系，分析上显然不为真，而其所依靠的是法律系统如何对环境的改变作出响应。⑱

⑯ 罗纳德·J·艾伦、拉里·劳丹：《致命困境》，载《得克萨斯技术大学法律评论》，第 41 卷，2008 年，第 65～92 页；拉里·劳丹、罗纳德·J·艾伦：《致命困境之二：保释与犯罪》，载《芝加哥肯特法律评论》，第 85 卷，2010 年，第 23～43 页；罗纳德·J·艾伦、拉里·劳丹：《致命困境之三：对预防性监禁的一些溢美之词》，载《刑法与犯罪学杂志》，第 101 卷，2011 年，第 781 页。

⑰ 例如，使用概率的概念，我们需要知道责任概率的发现与实际责任间的关系。传统分析进路中所隐含的是，责任概率的发现是 0.8，意味着 10 个中有 8 个相似的案例，此真实事实与责任概率相一致。然而，在所有事实发现者的概率发现与真实事态之间可以存在任何关系，由事实发现者发现存在 0.8 的责任概率的所有案例组成的集合中，可以发现由无责任案例组成的子集。

* 译注：这在分析上可能，但在经验上不可能。

⑱ 劳丹与费雷尔·贝尔特伦的主张恰好相反，然而清楚的错误概率并不能仅仅从决策规则中演绎推导得出。参见费雷尔·贝尔特伦，前引③，第 14 页。他主张决策规则处于错误类型 I 与错误类型 II 之间的概率。劳丹则认为这在法律语境中分析地不为真，参见劳丹，前引⑯，第 9～11 页。

常规分析模式更加根本的问题在于，审判判决仅仅是法律系统结果输出的一部分，民事案件和刑事案件中的当事人各方对结论进行协商，并且这种协商是在法庭审判的影响下进行，除此以外，这些案件中的协商结论显然是法律系统影响的社会总福利的一部分。简单地说，审判中高度随机的审判结论或者说相对高的审判成本可对社会成本最优化，因为这样可以鼓励当事人各方对争议进行协商。⑲

对于说服责任的常规理论解释所产生的经验不足，最近有三个理论进路尝试进行替代。其中两个理论分别由拉里·劳丹和乔迪·费雷尔·贝尔特伦创建，两者明显是规范性研究而非实证性研究，但他们在研究中都对证明责任概念化的含义感兴趣。第三个理论，是麦克·普拉多与笔者所进行的研究，主要是根据笔者的观点提出的实证性研究，但有一些有趣的限制条件。笔者将对三种理论作简要阐述，并转而讨论常规法律分析方法的不足。

拉里·劳丹最近的研究体现了他对“确信无疑证明”这样的概念的诸多不满。⑳ 确切地说，他抱怨这个概念相当含混，并且指出此概念的“荒唐”是由于这个标准的主观性所致。㉑ 他告诉我们，他先前对“确信无疑证明”的理解方式应该是：

建立在统计学与科学哲学之上，可对任何经验假设 H 的真值进行有力测试，此测试能清晰地对事实进行解释，如果假设 H 为假，被解释的数据则看上去完全是晦涩难懂的。在法律语境中运用，其思想是公诉人主张被告有罪所需某种程度的高度似真性只需有关证据初步确定为真，被告如果被判有罪，这些证据可以轻易地进行解释，但如果被告人无罪，能否解释则很难预料。如果案件的某些重要特征使得有罪假设具有意义，并与无罪假设一样作出解释，那么公诉人参与的案件就不可能作出充分保证的判决，同样地，只有基于无罪假设的任何有关证据才有意义，因为这样无罪裁决才是可能的。简单地说，劳丹所主张的证明标准要求判决被保证，当且仅当：a）有罪假设可以解释案件中大部分显见的事实，并且 b）无罪假设可以解释有罪假设解释不了的独特经验证据。正如我们所说，不会令人惊讶且可以被确证的科学预测其实非常不可

⑲ 对于此问题的讨论，参见罗纳德·J·艾伦：《理性与对复杂性的驾驭》，载《亚拉巴马法学评论》，第 62 卷，2011 年，第 1047 页；艾伦、劳丹：《致命困境之三：对预防性监禁的一些溢美之词》，载《刑法与犯罪学杂志》，第 101 卷，2011 年，第 781 页。

⑳ 拉里·劳丹：《将“确信无疑证明”拿出领地的最后时刻到了吗?》；拉里·劳丹：《真理、错误与刑法》，第二章，剑桥大学出版社，2006 年版。

㉑ 同上，第 6 页。

信，但其竞争的替代理论对此没有料想到。因此，有罪假设并没有基于非常令人意外的证据，却倾向于给出缺乏强有力经验支持的解释，然而这种经验支持对于判决又是必不可少的。[22]

劳丹进而承认，确信无疑标准的定义所产生的分配式结论，必须连同此定义的抽象意义一同考虑进来。尽管如此，我将关注的仅仅是这个主张的定义，而非其创新之处，我相信此定义是常规分析具有局限的进一步证据。正如上文指出，在任何事件中，任何规则或规则改动的分配式结论是经验问题而非分析性问题。

劳丹的分析研究的实质是，尝试从相关的学科中寻找决策规则替代不充分的法律决策规则，在这里，他从关于科学进步的一般概括中寻找支持。然而此进路有两方面的困难，第一，代表性的科学探索活动与代表性的法律系统活动之间仅仅存在因果关系；第二，劳丹不当地关注了科学活动中的探索阶段，而非更加类似的运用阶段。笔者将依次对这两方面的困难进行讨论。

仔细考虑标准审判与大部分科学研究活动之间的区别。[23]在法庭审判中，所有努力实际上总是在决定发生了什么，此目的并不在于揭示一般因果规律，虽然一般因果规律可能经常作为证据出现在某个事件之中。在大多数科学探究中，尽管数据产生的原因常常令人困惑，但所得到的数据却是很清楚的，实际发生了什么是尝试解释为何发生的出发点，比如微粒具有质量或者与其他微粒产生吸引力（如对希格斯玻色子的寻找），换句话说，是对一般因果规律的寻找。科学实验可以重复进行，并且可以在实验中对各项参数进行调校，以确保得到可能的解释。在法律中，情况恰恰相反，是以不一致的基础数据（“这个灯是红的”；“这个灯是绿的”）作为争点，复制科学实验中的方法显然行不通，争议的解决总是基于发生了什么之上。为何某事的发生（不论发生何事）可能导致争议？且各方当事人可能提出不同的和矛盾的一般概括、科学证据或者其他以帮助事实发现者进行事实发现，然而这些意在提出指向结论关于事实或一系列事实的推论结构，而非普遍适用的原则或理论。

在科学与法律之间还存在其他两方面重要差异。科学知识以自上而下、演绎方式构建，科学探索所关注的要么是通过（经验地或理论地）消除反例，使先前存在知识的演绎结构系统化，要么是对科学领域的概念结构进行修改或替

[22] 同上，第 7～8 页。

[23] 以下几段依据罗纳德·J·艾伦：《事实的含混与证据理论》，载《西北大学法律评论》，第 88 期，1994 年，第 604 页。

代。半个世纪前，两者间的差异在科学哲学界引起了热烈讨论[24]，但是两个领域实践的相似之处是值得关注的，因为他们对实质知识的良构主体和方法论进路共享，虽然他们在完整定义的问题上存在分歧，对法学领域内的概念基础的攻击通常使用了在方法论领域和数学原则中的攻击方法，但是此攻击对什么算作证据保持一致，并且能清楚地表达分歧的范围。

对科学研究活动的描述未能描述法律过程中的事实发现，两者间的差别不在于科学研究具有高度复杂性而日常生活判断非常简单，情况正好相反。科学探索中的标准操作是将问题简化，特别是对尽可能多的变元进行控制，而日常事件的判断则刚好相反，并实际上从来没有也不可能在可控的实验中得到重复的结论，大量变元连续且必要地产生作用。而且对审判中的事实判断更难进行控制，因为审判过程的复杂特征如同悬浮在真实生活的泡泡瓶之中。

我几年前举的一个简单例子：

假设某个证人开始作证，因此事实发现者必须决定哪些部分组成了证言，哪些是相关变元？首先，这些变元应该都是规范的可信性问题，但需要考虑这些变元的复杂性，行为表现反映的不仅仅是行为表现，而是变元的复杂集合。证人是否流汗或抽动？这些行为，是否是因为无辜而产生的紧张？是说谎时的压力所致？是药物问题所致？还是懊恼的童年养成的坏习惯？身体语言是否支持诚实或逃避，放松状态下所作证言是谎言还是清晰自在地说出的故事？证人作证时目视询问人，这是值得赞许的品格证据还是油嘴滑舌的销售员的自信呢？声调的变化反映了证人正直的品德还是紧张？紧张的声音是指明对案件结果的伪造或担忧？等等。

对相关变元列表远远超出了行为表现只是一种可信度问题。当证人表达命题时，事实发现者必须决定什么命题是作出的断言，以及事实发现者相信所断言的内容，而这个任务包含了对大量变元的处理，另外，事实发现者需要处理的信息还包括证人表达命题前的行为观察，比如通过律师的询问获取此类信息，可以说明此类信息的例子很多。将法律作为自然科学来处理，将需要对大量的变元在演绎结构以及其必要和充分条件中清楚说明，然而实际上没有这样的结构可以创造，这样做将会相当复杂。[25]

㉔ 该故事中的主角是汤玛斯·库恩：《科学革命的结构》（1962 年）；卡尔·波普尔：《科学发现的逻辑》（1934 年）。关于此问题观点的概要，参见弗雷德里克·祖佩（主编）：《科学理论的结构》，2 版，1997。

㉕ 同前引⑤，第 626 页。

第二个差异同样关键，科学探索关注的是运用现代科技手段可以发现什么样的成果，若某个问题不是通过科技手段进行的探索发现，比如宇宙大爆炸后发生了什么，则会完全被忽略。此外，回答科学实验的追问没有太多必要，如果科学实验得出了含混的结果，或者担忧某些不可控变元，或者任何其他，那么可以进行更多的改进，直至研究员得到相对满意的实验结果。然而法律并没有这样的办法来挑选争议，不论出现什么样的问题，法律都必须去解决，也不能像科学探究一样，有各种理由可以无限期的推迟决定，因为不决定本身就是一种决定，法律争议包括对现状是否修改或保留的论证，不作出决定通常是为了保持现状不变且一方当事人的诉求得到了满足。

总而言之，将这样完全属于不同学科体系的决策规则引进到法律中予以使用的原因并未完全清楚，即使倾向这样的做法——劳丹教授主张从科学发现中寻求法律决策规则，虽然这样做似乎不正确。劳丹教授识别的变元种类，同样是科学家和科学哲学家认为最能帮助新科学知识探索的变元种类，如果提出的某个解释被认为新且更好，并且依此解释作出令人惊讶的预测最终被证实，则此解释具有说服力，如爱因斯坦提出的光在太阳周围将折曲的解释。[26] 然而审判中大多组成部分没有包含令人惊讶的预测；而大部分是日常生活的争议，比如谁在说真话以及谁在说谎。[27]法律判决依据“令人惊讶的证据”的举证，即此判决可解释为创造性的、惊奇的或反直观的假设，或任何普通假设之外的类型，将使公诉人在实际判决中没有作用，而且还会从根本上误解审判过程的本质。另外，对于不同的被告应当接受相同证明标准的理由没有说明清楚，这种情况下，不论被告提供了多么有力的辩护，无罪判决也只会越来越少。几乎没有“有罪裁决”和“无罪判决”会在科学语境中使用，而在审判语境中却比比皆是（其取决于当事人一方对现状是否存在异议）。

希望案件中的公诉人与被告相对严格地分离开来同样是相当严格的责任，虽然这样限制了任何“重要特征”的引入（并且此表述非常含混；何为“重要”与案件的特质有关，并取决于当事人的断言）。审判中的案例往往包含了

㉖　波普尔认为科学的进步包括作出大胆预测并因此尝试证明预测为假。参见波普尔，前引 25。对一般关联性预测的其中一个经验测试，参见［美］F. W. 戴森、A. S. 爱丁顿、C. 戴维斯：《关于太阳重力场对光线的折曲的决定，来自 1919 年 5 月 29 日日全食的观察》，载《英国皇家学院哲学会报》，第 220A 卷，1920 年，第 291 页 。

㉗　参见罗纳德·J·艾伦、理查德·B·库恩斯、埃莉诺·斯威夫特、戴维·S·施瓦茨：《证据法：文本、问题以及案例》，第 4 版，第 2～75 页，2006 年。

存有少量明显异议的大量重叠证据[28]，事实发现者的任务是决定哪些人或哪些内容可以相信以解决这些不一致，从而作出对应判断。重申一次，此证明标准满足无罪裁决，即某些公诉人案件与无罪兼容吗？如果大部分公诉人案件将总与无罪兼容，那么有罪裁决可能不会存在。在审判中没有什么是“完全不能理解”的，证据间出现的冲突是因为某人希望说谎以获得其利益，而并非对此不能理解。尽管本人是劳丹教授著作的忠实拥护者，特别是他使得法学领域的学者开始认真思考基础概念问题，但是在此笔者坚持认为他没有注意到法律与多数科学领域间的根本差异。

乔迪·费雷尔·贝尔特伦，较劳丹更加明显地受到了科学哲学的影响，他主张对确信无疑证明标准进行测试，与劳丹的观点有所类似。

根据这个证明标准，作为证明有罪的假设，必须同时满足以下两个条件：

1. 此假设应该能以融贯的方式解释可用的信息，并且假设对新信息所作的预测必须被证实。

2. 解释相同信息（此信息与被告的无罪相兼容）的所有其他似真假设应当被反驳，但特定的假设除外。[29]

尽管此理论概貌较劳丹的理论，没有那么明确的定义，但是我们可以看到类似的概念争议。对于此定义的第一部分，审判（至少在美国）不包含“预测”新信息的假设，而是对所有信息加以考虑以决定发生了什么。这个测试似乎包含了将法律语境与科学语境无意义地混合，正如以上的讨论，在科学探索中，理论成功的一个标准是其所作的预测，但实际上法律事实发现的过程中没有应用这样的预测。对于此定义的第二部分，它有两方面未说清楚。回顾一下不同证人作出了相反的观察证言的典型案例，很明显一个证人说的是真话，另一个则没有。如果事实发现者得出被告证人说谎的结论，那么事实发现者有完美的被告有罪假设；如果事实发现者得出被告证人没有说谎的结论，那么事实发现者则需要好的被告无罪假设。“信息”与不同断言的兼容程度取决于事实发现者如何对待此种信息，如果事实发现者认为被告说谎，那么被告对自己无罪的证言将被“反驳”。

这个主张的第二个困难是其规避方法，其对“特定”假设的排除似乎本身完全是特定的。例如，刑事被告所作主张是被“陷害和逼供”的情况下作

㉘ 参见前引㉔。

㉙ 参见费雷尔·贝尔特伦，前引②，第19页。

出。[30] 此情形下这个标准仅仅等同于无罪主张以及对状态证据的解释，其似真性将取决于案件中的其他部分，这对于所有主张都为真，不论是通过状态还是通过被告人，但是不可能看到为何这种无罪主张与任何其他无罪主张不同。例如，不在犯罪现场是特定的？或者正常心理状态缺失是特定的？还是心智不正常是特定的？此标准等同于一个测试，包括了第一个标准以及第二个标准的前半部分，将此测试使用在某个未定义的子集上不产生作用时，则称任何推论问题是特定的。如果被告提出的争议由于某个原因不能被反驳，此争议就会被标记为特定的，即便此争议常常与直接无罪主张同构。或许欧洲的刑事案件与美国的刑事案件有所区别，但此提议显然不能对美国的情况作出准确描述，而且作为规范性理论似乎也缺乏吸引力。

麦克·普拉多与笔者，在早先的“相对似真理论”研究中已经探讨了说服责任最好的理解为推论出最好解释的例子[31]，用推论出最好解释与认知过程关联，而非视其为对知识是什么的回答。此概念的核心思想是，案件总是包括了各种可选择故事的比较以及事实发现者对这些故事的选择，或者这些故事驱使事实发现者作出选择，选择有更多似真性的解释作为真的解释以满足审判的目的。在刑事案件中，公诉人必须对有罪或损失给出似真的解释，如果公诉人提出了似真的解释，则被告必须提出无罪或损失的解释。[32]

上述提出的概念化不是规范性概念而是实证性的概念，并且我们多年来尝试展示实际的审判过程，推论出最好解释目前是对实际审判过程最好的解释。此概念的显著优点是与我们所知道的事实发现者如何推理相一致，而不是所有现有的那些如同劳丹和费雷尔·贝尔特伦那样的概率解释。另外，这个概念还整理和解释了审判过程中的诸多方面，从各类证据规则[33]到证据过程中实际给陪审团的指令（“使用你的常识”、“倾听其他陪审员”、“你不必相信所有的证据，但需要尝试去理解”），除了没有给出说服责任确定的形式定义。但是正如笔者前文所述，将说服责任的形式定义理解为概率衡量没有任何意义[34]，劳丹与费雷尔·贝尔特伦提出的全新理解，对相对似真性理论不能解释的内容的解释并未使得其他的责任理论受益。

㉚ 同前引⑱。

㉛ 参见罗纳德·J·艾伦：《事实的含混与证据理论》，载《西北法律评论》，第88卷，1994年，第604页。

㉜ 罗纳德·J·艾伦、迈克尔·帕多：《司法证明以及最佳解释》，载《法律与哲学》，第27期，2008年，第223页。

㉝ 罗纳德·J·艾伦：《司法证明的本质》，载《卡多佐法律评论》，第13卷，第373期，1991年，第413～420页。

㉞ 还有大量的其他问题——联合效应、难解性，等等。

可以确定和清楚的是，许多评论者包括劳丹与费雷尔·贝尔特伦从事的都是规范性研究，而非实证性研究，然而我们的研究几乎完全是实证性研究。我们只不过是在相对狭窄的观察范围内尝试对观察到的现象进行理解，例如，我们不尝试解释审判过程如何符合更大的社会过程，我们也没有尝试预计实际观察的司法过程中可以得到什么样的结果。我们想要说的这些问题多半是经验问题，而非分析问题，并且只能经验地回答，简言之，像劳丹与费雷尔·贝尔特伦等人所提出的宏大问题超越了我们分析研究的范畴。

我现在概括一下关于说服责任的分析方法在理论上的定位。常规的、概率的理解非常有趣然而显然是错的，这个替代方法，要么是无望的愿望，要么此运用非常有限而留下的更大问题，拉里·劳丹等人并未回答。如何对此作出解释呢？我想在本文中作出可以定论的解释，即此结论是用分析的方法对法律进行研究是有问题的。[35] 此进路的标准法律研究方法是将问题分成可控的大小并用现代逻辑的标准工具进行分析，特别是用演绎的方法分析。[36] 本人是逻辑演绎方法的忠实崇拜者，但是其用途具有局限性，或者演绎方法被使用在广阔的领域过于有限。无论因为这样还是那样的原因，法律分析的标准形式在逻辑上遭到了批判，并因此试图以新的和更好的规则替代遭受批判的法律分析形式，而这正是劳丹与费雷尔·贝尔特伦所做的工作。我和普拉多的工作却不具有这种特征，而是仅仅处理相关领域的很小部分。

大量的常规分析进路都有一个隐含假设，即其所在的环境是静态的，但在这个问题上我认为这个假设是非常错误的，与静态规则系统相比，更确切的法律系统概念应当是庞大的最优化问题中的很小部分。首先考虑证据法，其由必要和充分条件构成的相对自由裁量权规则组成，一定数量的判例连同自由裁量权被留给了审判法官，将这些规则适用在“审判证据”上，这意味着证人证言和实物在审判中被提出并在演绎推导出责任的推论中作为全部前提，但这是错误的。证据如果没有语言和逻辑的规则，其字面上无法理解，然而此研究进路只是简单地认为事实发现者可以处理证据信息并进行审议。而事实上，如果没有庞大的知识储备以及如何合理使用语言和逻辑的智慧，则这个工作很难完成。证据法毫无疑问是规章性文件，其必须规范审判中所提出的证据，并依靠

[35] 这是笔者本年度一次讲座中的核心理论。罗纳德·J·艾伦：《理性与复杂性的驾驭》，载《阿拉巴马法律评论》，第62期，2011年，第1047页。

[36] 拉里·劳丹的诸多工作不是完全描述性的，他所做的尝试是突破概念上的界限，特别是在其著作《真理、错误与刑法》（剑桥大学出版社，2006年版）中。然而在上述《论说服责任》一文中忽视了其他著作中的一些教训。

与事实发现者的知识和信念的推论过程间的相互作用，也正是这个差异才产生了上述关于证人作证的例子。

以上概念衍生出的背景也与理解劳丹提出的替代方式相关。劳丹博士对本文的初稿给出了慷慨的、有益的点评，尽管他坚持将其主张中的具体术语包含在运用的语境而非发现的语境中，并且在他心中判断证据的过程与诊断疾病的系统科学诊断方法类似。这个行动明显地使得他与我和普拉多的相对似真性理论在方向上保持一致，同时加强了其与推论出最好解释的理论联系，共同构成了关于司法证明目前最好的解释。系统科学的诊断方式与定量化学分析高度类似，都包含了基于不同数据点假设的排除和算入（例如，石蕊试纸为蓝色，此为参照色；如果变红，则表示为酸性），这在某种程度上与故事的形成类似，但概念上的差异包括证据的本质以及上述科学研究的独特语境。对于系统科学的诊断方法或者定量化学分析，正如在发现的语境中（事实上不只如此）数据是清楚的——如石蕊试纸到底是红色还是蓝色，反对方在批判性变元上进行反驳，比如，一个证人作证石蕊试纸是红色，另外一方证人作证石蕊试纸为蓝色，或者证人作证石蕊试纸是红色而反对方提出证据或者指出证人在说谎的情形（例如存在偏见或利益），或者事实发现者完全凭自己对证人的观察作出结论。审判中包含了不受控制的复杂性和含混，而这些并不存在于标准的科学研究领域，不论在发现还是在应用阶段。在科学探究中，科学家不必获得某些决策者据其人生经历而产生的认同；相反，正如先前提到且同样在此适用的，事实上在法律过程中每个人都分享知识和方法。然而系统科学的诊断方法在一定程度上包含了对可能解释的创造性表述，其的确充当相对似真理论与推论出最好解释间的一种关系，但正如我与普拉多的研究所指出的，系统科学的诊断方法仍然只解释了相关概念领域中很小一部分。

有效法律规则的挑战反映了更加深刻的问题。考虑一下基本行为与诉讼行为间的区别，基本行为是日常活动，包括经济行为和个人行为（以及任意其他类型）；诉讼行为是主张法律权利的行为，大多数法学评论者似乎认为投入到诉讼中的资源对社会没有增加任何价值，是社会沉没成本，因而需要将其控制到最小水平，然而这个想法可能显然是错的。诉讼行为影响基本行为并为基本行为提供激励，比如，诉讼的诸多困难创造了使人们合理安排自己的基本行为的激励因素，从而避免诉讼的发生，并因此优化了社会生产率。另一方面，诉讼成本也可能产生不当的激励因素阻碍有价值的基本行为。理解诉讼行为与基本行为之间关系的关键点在于它们都是庞大最优化问题中的一部分，并且需要用精准的方式进行思考。[37] 在这个思考过程中，包括了用分析术语对系统中的事物进行思考，而非一般的一阶谓词逻辑或法学研究中普遍使用的三段论术语。

我最近在米德讲座中就这个题目作了演讲：

法律制度的现实并不是美好、整齐、简单和静态的，其情境如同煮皂锅中的肥皂泡，是一个凌乱、复杂、有机和进化的过程。用来规制这种乱象的标准化工具是规则，正是该工具与其诸多用途之间的摩擦力，大体上解释了为什么事实认定与法律规范之间看起来总是存在问题。这种相同关系解释了很多法律谜题，例如，重要性升序，标准化法律错误分析的奇怪含义，规则与标准之间的争论，以及“法律”的含义。

作为设置必要或充分条件之规则的简单概念，其结果可从中演绎出来，这是单调逻辑的例子。其中，假定或假设的增加，仅仅增加了可从先前假设中演绎出来的东西。正如现代数学的出现以及很多科学领域的成就所表明的，单调逻辑是强大的工具。当它们的操作性假设准确捕获其领域时其运行最佳，在哈耶克著名的二分法中，这意味着它们在诸如游戏等即成系统中运行良好，而在成长型或组织化系统中运行稍差，这代表了人类的大部分情况。[38] 关于规则及其局限性的很大一部分争议，通常暗含着相关领域的复杂性，以及人们对不同种类错误的容忍程度。随着相关变量的数目增加，或者当其中某些变量连续而非不连续增加的时候，即使对计算机来说，演绎问题也会迅速变成无法计算的难题，更不用说人类了。当然，如果一个新变量突然出现，且其之前没有预料到，所有演绎赌注就结束了，就像原来一样。在任何一种情况下（计算性难解或想象的失败），依赖现存规则的算法、方法，将产生对规则不确定性的标准化批判。在现实中，规则并不是不确定的，相反，它们被用于去完成并非最理想的任务。[39]

我在那个讲座中斗胆主张，法律制度的核心问题与理性的核心问题是相似的，即驯服复杂性。在两种情形下，所运用的简单演绎工具都是次佳的。这就产生了一个重要问题，到底什么方法才是更有成效的？受到我多年前偶然读到的蒂姆·范·哥德尔一篇杰出文章的启发，我破天荒地提出的一个可能答案是：理性对复杂性的驯化斗争，可能更类似动态调节器而非数字计算，就如同瓦特离心调速器成为工业革命的关键部件。[40] 类似地，法律分析可能也需要在

[37] 拉里·劳丹在《真理、错误与刑法》（剑桥大学出版社，2006 年版）中开始此过程，并且此过程给予我们某些合著的动机。

[38] 弗雷德里希·A·哈耶克：《法律、立法、自由：规则和命令》，第 35～54 页，1973 年版。

[39] 同前引⑥。

[40] 蒂姆·范·哥德尔：《如果没有计算法，认知可能会是什么样?》，载《哲学杂志》，第 92 卷，1995 年，第 348 页。

演变中处理制度复杂性问题。范·戈尔德的例子是一个隐喻，而不是就我的目的而言的一种论证，因为它只提供了可能性建议而非一项已界定的研究项目，不过该提法还是很有趣的。

英国纺织工业的发展依赖于一种变量极其有限的持续能量。蒸汽机提供了这种能量，但其活塞提供了短促的能量爆发，而不是一种平缓的持续流。飞轮有帮助作用，但仍不充分。正如范·歌德尔所指出的，人们对该问题的潜在解决方案是计算性的：

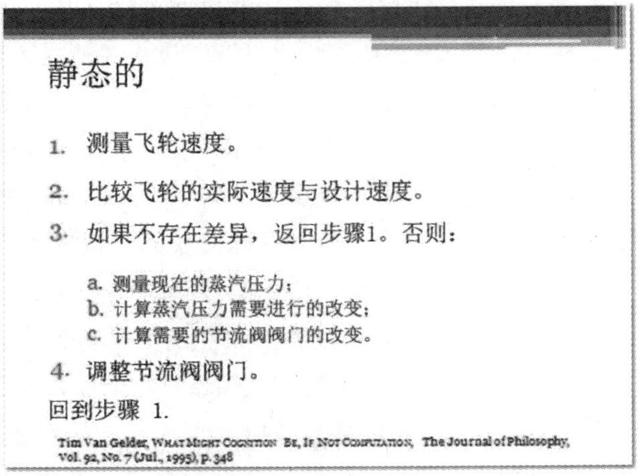

不幸的是，这种计算解决方案要求昂贵的人力成本来完成，而且难以生产出足够顺畅的能源。詹姆斯·瓦特通过在飞轮中心的轴承上安装活动机械臂解决了这一问题，其运动被即刻传送至控制蒸汽流动的阀门上。当飞轮转速提升时，机械臂会伸长而传送到阀门上，并关闭它，直至达到适当平衡，反之亦然：

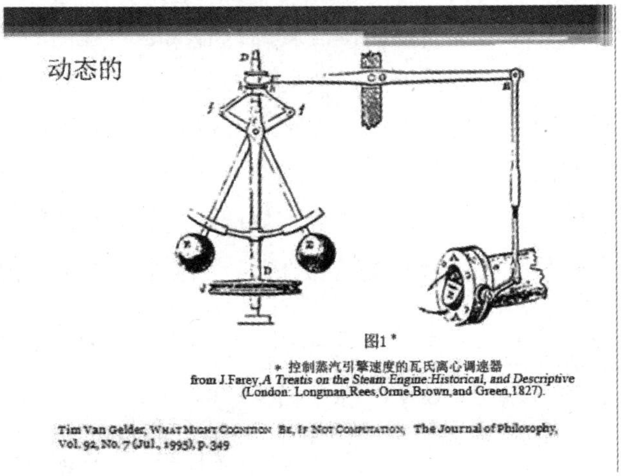

无论离心调节器是否捕获了关于合理性的某些重要内容，以这种比喻来看待法律制度也许是富有成效的。最引人注目的一点是：一些问题能够不通过演绎论证而被解决。[41] 那就是上文所讨论的致命的操作局限性，并且那也是对法学界的一种持续约束。[42] 把问题分解为更小的部分对其解决无疑是有用的，但与此同时，这个过程也可能导致问题的无法解决，从而掩饰而不是凸显了所考察实体的性质。包括我们自己在内所进行的说服责任研究，也证明了这一点。替代的做法也许像流体力学对待液体、气体的流动那样，对法律制度进行了更多的思考，换句话说，我们必须去拥抱现实生活的混乱，而不是将其抽象掉。

我目前正在自己的研究中探索另一种可能性，这涉及将法律制度概念化的经验充分性视为一种最优化问题，包括本质上类似于神经网络的东西。“法律制度”的传统概念化在很大程度上是建立在规则概念的基础上的。这对大多数学术领域来说显然是对的；确实，“学说”和“学术领域”在很大程度上是指规则和规则集，尽管它们的模糊性和缺点也是众所周知的。甚至过去 50 年，哈特、德沃金及其支持者之间的重大法学争论，在很大程度上是一场关于规则及其局限性的争论，即把它们概念化并以一种层级严明的方式进行裁决，包括论辩、适用以及被高级法院复审。

我的直觉是，经验地对法律制度进行更充分的概念化，在于它包含巨大数量的裁决节点或轨迹，就如同在神经系统网络中一样，与未知数量的其他节点发生着即时通信。例如，当审判法院达成一项裁决时，它就被传输给全国很多有着类似关注的其他人们，而不仅是位于该审判法院之上的上诉法院。如果案件被提起上诉，其结果便又被传输给整个利益相关方网络。即便某一特殊案件是终审，其他当事人亦能在其他司法辖区直接抨击它，或者以几乎无限多样的方式对其作出回应。任何特定裁决之潜在破坏性越大，对该系统中其他“结点”回应它、试图修正、限制或拒绝它的刺激就越强。因此，规则或规则适用就成为一种引起波及效应的制度性干扰，引起反应，直到最终达到某种新的平衡。因此，对于某一规则或其运用所要问的问题，不是其是否“正确”，而是其是否最佳，而最佳是指对平衡之破坏效果的判断。

我认为，这种将法律制度概念化的方式具有巨大解释力。例如，它解释了上面提到的许多说服责任的困难。它们从将说服责任视为演绎规则而非复杂系

[41] 关于同情本文观点的一个讨论，参见苏珊·哈克：《法律中的逻辑：“有一些但非全部”》，载《比率法学》，第 20 卷，2007 年，第 1 页。

[42] 美国法学院中的经验研究的兴起，在一定程度上回应了这个问题。

统之成分的观点中浮现出来。应当问的问题不是“说服责任是什么”，而是不同表达有什么效果。

我认为，这种概念化的解释力延伸到了更广泛的领域。例如，它解释了德沃金议程为什么简直是不可能的，无论其是关注法律制度还是道德。[43] 正如没有算法能预测一个水分子将如何在山溪中向下滑落（尽管那显然是一个完全的决定论过程）一样，没有人能知晓什么是法律或道德的最佳重建。相比之下，人们可从事一场超越规则（或其他无论什么）不同表达之不同效果的永无止境的谈判。现在，对我而言，法律制度的最佳解释，恰恰是一个超越那些效果的永无止境的谈判过程，持续于大量相互联系的节点，其中，证明责任推进其朝向一方或另一方的结局。

[43] 例如，参见罗纳德·德沃金：《法律的帝国》（1986年）和《刺猬正义》（2011年）。

Standards of Proof and the Limits of Legal Analysis

Ronald J. Allen *

Generally speaking, three burdens can be imposed upon a party at trial: the burden of pleading, the burden of producing evidence, and the burden of persuasion. Burdens of pleading specify the conditions under which factual/legal issues will be deemed to be included within a litigated case. They can be distributed any way the law maker prefers, although usually they are allocated to the party asking for a change in the status quo. There are exceptions to this general rule designed to respond to this or that policy concern, such as the requirement that criminal defendants plead specifically an alibi even though an "alibi" is nothing but a general denial. Burdens of pleading are significant in that they create the scaffold of the trial; but they pose no interesting conceptual challenge, and thus they can be put aside. ①

The remaining burdens—burdens of production and persuasion—together comprise what is normally meant by the phrase "standards of proof." Various countries give differing names to these two concepts, such as the evidential burden and the standard of proof, but whatever their titles the underlying concepts are clear. Parties can be required to produce evidence or face losing an issue or the entire case. Once a satisfactory evidentiary base is compiled, decision has to be reached in the face of uncertainty, and the burden of persuasion

* I am indebted to my good friends, co-authors, and somewhat in this article good humored foils, Larry Laudan and Michael Pardo, for commenting on an earlier draft of this paper.

① The *Twombly* revolution in federal pleading practice actually brings burdens of pleading under the coverage of the central thesis offered in this article by directly making the adequacy of the pleadings depend on a cost/benefit analysis of allowing the case to proceed, where part of the analysis is the probability of success on the merits. Ronald J. Allen & Alan E. Guy, *Conley as a Special Case of Twombly and Iqbal: Exploring the Intersection of Evidence, Procedure, and the Nature of Rules*, 115 Penn. St. L. Rev. 1 (2010).

specifies the decision rule to be employed. These are universal analytical requirements that are entailed by the conceptual nature of litigation. [②]Evidence must be produced if a disinterested third party is to decide the facts of the matter, and decision is virtually always under uncertainty.

Although it remains conventional to distinguish the burden of production from the burden of persuasion, Prof. McNaughton long ago demonstrated that the burden of production is a function of the burden of persuasion. [③]The measure of whether a burden of production is satisfied is, following the presentation of evidence, there remains a triable factual question—whether, in other words, further proceedings regarding that fact are in order. That depends both on the state of the evidence, but critically as well on the burden of persuasion. If a party with the burden of production produces some evidence of a factual issue, but no reasonable person could find for that party, given the burden of persuasion, then it is pointless to expend further resources on that factual issue and judgment should be entered accordingly (however this is done in each idiosyncratic procedural context). Thus, the critical conceptual issues of "standards of proof" reduce to the meaning and application of the burden of persuasion.

I intend to examine those conceptual issues in this article. First, I will demonstrate that the legal significance, and explanatory power, of the burden of persuasion ranges far beyond simply determining the implications of burdens of production. In this first part of the article, I will assume that the conventional understanding of burdens of persuasion as being probability measures is accurate. With the aid of that assumption, I will show that the burden of persuasion is one of the critical conceptual tools for understanding the litigation process. Second, I will address the current controversy over the substantive content of the burden of persuasion and the related controversy over the rela-

② Some continental theorists have tried to deny this on the ground that the standard of "intime conviction" avoids error, but this is literally impossible unless appointment as a judge in Europe creates omniscience, which I doubt. It is thus a positive development to see astute observers such as Jordi Ferrer Beltrán notice the limits of the slogan. See, e. g., *Legal Proof and Legal Truth* (Bentham Revisited), ms. p. 18.

③ John T. McNaughton, *Burden of Production of Evidence: A Function of Burden of Persuasion*, 68 Harv. L. Rev. 1382 (1955).

tionship between burdens of persuasion and errors. This analysis will include critically examining the assumption that the burden of persuasion is a probability measure. Indeed, I will attempt to demonstrate that the conventional understanding of the burden of persuasion and the recent efforts to respond to its shortcomings are inadequate as empirical descriptions of the relevant phenomena, and further that this inadequacy suggests that the analytical tools being employed misconceive rather than enlighten the object of inquiry.

One final introductory word. Much of the legal scholarship on burdens of persuasion, as on virtually all topics, is not meant to be descriptively adequate or contribute to discovery of knowledge, but instead is normative. My effort here is to the contrary. I will try to uncover certain interesting aspects of the problem to advance knowledge about them, and I will not editorialize about these matters. To be sure, a clearer understanding of the facts of the matter may yield more compelling normative analyses, but my objective here remains understanding not editorializing about the matters under investigation. Perhaps ironically, one implication of this analysis will be that different tools of legal analysis must be employed if one is to gain deeper understanding of legal phenomena. Of course, whether a deeper understanding is a desideratum is entirely subjective, and my argument will be IF this is a desideratum, THEN certain things follow.

I. The Significance of the Burden of Persuasion

As we have already seen, the burden of persuasion determines the meaning of the burden of production. It is also the key to understanding discrete jury control devices, such as affirmative defenses, presumptions, inferences, and judicial comment and notice, as well as more macro control devices such as, directed verdicts, summary judgments, and judgments as a matter of law. In each case, a burden of persuasion is directly or indirectly being imposed on a party or modified as it applies to a party. For reasons that will soon become clear, it is useful to sort out direct manipulations of the burden of persuasion from indirect manipulations. I begin with the former.

There are numerous direct allocations of the burden of persuasion. The substantive law determines who has the burden of persuasion through its articulation of elements and defenses, the only difference between the two being who has the burden of persuasion. In the Anglo-American realm, this allocation often occurs explicitly in statutory or common law rules. There is nothing conceptually difficult about this process, although there can be reasonable disagreements as to who should bear what burden. For example, should lack of contributory negligence be an element of a negligence cause of action or a defense to it? Should criminal defendants have to prove their own insanity or should the government have to prove sanity beyond reasonable doubt? There can be both moral and practical considerations favoring either, but once the decision is made its implementation is straight forward. If the plaintiff or state bears the burden of persuasion on an issue, it is labeled an element; if the defendant does, it is labeled a defense (sometime an "affirmative defense" to distinguish such things as contributory negligence from a straight forward denial) . In addition, the law can mix and match burdens of production and persuasion. There is nothing incoherent about requiring the defendant to bear a burden of production on an issue and the plaintiff to then bear the burden of persuasion. Of course, while coherent, it is unclear what is accomplished by this, as again the burden of production is a function of burdens of persuasion. Thus, only cases literally in equipoise should come out different, which is surely an exceedingly small set. ④

Allocations of burdens of persuasion, and thus the creation of defenses, also occur somewhat obscurely but still directly through the use of presumptions. This is done with legal language to the affect that "upon proof of X, a presumption of Y arises that must be rebutted" by one party or the other. The language of "presumptions" is ubiquitous but pointless; all this amounts to is the direct allocation of a burden of persuasion. There are other uses of "presumption" language, but in each case the language is truly epiphenomenal, merely obfuscating rather simple relationships. In general, presumptions serve

④ The way things work out in practice may differ from theory. Some studies suggest that preponderance of the evidence is understood as considerably higher than 0. 5 probability. Unfortunately, these studies do not show any operational consequence to the verbal descriptions. See, e. g. , Rita Simon and L. Mahan, *Quantifying Burdens of Proof: A View from the Bench, the Jury and the Classroom*, 5 Law and Soc. Rev. 319 (1971); D. Kagehiro & W. C. Stanton, *Legal vs. Quantified Definitions of Standards of Burden of Proof*, 9 L. & Hum. Beh. 159 (1985) . Mention empirical studies on how fact finders interpret burdens.

four different functions, three of which directly allocate or affect burdens of persuasion. They are used to articulate legal rules—these are the so-called irrebuttable presumptions, as just mentioned to allocate directly burdens of persuasion, and to allocate burdens of production, which as we have seen involve burdens of persuasion. [⑤]I will discuss these three uses of "presumption" language immediately below, and will then turn to the fourth use of presumptions—to provide for inferences and comments on the evidence. This use of the term involves indirect manipulations of the burden of persuasion and will be discussed in that context.

For various reasons, the law provides direct resolution of what might otherwise be contested facts. For example, proof that a person drove faster than the speed limit or with more than a certain amount of alcohol in his veins or evidence that a person violated a safety statute were at one time said to create an irrebuttable presumption of negligence. All this meant, however, is that the proof of the underlying condition—speeding, drunk driving, violating a safety statute—satisfied the elements of the cause of action, and thus satisfied whatever burden of persuasion might otherwise have been a play. In other instances, similar proof was held to create a rebuttable presumption, such as the presumption that a mailed letter was received by the addressee. This conclusion could be rebutted either by showing by a preponderance to the contrary, or by showing that a reasonable person could conclude by a preponderance to the contrary—and this is the critical distinction between the allocation of a burden of persuasion and a burden of production. In each instance, though, plainly the central feature is one or another type of direct manipulation of the burden of persuasion.

This exact same point applies to the various macro control devices, such as directed verdicts, summary judgments, judgment notwithstanding the verdict, and new trial orders, as has recently been demonstrated by Michael Pardo. [⑥]Each of these should be entered only when there is no jury issue or a jury reached an indefensible result, but when that is the case will depend on the burden of persuasion. New trial orders allow some greater latitude to the trial judge to handle second order proof problems—how confident is the judge that

⑤ Ronald J. Allen, *Presumptions in Civil Actions Reconsidered*, 66 Iowa L. Rev. 843 (1981).

⑥ Michael S. Pardo, *Pleadings, Proof, and Judgment: A Unified Theory of Civil Litigation*, 51 B. C L. Rev. 1451 (2010).

only one result is defensible or an indefensible result was reached? If quite confident, directed verdicts, summary judgments, or judgment notwithstanding the verdict are entered. If less but still reasonably confident, a new trial order permits the check of a second jury. The important point here, though, is that this entire analysis is driven directly by burdens of persuasion.

There are indirect manipulations of the burden of persuasion as well. Many evidentiary devices as well as the admission or exclusion of evidence can affect the relative burden of persuasion even though the explicit burden of persuasion may remain unaffected. ⑦Comment on the evidence, instructions on inferences (which are comments on the evidence), exclusion of relevant evidence or the admission of misleading evidence all change the relative burden of persuasion. ⑧ The fourth form of presumptions noted above does as well. It is used to create disguised comments/inference instructions through "presumption" language. A typical instruction is that "on proof of X a presumption of Y arises that is evidence of Y." There is no possible meaning of "a presumption is evidence of some fact" except to encourage the fact finder to find the fact upon finding the basic fact of the presumption. This, obviously, is a comment on the evidence.

The effect of these various evidentiary manipulations on burdens of persuasion can be seen by comparing two cases in which the only distinguishing feature is that one does not contain one of these manipulations and the other does. Assume two cases with essentially identical facts that involve the crime of knowing possession of stolen goods where the only evidence of knowledge is the fact of possession of recently stolen goods. Assume further that the judiciary has come to believe that the possession of recently stolen goods is very highly correlated with knowledge of the nature of the goods, but the judges also believe this knowledge is not widely possessed by the general populace who make up juries. And last, assume that in one case the judge provides a judicial

⑦ This phenomenon was first identified in Ronald J. Allen, *Structuring Jury Decisionmaking in Criminal Cases: A Unified Constitutional Analysis*, 94 Harv. L. Rev. 321, 331 (1980). Larry Laudan refers to this in "Is It Finally Time to Put 'Proof Beyond a Reasonable Doubt' out to Pasture?" at ms. p. 11.

⑧ See, Allen, supra n. 8, at 332-339. Some of what follows borrows heavily from that source.

comment on the evidence or an inference instruction on the relationship between possession and knowledge, while in the other the judge says nothing about the matter.

In the case without judicial comment, the jury might conceivably convict, but the chance of acquittal is higher than in the second case, in which the judge explains the implications of possessing recently stolen goods. The judge's comment increases the chance of conviction by enhancing the effect of the state's evidence. In order for the defendant to have the same chance of acquittal in the second case as in the first, the defendant would have to produce more persuasive rebuttal evidence than that advanced in the first case. Although the formal relationship between the state and the defendant has remained the same—the jury has applied the reasonable doubt standard in each case—the comment has modified the relative burdens of persuasion by altering the factual matrix within which the jury reached its decision. This demonstrates that the effect of judicial comment is to change the relative positions of the parties by modifying the relative burden of persuasion that a party bears on an issue, just as with affirmative defenses and placement of the burden of production. The exclusion of relevant evidence and the admission of irrelevant but misleading evidence has exactly the same consequence, as whoever is adversely affected by the evidentiary decision must do more to meet the burden of persuasion. ⑨

One objection to this analysis should be noted and resolved. That objection is that the burden of persuasion is on one party and not the other, and thus it may seem to make no sense to talk about shifting the relative burden of persuasion. This conventional view is false. Burdens of persuasion are reciprocal. To say that the plaintiff bears the burden of proving the case by a preponderance is isomorphic to the defendant having to show that the evidence does not show by a preponderance that the plaintiff deserves to win, or, taking out the negative, that there is at least 0.5 chance that the defendant's case is true. Even in criminal cases where it is said, erroneously, that defendants bear no burden of persuasion on elements, they actually do. Again, the statements are equiva-

⑨ So, too, does the admission of relevant evidence and the exclusion of irrelevant evidence, but presumably these activities move the decision maker to the idealized correct decision.

lent that the prosecution must prove an element beyond reasonable doubt and that the defendant must show there is a reasonable doubt.

In sum, the burden of persuasion conceptualized as a conventional probability measure has enormous explanatory power. It allows for the meaning of the term "presumption" to be unpacked[10]; it allows a unified analysis of evidentiary and procedural devices[11]; and it even permits order to be given the complexities of the constitutional requirement of proof beyond reasonable doubt in the United States. [12]However, it is increasingly clear that there are limits to the accuracy and utility of modeling the burden of persuasion as a conventional probability measure. That, in turn, raises doubts about the tools of legal analysis that are ubiquitously employed by legal analysts, or alternatively about the adequacy of the conception of the phenomenon they are studying. I turn now to these issues.

II. The Limits of Legal Analysis

The attraction of a probabilistic analysis of burdens of persuasion is obvious. It is consistent with an equally attractive conceptualization of the evidentiary process as the updating of probabilities in the light of new evidence. Together, the two appear to explain both the evidentiary process at trial and the application of the decision rule at the end of the trial. Notwithstanding their appeal, the empirical and analytical inadequacy of these conceptualizations has become quite clear. For example, burdens of persuasion can play their allotted role in these conceptualizations only if they involve relative frequencies (how else can one say anything about errors?), yet the only interpretation of probability theory that has any possible explanatory power for juridical proof is subjective belief states. There is virtually never knowledge of relative frequencies at trial, DNA being an interesting exception to be sure; nor do either the propensity or logical theories of probability have any application. [13]The subjective theory is obviously false as a descriptive mat-

[10] Allen, supra n. 5 .

[11] Pardo, supra n. 6.

[12] Allen, supra n. 5.

[13] For a discussion of theories of probability, see Donald Gillies, *Philosophical Theories of Probability* (2000) .

ter in the United States; no fact finder is instructed to consult his or her subjective belief states or personal utilities. They are instructed, sensibly enough one might think, to find the facts. Moreover, the structure of trial is radically inconsistent with the demands of subjective probability theory. Fact finders are instructed not to update in the light of new evidence, and in any event the updating would be computationally intractable.[14] Whatever the normative attraction of subjective theories of probability, or other uses they may serve (such as heuristics), they are empirically inadequate descriptors.

There are further difficulties. Larry Laudan has launched a multi-faceted attack on the meaning of proof beyond reasonable doubt, in which it is conceived as a high probability.[15] Part of his attack makes use of joint work that he and I have done that establishes that the common understanding of the justification of burdens of persuasion generally (not just in criminal cases) is completely unconvincing.[16] That justification is to allocate errors consistent with various policies. In civil cases, the normal policies are to treat the parties equally and to reduce the total number of errors. In criminal cases, the policy is to protect innocent people by making it hard to convict anyone, and this supposedly is done through skewing errors in favor of acquitting the guilty (the mantra being that it is ten times worse to convict an innocent person than acquit a guilty person).

Although these slogans and ways of thinking have been around for perhaps centuries, it is plain that they suffer from irremediable defects. First, there are four decisions that can be made at trial, and all have social benefits or costs. In addition to errors, correct decisions can be made. Neglecting correct decisions is perverse. For example, in civil cases, the error equalization policy is satisfied by making errors in every single case, so long as the base rates of cases that go to trial include roughly the same number of deserving plaintiffs

⑭ Ronald J. Allen, *Rationality, Algorithms, and Juridical Proof: A Preliminary Inquiry*, 1997 International Journal of Evidence and Proof (Special Issue) 254.

⑮ Larry Laudan, *Truth, Error and Criminal Law* (Cambridge University Press, 2006).

⑯ Ronald J. Allen & Larry Laudan, *Deadly Dilemmas*, 41 Texas Tech. L. Rev. 65-92 (2008); Larry Laudan & Ronald J. Allen, *Deadly Dilemmas II: Bail and Crime*, 85 Chi. Kent L. Rev. 23-42 (2010); Ronald J. Allen & Larry Laudan, *Deadly Dilemmas III: Some Kind Words for Preventive Detention*, 101 J. Crim. L. Crim. 781 (2011).

and defendants. Similarly, in criminal cases, the ratio of 10 incorrect acquittals to one incorrect conviction is satisfied by 99 out of every 100 cases being wrongly decided. Furthermore, without knowledge of the bases rates of deserving parties that go to trial and the relationship between the assessments of fact finders and true states of affairs⑰, there is literally no way to predict the effect of a burden of persuasion on correct or incorrect decisions. If everyone who goes to trial is guilty, for example, there can be no convictions of the innocent, no matter how low the standard of proof. The conventional discourse on burdens also assumes a static system, whereas in fact it is dynamic. One aspect of this dynamism is that parties decide which cases to take further into the procedural system, and can adjust their decision in light of changes in the rules. Thus, the simple assumption that lowering the standard of proof in criminal cases will cause more errors of convicting the guilty, or any other suggested cause and effect relationship between burdens and outcomes, is obviously not analytically true; it depends on how the system responds to the change. ⑱

The problems with these conventional modes of analysis press even more deeply. Trial decisions are only one part of the output of the legal system. Parties negotiate outcomes in both civil and criminal cases. They do so in the shadow of trials, among other things, but the outcomes in those cases are obviously part of the total social welfare effects of a legal system. More plainly put, it could be the case that quite random outcomes at trial or relatively high costs are socially optimal because they encourage party settlement. ⑲

⑰ For example, working with a probabilistic conception, one needs to know what the relationship is between findings of the probability of liability and actual liability. Implicit in the conventional discourse is that a finding that the probability of liability is 0. 8 means that in eight out of ten similar cases, the true facts are consistent with liability. However, there could be any relationship at all between fact finders' findings of probability and true states of affairs. In the set of all cases where fact finders find there to be a 0. 8 probability of liability, it could be true that all cases in that subset are cases where no liability should be found.

⑱ Laudan and Ferrer Beltrán assert to the contrary, but plainly error rates cannot be deduced from the decision rule alone. See Ferrer Beltrán, supra n. 2, at ms. p. 14, in particular n. 12, asserting that the decision rule mediates the probability of Type I and Type II error. This is not analytically true in the legal context. See also, Laudan, supra n. 7, at ms. pp. 9-11.

⑲ For discussion of this point, see Ronald J. Allen, *Rationality and the Taming of Complexity*, 62 Ala. L. Rev. 1047 (2011); Allen & Laudan, *Deadly Dilemmas III: Some Kind Words for Preventive Detention*, 101 J. Crim. L. Crim. 781 (2011) .

The empirical inadequacy of the conventional accounts of burdens of persuasion has generated three recent efforts to substitute an alternative theory. Two of those, created respectively by Larry Laudan and Jordi Ferrer Beltrán, are explicitly normative rather than positive, but they nonetheless are interesting in their implications for present conceptualizations of burdens of proof. The third, by Michael Pardo and myself, is explicitly positive, and while that is a virtue from my perspective, it has other interesting limitations. I will briefly explore these three theories and then turn to the limits of conventional legal analysis.

Larry Laudan's recent work extends his many complaints about the concept, such as it is, of proof beyond reasonable doubt. [20] He complains, accurately, about its remarkable ambiguity and that in addition notes that it is "preposterous" because of its subjectivity. [21]He reminds us of his previous proposal of a way to understand what proof beyond reasonable doubt should mean:

It rests on the insight emerging from statistics and the philosophy of science that a powerful test of the truth of any empirical hypothesis, H, is its ability to account for apparent facts or data that seem utterly unintelligible if H were false. Applied to the legal context, the idea would be that the prosecution's claim that the defendant is guilty acquires high plausibility just to the extent that some pertinent evidence has been established as prima facie true that can be readily accounted for if the defendant is guilty but that would be highly unexpected if the defendant were innocent. If some of the important features of the case that the guilt hypothesis can make sense of are likewise compatible with an hypothesis of innocence, then the prosecution's case is insufficiently strong to warrant a conviction. Likewise, if there are any pertinent facts that make sense only on the hypothesis of innocence, then an acquittal is called for. In short, this proposed standard demands that a conviction is warranted if and only if a) the hypothesis of guilt can explain most of the salient

⑳ Larry Laudan, *Is It Finally Time to Put "Proof Beyond a Reasonable Doubt" out to Pasture?* . See also chapter two of Larry Laudan, *Truth, Error and Criminal Law* (Cambridge University Press, 2006) .

㉑ Laudan, ms. p. 6.

facts of the case, and b) the innocence hypothesis can account for no important evidence that is inexplicable on the guilt hypothesis. Just as we say that a scientific hypothesis that makes no surprising, corroborated predictions—unanticipated by its rivals—is not very credible, so a guilt hypothesis not backed up by very surprising evidence in its favor lacks the strong empirical support that should be a sine qua non for a conviction. [22]

Laudan proceeds to acknowledge that the distributional consequences of a proposed definition of beyond reasonable doubt must be taken into account in addition to the attractiveness of the definition in the abstract. Nonetheless, I will focus just on the proposed definition, for, notwithstanding its creativity, I believe it is further evidence of the limits of conventional analysis. And in any event, as noted above, the distributional consequences of any rule or rule change is an empirical rather than analytical question.

The essential analytical move Laudan makes is to search for a decision rule from a related discipline to substitute for the inadequate legal decision rule, and in this case he takes it from generalizations about the progress of science. There are two difficulties. First, there is only a casual relationship between the typical activities of scientific inquiry and that of the legal system. Second, Laudan looks to the wrong phase of science, that of discovery or justification, rather than to the more analogous phase of application. I discuss these two points in turn.

Consider the differences between the standard trial and the research activities of most scientific fields. [23]At trial, the effort virtually always is to determine what happened. The purpose is not to uncover general causal laws, although general causal laws may be and often are invoked as evidence that some event occurred. In most scientific efforts, the data are not ambiguous, although their causes are generally puzzling. What actually happens, such as particles have mass or are attracted to each other, is the starting point for attempting to explain why it happened (such as the search for the Higgs boson) —the search for the general caus-

[22] Laudan ms. at 7-8.

[23] The next few paragraphs rely on Ronald J. Allen, *Factual Ambiguity and a Theory of Evidence*, 88 Nw. Univ. L. Rev. 604 (1994) .

al law, in other words. Experiments can be run and rerun, and often tweaked along the way, in order to uncover a possible explanation. In the law, exactly the opposite obtains. Inconsistent primary data ("the light was red" — "no, it was green") are the norm, and replication is generally impossible. Controversy always settles on what happened. Why something happened (whatever did happen) may be disputed, and parties may advance varying and conflicting generalizations, scientific or otherwise, for the benefit of the fact finder, but they will be advanced in an inferential structure leading to a conclusion about a fact or series of facts rather than about a universal, a principle, or a theory.

Two other significant differences between science and law obtain. Scientific knowledge is organized in a top-down, deductive fashion. Scientific inquiry focuses on either systematizing further the deductive structure of preexisting knowledge through the elimination of anomalies (empirically or theoretically) or on the modification or replacement of the conceptual structure of the field. The differences between these activities caused quite a stir in the philosophy of science half a century ago[24], but the similarities of their respective practitioners is remarkable. They share a well-organized body of substantive knowledge and methodological approaches. They disagree, but over well-defined issues. Even those assaulting the conceptual foundations of a field typically share with those doing work within a field methodological and mathematical principles, agree on what counts as evidence, and are able to express their scope of disagreement comprehensibly.

This description of the activity of scientific research does not describe factual inquiry in the legal process. The difference is not that scientific inquiry is highly complicated and lay judgments about ordinary life quite simple, but the exact opposite. Scientific progress in large measure proceeds through the simplification of problems, in particular through controlling as many variables as possible. Judgments about ordinary events, by contrast, virtually never are and cannot be recast as the results of controlled experi-

[24] The major players in this drama were Thomas Kuhn, *The Structure of Scientific Revolutions* (1962); Karl Popper, *The Logic of Scientific Discovery* (1934). For a compendium of perspectives on the problem, see Frederick Suppe (ed.), *The Structure of Scientific Theories* (2nd, 1977).

ments. Too many variables are constantly and necessarily in play. And factual judgments at trial are even more resistant to domestication because the complicating features of the trial process are draped over the bubbling cauldron of real life.

Consider a simple example I constructed some years ago：

Suppose a witness begins testifying，and thus a fact finder must decide what to make of the testimony. What are some of the relevant variables? First，there are all the normal credibility issues，but consider how complicated they are. Demeanor is not just demeanor；it is instead a complex set of variables. Is the witness sweating or twitching，and if so is it through innocent nerves，the pressure of prevarication，a medical problem，or simply a distasteful habit picked up during a regrettable childhood? Does body language suggest truthfulness or evasion；is slouching evidence of lying or comfort in telling a straight forward story? Does the witness look the examiner straight in the eye，and if so is it evidence of commendable character or the confidence of an accomplished snake oil salesman? Does the voice inflection suggest the rectitude of the righteous or is it strained，and does a strained voice indicate fabrication or concern over the outcome of the case? And so on.

The list of relevant variables goes far beyond credibility issues，of which demeanor is only one. When a witness articulates a proposition，the fact finder must determine what the proposition is designed to assert and what the fact finder believes it asserts. That task，too，involves an immense number of variables. In addition，the fact finder will possess some knowledge based on its observations leading up to the first articulated proposition by a witness，acquired from the lawyers for example. And there are many more examples. For the law to proceed as a science would require that many of these variables be in a deductive structure with their necessary and sufficient conditions spelled out. No such structure could be created；it would be too complex. ㉕

The second difference is equally critical. Scientific inquiry focuses on what fruitfully can be explored with the techniques of modern science. If a question does not yield to those techniques，such as what happened before the Big

㉕ Allen，supra n. 5，at 626-626.

Bang, it is simply ignored. Moreover, there is no need to decide the answer to an experimental question. If the experiments render ambiguous results, or there is worry about some uncontrolled variable, or whatever, more work can be done until the investigators are more or less satisfied with the results. The law does not have the luxury of picking its disputes. Whatever the problem is, it must be dealt with. Nor does it have the luxury of postponing decision indefinitely, because not to decide is to decide. Legal disputes involve arguments over whether to modify or preserve the status quo. Not to decide typically leaves the status quo unmodified and thus one side obtains what it desires.

In sum, it is not at all obvious why a decision rule from such a radically different intellectual enterprise can usefully be imported into the law. Even were one inclined to do so, the decision rule from the enterprise of discovery, which is what Prof. Laudan proposes, seems to be the wrong one. The sorts of variables that he identifies are the ones many scientists and philosophers of science think best assist in the discovery of new scientific knowledge. If a new and purportedly better explanation of some phenomenon is offered, it is persuasive if that explanation makes surprising predictions that are then confirmed, such as Einstein's that light will bend around the sun. [26] But for the most part trials do not involve surprising predictions; they involve the most mundane of disputes such as who is telling the truth and who is lying. [27] To make a conviction depend on the production of "very surprising evidence" that is explained by creative, startling, or counter-intuitive hypotheses, or any other type of out of the ordinary hypothesis, is to doom prosecutors to virtually no convictions and more fundamentally to misconceive the nature of the trial process. And it is unclear why defendants should not be subject to the same standard, in which case there will be fewer acquittals whenever an affirmative defense is offered. Few

[26] Popper argued that the progress of science include making bold predictions and then attempting to falsify them. See Popper, supra n. 24. For one of the empirical tests of the prediction of general relativity, see F. W Dyson, A. S., Eddington, C. Davidson, *A Determination of the Deflection of Light by the Sun's Gravitational Field*, from Observations Made at the Total Eclipse of 29 May 1919, 220A Philos. Trans. Royal Soc. London 291 (1920).

[27] See transcript in Ronald J. Allen, Richard B. Kuhns, Eleanor Swift & David S. Schwartz, *Evidence: Text, Problems and Cases* (4th ed., 2006), pp. 2-75.

“convictions” and “acquittals” works in the context of science, but may not in the context of trials (that depends on whether one thinks the status quo is objectionable) .

It is also too rigorous a burden to expect the cases of the prosecution and defendant to be more or less hermitically sealed from each other, even if this is limited to whatever “important features” may refer to (and the phrase is quite ambiguous; what is “important” will be intensely idiosyncratic and dependent on what the parties assert) . The typical case at trial involves massive overlap of evidence with a few salient disagreements. [28] The fact finder's task is to decide who or what to believe to resolve those few disagreements, and provide judgment accordingly. Again, were it satisfactory for an acquittal that some of the prosecution's case is compatible with innocence, there would be no convictions, for most of a prosecution's case will always be compatible with innocence. And nothing is “utterly unintelligible” at trial. Evidentiary conflicts can come about because someone is lying to advance his or her interests. There is nothing unintelligible about that. Although I am a great admirer of Prof. Laudan's work, and in particular his forcing us within the law to engage seriously with fundamental conceptual problems, here I think he has not attended to the fundamental differences between the law and most scientific fields.

Jordi Ferrer Beltrán, more implicitly than Laudan under the influence of philosophy of science, proposes a test for proof beyond reasonable doubt that is somewhat analogous to Laudan's:

According to this standard of proof, to consider a hypothesis as proving guilt, it must meet both of the following conditions:

1. The hypothesis should be able to explain the available information in a coherent way, and predictions about new information that the hypothesis manages to outline must have been confirmed.

2. All other plausible hypotheses which offer an explanation about the same information which are compatible with the defendant's innocence should have been refuted, except for ad hoc hypotheses. [29]

[28] See Supra n. 24.

[29] Ferrer Beltrán, supra n. 2, at ms. p. 19

Although the contours of this proposal are less sharply defined than Laudan's, one can see analogous conceptual issues. With regard to the first part of the definition, trials (in the United States at least) do not involve hypotheses that "predict" new information; they involve deciding what happened in light of all the information. This test seems to involve an unhelpful conflating of the legal and scientific contexts; as discussed above, in scientific endeavors, one criterion of a theory's success is its predictions, but that has literally no application to legal fact finding. As to the second part of the definition, it is unclear what it means in two respects. Take again a typical case of witnesses testifying to opposite observations. Obviously one is telling the truth and one is not. If one concludes that the defendant's witness is lying, one has a perfectly good hypothesis of guilt; if one concludes the opposite, then one has a good hypothesis of innocence. The extent to which "information" is compatible with different assertions depends upon how that information is treated by the fact finder. A defendant who testifies to his innocence is "refuted" if the fact finder concludes that he or she is lying.

The second difficulty with this proposal is that the escape hatch that excludes "ad hoc" hypotheses seems itself to be entirely ad hoc. An example given is the claim that a criminal defendant has been "setup and framed."[30] That simply amounts to a claim of innocence and an explanation for the state's evidence. Its plausibility will depend upon everything else in the case. That is true of all claims, whether by the state or the defendant. It is impossible to see why this possible claim of innocence is different from any other. Are alibi's ad hoc? Or the claim of the lack of the proper mental state, or insanity? This amounts to a test, contained in the first criterion and the first part of the second, to be applied in some undefined subset when it does not work by claiming any interfering problem is ad hoc. If the defendant raises an issue that cannot be refuted for some reason, it can be labeled ad hoc, even though it often will be isomorphic to a direct claim of innocence. Perhaps European criminal cases are different from American criminal cases, but this proposal is obviously not an accurate description of what occurs in the United States; nor does it seem norma-

[30] Id., at n. 18.

tively attractive.

Michael Pardo and I, building on earlier work of mine on "the relative plausibility theory,"[31] have explored whether the best understanding of burdens of persuasion is that they are an example of inference to the best explanation, using that phrase to refer to cognitive processes rather than as a solution to the question of what is knowledge. The central idea is that cases involve the comparison of alternative stories and the fact finder's choice is over them or driven by them, with the more plausible of the accounts being accepted as true for purposes of the trial. In criminal cases, the prosecution must advance a plausible account of guilt or lose; if the prosecution advances a plausible account, then the defendant must advance a plausible account of innocence or lose.[32]

This conceptualization is advanced not normatively but positively, and we have tried to show over the years how it is, actually by far, the best account of the actual trial process so far identified. It has the obvious virtue of being consistent with what we know about how fact finders reason, unlike all extant probabilistic accounts as well as Laudan's and Ferrer Beltrán's accounts. It also orders and explains many aspects of the trial process, from various evidentiary rules[33] to virtually all jury instructions on the evidentiary process ("use your common sense," "listen to your fellow jurors," "you do not have to believe all the evidence but try to make sense of it,"), except the formal definition of burdens of persuasion to be sure. But as I showed above, the formal definition makes no sense at all understood as a probability measure[34], and Laudan and Ferrer Beltrán propose a completely new understanding, and so no other theory of burdens benefits from its ability to explain what the relative plausibility theory cannot.

To be sure, and to be clear, many of the commentators, including

[31] See, e. g., Ronald J. Allen, *Factual Ambiguity and a Theory of Evidence*, 88 Northwestern Law Review 604-640 (1994).

[32] Ronald J. Allen & Michael Pardo, *Juridical Proof and the Best Explanation*, 27 Law & Philosophy 223 (2008).

[33] Ronald J. Allen, *The Nature of Juridical Proof*, 13 Cardozo L. Rev. 373, 413-420 (1991).

[34] There are a host of other problems—conjunction effect, computational intractability, and so on.

Laudan and Ferrer Beltrán, are engaging in normative rather than positive efforts, whereas our is virtually exclusively positive. We are simply trying to understand what we observe over a relatively narrow observational range. We were not trying to explain, for example, how the trial process fits into larger social processes; we were not even trying to estimate what kind of results obtain from the kind of judicial process we actually observe. We would say that those are empirical questions, for the most part, not analytical ones, and can only be answered empirically. In short, the large questions posed by people like Laudan and Ferrer Beltrán are beyond the scope of our analytical efforts.

Let me now recapitulate the lay of the analytical land concerning burdens of persuasion. The conventional, probabilistic understanding is obviously false in every interesting way; the alternatives that have been advanced are either hopelessly aspirational or very limited in their implications, leaving the larger issues focused on by people like Larry Laudan unaddressed. What could explain this? One possible explanation that I wish to explore to conclude this essay is that it is a consequence of the very method of analysis that is endemic to legal research. [35]The standard method of legal research is to break problems down into manageable size and analyze them employing the standard tools of modern logic, in particular deduction. [36] I am a great fan of logical deduction, but its utility has its limits, or perhaps it is being employed in domains that are themselves too capacious for such limited tools. In either event, the standard form of legal analysis is to engage in a logical critique and then to argue for substituting a new and better rule for the critiqued one, much as Laudan, Ferrer Beltrán, have done. Allen and Pardo's work, while not quite in the same vein, nonetheless dealt with only a very small slice of the relevant universe.

Much of this work makes the implicit assumption that it is engaging with a static environment, and here is where it goes radically wrong, I believe. A

[35] This is the central theme of the Meador Lecture I gave this academic year. Ronald J. Allen, *Rationality and the Taming of Complexity*, 62 Ala. L. Rev. 1047 (2011).

[36] Much of Larry Laudan's work is not so describable; he is attempting to burst conceptual boundaries, in particular his majestic book, *Truth, Error and Criminal Law* (Cambridge University Press, 2006). This is not true, however, of his article on burdens of persuasion, supra, which neglects some of the lessons of his other work.

more accurate conception of the legal system than a system of static rules is that itis a small part of a huge optimization problem. Consider first the law of evidence, which is comprised of relatively discrete rules of necessary and sufficient conditions, leavened in a number of instances with allocations of discretionary authority to trial judges. These rules are applied to the "trial evidence," which means the testimony and physical objects proffered at trial, which supposedly provides an exhaustive basis for deducing liability. But this is false. The evidence is literally incomprehensible without rules of language and logic, yet it is simply accepted that a fact finder can process information and deliberate on it. That cannot be done without a vast storehouse of knowledge and the intelligence to use it appropriately. For the law of evidence truly to be regulatory, it must regulate the interaction between what is adduced at trial and the ensuing inferential process that depends upon fact finder's knowledge and beliefs. It is precisely this gap that generated my example above about the witness testifying.

A derivative of the conceptual point above is also pertinent to an alternative way of understanding Laudan's proposal. Dr. Laudan in graciously and helpfully commenting on a draft of this article asserted that, notwithstanding the exact wording of his proposal, he intended it as involving the context of application rather than discovery, and that what he had in mind was something like differential diagnosis in medicine. This moves his proposal significantly in the direction of the relative plausibility theory of Allen and Pardo, as well as undergirding it with inference to the best explanation, which together comprise the best explanation of juridical proof to date. Differential diagnosis, highly akin to qualitative chemical analysis, involves the elimination and inclusion of hypotheses based upon differentiating data points (e. g. if the litmus paper is blue, it's a base; if red, it's an acid). To some extent this is like story formation, but the conceptual gaps involving the nature of evidence and unique context of scientific endeavors noted previously remain. In differential diagnosis or qualitative chemical analysis, just as in the context of discovery (indeed, even more so) the data are clear—the litmus paper really was red or blue. The opposite obtains on the critical variables. One witness testifies the litmus paper was red and another blue. Or one witness testifies it was red and the other side offers evidence or points out circumstances (such as bias or interest) indicating the witness was lying. Or the fact finder simply reaches that conclusion itself based on its observations of demeanor. Trials involve untamable complexity and ambiguity that simply does not exist in standard scientific enterprises, whether in the discovery or application phase. In scientific endeavors, one does not have to gain the assent of some decision makers that is driven by that person's entire life experiences; rather, as previously noted above but equally applicable here, virtually everyone shares knowledge and methodology. Nevertheless, to the extent that differential diagnosis involves the creative articulation of possible explanations, it does indeed bear a relationship to the relative plausibility theory and inference to the best explanation, but it, like Allen & Pardo's work, would still only explain a small part of the relevant conceptual universe.

The challenge of effective legal regulation presses even more deeply. Consider the distinction between primary and litigation behavior. Primary behavior is every day activities, including economic and private behavior (and any other sort). Litigation behavior is behavior dedicated to vindicating legal rights. Resources spent on litigation appear to most legal commentators as dead weight social losses that add nothing of value to society, and thus should be kept to a minimum, yet this could obviously be false. Litigation behavior affects primary behavior and creates incentives for it, just as primary behavior affects litigation behavior and creates incentives for it, as well. For example, perhaps difficulties of litigation create incentives for people to order their primary behavior in ways to avoid litigation, and thus to optimize social productivity. Alternatively, litigation costs could create perverse incentives that overdeter productive primary behavior. The point is that that litigation and primary behavior are parts of huge optimization problems that need to be thought of in precisely that fashion. [37]This involves thinking of things in system analytic terms rather than the common first order predicate logic or syllogistic terms common to legal research.

I recently addressed this topic in my Meador Lecture:

The reality of the legal system is not nice, tidy, simple, and static, con-

[37] Larry Laudan begins this process in *Truth, Error and Criminal Law* (Cambridge University Press, 2006), and this also motivates some of our joint work.

texts but instead bubbling cauldrons of messy, complicated, organic, evolutionary processes. The standard tool used to regulate this bubbling mess is rules, and it is the friction between that tool and many of the uses to which it is put that explains in general why fact finding and legal regulation are viewed as so often problematic. This same relationship is explanatory of many legal puzzles, such as, in ascending order of importance, the curious implications of standard legal error analysis, the rules v. standards debate, and the meaning of "law."

The simple concept of a rule as setting necessary or sufficient conditions from which outcomes may be deduced is an example of monotonic logic, in which the addition of postulates or assumptions simply adds to what may be deduced from the previous assumptions. Monotonic logics are powerful tools, as the rise of modern mathematics and the success of many scientific fields demonstrate. They work best when their operant assumptions accurately capture their domains, which means they work quite well, in Hayek's famous dichotomy, in made systems such as games and less well in grown or organic systems, which typifies much of the human condition. [38] A large part of debate over rules and their limits is often implicitly about the complexity of the relevant domain and one's tolerance for mistakes of different kinds. As the number of pertinent variables increases or when some of them are continuous rather than discrete, the deductive problem quickly becomes computationally intractable, even for computers let alone humans. And of course if a new variable pops up that was not previously anticipated, all deductive bets are off, as it were. In either case (computational intractability or failure of imagination), algorithmic approaches that rely on extant rules generate the standard critiques of the indeterminate nature of rules. In reality, it is not that rules are indeterminate but that they are being put to a task for which they are not optimal. [39]

I ventured in that lecture to suggest that the central problem of the legal system is similar to the central problem of rationality, which is the taming of complexity. In both cases, simple deductive tools were being put to uses that

[38] Friederich A. Hayek, *Law, Legislation, Liberty: Rules and Order* 35-54 (1973).

[39] Allen, supra n. 5.

were suboptimal. That raises the important question what other approaches may be more fruitful. Inspired by a brilliant article by an artificial intelligence researcher, Tim Van Gelder, that I came across many years ago, one possible answer I ventured was that the struggle of rationality to tame complexity may be less like digital computation and more akin to a dynamic regulator, such as the Watt Centrifugal Governor that was a critical part of the industrial revolution.[40] Analogously, legal analysis may need to evolve to deal with the complexities of systems. Van Gelder's example is a metaphor rather than an argument for my purposes, for it provides just the suggestion of possibilities rather than a defined research program, but it is nonetheless interesting.

The growth of the textile industry in England depended upon a consistent energy source with very limited variability. The steam engine provided the energy but its pistons provided episodic bursts of energy rather than a smooth, continuous stream. Fly wheels helpful, but still not adequate. As Van Gelder pointed out, one potential solution to this problem is computational:

Static

1. **Measure the speed of the flywheel.**
2. **Compare the actual speed against the desired speed.**
3. **If there is no discrepancy, return to step 1. Otherwise,**
   a. Measure the current steam pressure;
   b. Calculate the desired alteration in steam pressure;
   c. Calculate the necessary throttle valve adjustment.
4. **Make the throttle valve adjustment**

Return to step 1

Tim Van Gelder, WHAT MIGHT COGNITION BE, IF NOT COMPUTATION, The Journal of Philosophy, Vol. 92, No. 7 (Jul., 1995), p. 348

Unfortunately, this computational solution requires a costly person doing it, and it will rarely produce a smooth enough source of energy. James Watt solved this problem by placing movable arms on a spindle at the center of the flywheel, whose motion was transmitted instantaneously to the valve regula-

[40] Tim Van Gelder, *What Might Cognition Be, If Not Computation*, 92 J. of Philosophy 348 (1995).

ting the flow of steam. As the rotation of the fly wheel speeds up, the arms extend, which transmits to the valve and closes it until the proper equilibrium is reached, and vice versa:

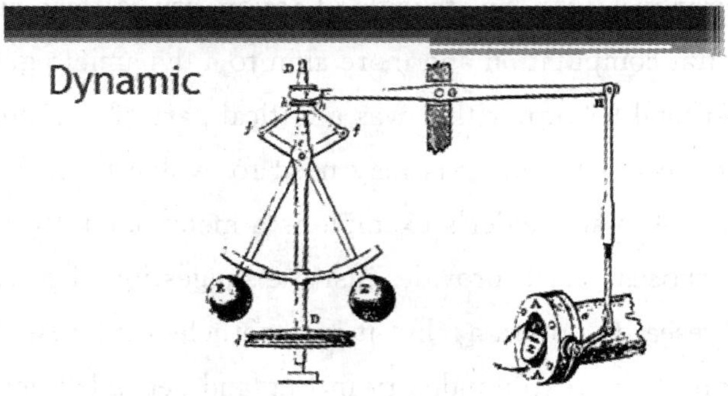

Figure 1*

*The Watt centrifugal governor for controlling the speed of a steam engine—from J. Farey, *A Treatise on the Steam Engine: Historical, Practical, and Descriptive* (London: Longman, Rees, Orme, Brown, and Green, 1827).

Tim Van Gelder, WHAT MIGHT COGNITION BE, IF NOT COMPUTATION, The Journal of Philosophy, Vol. 92, No. 7 (Jul., 1995), p. 349

Regardless whether the centrifugal regulator captures something important about rationality, viewing the legal system with this metaphor in mind may be fruitful. The most dramatic point is that some problems can be solved other than through deductive arguments. [41]That is the crucial limitation of the work discussed above, and a consistent constraint on legal scholarship generally. [42]It is undoubtedly useful to break problems down into smaller parts, and so on, but at the same time that process can be counterproductive, disguising rather than highlighting the nature of the entity under examination. The work on burdens of persuasion, including our own, demonstrate that point. The alternative is to think of the legal system more, perhaps, like fluid dynamics treats the flow of liquids and gases, to embrace, in other words, the messiness of real life rather than abstract it away.

Another possibility, which I am presently exploring in my own work, involves the empirical adequacy of a conceptualization of the legal system as an optimization problem involving what is in essence something analogous to a

㊶ For a discussion sympathetic to the textual point, see Susan Haack, *On Logic in the Law: "Something but not All"*, 20 Ratio Juris 1 (2007).

㊷ The rise of empirical research in the American law schools is to some extent a reaction to this problem.

neural network. The conventional conceptualization of the "legal system" remains one largely based on the concept of rules. This is obviously true of most doctrinal areas; indeed, "doctrine" and thus "doctrinal area" largely refer to rules and sets of rules, although their ambiguity and shortcomings are well known. Even the great jurisprudential debate of the last fifty years between Hart, Dworkin, and their respective adherents is largely a debate over rules and their limits that conceptualizes them as decided in a largely hierarchical way involving articulation, application, and review by higher courts. My intuition is that an empirically more adequate conceptualization of the legal system is that it involves an enormous number of decision nodes or loci, as in a neural network, with almost instantaneous communication with untold numbers of other nodes. When, for example, a trial court reaches a decision, it is transmitted to many other people across the country with analogous concerns, and not just to the appellate court that sits atop the trial court. If the case is appealed, again the result is transmitted across a network of interested parties. Even when that particular case is final, other parties can attack it directly in other jurisdictions, or respond to it in an almost infinite variety of ways. The larger the potential disruption of any particular decision, the greater incentive for other "nodes" in the system to respond to it, to attempt to modify, cabin or reject it. Thus rules or applications of rules are disturbances of a system that cause ripple effects across it, leading to reactions until finally some new equilibrium is reached. Thus, the question to ask about a rule or its application is not whether it is "correct," but whether it is optimal, where optimality is judged by reference to its disruptive effects on equilibria.

I believe this way of conceptualizing the legal system has enormous explanatory power. It explains, for example, many of the difficulties of burdens of persuasion noted above. They emerge from viewing burdens of persuasion as deductive rules rather than part of a complex system. The question that should be asked is not "what is the burden of persuasion," but instead what effects do different articulations have.

I think the explanatory power of this conceptualization goes considerably further, as well. For example, it explains why the Dworkin agenda, whether focusing on the legal system or morality，is literally impossible. [43]Just as no algorithm could predict how a water molecule will actually tumble down the mountain in a mountain stream (although obviously that is a completely determined process)，no one could possible know what the "best" reconstruction of either law or morality is. One can，by contrast，engaging in a never ending negotiation over the differing effects of differing articulations of rules (or whatever). Right now，it seems to me that the legal system's best explanation is precisely a never ending negotiation over those effects，carried on across a huge number of interconnected nodes，in which burdens of proof nudge outcomes in one direction or the other.

㊸ See，e. g.，Ronald Dworkin，*Law's Empire* (1986) and *Justice for Hedgehogs* (2011).

美国证据排除规则*

郑飞　王磊　译**　张保生　校

昨天，我和你们讨论了美国宪法性裁判的某些方面，我特别强调了困扰宪法解释的某些难题。我这样做的目的，部分是为今天有关美国排除规则的讲座做一些铺垫。当其他国家的人提及“美国排除规则”（请注意，我说的是单数“规则”而非复数“规则”）时，他们一般是指，发源于美国最高法院诸如米兰达诉亚利桑那州案（1966 年）和马普诉俄亥俄州案（1961 年）裁定的著名排除规则。由于这些案件常常具有对非法获取的证据明令排除的特征，世界上许多人认为，在美国有一个对非法获取的证据明令排除的规则。然而，这个信念是错的，这就是为什么我在这个讲座的标题中没有提到非法证据的排除，以及为什么我提到的是复数“规则”而不是单数“规则”。在美国，不是只有一个排除规则，还有为数众多的排除规则。某些规则对非法获取的证据明令排除，某些则没有。某些规则明令排除是由于其他原因，非法获取的证据有时候反而是可采的。

在讨论这些各式各样排除规则中的某个规则之前，我要解释一下，为什么排除规则并不像世界上许多人所想的那么简单——换句话说，为什么我们不得不讨论排除规则中的许多不同规则和原则，而不是仅仅讨论在法庭上非法证据必须被排除这样一个简单规则。那种解释的某些部分已包含在我去年给你们做的一个讲座中，题目是“证据法、诉讼法和实体法之间的关系”，如果它还未发表，我相信它将会发表在《证据科学》杂志上。让我来提示一下那次讲座的一些重要观点。

首先，在主要行为和诉讼行为之间有一个重要区别。主要行为涉及一个社会把什么看作是对的和错的，什么行为应当被鼓励，什么行为应当被阻止。这涉及为高效经济行为创造环境，规制社会交往和社会制度，等等。实体法各式各样的正当理由，几乎与其所规制的行为一样变化多端、纷繁复杂，但总的来

* 本文是艾伦教授 2010 年 12 月 1 日在中国政法大学所作的讲座。本译文原载于《证据科学》，第 20 卷，2012 年第 1 期。

** 郑飞，中国政法大学博士研究生；王磊，中国政法大学硕士研究生。

说，与一个社会认同的符合道义和经济上高效的行为有关。促进这种行为是社会组织尤其是法律的典型目标。相比之下，诉讼行为涉及试图解决争端的当事人，这些争端是由于诉诸不适当的主要行为而产生的，或者是要矫正所称违反实体法而发生的社会破坏。[①]

在世界许多地方，通常认为，主要行为和诉讼行为因其各自内在逻辑而被区分为截然不同的领域。在美国，我们已经达成了这是错误的共识，并认为主要行为和诉讼行为之间有密切联系，不能脱离诉讼程序对主要行为的影响而对其单独进行分析。主要行为和诉讼行为不是彼此隔绝的，它们相互影响，而且它们的相互影响必须被认真考虑。主要行为显然影响诉讼行为，但诉讼行为也会影响主要行为，且影响方式比传统上认为的更加微妙。例如，也许有一些类型的诉讼，其中的行为（包括主要行为和诉讼行为）是通过低成本或零成本的诉讼程序来优化的。然而，也许有另一些类型的诉讼是由极高成本来优化的——换言之，这类案件不宜提起诉讼。其他案件可能介于两者之间，在这类案件中，行为是通过强加某些成本来进行优化的。法律制度的任务包括，尝试决定如何回应所面对的这种复杂性——哪些案件应当被鼓励提起诉讼，哪些不应当被鼓励。

现在，让我简单地提示你们，我去年在这儿做的另一个讲座的重要观点，该讲座的题目是“证据法的理论基础和意义”[②]。在这次演讲中，我展示了理性法律体制所面对的许多复杂性。例如，事实的准确性是审判最重要的目标，但绝非唯一目标，这一观点是被人们普遍接受的。事实的准确性有一个成本，并且这个成本有时候可能太高了。一个过于关注事实准确性的法律制度，可能恰恰会侵蚀这一法律制度试图促进的社会环境。一个只值一美元的纠纷，却要花费一千美元起诉去追求一个事实准确的结论，可能就不应该被起诉。这种诉讼可能正好减少了总体社会福利并阻止了争端的私人和解。

事实的准确性不仅与成本具有竞争关系，而且与政府合理追求的其他政策也有竞争关系。这类政策的清单很长，而且具有文化上的随附性。特免权法可以培育和保护很多关系（配偶关系、法律关系、医疗关系、心灵关系、政府关系等等）。一个事故的诉讼不应当阻碍风险的减少（事后补救措施规则）。纠纷的和解可能比诉讼更好，这将导致在和解谈判中作出的陈述被排除。鼓励纠纷

① 罗纳德·J·艾伦：《证据法、诉讼法和实体法的关系》，张保生、张月波、汪诸豪译，载《证据科学》，2010年第6期。

② 罗纳德·J·艾伦：《证据法的理论基础和意义》，张保生、张月波译，载《证据科学》，2010年第4期。

和解，也是不能将诉讼费降得太低的一个原因。诉讼的公共补贴越多，诉讼就可能越多，私了谈判就会越少。这里仍然有其他可以追求的政策。在美国，基于对警察调查行为规制之需要的认识，我们设置了一个庞大的排除规则体系——实际上，这将回到我刚刚提及的那个话题。证据规则还可鼓励或阻止某些类型的法律诉讼的提起。同样是在美国，我们经历了这样一个时期，即认为强奸受害人对违背她们意志之犯罪行为的举报受到了过分阻碍，对此的一个回应是，我们创造了一些证据规则，这些规则减少了这些个人可能在法庭上受到的伤害。

审判还涉及其他重要社会问题，比如，对公正的总体考量。例如，应当要求一个人在什么程度内披露令人难堪的信息。当然，一个免于犯错误的法律制度是不可能的。正如我去年夏天的讲座在细节上所做的探究一样，极为重要的是，要认识到两种可能犯的错误：一是对原告的错判（包括判无辜者有罪），对此我们称之为Ⅰ型错误，或积极错误；二是对被告的错判（包括判有罪者无罪），对此我们称之为Ⅱ型错误，或消极错误。资源配置和其他决定将影响这两种错误类型之间的关系。正常人可能对这两种错误类型的重要意义存有争议，但这两者必须在法律制度的建构中被加以考虑。另外，可能作出的是两种正确的裁决，而正确的裁决在评价一个法律制度之公正性方面也是重要的。

总之，一个纠纷的审判不仅涉及解决纠纷的最有效的方式，而且涉及一些攸关存亡之社会政策的复杂问题。在美国，我们认为审判发挥着促进那些利益的作用。包括排除规则在内的许多证据法律，都在相应地构建那些目标。然而，最重要的一个观点大概是，那些目标经常相互冲突，而且，对一个目标的追求可能抑制对另一个目标的追求。在这种情况下，就一个特定目标而言，问题常常是何为最佳做法，而不是何为正确做法。

请记住这些观点，现在我们可以回到今天晚上的核心问题了，即非法获取的证据之排除规则。我将特别关注美国众多排除规则中的两个规则，它们是两个最著名的规则：一个规则是，警察通过侵犯美国宪法第 5 条修正案所规定的免于强迫自证其罪的权利，进行非法讯问而获得的供述，应该被排除；另一个规则是，通过侵犯美国宪法第 4 条修正案所规定的免受无理搜查和扣押的权利而获得的证据，应该被排除。正如我们将看到的，这两个领域确实都有许多排除规则，但它们是复杂而微妙的，而不是简单直接的。

众所周知，米兰达诉亚利桑那州案中法庭主张，在警察可能采取羁押讯问前，警察必须给犯罪嫌疑人四个警告，并获得对这些警告涉及权利的放弃。特别是，犯罪嫌疑人必须被警告：（1）他有权利保持沉默。（2）他所说的任何话都可能或者将会被用来反对他。（3）他有权利要求律师在场。（4）如果他请不起律师，他有权利要求指定律师。

如果没有给出警告，又没有获得弃权，据信任何供述都将被排除。我说的是“据信”，因为事实上最高法院已经开创了许多例外，并且对米兰达规则的某些核心条款进行了限制性解释，这引起了一些人的反对，他们认为最高法院是在“削减”（cutting back）或者不尊重自己先前的判决。我认为这是误解。相反，法院试图做的是，以这种方式适用米兰达规则，旨在优化各种社会价值，而不仅仅是让犯罪嫌疑人不与警察合作的可能性最大化。为了理解这一动态，需要我们回顾一下米兰达案的历史先例。

在免于强迫自证其罪权利的第 5 条修正案通过之前，就存在各种据信昭示其意义的相互抵触的历史解释。[③] 这些解释有的关注一个人忏悔之宗教义务不应使公民受到伤害；有的关注维持普通法抗辩和审判的方式；有的关注非律师外行没有能力对抗由娴熟职业律师进行的讯问；当然，还有的关注刑讯的使用和认罪书效力的有限性。[④] 引人注目的是，第 5 条修正案的直接历史记录非常稀缺且含混不清，以至于在这些不同的解释中，究竟哪一个才是制定和通过第 5 条修正案的人们头脑中至上的东西，立法史并未给出多少启示。无论是什么原因，两种相关却存在分歧的学说，都源于对强迫自证其罪中潜在利害关系的回应。一个是排除强迫性供述的普通法规则，其理由是，以痛苦或许诺方式获取的证据是不可靠的；另一个是将第 5 条修正案的含义凝练化的宪法性规则，即一个人不能因为受到藐视法庭的威胁而“被迫”作证。

尽管这两种法律学说存在不同，但它们显然都是对相似关注点的回应，即对个人动机的影响，其中一种理论更关注对身体的影响，另一种理论更关注对心理动机的影响。在最高法院早期的宪法刑事诉讼程序中，有一个值得注意的观点：最高法院将这两种学说一并考虑，从而得出结论说，通过威胁或者许诺获得的供述违反了第 5 条修正案，因而不得在审判中使用。[⑤] 当然，排除证据

③ 约翰·H·郎本：《普通法中反对自我归罪特权的历史起源》，载《密歇根法律评论》，第 92 期，1994 年，第 1047 页；E. M. 摩根：《反对自我归罪特权》，载《明尼苏达法律评论》，第 34 期，1949 年，第 1 页。也可参见 R. H. 赫姆霍尔兹等：《反对自我归罪特权》（1997 年）。

④ 参见查尔斯·理查德·道尔：《第三等级——及其历史背景、当代法律和建议》，载《肯塔基法律杂志》，第 43 期，1954—1955 年，第 392 页；保罗·G·考珀：《被告的司法审查——给第三等级的救济》，载《密歇根法律评论》，第 30 期，1932 年，第 1224 页；蒙拉德·G·保尔森：《第 14 条修正案与第三等级》，载《斯坦福法律评论》，第 6 期，1954 年，第 411 页。

⑤ 布拉姆诉美国案，168 U. S. 532，543-49（1897 年）。

的目的是，通过剥夺警察从他们非法行为中获取的利益，来鼓励警察尊重犯罪嫌疑人的权利。同样引人注目的是，*Bram* 案裁决实际上没有任何效力。20 世纪下半叶，在州和联邦诉讼中，所谓非自愿性供述继续受到正当程序检验，自证其罪条款几乎没有或没有发挥什么作用，并且自证其罪条款仍然在很大程度上被限制于解决法律强制而非身体强制方面的问题。[6]

一系列因素共同促成了所有这种改变，特别是警察的暴虐行为和南部各州刑事司法制度中的种族主义这两个问题。[7] 被最高法院复审的州案件不断增加，最高法院开始实验规制警察行为的不同方法。古老的普通法自愿检验（voluntariness test）方法被宪法化了，警察的行为要被审查，正式程序机制被用来试图限制这一问题[8]，律师的这一权利开始被用作限制警察暴虐行为的手段。对供述问题多管齐下的遏制之驱动力在于，把一个人自愿、乐意的行为和被迫的行为区分开来很难，但在最低限度上来说，这一要求几乎是不可能的——它需要作出陈述的人有一个可靠或近似合理的动机。一个人在被讯问时立即作出供述，是出于“自由意志”，还是因为受到警察恐吓？一个经过长时间讯问的人作出供述，是因为他最终被击溃了，还是因为他最终得出结论认为合作才是最正确的做法？

正如我刚才所问，先前存在的法律检验并未提供解决问题的有效手段，并且这些努力所产生的米兰达诉亚利桑那州案中警告和弃权制度的替代品，并不令人满意。核心观点是，羁押讯问天生会给犯罪嫌疑人压力而迫使其供述，这种压力可轻易击溃其意志。[9] 因为，什么是“非自愿的供述”，怎样检验它，本身就是模棱两可的，所以，自愿检验规则并不能从警察讯问的非自愿供述中分辨出真正自愿。最高法院的创造性回应，是试图通过要求一个有权保持沉默和作出陈述之后果的警告，以及如果愿意则要求律师在场提供帮助，来支撑自由意志。总之，最高法院认为，这些警告将有助于打破监狱环境中的平衡，从

⑥ 参见布朗诉密西西比州案，297 U. S. 278，285-86（1936 年）（把自愿性当作一个正当程序问题来讨论。）以及阿什克拉夫特诉田纳西州案，322 U. S. 143，154-55（1944 年）（同上）。

⑦ 参见耶鲁·卡密萨：《在警卫室的平等司法与美国刑事诉讼大厦：从鲍威尔到吉迪恩，从艾斯克维多到……》，载 A. E. 迪克·霍华德主编：《我们时代的刑事司法》，1965 年，第 1 页。

⑧ 例如 McNabb-Mallory 规则。参见麦克纳布诉美国案，318 U. S. 332，339-40（1943 年）（支持最高法院有权在联邦刑事诉讼中行使“监督权力”，这超越了反对联邦的正当程序的最低限度保护。）；马洛里诉美国案，354 U. S. 449，452-55（1957 年）（重申了该规则）。对该规则发展历程的讨论，参见耶鲁·卡密萨等：《模范刑事程序：案件、评论和问题》，第 457-458 页，1999 年第 9 版。

⑨ 正如米兰达案中法院的观点所述，“事实仍然是，在这些案件中没有一个案件警察是在讯问一开始就承诺给予适当的保障措施以保证陈述真正是自由选择的结果。”米兰达诉亚利桑那州案，384 U. S. 436，457（1966 年）。

而维护只在不约束自由意志的活动中才作出陈述的权利。

相反，从法律实施的角度看，米兰达案相当于排除了供述。神智正常的人谁会放弃行使保持沉默和要求律师在场的权利？如果行使了其中任意一个权利，结果将是警察得不到任何陈述，因而供述便终结。反过来，供述的终结将是对法律实施的一个实质性打击。

引人注目的是，最高法院支持被讯问犯罪嫌疑人意志自由的希望，与批评者们关于供述之终结的担心一样，都未能实现。反之，局面和从前差不多，其中主要差别是，从此以后，警察在获得弃权和进行讯问前必须朗诵该警告。具有讽刺意味的是，最高法院裁决自愿问题的解决办法，仅仅是对其试图回避的同一问题的简要重述。请记住，自愿检验的实质性问题是其模糊性。讯问时间长达 36 个小时的阿什克拉夫特诉田纳西州案⑩，提供了一个范例。经过 36 个小时的讯问，怎么能说阿什克拉夫特的意志没被击溃？如果连这样的遭遇下也能在该供述是否自愿的问题上产生分歧⑪，那么，自愿检验几乎就毫无用处了。但是，它毫无用处的原因，恰恰是我们不能有效获得犯罪嫌疑人的动机；我们缺乏辨别是什么原因使人坦白的检测手段。但是，如果我们缺乏对什么可以征服意志的判定手段，那么，给予警告和获得弃权将有助于阻止这一相同意志被击溃。说这句话的理由是什么？答案是，也许没什么理由，但它将增强意志，增加只有那些真正想坦白的人才会供述的可能性。但是，那将可能会怎样呢？如果拘留所的气氛如此具有强迫性，如果它强大到足以击溃意志而强迫一个完全清白的人作出重罪供述，那么，（犯罪嫌疑人）为什么不会被迫放弃米兰达警告中的抽象法律权利呢？对这些问题缺乏一个解释，所以，人们将准确预测近 40 年的经验已证明了什么，这是有或者没有米兰达规则均无不同的地方。它试图压制的相同力量，将压倒它的解决办法。回顾一下，这可能没有什么令人惊奇的。米兰达案及关于这个案子的争论，完全忽视了其解决方案要依赖裁决心理学，对任何此类心理学著作都没有引用。其意见是，先验推理没有认真对待它自己的假定前提。

因此，今天的情形是，米兰达规则没有彻底改变什么，如果它改变了什么的话，部分是因为它对法律实施是一个重大打击，这个过程是我们今晚早些时候谈到的具有重要意义的一个完美例子——法律裁决者，当然是法院，一般都要在其裁决中使众多问题得到优化。对这些观点的某种程度上的回应是，最高

⑩ 阿什克拉夫特诉田纳西州案，322 U. S. 143（1944 年）。

⑪ 在异议中，大法官杰克逊没有考虑陈述的非自愿性。同上，第 156－174 页（大法官杰克逊的异议）。

法院从未极力支持该案。一些例子是，羁押被狭义地界定为：一个正常人必定会感觉到不能自由离开，而不论犯罪嫌疑人是否实际上感觉到这一点。可以参见明尼苏达州诉墨非案。对米兰达案裁判所阐释的警告之细微偏离是可接受的。参见加利福尼亚州诉普里索克案，以及佛罗里达州诉鲍威尔案。“讯问”意味着，采取一些行为暗示犯罪嫌疑人，一个回答是被期待的。仅仅做些偶尔引起犯罪嫌疑人回答的事情，并不能构成讯问。参见罗达岛诉英尼斯案，以及布鲁尔诉威廉姆斯案。关于弃权，犯罪嫌疑人的任何与弃权相符的行为都会被认为是放弃了权利，比如回答问题；如果关于犯罪嫌疑人是否试图使讯问停止存有争议，该犯罪嫌疑人就必须证明他随后将援引其权利。参见俄勒冈州诉伯拉萧案和伯格休斯诉汤普金斯案。

我想以一个关于现在最紧要问题的简短讨论，来结束这个关于来自强迫自证其罪权利的讨论，即被称作“衍生果实”（derivative fruits）的问题。该理念是，有罪的其他证据可能是作为被告被迫陈述的结果而被发现的，该有罪的其他证据就是被称为来自强迫本身的“毒树之果”，在这个比喻中，强迫就是“毒树”。正如我早些时候提到的，第 5 条修正案排除规则的主要目的之一，就是给警察一个尊重犯罪嫌疑人权利的理由。然而，为了对警察的非法行为产生一个威慑，从主要非法行为所获得的利益必须被排除，似乎也是正确的。这种观点应该被推进多远，是现今关于免于自证其罪权利之意义的最紧迫问题。在波塔什诉新泽西州案中，最高法院说，对非自愿陈述及其果实的任何运用都是被禁止的；同时，最高法院认为如果被告作证的话，一个违反了米兰达规则但事实上没有被强迫的陈述可以用来指控被告人。我们又一次看到，最高法院试图优化的各种担忧，引起了一系列复杂而微妙的学说，而非简单的一个排除规则。

一个相关的问题是免于起诉的范围，这也是一个重要问题，因为它澄清了一个对第 5 条修正案的普遍误解。有时，人们会说，在美国有一个保持沉默的权利。这是错误的。应该是有一个不被强迫自证其罪的权利。这两者是不同的。如果政府方同意对你免于起诉，就可能让你作证，如果你拒绝作证，就可以你藐视法庭而监禁你，直到你出来作证。因而，第 5 条修正案并不保护隐私、自治或尊严；它仅仅保护免于强迫自证其罪。参见卡斯蒂加诉合众国案。

在美国，我们正在努力理清这些规则之间的关系。假设，一个人被命令写一个书面证言。这个书面证言本身并没有特权，因为它们在这个命令发出之前就存在了。因而，根据它们进行的任何归罪都不是被迫的。但是，写这个书面证言的行为是被迫的，并且它向当局传达了其他信息，如这些上交的书面证言的存在、同一性和真实性等。反过来，可以在审判中作为证据对该书证鉴真，因而，该强迫行为潜在地具有通讯和归罪的双重属性。在费希尔诉合众国案中，最高法院因而主张，写该书面证言的行为不能被用于对该书证的鉴真，但这些书证能以其他方式被鉴真吗？问题是，这些书证实质上是强迫书写行为的直接产物。最高法院已经开始与这一问题作斗争了，并指出，如果书写行为需要实质认知结果，那么文件内容本身可以在审判中被排除。参见合众国诉哈贝尔案。但是，我们不知道“实质认知结果”是什么，与任何认知结果相比而言，为什么这些规则要求实质性。这一差别的实际后果是巨大的。它将决定，通过传票的使用，一个人能否被调查，以及是否仍被谋求调查任何犯罪行为。

但愿，这澄清了第 5 条修正案免于强迫自证其罪权利的某些方面，以及为什么关于那一权利的裁决是如此复杂。现在，我将转到第 4 条修正案免于无理搜查和扣押权利的讨论，并且我们将看到发挥作用的是同样的动力——我们将看到，通过一系列非常复杂的裁决而非一个简单的排除非法获取证据的规则，在规制一个非常复杂的问题。

第 4 条修正案的文本并不复杂：

公民的人身、住宅、文件和财产不受无理搜查和扣押的权利，不得侵犯。除依合理根据，以宣誓或宣言作为保证，并具体说明搜查地点和扣押的人或物，不得签发搜查和扣押状。

请注意，该修正案第一款所界定的禁令——不允许“无理搜查和扣押”。第二款对搜查令的签发作了一些限制，最重要的是合理根据的要求。这两款之间的关系是不明晰的。是免于无理搜查和扣押的权利条款，还是搜查令条款居支配地位？因而，使一项搜查具有合理性的，是搜查令的签发还是合理根据？直到最近人们把合理根据和搜查令看作是一项“合理”搜查或扣押的通常条件之前，对该文本的传统解读几乎都是采用最高法院的观点。今天的趋势是，把合理性看作独立概念，而不是对搜查令或合理根据的必要支撑。我想在余下的讨论中探究为什么这种转变正在发生，而一个简短的回答是，因为裁决的复杂性是最高法院面临的问题，也是任何解释简单文本以将其适用于极其复杂之社会动力的人面对的问题。

这一相对简单的文本有一个相对简单的历史，尽管它也有一个非常复杂的现代存在。第 4 条修正案产生于 18 世纪的三个著名案件，其中两个来自英格兰，一个来自其殖民地。两个英国案件中名气稍小一点儿的是恩泰克诉卡灵顿案。恩泰克是一个对国王的大臣们不满的英文时事评论家。作为一项煽动性诽谤调查的一部分，一个授权逮捕恩泰克并扣押他所有书籍和文件的搜查令被签发了。这一搜查令被执行了；恩泰克提起非法入侵之诉，并赢得一项300英镑的裁决。另一个英国案件是威尔克斯诉伍德案。威尔克斯同样是一位时事评论家，而且是一位著名议员，他可能是当时英国最受欢迎的人。他也是一位政府的批评者，并且遭到了逮捕、住宅被搜查、书籍和文件被扣押的对待（威尔克斯的49个朋友也遭到了同样对待）。所有这些搜查和扣押，依据的是一个搜查令，在这个搜查令中既没有犯罪嫌疑人的名字，也没有要搜查的具体地点。像恩泰克一样，威尔克斯和他的朋友们起诉了这一非法入侵，并获胜；在威尔克斯案中，判给他1 000英镑，这在当时是一笔可观的数额。恩泰克和威尔克斯这两个案子在美国都赢得了名声，并在若干年后导致美国的变革；主持审判的法官卡姆登勋爵是一位被美国众多城市和县铭记的殖民地英雄。

第三个案件出自殖民地马萨诸塞州，那里的海关稽查员正在打击当时控制着波士顿经济的走私活动。为了帮助他们完成这项任务，稽查员们使用了“协助令状”，它是由国王签署的，并授权稽查员既可以征用协助（因而成为令状的名字），也可以搜查任何可能藏匿走私物品的场所。在1761年的协助令状案中，詹姆斯·奥蒂斯代表一些走私者辩护说，这些令状并未传达任何法律授权。尽管奥蒂斯输了，但按照约翰·亚当斯所说，他的辩论是革命的开端——按照亚当斯的话说：“从此，独立之子诞生。”

不管第4条修正案是关于其他什么的，它都可能作为恩泰克案和威尔克斯案的成果而制定，并推翻了协助令状案的成果。请注意，这三个案件中没有任何一个是有关刑事法律执行的典型例子：没有关于杀人、强奸或者抢劫的调查。确实，这三个案件中的两个——恩泰克案和威尔克斯案——来自今天不可能发生的调查，因为它们将明显违反第1条修正案。如果英国法中有一个与我们第1条修正案等效的规则，如果恩泰克案和威尔克斯案中的搜查因此而不会发生，那么第4条修正案可能就不会存在了。同时请注意，在恩泰克案和威尔克斯案中，那些进行搜查的官员不是普通警官，他们是“信使”，即国王的特工；在协助令状案中，他们是海关稽查员。那不是偶然的，因为在18世纪，不管是英格兰还是殖民地，普通警官都不存在。第一支警察力量建立于1829年的伦敦；美国警察力量则是1829—1870年间一个个陆续产生的。因而，第4条修正案——对警察施加法律限制的主要渊源——制定于警察存在之前，至少在像他们今天所采取的形式方面。当试图确定对当代各种关于第4条修正案争议的原意的理解时，这一事实可能使人必须谨慎对待。

今天，在对普通刑事禁止——谋杀、强奸、盗窃，特别是毒品犯罪——进行调查或执法过程中，第4条修正案诉讼不可避免地陷入许多由警察实施搜查和扣押所带来的挑战。这些挑战大多发生在刑事案件中，如被告寻求废止他们控诉警察违反第 4 条修正案扣押的证据。对第 4 条修正案的违反还有其他救济方法，但最主要的，也是最常被援引的是排除规则。有 5%的刑事案件提出了抑制非法扣押物证的动议（被告方赢得其中 17%的动议）。即使全部逮捕中只有四分之一生成刑事案件，那也意味着全国每年大约有 175 000 个抑制动议。针对警察违反第 4 条修正案的民事诉讼数量，每年最多有几千个。刑事起诉的数量有几十个。这对第 4 条修正案法律产生了很大的影响。排除规则塑造了法官们所见的第 4 条修正案的案件种类。所有排除规则都主张寻求抑制归罪性证据；如果没有发现归罪性证据，对被告来说就没有什么要排除了。

这个简史表明，为什么第 4 条修正案排除规则的现代问题是如此棘手。首先，无论法院何时被要求排除证据，如果没有执行刑法的更严肃的目标，那么，实现遵从第 4 条修正案的目标应该被相对方平等提出。其次，现代社会环境与两个世纪以前的社会环境完全不同。将一个文件的“原始意义”适用于连起草该文件的人也未曾考虑过的情形，能产生什么意义？警察、汽车、大量人口密集的城市、通信的电子方式、恐怖威胁——这些事物在起草宪法的那个时代都不存在。

两个多世纪前的原始环境和现代环境之间的不匹配，可以在对第 4 条修正案的理解中看到，如上所述，没有搜查令的搜查被推定为不合理。尽管最高法院常常这样说，但它已经创制了一个搜查实际上不是根据搜查令而进行的法律。解释这一现象最容易的方式是，简单地想一想现代城市中的警察。当他们发现一些事情在他们面前发生时，他们没有时间去申请搜查令。这是为什么有关第 4 条修正案的现代案例已开始设想它直接涉及合理性的例子，结论是：基于合理根据而签发一项搜查令，是一种但只是一种进行合理搜查的手段。

同样，最高法院从未开发出一个真正健全的排除规则，恰恰是因为成本太高。它将从巡逻和调查功能中转移出资源，降低有效性并增加警察活动的风险，并使刑事起诉变得过于困难。相应地，从一开始，最高法院已通过例外或者通过坚持第 4 条修正案不能简单适用于特定情况，限制了排除规则的范围。考虑一下这些观点：

1. 马普诉俄亥俄州案判决不久之后，最高法院断言，基于“犯罪活动可能正在实施”的合理怀疑，没有搜查令，警察也可以强制阻拦并搜身。

2. 大约同时，最高法院断言，任何紧急情况——最高法院称为“急需”情况——都可以免除对搜查令的要求。

3. 一位执勤警官“清晰察觉”的任何东西，在没有搜查令的情况下，他也同样有权进行扣押。

4. 因为人们对汽车的隐私期待不高，所以，在没有得到搜查令的情况下，汽车可基于合理根据被阻拦。

5. 无数不同种类的行政搜查，包括住宅、汽车和企业，都不以刑法实施为直接目的，也许是在无视搜查令或合理根据的情况下作出的。

6. 在马路上行驶的每一辆汽车都可在路障处被拦下来，进行安全违规检查。

7. 在某些没有合理根据和搜查令的情况下，学校学生的有锁寄物柜可能被搜查，学生可能被要求接受毒品检测。

8. 诸如无线追踪器、GPS 追踪器、飞机和直升机等感官增强设备，可能被使用。

9. 不像第 5 条修正案，最高法院还没有为第 4 条修正案创建一个健全的毒树之果规则。明显违反第 4 条修正案的目击证人仍然可能作证，参见合众国诉切克利尼案，最高法院已创建了一系列限制排除规则范围的学说。如果证据有“独立来源”，或者，如果该证据不可避免地将被发现，那么，即使它是非法搜查的结果，也不需要被排除。

10. 被第 4 条修正案掩盖的是我们所知道的“排除规则的善意例外”。其实，如果警察以善意从事活动，且没有意识到他们正在违反犯罪嫌疑人的权利，那么，证据将不需要被排除。

我应该强调，这里还有另一个同样长的案件清单，在这些案件中，最高法院已扩展了第 4 条修正案的适用范围，并因此使排除规则至少在理论上具有了可能性。最引人注目的是，最高法院理清了第 4 条修正案在电话电子监听中的适用。尽管在卡茨诉合众国案中，关于第 4 条修正案怎样适用于电子邮件和类似“推特”等事情还不太清晰。它也适用于警察参与正常刑事调查而非行政事务的任何时候。参见印第安纳州波利斯市诉埃德蒙案。

让我总结一下今晚的讲座。我被要求讨论排除非法证据的规则。但愿你们现在明白了，我为何不能这么做，因为实际上不存在这样的规则。有很多规则，是为在不同领域的适用而量身定作的。然而，每一个这样的规则都反映了一系列极其复杂而需要优化的变量，因而在每一个领域都会发现这样一个有着大量例外和限制性条件的规则。换句话说，在美国，没有一个排除非法获取证据的简单规则；反而，像所有法律规制的领域一样，在这一领域人们发现，在强调简单、直截了当的规则，与简单规则旨在规制的异常复杂和动态的社会环境之间有一个博弈。顺便提一下，这种关系恰恰提出了有关法治的最有意义的问题。然而，尽管我很高兴被邀请来中国做这次讲座，但这确是一个复杂话题。

The American Exclusionary Rule(s)

Ronald J. Allen

Yesterday I discussed with you certain aspects of constitutional adjudication in the United States, and I particularly focused on certain difficulties that beset constitutional interpretation. I did so in part in order to lay the ground work for today's lecture on the American Exclusionary Rule (s). When people from other countries refer to the "American Exclusionary Rule," and I note I said "rule" not "rule (s)," they normally have in mind the famous exclusionary rules that emanate from rulings of the United States Supreme Court such as *Miranda v. Arizona*, 384 U. S. 436 (1966), and *Mapp v. Ohio*, 367 U. S. 643 (1961). These cases in turn often are characterized as mandating the exclusion of illegally obtained evidence, and many people across the world think that there is an exclusionary rule in the United States that mandates the exclusion of illegally obtained evidence. This belief, however, is false, and this is why I do not refer in my title to the exclusion of illegal evidence and why I refer to "rule (s)" rather than "rule." There is not just one exclusionary rule in the United States; there are numerous exclusionary rules. Some mandate the exclusion of illegally obtained evidence and some do not. Some mandate exclusion for other reasons, and oftentimes illegally obtained evidence is admitted.

Before I discuss some of these various exclusionary rules, I need to explain why the matter is not as simple as many people across the world think—why, in other words, we have to talk about numerous differing rules, and principles for that matter, rather than simply one simple rule that illegal evidence must be excluded at trial. Part of that explanation is contained in one of my lectures to you last year, which was entitled *The Relationships among Evidence Law, Procedural Law, and Substantive Law*, and which I believe will be published in the journal Evidence Science if it has not already been published. Let me remind you of some of the important points from that lecture.

First, there is a critical distinction between primary and litigation behavior. Primary behavior deals with what a society thinks is right and wrong, what behavior should be incentivized and what behavior should be discouraged, with creating the conditions for efficient economic behavior, regulating social interactions and institutions, and so on. The various forms of justification for substantive law are almost as varied and as complex as the behavior they regulate, but in general have to do with what a society believes to be morally correct and economically efficient behavior. Facilitating such behavior is the typical objective of social organization, and the law specifically. Litigation behavior, by contrast, involves parties attempting to resolve disputes that have arisen over claims about inappropriate primary behavior or to rectify social disruptions that have occurred through alleged violations of substantive law. ①

In many parts of the world, it is conventionally believed that primary and litigation behavior are separate and distinct areas with internal logics of their own. In the United States, we have come to the conclusion that this is wrong, that there is an intimate connection between primary and litigation behavior, and that the litigation process cannot be analyzed separately from its effects on primary behavior. Primary and litigation behavior are not hermetically sealed off from each other; rather, they affect each other, and their interactive effects must be taken into account. Primary behavior obviously affects litigation behavior, but so too does litigation behavior affect primary behavior and in more subtle ways than conventionally is believed. For example, there may be some types of litigation where behavior (both primary and litigation) are optimized by a low or zero cost litigation process. However, there may be other types of litigation that are optimized by infinitely high costs—in other words, cases that should not be brought. Other cases may be somewhere in between in that behavior is optimized by the imposition of some costs. The task for the legal system includes trying to determine how to respond in the face of such complexity—which cases should be encouraged to be brought, and which should not.

Now let me briefly remind you of the critical point of another lecture that I

① Ronald J. Allen, *The Relationships among Evidence Law, Procedural Law, and Substantive Law*, Evidence Science Dec. 2010 Volume 18 No. 6.

gave here last year, *The Theoretical Foundations and Implications of Evidence*[②], in which I laid out many of the complexities facing rational legal organization. For example, it is generally accepted that factual accuracy is the most significant objective of trials, but it is by no means the only one. Factual accuracy has a cost, and the cost can sometimes be too high. A legal system overly preoccupied with factual accuracy may undermine the very social conditions that the legal system is trying to foster. A dispute worth only a dollar that would take a thousand dollars to litigate to a factually accurate conclusion perhaps should not be litigated. Such litigation may very well reduce overall social welfare and discourage private settlement of disputes.

Factual accuracy competes not just with cost but with other policies that a government reasonably may pursue. The list of such policies is long, and culturally contingent. The law of privileges may foster and protect numerous relationships (spouses, legal, medical, spiritual, governmental, etc.). Litigation of an accident should not discourage reduction of risk (the subsequent repair rule). Perhaps settlement of disputes is preferred to their litigation, which leads to the exclusion of statements made during settlement talks. The encouragement of settlement is also a reason not to price litigation too low. The more the public subsidizes litigation, presumably the more of it there will be, and the less of private negotiation. There are still other policies that can be pursued. In the United States, we rest a vast body of exclusionary rules on the perceived need to regulate police investigative activities—this is the topic that I will turn to in just a moment, in fact. Rules of evidence also can encourage or discourage certain kinds of law suits from being brought. Again in the United States, we went through a period in which we thought rape victims were being overly discouraged from reporting crimes against them, and one response was to create rules of evidence that reduced the abuse at trial that such individuals may have been exposed to.

Trials involve other important social matters, as well, such as general considerations of fairness. For example, to what extent should a person be re-

② Ronald J. Allen, *The Theoretical Foundations and Implications of Evidence*, Evidence Science, Aug. 2010 Volume 18 No. 4.

quired to disclose embarrassing information? And of course, a mistake free legal system is not possible. As I explored in detail last summer, it is critically important to recognize that two types of errors can be made—a wrongful verdict for a plaintiff (including a conviction of an innocent person), which we call a Type I or false positive error, and a wrongful verdict for a defendant (including an acquittal of a guilty person), which we call a Type II or false negative error—and resource allocation and other decisions will affect the relationship between these two types of errors. Reasonable people can disagree as to the significance of these two types of errors, but both must be taken into account in the construction of the legal system. In addition, two kinds of correct decisions can be made, and correct decisions also matter in appraising the justness of a legal system.

In sum, the trial of a dispute does not just involve the most efficient means of resolving a dispute, but in addition involves complex issues concerning numerous social policies that are at stake. In the United States, we view trials as serving the role of advancing those interests. Much of the law of evidence, including exclusionary rules, is accordingly structured to further those goals. However, and perhaps this is the single most important point, often those goals conflict, and the pursuit of one goal can inhibit the pursuit of another. In such cases, the issue invariably is what is the optimal course of action to take rather than what is the correct course of action, given one particular goal.

With these thoughts in mind, we can now turn to the central question of tonight, which is the exclusion of illegally obtained evidence. I will focus in particular on two of the many exclusionary rules in the United States, and they are the two most famous such rules: the exclusion of confessions following wrongful police interrogations that violate the right to be free from compelled self-incrimination contained in the Fifth Amendment to the U. S. Constitution, and the exclusion of evidence resulting from a violation of the right to be free from unreasonable searches and seizures contained in the Fourth Amendment to the U. S. Constitution. As we shall see, both areas do indeed have exclusionary rules, but they are complex and nuanced rather than straightforward and simple.

As is well known, *Miranda v. Arizona* held that, before the police may conduct a custodial interrogation, the police must give suspects four warnings and get a waiver of the rights that the warnings refer to. In particular, the suspect must be warned that:

1. He has a right to remain silent.
2. Anything he says can and will be used against him.
3. He has a right to counsel present.
4. He has a right to have counsel appointed if he cannot afford counsel.

If the warnings are not given, and a waiver obtained, any resulting confession supposedly will be excluded. I say "supposedly" because in fact the Supreme Court has also carved out a number of exceptions and given limiting interpretations of some of the key terms in its *Miranda* ruling causing some people to say that the Supreme Court is "cutting back" or not respecting its prior decision. I think this is wrong. Rather, what the Court is trying to do is apply *Miranda* in such a way as to optimize various social values, and not just maximum the probability of a suspect not cooperating with the police. To understand this dynamic requires that we address the historical antecedents of the *Miranda* case.

There are many competing historical explanations of the relevant developments that preceded the adoption in the Fifth Amendment of the right to be free from compelled self-incrimination that supposedly inform its meaning. ③There were concerns that one's religious duty to confess not result in civic harm; there were concerns about maintaining the common law forms of pleading and trial; there were concerns about the inability of uncounseled laymen to withstand interrogation by skilled professionals; and of course there were concerns about the use of torture and to a lesser extent of the effect of promises. ④Remarkably, the direct historical record of the Fifth Amendment is sparse and ambiguous, with little in the way of enlightening legislative history

③ John H. Langbein, *The Historical Origins of the Privilege Against Self-incrimination at Common Law*, 92 Mich. L. Rev. 1047 (1994); E. M. Morgan, *The Privilege Against Self-incrimination*, 34 Minn L. Rev. 1 (1949). *See also* R. H. Helmholz et al., *The Privilege Against Self-Incrimination* (1997).

④ *See* Charles Richard Doyle, *The Third Degree-Its Historical Background the Present Law and Recommendations*, 43 Ky. L. J. 392 (1954—1955); Paul G. Kauper, *Judicial Examination of the Accused-A Remedy for the Third Degree*, 30 Mich. L. Rev. 1224 (1932); Monrad G. Paulsen, *The Fourteenth Amendment and the Third Degree*, 6 Stan. L. Rev. 411 (1954).

as to which of these various matters were uppermost in the minds of the many individuals who fashioned and adopted the Fifth Amendment. Whatever the cause, two related but separate doctrines arose to respond to the interests underlying compelled self-incrimination. One was the common law rule that excluded coerced confessions on the ground that evidence extracted through pain or promises was unreliable, the other a constitutional rule that crystallized the meaning of the Fifth Amendment into a rule that a person could not be "compelled" into testifying by the threat of being held in contempt.

Notwithstanding the differences between these two legal doctrines, plainly they were responding to similar concerns about the effects of incentives on individuals, with one focusing more on physical and the other more on psychological incentives. In a remarkable opinion early in the Supreme Court's career in constitutional criminal procedure, the Court brought the two lines together in concluding that any confession obtained by threat or promise violated the Fifth Amendment and as a result could not be used at trial. [5]The point of excluding the evidence, of course, is to give the police an incentive to respect the suspect's rights by depriving the police of the benefit flowing from their illegal behavior. Equally remarkable, the *Bram* decision had virtually no apparent impact on anything. For the next half-century, allegedly involuntary confessions continued to be tested by due process in both state and federal cases, with little or no help from the self-incrimination clause, and the self-incrimination clause remained largely limited to dealing with legal compulsion rather than physical coercion. [6]

A number of factors conspired to change all this, in particular the twin problems of police brutality and racism in the criminal justice systems of the southern states. [7]An increasing number of state cases were reviewed by the Supreme Court, and the Court began to experiment with different means of regu-

⑤ Bram v. United States, 168 U. S. 532, 543-49 (1897).

⑥ *See* Brown v. Mississippi, 297 U. S. 278, 285-86 (1936) (discussing voluntariness as a due process issue) and Ashcraft v. Tenn., 322 U. S. 143, 154-55 (1944) (same).

⑦ *See* Yale Kamisar, *Equal Justice in the Gatehouses and Mansions of American Criminal Procedure: From* Powell *to* Gideon, *From* Escobedo *to* ... *in* Criminal Justice in Our Time 1 (A. E. Dick Howard, ed., 1965).

lating police behavior. The old common law voluntariness test was constitutionalized, police practices were scrutinized, formal procedural mechanisms were employed to attempt to limit the problem⑧, and the right to counsel began to be used as a means of limiting police brutality. The driving force behind this multi-prong attack on the problem of confessions was the difficulty of sorting out voluntary, willful acts from those that an individual is coerced into doing, but at a minimum this requires the near impossible—it requires reliable access to or a reasonable approximation of the motivations of the individual who makes a statement. Did a person confess immediately upon interrogated out of "free will" or because he was petrified of the police? Did a person confess after a long interrogation because his will was eventually broken or because he finally concluded that cooperating was the right thing to do?

The pre-existing legal tests did not provide effective means of getting at questions like I just asked, and dissatisfaction with these efforts led in turn to *Miranda v. Arizona*'s substitution of a warning and waiver regime. The central idea was that custodial interrogation inherently puts pressure on the suspect to confess, pressure that can easily overwhelm the will. ⑨Because of the ambiguity in what an "involuntary confession" is, and how one can be identified, the voluntariness test did not suffice to sort out truly voluntary from involuntary confessions resulting from police interrogation. The Court's creative response was to attempt to bolster the will by requiring a warning of the right to remain silent and the consequence of making statements and by providing assistance if desired in the form of counsel. Together, in the Court's view, these warnings would help strike the balance in the jail house setting, thus preserving the right to make statements only in the unfettered exercise of free will.

⑧ The McNabb-Mallory rule, for example. *See* McNabb v. United States, 318 U. S. 332, 339-40 (1943) (upholding the Court's power to exercise "supervisory authority" in federal criminal proceedings that go beyond the minimal protections of due process enforced against the states); Mallory v. United States, 354 U. S. 449, 452-55 (1957) (reaffirming this rule). For a discussion of the development of the rule, see Yale Kamisar et al., *Modern Criminal Procedure: Cases, Comments, and Questions* 457-58 (9th ed., 1999).

⑨ As the *Miranda* Court put it, "[t] he fact remains that in none of these cases did the officers undertake to afford appropriate safeguards at the outset of the interrogation to insure that the statements were truly the product of free choice." Miranda v. Arizona, 384 U. S. 436, 457 (1966).

In the view of law enforcement, by contrast, *Miranda* was tantamount to the elimination of confessions. Who in their right mind would fail to exercise both their right to remain silent and their right to counsel? If either were exercised, the result would be no statement to the police, and thus the end of confessions. The end of confessions, in turn, would be a substantial blow to law enforcement.

Remarkably, neither the Court's hope of bolstering the will of interrogated suspects, nor the critics' fear of the end of confessions, came to pass. Instead, things went on more or less as before, with the primary difference that the police henceforth had to recite the warnings before obtaining waivers and proceeding to the interrogation. Ironically, the Court's solution to the problem of determining voluntariness merely recapitulates the very same problem it was attempting to avoid. Remember that the substantive problem with the voluntariness test is its ambiguity. *Ashcraft v. Tennessee*[10], which involved a thirty-six hour interrogation, provides an excellent example. How can one say Ashcraft did not have his will overborne after thirty-six hours of interrogation? If even that kind of treatment can generate disagreement about whether an ensuing confession is voluntary[11], then the voluntariness test appears fairly useless. But the reason it is useless is precisely that we do not have effective access to the motivations of the suspect; we lack the means of identifying what made the person confess. But, if we have no means of determining what overbears the will, what reason is there to think that giving warnings and obtaining a waiver will suffice to stop this very same will from being overborne? Maybe it will not, so the answer goes, but it will strengthen the will, increasing the probability that only those who truly wish to will confess. But how can that be? If the atmosphere of the jail house is so compelling, if it is powerful enough to overbear the will to compel confessions to serious felonies by even innocent people, why will it not compel waivers of the abstract legal rights contained in the *Miranda* warnings? In the absence of an explanation of

⑩ Ashcraft v. Tenn., 322 U.S. 143 (1944).

⑪ Justice Jackson, dissenting, did not think the confession involuntary. *Id.* at 156-74 (Jackson, J., dissenting).

such matters, one would predict exactly what close to forty years of experience has demonstrated, which is that *Miranda* did not make much of a difference. The very same forces it was trying to quell would overwhelm its solution. In retrospect, perhaps this is not much of a surprise. *Miranda*, and for that matter the ensuing debate over the case, completely neglects that its solution is dependent upon the psychology of decision making, and there are no cites to any such work. The opinion is all *a priori* reasoning that fails to take seriously its own presuppositions.

As a result, the situation today is that *Miranda* did not revolutionize things, partly because, if it had, it would have been a significant blow to law enforcement, which of course is a perfect example of the significance of my earlier remarks tonight—legal decision makers generally, and certainly the courts, have a multitude of issues to optimize in their decisions. To some extent responsive to these points, the Supreme Court has never vigorously tried to bolster the case. Some examples are that custody is narrowly defined to mean that a reasonable person must have felt not free to leave, regardless of whether the actual suspect felt that way. *Minnesota v. Murphy*, 465 *U. S.* 420 (1984). Minor deviations from the warnings laid out in the *Miranda* decision are acceptable. *California v. Prysock*, 453 *U. S.* 355 (1981); *Florida v. Powell*, 130 *S. Ct.* 1195 (2010). "Interrogation" means taking action that would suggest to the suspect that an answer is expected. Merely doing things that incidentally cause a suspect to respond does not constitute interrogation. *Rhoda Island v. Innis*, 446 *U. S.* 291 (1980); *Brewer v. Williams*, 430 *U. S.* 387 (1977). With regard to waivers, any actions of the suspect consistent with a waiver will be taken as waiving the rights, such as answering questions, and the suspect has to prove that he subsequently invoked his rights if there is a dispute about whether the suspect attempted to bring the interrogation to a halt. *Oregon v. Bradshaw*, 462 *U. S.* 1039 (1983); *Berghuis v. Thompkins*, 130 *S. Ct.* 2250 (2010).

I want to end this discussion of the right to be from compelled self-incrimination with a brief discussion of the most pressing current issue, and that is called the "derivative fruits" problem. The idea is that other evidence of guilt might be found as a result of coercing statement from the defendants, and that other evidence of guilt is said to be the "fruit of the poisonous tree" flowing from the coercion itself, which in this metaphor is the "poisonous tree." As I mentioned earlier, one of the primary motivations of the Fifth Amendment exclusionary rule is to give the police a reason to respect a suspect's rights. However, in order to have a deterrent effect on police illegality, it is plausible that benefits that flow from the primary illegality must be excluded, too. How far that idea should be pushed is the most pressing issue today concerning the meaning of the right to be free from compelled self-incrimination. The Court has said that any use of an involuntary statement and its fruits is forbidden, *Portash v. New Jersey*, 440 *U. S.* 450 (1979); at the same time, the Court has said that a statement that violates *Miranda* but is not actually coerced may be used to impeach a defendant if the defendant testifies. *Harris v. New York*, 401 *U. S.* 222 (1071). Again, we see how the various concerns that the Court is attempting to optimize causes a complex and nuanced set of doctrines rather than just a simple exclusionary rule.

A related problem is the scope of immunity from prosecution, which is also important because it clarifies a common misconception about the Fifth Amendment. Sometimes people say that there is a right to silence in the United States. This is false. There is a right not to be compelled to incriminate yourself. The two are different. If the government grants you immunity from prosecution, it can make you testify, and imprison you for contempt if you resist until you do testify. Thus, the Fifth Amendment does not protect privacy, autonomy, or dignity; it simply protects against being compelled to incriminate oneself. *Kastigar v. U. S.*, 406 *U. S.* 441 (1972).

In the United States we are struggling over the relationship between these rules. Suppose a person is order to produce his paper. The papers themselves are not privileged because they preexisted the order to turn them over. Thus, whatever is incriminating about them was not coerced. But the act of producing the papers is coerced, and it communicates various things to the authorities, such as the existence, identity and authenticity of the papers turned over. That, in turn, can be used to authenticate the papers for use as evidence at trial, and thus the compelled act potentially has both communicatory and incriminatory attributes. The Supreme Court has thus held that that act of production cannot be used to authenticate the papers, *Fisher v. U. S.*, 425 *U. S.* 391 (1976), but can the papers be used in they are authenticated in some other way? The problem is that the substance of the papers are a direct product of the compelled act of production. The Supreme Court has begun struggling with this problem and has said that if the act of production requires substantial cognitive effort, the content of the documents themselves may be excluded at trial. *United States v. Hubbell*, 530 *U. S.* 27 (2000). But, we do not know what "substantial cognitive effort" is and why the rule requires substantial as compared to any cognitive effort. The practical consequence of this distinction is enormous. It will determine whether a person can be investigated through the use of subpoenas and still be tried for any criminal acts that the investigation turns up.

Hopefully, this clarifies something about the Fifth Amendment right to be free from compelled self-incrimination, and why the decisions concerning that right are so complicated. I now turn to the Fourth Amendment right to free from unreasonable searches and seizures, and we will see the same dynamic at play there as well—we will see a very complicated problem regulated through a very complicated set of decision, rather than a simple rule that excludes illegally obtained evidence.

The text of the Fourth Amendment is uncomplicated:

The right of the people to be secure in their persons, houses, papers, and effects, against unreasonable searches and seizures, shall not be violated, and no warrants shall issue, but upon probable cause, supported by oath or affirmation, and particularly describing the place to be searched, and the persons or things to be seized.

Notice that the first clause of the Amendment defines the prohibition—no "unreasonable searches and seizures." The second clause places some restrictions on the issuance of warrants, the most important being the requirement of probable cause. The relationship between the two clauses is unclear. Is the right to be free from unreasonable searches and seizures the dominant clause, or is the warrant clause dominate, and thus what makes a search reasonable is the issuance of a warrant on probable cause? The conventional reading of the text adopted in nearly all Supreme Court opinions until recently treats probable cause and a warrant as defining the usual conditions for a "reasonable" search or seizure. Today, the trend is to treat reasonableness as a freestanding concept, not necessarily anchored to warrants or probable cause. I want to explore in the remainder of my remarks why this transformation is occurring, and again the short answer is because of the complexity of the decision making problem facing the Supreme Court, or anyone who interprets simple texts such as this for application to the infinitely complex social dynamic.

This relatively simple text has a relatively simple history although it also has a very complicated modern existence. The Fourth Amendment arose out of a trio of famous eighteenth-century cases, two from England and one from the colonies. The less famous of the two English cases was *Entick v. Carrington*, 19 *Howell's State Trials* 1029 (*C. P.* 1765). Entick was an English pamphleteer critical of the King's ministers. As part of a seditious libel investigation, a warrant was issued authorizing Entick's arrest and the seizure of all his books and papers. The warrant was carried out; Entick sued for trespass, and he won a verdict of 300 pounds. The other English case was *Wilkes v. Wood*, 19 *Howell's State Trials* 1153 (*C. P.* 1763). Wilkes was likewise a pamphleteer, and also a well-known Member of Parliament, perhaps the most popular man in England in his day. He too was a critic of the government, and he too was rewarded with arrest, search of his home, and the seizure of his books and papers (some 49 of Wilkes's friends received the same treatment). All these searches and seizures were made pursuant to a warrant that neither named suspects nor specified places to be searched. Like Entick, Wilkes and a number of his friends sued for trespass and won; in Wilkes's case the verdict was 1 000 pounds, a considerable sum at the time. Both *Entick* and *Wilkes* won renown in the American colonies in the years leading up to the American Revolution; the judge who presided over both their trials, Lord Camden, was a colonial hero for whom a number of American cities and counties were named.

The third case arose in colonial Massachusetts, where customs inspectors were seeking to crack down on the smuggling that then dominated Boston's economy. To aid them in that task, inspectors used "writs of assistance," which were issued by the King and which authorized the inspectors both to draft assistance (hence the name of the writs) and to search any place where smuggled goods might be concealed. In 1761 in *The Writs of Assistance Case*, James Otis argued, on behalf of some of the smugglers, that these writs conveyed no legal authority. Otis lost, but according to John Adams, his argument was the beginning of the Revolution—in Adams's words, "Then and there was the child Independence born."

Whatever else the Fourth Amendment was about, it was probably designed to enact the results in *Entick* and *Wilkes* and to overturn the result in *The Writs of Assistance Case*. Notice that none of the three cases involved a typical instance of criminal law enforcement: These were not investigations of murders, rapes, or robberies. Indeed, two of the three cases—*Entick* and *Wilkes*—arose out of investigations that could not happen today, because they would be clear violations of the First Amendment. Had English law had an equivalent to our First Amendment and had the searches in *Entick* and *Wilkes* therefore not happened, the Fourth Amendment might not exist. Notice too that the officials who conducted the searches in these cases were not ordinary police officers—in *Entick* and *Wilkes*, they were "messengers," special agents of the Crown; in *The Writs of Assistance Case*, they were customs inspectors. That is no accident; ordinary police officers did not exist, either in eighteenth-century England or in the colonies. The first police force was established in London in 1829; American police forces were born, one by one, between that date and about 1870. Thus, the Fourth Amendment—the prime source of legal restraint for the police—was written before the police existed, at least in anything like the form they take today. That fact might lead one to be cautious when seeking to determine the original understanding of various contemporary Fourth Amendment issues.

Today Fourth Amendment litigation overwhelmingly involves challenges to searches and seizures conducted by the police in the course of investigating or enforcing ordinary criminal prohibitions—homicide, rape, theft, and, especially, drug violations. The large majority of those challenges occur in criminal cases, as defendants seek to suppress evidence they claim the police seized in violation of the Fourth Amendment. There are other remedies for Fourth Amendment violations, but the dominant one, the one that is invoked most often by far, is the exclusionary rule. Motions to suppress illegally seized physical evidence are filed in 5 percent of criminal cases (defendants win 17 percent of those motions). Even if only a quarter of all arrests produce a criminal case, that would mean roughly 175 000 suppression motions per year, nationwide. The number of civil lawsuits against police for Fourth Amendment violations is, at most, a few thousand per year. The number of criminal prosecutions is a few dozen. This has a large effect on the substance of Fourth Amendment law. The exclusionary rule shapes the kinds of Fourth Amendment cases judges see. All exclusionary rule claims seek to suppress incriminating evidence; if no incriminating evidence is found, there is nothing for the defendant to exclude.

This brief history suggests why the modern problem of the Fourth Amendment exclusionary rule is so intractable. First, whenever a court is asked to exclude evidence, the goal of achieving compliance with the Fourth Amendment is counter-posed by the equally if not more serious goal of enforcing the criminal law. Second, modern social conditions simply are radically different from the social conditions of two centuries ago. What sense can be made of applying the "original meaning" of a document to things that no one involved in writing that document ever thought about? Police, cars, large densely populated cities, electronic means of communication, terrorist threats—none of these existed at the time that the Constitution was drafted.

The mismatch between the original conditions pertaining two centuries ago and modern conditions can be seen in the understanding of the fourth amendment, noted above, that searches without a warrant are presumptively unreasonable. Although the Supreme Court often has said that, it has created a law in which virtually no searches are on warrants. The easiest way to explain this is simply to think about police in modern cities. They do not have time to get warrants when they observe something happening in front of them. This is an example of why the modern cases concerning the Fourth Amendment have begun conceiving of it has involving reasonableness directly, and concluding that a warrant issued on probable cause is one but only one means of making a search reasonable.

Similarly, the Court has never developed a truly robust exclusionary rule, precisely because the costs would be too high. It would divert resources from patrol and investigative functions, decrease the effectiveness and increase the risk of policing activity, and make the prosecution of criminals too difficult. Accordingly, from the very beginning, the Court has limited the scope of the exclusionary rule either through exceptions or through holdings that the Fourth Amendment simply does not apply in certain circumstances. Consider a number of these:

1. Not too long after *Mapp v. Ohio* was decided, the Court concluded that the police could make a forcible stop and frisk without warrants based on reasonable suspicion that "criminal activity may be afoot." .

2. At about the same time, the Court concluded that any emergency situations—what the Court referred to as "exigent" circumstances—excused the requirement of a warrant.

3. Anything that is within the "plain view" of an officer who is in a position he has a right to be in likewise may be seized without a warrant.

4. Because automobiles involve a lesser expectation of privacy, cars may be stopped on probable cause but without getting a warrant.

5. Innumerable different kinds of administrative searches not directly aimed at criminal law enforcement involving houses, cars and businesses may be done without regard to warrants or probable cause.

6. Every single car on a road may be stopped at a roadblock to check for safety violations.

7. School children can have their locker searched and be required to undergo drug testing under certain circumstances without regard to probable cause and warrants.

8. Sensory enhancing equipment such as tracking beepers, GPS trackers, airplanes, and helicopters may be employed.

9. Unlike the Fifth Amendment, the Supreme Court has not created a robust fruit of the poisonous tree rule for the Fourth Amendment. Live witnesses found as a result of fourth amendment violations apparently may still testify, *U. S. v. Ceccolini*, 435 *U. S.* 268 (1978), and the Supreme Court has created a series of doctrines that limit the scope of the exclusionary rule. If there is an "independent source" for the evidence, or if the evidence would have been inevitably discovered, it need not be excluded even though it is the fruit of an illegal search.

10. And overlay over the entire Fourth Amendment is what we known as the "good faith exception to the exclusionary rule." In essence if the police were acting in good faith and unaware that they were violating the suspect's rights, the evidence need not be excluded.

I should emphasize that there is another equally long list of cases in which the Supreme Court has extended the reach of the Fourth Amendment, and thus made the exclusionary rule at least a theoretically possibility. Most dramatically, the Supreme Court made clear that the Fourth Amendment applies to electronic surveillance of telephones. *Katz v. U. S.*, 389 *U. S.* 347 (1967), although it is quite unclear how the Fourth Amendment applies to emails and things like *Twitter*. It also applies whenever the police are engaged in normal criminal investigative functions rather than administrative matters. *Indianapolis v. Edmund*, 531 *U. S.* 32 (2000).

Let me sum up tonight's lecture. I was asked to talk about the rule of excluding illegal evidence. Hopefully, you now see why I could do not do so, because in reality there is no such rule. There are many rules, individually fashioned for application in different areas. However, each such rule reflects an enormously complicated set of variables that need to be optimized, and thus each area within which one finds such a rule also has numerous exceptions and qualifications. There is no simple rule of excluding illegally obtained evidence in the United States, in other words; instead, in this area like all areas of legal regulation one finds the struggle between the rule of law with its emphasis on simple, straight forward rules and the incredibly complex and dynamic social environment that simple rule is designed to regulate. It is precisely that relationship, by the way, that raises the most profound issues concerning the rule of law. That is a complicated topic, however, although I would be happy to be invited back to China to lecture on it.

排除规则的困难*

郑飞　强卉　译　张保生　校

今晚演讲的题目——排除规则的困难，是在我去年 12 月讲座《美国证据排除规则》[①] 基础上的继续深入。在那次演讲中，我关注的是米兰达诉亚利桑那州案（1966 年）和马普诉俄亥俄州案（1961 年）这两个案件，它们涉及旨在保护美国宪法中权利法案有关免于自证其罪与不合理搜查和扣押之权利的排除规则。美国最高法院还有其他授权在个人权利受到侵犯时予以排除的案例；这使许多人包括资深法学家认为，在美国存在着授权排除非法获取证据的排除规则。正如我在那场演讲中指出的，这个观点是错误的。在美国有许多复杂的证据规则。某些规则授权排除非法获取的证据，而另一些则没有。某些授权排除是因为其他理由，与证据获取方式的合法性没什么关系，而且，非法获取的证据常常是可采的。

尽管“排除规则”常被认为是美国特有的现象，但这是错误的；不能将今晚的演讲放入某种语境，并强调该题目对任何国家学习证据法的学生都同样重要。理由既简单又深刻：任何诉讼或争端解决制度都有大量的排除规则。实际上，所有证据规则和许多程序规则都规定了什么能够在法庭上出示。所有这类规则都区分了什么可采、什么不可采以及证据排除的可能后果。只有在当事人被允许在他们喜好的任何时间和以他们喜好的任何方式提供任何证据的情况下，才没有“排除规则”，但据我所知，世界上没有这样的制度存在。因为证据的采纳对于所有法律制度的构建和运行都是至关重要的，所以其反面即证据排除，对一个法律制度来说，二者是缺一不可的。与其说排除规则是美国的发明，不如说它是任何良好的法律制度的基础成分。此外，法律制度是复杂的，任何国家的排除规则也是如此，不管它们在这些国家的称谓如何。

两年前在这里的一个讲座中，我罗列了许多理性法律组织的复杂性。我们

* 本文是艾伦教授 2011 年 12 月在中国政法大学的演讲，原载于《证据科学》，第 20 卷，2012 年第 6 期。

① 罗纳德·J·艾伦：《美国证据排除规则》，郑飞、王磊译，张保生校，载《证据科学》，2012 年第 1 期。

将这些内容快速回顾一下，因为它们对理解某些排除规则的困难来说是基础知识。[②] 到目前为止，最重要的观点是关于法律制度的目的。一般认为，事实的准确性是审判最重要的目的，但准确性并非唯一目的。事实的准确性至关重要，因为它通过保护个人的权利价值而产生社会最佳效果。的确，没有事实的准确性，权利将变得毫无意义。你们中的一些人可能已听过我先前讲座中阐述的这个观点，因为每次我来中国演讲都会强调准确的事实认定比实体权利更重要；权利完全取决于事实认定。当你认为自己拥有某物即你的财产时，那意味着你有权占有、使用和处分那件物品。如果你做这些事情的权利受到挑战，争议将会由该事项之事实来决定。你能证明你制作、购买、发现或被赠与该物品的争议吗？只有回答“是”，你才能够享有其利益。财产权的真实性意味着所有权利的真实性，包括政治和公民的权利。这就是为什么我对中国各地的听众说，中国未来的持续成功完全掌控在像你们这样致力于从事证据法和理性法律制度建构的人手里。

回到今晚的主要论题——准确性问题上，它是相互竞争又彼此包容之利益复杂集合的一部分。其中每一个都是有成本的。诉讼不是免费的；有人必须为此付出，或是诉讼当事人，或是国家。可以想象的是，在特定案件中过高的诉讼费用可能超过了试图保护的价值。如果一个价值 100 元的案件将花费 1 000 元去诉讼，那就完全可以合理地得出这样的结论：这样一个争议不应当被提起诉讼，大概应当以其他方式去解决。这类案件的诉讼可能减少社会福利，这不仅是因为其成本高于价值，还因为允许这类案件进入诉讼程序可能阻碍纠纷的私人解决。所有这些考量都对法律制度的构造产生影响，人们对它们的重要性可能产生合理分歧。在某些社会中，诉讼大概是不受欢迎的；在另一些社会中，对权利的官方裁判可能被认为是至关重要的，无论其代价如何。

如我所说，像成本的例子所显示的那样，事实的准确性与一个法律制度可能追求的各种政策是竞争性关系，这些政策的实现可能确实涉及排除规则。特免权可以鼓励特定关系，比如配偶之间、患者与医生之间的关系，但要通过证据排除来实现。如果纠纷的私人解决比诉讼更好，那么这可能通过排除和解谈判期间所作陈述来得到鼓励。许多其他政策可以通过证据规则来促进。想想我前面提到的两个涉及口供、搜查和扣押的美国著名的排除规则。它们是排除规

② 罗纳德·J·艾伦：《证据法的理论基础和意义》，张保生、张月波译，载《证据科学》，2010 年第 4 期。

则的典型，旨在通过激励警察尊重个人权利来规制警察调查活动；如果该权利没有得到尊重，任何随之而产生的证据都不能在审判中使用。证据规则还能影响被提起的各种诉讼。通过使强奸被害人免于必须对其先前性行为作证的证据规则，通过排除那些可能使声称的被害人难堪的证言，来鼓励所称被害人对所称强奸犯提起民事或者刑事诉讼。对品性证据的排除，使起诉某些特定类型的犯罪更加困难，这些犯罪可能很少产生其他类型的证据，比如毒品犯罪就是一种私下从事的犯罪，不会产生一般意义上的“被害人”。

审判，以及排除规则，涉及常常被贴上“公正”标签的格外重要的事项。某些社会信奉，不应当要求一个人披露令其难堪的信息，这导致大量不允许审判的隐私领域的创立。在一个甚至更基本的层面，至关重要的是意识到，法律制度将犯错误，而证据规则将影响所犯错误的类型和方式。某些制度斥巨资以维持现状，而另一些制度则更关心任何心怀不满的人都能有一个法庭来宣泄其冤屈。总的说来，一个法律制度能试图影响可能犯的两种错误：一是对原告的错判（包括判无辜者有罪），这称为积极错误；二是对被告的错判（包括判有罪者无罪），这称为消极错误。资源配置和证据规则都将影响这两种错误之间的关系。谢天谢地，法律制度还能作出正确裁决。与错误相比，两种（对原告和被告的）正确裁决都可能作出，而且，正确裁决在对一个法律制度进行评估时也非常重要。当然，在这些事项如何从属于法律制度的建构，以及正确和错误的裁决应适当匹配的程度等问题上，理性人可能存在着分歧，但就这种复杂性事项本身可能不存在着合理的分歧。

我需要提醒你们，我去年的讲座也提到了这一点③，存在着另一个层面的复杂性，它涉及主要行为和诉讼行为的区别。主要行为涉及何为正确和错误，什么应当鼓励或劝阻，鼓励有经济效益的行为，规制诸如婚姻等社会制度的其他事项——所有组成复杂社会的事项。尽管这有点过于简化，但促进适当和具有经济效益的行为是社会的典型目标，而先进社会的法律是实现这些目标的最重要的工具之一。相比之下，诉讼行为涉及纠纷解决，这些纠纷产生于所称不适当的主要行为。在某些社会，依据主要行为和诉讼行为的内在逻辑将其概念化地分为截然不同的领域，但这种概念化是错误的，错在一个非常重要的方法上。主要行为和诉讼行为相互影响；的确，它们紧密相连，这意味着不能割裂法律制度对主要行为的影响而单独对其进行分析。我在前面已经给了一个例

③ 罗纳德·J·艾伦：《证据法、诉讼法和实体法的关系》，张保生、张月波、汪诸豪译，载《证据科学》，2010年第6期。

子；可能存在某种诉讼，即行为（包括主要行为和诉讼行为）被一个低成本或零成本的诉讼程序所优化，但也可能存在其他类型即行为被极高成本所优化的诉讼——换句话说，这些是不应当被起诉至法官面前的案件。一个社会大概应当特别慎重地让家庭关系成为法律诉讼的主题或意见表达的内容。一般观点是，诉讼能够决定权利的价值，即什么权利可被剥夺，哪些权利是没有价值的。像我们所讲的诸如专利权和著作权等知识产权之全球性纠纷的例子，就是当代具有紧迫性的实例。在当今中国，你们正在为之斗争的另一个例子，涉及财产能被个人拥有的进化概念。

我这里的主要观点是：某种具有讽刺意味的是，审判不只是关于审判的！法律制度的构造不仅是关于诉讼之最有效的形式。相反，法律制度的构造涉及大量社会政策之间高度复杂的相互作用。证据法的大量内容特别是排除规则，均服务于这些目标，但这些目标常常是相互冲突的。促进一个目标可能会损害另一个目标。因此，标准的社会问题不是如何追求一个单一目标，比如准确性或有效裁判，而是如何优化一系列冲突性目标的极其复杂的问题。证据法以及相关的排除规则，都肩负着这一复杂的任务，这就是我将今晚的演讲题目定为排除规则的困难的原因。

现在，我将转入对这些困难的论述。

一、第一部分定义中的困难：在“排除规则”短语中什么都未被排除

正如迄今为止我讲的内容所暗示的，存在定义上的困难——“排除规则”到底是什么？在美国，有许多著名证据排除案例，如我早些时候提到的米兰达案和马普案，但正如我已经说过的，没有什么独特的关于非法搜查和扣押的第4条修正案排除规则，也没有什么独特的针对违反米兰达案要求的第5条修正案排除规则，米兰达规则要求，犯罪嫌疑人必须被告知他有保持沉默的权利和放弃此项权利的后果。存在着大量不那么知名的排除规则，旨在实施宪法的其他规定。第6条修正案对质权和获得律师辩护的权利就是典型例子。来源于一个不能被交叉询问之人的言词证据将被排除以维护对质权；从一个获得律师辩护的第6条修正案权利已通过正式诉讼程序启动的人那里谨慎引出的陈述，也是如此。关键点在于，所有这些规则都在维护一个特定审判场景。这个场景可能是特别美国化的，但在任何其他社会中无论它拥有什么场景，在很大程度上都将通过证据排除规则来构成。

然而，排除规则的范围将进一步大大扩展。实际上，所有的英美证据规则

都是排除规则，而这也是任何法律制度的真实情况。请思考几个例子：

1. 相关性：所有组织良好的法律制度都要求，证据与要在法庭上提交的一个实质性主张是相关的。所有其他证据均被排除，这意味着，构成一个理性证据法的最基本的主张实际上是一个排除规则。除了具有相关性之外，大多数制度还施加了其他限制条件，比如证据必须不是重复的、误导的或费时的，而这又意味着许多潜在的证据被这个基本概念排除了。

2. 许多但并非所有的法律制度，还通过排除不适当的偏见证据来限制相关证据的可采性。如你们所知，这包括诸如具有煽动性或成见性的证据，典型情况下某种平衡检验将被启用，如《联邦证据规则》规则 403 允许排除相关证据，如果该证据的偏见性影响实质上超过其证明价值的话。有趣的理由很多，最重要的是它将一种明确的成本\收益分析引入了证据法的核心内容，而通过一个排除原则得以实现。

3. 排除具体证据形式的特殊相关性规则是很普遍的，特别是在普通法制度中。这些在我先前的讨论中已提到很多，但还有更多其他情形。一种医疗协助的提供对于责任来说不具有可采性；保险的存在也是如此。特殊规则常常为照片或录像带的采纳而设置，当这些规则未被遵循时，结果就是那个证据被排除。

4. 像一般排除规则一样，传闻证据被认为是一个特殊的英美法问题。正如我在昨晚的讲座中试图说明的那样④，传闻证据规则比那些要丰富得多；它是一个研究推论过程的天然实验室。正如我也试图揭示的那样，它的排除属性被夸大了，但它们仍然存在。

5. 实际上，所有法律制度都在与品性和倾向证据作斗争。其原因比较复杂，但简略地说，品性和倾向证据是一种证据拥有积极和消极两种属性的一个例证。从积极方面说，几乎没人怀疑品性和倾向证据对行为具有预测性，这意味着那种证据是相关的，但同时这种证据又可能带来巨大的成本。这种证据由于分散了审判关于一个特定控告是否发生的注意力，因而可能产生误导性；这种证据由于减少事实认定者对该主张之准确性的关注，因而被指控的人若是一个坏人（对事实认定者的效用功能会产生不利影响，是一个技术性概念），就可能会引起偏见。然而，一个制度要解决这些关于其性质的深层问题，将通过一个排除规则来实现。

④ 《传闻证据的理论阐释，及其对中国产生的影响》，系艾伦教授 2011 年 12 月在中国政法大学的演讲。

6. 在和伪造和欺骗行为作斗争的过程中，各种最佳证据规则已得到发展：对文件可采性条件的规定比一般鉴真规则更加详细（尽管信息技术的创新已从根本上改变了“文件”的含义）；不能满足各种检验的文件被排除。与服务于相关性的规则形成鲜明对照，这是具有排除性的证据规则的另一个例子。

7. 构造诉讼却伴随一个排除因素的其他例子，是外行和专家意见规则。外行意见规则排除包含证人太多积极认知的证据。证人只对他的感知记忆作证，而不是别的东西。当他开始重建那种记忆或从它得出推论时，他就超出了自己的适当角色，他的证据就是不可采的，这当然就意味着它被排除。类似的情况，专家可根据经过验证的专业知识而作证，但不能提供超出他们训练和知识范围的意见。通过排除，审判的一种特别方式得以维持。

并非所有证据规则都属于上面讨论的类型。与其说采纳或排除证据，不如说某些规则处理的是提问形式，比如，禁止在直接盘问中提出诱导性问题，以及通常的辩论性或纠缠性提问。其他规则涉及提问的回答问题，比如没有回应或者叙述性的回答。还有一些规则涉及管理问题，大部分但并非都是审前排除的问题。例如，在美国联邦法院诉讼中，《联邦证据规则》规则 412 是关于打算使用先前恶行证据的通知要求。《联邦证据规则》规则 613（b）要求，给予证人一个解释明显不一致先前陈述的机会。各种证据规则都涉及法律选择问题，比如《联邦证据规则》规则 302、501、601 和 903，其他规则涉及审判程序（《联邦证据规则》规则 103 建构异议，《联邦证据规则》规则 104 涉及附条件的相关性和附条件的可采性）。我相信，在中国法律中，也有与这些规则相对应的规定。尽管它们并非以排除规则的面目出现，但大多数都有排除作用。如果一方当事人没有给予适当的通知，证据就不能被使用；如果证人坚持不以适当方式回答问题，该回答可被排除；法律规则的选择决定着依据哪一项国内法来决定排除；而许多审判程序，比如异议，就是用于排除的。

本讲座这部分的要点是，“排除”仅仅是“采纳”的反面。因而，排除规则的第一个困难是，它们并非美国的独特创造，而是任何法律制度建构中一个完整且相当复杂的部分。

二、第二部分定义中的困难：各种排除规则并不依其目的而区分，因为实际上所有证据规则都包含激励

有时人们认为，排除规则的区分，特别是美国各种排除规则的变体，在于其具有控制警察之目的。“美国排除规则”的传统却错误的观点是，用排除作为一种惩罚动机去强制人们遵守某些法律标准，这是排除规则所特有的，特别

是美国宪法之权利法案的规定。这种界定努力也失败了。除了那些强制执行宪法权利的规则外，许多排除规则还像宪法基础规则那样，作了激励主要行为的规定。以上提到的特殊相关性规则，如提供医疗协助的规则和特免权规则，显然旨在影响主要行为。有趣的是，甚至品性证据规则都能以这种方式来理解，由于其不纠缠一个人的过去，而是激励改进和悔过。排除规则特定子集的宪法来源是不相关的。

其他排除规则为证据的产生提供了激励，这模糊了主要行为和诉讼行为的界限。这里明显的例子是最佳证据规则，以及详细规定以前的证言、先前记录的回忆和业务档案何时可采的规则。的确，“主要行为”和“诉讼行为”之间的区别，对于隐含在我本次讲座开场白中的理由来说，无论如何都没有什么帮助作用。通过参考最糟糕的诉讼情景，谨慎的当事人将规划他们的“主要行为”。这是诉讼行为和主要行为之间存在密切关系的一个例证。谨慎的当事人将规划他们的主要行为，以至于任何诉讼无疑都将回报给他们一个满意的裁决。合同将被签署并按最佳证据规则来保存；文件将被创建并按业务档案例外规则来保存，等等。这种行为仅涉及减少长期交易成本包括诉讼成本（毕竟只是一种经商成本）的明智努力，但要点是这种策略行为模糊了主要行为和诉讼行为的界限。

三、民事/刑事差异中的困难

美国排除规则的部分神话是，它是一个仅涉及刑法中强制遵从事项的工具。人们从我已讲的内容可以推知，对排除规则而言，刑法和民法的分野并不那么重要。二者之间显然存在区别，但这些区别并未以任何重要方式清晰地显现出来。民法和刑法都明确表达了权利与义务的存在。二者都影响着人们以适当方式而行为的社会福利。例如，非正常死亡法和谋杀法就有高度类似的正当理由。一般来说，让人们承担自己行为的真实成本，鼓励了他们去优化自己的行为。对今晚讲座的目的而言，更重要的是，证据规则影响两种制度行为。准确性的成本对主要行为和诉讼行为都具有极为类似的影响。归根结底，无论是“民事规则”还是“刑事规则”的价值，都是由期待优化诉讼行为和主要行为之和的成本/收益分析来决定的。

鉴于它们实质上的相似性，为了强制实施程序性权利和证据性权利，在民事和刑事案件中存在高度类似的诉讼机制就没有什么可奇怪的了，当然这主要是通过证据排除规则来实现的。事实上，在民事案件中，甚至还有针对错误行为的证据排除。一个范例是，对于没有遵守诉讼的证据开示阶段（“诉讼的证据开示阶段”是指，在民事案件中，双方为了促进高效审判而互相披露他们已知案件情况的过程）期限而施加惩罚的情况。美国联邦第七巡回上诉法院在 *Banco del Atlantico*，*S. A. v. Woods Indus.*，*Inc.*，No. 07—2238（7th Cir. Mar. 7，2008）案中的裁决，就是一个很好的例子，它维持了驳回诉讼的原判，作为对原告失于提供证人为公司文件作证的制裁。未尽到自己应尽的义务，原告受到了被驳回诉讼的制裁。

还有由于未遵守有关证据规则而受到制裁的其他例子。最重要的是所谓毁灭证据。毁灭证据这一术语用于形容一方当事人毁灭或藏匿其明知与诉讼案件有关的证据的行为。如果一方当事人“毁灭”证据，该方当事人就不能对与已毁灭证据有关的争点提出质疑。实质上，该方当事人就被迫承认了与已毁灭证据相关的任何主张中对其不利的事实真相。例如，如果一方当事人毁灭了有争议的合同的唯一副本，法院就将假定，该合同的条款正好是对方所主张的内容。

另一个在某种程度上与宪法性排除规则概念上适用一致、旨在影响行为的重要制裁领域，是基于错误行为的特免权例外。采纳而非排除其他特免权证据，被用来制裁相关行为。例子包括，律师—委托人特免权中的犯罪或诈欺例外，这揭开了律师—委托人在促成犯罪和欺诈上交流秘密性的面纱；患者—精神诊疗师特免权的危险性例外要求，精神诊疗师披露其患者对他人构成危险的信息；而夫妻特免权的共谋例外，则在配偶一起故意从事犯罪时，消弭了夫妻特免权。

四、实施中的困难

大家从我到目前为止所讲的内容中可以看出，我对盛行的“美国排除规则”神话持相反的态度，排除规则在美国实际上是千变万化的。它们在程序上是同样复杂的。在证明责任这一最重要的程序问题上，各种宪法性排除规则之间甚至没有一致性。例如，一个刑事被告人有责任证明，根据第 4 条修正案，一份搜查令状是有缺陷的；而国家机关有责任证明一个未经授权的搜查是正当合理的；国家机关还有责任证明，一项列队指认没有侵犯第 6 条修正案获得律师帮助的权利；但被告人又有责任证明，（列队指认过程中）不必要的暗示违反了第 14 条修正案关于法律正当程序的规定。⑤

因为大多数“排除规则”并非基于宪法而设立，所以其程序设置甚至比我

⑤ 参见卡密萨等：《现代的刑事诉讼程序》，第 11 版，第 938～944 页。

上面描述的还要复杂。它们的程序设置可能是由制定法和法院规则而非宪法性裁判所决定的，所以在适用中出现相当大的变化也不令人吃惊。例如《联邦证据规则》规则 104 有一个复杂的排序机制，以确定一个证据规则适用的证明标准是“优势证据”，还是在特定规则适用条件下的“足以支持一项认定的证据”。还有其他复杂情形，《联邦证据规则》规则 401 有自己的适用于相关性初步判定的“任何影响”（any effect）* 的说服责任，但与《联邦证据规则》规则 403 相比，却似乎对偏见影响实质上超过证明力这一如何可能的问题未作回应。贯穿于各种证据规则之中，还潜藏着众多的一项一项分散的规则，它们都影响着程序语境。《联邦证据规则》规则 602 的证明标准要求证人拥有亲身知识（足以支持一项认定的证据），是对《联邦证据规则》规则 104（a）所说的证人资格应当由一项优势证据来确定的背离。这里并没有什么问题，因为美国有一个很强的传统，即在规则或法律之间存在冲突时适用更特殊的一个，但尽管如此，其复杂性本身却很有趣（我将用几分钟解释一下它存在的原因）。的确，一个规则，即《联邦证据规则》规则 609 利用四个不同的证明标准来处理先前定罪的可采性问题，这些证明标准取决于该先前定罪的性质及发生时间。

因为考虑到排除证据的社会成本，宪法性排除规则的实施就变得甚至更为复杂了。即使宪法性排除规则遏制错误的国家行为，这种遏制的代价却是增加了有罪的人将未被定罪的概率。还有就是对证据排除作为一种威慑力之效力的怀疑。这两种关注点的联合作用，产生了一系列缩减排除规则范围的裁决。例如，在第 4 条修正案的领域，仅当一个人对隐私权的合法期待被侵犯时，他才能投诉一项不合理的搜查和扣押。例如假定，一名警察未获得批准令状就搜查了一栋房屋。进一步假定，该警察找到了可将该房主和第三方归罪的证据。在这种情况下，该房主能够排除该证据，而第三方却不能。法院得出的结论是，将排除规则扩展适用于第三方，将导致一个没有任何补益的错误无罪开释。还有大量类似的规则。检控方不能在其主诉中使用非法获取的证据，以反对在获取该证据过程中其权利遭受侵害的人；但如果该人出庭作证，非法取得的证据就能被用于弹劾该被告人。即使证据是非法取得的，但如果检控方证明了它将被以一种合法的方式“必然发现”，或者能够通过另一个独立来源获得这些证据，那么，这些证据仍可为检控方所用。同样，间接来源于非法行为的证据也可为检控方所用。

* 译注：艾伦教授说，这里的“any effect”与《联邦证据规则》规则 401 原文中的“any tendency”（任何趋向性）是同义词。

另一个造成排除规则适用范围缩减的因素是，执法官员能通过调整自身行为来努力消减排除规则的影响力。[⑥] 例如，警察知道，通过对米兰达权利的生搬硬套和机械性复述，几乎就可以导致不会有人援用沉默权或者获得律师帮助的权利。律师只能在控诉后、列队指认发生前提供法律帮助，但警察控制着列队指认的时间，并且如果他们愿意的话，还可以提起一个预控诉。即便警察因为嫌疑人援用其米兰达权利而不能对其进行讯问，警察仍能通过在嫌疑人的监房安插线人来获取嫌疑人所作的有罪陈述。最重要的是，所有宪法权利均可被放弃，并且没有什么能够阻止执法官员要求个人放弃他们的权利，而让警察按照他们喜欢的方式进行调查。由于显而易见的心理原因，很多人不能拒绝警察为所欲为的要求，而他们的宪法权利便以这种无法阻止调查的方式而告消亡。

五、为什么会产生所有这些困难

我在解释“排除规则”为何如此复杂的时候已经暗示了原因。这是因为“排除规则”与审判构造密不可分。人们构造并定制了审判。反过来说，审判以两种不同的方式体现出其为复杂事件。首先，审判涉及大量参与人包括法官、陪审团（如果有的话）、律师、当事人和证人之间关系的排序。有趣的是，即使审判法院常被认为处于强势地位，但其权力相当有限。审判法官不能掌控审判过程的细节，而不得不由当事人或他们的律师来掌控。复杂性的第二个来源在于审判是具有教育意义的事件。在这样的情境下，要“规制”证据的出示，就要求对推论过程进行规制，否则便徒劳无益。法官能做的，最多是以其认为正确的推论方向来推进当事人及整个程序。法官也能施以多种激励手段，主要手段是通过相关证据的采纳和以任何理由而提出的异议证据的排除，来推进当事人和整个程序。当然，还有其他的工具，比如，实质性裁定和对法院认定的无视，但确保审判中证据适当出示的主要工具，还是排除规则的某种适用。

还有另外两个复杂特征，那就是证据规则既构建上下级法院（审判法院与上诉法院）之间的关系，又构建立法机关和司法机关之间的关系。有关证据规则及其排除成分的裁定，是上级法院规制下级法院的主要手段之一。同样，证据规则也是立法机关制衡法院的一种方式。这些变量为本来就颇为复杂的法律制度基础增加了行政和政治的变量，并导致证据规则及其排除特征更加复

⑥ 相关讨论，参见威廉·J·斯塔茨：《刑事司法中的政治宪法》，载《哈佛法律评论》，第119卷，2006年，第780页。

杂化。

六、什么是最佳规制形式：排除还是惩罚

这是一个极难回答的问题，并且很难说何为最佳。证据排除不是实施证据规则和程序规则的唯一可取方法。惩罚可能具有替代作用；可以对违背相关实质标准的人施以制裁，无论其是侵犯个人权利的政府官员，还是没遵循证据规则的律师。的确，美国排除规则的神话通常有一个考虑因素，就是排除规则的成本较之收益过高，也许实施制裁是一个更好的办法。然而，个人制裁和排除证据之间的选择也颇为复杂。正如两位著名学者所言："排除规则或追缴非法所得而非损害赔偿，有两种……管理上或实际的好处：易于评估和程序便利。"⑦ 正如他们继续指出的，实际损害是难以评估的。国家应当为一项不合理的搜查和扣押赔偿多少？同样麻烦的是，这些对个人的损害赔偿恰好会导致对官员的过度威慑。如果一名政府官员因为犯了一个错误而面对个人损害赔偿，他将尽量避免去犯错误；为什么要对没有私利的事情承担个人风险？这会使司法人员个体过于谨慎，而在阻止犯罪行为发生或认定并给那些违法之人定罪时不能采取应有的积极行为。

证据排除还有另一面的风险。如果一个人知道自己不会受到制裁，他可能会更倾向于采取侵犯他人权利的行为，这将导致威慑力丧失。当然，只有在一个人具有良好动机的情况下，审判中的证据排除才能发挥作用。如果警察不在乎是否定罪，排除证据是唯一的制裁，那么，警察简直就没有动机去关心他们也许正侵犯的他人权利。他们就会只为侵扰人们而对他们进行搜查或逮捕，而不是为了寻找罪证。在何种补救措施为最佳的问题上，还存在另一个有趣的社会维度："宪法性侵犯所导致的损害赔偿责任的缩减，对美国宪政具有深层的结构性裨益。从本质上说，对金钱损害赔偿的限制，将社会资源从对过去伤害的赔偿中转移到对未来福利的投资，继续把社会资源从老年公民转向对年轻公民的重新分配。"⑧ 这就是说，损害赔偿是着眼于过去的，而排除性制裁则着眼于影响未来的行为。

受其他因素的影响，最佳救济机制的塑造变得复杂了。这其实是个经验问题，而不仅仅属于逻辑分析，实际上也没有关于各种救济措施的数据以供分

⑦ 莱夫莫尔、斯塔茨：《私法和公法之中的救济与激励：一篇比较研究的文章》，载《威斯康星法律评论》，1990 年卷，第 483 页。

⑧ 杰弗里斯：《宪法性法律中的权利救济差距》，载《耶鲁法学杂志》，第 109 卷，第 87 页。

析。正如我上面提到的，部分原因是，在一个真实世界中，人们能对任何新规则作出响应，因而创造一种无意识的结果。想想那些著名的宪法性裁定，如我在演讲开始时提到的“马普规则”和“米兰达规则”。如果没有其他理由，而只是因为存在过多的犯罪，这些规则到底有什么影响其实并不完全清楚。这看起来似乎是一个奇怪的论调，但却极为重要。任何社会中的犯罪都比官员能够处理的要多得多。因此，执法官员就有巨大的自由裁量权来决定对哪些案件要进行调查和追诉，对哪些案件可以不予理睬。选择理由之一是相对胜诉率，即作出此选择，而非彼选择。对四起案件起诉并获得有罪判决比对一起案件起诉要好。但这意味着，警察和控诉方将更倾向于对易于取胜和成本较小的案件进行追诉，而案件花费多少的一个决定因素是人们能雇到多么优秀的辩护律师。反过来说，在某种程度上也取决于，检控方主诉的案件是否存在导致证据排除的问题，以及人们是否有经济实力将那些争点对簿法庭。如果是这样，检控方也许选择不起诉此类案件，但这样选择会导致这样的后果，即检控方无论何时对能承担更多诉讼费用的富人被告采取的一种逃避态度，都是对穷人的歧视。[9] 当然如果这种情况发生，任何排除规则对警察行为的实际效果都会被打折扣，因为这类案件中胡作非为的事情将永远不为人知。因此，像“马普案”和“米兰达案”中所奉行的原则，其实际效果不会减少这类胡作非为的发生率，而只能促使检控方选择起诉何种案件。

非常值得注意的是，排除规则还会以另一种方式对穷人不利。排除规则的存在会使有限的防御资源转而制造法律动议，而使这些资源背离事实调查。这也许意味着，排除规则会增加错误定罪的概率。[10]

关于排除规则的复杂性和最佳救济机制还有最后一点值得一提，这类似剩余犯罪问题。在美国和中国，立法机关控制着实体法参数，它们能或多或少地凭自己的喜好修改实体法。这意味着，即便在美国，立法机关也能通过改写支配性实体标准而使程序性裁定实质上失效。我给你们讲一个美国的例子。法院将宪法第 4 条修正案关于禁止不合理搜查和扣押的禁令解释为，禁止警察任意截停汽车进行检查。法院合理地考虑到所谓“任意”选择可能并不真是任意的，反而可能隐藏着不可能予以规制的差别对待决定。相比之下，警察当然非

⑨ 斯塔茨：《辩诉交易和刑事法律消失的影子》，载《哈佛法律评论》，第 117 卷，2004 年，第 2548 页。

⑩ 斯塔茨：《排除规则的美德与罪恶》，载《哈佛法律与公共政策期刊》，第 20 卷，第 443 页；还可参见斯塔茨：《刑事诉讼程序与刑事司法间的紧张关系》，载《耶鲁法学杂志》，第 107 卷，1997 年，第 1 页。

常希望，能在他们怀疑可能发生某些犯罪行为的任何时候都截停汽车。立法机关或多或少会同意警察的说法，并以扩展机动车法律覆盖范围的方式来回应，使驾驶行为实际上不可能不触犯一项法律。作为法律改变的结果，如果警察想要截停一辆汽车，他们仅需花足够时间跟着它，直到其驾驶员违反众多有关车辆法律中的一款。一旦出现这种情况，警察便有理由将该车截停。

这个例子可能具有普遍性，据我所知，每个立法机关都采取了相似的策略。“9·11”事件刚发生后，全世界的立法机关都扩张了大量的犯罪界定，以促进对所称恐怖活动的调查。如果立法机关担忧某个特定企业存在腐败，一个常用的策略是要求该问题企业保存详细档案以备政府进行有效核查。我要指出，这也是我今晚讲座主题的另一个例证，即社会有机特性。它成长并进化着，而非静止不动。它以不可预知的方式对变化作出回应。

七、结论

我今晚的讲座试图解释很多事情。首先，我试图让你们对与排除规则问题有关的美国审判过程的真面目，有更准确的理解。特别是，我试图说明，其他国家对美国排除规则的传统理解是非常不准确的。然而，更重要的是，我试图表明，排除规则——不只是美国排除规则——就审判的全部概念而言，实际上是不可或缺的。我最后讲的主题，即不同救济机制的选择是复杂且不确定的，值得再用一个单独的讲座来专门探讨。当然，这些课程对中国和美国都同样重要。

谢谢你们耐心听讲，我期待着你们的提问。

Difficulties of Exclusionary Rules

Ronald J. Allen

My topic tonight, Difficulties of Exclusionary Rules, builds on the lecture that I gave last November, which was entitled The American Exclusionary Rule (s). [①]I focused in that lecture on the famous cases of Miranda v. Arizona, 384 U. S. 436 (1966), and Mapp v. Ohio, 367 U. S. 643 (1961), which involve exclusion of evidence in order to protect the rights to be free from self-incrimination and from unreasonable searches and seizures that are in the Bill of Rights of the United States Constitution. There are other cases from the U. S. Supreme Court that mandate exclusion if an individual right is violated, and this has led many people, including sophisticated legal scholars, to believe that there is an exclusionary rule in the United States that mandates the exclusion of illegally obtained evidence. As I pointed out in that lecture, this belief is false. There are many complicated rules of evidence in the United States. Some mandate the exclusion of illegally obtained evidence and some do not. Some mandate exclusion for other reasons that have nothing to do with the legality of the manner in which the evidence was obtained, and quite frequently illegally obtained evidence is admitted.

Although the "exclusionary rule" is often thought of as peculiarly American phenomenon, again this is not true; and the reason that is not true both puts tonight's lecture into context and highlights why tonight's topic is important for the student of evidence in any country. The reason is simple but profound: Any organized system of litigation or dispute resolution will have numerous exclusionary rules. Virtually all rules of evidence and many rules of

① Ronald J. Allen, *The American Exclusionary Rule* (*s*), Evidence Science, Feb. 2012 Volume 20 No. 1.

procedure determine what can be presented in court. All such rule sort out what is admissible from what is not, which in turn may result in the exclusion of evidence. Only if the parties were permitted to produce any evidence they liked whenever they liked in any form that they liked would there be no "exclusionary rule," but no such system exists anywhere in the world, to my knowledge. Because admission of evidence is critical to the construction and operation of all legal systems, so too is its mirror opposite—the exclusion of evidence—because a legal system cannot have the one without the other. Rather than being a peculiar American invention, then, exclusionary rules are part of the foundation of any organized legal system. Moreover, legal systems are complicated, and so too are the exclusionary rules in any country, whatever names they may go by in those countries.

I laid out many of the complexities facing rational legal organization in a lecture I gave here two years ago. We should review these quickly, for they lay the ground work for understanding some of the difficulties of exclusionary rules. ②By far the most important point concerns the objective of legal systems. It is generally accepted that factual accuracy is the most significant objective of trials, but accuracy is not the only objective. Factual accuracy is crucial because it leads to socially optimal results by securing to individuals the value of their rights. Indeed, without factual accuracy, rights are literally meaningless. Some of you may have heard me make this point in previous lectures, because each time I come to China to lecture, I emphasize that factually accurate findings are as if not more important than substantive rights; rights are completely dependent upon the findings of fact. When you think you own something, that it is your property, you mean that you have the right to possess, consume, and dispose of that object. If your rights to do those things are challenged, the controversy will be decided by the facts of the matter. Can you prove that you made, bought, found, or were given the object in question? Only if the answer is yes will you be able to enjoy its benefits. What is true of property rights is true of all rights, including political and civil rights. This why I say to audiences like this throughout China that the future of the conti-

② Ronald J. Allen, *The Theoretical Foundations and Implications of Evidence*, Evidence Science, Aug. 2010 Volume 18 No. 4.

nuing success of China rests in good measure in the hands of people like you are dedicated to the study of evidence and the construction of a rational legal system.

To return to the primary topic of tonight, accuracy matters, but it is part of a complex set of competing interests that also much be accommodated. One of those is cost. Litigation is not free; someone pays for it, either the parties to litigation or the State. It is conceivable that litigation in particular cases can be too expensive given the value it is trying to secure. If a case worth 100 yuan would take a thousand yuan to litigate, it is perfectly sensible to conclude that such a case should not be litigated and perhaps should be resolved in some other fashion. Litigating such cases could reduce social welfare both because the cost is more than the value and because allowing such cases to proceed might discourage private settlement of disputes. All of these considerations bear upon the structure of a legal system, and people can reasonably disagree about their significance. In some societies, perhaps litigation is frowned upon; in others, an official adjudication of rights may be viewed as critically important, no matter what the stakes may be.

As I say, and as the example of cost indicates, factual accuracy competes with various policies that a legal system could pursue, and the achievement of which could very well involve exclusionary rules. Privileges may encourage certain relationships, such as that between spouses or patients and doctors, but do so through the exclusion of evidence. If private settlement of disputes is preferred to litigation, this can be encouraged through the exclusion of statements made during settlement negotiations. There are numerous other policies that can be advanced through evidence rules. Consider the two examples I gave above of famous American exclusionary rules involving confessions and search and seizure. These are examples of exclusionary rules that are designed to regulate police investigative activities by giving the police an incentive to respect individual rights; if the rights are not respected, any ensuing evidence cannot be used at trial. Rules of evidence also can affect the kinds of law suits that are brought. Evidence rules insulating rape victims from having to testify to their prior sexual behavior encourages alleged victims to bring civil or criminal actions against alleged abusers by excluding what could be embarrassing testimony of the alleged victim. Excluding character evidence makes it more difficult to prosecute certain kinds of crimes that are less likely to generate other kinds of evidence, such as drugs crimes that are conducted in secret and that do not produce "victims" in the normal sense of the word.

Trials, and thus exclusionary rules, involve additional important matters that often go under the label of "fairness." Some societies believe a person should not be required to disclose embarrassing information, which results in the creation of large zones of privacy that are off limits at trial. At an even more fundamental level, it is critical to realize that legal systems will make mistakes, and evidence rules will affect how and what kind of mistakes are made. Some systems are heavily invested in maintaining the status quo, whereas others are equally concerned that anyone with a complaint be able to have the grievance aired by a court. In general, a legal system can try to affect the two types of errors that can be made—a wrongful verdict for a plaintiff (including a conviction of an innocent person), which is called a false positive, and a wrongful verdict for a defendant (including an acquittal of a guilty person), which is called a false negative. Both resource allocation and evidentiary rules will affect the relationship between these two types of errors. Legal systems also make correct decisions, thankfully. As with errors, two kinds of correct decisions can be made (for plaintiffs and defendants), and correct decisions also matter in appraising a legal system. Reasonable people can disagree as to how these matters pertain to the construction of a legal system, of course, and what the proper mix of true and false decisions should be, but there can be no reasonable disagreement that such complexities matter.

There is another layer of complexity that I need to remind you of, and which I lectured on last year as well③, and that involves the distinction between primary and litigation behavior. Primary behavior deals with what is right and wrong, what should be encouraged or discouraged, with encouraging efficient economic behavior, regulating social institutions such as marriage, and many other things—all the things that make up a complex socie-

③ Ronald J. Allen, *The Relationships among Evidence Law, Procedural Law, and Substantive Law*, Evidence Science, Dec. 2010 Volume 18 No. 6.

ty. Although it is a bit of an oversimplification, facilitating appropriate and economically efficient behavior are the typical objectives of society, and the law in advanced societies is one of most important tools to accomplish these goals. Litigation behavior, by contrast, involves resolving disputes that have arisen about allegedly inappropriate primary behavior. In some societies, primary and litigation behavior are conceptualized as separate and distinct areas with internal logics of their own, but this conceptualization is false, and it is false in a very important way. Primary and litigation behavior affect each other; indeed, they are intensely interconnected, which means that the legal system cannot be analyzed separately from its implications for primary behavior. I have already given one example above; there may be some types of litigation where behavior (both primary and litigation) are optimized by a low or zero cost litigation process, but there may be other types of litigation that are optimized by infinitely high costs—in other words, cases that should not be brought before judges. Perhaps a society should only cautiously let family relationships be the subject of law suits, or the content of expression of opinions. The general point is that litigation can determine the value of rights, and thus what rights are exploited and which are valueless. A modern, pressing, example of this is the global dispute occurring as we speak over intellectual property such as patents and copyrights. You here in China are now struggling with another example of this with your evolving conceptions of property that can be personally owned.

My primary point here is the somewhat ironical one that trials are not just about trials! The structure of the legal system is not just about the most efficient form of litigating. Rather, the structure of the legal system involves highly complicated interactions between the numerous social policies that are at stake. Much of the law of evidence, and in particular exclusionary rules, serves those goals, but often those goals conflict. Furthering one goal can disadvantage another. Thus, the standard social problem is not how to pursue a single goal, such as accurate or efficient adjudication, but instead the infinitely more complicated problem of optimizing a set of conflicting objectives. Evidence law, and thus exclusionary rules, pursue this complicated task, which is why I have titled tonight's lecture Difficulties of Exclusionary

Rules.

I will now turn to some of those difficulties.

Ⅰ. Difficulties in definition Part I: Virtually nothing is excluded by the phrase "exclusionary rule":

As is implicit in what I have said so far, there are definitional difficulties—what exactly is an "exclusionary rule"? There are many famous examples of exclusion of evidence in the United States, such as the Miranda and Mapp cases that I mentioned earlier, but as I have already said there is nothing unique about either the fourth amendment exclusionary rule as a result of an illegal search and seizure or the fifth amendment exclusionary rule if the requirements of the Miranda case are violated that a suspect must be warned of his right to remain silent and waive that right. There are numerous less well-known exclusionary rules that are designed to enforce other constitutional provisions as well. The sixth amendment rights to confrontation and counsel are perfect examples. Testimonial evidence from a source who cannot be cross-examined is excluded to preserve confrontation rights, as is a statement deliberately elicited from a person whose sixth right to counsel has been initiated through formal proceedings. The critical point is that all these rules are preserving a certain vision of a trial. That vision may be peculiarly American, but whatever vision is held in any other society it, too, will be constituted in large part through exclusionary rules of evidence.

The reach of exclusionary rules goes considerably farther, however. Virtually all Anglo-American rules of evidence are exclusionary rules, but this is true of any legal system. Consider some examples:

1. Relevance: All organized legal systems require that evidence be relevant to a material proposition in order to be offered at trial. All other evidence is excluded, but that means that the most fundamental proposition constituting a rational law of evidence is in fact an exclusionary rule. In addition to being relevant, most systems impose other constraints, such as the evidence must not be cumulative, misleading, or a waste of time, but again that means much potential evidence is excluded by this fundamental concept.

2. Many but not all legal systems also qualify the admissibility of relevant evidence by excluding unduly prejudicial evidence. As you all know, this in-

volves such matters as evidence that would be inflammatory or biasing, and typically some sort of balancing test is employed, such as that of Federal Rules of Evidence 403 that permits the exclusion of relevant evidence if its prejudicial effect substantially outweighs its probative value. This is interesting for many reasons, not the least of which is that it imports an explicit cost/benefit analysis into the heart of the law of evidence that is enforced through an exclusionary principle.

3. Specialized relevancy rules that exclude specific forms of evidence are common place, especially in common law systems. I have mentioned a number of these in my earlier remarks, but there are many more others. An offer to provide medical assistance is not admissible on liability; neither is the existence of insurance. Special rules often exist for the admission of photographs or videotapes, and when the rules are not followed, the result is the exclusion of that evidence.

4. Hearsay is, like exclusionary rules generally, thought to be a peculiarly Anglo-American problem. As I tried to demonstrate in last night's lecture④, the hearsay rule is much more than that; it is a natural laboratory to study the inferential process. As I also tried to show, its exclusionary attributes are overstated, but they nonetheless exist.

5. Virtually all legal systems struggle with character and propensity evidence. The reasons are complicated, but briefly character and propensity evidence is a paradigmatic case of evidence that has both positive and negative attributes. On the positive side, few doubt that character and propensity evidence are predictive of behavior, which means evidence of that sort is relevant, but at the same time such evidence can have significant costs attached to it. The evidence can be misleading by distracting trials from whether a particular accusation happened, and the evidence can be prejudicial by reducing a fact finder's concern about the accuracy of this allegation because the person accused is a bad person (adversely affecting the fact finder's utility functions, is the technical concept) . However a system works out these deep problems about its na-

④ Ronald J. Allen, *A Theoretical Account of Hearsay, and Why It Matters for China*, presentation at China University of Political Science and Law in December 2011.

ture, the resolution will be enforced through an exclusionary rule.

6. In the struggle again forgery and fraudulent practices, various best evidence rules have been developed that specify in greater detail than general authentication rules the conditions of admissibility of documents (although innovations in information technology have radically changed the meaning of "document"); documents that do not meet the various tests are excluded. This is another example of an evidence rule with its exclusionary counterpart being put to the service of relevancy.

7. Other examples of rules that structure litigation but with an exclusionary component are the lay and expert opinion rules. The lay opinion rule excludes evidence that involves too much of the active cognition of the witness. A witness is to testify to his memory of his perceptions, and nothing else. When he begins to reconstruct that memory or draw inferences from it, he goes beyond his proper role and his evidence is inadmissible, which of course means it is excluded. Somewhat similarly, experts can testify on the basis of validated specialized knowledge but may not offer opinions that leap beyond their training and knowledge. Through exclusion, a particular form of trial is maintained.

Not all evidence rules appear to be on the type discussed above. Rather than admitting or excluding evidence, some rules deal with form of questions, forbidding for example leading questions on direct examination, and argumentative or badgering questions in general. Others deal with problems with answers to questions, such as a nonresponsive or a narrative answer. Still others deal with housekeeping issues, mostly but not exclusively pre-trial. In litigation in federal court in the United States, for example, FRE 412 requires notice of the intent to use prior bad acts; FRE 613 (b) requires that a witness be given the opportunity to explain an apparently inconsistent prior statement. Various evidence rules deal with choice of law problems, such as FRE 302, 501, 601, 903, whereas others deal with trial procedure (FRE 103 structures objections, and FRE 104 deals with conditional relevance and conditional admissibility). You have counterparts to all these rules in Chinese law, I believe. Although these do not appear on their face to be exclusionary rules, most have an exclusionary impact. If a party fails to give proper notice, the evidence cannot be used; if a witness persists in not answering questions in an appropriate fashion, the answers may be excluded; the choice of law rules determine which domestic law determines exclusion; and much trial procedure, such as objections, is directed at exclusion.

The primary point of this part of the lecture is that "exclusion" is simply the inverse of "admission." Thus, the first difficulty with exclusionary rules is that they are not a unique American creation but instead are an integral and quite complex part of the construction of any legal system.

Ⅱ. Difficulties in definition Part II: The various exclusionary rules are not distinguishable on the basis of their purpose, as virtually all evidence rules involve incentives.

Sometimes it is thought that what distinguishes exclusionary rules, especially the American variant, is that they have as their purpose controlling the police. The conventional, but erroneous, view of the "American exclusionary rule" is that it is unique in its motivation of using exclusion as a sanction to coerce compliance with some legal standard, in particular the provisions in the U. S. Constitution's Bill of Rights. This definitional effort fails, also. Many exclusionary rules in addition to those enforcing constitutional rights provide incentives for primary behavior similar to the constitutionally based rules. The specific relevance rules mentioned above, such as the rule about offers to provide medical assistance and the privilege rules, are obviously designed to affect primary behavior. Interestingly, even the character evidence rules can be understood in this manner, as they give incentives to reform and repent by not trapping a person in the past. The constitutional provenance of a certain subset of exclusionary rules is an irrelevancy.

Other exclusionary rules provide incentives for the creation of evidence, which blurs the distinction between primary behavior and litigation behavior. Here the obvious examples are the best evidence rule, and the rules detailing when former testimony, prior recollection recorded, and business records are admissible. Indeed, the distinction between "primary" and "litigation" behavior is unhelpful in any event for reasons implied in my opening remarks in this lecture. Well advised parties will plan their "primary behavior" by reference to the worst case scenario of litigation. This is an example of the intimate relationship between litigation and primary behavior. A well advised party will plan their primary behavior so that there is little doubt that any litigation will return a verdict in their favor. Contracts will be signed and kept in accordance with the best evidence rule; documents will be created and kept consistently with the business records exception, and so on. Such behavior simply involves sensible efforts to reduce long term transaction costs, including litigation costs (which after all are just a cost of doing business), but the point is that such strategic behavior blurs the distinction between primary or litigation behavior.

Ⅲ. Difficulties in the civil/criminal distinction

Part of themyth of the American exclusionary rule is that it is a tool to coerce compliance in matters uniquely dealing with the criminal law. As one can infer from what I have already said, the distinction between criminal and civil law is not very important with respect to exclusionary rules. While there are obvious distinctions between the two, it is not at all clear that those distinctions matter in any significant way. Both civil and criminal law exist to articulate rights and obligations. Both affect the social interest in people behaving appropriately. For example, wrongful death statutes and murder statutes have highly analogous justifications. In general, making people bear the true cost of their behavior encourages them to optimize their actions. More importantly for the purposes of tonight's lecture, rules of evidence affect behavior in both regimes. Costs of accuracy have highly analogous implications for both primary and litigation behavior. When all is said and done, the value of a rule, whether "civil" or "criminal," is determined by a cost/benefit analysis that looks to optimize the sum of litigation and primary behavior.

In light of their substantive similarities, it should come as no surprise that there are highly analogous procedural mechanisms in civil and criminal cases for enforcing procedural and evidentiary rights, which of course is largely through exclusionary rules of evidence. In fact, there is even exclusion of evidence for wrongdoing in civil cases. A perfect example are the cases that impose sanctions for the failure to abide by time limits in the discovery phase of litigation (the "discovery phase of litigation" refers to the process by which parties in civil cases turn over to each other what they know about the case in order to facilitate efficient trials) . A good example of this is the decision of the U. S. Seventh

Circuit Court of Appeal, in Banco del Atlantico, S. A. v. Woods Indus., Inc., No. 07—2238 (7th Cir. Mar. 7, 2008), that affirmed the dismissal of a case as a sanction for plaintiffs' wrongful failure to produce witnesses that could testify to corporate documents. Having failed in their obligations, they were sanctioned by having their case dismissed.

There are other examples of sanctions due to the failure to follow the rules concerning evidence. The most important one is known as spoliation. Spoliation is the term applied to a party's action of destroying or hiding evidence that the party knows is relevant and pertinent to a litigated case. If a party "spoliates" evidence, that party cannot contest issues pertinent to the spoliated evidence. In essence, the party is forced to admit the adverse truth of any proposition to which the spoliated evidence is relevant. If a party destroys the only copy of a contested contract, for example, the court will assume that the provisions of the contract are precisely what the adverse party asserts them to be.

Another important area where sanctions are applied in a manner conceptually consistent with the constitutional exclusionary rules that are designed to affect behavior is the exceptions to privileges that are based on wrongdoing. Admission rather than exclusion of the otherwise privileged evidence is used to sanction the behavior. Examples include the crime/fraud exception to the attorney-client privilege that lifts the veil of confidentiality on lawyer-client communications in furtherance of a crime or fraud; the dangerousness exception to the patient-psychotherapist privilege that requires the psychotherapist to release information that his client is a danger to others; and the common scheme exception to marital privileges that lifts the marital privileges when the spouses are engaged together in criminal purposes.

Ⅳ. Difficulties in administration

As one can tell from what I have said so far and contrary to the prevailing myth about "the American exclusionary rule", exclusionary rules in the United States are tremendously varied substantively. They are equally complicated procedurally. On the most important procedural issue—the burden of proof—there is not even uniformity among the various constitutionally based exclusionary rules. For example, a criminal defendant has the burden to prove that a warrant was defective under the fourth amendment; the state has the burden to prove that a warrantless search was justified as reasonable; the state has the burden to prove that alineup did not violate the 6th amendment right to counsel, but the defendant has the burden to prove that it violated the 14th amendment due process of law by being unnecessarily suggestive. ⑤

The procedural setting is even more complicated than I have described above, because most "exclusionary rules" are not constitutionally based. Their procedural setting consequently may be determined by statute or court rule, rather than constitutional adjudication, and not surprisingly the result is considerable variation in application. FRE 104, for example, has a complicated sorting mechanism to determine whether the standard of proof for the application of a rule of evidence is "a preponderance of the evidence" or instead "sufficient evidence to find" that the conditions of a particular rule apply. Adding yet another complication, FRE 401 has its own burden of persuasion of "any effect" that applies to the initial determination of relevancy, but by contrast FRE 403 seems silent on the issue of how likely must it be that prejudicial effect substantially outweighs probative value. Throughout the various rules of evidence also lurk numerous discrete rules that affect the procedural context. FRE 602's standard of proof for the requirement that a witness possess first-hand knowledge (evidence sufficient to support a finding) is a deviation from FRE 104 (a) that says the qualification of a witness should be established by a preponderance of the evidence. There is not problem here, because in the United States there is a strong tradition that, in a conflict between rules or laws, the more particular one applies, but nonetheless the complication is interesting in its own right (and I will explain why it exists in a few minutes) . Indeed, one rule, FRE 609 dealing with the admissibility of prior convictions, employs four different standards of proof depending on the nature of the prior conviction and when it occurred.

The administration of the constitutional exclusionary rules is made even more complicated because of concerns about the social costs of exclusion. Even if constitutional exclusionary rules deter wrongful state behavior, the deterrence comes at the cost of increasing the probability that guilty people will not

⑤ See Kamisar, et al., Modern Criminal Procedure (11th ed.), pp. 938-944.

be convicted. There are also doubts about how effective exclusion is as a deterrent. The combined effect of these two concerns has resulted in a series of decisions that reduce the scope of exclusionary rules. In the fourth amendment area, for example, a person may complain about an unreasonable search and seizure only if his legitimate expectations of privacy were violated. For example, assume the police search a house but failed to get a warrant. Assume further that the police find evidence incriminating both the owner of the house and a third party. The owner can suppress the evidence, but the third party cannot. The courts have concluded that extending exclusion to the third party would result in a wrongful acquittal with no compensating benefit. There are numerous similar rules. Illegally obtained evidence cannot be used by the government in its case in chief against a person whose rights were violated in obtaining the evidence, but the illegal obtained evidence can be used to impeach the defendant if he takes the stand to testify. Even if evidence is illegally seized, it may be used by the state if the state shows that it would have "inevitably discovered" the evidence in a legal fashion or if the state got possession of the evidence through a source independent of the illegality. Similarly, evidence indirectly derived from the illegality may be used by the state.

Yet another factor that reduces the scope of exclusionary rules is that law enforcement officials can modify their behavior to attempt to reduce the impact of exclusionary rules. [⑥]For example, the police have learned that a rote and mechanized recitation of the *Miranda* rights results in few individuals invoking their right to remain silent or their right to counsel. Counsel has to be provided before a post-indictment lineup occurs, but the police control the time of lineups and can conduct one pre-indictment if they wish. Even if the police may not interrogate someone because he has invoked his *Miranda* rights, the police can still place an informant in the jail cell with the suspect to see if the informant can get the suspect to make incriminating statements. Most importantly of all, all constitutional rights may be waived, and nothing stops law enforcement officials from asking individuals to waive their rights and let the police investigate

⑥ For a discussion, see William J. Stuntz, *The Political Constitution of Criminal Justice*, 119 Harv. L. Rev. 780 (2006).

as they like. For obvious psychological reasons, many people are unable to refuse their consent to what the police want to do, and in this fashion their constitutional rights end up not obstructing investigations.

Ⅴ. Why all the Difficulties?

I have already hinted at the explanation of why "exclusionary rules" are so complicated. It is because "exclusionary rules" are indistinguishable from the structure of trials. They structure and order trials. Trials, in turn, are complicated events in two different ways. First, they involve the ordering of relationships between a large number of participants, including judge, jury (if there is one), lawyers, parties, and witnesses. Interestingly, the trial courts powers are rather limited, even though they are often thought of as powerful figures. The trial judges cannot control the details of the trial process; that has to be done by the parties or their lawyers. The second source of complexity is that trials are educational events. To "regulate" the presentation of evidence in such a context would require the regulation of the inferential process, which isa futile effort at best. The most that judges can do is nudge the parties and the process in what the judges believe to be the correct direction inferentially. The judges can also implement various incentives, and the primary means of doing both is precisely through the admission of relevant evidence and the exclusion of evidence objectionable for whatever reason. There are other tools, of course, such as substantive rulings and contempt of court findings, but the primary tool to ensure the proper presentation of evidence at trial is some version of an exclusionary rule.

There are two other complicating features, and those are that the rules of evidence structure both the relationship between higher and lower courts (appellate v. trial courts) and between the legislature and the judiciary. Rulings on rules of evidence and their exclusionary component are one of the primary means by which higher courts regulate lower courts. Similarly, rules of evidence can provide a means by which legislatures regulate the courts. These variables add administrative and political variables to the already complicated foundation of the legal system, and lead to further complications in evidence rules and their exclusionary features.

Ⅵ. What is the optimal form of regulation: Exclusion or punishment?

This is a very difficult question, and it is hard to say what is optimal. The exclusion of evidence is not the only method available to enforce evidentiary and procedural rules, whether of a constitutional dimension or not. Punishment could be used instead; sanctions could be imposed on the individuals who violate the pertinent substantive standards, whether this is a state official who violates individual rights or a lawyer who does not follow the rules of evidence. Indeed, the myth of the American Exclusionary Rule often has as one of its components that the costs of the exclusionary rule are too high, given its benefits, and that perhaps a better approach would be to employ sanctions. However, the choice between personal sanctions and exclusion is complicated. As two well-known scholars have elaborated, "There are two... administrative or practical advantages of exclusion, or disgorgement, rather than damages: ease of valuation and procedural convenience."⑦ As they go on to point out, actual damages are hard to appraise. How much should the state pay for an unreasonable search and seizure? Equally troubling, damages applied to individuals could very well lead to overdeterrence of the officer. If a state official faces personal damages if he makes a mistake, he will be reluctant to make a mistake; why take a personal risk for no personal gain? This may lead to individual policeman being too cautious and failing to take aggressive enough action to stop criminal acts from occurring or to find and convict those who have violated the law.

Exclusion of evidence has the obverse risk. If a person faces no personal sanction, they may be too much inclined to violate the rights of others, which will lead to underdeterrence. And of course exclusion of evidence at trial only works if a person has the correct motivation. If the police do not care about a conviction, and exclusion of evidence is the only sanction, then the police have literally no incentive to be concerned about a person's rights that they may be violating. They may arrest and search people just to harass them rather than to solve or search for evidence of crime. There is another interesting social dimension to the question of what kind of remedy is optimal: "the curtailment of damages liability for constitutional violations has deep

⑦ Levmore and Stuntz, Remedies and Incentives in Private and Public Law: A Comparative Essay, 1990 Wisc. L. Rev. 483.

structural advantages for American constitutionalism. In essence, the limitation on money damages shifts societal resources away from reparation for past harms and toward investment in future welfare, continually redistributing societal resources from older to younger citizens."[8] What this means is that a damages action looks to the past, whereas an exclusionary sanction looks to affect behavior in the future.

Fashioning the optimal remedial regime is complicated by other factors. The question in essence is empirical, not just analytical, and there is not good data on differing kinds of remedial measures. In part this is because in the real world, as I noted above, people can respond to any new rule, and thus create unintended consequences. Consider in this regard the famous constitutional rulings that I noted at the beginning of this lecture, the *Mapp* and *Miranda* rules. It is not at all clear what effect these rules had, if for no other reason than that there is surplus criminality. This seems like a strange idea, but it is terribly important. There is more crime in any society that officialdom can deal with. As a result, law enforcement officials have enormous discretion as to which cases to investigate and prosecute and which to ignore. One reason to choose is the relative productivity that will result from one choice rather than another. It is better to prosecute and obtain convictions in four cases rather than one. But that means that police and prosecutors will have an incentive to prosecute cases that are easier and less expensive, and one determinate of how expensive a case is will be how good of a defense the person can offer. That, in turn, will be determined in part by whether there are problems in the state's case that may result in the exclusion of evidence and whether the person has the financial means to litigate those issues. If so, the state may chose not to litigate that kind of case, but that choice results in discrimination against the poor whenever the state substitutes away from wealthy defendants who can mount more of a fight. [9]And of course if this occurs, the actual effect on police practices of any exclusionary rule will be blunted because the cases involving abuses will simply never come to light. Thus, the actual effect of the holdings in cases like *Mapp* or *Miranda* may not be to reduce the incidence of abuse but

⑧ Jeffries, *The Right Remedy Gap in Constitutional Law*, 109 Yale L. J. 87.

⑨ Stuntz, *Plea Bargaining and Criminal Law's Disappearing Shadow*, 117 Harv. L. Rev. 2548 (2004).

instead just to cause the state to choose which cases to litigate.

Quite remarkably, there is another way in which exclusionary rules may disadvantage poor people. The existence of exclusionary rules may shift limited defense resources to making legal motions and away from factual investigation. That may mean that exclusionary rules increase the probability of erroneous convictions. [10]

There is one final point worth noting about the complexity of exclusionary rules and the optimal remedial regime that is analogous to the problem of surplus criminality. Legislatures control the parameters of the substantive law, and they can modify the substantive law more or less as they like in my country and yours. That means that, even in the United States, legislatures can essentially make nullities of procedural rulings by rewriting the governing substantive standards. I will give you an example from the United States. The courts interpreted the fourth amendment ban on unreasonable searches and seizures to forbid the police from randomly stopping cars to inspect them. The courts were legitimately concerned that "random" selection might not truly be random and might instead hide discriminatory decision making that would be impossible to regulate. The police by contrast very much want the ability to stop cars whenever they suspect some illegality may be occurring. The legislatures more or less agreed with the police and responded by expanding the coverage of vehicular laws to make it essentially impossible to drive without committing a violation of the law. As a result of the change in the law, if the police want to stop a car, they merely have to follow it long enough until the driver violates one of the many vehicular laws. Once that happens, the police have probable cause to stop the car.

This example can be generalized, and every legislature that I am aware of has engaged in similar tactics. Immediately following 9. 11, the legislatures across the world expanded the definition of numerous crimes, which facilitated the investigation of allegedly terrorist activities. If legislatures are concerned

[10] Stuntz, *The Virtues and Vices of the Exclusionary Rule*, 20 Harv J. L. & Pub. Pol. 443. Also see Stuntz, *The Uneasy Relationship Between Criminal Procedure and Criminal Justice*, 107 Yale L. J. 1 (1997).

about corruption in a particular industry, an often employed tactic is to require that the industry in question keep detailed records and make them available to the government for inspection. This, I should point out, is yet another example of one of my major themes tonight, which is the organic nature of society. It grows and evolves and is not static. It responds to changes in unpredictable ways.

Ⅶ. Conclusion

I have tried to explain a number of things tonight. First, I have tried to give you a more accurate understanding of the reality of the trial process in the United States as it bears on the question of exclusionary rules. In particular, I have tried to explain how the conventional understanding in other countries of the American exclusionary rules is quite inaccurate. More importantly, however, I have tried to show how exclusionary rules, not just American exclusionary rules, are integral to virtually all conceptions of trials. And last I introduced the topic, which is deserving of a complete lecture in its own right, that the choice of differing remedial regimes is a complicated and uncertain one. These lessons apply just as much to China as they do to the United States, of course.

Thank you for your patience, and I look forward to your questions.

专家证言的概念性挑战*

汪诸豪　译

每次回到中国与学生们相聚，看到他们所取得成绩，我都会倍感欣慰。正如我今天所要谈的，学习证据法和诉讼法的你们对于中国的持续发展而言至关重要。本文的主题是关于专家证言的概念性挑战。这个议题本身非常重要，因为如果不能理解专家证言所引发的问题，你们就无法很好地运用这项规则。但同时这也意味着你们必须要深入地思考法律制度的本质，以及专家证言会如何推进或者挑战法律制度的理想状态。我将尝试对所有这些问题以某种系统的方式进行讨论。

各国法律中关乎于法律争议解决的信息都有着相对复杂的分类法。举例来说，美国证据法涉及科学、技术及其他专业知识。①《联邦证据规则》进一步增加了这个问题的复杂性，明确规定了专家资格的各种要求，其中包括通过任何方式所获得的“知识、技能、经验、训练或教育有助于案件事实认定者理解证据或决定某项事实争点”②。如果上述条件中有一或多项得以满足，在依据相关行业标准行事的前提下，专家便可在法庭上就案件中争点发表自己的意见或评论。

相较于《联邦证据规则》在认识论上的复杂性（因为不胜枚举的知识类型或关乎争议的解决），实际操作中的复杂性有过之而无不及。巨大的资源耗费在分析和评断一份显然无法穷尽的专业知识类型清单上，用于判断专家证言的可采性，并确保专家的确会基于某种知识作证。如果满足了条件，专家便可出庭作证，但事实上却不被要求要以其专业知识作证。比如说，专家亦可基于有关案件关键主张上的知识来提供意见。③ 然而，对方的专家证人也可以这么做——并且在一般情况下，如果没有反方专家证人，也就没有了诉讼的争点。

* 本文系艾伦教授 2014 年 1 月在中国政法大学所做的演讲。感谢美国西北大学法学院学生蒋雨佳对我研究的帮助。本译文原载于《证据科学》，第 22 卷，2014 年第 1 期。本译文系国家“2011 计划”司法文明协同创新中心研究成果。

① 美国《联邦证据规则》规则 702。

② 美国《联邦证据规则》规则 702。

③ 美国《联邦证据规则》规则 702、703。

因此，在将巨大的精力耗费在规制诉讼中的专家证言后，事实裁判者也许会发现自己所面对的是两种截然相反的专家意见，且其关乎于超出一般事实认定者认知范畴的问题。

刚才的描述有许多非常规之处，揭示了不同类型的知识之间存在着显著的差异，而一旦其被认定符合了专家证人可对所擅长专业领域与案件争点间联系发表看法之标准后，这些差异是可以为了诉讼目的通过对证据的内在分析而予以调和的。我认为，这种描述是怪异的，因为上述每一个命题都有问题，且总体来看，尽管其合乎传统，却与诉讼的核心目标背道而驰。为了证实我的观点，我将首先对诉讼的核心目标进行界定，然后会分析规制专家证人的传统方法会给此诉讼目标造成的遗憾影响，最后会提出一个替代性解决方案。我将在下文中对此三点依次进行讨论。

自由法律制度的理想状态

关于诉讼的目的尚存争议，尤其是在那些拥有陪审团制度的司法体系中（陪审团制度或造成了违法事实裁决可能性的上升）。④ 但可以肯定的是，缺少了合理准确的事实认定，诉讼便毫无意义。岂止是毫无意义；其是对自由社会基石的践踏。为那些忽视准确事实认定重要性的诉讼所进行的辩解都受一种错误认知的影响。这种错误的认知认为启蒙运动中的根本政治观点，以及西方政府所赖以存在的根本要件，都与权利和义务有着某种重要联系。从孟德斯鸠到卢梭，法学界盛行着对政治哲学家的讨论。诉讼确实与此有关，其是众多权利——譬如辩解、对质以及反对的权利——得以行使的工具。在拥有陪审团的国家，个人可以通过诉诸陪审团的良知和人道主义精神来直接对抗政府。

显然，权利和义务至关重要且必不可少，但仅仅停留在权利义务上是不够的。启蒙运动对法律制度更为基本的贡献在于认识论上的革新，以经验性知识取代了教条性知识。其改变了人们对知识的认识。在过去，知识被认为是关于宗教和政治权威的学说，而启蒙运动让人们逐渐接受了内心之外的世界可以通过证据来客观认识。⑤ 毫不夸张地说，若没有准确的事实认定，权利和义务便失去了意义；因此，可以说现代西方文明最为重要的组成部分即是准确的事实认定。请注意我这里所说的是“现代西方文明”。关于中国的经验我会在下文中进行讨论。

④ 参见罗伯特·伯恩斯：《审判的理论》（1999 年）。

⑤ 关于对启蒙运动的介绍，请见《斯坦福哲学百科》，详见 http：//plato. stanford. edu/entries/enlightenment。

事实上，即便是“陪审团否弃权”概念在脱离了准确事实认定的情形下也会变得毫无意义；否弃权是准确事实裁决规则的一种例外情况。[⑥] 更深层次而言，无论考察哪一种权利，人们都会很容易地发现权利是附生在其认识论基础上的。请考虑一项在西方曾经并且仍然是最为根本的权利——财产权。为了让讨论更加生动，就以你手中的手机为例。你对手机的所有权赋予你“权利”去拥有、使用，并处置该财产。但现在假设我走向你，夺走了你所谓属于你的手机并拒绝归还，并声称该手机为我所有。你会怎么做？你会去找那些拥有裁决权的人，譬如法官或者陪审团，然后你会怎么做？要求归还你的手机？那样行不通，因为我自然也会声称该手机属于我。你会出示有关你是如何得到这部手机的证据，提供来自于手机公司的发票或者账单，以证明这部手机与你（而非我）相关。然后你也许会开机演示手机中各种内容，譬如手机中保存着的那些发送给你而非我的短信或邮件，以便说服理性人这部手机的确属于你而非我。

若能成功证明这些事实，裁决者将会切实赋予你拥有、使用和处置该部手机的权利——将其归还至你手中，同时施加于我相应的义务。但此处的关键在于：财产权完全依附于认定了什么样的事实，并且是事实认定的连锁反应。这一点的重要性毋庸置疑，并且颠覆了传统概念上事实与权利二者的关系。事实决定权利和义务。决断事实的人决定着权利的内涵与外延，无论是财产权还是生命权。

一种潜在的怀疑观点认为——即使事实认定确如我所讨论的那般重要，将其称之为现代自由民主之基石是不是有些夸大其词了？我想说这非但毫不夸张，而且西方民主的成功正是与这样的司法安排有着紧密关联。将法律与真实的世界紧密联系在一起会将权利和义务锚定于可知事物之上，并且摆脱了冲动和反复无常。享用财产的权利并不取决于易犯错误的人类所拥有的慈悲、情绪或偏见。你无须受到他人的特殊照顾以便以你认为最好的方式去拥有房子、享受假期或培养孩子。这些权利植根于任何人内心世界之外的客观存在，并且正如伟大的启蒙运动认识论所预言的那样[⑦]，这一点可以通过不依赖于任何个人思想而存在的证据予以高度规律性的证明。

除了确定权利所有者，将权利系于事实之上也使得人们能够围绕着权利在许多不同且重要的方面进行谈判。植根于事实中的权利为所有者与其他人提供

⑥ 应注意陪审团虽然可以拒绝使用法律而赦免被告人，但同样也可以拒绝使用法律而认为被告人有罪。参见托马斯·安德鲁·格林：《根据良心来断案：英国刑事审判陪审团角度》，1988 年，第1200～1800 页。

⑦ 参见脚注④。

了清晰的界定，将权利在法律上的潜力与限制告知于每个人。基于这种认识，人们可以作出选择并将更有保障地来安排生活。同等重要的是，权利的事实基础保障使得其下市场的出现成为可能——权利可以通过市场经济所认可的各种方式转让出去——这让世界上那些恪守该原则的国家在财富上取得了惊人的增长。

当然，有时候证据会缺失，有时候错误难以避免，但在通常情况下，世界在向前发展的过程中总能留下一些蛛丝马迹，可以用来重建过去——足以用于当前案件审理中的过去构建。这就是为什么尽管诉讼的数量越来越多，现代社会却仍运转得很好。这就是为什么你可以购买并预期享用商品，比如手机或者房子。这就是为什么在任何尊重我所谈上述基本概念的国家，你可以合理地预期不会受到来自政府的干涉。这就是为什么绝大多数时候生活是有章可循的而不是随机的。这也就是为什么相关性和实质性的概念对于一个自由法律系统的构建而言具有根本性的重要意义。[⑧] 这二者将法律系统附着于事实准确性的基石上，并随之生成如上所述的连锁反应。

基于我刚才所谈思路，请回顾中国过去发生的一段历史。西方观察家们从中国“文化大革命”中得出的最直观推论是：当法律制度遭到破坏时，经济也会随之遭受毁灭性打击，而这正是当时真真切切发生的情况。随着 20 世纪 70 年代末和 80 年代初开始的经济改革，中国进入了一场天然的试验，事关强劲的经济发展在缺少有效法律体系保驾护航的情况下能否予以维持，结果显然是否定的。这也就是为什么今天的中国政府如此专注于建立诸如西方法治理念的原因。但是建立法治的前提是要认识到准确事实认定在司法裁判中的重要性。这也就是为什么我说正在对中国证据法快速发展作出贡献的你们正是中国持续发展的关键组成部分。若没有你们正在开展的工作，中国的法律制度改革就会失去意义，并将无疾而终。因为，没有准确的事实认定就没有权利可言。[⑨]

总而言之，权利和义务取决于事实，并且只有在对实际、相关的事实情况了解的前提下，权利和义务才能系统地落实——这个结论无论在美国或中国都适用。至于法律系统如何规定事实认定，何种方法最为准确且/或有效，哪些政策考虑可以削减事实认定准确的重要性，那都是可以存在合理分歧的领域。因此，在任何法律传统下要理解专家证据所带来的问题，就必须要先考量审判的基本概念以及其下知识构建的途径。接下来，我将描述我所最熟知的审判体

⑧ 例如，参见《联邦证据规则》规则 401、402、403。

⑨ 参见罗纳德·J·艾伦：《证据法的理论基础和意义》，张保生、张月波译，载《证据科学》，2010 年第 4 期。

系——英美模式。请允许我再快速重申一遍，尽管英美模式在一些方面有其独特性，而知识对于权利的重要性则是普适的。我将在英美法传统的框架下详细地探讨该问题，但是正如我将在本文末尾中提及的——这个探究过程中所收获的经验教训具有普遍的意义。

从最直观的方面说，审判在英美传统中所解决的是社会争议。这些争议多为常规性的，而非高度复杂，因为社会本身便是如此。实际上，作为陪审团制度的发端，原始模式的审理是将那些通晓本地事物的人聚集在一起，请他们根据已有的知识和经验来对争议进行决断——而与传统相悖的观点却错误地认为现代陪审团事先必须要对诉讼相关的情况完全不知情。悬而未决的争议本身就是社区情况的一部分。更为重要的是，同样，为解决这些争议所必备的知识也是其中一部分。举例来说，许多争议涉及譬如道路权、地役权等当地惯例，意味着这些争议很有可能就是相关社区中人们茶余饭后的谈资。类似的，关于社区中某人对他人做了什么之类的情况也会在小范围内广为人知，加上对当地习俗的了解，共同构成了解决争端的基础。

然而，即便是在相对早期的发展阶段，偶尔也会有不涉及公众常识的案件，其中证人开始被传唤，但这更像是例外情况而非主流规则。随着社会的进化，尤其是经济的发展，问题变得越来越复杂，认知也开始被区分出更多层次。随着商业的发展，案件的审理开始走向专业化和规范化，比如说，需要提供关于当地习俗的证据。外语可能需要翻译，或者案件可能会涉及某些近似于外语的技术性词汇，必须要让那些没有相关专业知识的案件审理人设法理解。有趣的是，在陪审团日益剧增的政治影响力下，尽管这些复杂案件越来越普遍，英美法系统仍然遵循着传统意义上的事实认定模式。案件双方需要做的仅仅是稍加解释，以便事实认定者可以理解证人陈述，明智地裁决案件，但是说到底，案件事实仍然是需要本地人士不偏私地以常识来进行认定。

随着审判中开始引入证人制度，理想状态是事实认定者可以接触到每位证人的背景和经验，以便事实认定者清晰地理解证人证言。在对案件事实作出了最接近于真实发生的认定后[10]，责任义务便可以依法进行判定。因为天衣无缝地将证人与事实认定者的思想合二为一是不可能完成的任务，普通法系设计了一套方法来缩小这二者在思想上的差异，以便接近于达到合二为一的最佳状态。这正是证人意见规则的来源，即要求证人只对自己的观察进行作证，而不

⑩ 参见罗纳德·J·艾伦：《司法证明的本质》，载《卡多佐法律评论》，第13期，1991年，第373页。

能给出其推论（意见）。“事实”与“意见”的区别在理论上非常难界定[11]，但作为一项准则其给证人施加了压力，迫使证人尽可能地就自身感知作证，以便事实认定者能够身临其境般地去决断案件事实。同样，这也解释了为何交叉盘问规则会允许对证人证言形成的基础进行探究。

在诸多方面，这套规则实现了设计初衷，尽管也付出了一定的代价。通常而言，审判中各方（法官、陪审员、证人）会共享充分的背景信息，使得有效的交流和理解成为可能。交流与理解的可行性会随着案件审判成员规模的扩大而增长，因为每一个新增成员都会给审理团队评判证据带来自己的经验和知识。而另一方面，小规模的人员组成则具有更为精确的信息处理能力。总之，任何决策组织形式都伴随有相应的成本代价。

最终，证人与陪审员（证人与法官）被鲜明地进行了区分，而这在普通法审判发端之际并不存在。陪审员仅可根据审判中所呈现的证据（而非其个人知识）作出裁定。有人也许会质疑这样的描述在今天是否仍然准确，尤其是在美国这样充分运用陪审员审判的国家（传统媒体常常报道在一些案件中，尤其是那些臭名昭著的丑闻案件中，要找到预先不知情的陪审员是多么困难）。对于这种质疑，简短的回答是：传统上认为潜在陪审员必须要对案件（预先）不知情的观点是错误的。而这种传统观点之所以错误的原因对于理解专家证言的概念性挑战至关重要。

从技术层面而言，传统观念的错误在于，对诉讼事件拥有知识并不意味着就失去了担任陪审员的资格；只有当这些知识会使得陪审员满足了作为证人的条件后其才会失去陪审员资格。[12] 在更深层次且更为重要的意义上，传统观念认为陪审员必须要对案情不知情的观点也是错误的。正如我上文中提及的，认识到此错误对于理解专家证言的真正概念性挑战极为重要。一个必要的预备性概念要点是：事实认定者都是带着已有的知识体系、信念以及推理方式进入审判程序，而这恰恰是快捷、高效交流的前提。（在美国）只要每个人的英语都合格，除了例外情况，用词不需要进行定义。全体审判参与者都被假定已经悉知了关于现实本质与因果关系存在的传统信念，几乎从来不会是证据所证明的对象。每个人都被假定在进行有序推理，使用各种必要或合适的推理形式——演绎推理、归纳推理、回溯推理以及统计推理。通过某种共通的语言，或者必

[11] 参见罗纳德·J·艾伦、理查德·B·库恩斯、伊琳诺·斯威夫特、大卫·S·施瓦茨：《证据：文本、问题与案例》，4版，2006年，第609～620页。

[12] 这是由《联邦证据规则》规则606禁止陪审员作为证人所解释。

要的翻译，对证人的理解也被假定，同样被假定的还有对证据与审判之间联系的感知能力。每个人都被假定了解人证的弱点与潜在偏见的负面影响，并能够判断证言的可信性。相对而言，不那么广为人知的是，每个人都被期望能够通过自身知识推论来填补审判中的证据性空白（这些证据性空白源自于诸多因素，包括个体证人所知道的事情却不一定能够完整表达出来）。

事实上，“证据”的准确概念不能简单地理解为就是审判中呈现的证人证言和展示件，而是还应当包括人与其所观察到情况之间的互动，此种互动将审判的“自我知会”本质推进到了更深的层次。我曾经对此做过如下总结：

> 假设某个证人开始作证，事实认定者必须要判断能从该证言中得出什么结论。相关的变量都有哪些呢？首先，有各种常规的可信性问题，但是要到考虑这些问题的复杂性。言谈举止不仅仅是表面化的举止行为，其背后是复杂的变量集合。证人在作证时是否有流汗或颤抖的状况？如果有的话，这是由于无辜的紧张，还是出于搪塞的压力？是药物作用，还是仅仅是在不幸的童年所养成的不良习惯？肢体语言是表明了真实情况，还是一种逃避？无精打采是说谎的证据，还是说出真实情况的坦然表现？证人是否在直视检察官的眼睛？如果是的话，此种证据所表达的是值得称道的品格还是油腔滑调的自信呢？语调的起伏体现了正直的品格还是牵强附会的态度？牵强附会的声音所表明的是证人在捏造证言，还是一种对案件结果的顾虑呢？诸如此类。
>
> 相关变量的清单远超出了可信性的范畴，言谈举止仅是其中一项而已。当证人提出某种主张，事实认定者要判断该主张所要表达的是什么，以及事实认定者从中所得出的又是什么。这项任务也同样包含了大量的变量。此外，事实认定者基于自身观察会产生一些特定知识，先于证人所作陈述，例如从律师那里获取的知识。还有许多类似的例子。为了法律（以规则为基础方式）的执行，许多这些变量需要在演绎推理结构中以必要且充分的条件予以说明。然而我们不可能创造出这样的结构，因为其过于复杂了。[13]

事实认定者的重要属性并非是预先要对案件不知情，正如我们所见，那是

⑬ 罗纳德·J·艾伦，《事实的模糊性与证据理论》，载《西北大学法律评论》，第88期，1994年，第604、625～626页。道格拉斯·沃顿：《法律论证与证据》，2002年，第200页，此书论述了相似的法律证据分析。真实生活的复杂性是人工智能与法研究者所面临的中心问题，参见罗纳德·J·艾伦：《人工智能与证据过程：形式主义与计算的挑战》，载《人工智能与法》，第9期，2001年，第99页。早期关于人们可能对于证据所推导出事实持不同意见的哲学讨论，参见G. 波利亚：《数学与似真推理：似真推论的型式》，2版，1954年。

不可能的。真正重要的是事实认定者无私、公正的心态，能够以开放的心态全盘考虑证据。我所描述的这两方面可以合并为一个融贯的标准，其描绘了任何自由法律系统中最为深刻的愿景，即：将裁决权交给有能力、无偏私的事实认定者，由其对证据进行处理和审议以便对案件事实作出理性的判断，进而对当事人各方的权利和义务作出准确的判决。

专家证言相悖于审判的理想状态

当对证言的理解需要运用到事实认定者们所不具备的知识或技能时，事实认定者对于这种证人证言所欲表达之意的理解力就几乎为零，或至少无法有效地评估其所述内容之真伪性。我们现在接触到了专家证言所带来的核心概念性困境，而且对此只有两种可能的解决途径——要么必须以某种方式提供出必要的背景信息，要么事实认定者必须要遵从于他人的判断。此处“遵从”是指采纳他人的意见作为正确的意见，并非因为你对该意见表示理解或赞同，而仅仅是由于你将事实认定的决定权移交给了他人。通常，英美法系会选择要求以可理解的方式向事实认定者提供信息。如果证人说的是外语，那么将提供翻译。如涉及常规性商业操作或惯例，那么需要提供与该主题相关的证据以便事实认定者能够自行判断该常规操作或惯例的实际情况。要求证据与社区中一般成员的背景和经验相对接是一种近似于理想的审判模式。

专家证言的核心概念性问题在于其在审判中的应用常常有悖于审判的一般概念。专家们往往接受过多年的专业化训练，而这种经历反而可能会使其很难就审判中的相关争议对事实认定者进行教育。尽管有关专家证言的争议常见于可靠性方面的顾虑，但实际上的争议在于当证人以专家的身份作证时，事实认定者是否应直接遵从其意见而非采用传统性的教育模式。下文中将着重探讨解决这个问题。⑭

显然，首先要提出的问题是这种对专家证人的“遵从”是否为绝对必要？是否存在任何传统模型（教育模式）所不能兼容的情况？某些案件中所呈现的争议是否为事实认定者认知能力所不能企及的？应该来说，对于这些问题的回答都是否定的。事实认定者的缺陷并非源自其认知能力上的不足而是信息量的不足所致。法官和陪审员对许多事物都缺乏相关的知识，比如科学和技术领域，但是没有理由认为他们就不能充分掌握这些相关领域。这并不意味着事实

⑭ “教育—服从”模式的区别由罗纳德·J·艾伦和约瑟夫·S·米勒首先提出于《专家的普通法理论：服从还是教育》，载《西北大学法律评论》，第87期，1993年，第1131页，以及罗纳德·J·艾伦：《专门知识与道伯特决策》，载《刑法与犯罪学杂志》，第84期，1994年，第1157页。本文是这些论文的进一步补充。

认定者非要成为诸如肿瘤学家、放射学家之类的专家。事实认定者无须全盘通晓特定专业领域的知识，反之，其目标在于掌握足够多的知识，从而能够理性地对当前案件进行审议。从这个角度来说，多人组成的决策团队（陪审团或者由法官组成的合议庭）实际上优于个体的决策者。决策团队中无须每一个成员都能深入地理解案件中的每一个争议。真正需要关心的问题在于决策团队作为一个整体是否充分理解了争议。如果一个案件的事实部分超出了从社会大众中即兴挑选出的决策团队认知能力，那将是令人震惊的，更何况法官和陪审团成员都是经过严格甄选的。

超出当前普通理解力的观念或领域的确是真实存在的。物理学中的许多概念在社会大众中的普及速度十分缓慢，甚至在科学家群体中也是如此。或许对于事实认定者而言，要求其学习狭义相对论或者量子理论实属过分，然而据我所知，这些理论都未曾切中过任何过往的诉讼。无可否认，物理学并非是唯一难以掌握的学科。很多人认为高等数学也难以掌握（或许这就是为何他们认为物理学很难）。微积分和概率论是高等数学领域中与现代审判有关的两个例子。尽管有人认为其很抽象，但其他人并不这么认为——更为重要的是，有些人不认为其抽象到了无法学习以便作出理智决策的程度。这恰恰又是多人决策团队的价值。正如我上文中所述，真正重要的不在于每个决策者是否都能理解，而是在于作为一个整体，决策团队是否拥有或者能够学习掌握作出理智决策所需要的知识。

对事实认定者进行教育的真实障碍并非在于其无法实现，而是这样做的代价过于昂贵。如果审判中涉及统计学，那么就不得不对其进行解释以便事实认定者能够理解，在某些案件中甚至需要耗费可观的资源。在医学等其他众多领域中同样也是如此。在某些案件中，这样的教育过程并非难以承受，但在另一些案件中，这种教育过程则异常困难并且需要大量指导。所以，综上所述，该教育过程十分昂贵，但在实际操作中我本人并没有遇到过无法（对事实认定者）进行教育的案件。

一个待思考的重要问题是，对事实认定者就“专家”证言基础进行教育的额外成本是否足以构成了我们放弃理想审判模式而以遵从模式取而代之的理由？这个问题反映出了关于专家证人证言之传统论述的不合理之处。在大量并不涉及科学或者技术问题的案件中，证人证言的提取亦需数月的时间。在我所熟知的西方法律系统中，此类案件审理中对证人并没有采用遵从模式；当事人双方都被要求以事实认定者可以理解的证据去证明案件事实。仅仅因为当事人一方所供证据被标榜为“专家证言”便要采用遵从模式诉讼程序，这是令人费解的。两类案件中的认知性问题在本质上是相同的，经济上的考量也是相同的。在所有案件中之于所有证人，提出主张的当事人一方应负责承担证人出庭作证及回应对方当事人提问的成本。就这一点而言，专家证人不存在特殊性。耗费在长年累月涉及放射学之审判中的公共补贴与耗费在长年累月证券诉讼中的公共补贴并没有实质区别。事实上，如果的确存在差异的话，这种差异反而有利于放射学公共补贴，因为与那些全然无用的证据相比，学习放射学还可能给事实认定者带来实实在在的收获。因此，反对教育事实认定者的“成本说”存在着自相矛盾之处。

解决方案

若要实现审判的理想状态，当事人就必须要在所有情形下对事实认定者进行教育。这样一来可以消除有关“专家”证言的法律问题，因为此分类将不复存在。这看起来像是在定义上做手脚来解决问题，其实不然；其所触及的要深刻得多。伴随“遵从”模式审判的一个可悲结果就是：如果事实认定者选择遵从于所谓的专家，而该专家事实上并未基于专业知识作证而是在法庭上提供了在美国被称作是“垃圾科学”的信息，那么错误就会发生。当事实认定者不理解专家的证言基础时，垃圾科学和不可靠的专家就会引爆法律的信息性弱点。让所有的证人（包括所谓的专家证人）对其证言进行解释，将会在很大程度上消除这个问题，因为要对虚假主张进行清晰的解释是件极其困难的事情。我不是说弄虚作假没有了可能，而是这样一来呈现不可靠证据将会变得困难得多。

然而，这枚认识论的硬币还有其另一面。我所主张的事实认定者之主要限制来自于信息而非认知的观点也许存在缺陷；或许有一些案子中涉及法官和陪审团确实无法理解的严格意义上“知识”（真实合理的信念）。显然，现实中的确有一些与法律争议相关的，涉及诸多领域（如数学和医学）的专门性非常规知识。一旦存在这样的知识但在审判中却无法被传递理解，那么在任何一种强调由利益无涉个人来理性地处置分析证据之法律传统中，开展涉及这些知识的审判便会失去意义；这种理想的审理状态不可能发生在遵从专家证言的模式中。相反的做法是，如果审判涉及专业的知识形式但却无法在审理中予以表述的话，解决的办法就是不要去审这些案子。如果专业知识存在，并且能够以确定的方式进行表述（比如我们确定知道自己现在在中国），这种教育就值得在法庭上进行并作为定案的依据。然而，如何操作却是另一个问题，通常会是通过制定法律或规则来完成。

相比之下，毫不夸张地说，维持现在这种涉及事实认定者无法理解之专门知识的审判模式没有意义。在案件审理中，双方当事人都会提供事实认定者可遵从的专家意见；而这些专家意见几乎总是截然相反的，倾向于各自的当事人方。如果不存在相反的意见，那就不会有可裁判的争议，拥有无懈可击（或是最少受到攻击的）专家的一方将会赢得审判。当专家们的意见不一致时，“遵从”模式中的事实认定者们不会将注意力集中在事实上，而仅仅会去决定该采纳哪一方专家的意见。现在，关键的问题是：在对相关领域缺乏了解的情况下，事实认定者又如何能明智地决定该遵从哪一方专家的意见呢？本质上来说，得以确认该相信哪一方专家的唯一途径就是：先充分地了解该领域，再结合案件中的具体情况来评价专家意见。在对相关领域知识缺乏探究的情况下，事实认定者对于选择该遵从哪一方专家的判断就缺少了理性的基础。这一点贯穿于审判中对专业知识的使用，并强调了当前的专家证言形式是对英美法制度之最深层次愿景的背离。重申一下这种显然性：缺乏足够背景知识来通过证据得出正确推理的事实认定者（或其他任何人），无法就该选择遵从哪一方专家意见进行理智的判断。反之，如果事实认定者能够理智地判断该相信哪一方专家证人，那么对于专家意见的遵从也就没有必要性了。在该种情况下，事实认定者能够自己理解专家的思路，即通过案件中所提供的证据，基于专门知识来得出最后的结论。

理性决策可能性的降低违背了审判的深层次愿景（即通过理性的思考以追求事实认定的准确性）。当然，这里面有着很重的讽刺意味。审判法官在不要求专家对观点进行解释的情况下就采纳不一致或相互矛盾的各种专家意见，其做法是不理性的。只有当事实认定者能够清楚地认识到一方专家意见为正确而另一方为错误时，其才能作出理性的决定。但如此一来，法官就会仅采纳一方专家的意见，同时排除另一方专家意见。如果理性人在究竟哪方专家是正确的问题上存有合理分歧，那么就说明他们能够理解其背后的争议，这样一来，遵从模式也就没必要了。另需注意的是，证据相关性原则的条件限制在遵从模式下也会大打折扣。通常来说，在当事人一方解释证据相关性的过程中需要将证据与事实认定者的理解进行充分对接。但是，在对证言基础缺乏理解的情况下这是不可能做到的。

还有一种说法称：从分析的角度来说，遵从和教育并没有区别，而只是同一个范畴的两极；原始数据几乎从来不会在庭审中出现（偶尔会在法庭上进行演示，但是这种情况极其罕见）；在决定一位证人是否真实作证时，都需要一定意义上的“遵从”。但在我看来，即便遵从和教育都是普遍存在的变量，其是能够以不同程度进行呈现的。请比较听闻感官经历证据（“被告打了原告”）和作出推理（“根据这些研究，我认为吸烟会导致癌症”）。关键的变量在于事实认定者是否能够理解证人从观察到得出结论之间的推理过程。如果没有此等理解，那么就不可能理性地评价证据。在有专家证人出席的场合，人们往往不会期待其推理过程能够被普通人所理解。因此，人们往往无法通过行使自身判断力来决定接受或排除一项专家意见，在这一点上，可以说，对专家证人的遵从有别于决定是否要相信外行证人的遵从。

总而言之，处理专家证据的方法仅有两种，再退一步说，处理证据的方法只有两种。第一种就是把专家证言作为一般证言对待，即采纳专家证言的前提须为事实认定者能够对其理解。要理解专家证言，则需要对事实认定者就相关事项进行教育。困难之处在于成本，尤其是，高昂的成本可能会使得判决的结果倾向于拥有更多资源的一方当事人。因为一方当事人越是贫穷，则越没有能力向事实认定者提供必要的教育，或回应对方当事人的主张。该问题也反映出了美国法律体系的一个缺陷，即未能实现当事人真正承担本方在案件中的成本费用，尤其是对方就本方主张进行回应的费用。若不能转嫁成本，则更富有的当事人一方可将诉讼的成本费用故意推高，致使对方当事人无法承受。采用常规方法来对待专家证言，会因涉及专业知识而致使案件审理被拖延，进而加剧上述问题。⑮ 然而，该种方法保持了由利益无涉的个人来处理和考量证据，并以此作出决定。

另一种替代方法就是遵从模式：事实认定者可以被要求选定信任一位专家，即便其并没有能力理性地作出这样的选择；或者，政府可以明确决定一个结果。审判中采用遵从模式的唯一可能优点在于费用开支的降低，但是随之而来的是非理性决策几率的上升。

通过制定法律或规则等确定性政府方案，处置专家证言的决定权与事实认定者相脱离，转而有希望交给那些真正有能力理性决策的人，并可提高决策的一致性。如果对于专业知识的判断是正确的，那么最终判决的准确率也能够相应提高。但此种模式有两处缺陷：第一，该模式视官方的说法为真理，但什么能够保证官方的答案就一定是正确的呢？诉讼的优点之一就在于其允许人们在某一时刻对各种信念的真实性进行反复的考量。如果存在官方的结论且该结论是错误的话，决策的结果仍然会具有一致性，但却会一直错下去。当然，诉讼的这种优点只有在教育模式而非遵从模式中才能得以体现。

⑮ 尽管这一问题太复杂，现在难以深究，为了部分抵消这方面的因素，提高诉讼费用是一个值得赞赏的做法，或者采取同样值得赞赏但更为经济一些的讨论会方式。如何在这些问题中寻求平衡是现代法律制度的最大挑战之一。

也许有人会认为我所叙述的并非是一个真正的问题。在美国，关于对抗制和社会争议私了化的强调使得当事人可以自主选择是否要教育事实认定者或是转而说服他们去遵从专家的意见。（这个问题由当事人双方自行决定，而仅将证据可采性的决定权留给法官。）当事人双方比其他任何人都更清楚他们自己的争议及所掌握的资源，并且处于作出优化其自身利益选择的最佳位置。然而，需要指出的是，遵从模式通过引入功能性成本转嫁，加剧了成本费用问题。如果审判法官采纳了一方当事人的专家证言并且该方当事人仅展示了专家的结论或者意见，那么事实上对这些专家结论或意见进行解释的成本费用将会转嫁给另一方当事人。这会增加对方的交易成本，并加剧（诉讼中的）策略性博弈，破坏当事人承担自身费用这一诉讼基本原则。

以上我在试图说明，专家证言的使用对于任何司法审判体系来说都是根本性的挑战。这也在一定程度上解释了为什么当专家证言在审判中的应用更为普遍时，相关争议也日益增多。潜藏其中的是当前涉及专家之诸多操作中所遭遇尴尬的问题：理性的思考在审判中究竟有多重要？在何种程度上人们可以期待事实认定者会倾听、处理、仔细思量证据，并依据对事实的真实认定来裁定合法权利和义务？任何专注于权利和义务的体制均暗示或明示地采用了这种司法模式。事实上，这也正是本文开头所述，强调事实认定的准确性对于所有专注于法治的体系都具有根本重要性。在某种程度上，无法应对所有困难的深层次原因（即对专家证言所采取的遵从模式与审判的理想状态之间不兼容）加剧了有关专家证言的争议。接下来我将会就这一点展开讨论，但在此之前还是要先带大家来感受一下过度依赖教条式的知识论断是个多么严重的问题。请考虑下列美国案件审理中曾被惯常性采纳的证据，其后都被陆续证实要么存在问题、要么高度不可信：

- 摇晃婴儿综合征——是否存在有效的标记可以将无辜的婴儿猝死症和虐待行为区分开来？
- 笔迹分析——这个领域存在真正的专家吗？专家们自己对笔迹的判断均可保持一致吗？
- 指纹分析——其独特性从未经受过实践的检验，专家的准确性也从来没有被认证过
- 危险预测——不可靠、未经证实的有关精神病的证言把人送入监狱遭受长期监禁
- 被压抑的记忆——同样，不可靠、未经证实的有关精神病的证言把

人送入监狱遭受长期监禁

- 毛发和纤维分析已被证明是不可靠的
- 对疾病起因的鉴定——往往是不可靠的
- 硅对自体免疫系统的有害影响——完全错误
- 纵火调查使用了完全不可信的方法论
- 数十年来，显示吸烟会引发癌症的科学证据已被禁止使用

美国的经验表明，在对待专家证言的问题上出现了严重的谬误。[16] 我认为其主要问题在于：美国法律忽视了专家证言中的核心概念性问题。美国法律一直在尝试对专家证言的遵从模式进行修补以求对其完善，而没有直接正面地去处理问题。修修补补的动力是可以理解的。许多专门性知识在解决争议时非常有用。但是，即便其并非无法被事实认定者所理解，也常常会带来认识上的挑战和困难。如果能够正确处理好遵从模式的问题，我们就可以低成本且高效地将专家知识引入审判，从而提高裁决的准确性。

然而，正如上文所举例子表明的，对于遵从模式的修补并没有很成功。也许有人会认为这是由于“科学性”知识与普通外行人知识之间的不兼容性，但这并非是造成困难的真正原因。不同形式的知识之间并不存在所谓的不兼容性，仅存在是或者不是知识的界分。诚然，在很多已知领域内对知识的探究只是概然性的，但确实会以普通和专业的形式出现。许多“科学性”知识是高度复杂的，然而，日常生活也是如此——事实上，常规的生活比任何专业知识体系都要复杂。科学的进步就在于对可以研究的事物进行简化和学习。[17] 科学探究与诉讼最大的区别就在于法律体系无法为了等待知识的精进而延迟作出判决——总是在作出偏向于某一方当事人利益的判决——但是这一点对于在审判中应用专家证据而言不存在程序性的影响。

在我看来，美国法律体系在引入专家证言问题上的挣扎，很大程度上是由于忽视了审判中遵从和教育模式之间的不兼容性，而非科学性知识与其他形式知识之间的不兼容性。这一点对世界上许多其他法律系统也有教育意义，尤其是对中国而言。美国专家证言采纳的一系列测试标准在中国也受到了广泛的探讨，如弗莱伊案和多伯特案测试标准。然而，在审判中使用专家证据所带来的

⑯ 为了系统地讨论有关科学证据和法律的问题，参见美国国家科学院、国家研究委员会：《加强美国法庭科学之路》（2009 年）。

⑰ 罗纳德·J·艾伦：《事实的模糊以及一项证据理论》，载《西北大学法学评论》，第 88 期，1994 年，第 604、616～630 页。

概念性挑战方面，我还没有在中国见到任何相关的讨论，目前对其重要性的理解也还不够。[18] 中国的法院和法学家有待于去探究专家证言的概念性基础及其困境。如果不这么做，你们便无法明智地决定该如何最优化专家证据的使用，也无法去评价作为解决方案的弗莱伊案或者多伯特案之优劣。事实上，正如我接下来要展示的，这两个案件判决都不能算是好的解决办法。相较于弗莱伊案标准而言，多伯特案标准稍好一些，但也是在回避而非解决了最核心的问题。在中国，你们不应仅停留在探讨这些途径的优劣性上，或是否有其他更好的途径。你们应当紧扣中国法律体系的概念性基础，并追问处理专家证言的各种不同模式如何才能与中国法律体系之理想状态相协调。所以，在此我的主要观点就是，美国所使用的两种主要测试标准均未能很好地解决专家证言与法律体系理想状态之间的冲突。这对中国来说是种警示。

弗莱伊案和多伯特案测试标准在中国都有很高的知名度，所以有关其内容的介绍我就尽量简短一些，而用更多的时间来解释其缺陷。众所周知，在美国，对科学证据的系统化处理始于弗莱伊诉合众国案。该案中，辩方试图引入某种早期型号测谎仪所做的测试结果作为证据——某种血压收缩压测试。在维持审判法院对证据的排除决定时，本案上诉法院采用了一套决定科学证据可采性的专门规则，规定如下：

> 当一项科学原理或发现同跨实验和论证两个领域时，其界限就很难界定。在这个模糊的区域中，该原理具有怎样的证明力须予以确定；尽管法院需要经历复杂的过程才会采纳从受到普遍认可的科学原理或发现中推导出的专家证言，推理所得之事必须是充分成立的，并且已经获得其所属领域的普遍认可。[本案，第 1014 页]

弗莱伊案并未说明必须获得“普遍认可”的“事”确切指什么。是说真话与血压之间的关系吗？还是专家测量、解释血压变化的能力？或者两者的结合？但该案意见终被证明具有强大的影响力，美国多数法院采用了这种“普遍认可”（或称“弗莱伊”）测试标准。

从上文我所描述的认识论架构视角来看，弗莱伊案测试标准的吸引力显而

⑱ 参见易延友：《英美证据法上的专家证言制度及其面临的挑战》，载《环球法律评论》，2007 年第 4 期，第 67 页。刘晓丹：《如何建立我国鉴定结论采纳规则》，载《现代法学》，2009 年第 4 期，第 187 页（讨论了《联邦证据规则》规则 702、弗莱伊测试和多伯特测试，并就中国如何从美国的实践中受益提出了建议，但是没有探讨认识论的问题）；爱德华·J·伊姆文考瑞德：《从过去 30 年美国使用专家证言的法律经历中应吸取的教训》，王进喜、甄秦峰译，载《证据科学》，2007 年第 6 期，第 181 页（对专家证言体系的一般介绍，而没有讨论认识论的问题）。

易见。我们确信，的确存在一些经过整理的知识体系超出了日常生活知识的水平；我们也明白，司法程序中需要有途径能获取这些知识以便正确地裁判案件。然而，我们假定司法事实认定者们并没有预备的途径接触到这些知识。这便是我先前所提及的法律信息性弱点——我们知道我们亟须某些所不了解的知识，因此，对于那些声称已经掌握有这些知识的人来说，我们是脆弱的。在此情形下，认定已获认可的知识体系并随之遵从于那些真正掌握有该些知识的专家是非常明智之举——如果你们确有能力那样做的话。这恰恰是弗莱伊案测试标准（及其对“普遍接受”原则的强调）规定的内容。该测试标准试图辨别出无争议的专家知识，并安排那些掌握有这些知识的专家作为相关事实的裁判者。该问题同样也是法律的弱点——对未知一无所知，因此只能听从他人的说法。然而，那些提供援助的人却有着自己的动机，有别于利益无涉的事实追求。这也就是为什么弗莱伊案测试标准非但未能实现其总体设计目标，反而招致了相当的不满。

美国联邦最高法院在多伯特诉梅里尔道制药有限公司一案[19]中否定了弗莱伊测试标准，在其影响下，弗莱伊案测试标准在美国许多司法辖区中也相继被否定了。[20] 该测试标准最根本的问题在于，如果拥有着骄人资历的专家们能够被雇佣来就任何事项作证的话，那么遵从模式也就彻底失败了。与此同时，该测试标准也饱受业内人士的批评，指出其无法顺应现代科学的进步，对新兴学科或者交叉学科领域的研究存有偏见，并对复杂领域内的普遍一致认可有着过于严苛的要求。在一个诸多学科正在以惊人速度增长并细分出更多精细专业的时代，弗莱伊案标准的提出显然不合时宜。在将该标准适用于专业化的非科学性学科过程中，法院也遭遇到了困境。

最高法院恰如其分地总结道：形式化的标准不合适；取而代之，审判法院需要在实质层面上经手所提供的证言，确保只有相关并可靠的证据才在审判中被采纳。用眼下时髦的术语来说，审判法院要扮演好“守门员”的角色以确保审理在认识上的稳健性。

尽管多伯特案在要求审判法院实质性接触专业知识领域的问题上走上了正确方向，但其所表明的要遵从公认专家的做法为美国的法律体系蒙上了阴影。最高法院在阐述“科学知识”标准时的业余努力凸显了这一点。事实上，多伯特案

⑲ 509 U. S. 579 (1993) .

⑳ 绝大多数人拥护“多伯特案规则”。参见克里斯托弗·B·穆勒、莱尔德·C·柯克帕特里克：《证据法》，4版，2009年，第639页。需要牢记的是美国各州有其各自的证据法。美国联邦最高法院仅为联邦法院系统决定证据性问题。

的“科学知识”标准与弗莱伊案的普遍接受标准大同小异。最高法院在该案中确认了决定专家证言可采性的四个相关因素，其中三项直接来源于弗莱伊案：

——主要内容是否已经过证伪实验的检测？证伪实验需要按照常规普遍接受的科学标准进行。

——“理论或技术是否经受过同行的审查并已公开发表”？很少有不符合普遍接受标准的结果能够得以发表。

——在决定数据是否充分可靠以便采纳时，法院也会参照普遍接受原则。在这一点上明确适用普遍接受标准。

最高法院所确认的第四项标准仅仅是在说科学技术中存在的错误发生率应当被予以考虑。毫无疑问，不考虑错误发生率势必会严重损害任何科学性工作。

最为令人惊讶的是，在否定科学证据采纳之形式化旧标准的过程中，法院退回到了某种同样形式化的怪圈之中。换句话说，这正是我先前所提到的信息性弱点之直接结果。要求审判法院要接触科学基础是一回事，可实际操作起来却是另一回事，且绝非易事。在任何真正的专业领域中，只有通过长期的学习研究和努力才能成为专家。最高法院的这份清单含蓄地默认了其对下级法院所提要求的难处，并建议通过遵从模式来简化所需付出的努力。

有意思的是，下级联邦法院将多伯特案解读为最高法院的一种引导（引导众法院在采纳专家证言的问题上应采取更为谨慎的态度），并积极地进行了回应。鉴于此，多伯特案显著地改变了专家证言在联邦诉讼中的应用。此外，最高法院还认定了“多伯特案四要素”仅为建议而非命令，并明确了多伯特案规则适用于所有形式的专业性证据；审判法院必须要提防采纳不可信的证据，无论专业知识的性质是什么。[21]

审判法院该怎么做取决于待决事项的性质；简而言之，只要是可采性问题，最高法院便不允许遵从模式，而是坚持审判法院必须要接受相关主题的充分教育，直到法院能够独立地判定专家证言是（或不是）真正基于知识而作出。对于关注于实现事实认定准确结果的审判核心愿景而言，这毫无疑问是一项积极的进步。[22]

[21] 后续案件判决明确表明了多伯特案标准仅仅是建议，锦湖轮胎公司诉卡迈克尔案，526 US 127（1999），并且应用可靠性测试的责任主要在下级法院。通用电气公司诉结合者案，522 US 136（1997）。

[22] 美国联邦法院的经验也许不同于州法院。一些观察者认为从弗莱伊案测试到多伯特案测试的变化在若干州内并未引起实践中的不同。特别参见爱德华·成、阿尔伯特·尹：《弗莱伊测试或者多伯特测试重要吗？关于科学的可采性标准研究》，载《弗吉尼亚法律评论》，2005 年。

但是，最高法院的做法存在着一个明显的问题，而且该问题同样存在于联邦法院使用专家证言的程序中。别忘了美国案件审理中陪审团的使用频率是很高的，而多伯特案及后续案例中却并未要求审判法官坚持专家要像教育法官一样的去教育陪审团。许多专家仍然只是就他们的结论进行作证而非在真正意义上去教育陪审团（《联邦证据规则》实际上鼓励这么做）。[23] 这就把陪审团留在了原地，面对着无法理解的专家意见去不理性地决定选择相信一方或者另一方（专家证言）。这是美国在处理专家证言问题上的一个巨大错误。多伯特案有一个好的开始，但却没有一个好的结局。最高法院意识到了认识论的深邃，弥合了其中一部分，但却在一项要求面前停了下来，即证据只有在能够被理解的基础上才可以被采纳。如果证言没有在充分的细节上进行解释以便事实认定者进行理解，那么审理中的裁决就不可能是理性的。

有趣的是，或许中国能够避免目前美国所犯的错误，而这恰恰是因为你们不使用陪审团制度。即便如此，中国法官依然会对要去学习其他学科的知识而感到不适，并会本能地被遵从模式吸引，因为从其角度出发遵从模式将问题简化了。对此，你们应当予以抵制。你们应当坚持，无论诉讼标的是什么，庭审中所呈现的信息都应该是能够被理解的。只有当审判成为真正意义上的教育性活动时，其理想状态才能实现。

[23] 例如，参见《联邦证据规则》规则 703、703、705。

Conceptual Challenge of Expert Testimony

Ronald J. Allen *

It is a great pleasure each time I return to China to see my many students and how well they are doing. As I will discuss later in this paper, those of you studying evidence and procedure are critical to the continued progress of your country. My lecture tonight involves the conceptual challenge of expert testimony. This is important in its own right, because you cannot decide how to use expert testimony without understanding the difficulties that it poses, but that in turn means you must think about the nature of the legal system and how expert testimony advances or challenges the deepest aspirations you should hold for your legal system. The challenge will be to address all these issues in a systematic way, so let us begin.

The law of all countries of which I am aware contains relatively complex taxonomies of the types of information that conceivably may be pertinent to the resolution of a legal dispute. For example, American evidence law refers to scientific, technical and other specialized knowledge. ① The Federal Rules of Evidence, compounding the complexity, go on to specify various ways in which a person might become an expert, which involves the acquisition in any manner of "knowledge, skill, experience, training, or education" that may "assist the trier of fact to understand the evidence or determine a fact in issue."② If at least one of these criteria is met, an expert may express opinions or otherwise comment about the issues in a case, so long as the expert does so more or less consistently with the standards of the particular expert's field of knowledge.

* I am indebted to Jiang Yujia, a law student at Northwestern University, for her research assistance.

① Federal Rules of Evidence (FRE) 702.

② FRE 702.

The suggestion in the Federal Rules of significant epistemological complexity because of the numerous forms of knowledge that might be pertinent to resolve a dispute is matched if not exceeded by complexity in practice. Enormous resources are spent analyzing and critiquing an apparently endless list of purported forms of expertise to determine the admissibility of testimony, to ensure that the expert is indeed going to testify on the basis of knowledge of some sort or another. If so, the expert is allowed to testify, but is not required actually to testify to that specialized knowledge. Instead, the expert may offer an opinion based on that knowledge about material propositions in the case. [③] Unfortunately, opposing experts can do the same thing—and normally if there is not an opposing expert there is not a triable issue. Thus, after all the effort put into regulating expert testimony at trial, the trier of fact might find itself with two opposing opinions about what to do about matters that are beyond the knowledge of the typical fact finder.

The picture I painted above is odd in many respects. It suggests that there are critical differences between different forms of knowledge, that those differences can be accommodated for trial purposes by taking an internal perspective on the evidence being offered, and if that passes muster letting the expert opine about the relationship between the expert's field and the issues being tried. This is odd because each of these propositions is high problematic, and collectively, while conventional, are quite counterproductive to the central purpose of trial. To justify that assertion requires that the central purpose of trial be identified, that the regrettable consequence of the conventional approach to expert testimony on that purpose be identified, and an alternative offered. I discuss these three points in turn below.

THE FUNDAENTAL ASPIRATION OF LIBERAL LEGAL SYSTEMS

There is controversy about the purposes of trial, especially in those jurisdictions with juries which may increase the possibility of a verdict against the law, [④] but trials without reasonably accurate fact finding are pointless. They are worse than pointless; they are destructive of the foundations of liberal socie-

③ FRE 702, 703.

④ See Robert P. Burns, *A Theory of the Trial* (1999).

ties. The justifications of trials that neglect the significance of accurate fact finding are uniformly influenced by the misconception that the fundamental political insight of the Enlightenment, and thus the critical element upon which modern western governments rest, has something important to do with rights and obligations. Discussions of the political philosophers from Montesquieu to Rousseau are quite prevalent in legal scholarship. Trials bear upon this because they can be the vehicle by which various rights can be exercised, such as the right to be heard or to confront or resist. In countries with juries, an individual can defy government directly by appealing to the jury's common sense and humanity.

Obviously rights and obligations are important and necessary, but they are not sufficient. The more fundamental contribution of the Enlightenment to the legal system was the epistemological revolution that supplanted dogmatic knowledge with empirical knowledge. It replaced knowledge as the doctrines of the religious and political authorities with the concept that the world external to our mind may be known objectively through evidence. ⑤ It is not an exaggeration to say that without accurate fact finding, rights and obligations are meaningless, and thus it is not an exaggeration to say that the most critical component of modern western civilization is accurate fact finding. Note that I say "modern western civilization." I will discuss below the Chinese experience.

In fact, even the concept of jury nullification is literally meaningless without generally accurate fact finding; nullification is the exception to the rule of factually accurate verdicts. ⑥The point presses considerably more deeply. Examine any example of a right and it becomes immediately apparent that it is parasitic upon its epistemological foundation. Consider what was originally and still is one of the most fundamental rights in the West, the right to property. To make the exercise concrete, consider the simple case of ownership of your cellphones. Your ownership of a cellphone allows you the "right" to pos-

⑤ A good introduction is Enlightenment, Stanford Encyclopedia of Philosophy, available at http: //plato. stanford. edu/entries/enlightenment.

⑥ It also neglects that a jury that can acquit against the law can equally well convict against it. Thomas Andrew Green, Verdict According to Conscience: Perspectives on the English Criminal Trial Jury, 1200—1800 (1988) .

sess, consume, and dispose of those assets, but suppose I walk up to you and grab what you say is your cellphone and refuse to return it, claiming that it is mine. What will you do? You will go to someone with the power to adjudicate rights, to be sure, a judge or a jury, but what will you do next? Demand the return of your cellphone? No, of course not because I will respond that the phone is mine. You will present evidence about how you came into possession of that cellphone, by presenting a receipt or a bill from the phone company that associates you with that cellphone instead of me. Then you might turn it on and demonstrate all kinds of things that would convince a reasonable person that it is your cell phone rather than mine, such as text messages or emails addressed to you and none to me, and so on.

If successful in this effort to show the facts, the decision-maker will grant you the right to possess, consume, and dispose of the cellphone—return it to your possession, in other words—and that will impose upon me reciprocal obligations. But here is the absolutely critical point: the right to property is completely and utterly dependent upon the facts that are found and are derivative of them. This point cannot be overemphasized, and it inverts the conventional conception of the relationship of facts and rights. Facts determine rights and obligations. Whoever finds the facts determines the meaning and scope of a right, whether it is the right to property or the right to life.

A potential skeptical note—even if fact finding is important in the way I have described, isn't it a rather large stretch to suggest that it is one of the most fundamental planks of modern liberal democracies? Not only is it not a stretch, but the success of the western democracies is intimately tied to this set of juridical arrangements. Tightly binding the rule of law to true states of the world anchors rights and obligations in things that can be known and are independent of whim and caprice. The right to the enjoyment of property does not depend upon the good graces of fallible human beings, or on their moods or prejudices. You do not have to be in someone's favor to possess a house or travel on a vacation or raise your children in the manner you think best. Quite to the contrary, these rights are grounded on things that have an existence outside the mind of any particular human being and that, as the great Enlightenment epistemologists saw, [7] can be proved with a high degree of regularity by evidence that itself tends to exist without regard to the mind of any particular individual.

In addition to securing rights for their holders, grounding rights on facts permits people to negotiate around them in many different and important senses. Rights grounded in facts provide clear landmarks for both the holder and others, informing every one of the legal potentiality and limits of rights. Choices can be made and lives planned with greater security with such knowledge. Equally important, the secure foundation of rights makes possible the emergence of markets in them—they can be alienated in the various ways permissible within market economies—which has led to the astonishing growth of wealth in those parts of the world that adhere to such commitments.

To be sure, sometimes evidence is lacking and other times mistakes can be made, but normally the progression of the world leaves very traceable marks that permit the reconstruction of the past that is more than adequate to establish the past for the purpose of adjudicating the present. This is why, notwithstanding the complaints about ever increasing litigiousness, modern life works so amazingly well. It is why you can buy and expect to enjoy the use of your cellphones, houses, whatever. It is why you can reasonably expect not to be harassed by government in any country that actually aspires to the fundamental concepts that I have been discussing. It is why life is orderly for the most part rather than random. And this is why relevance and materiality are so fundamentally important to the construction of a liberal legal system. [8]They tie the legal system to the bedrock of factual accuracy, and generate the consequences identified above.

Consider China's recent history from the perspective I have just developed. The most obvious inference any western observer would draw from the destruction of the legal system as occurred during the Cultural Revolution is that the economy would die with it, which is precisely what happened. With the unleashing of economic reform in the late 70's and early 80's, China en-

⑦ See n. 6, supra.

⑧ See, e.g., FRE 401, 402, 403.

gaged in a natural experiment about whether robust economic growth could occur and be sustained without a functioning legal system, and again the verdict was clear that it cannot. That, of course, is why your Government is so concerned with establishing something that approximates the western concept of the rule of law today, but establishing the rule of law requires a recognition of the primacy of factual accuracy in adjudication. This is why people like you in this room who are contributing to the fantastic growth of the field of Evidence in China are one of the most important components of China's continued progress. Without the work that you are doing, the reform of China's legal system is pointless and will be of no consequence whatsoever. Without factual accuracy, there are no rights. ⑨

In sum, rights and obligations depend on facts, and can only be implemented systematically with knowledge of the actual, relevant states of affairs—and this is true whether we are talking about China or the United States. How legal systems find facts, what is the most accurate and/or efficient methodology, and critically what policies may offset the significance of factual accuracy, can be matters of reasonable disagreement. Thus, to understand the problems posed by expert evidence in any legal tradition, one needs to address the basic conception of a trial and the way in which knowledge is constructed in that conception. I will thus next describe the system of trials that I know best, the Anglo-American approach. Let me hasten to reiterate that, although there are aspects of the Anglo-American approach which are idiosyncratic, the significance of knowledge for rights is universal. I will explore that problem in detail within the context of the Anglo-American tradition, but the lessons of that exploration generalize, as I will briefly discuss at the end of this lecture.

To begin with the obvious, trials in the Anglo-American tradition resolved social disputes. These disputes were conventional and not highly complicated because society itself was not highly complicated. Indeed, the original mode of trial, from which trial by jury emerged, gathered together individuals

⑨ See Ronald J. Allen, Baosheng Zhang & Yuebo Zhang trans., *The Theoretical Foundations and Implications of Evidence*, 18 Evidence Sci. 485, 487 ("Facts are prior to and determinative of rights and obligations. Without accurate factfinding, rights and obligations are meaningless").

with knowledge of local affairs to decide disputes based on their pre-existing knowledge—the exact opposite of the conventional, although, mistaken belief that modern juries must be completely ignorant of anything connected to the litigation. Ongoing disputes were part of community knowledge. More importantly, so was the knowledge of the facts necessary to resolve them. Many disputes, for example, involved truly local conventions, such as rights of way or easements, which meant they were known throughout the relevant community. Similarly, knowledge of who did what to whom was likewise notorious and, along with knowledge of local conventions, formed the basis of dispute resolution.

Even at a relatively early stage of development, situations arose that did not involve common knowledge, and witnesses began to be heard, but this was more the exception than the rule. As society, and in particular the economy, evolved, matters became more complex and knowledge began to be more stratified. As commerce developed, cases could turn on the practices of professions, for example, which require evidence of those conventions. Foreign languages may need translation, or the case may involve a technical vocabulary that, like a foreign vocabulary, must be made accessible to those lacking the pertinent knowledge. Interestingly and under the influence of the growing political importance of the jury, as such cases became more common the Anglo-American legal system continued to adhere to the traditional model of fact finding. The parties were merely obligated to explain a little bit more, to put the fact finder in a position to understand what the witnesses were saying, and thus to decide the case in an intelligent fashion, but the facts were still to be found by the disinterested application of common sense by members of the community.

With the introduction of witnesses at trial, the ideal would be to give the fact finders access to the background and experience of each witness so that the fact finder would know precisely why a witness testified as he or she did. After determining the most plausible account of what actually happened,[10] liability would be determined consistent with the law. Because it is not possible literally to merge the minds of witness and fact finder, the common law systems developed methods to approximate that result. This is the source of the opinion rule

[10] See Ronald J. Allen, *The Nature of Juridical Proof*, 13 Cardozo L. Rev. 373 (1991).

that requires that witnesses restrict testimony to their observations and not the inferences (opinions) witnesses may draw. The distinction between "fact" and "opinion" is analytically insupportable,[11] but as a guideline it puts pressure on witnesses to relate as much as possible their sensory impressions, leaving the fact finder to decide the facts as though the fact finder had actually observed them rather than just heard about them. This also explains the rise of liberal rules of cross-examination that allow witnesses to be probed concerning the basis of their testimony.

In many respects, these rules accomplish their purposes, although with certain costs, of course. Typically, everyone at trial—judges, jurors, witnesses—have shared enough backgrounds so that effective communication and comprehension are possible. The probability of both increases with the size of the body deciding a case, because each person added to the group brings a lifetime of experience and knowledge by which to judge the evidence. Small groups of people are enormously powerful and accurate processors of information, although again there are costs attached to any form of decision-making.

Eventually, a sharp distinction was made between witnesses and jurors (and judges for that matter) that did not exist in the common law origins of trials. Jurors were to base decision solely on the evidence presented at trial, and not on their own private knowledge. Some may be wondering how accurate this description is today, especially in the United State where a fairly robust use of jurors continues and the conventional media are filled with stories about how difficult it is in some cases to find jurors who are ignorant of a case to be tried—a difficulty that compounds dramatically with notorious or scandalous cases. The short answer is that the conventional view that potential jurors must be ignorant of the case is false. Why it is false is very important to understanding the conceptual challenge of expert testimony, however.

The conventional belief that fact finders must come with a blank slate is false in every respect save one. The belief is false in the technical sense that knowledge about the litigated event is typically not a disqualification; only

[11] See Ronald J. Allen, Richard B. Kuhns, Eleanor Swift, David S. Schwartz, *Evidence: Text, Problems, and Cases* 609-620 (4th ed., 2006).

knowledge that would qualify a person as a witness disqualifies the person as a juror. [12]The conventional belief about the necessary ignorance of jurors is false in a deeper and more important sense, and as I say one that is essential to understanding the true conceptual challenge of expert testimony, to which I will soon turn. Here is the necessary preliminary conceptual point: Fact finders come to trial with a vast storehouse of knowledge, beliefs, and modes of reasoning that are necessary to permit communication to occur simply and efficiently. So long as everyone is qualified in English (in the United States), words are not defined except in exceptional cases. Conventional beliefs about the nature of reality and the existence of causal relationships are just assumed to be held by all participants, and virtually never are the subject of evidence. Everyone is just assumed to engage in orderly reasoning, employing all the necessary forms—deductive, inductive, abductive, statistical—as necessary or appropriate. Given a common language, or translations if necessary, comprehension of witnesses is just assumed, as is the ability to perceive the connection between the evidence and the trial. Everyone is assumed to know about the foibles of human testimony and the perverse effects of potential biases, and thus to be able to judge the credibility of the testimony. Less well known, everyone is expected to be able to fill in the evidentiary gaps at trial that result from many factors (including that individual witnesses always know more than they can express) by drawing inferences based on one's own.

In fact, the very concept of "evidence" cannot be understood as simply the testimony and exhibits produced at trial, and instead must involve an interaction between a human being and their observations, which presses the self-informing nature of the trial to an even deeper level. I once summarized this point in the following way:

> Suppose a witness begins testifying, and thus a fact finder must decide what to make of the testimony. What are some of the relevant variables? First, there are all the normal credibility issues, but consider how complicated they are. Demeanor is not just demeanor; it is instead a complex set of variables. Is the witness sweating or twitching, and if so is it

[12] This is implied by FRE 606's prohibition on jurors being witnesses.

through innocent nerves, the pressure of prevarication, a medical problem, or simply a distasteful habit picked up during a regrettable childhood? Does body language suggest truthfulness or evasion; is slouching evidence of lying or comfort in telling a straightforward story? Does the witness look the examiner straight in the eye, and if so is it evidence of commendable character or the confidence of an accomplished snake oil salesman? Does the voice inflection suggest the rectitude of the righteous or is it strained, and does a strained voice indicate fabrication or concern over the outcome of the case? And so on.

The list of relevant variables goes far beyond credibility issues, of which demeanor is only one. When a witness articulates a proposition, the fact finder must determine what the proposition is designed to assert and what the fact finder believes it asserts. That task, too, involves an immense number of variables. In addition, the fact finder will possess some knowledge based on its observations leading up to the first articulated proposition by a witness, acquired from the lawyers for example. And there are many more examples. For the law to proceed [in a rule-based fashion] would require that many of these variables be in a deductive structure with their necessary and sufficient conditions spelled out. No such structure could be created; it would be too complex. ⑬

The critical attribute of fact finders is not that they are ignorant, for as we have seen that is impossible; rather, it is that they are disinterested and fair minded, and thus will consider the evidence with an open mind. These two strands of what I have described so far can be pulled together into a coherent whole that describes the deepest aspirations of any liberal legal system, and that is to vest decision in competent, disinterested individuals able to process and deliberate upon the evidence to reach a

⑬ Ronald J. Allen, *Factual Ambiguity and a Theory of Evidence*, 88 Nw. U. L. Rev. 604, 625-26 (1994). Douglas Walton, *Legal Argumentation and Evidence* 200 (2002), has articulated a similar analysis of legal evidence. The complexity of real life is the central problem that AI and the law researchers face. See Ronald J. Allen, *Artificial Intelligence and the Evidential Process: The Challenges of Formalism and Computation*, 9 Artificial Intelligence & Law 99 (2001). For an early philosophical discussion to the effect that people can disagree about the implications of evidence, see G. Polya, 2 *Mathematics And Plausible Reasoning: Patterns of Plausible Inference* (1954).

rational judgment as to what occurred—and thus reach an accurate judgment as to the rights and obligations of the parties.

EXPERT TESTIMONY AS A REPROACH TO THE ASPIRATIONS OF TRIALS

But what if testimony can only be understood with knowledge or experience that the fact finder lacks so that the chances are virtually zero that the fact finder will understand what the spoken words are intended to convey, or at least will be unable to intelligently appraise the truth of what is spoken? We have now gotten to the central conceptual difficulty posed by expert testimony, and there are only two possible solutions to it. Either the necessary background information must be provided somehow, or fact finders must defer to the judgment of others. Here "to defer" means to adopt someone else's views as correct, not because you understand and agree, but because you are simply delegating that decision to someone else. Virtually always, the Anglo-American legal system has chosen to require that information be provided in a comprehensible fashion to the fact finder. If a witness speaks a foreign language, translations will be provided. When routine business practices or conventions matter, for example, evidence is adduced on the topic so that the fact finder may judge what the actual routine practices or conventions are. Requiring that the trial evidence be connected to the background and experience of typical members of the community approximates the ideal vision of a trial.

The central conceptual problem of expert testimony is that its use at trial is often inconsistent with the normal conception of a trial. Experts often engage in years of specialized training, which can make it difficult to educate the fact finder about the relevant issues at trial. Although the controversies over expert testimony explicitly are typically about such things as reliability, they in fact are controversies over supplanting the norm of education by deference when someone qualified as an expert speaks, and thus can only be resolved by addressing that issue. [14]

---

⑭ The education-deference distinction was first introduced into the literature in Ronald J. Allen & Joseph S. Miller, *The Common Law Theory of Experts: Deference or Education*, 87 Nw. U. L. Rev. 1131 (1993), and Ronald J. Allen, *Expertise and the Daubert Decision*, 84 J. Crim. L. & Crim. 1157 (1994). This article is an extension of those articles.

The obvious first question to ask is whether deference is ever an absolute necessity, whether there any cases that cannot be accommodated within the traditional model. Do some cases present issues for decision that defy the ability of fact finders to understand them? Perhaps the answer to these questions is "no." The deficits of juridical fact finders are not cognitive; they are informational. Judges and jurors lack knowledge about many things, like science and technology, but there is no reason that they could not adequately master the relevant fields. This does not mean that a fact finder would have to become an oncologist or radiologist, or whatever. The objective is not to understand any particular field in its entirety. Rather, the objective is to learn enough so that rational deliberation can occur. In this respect, multi-body decision makers—either juries or panels of judges—are actually superior to single person decision makers. Not every member of a panel needs to understand deeply every issue. The question is whether the panel adequately understands. It would be astonishing if a legal case actually defied the cognitive capacities of a small group even randomly picked from society at large, let alone vetted as both judges and jurors are.

Obviously, there are examples of ideas and even fields of inquiry that may defy common understanding at present. Many ideas in physics seep only slowly into the general population, even the general population of scientists. Maybe it would be asking too much for a judicial fact finder to learn special relativity or quantum theory, but to my knowledge these theories are not pertinent to any litigation that has ever occurred. Admittedly, physics is not the only difficult science to learn. Many individuals find higher mathematics difficult (which is probably why they find physics difficult). Examples of two areas of somewhat higher mathematics that are pertinent to modern trials are calculus and probability theory. Still, while some people do, others do not find mathematics at this level obscure—or more importantly would not find it impossible to learn sufficiently for intelligent decision. Here again is the value of a multi-body decision maker. As I said above, what matters is not whether everyone understands but whether the body as a whole does or could learn what is needed for intelligent decision.

The real objection to educating the fact finder is not that it is impossible but that it would be too costly. If statistics plays a role in the trial, it would have to be explained so that the fact finder can understand, which in some cases might require some considerable instruction. The same would be true of various areas of medicine, and so on. In some cases, this educational process would not be terribly burdensome, but in others it would be difficult and require extensive instruction. So, yes, it would be costly, but I literally do not know of any cases actually litigated that would seem to defy this educational process.

The important question is whether the increased cost of educating the fact finder about the basis of "expert" testimony is a good enough reason to forego the normal ideal of a trial and substitute a form of deference. The very question is one of the bizarre aspects of the conventional discourse over expert testimony. There are many cases without scientific or technical questions that nonetheless involve months of testimony. No legal system in the west of which I am aware defers to experts in such cases; the parties are required to prove the case with evidence that is comprehensible to the fact finder. It is difficult to understand why a deferential procedure should be followed merely because a party produces something labeled "expert testimony." The cognitive questions are essentially identical in both sets of cases, and the economic issues are truly identical. In all cases and for all witnesses, the parties in fashioning strategy account for the costs of presenting witnesses and responding to the other side. There is nothing unique about expert witnesses in that regard. An objection on the ground that the public subsidy to trials should not be wasted by requiring more detailed examination of the basis of expert testimony highlights the bizarre nature of the controversy. The public subsidy to a year long trial involving radiology is not substantively different from the subsidy to a year long securities trial. Indeed, if there is a difference, it favors the subsidy for radiology, as the fact finder might actually benefit from learning about radiology, as compared to the utter uselessness of the evidence that fact finders have to process about the unique and idiosyncratic facts of various disputes. The objection on the ground of cost to educating the fact finder has it exactly backwards.

THE SOLUTION

If the central aspiration of trials is to be achieved, the parties must educate the fact finder in all instances. This would eliminate the legal problem of "expert" testimony, because the category would no longer exist. That may seem like solving a problem by definitional fiat, but it is not; the point cuts much more deeply than that. The lamentable consequence of conducting trials through deference is that mistakes will be made because fact finders choose to defer to a purported expert who is in fact not testifying on the basis of knowledge but instead is providing what is called in the United States "junk science." Junk science and unreliable expertise exploit the informational vulnerability of the law, the necessary condition of which is that the fact finder does not understand the basis of the expert's testimony. Making all witnesses, including what are now called expert witnesses, explain their testimony will largely eliminate this problem because false propositions resist comprehensible explanations. I do not say make them impossible, but the presentation of unreliable evidence would be made considerably more difficult.

But there is another side to this epistemological coin. Perhaps I am wrong that the primary limitation of fact finders is informational rather than cognitive; perhaps there are cases that involve "knowledge" in a strict sense—true justified belief—that judges and jurors are not able to comprehend. Obviously, there is specialized nonconventional knowledge pertinent to legal disputes about many fields such as mathematics and medicine. If such knowledge exists and cannot be conveyed at trial, then it is pointless to hold trials involving it in any legal tradition that emphasizes decision by disinterested individuals who rationally process the evidence; that simply cannot occur with a deferential mode of presenting evidence. Quite the contrary, if there are forms of expertise that are pertinent to trials but cannot be explained at trial, the solution is to not try those cases. If expertise exists and can be identified with the certainty that we know that we are presently in China, its lessons should be embraced and the case so decided. How to do so is a different question, and it would usually be done through legislation or regulation.

By contrast, maintaining the present form of trial that involves expertise that is not comprehensible to the fact finder is, literally, nonsensical. In trials, both sides offer expert opinions to which fact finders can defer; these opinions are virtually always diametrically opposed, with one favoring one party and the other favoring the other. If there are not opposing opinions, there is not a triable dispute, and the side with the unassailable (or at least unassailed) expert wins. If there are competing experts, fact finders in a deferential process do not grapple with the facts but simply decide which expert's opinion to accept. And now the critical question: How can fact finders defer intelligently without understanding the relevant fields? Essentially the only way that one could know which expert to believe is by knowing the field adequately enough to appraise the opinion in light of the facts of the particular case. Without knowledge of the field of inquiry, the fact finder has no rational basis to defer to either expert. This point reverberates over the use of expertise at trial, and emphasizes how much the present form of expert testimony is a reproach to the deepest aspirations of the Anglo-American legal system. To restate the obvious, fact finders (or anyone else) who do not know enough to draw the correct inferences from the evidence cannot decide intelligently which expert opinion to choose as correct. If, by contrast fact finders can decide intelligently about which expert to believe, deference to the expert is not necessary. The fact finders could see for themselves the progression of the expert's thought leading from the specialized knowledge through the evidence of the case to the conclusion being offered.

The reduction in the likelihood of rationality is at odds with the deepest aspirations of trials, which again is the pursuit of factual accuracy through rational deliberation. Indeed, there is a high irony here. The mere admission by the trial judge of competing expert opinions without requiring an explanation of the experts' views, including testimony on the underlying field of inquiry, ensures that decision will be rational if not irrational. Only if a fact finder could see clearly that one side was right and the other wrong would decision be rational; but if that were so, the judge would admit only the one version and exclude the other. If reasonable people could rationally disagree about which expert is right, they would be able to understand the underlying dispute, and thus deference would not be needed. Note also the dramatic qualification of the normal rules of relevancy that deference entails. Normally a party must explain the relevance of evidence by adequately connecting the evidence to the fact finder's understanding, but that is simply not possible without an understanding the of the basis of testimony.

An important qualification to explain one possible objection: deference and education are not analytically distinct but opposite points on a spectrum. Raw data is almost never presented at trial (once in a while a demonstration will occur in court, but such things are rare) . There is an element of deference in deciding that a witness has testified truthfully. Even if deference and education are ubiquitous variables, they can be present in differing concentrations. Compare hearing the evidence of sensory experience ("The defendant hit the plaintiff. ") to the drawing of inferences ("In light of these studies, I am of the opinion that smoking causes cancer. ") . The key variable is whether the fact finder understands the reasoning process that led the witness from observation to conclusion. Without that understanding, appraising rationally the evidence is literally impossible. Often with experts there is no expectation that the reasoning process can be understood. Thus, acceptance or rejection of an opinion cannot occur by the exercise of judgment, and in precisely that way deferring to an expert differs from the deference involved in deciding whether to believe a lay witness.

In sum, there are only two ways expert evidence can be dealt with because there are only two ways evidence can be dealt with. The first is to treat expert testimony just like any other testimony, which means for it to be admissible it must be understandable by the fact finder. To make an expert's testimony understandable will require the fact finder to be educated about the relevant matters. The difficulty is cost, and especially that cost may skew decision toward those with greater resources. The more impecunious a party, the less able he or she will be to provide the necessary educative function, or to respond to an opponent's case. The latter point is an aspect of the U. S. system's failure to make parties bear the true cost of their cases, which includes the opponent's cost of responding. Without cost shifting, a wealthier party can make the cost of suit too high for the opponent. Adopting the normal approach to expert testimony would exacerbate this problem by tending to make cases involving expertise more protracted. [15]It would, however, maintain decision by disinterested individuals who have processed and deliberated upon the evidence.

⑮ Although the matter is too complicated to pursue now, offsetting this factor in part is that higher costs are a laudable disincentive to sue or an equally laudable incentive to agree to resolution in other, less costly, forums. How to balance these matters is one of the largest challenges of modern legal systems.

The alternative to education is deference: Fact finders can either be asked to choose which expert to believe even though the fact finder is incompetent to do so rationally, or the state can definitely determine an outcome. The only possible advantage of a deferential model at trial is the potential reduction of cost, but those savings are secured by increased irrationality in decision.

Removing issues from fact finders through definitive state resolution through legislation or regulation has the potential to vest responsibility in those with the ability to decide rationally and consistency in decision is advanced. If the decisions about expertise are correct, accuracy in decision should be advanced as well. There are two disadvantages to this approach. First, it amounts to imposing an official orthodoxy on truth, and what guarantees does one have that the official answer—the official dogma, as it were—is correct? One of the advantages of litigation is that it permits a constant evaluation and reevaluation of the truth of various beliefs that are at certain moments in time taken for granted. If there is an official orthodoxy and that orthodoxy is incorrect, consistency of decision will remain, but the decisions will be consistently wrong. Of course, this advantage of litigation requires an educational, not a deferential, mode of trials.

Some may think that what I have been describing is not really a problem. The great emphasis on the adversary system and the privatization of social disputes in the United States let parties choose whether to educate the fact finders or convince them to defer to an expert. This leaves the whole matter up to the parties, save only for the admissibility decision of judges. The parties know their dispute and their resources better than anyone else, and are in the best position to make choices that optimize their interests. There is one last critical point, though. A deference model exacerbates the problem of cost by introducing functional cost-shifting. If the trial judge admits one party's expert testimony, and that party simply presents the expert's conclusions or opinions, the actual cost of explaining those opinions can be shifted to the other side. This raises the opponent's transaction costs, and facilitates strategic game playing by undermining the normal rule that parties bear their own costs.

I have tried to demonstrate that the use of expert testimony poses fundamental challenges to any system of adjudication, which explains in part the growing controversy over expert testimony even as expert testimony is becoming ever more prevalent at trial. Lurking here is the question embarrassing to much current practice involving experts：To what extent is rational deliberation the hallmark of adjudication? To what extent are fact finders supposed to listen to，process，deliberate upon the evidence，and decide legal rights and obligations consistently with true determinations of facts? Any system dedicated to rights and obligations implicitly if not explicitly adopts just such a juridical model. Indeed，that is precisely why I began this article as I did，with an emphasis on how fundamentally important factual accuracy is to any system dedicated to the rule of law. In part，the controversy over expert testimony is fueled by failing to treat the underlying cause of all the difficulties，which is the incompatibility of the deferential mode of treating expert testimony with the fundamental aspirations of trials. I will develop that point below，but first to get a sense of just how big a problem the unreflective reliance on dogmatic assertions of knowledge can be，consider some of the categories of evidence that have been routinely admitted at trial in the United States，only subsequently to be shown to be anywhere from questionable to highly unreliable：

● Shaken baby syndrome—are there effective markers sorting out innocent Sudden Infant Death Syndrome from abusive behavior?

● Hand writing analysis—is there truly an expertise here? And are experts even consistent in their judgments about hand writing?

● Finger prints analysis—uniqueness has never been subjected to

● Predictions of dangerousness—unreliable and unvalidated psychiatric testimony has sent people to jail for extensive periods of time

● Repressed memories—again unreliable and unvalidated psychiatric testimony has sent people to jail for extensive periods of time

● Hair and fiber analysis has been shown to be unreliable

● Identification of causation of diseases—often unreliable

● Silicone's deleterious effect on the autoimmune system—completely false

● Arson investigation used completely discredited methodologies

● For decades，the scientific evidence showing smoking causes cancer was suppressed

The experience in the United States suggests that something is seriously amiss in its treatment of expert testimony. [16] I believe and will attempt to demonstrate that the major problem is that the U. S. law has neglected the central conceptual problem posed by expert testimony. Rather than directly dealing with the deferential aspects of expert testimony, the law in the United States has tried to tinker with deference to improve it. The impulse lying behind the tinkering is understandable. Much specialized knowledge is useful in resolving disputes, but even if it is not impenetrable it is often challenging and difficult. If we could just get deference right, we could cheaply and efficiently import that knowledge into trials and improve the accuracy of verdicts.

As the above examples indicate, however, tinkering with deference has not been terribly successful. Some may think this is because of the incompatibility between "scientific" knowledge and lay knowledge, but that is not the cause of the difficulties. Incompatibilities between forms of knowledge do not exist; there simply is or isn't knowledge. To be sure, knowledge in many organized fields of inquiry is probabilistic, but this is true of general and specialized forms. Much of "scientific" knowledge is highly complicated, but so, too, is ordinary life—indeed, ordinary life is more complicated than any specialized body of knowledge. Science proceeds by simplifying and studying what is amenable to study. [17] The biggest difference between scientific inquiry and litigation is that the legal system cannot delay decision while it waits for knowledge to advance—maintaining the status quo is a decision on the merits for someone—but this has literally no programmatic implications for the use of expert evidence at trial.

In my opinion, the struggle of the American legal system to domesticate expert testimony is largely if not entirely due to its neglect of the incompatibility of deference and education at trial rather than the incompatibility of scientific

[16] For a systematic discussion of the problems with forensic sciences and the law, see the report of The National Academy of Sciences, National Research Council, *Strengthening Forensic Science in The United States: A Path Forward* (2009).

[17] Ronald J. Allen, *Factual Ambiguity and a Theory of Evidence*, 88 Nw. U. L. Rev. 604, 616-630 (1994).

and some other form of knowledge. This, though, is a lesson that generalizes to many other legal systems, and in particular China. There is considerable discussion in China about the various tests for the admission of expert testimony in the United States, such as the *Frye* and *Daubert* tests, but there is literally no discussion of the conceptual challenge posed by the use of expert evidence at trial, nor so far as I can tell much comprehension of its significance. [18]Your courts and legal scholars have yet to probe the conceptual foundations and difficulties of expert testimony. Without doing so, you cannot intelligently decide how best to accommodate expert evidence, nor can you appraise how good a solution either *Frye* or *Daubert* is. In fact, as I will show, neither is a very good solution. *Daubert* is slightly better than *Frye* but it, too, avoids rather than resolves the central problem. You in China should not just be having a discussion as to which of these approaches is best, or whether some other approach is better still. You should be grappling with the conceptual underpinnings of your legal system and asking how different models of handling expert testimony can be reconciled with the aspirations you have for your system. So, my main point here is going to be that neither of the main tests used in the United States satisfactorily resolve the conflict between expert testimony and the aspirations of the legal system, which should be a cautionary lesson for you in China.

Both the *Frye* and *Daubert* tests are well known in China, so I can be quite brief in their description and spend a bit more time explaining their limitations. As is well known, the systematic treatment of scientific evidence in the United States began with Frye v. United States. The defendant sought to intro-

⑱ See Yanyou Yi, Yingmei Zhengju Fa Shang de Zhuanjia Zhengyan Zhidu Jiqi Mianlin de Tiaozhan（英美证据法上专家证言制度及其面临的挑战）[*Expert Testimony System in Western Evidence Law and Its Challenges*], 4 Global L. Rev. 67 (2007) (discussed the Frye and Daubert tests and the Kumho Tire Company case, but did not address the conceptual challenges of expert testimony); Xiaodan Liu, Ruhe-Jianli Woguo Jianding Jielun Caina Guize（如何建立我国鉴定结论采纳规则）[*How to Develop the Rules of Admissibility of Judicial Appraisal Evidence in China*], 32 Modern L. Science 187 (2009) (discussed FRE 702, the Frye and Daubert tests and made suggestions on how China can benefit from the U. S. practices, but did not discuss epistemological questions); Edward J. Imwinkelried, Jinxi Wang & Qinfeng Zhen trans., *The Lessons to Be Learned from the Last Three Decades of American Legal Experience with Expert Testimony*, 15 Evidence Science 181 (2007) (general introduction to the expert testimony system without any discussion on epistemological issues).

duce into evidence the results of an early type of lie detection device—a systolic blood pressure test. In upholding the trial court's exclusion of the evidence the Court of Appeals adopted a special rule for the admissibility of scientific evidence, stating:

> Just when a scientific principle or discovery crosses the line between the experimental and demonstrable stages is difficult to define. Somewhere in this twilight zone the evidential force of the principle must be recognized, and while courts will go a long way in admitting expert testimony deduced from well-recognized scientific principle or discovery, the thing from which the deduction is made must be sufficiently established to have gained general acceptance in the particular field in which it belongs. [Id., at 1014.]

The Frye opinion is unclear about precisely what "the thing" is that must have gained "general acceptance." Is it the relationship between truth-telling and blood pressure, or the ability of an expert to measure and interpret the changes in blood pressure, or both? Still, the opinion eventually proved very influential, and a majority of courts in the United States adopted the "general acceptance" or "Frye" test.

The attraction of the *Frye* test is immediately apparent from the perspective of the conceptual framework I have developed above. We are confident that there are organized bodies of knowledge that transcend everyday knowledge, and we know further that the judicial process needs access to that knowledge to decide cases correctly. Yet, by hypothesis, the juridical fact finders do not have ready access to that knowledge. This is the informational vulnerability of the law I mentioned before—we know we need knowledge that we do not have, and thus we are vulnerable to those who claim to possess such knowledge. In those circumstances, it is perfectly sensible to identify accepted bodies of knowledge and then defer to those who in fact do possess that knowledge—if you able to do so. That is precisely what the *Frye* test, with its emphasis on "general acceptance," does. It tries to identify uncontroversial expert knowledge and sets up those experts in that knowledge as the arbiters of the relevant facts. The problem is again the law's vulnerability—it doesn't know what it doesn't know and can only take someone else's word for it. Those offering assistance, however, have their own agendas which go beyond a disinterested pursuit of the truth. This is why the test failed in its overall objectives, which in turn led to considerable dissatisfaction with it.

The United States Supreme Court rejected *Frye* in Daubert v. Merrell Dow Pharmaceuticals, Inc,[19] and under its influence *Frye* test has been rejected in many jurisdictions in the United States.[20] The most fundamental problem with the test was the painfully obvious point in retrospect that, if purported experts with impressive credentials can be recruited to testify to just about anything, deference fails utterly. The test was also the subject of extensive internal criticism that it was not responsive to modern scientific developments. It was biased against emerging disciplines or cross-disciplinary studies and in one sense had too stringent of a requirement of general unanimity within complex fields. The test was rendered anachronistic by the astonishing increase in and the splintering of disciplines into subspecialties. Courts also struggled to apply it to specialized but nonscientific disciplines.

The Supreme Court, quite appropriately, concluded that a formal standard was inappropriate and that instead the trial courts had to engage substantively with proffered testimony to ensure that only relevant and reliable evidence is admitted at trial. In the now famous phrase, the trials courts are to act as "gatekeepers" ensure the epistemological soundness of trials.

Although the holding in the case goes decidedly in the right direction of requiring the trial courts to engage substantively with fields of expertise, the *Daubert* opinion nonetheless demonstrates the remarkable shadow that the urge to defer to acknowledged expertise casts in the American system. This is most clear in the Court's amateuristic effort to articulate the criteria of "scientific knowledge," virtually all of which reflected backwards on *Frye's* general acceptance standard. The Court identified four factors relevant to the determination of the admissibility of expert testimony, three of which derive directly

⑲ 509 U. S. 579 (1993).

⑳ All but a handful have embraced Daubert. See Christopher B. Mueller & Laird C. Kirkpatrick, *Evidence* (4th ed., 2009) 639. It is important to bear in mind that each state within the United States provides its own law of evidence. The Supreme Court of the United States only decides evidentiary questions for the federal courts.

from Frye:

—Has the subject matter been subjected to falsifying tests? Falsifying experiments take place within normal generally accepted scientific canons.

—Has "the theory or technique has been subjected to peer review and publication." Rarely do results not within generally accepted paradigms get published.

—In determining whether data is sufficiently reliable to be admitted, a court may also look to general acceptance. This adopts general acceptance explicitly.

The fourth criterion identified by the Court is merely that rate of error in scientific techniques should be taken into account. Of course, failing to take into account error rates would seriously undermine any work purporting to be scientific.

What is most startling about this list is that while in the very process of rejecting formal standards for the admission of scientific evidence, the Court retreated to a set of equally formal standards—the Court went in a circle, in other words, which is a direct consequence of the informational vulnerability I referred to earlier. It is one thing to say that the trial courts should engage with the underlying science; it is another to do it, and it will not be easy. In any truly specialized field, there are reasons why it takes long study and effort to become an expert. The Court's list implicitly acknowledged the difficulty of what it was asking the lower courts to do, and offered suggestions as to how to simplify the effort through a form of deference.

Interestingly, the lower federal courts saw in *Daubert* the invitation to be much more careful in admitting expert testimony, and they accepted the invitation with some enthusiasm. As a result, *Daubert* has significantly changed expert testimony in federal litigation. The Supreme Court has encouraged this process by recognizing that the *Daubert* factors are suggestions not mandates, and also made clear that *Daubert* applies to all forms of specialized evidence; the trial courts must guard against the admission of unreliable evidence, regardless of the nature of the expertise. [21]

[21] Later decisions made it clear these were only suggestions, Kumho Tire Co. v. Carmichael, 526 US 127 (1999), and that the responsibility for implementing the reliability test lay primarily in the lower courts. General Electric Co. v. Joiner, 522 U.S. 136 (1997).

How the trial courts are to do that depends upon the nature of the subject matter; the Court, in short, has rejected a deferential mode of proceeding so far as the admissibility decision is concerned, and now insists that trial courts must be educated enough about the relevant subject matter so that the court can independently conclude that the expert's testimony is actually based upon knowledge. This is unmistakably a very positive development, to the extent one cares about the central aspiration of trials to reach factually accurate results. ㉒

But there is one glaring and remarkable problem in what the Court has done, and thus in the use of expert testimony in federal court. Remember that juries are still used frequently. The *Daubert* line of decisions most emphatically does not require that the trial judge insist that the experts educate the jury as well as the judge. Many experts still testify to their conclusions without truly educating the jury, a process that is actually encouraged by the Federal Rules of Evidence. ㉓That leaves the jury exactly where it was before, with, incomprehensible opinions and the irrational mandate to choose one or the other. This is the great mistake of the United States' approach to expert testimony. *Daubert* started well but ended badly. The Court saw the epistemological abyss, bridged it in part, but stopped short of a requirement that evidence can only be admitted if it was capable of being understood. If testimony is not explained in sufficient detail to allow the fact finder to understand it, trial verdicts cannot be rational.

Interestingly, perhaps China can avoid the mistake so far being made in the United States, precisely because you do not use juries. Still, your judiciary will feel uncomfortable in having to learn about other disciplines and will intuitively be attracted to a form of deference because it simplifies things from their perspective. You should resist this. You should insist that information presented at trial be comprehensible, no matter what its subject matter is. Trials cannot fulfill their aspirations unless they are truly educational events.

㉒ The experience in the federal courts may differ from that in state courts. Some observers think that the change from *Frye* to *Daubert* within various states did not make much of a difference in practice. See in particular Edward Cheng and Albert Yoon, *Does Frye or Daubert Matter? A Study of Scientific Admissibility Standards*, 91 Va. L. Rev. 471 (2005).

㉓ See, e.g., FRE 703, 703, 705.

证据与推论/概率与似真性*

张月波 译 张保生 校

今天的讲座和前四讲有一些不同。在前四讲中，我所分析的都是证据法的公认领域，试图说明我们何以能够通过运用各种分析工具来更深刻地理解它们。今天我不想讨论证据法的传统领域，而要讨论在美国和其他几个国家正在进行的一项重要研究工作，这涉及我们所称的“司法证明的性质”。该研究领域并不论及像传闻规则那样的证据法特定领域，而是关于证据法根基的探讨。但这就意味着它是关于理性思考根基的研究。在讲座第一部分，我将简短讨论一些我们本周已经接触到并与今天话题有关的内容。同时，我要介绍一些新概念，这些新概念是你们在从事证据领域研究时需要思考的。现在就让我们开始。

就从事法律研究而言，人们必须作出的最重要的区分，是被称为“实证性”与“规范性”研究的区分。“规范性研究”是对应然的探究：一个国家应当做什么，一个人应当做什么，司法制度应当做什么。例如，当你们对自己应当拥有一部宪法或权利法案进行论证的时候，就是在进行具有道德内涵的规范性论证。正是在这个意义上，法律中的很多学术和研究是规范性的。关于你们是否应当拥有一部证据法，是否应当有人权，是否应当这样做或者应当那样做，诸如此类的争论都属于规范性探究。

实证性探究相对于规范性探究而言，意味着这种研究旨在找出事物或世界真正的存在方式。例如，一位科学家，像正在寻找底夸克真实存在之证据的粒子物理学家，所从事的就是实证研究。因此，这里规范性研究和实证性研究的区分是，前者通常具有道德内涵，而某人在后者中的行为则更像科学家而非哲学家。

这两种研究都非常重要，并且，科学家和研究者在包括证据法在内的所有领域，都应当进行这两种研究。但是，当人们并未清晰辨别自己正在作出规范性主张还是实证性主张的时候，常常会产生混淆，因此，当一个人正在作出规

* 本文系艾伦教授 2009 年 12 月 4 日在中国政法大学所作的高级证据讲座第五讲。本译文原载于《证据科学》，第 19 卷，2011 年第 5 期。

范性主张，而另一个人正在作出实证性主张时，他们可能会各说各话。所以，你们必须记住这种区分。

我今天要讲的研究工作是实证性的而非规范性的，这是一项解释或者理解司法证明的工作，而非证明其正当性的工作。解释与理解作为一个方面，与作为另一个方面的正当理由之间几乎总有某种关系，但通常情况下，解释或理解是先于规范性探究的，因为在大多数情况下，人们如果不知道是什么，就无法对应当是什么作出有效的论证。

还有第二个重要区分，我需要做这种区分，而你们需要进行思考。这就是“实验工作”和“思维活动”。实验工作是通过观察和试验发现事物实际运行方式的工作。思维活动通常则在分析哲学语境中进行，其努力在于理解和重新定义我们概念的性质。因为概念分析试图重新定义我们概念的性质，它便成为实证研究的一种形式。

就你们自己的工作而言，这些是需要思考的非常重要的概念性区别。规范研究与实证研究之间存在着区别，思维活动与实验工作也有区别。我们今天所要谈论的内容，大部分属于司法证明性质中的实验探究，尽管其也有概念成分。

请记住这些区分，让我再回顾一下本周我们讲过的一些东西。首先且最重要的一点是，事实比权利和义务更为根本，因为权利和义务取决于事实的准确性。我相信你们都记得放在这里的公文包的例子。如果对其所有权存在争议，事物在某一特定时间点存在方式的证据就将被提出，而关于谁拥有该公文包的裁决将取决于被认定的事实。

我要重申一下第二点并做一些说明，因为我现在意识到这一点非常难于理解。有时候，在法律研究中有这样的断言，即法律制度并非专注于事实真相，经常所作出的断言是：存在一些比事实更为重要的事情。如果任何制度或者体系旨在发现事实，我们称其为“求真”（从证实一词而来）或者“求真主义”。

目前，关于事实真相是否存在，我们能否真正知道事实，求真主义是否有意义，在这些问题上都有深刻的哲学争论。这方面的一个例子是，当我的讲座讲到中国证据的某些方面并对事实的含义加以评论时，听众中曾有人提出异议，并说“正义比事实更重要”。然而，这是不正确的，因为正义也要依赖于事实。设想你拥有一种正义观，这意味着你对权利和义务应以何种方式在社会中进行分配持一种观念。但是，要实现对权利和义务的正确分配，则取决于准确弄清实情。这是看似简单却非常深刻的观点，因为这意味着，一切的事情，包括宪法权利和人权，都取决于事实的准确性。因此，求真主义和相对主义以及其他各种事物之间这种存在于哲学思想中的区分，并没有给法律制度造成什么区别。在对这些关于事实认定或事实认定科学中的难题做了绪论性的说明之后，我将进入本次讲座的内容。

所要介绍的第三点，也是我们本周已经简单讨论过的一点是，不能把证据局限于审判中提出的证言、展示件和行为举止，而要看到更加广阔的证据领域。审判中所出示的东西本身没有意义，而是必须经过智慧的观察者运用其关于这个世界的经验和知识来对其进行评价，它们才产生意义。这就是为什么我说，证据成分中包括着语言含义、逻辑规则、常识和经验等等。这一点之所以重要，是因为司法证明的核心问题是复杂性。对一个法律制度而言，问题在于驾驭和驯化复杂性。

要作为绪论讲述的第四点也反映了我们本周一直在谈的东西，那就是成本问题中的经济问题。正如我说过的，对于西方文明及其法律制度来说，事实真相是带有根本性的问题，但决定实体法主张的事实真相是代价高昂的东西，而且不是唯一的价值，这一点正是我现在所从事的研究工作的一部分。社会组织的一个重要方面，是去决定不同种类权利之间的关系。请再考虑一下公文包和物权法的例子。事实对于理解什么是财物以及是谁的财物是至关重要的，但这并不意味着社会在作出这种决定时应当扩张资源。

成本的意义和竞争性权益的意义，在我和科学哲学家拉里·劳单的一些文章中正得到了验证。我们把这项研究称作“致命困境”考察。我们做这项研究的原因是，事实上每一项政府选择，都对谁将生存谁将死亡产生影响。这乍听起来是个奇怪的想法。当然，政府的某些选择只是阻止人们死亡。也许它们起到了这样的作用，但即便它们总是可以阻止一些人死亡，实际上它们却将造成另外一些人死亡。因此，所有政府行为实际上都包含着效益悖反的致命困境，即以一些人的死亡换取另一些人的死亡，或者以一些人的利弊换取另一些人的利弊。

举一个致命困境的简单例子——一条公路建在何处。政府可以在这儿建一条公路，也可以在那儿建一条公路。如果政府在这里而非在那里建公路，那么，特定的人民将会从这条路获利。某位重病人将因为公路建在这里而被送到医院，某位重病人将因为公路建在了别的地方而不能被送到医院。建了公路的地方将会有人出车祸受伤，而没建公路的地方的人民则免遭车祸，所以，不同的人将会受伤与不同的人会将会受益——这些全是致命困境。

请考虑一下医学研究。你可能会认为，医学研究一定是个没人受伤的例子，但是，投入医学研究的资金是有限的。如果在癌症研究方面投入更多，那么投入心脏研究的钱就会更少。如果把所有投到心脏研究的钱都拿来投到癌症研究，人们将会更快治愈癌症。但那些将从心脏研究受益的人，现在的情况就会更糟。今天在美国，这个问题由于死刑而成为一个关键问题。死刑的最大问题是存在着处决一个无辜者的可能性；一些人说我们不应该有死刑，因为我们可能杀掉一个无辜者。但如果死刑对实施谋杀的人有威慑作用，情况又会如何？如果限制死刑，可能会从错误处决中挽救无辜的人，但由于威慑作用减小将会使更多的人被杀。我不再花更多时间谈这个问题，但这段话对我们目前正从事的研究工作是非常重要的。各种权利在稀有资源中存在竞争关系。

最后一个我预先要讲的问题是，我们不得不忍受错误，并且我想再次提醒大家我们本周讨论过的一些事情。在很多车祸中，有责任的人并没有赔付，因为不知道是谁干的；这些全是错误。问题在于，这些案件中只有一些进入了审判。就所有人类活动来说，审判裁决只是非常之大的社会决策体系中的一个非常之小的体系。但在审判裁决和更大规模的社会决策之间确实存在一种关系。当你们对自己法律制度的性质进行研究时，请记住审判和激励之间的关系，激励被创造出来用于优化制度整体中的正确结果。人们容易痴迷于或仅仅关注审判和争端的法律解决，但这只是更大规模社会问题中的一个很小的部分。

我们现在就开始讨论我想要谈的研究项目。记住我 15 分钟前所说的，法律制度的关键问题是“驾驭和驯化复杂性”。要达到驾驭复杂性的标准，就要以概率方式思考问题。比如我们在本周前面所谈到的，在民事案件中，说服责任是超过 50%的概率；在刑事案件中，“确信无疑”是犯罪的高概率。对这些事情以概率方式进行思考，是很自然的事情。

与这种思考方式同样自然的是，它有严重的困难。我今天要讨论很多这种困难，这些困难对当今美国正在进行的研究是极为重要的。让我们从思考这项研究中的一些构成要素开始。我们需要对自己想要驾驭的复杂性的性质有一个了解，因为除非你知道自己想要解决的问题是什么，否则就不能为其规定规则。对法律来说，问题在于法律与现实之间的相互作用，但二者都非常复杂。首先考虑法律，法律提供了多重规则之网，实际上包含所有（很可能刚好是所有）人际关系。我们倾向于把法律考虑为一套狭义和周密的规则。事实上它不仅无所不包，而且还有无所不包的规则之多重网络。所以，这里有两个不同要点：一是法律实际上规制所有人际关系，二是治理那些相互关系的法律有多重之网。

我们先谈论第一点：法律治理所有人际关系。你们皆因法律才待在这个房间里，拥有在特定情况下成为学生的权利，法律创造了这项权利。你们穿的衣服全都受到严格规制；特定种类的材料被允许使用，特定种类的材料不允许使用。你们坐的座位，事实上是作为法律决定的结果而建造的。雇佣关系、家庭关系，所有关系都受法律规则的规范。我认为情况确实如此，你不能找出哪怕一个不受法律支配或不能作为法律争端而终结的人类行为。即使最亲密的关系，像性关系，也是如此。婚姻的范围是什么？什么是适当的性行为？因此，法律所及，实际上是你能够设想的每一种相互作用。从生命开端，法律就规制医院及医生在生育过程中必须遵循的行为方式。到生命终点，法律规制死者遗体被处理或处置的方式。这就是我所说的意思：规则之网处于一个大蜘蛛网式的法规之中。

另外，存在着包罗万象、相互联系的多重法规网络。联邦政府规制、州政府规制、市政府规制、县规制、社区规则，还有可能规制国家之间关系的条约。不知道在中国你们有多少种规制。有些是城市法规，有些是国家法规，也许你们有一些省级法规。这些是重叠交错的规则之网。请记住我们正在讨论复杂性的驯化问题；我们不得不了解自己想要驯化的复杂性，而复杂性的主要根源之一便是这些多重规则之网。

这里要讲的第二点是：潜在事实以及它们的证据是无限变化的。例如，你需要知道哪些证人在说实话，你需要考虑他们不得不说什么，但每一位证人在不同情况下都将说不同的事情。由于个人之间潜在的相互作用，法律争端本质上便以无限多样的方式产生，想必在这些争端中的证据也是相应变化的。那有什么重要呢？因为你驾驭或驯化复杂性的通常方法是依据规则，但这些规则必须能抓住它们所要控制的复杂性。我们通常试图去做的是，创造公式或被称为法则的东西，如 $E=mc^2$。在科学中，我们试图通过简化为公式和简单规则，来理解事物的复杂性。这是极其强大的处理方法。这也是我们尽力为法律所做的事情。我们试图以科学对现实进行描述的相同方式，制定可行的证据规则，或其他种类可行的法律规则。同样，在证据语境中，这里最重要的方法是概率性的，我将要简短地描述一下这种方法所具有的一些严重和深层的困难。

但是，现在我想让你们思考与法律研究有关的某些别的事情。试图把计算方法应用于日常生活领域，是比“科学”更复杂的，而且经不起对照研究的检验，无论如何都缺乏应用价值。对于科学处理难题的能力有一种误解，即认为日常生活的复杂性比科学家的探索更简单一些。这是完全错误的看法。科学之所以能像它所做的那样处理许多复杂性问题，唯一的原因是它实际上能简化其所考察的现象。所以人们能够清楚表达像 $E=mc^2$ 那样的公式，它描述了物质与能量的关系。类比到法律中，就是对照研究将告诉我们，证人何时在说谎或在说实话。为什么没有这么做？因为日常生活比科学更复杂；这就是法律研究在证据领域的主要困境。假定你做了一项关于某证人是否说谎的研究，那么，何种原因会迫使你相信，这将同样适用于某个其他证人？相比之下，当人们做电子聚变或裂变实验时，它们的反应总是一样的。人比电子更复杂。这是你们作为证据领域研究学者将面临的核心问题。

在第一天的课程中，当我试图说明你们听这个讲座之前所持的一个信念是错的时候，就已经简单讨论过这个问题。在听这些讲座之前，你们很可能以为，我们在民事诉讼中采用优势证据标准，是为了减少随时间推移所产生的错误。我举过一个例子说明，概率论并不像它被期望的那样有效。这在当今美国之所以如此被看重，原因是由于科学的成就，每个人都认为概率方法总是所遵循的最佳方法。所以在美国，证据法研究曾经被概率论所统治，而现在我们正开始考察这些理论在自己研究中的局限性。

这里还有其他简单的例子可以向你们说明存在的问题。如果在一个民事案件中有两个要件，每个要件被证明到 0.6 的概率，那么原告将赢得诉讼。但是，两个要件同真的概率是 0.36。这是我们在另一天所谈到的。请考虑一个十分奇怪的相关例子。假定一个要件被证明到 0.9，第二个要件被证明到 0.5 的概率，这是被告获胜的案件，因为 0.5 没有达到优势证据标准，“优势证据”意味着大于 0.5 的概率。但现在来看这两个例子的反直观含义。在第二个案件中原告应当赢的概率高于第一个案件。在第一个案件中两个要件同真的概率是 0.36，那是原告获胜的案件；在第二个案件中两个要件同真的概率是 0.45，比第一个案件的概率要高，但被告却赢了。这就提出一个问题。这被称作合取难题。合取难题也是刑事案件中存在的问题。只要刑事案件中有多个要件，就会出现同样的问题。

解决合取难题的一种尝试是，建议应当忽略单个要件的概率，而用它们的合取概率来取代。合取概率而非单个要件的概率，应当超过说服责任。这种解决方法有什么错误呢？请考虑一下有四个要件的谋杀和有六个或七个要件的盗窃。为给某个盗窃者定罪，合取概率将要求必须达到确信无疑，即这些要件中的每一个都被证明到比谋杀要件更高的概率。证明杀人故意的概率，将低于证明盗窃故意的概率，这是令人匪夷所思的。这正是我的观点。令人匪夷所思的是，这表明存在着证据概率的解释难题。请记住，这是被称为高级证据法系列讲座的最后一讲。如果这个讲座很简单，就称不上高级了。对这些难题我很抱歉，但我确实想让你们了解，在世界的另一个地方，对这些问题的研究正在如何进行。

针对合取难题提出的另一种解决方法是，问题均非孤立；相反，它们相互依赖。独立要件的概率是各自独立概率的乘积。因变量X和Y的概率，是对Y而言的X的概率，再乘以Y的概率。它们共同的概率，不是两个要件各自被证明到0.6故而为0.36，而是取决于这两个要件之依赖度。我们所说的依赖度是指，一个要件之概率影响另一个要件之概率的程度——青草是否生长，取决于天是否下雨。但是，所有这些只是将合取难题最小化，而并没有消除它。另外，使依赖程度难题最小化，还有其自身的其他逻辑问题。我只提及这些，不再继续深入探讨下去。依赖度造成了“辛普森悖论”问题，有时候也称为“确证悖论”，这个问题你们需要自己去研究。

我将举一个辛普森悖论的简短的例子。这也是不可思议的，但它确实是真的。事物可以有无数种划分方法。考虑一下失业率——有多少人没有工作。失业率由受过教育而没有工作的人和未受过教育而没有工作的人而决定。假定你阅读的统计数据说，失业率已从12%降到了10%。那就不可思议了。尽管在一个更大集合内你得到这个事实，但失业率仍可能在两个子集都是上升的。失业率可能在两个子集中都上升，或在整个集合中上升。假设受过教育人群的集合比未受过教育人群的集合大，并假设受过教育人群的失业率先前为8%，现在升到9%，在较小集合（未受过教育人群）中失业率从12%上升到13%。如果受过教育人群足够大，受过教育人群失业率的影响，将左右未受过教育人群的失业率。所以，这里的教训是，个别部分和整体之间没有必然关系。如我所说，这些称作确证悖论或辛普森悖论。

在试图理解司法证据的过程中，我们所面临问题的症结就在这里。证据概率论的主要问题在于，它需求太多信息；在能够计算概率之前，人们必须已知结果。我们今天一直在做的，就好像我们知道它可能意味着什么。比如说，原告必须将其案件证明达到优势证据标准，而这意味着大于0.5的概率，但这究竟是什么意思呢？确切地说，这意味着原告必须以超过0.5的概率证明自己的案件吗？这意味着原告必须对争议中的事情在发生那天的所有各方面，证明达到超过所有各方面的一半，被告就将承担责任吗？这是十分苛刻的标准。它是一个实际上不可能达到的标准，那就是为什么法律没有坚持这个标准的原因。相反，在这里也是关键点，证据规则处处支持所谓整体解释或整体说明。整体说明本质上是一个故事。一味要求特定证据，就不能在构建推论方面下工夫了；证据的相关性和分量是情境性的，而人们却对竞争性故事作标准化比较。

对此又怎么解释呢？就我们本周所讨论的意义而言，解决办法是，司法证明不是概率性的，而是包含着解释，这在哲学中的专业术语是最佳解释推论

(IBE)。这是对此种理论的核心解释。这是很复杂的，我并不指望你们今天就理解，但我想让你们至少接触它一下。概率解释的主要错误在于，把证据模型化为赋予证据的假设概率。事实上，更好的解释是，赋予假设的证据概率。这是什么意思呢？优势证据是显而易见的。原告的故事是否比被告的故事好？还是被告的故事比原告的故事好？哪一个故事更似真，哪一方便赢。

我们该如何理解确信无疑呢？如果没有似真犯罪案情，此人就是无罪的；如果有似真犯罪案情，且没有似真无罪案情，此人就是无罪的。如果有似真犯罪案情和似真无罪案情，此人就是无罪的。这就是对最佳解释之推论的主要解释。它表明了合取悖论的解释方式。如果最佳解释之推论是正确的，合取悖论便因案件双方有同样的合取问题而得到解释。关于这个理论有很多东西可讲，你们可以在各种法律学术文章中找到有关论述。

这种理论性解释也有弊端，请记住我是一位科学家，因此我必须审视我正在探索的这个理论性解释的弊端。一个困难是，我们需要知道解释是什么。同样，这在美国方兴未艾的研究中有很多探讨。

我想简短地讨论一下最后一个难点。这再次表明，证据概率解释的困难以及最佳解释之推论如何可以解决其中的一些问题。我指的是参照组问题。假定你们认为，我今天所说的很多难题有一个解决方法，就是把概率考虑为相对频度。相对频度是在一个更大集合中的子集的出现。这就是为什么我们说，抛硬币得到头像面的相对频度是50对50。在一长串抛硬币的活动中，有一半将是头像而另一半是文字，这就是相对频度。这种方法被用于解释证明的一些难题。举个例子，假设一位证人看到一辆公交车撞了一辆小轿车，但记不清公交车颜色了；蓝色公交车公司拥有镇上75%的公交车，红色公交车公司拥有余下的25%。对证人报告之证明力的惯常看法是，它将取决于蓝色公司公交车与红色公司公交车的比例。这是思考该事件的自然方式。但是，它所表明的是概率，这是由参照组决定的。为什么该城的参照组是适当的？如果红色公司拥有该县75%（而蓝色公司占剩余的25%）的公交车呢？此时概率被翻转了。每次给定一个相对频度，都暗中确定了一个参照组。因此，现在问题变为：正确的参照组是什么？上帝不会给出正确答案，我们要自己决定。结果是，每一个事件都是无限数量参照组中的一部分。例如，假设在这个案件中，你说这是个很好的证据，因为该城是比县更小的单元，因此我们把该城作为参照组。但该参照组还包含更小单元时又该如何，比如，与红色公交车比，该街区上有多少辆蓝色公交车。你会说，好吧，就用这个街区做参照组。但是，究竟为什么公交车数量就是正确的参照组？我们想要认定的是可能造成事故原因的概率，换句话说，谁造成了事故？那才是我们想要知道的。也许正确参照组并不是蓝色公司或红色公司所拥有的公交车数量，而是别的东西。也许适当的参照组必须与安全标准和报告事故的规程有关。我知道这是新的复杂情况，所以这些是摧毁证明力之概率方法的假设。证明力不能概率化，因为要得出概率，就必须有正确参照组。但是，不存在正确的参照组，存在的只是无限数量的参照组。

什么是这里的解决办法？当事人决定他们想要主张的东西才是适当的参照组，因此，在任何特定审判阶段，当事人都决定分歧的范围。当事人也决定他们打算争论的参照组。甚至非常基本的争点，如证据的证明力，都要按照似真性和最佳解释推论而非概率才能得到最佳理解。总之，似真性决定概率，而非相反。实际上，不存在对所有案件事实都适用的客观真实的相对频度，因为不存在客观正确的参考组。证明力是最佳解释推论的功能，而非先前概率中的一种概率变化。

我举最后一个例子。假设我问，你们的平均寿命有多长？中国某个人的平均寿命与美国某个人的平均寿命不同，这些是不同参照组。北京人平均寿命与华盛顿特区人平均寿命不同。吸烟者寿命与不吸烟者寿命不同。受过教育的人与文盲的寿命不同；有无数参照组，因此并没有形式上正确的概率。这个例子的含义所支持的是，司法证明涉及似真性而非概率。

这是我的高级证据法五次讲座的最后一讲，今天的讲座在理论和观念上都是最具挑战性的。这次讲座也为证据研究在中国的发展指明了方法。我们今天讨论的问题，在理解司法证明本质的任何努力中都是必须面对的。我期待你们的学者解决它们，并与我们一道为揭示司法证明的本质而努力。

Evidence and Inference/ Probability and Plausibility

Ronald J. Allen

Today's lecture will be a little different from the previous four lectures. In each of the previous four lectures, I analyzed an accepted area of evidence law and tried to show how we can understand them even more deeply through the use of various analytical tools. Today I am not really going to discuss a conventional area of evidence law; instead I am going to discuss one of the major research efforts underway in United States and a few other countries, which involves what we call "the nature of juridical proof." This research area does not deal with a particular area of evidence like the hearsay rule but instead deals with the very foundations of the law of evidence. But that in turn means it deals with the very foundations of rational thought. I will briefly discuss in the first part of the lecture some of the things we have touched upon this week that bear on tonight's topic. At the same time I am going to introduce some new concepts that you need to think that facilitate doing research in the field of evidence. So let's begin.

The single most important distinction that one has to draw in terms of doing research in the law is between what is called "positive" and "normative" work. "Normative work" involves inquiry into what should be the case: what a country should do, what a person should do, what a judicial system should do. For example, when you make an argument that you should have a Constitution or A Bill of Rights, you are making a normative argument that has moral implications. Much of scholarship and research in the law is normative in just that sense. You have debates about whether you should have a law of evidence, whether you should have human rights, whether you should do this or you should do that, and these are all normative inquiries.

The alternative to normative inquiry is positive inquiry, and that means research designed to find out the way the universe or the world really is. A scientist, for example, like a particle physicist who is trying to find evidence that the bottom quark actually exists, is engaged in positive research. So the distinction here is between normative work that usually has moral implications and positive work in which the person is behaving like a scientist rather than a philosopher.

Both are very important, and both should be done by scientists and researchers in all fields, including the law of evidence. But there is often confusion when people don't clearly distinguish whether they are making a normative claim or a positive claim, and people can thus talk pass each other when one is making a normative claim and the other is making a positive claim. Thus, you must keep this distinction well in mind.

The research effort that I am going to talk about today is positive, not normative; it is an effort to explain or understand juridical proof rather than an effort to justify it. There almost always is a relationship between explanations and understanding on the one hand and justification on the other, but typically the explanation or understanding precedes the normative inquiry because one cannot make an effective argument about what ought to be without knowing what is in most cases.

There is a second important distinction that I need to make and you need to think about. It is between "empirical work" and "conceptual work." Empirical work is the effort to find out the way in which the universe actually is through observation and testing. Conceptual work is typically done in the context of analytical philosophy where the effort is to understand and refine the nature of our concepts. Because conceptual analysis tries to refine the nature of our concepts, it is a form of positive research.

These are very important conceptual distinctions that you need to think about in terms of your own work. There is a difference between normative work and positive work, and there is a difference between conceptual work and empirical work. What we are going to talk about tonight is mostly empirical inquiry into the nature of judicial proof, although it also has a conceptual component.

With these distinctions in mind, let me refresh your memory about some of the things we have talked about this week. The first and most important point is that facts are more fundamental than rights and obligations, because rights and obligations depend on factual accuracy. You all remember, I am sure, the example of the brief case that was sitting right here. If there is a dispute as to its ownership, evidence of the way the universe was at a particular point in time will be produced, and the decision as to who owns the briefcase will depend on what facts are found.

The second point I want to reiterate and to elaborate a little bit, because I now realize this next point is very hard to understand. Sometimes within legal research claims are made that the legal system is not dedicated to truth, and the claim is often made that there are things that are more important than the facts. If any institution or system is designed to find facts, we call it "veritistic" (from verify) or "veritisim".

Now, there are deep philosophical issues about whether truth exists, whether we can actually know facts, and whether or not veritisim makes sense. One example of this is when I have lectured on some aspects of evidence in China and commented on the significance of facts, some people in the audience objected and said "Justice is more important than facts" . However, this is not correct because even justice depends on facts. Imagine that you have a conception of justice; what you mean by that is that you have a conception of a way in which rights and obligations should be distributed over society. But to get the correct distribution of rights and obligations depends upon getting the facts correct. This is a deceptively simple but extraordinarily deep point, because it means that everything, everything, everything, including constitutional and human rights, depends on factual accuracy. So this distinction that exists in philosophical thought between veritisim and relativism and other sorts of things simply makes no difference for a legal system. What I will be talking about tonight after these preliminary remarks are the difficult problems in finding facts—the science of finding facts.

The third introductory point, which again we have discussed briefly this week, is that evidence cannot be restricted to testimony, exhibits, and demeanor presented at trial, but instead is much broader than that. Nothing presented at trial makes sense in its own right, but instead must be appraised by an intelligent observer employing one's experience and knowledge of the world. That is why I say that part of the evidence includes the meaning of language, rules of logic, common sense and experience, and so on. The reason this is important is because the central problem of juridical proof is complexity. The problem for a legal system is to tame and domesticate complexity.

My fourth preliminary remarks again reflects things we have talked about from time to time this week, and that is the economic question of the problem of cost. Truth is, as I have said, foundational to western civilizations and their legal systems, but determining the truth of substantive legal claims is costly and is not the only value, a point that is part of the research that I am doing now. An important part of social organization is to determine the relationship between different kinds of rights. Reconsider the example of the brief case and property law. Facts are critical to understanding what property is and whose property it is, but that does not mean that society should expand resources on making that determination.

The significance of cost and of competing interests is being examined in a number of articles by myself and Larry Laudan, the philosopher of science. We refer to this work as an examination of "deadly dilemmas." The reason we do so is that virtually every governmental choice affects who will live who will die. This seems like a strange idea at first. Surely some governmental choices simply stop people from dying. Perhaps they do, but virtually always even though they may stop some people from dying, they will actually cause somebody else to die. Thus, virtually all government action involves the deadly dilemma of trading off one set of deaths for another, or one set of advantages of disadvantages for another.

Take a simple example of deadly dilemmas—where a road is built. The government can build a road here, or can build a road there. If the government builds the road here, and not there, then certain people will get the advantage of that road. Somebody who was very ill will get to the hospital because the road was build here, somebody over here will not get to the hospital because the road was build over there. There will be car crashes here where people are injured instead of over there, and so again different people will be hurt and different people will benefit—these are all deadly dilemmas.

Think about medical research. You might think that medical research must be an example where nobody is hurt, but there are limited funds to invest in medical research. If you invest more in cancer research, then you will have less to invest in heart research. If you took all the money that goes into cardiac research and invested in cancer research, you will cure cancer more rapidly. But people who would have been benefited by the research in heart disease would now be worse off. This is a critical issue today in the United States because of the death penalty. The biggest problem in the death penalty is the possibility of executing an innocent person; some people say we shouldn't have the death penalty because we might kill an innocent person. But what if the death penalty deters people from committing murders? If you limited the death penalty, you might save innocent persons from wrongful execution, but you will kill many more because deterrence will be reduced. I am not going to spend more time on this, but this one little phrase is extraordinarily important to the research that we are presently engaged in doing. There is a competition among rights over scarce resources.

My last preliminary point has to do with errors, and again I want to remind you of some of the things that we have discussed this week. There are a lot of car crashes in which a person who is responsible does not pay for them because you don't know who did it; those are all errors. The point is that only some of those cases go to trial. With respect to any activity, trial decisions are a very small set of a very much larger social set. But surely there is a relationship between trial decisions and the larger social set of decisions. When you do research into the nature of your legal system, keep in mind the relationship between trials and incentives that are created to optimize correct outcomes in the system as a whole. It is easy to get caught up with and focused on just trials and the legal resolution of disputes, but that is only a one small part of the larger social problem.

We are now ready to begin addressing the research program that I want to talk about. Remember what I said fifteen minutes ago that the central legal problem is "taming or domesticating complexity". The standard approached to taming complexity is to think about things in a probabilistic way. So for example we talked earlier in the week about the burden of persuasion being more than a fifty percent probability in civil cases, and in criminal cases "beyond a reasonable doubt" is a high probability of guilt. It is natural; to think of these things in a probabilistic fashion.

As natural as this way of thinking is, it has serious difficulties. I am going to discuss tonight many of the difficulties, which is central to research going on today in the United States. So let's begin by thinking about some of the constituent elements of this research. We need to get an understanding of the nature of this complexity that we are trying to tame, because you can't prescribe rules for things unless you know what the problem is that you are trying to solve. The problem for the law is the interaction between law and reality, but both are enormously complicated. Think about law first: law provides multiple webs of regulation that encompass virtually all (and probably just all) human interactions. We tend to the think of the law as a set of narrow, discreet set of rules. In fact it is not only all encompassing, but there are multiple webs of all encompassing regulations. So there are two different points here: one is that law regulates virtually all human interactions, and the second is that there are multiple webs of law governing those interactions.

Let's take the first point first: the law governs all human interactions. You are in this room because of law, you have a right to be a student under certain circumstance, and law creates that right. The cloths that you are wearing are all heavily regulated; certain kinds of substances are allowed, certain kinds of substances are not allowed. The seats you are just sitting in are in fact constructed as a consequence of legal decisions. Employment relationships, family relationships, all relationships are governed by legal regulation. I think it is the case that you can not identify a single human act that is not governed by law or that could not end up as a legal dispute. Even the most intimate are and can, like sexual relationships. What is the scope of a marriage, what are proper sexual acts? So the reach of law is to virtually every single interaction that you can imagine. From the beginning of life, the law regulates hospitals and how doctors have to behave in the birthing process. At the very end of life, law regulates how the deceased bodies are to be disposed or to be treated. That is what I mean by a web of regulation in a big spider web of regulations.

In addition, there are multiple webs of overarching and interrelated regulation. The Federal government regulates, state government regulates, city government regulates, county regulates, neighborhoods regulate, and treaties can regulate between countries. I don't know how much of this you have in China. Some city regulations, some national regulations, maybe you have some provincial regulations; these are over lapping webs of regulations. Remember we are talking about domesticating complexity; we have to understand the complexity we are trying to domesticate and one of the major sources of complexity is these multiple webs of regulation.

Here is the second: the potential facts, and evidence of them, are infinitely varied. For example, you need to know which witnesses are telling the truth, and you need to think about what they have to say, but every witness will say different things in different cases. Because the potential interactions of individuals give rise to legal disputes in an essentially infinite fashion, so too does the evidence vary among those disputes. Why does that matter? Because the normal way in which you domesticate or tame complexity is by rules, but the rules have to be able to grasp the complexity that they are ordering. What we normally try to do is try to create formulas or what are called algorithms such as $E=mc^2$. In science, we try understand the complexity of the universe by reducing it to simple formulas and simple rules. This is a tremendously powerful method of proceeding. That is what we try to do for law, too. We try to determine rules of evidence that will work, or other kinds of legal rules that will work in the same way that science describes reality. Again in the context of evidence, the single most important approach here is probabilistic, and I am going to describe some serious and deep difficulties with that approach in just a second.

But now I want you to think of something else that is pertinent to legal research. Trying to apply algorithmic approaches to everyday life is MORE complicated than "science," less amenable to controlled study, and less likely to be worth doing in any event. There is a misconception that science deals with the difficult issues, and complexity in everyday life is much simpler than what scientists explore. This is exactly wrong. The only reason science can proceed as it has is because it can in fact simplify the phenomenon that it examines. So you can articulate formulas like E=mc2 that describes the relationship between matter and energy. In the law, the comparable goal would be to tell us when the witness is lying or telling the truth. Why isn't it done? Because everyday life is more complicated than science; that is the central dilemma of legal research in the evidentiary filed. Suppose you did a study of whether one witness is lying; what reason would you have to believe that it would apply to some other witness? By contrast, when we engage in fusion or fission of electrons, they all behave the same way. People are more complicated than electrons. That is the central problem that you as research scholars in the field of evidence will face.

We talked about this briefly the first day of class where I attempted to show that a belief that you held before you come into this lectures was false. Before these lectures, you probably believed that the reason we adopted the preponderance standard in civil cases is to reduce errors over time. I gave an example that shows that probability theory doesn't quite work it is supposed to. The reason this is so important today in the United States is, because of the success of science, everyone think a probabilistic approach is always the best path to follow. So research into evidence law in the United States has been dominated by probability theory, and now we are beginning to explore in our research of limits of these theories.

Here are other simple examples that show you that there is a problem. If there are two elements in a civil case and each was proved by 0. 6 probability, that will be a plaintiff's case. But the probability that they are both true is 0. 36. This is what we talked about the other day. Consider a related example that is really strange. Suppose one element is proved to 0. 9, and the second element is proved to 0. 5, this is a defendant's case because 0. 5 is not a preponderance of the evidence because "preponderance of the evidence" means more than a 0. 5 probability. But now look at the counter intuitive implications of these two examples. The probability that the plaintiff deserves to win is higher in the second case than in the first. The probability of both elements being true in the first case is 0. 36 and that is the case plaintiff wins; the probability of both elements being true in the second case is 0. 45, which is higher than the first, but the defendant wins. Now this poses a problem. This is called the conjunction problem. The conjunction problem is a problem in criminal cases too. Whenever there are multiple elements in criminal cases, the same problem arises.

One attempt to solve the conjunction problem has been to propose that the individual probabilities of elements should be ignored in favor of the probability of their conjunction. The conjunction should exceed the burden of persuasion rather than each of the individual elements. What is wrong with that solution? Think about murder that has four elements and theft that has six or seven elements. To convict somebody of theft where the conjunction has to be beyond unreasonable doubt would require that each of these elements be proved to a higher probability than the elements of murder. The probability to prove the intent to kill would be lower than the probability to prove the intent to steal, which is quite strange. That is exactly my point. That it is strange suggests that there are problems with the probabilistic interpretations of evidence. Now remember this is the last lecture of a series lectures called Advanced Evidence. If it were simple, it would not be advanced. My apologies for these difficulties, but I really want you to see what is going on out there in the world in terms of the research into these problems.

Another solution that has been proposed to the conjunction problem is that issues are not independent; rather, they are dependent. The probability of independent elements is the multiple of their independent probabilities. The probability of dependent variables, X and Y, is the probability of X given Y times the probability of Y. Rather than the probability of two elements when they are each proven to 0.6 being 0.36, their conjoint probability depends on the dependence of those two elements. What we mean by dependence is that the probability of the one influences the probability of the other—whether grass grows is dependent on whether it rains. But all that does is minimize the conjunction problem rather than eliminate it. In addition, minimizing the problem of dependence has other logical problems of its own. I can only mention and not go into these in great details. Dependency raises the problem of "Simpson's paradox," which is sometime referred to as "confirmation paradoxes," and which you will need to research.

I will give a brief example of Simpson's paradox. This is really strange, but it is true. There are infinite number of ways that world can be sliced up. Think about the unemployment rate— how many people do not have jobs. The unemployment rate is determined by the educated people who don't have jobs and the uneducated people who don't have jobs. And suppose you've read the statistic that the unemployment rate has gone from 12% to 10%. Now, this is where things get weird. Even though in a larger set you have this fact, it can also be the case that unemployment can go up in both subsets. Unemployment can rise in both subsets or in the set as a whole. Suppose the set of educated people is larger than the set of uneducated people, and suppose the previous unemployment rate in the educated people is 8% and it goes to 9%, and in the smaller set (uneducated people) the unemployment rate goes from 12% to 13%. If the group of educated people is large enough, the effect of the rate of educated people's unemployment will dominate the rate of uneducated people's unemployment. So the lesson here is that there is no necessary relationship between individual parts and the whole. As I said, these are called confirmation/Simpson paradoxes.

Here is a crystallization of the problems that face us in trying to understand juridical evidence. The central problem a probabilistic theory of evidence is that it demands too much information; you have to already know the outcome before you could compute the probabilities. We have been proceeding tonight as though we know what it might mean that, for example, the plaintiff must prove its case by a preponderance of the evidence, where that means greater than a 0.5 probability, but what exactly does that mean? What, exactly, does it mean that a plaintiff must proof his case by greater than a 0.5 probability? Does it mean the plaintiff must demonstrate all the various ways the universe might have been on the day in question, and that in over half of them the defendant would be liable? That is a pretty tough standard. It is an impossible standard in fact, which is why that is not what the law insists upon. Rather, and this is the key point here, the rules of evidence everywhere favor what is called holistic accounts or holistic descriptions. A holistic description is essentially a story. Rather than require particularistic evidence, there is very little effort to structure inference; relevance and weight of the evidence are contextual, and you standardly compare competing stories.

So what is the explanation for this? The solution is that judicial proof is not probabilistic, in the sense we have been discussing this week, but instead involves explanations, and the technical term in philosophy for this is inference to the best explanation (IBE) . This is the central account of this theory. This is complicated and I don't expect you to absorb it tonight, but I want you at least to be exposed to it. The central mistake of the probabilistic accounts is to model evidence as the probability of the hypothesis given the evidence. In fact, the better explanation is the probability of the evidence given the hypothesis. What does this mean? Preponderance of the evidence is obvious. Is the plaintiff's story better than the defendant's story? Or is the defendant's story better than the plaintiff's story? Whichever is more plausible wins.

How do we understand beyond a reasonable doubt? If there is no plausible story of guilt, the person is innocent; if there is a plausible story of guilt, and no plausible story of innocence, the person is guilty. If there is a plausible story of guilt and a plausible story of innocence, the person is innocent. So this is the central explanation of inference to the best explanation. It shows how the conjunction paradoxes are explained. The conjunction paradoxes are explained because, if IBE is correct, both sides of the case have the same conjunction issue. There is a lot more to be said about this theory, and you can find discussions in various articles of legal scholarship.

There are also disadvantages of this theoretical account, and remember that I am a scientist and thus I have to look at the disadvantages of the theoretical account that I am exploring. One difficulty is that we need to know what an explanation is. Again, much of this discussed in the ongoing research in the United States.

There is one last difficult point I am going to discuss for just a minute. It again shows the difficulties of the probabilistic account of evidence and how IBE may solve some of those problems. I am referring to the reference class problem. Suppose you think that one solution to many of the problems I have been talking about tonight is to think about probability as relative frequency. A relative frequency is the occurrence of subsets within a larger set. This is why we say the relative frequency of flipping a coin of getting heads is 50—50. In a long series of flips of coins, half of them would be heads and half of them would be tales, and that is a relative frequency. This approach has been used to explain some problems of proof. Here is an example. Suppose a witness saw a bus strike a car but cannot recall the color of the bus; the Blue Company owns 75 percent of the buses in the town and the Red Company owns the remaining 25 percent. The conventional view of the probative value of the witness' report is that it would be determined by the ratio of Blue Company buses to Red Company buses. That is a natural way to think about it. But what it shows is the probability is determined by a reference class. Why is the proper reference class the city? Suppose the Red Company owns 75 percent (and Blue the other 25 percent) of the buses in the county? Now the probability is flipped. Every time you give a relative frequency, implicitly you have identified a reference class. So now the question becomes, what is the right reference class? They are not given by God; they are determined by us. And it turns out that every single event is part of an infinite number of reference classes. Suppose in this case, for example, you say, well this is pretty good evidence because the city is a smaller unit than a county, so let's go with the city as the reference class. But what about the reference class involving still smaller units, such as how many blue buses are in that neighborhood as compare to red buses. You may say, ok, use the neighborhood reference class. But why is the number of buses the right reference class at all? What we are trying to find is probability of the possible causes of the accident—who caused the accident, in other words? That is what we want to know. Maybe the right reference class isn't the number of buses that owned by the blue company or the red company but something else. Maybe the proper reference class has to do with safety standards and protocols for reporting accidents. What this does, and again I know it is new and it is complicated, is destroy a probabilistic approach to probative value. Probative value can't be probabilistic because to be probabilistic you have to have the correct reference class. But there is no correct reference class; there is infinite number of reference classes.

What is the solution here? The parties determine what they want to claim is the proper reference class, and thus the parties determine the scope of disagreement at any particular trial. They also determine the reference classes that they are going to argue about. Even very basic issues like the probative value of evidence is best understood in terms of plausibility and IBE rather than probability. In sum, plausibility determines probability, not other way around. There is no objectively true relative frequency applicable to the litigation in virtually all cases because there are no objectively correct reference classes. Probative value is a function of IBE, not of a probabilistic change in prior probability.

I will give one last example. Suppose I ask you what is your life expectancy? The life expectancy of somebody in China is different from life expectancy of somebody in US; those are different reference classes. Life expectancy in Beijing is different from life expectancy in Wash. D. C. A smoker's life expectancy is different from a nonsmoker's life expectancy. An educated person has a different life expectancy than an illiterate person; there are an infinite number of reference classes, so there is no formally correct probability. The implication of this is to support that juridical proof involves plausibility not probability.

This concludes my five lectures on Advanced Evidence, and tonight's lecture was the most challenging theoretically and conceptually. It also points the way that evidence research must evolve in China. The issues I have discussed tonight must be addressed in any effort to understand the nature of juridical proof. I look forward to your scholars tackling them and joining with us in the efforts to uncover the nature of juridical proof.

证据法革新的框架*

汪诸豪　李吟　译**

很高兴再次为你们演讲，这无疑是一项殊荣。我与中国政法大学及其他中国高校教师之间的合作迄今已逾十年，这是我第十五次来中国做演讲，并与有着共同关切的同仁们会面。对我而言，当初一个短暂关注别国法律的机缘，而今俨然已经发展成了我生活的一部分。同时，作为一名教师和学者，我欣喜地看到通过许多我曾有幸在美国西北大学所指导过的学生，以及多年以来在美国和中国与我保持互动的学者们之贡献，中国已取得了巨大进步。

本次大会的主题可能会显得有些大胆。一个研究领域通过其会议主题暗示该领域的学者们相信其自身的努力将会有助于法治和文明进步，这并不常见。为了避免有人误认为组织本次大会的中国学者们有悖于他们日常的谦逊，我必须要抓紧指出，本次大会的主题是我本人建议的。之所以这么做的原因在于，这预示了一个重要真理——实际上是两个真理。第一，证据领域对于法治而言至关重要；第二，法治是社会进步的关键。进一步而言，我认为法治研究中最为重要的一个领域便是证据，并且社会只能在法治中发展进步。

十年“文化大革命”的浩劫已经让中国应验了上述真理。据我所知，在那个可悲的年代里，中国没有实质上的法律体系可言，全国绝大多数法学院也遭停课。显而易见，这种对法治的不尊重导致了经济上的灾难及中国本土制造业的大幅倒退。然而，“文化大革命”结束之后，中国政府主导市场经济以来，这一自然效应仍在继续应验。改革开放之初，生产力飙升的势头很快地就开始回落，造成这种现象的原因恰恰就是一个高生产力的社会必然需要一套行之有效的法律体系与之配套。财富的创造依靠交易，但若没有一个行之有效的法律体系，除了最基础的物物交换以外，交易将不会发生。正是因为意识到了这一真理的存在，中国政府走上了漫长的重建有效法律体系之路，一个持续至今的过程。

* 感谢美国西北大学法学院学生蒋雨佳对我研究的帮助。本文系艾伦教授于 2013 年 7 月在第四届证据理论与科学国际研讨会上的主题演讲。本译文原载于《证据科学》，第 21 卷，2013 年第 5 期。本译文系教育部人文社会科学研究项目 2013 年青年基金项目“证人弹劾制度研究”阶段性成果。项目编号：13YJC820073。

** 李吟，中国政法大学证据科学研究院博士研究生。

正如我接下来将谈到的，该过程的核心实际上就是证据法，为此我将重申之前来华时曾说过的：本会议大厅中正在学习探索并在深化证据领域研究以及相关配套诉讼领域知识的你们，正是中国这个持续进程中最为重要的一环。若没有你们和你们的努力，若没有证据和诉讼领域方面的不断完善，中国经济的发展将会迟滞，权利将会变得失去意义；若不能创造出财富，关于现代社会的种种期盼都只是泡影。更为重要的是，若没有准确的事实认定，无论是经济权利、人权，还是政治权利，从根本上来说就都失去了意义。这些正是我今天想要谈及的内容，我将先从法治说起。

当今的中国和世界对法治都有着浓厚的兴趣。然而，关于“法治”的定义有着许多不同的说法。我所指的“法治”，以及世界上所有关注“稳定”和“发展”这两大目标的国家会普遍认同的“法治”含义首先是指：要求、指令或命令对特定人群具有约束力的评价标准得到了普遍认同。哈特（H. L. A. Hart）将此称之为“承认规则”，参照该规则，一个人便能够判断在社会中什么是可信的。[①] 正如哈特所指出的，“法治”还包含了允许社会根据其自身进化中不可避免的连带大环境变化而改变其权威性指令（即“法律法规”）之规则。在现代，这些规则通常被置于宪法之中，正如中国和美国，宪法创设了拥有此种权力的特定机构。诚然，如哈特进一步所指出的，“法治”的含义还包含了执行权威性指令和解决有关其纷争的手段。在现代，这往往归属于法院和各种形式的裁判。当然，关于“法治”的哲学基础还有许多可以谈及的，包括约翰·奥斯汀（John Austin）所强调的指令执行机制[②]，汉斯·凯尔森（Hans Kelsen）所强调的法律层级本质[③]，以及致使过去四十年中现代西方法理学上著名的哈特—德沃金（Hart-Dworkin）之争的法律与道德之内在关系，但为了今天演讲的主旨，我将抛开这些深奥有趣的问题，而仅聚焦于哈特所确认的法治先决条件，因为我相信这些法治的先决条件切中了常规语境下“法治”的常规含义。

哈特观点的吸引力及其受世人追捧为社会变革方向的原因，既显而易见又深刻。哈特观念中的法律如同一种黏合剂成分，将社会各部分安稳地维系在一起。它给人们提供了途径，以便事先知晓权利和义务，并可围绕其进行协商。我拥有某样东西，你想要得到这样东西。你就需要与我就其价格进行洽谈而不

① H. L. A. 哈特：《法律的概念》。

② 约翰·奥斯汀：《法理学或积极法律哲学讲座》，两卷，第 4 版，R. 坎贝尔校订，伦敦：约翰·穆雷；再版，布里斯托尔：Thoemmes 出版社，2002 年。

③ 汉斯·凯尔森：《纯粹法律理论》，1934 年。

能肆意地侵占。因此，在这个重要意义上，法律实际上是赋予了人们自由，而非限制。法律开辟了人们赖以构建人生和追求美好生活的渠道，消除了不确定性和政府或他人对其私人空间不测侵犯的风险。

在这个大千社会中，人们习惯上将法治的价值主要归结于对权利及其相应义务的描绘。这种观点有一定道理，但其模糊了某些同等重要的因素，即：没有争议的准确解决——换言之，没有准确的事实认定——权利和义务便都失去了意义。过去我在中国的演讲中已经多次指出了这一点，但请让我再次提醒你们，因为这一要点无论如何去强调都不为过，即：事实先于权利和义务，并且是权利和义务的决定因素。举一个简单的例子，有关你们身上穿着衣服的所有权。你们对衣服的所有权赋予了你们拥有、使用和处置这些衣服的权利，但是，假设我要求你们归还给“我的”衣服。也就是说，我坚持你们所穿着的衣服实际上是属于我的。你们会怎么做？你们会找到一个裁决者，会将你们所购买、制作、捡到或被赠予了这件争议衣服的证据呈现给他，并且，如果这种努力成功的话，裁决者会切实赋予你们衣服的所有权并施加给我将相应的义务。这里的重点在于，这些权利和义务都依附于认定了什么样的事实，且是该事实认定的连锁反应。这一点的重要性不言而喻。把法治与真实世界的实际情况相联系的努力，锚定了可知事物中的权利和义务，并使其摆脱了反复无常和任性的支配。这就是相关性和实质性的理念对于法律制度构建具有根本重要性的原因。正是这些理念把法律体系牢牢地安置在了事实准确性的基石之上。这一点是真正具有普适性的。一方面，在对实际、相关发生状况缺乏了解的情形下，权利、义务或是政策选择都无从谈起。另一方面，将权利与事实相联系赋予了权利以可靠性和稳定性，使得其不会被专横地剥夺。

如你们中许多人所知，在强调事实的重要性时我经常会以财产权作为例子。而这次我要另外举一个人权的例子。在今天这样的场合谈论人权，大多数人通常会以为美国人又要对中国的人权纪录进行批评，但这并非是我所想讨论的。相反，这个例子是爱德华·斯诺登所揭露的美国政府对其本国公民、外国人甚至是别的主权国家所进行的间谍行为。我不确定斯诺登先生是该被当作英雄还是叛徒来对待，但我确信，如果没有他的揭露，我和我本国的同胞们可能完全注意不到奥巴马政权期间所发生的对我们权利之诸多侵害。若没有这个认识，我或其他任何人就绝不可能行动起来去维护我们的权利。若没有这些事实，人们很有可能会说过去没有侵害发生。

由是，事关紧要的并不仅仅是哈特的“三位一体”式裁判，更是准确的裁判。如同我在中国已经多次提及的，这就是为什么你们中那些正在学习并不断精进有关证据、诉讼和法律体系结构方面知识，并将这些知识运用于中国法律改革的人，对于你们国家的持续发展至关重要。随着你们已经从较不任意专断的法律体系过渡到了更具有可预判性的法律体系，中国繁荣兴旺与蓬勃发展的能力也相应提升了。我为你们惊人的成就而由衷地赞叹，为自己在其中所起到的微小积极作用而感到荣幸，并将为你们继续向前努力而助力。

因此，有关争议解决方面的法律——证据法和诉讼法——具有着普适的共性方面。准确的争议解决必然有斟酌可靠证据的理性人参与其中，这给争议的解决带来了更多普适的特征。然而，构建争议解决模式并不仅仅是一个优化普适共性（包括权利行使和理性意义等）的问题。其还有一个强烈的因地制宜因素。这里需要掌握三个要点：首先，所有构建证明过程的规则都源于且执行了某种争议解决理论。在美国，占主导性的争议解决理论是对抗程序理论，但对抗制并非普适的。第二个关联要点是，争议解决理论，如对抗制或大陆法系体制（也称纠问制），本身又发源于一国政府在民事案件私人之间及刑事案件公诉争议解决中所扮演角色的基础性理念。在英美法系传统中，政府在私人争议解决中所起的作用多是在提供便利。其为私人纠纷的公正解决提供了一个公平和利益无涉的法庭，这从本质上来说是所有政府有义务甚至是有权利去做的。这种争议解决的理念也在很大程度上影响到了刑事案件。政府在案件中提起公诉，但其在法庭上被视为与被告当事人处于平等地位的另一方个体当事人。法庭是中立的，换句话说，法庭并不是为了深化政府在某一特定审判中的特定政策利益而构建的政府机关；众所周知，美国法院向来是以通过排除规则之类的规定来阻碍美国政府政策目标的实现而闻名。同样，这也并非众法律体系间的普适特性。

第三个前置性要点则位于更深的概念层级。司法系统和其他政府机构都是为了实现国家的根本性文献（如美国宪法和中国宪法）和国家传统中所体现出的政治抱负而设计的。这为我们的分析注入了另一个变量因素，因为并非所有国家都有着分量相当的政治理念。比如说，美国政府管理中的核心政治性问题是一个“委托代理”问题：政府是人民的代理人，首要问题是委托人——人民——怎样能够掌控其代理人——政府。出于对中央政府集权的恐惧，形成了对控制和限制中央政府的高度关注，这解释了美国政治架构中的两大根本性特征，联邦制和三权分立。这与许多东方国家政权形成了鲜明对比。例如，你们长期以来有着共产党单一政权的理论，因此中心政治问题是政府政策目标的有效执行问题。这些政治理念上的差别直接影响到了其下所构筑起来的法律体系。有人可能会预言，为了有效落实其政策目标，中国政府将趋于在争议解决过程中行使更多权力和控制。相形之下，在美国，政府拥有的权力更为有限，法院则主要是一个无利害关系的平台。

在法律体系类型和政府理念上的区别并不一定都会形成鲜明对比，但会以形形色色、不同程度的方式显现出来。例如，即使在有着许多共性的代议制民主国家中，政府在争议解决中的角色定位也并不一致。例如，本在美国属于“私人”事务的争议在许多西欧国家并非如此，并且西欧国家政府在诉讼的绝大多数阶段都扮演着一个更为主动的角色。这些国家的政府常常会更主动地参与调查，庭审进程与美国相比更多地为法院所控制。这反映了公民之间的争议具有公共性特征，因此该争议的解决是一个共同关注的事件。对照而言，在美国，总的来说，私人间争议不被认为是社会所关注的事件，且政府在其中所扮演的角色要消极得多。当事人自己负责为调查和案件庭审做准备，并在很大程度上负责管控庭审中证据的呈交。类似地，上诉法院往往仅根据当事人所呈现给其的论证来决定案件，由此可能产生的结果是：事实几乎相同的两个案件由于所提出的法律论证不同而被作出了截然不同的判决。此处需要说明的是，法院的职责仅限于根据当事人的供述来正确地对案件进行裁判，而非在绝对意义上“正确地”对案件进行裁判。

法律体系的架构还受另外两个变量的影响。第一个变量包含法律认识论，即有关不同形式的争议解决方式在生成准确判决问题上效能如何之观念。在美国，尽管不无例外，但人们普遍认为对抗性调查和证据呈现比之一个由法庭支配的审判过程更有可能生成与事实真相一致的裁判。当事人比其他任何人都更了解自己的案件，并且有合理动机在争议解决中投入最优的资源。相比较于当事人更为详尽的知识和更为精细的动机，政府的职权主义通常是一种粗糙的替代品。那些更支持纠问制体系的人则强调，一个无偏私的法庭对证据滥用和操纵的几率更低，他们相信这会提高作出与事实真相一致判决的几率。

然而，社会利益涉及面很广，追求事实真相仅是其中一种，且如何权衡追求事实真相与其他社会利益（如隐私）之间的关系仍然是个争议话题。在美国，通行观点是，民事案件中的当事人在审理开始前应当有机会不受约束地获取有关争议的所有相关信息。获取该些信息的程序被称之为证据开示，且健全的证据开示制度是美国法律体系的标志性特征之一。其理念是审判应当真正地属于一种认识论活动且不应该充满意外或障碍。然而，正如我在中国的多次讲座中所谈及的，所有国家都会为了保护其他社会价值而在某些方面约束或限制对事实真相的追求。至于何种价值会在追求事实真相的价值之上则又是一个视社会具体情况而定的问题。

最后一个需要提及的前置性要点是陪审团或外行评审员对于法律体系架构的影响。在美国，陪审团一方面是被尊崇的，同时则又被视作是高度规范化法律职业者世界中的外来入侵者。美国证据法和诉讼法中相当一部分规定的形成正是源于法官与陪审团之分。在革新其他国家的证据法架构时应当牢牢记住这一点。

作为总结，当我们思考证据法的架构或革新时，须牢记以下五点：

（1）证据规则（及诉讼程序）是诉讼理论的一部分

（2）诉讼理论本身又是政府理论的一部分

（3）政府理论多种多样，区别巨大

（4）争议解决涉及事实认定，并且对于认定事实真相的最佳路径，以及当与其他社会利益相互竞争时事实真相价值之高低都是有争议的

（5）陪审员之类的外行事实认定者参与可能会影响到诉讼程序的建构。

我们上述所讨论的各种问题表明了证据概念基础及其内涵的深度和奥妙，并连同创设了架构和革新证据法的框架。我迄今所讲的可能在概念上是有用的、有趣的，且甚至是正确的，但在实际操作中并无多大帮助，不是吗？我仅仅是将证据领域置于更大的背景下来谈，但并没有提供出证据法改革者们可以跟随的路线图。在下文中，我将试图从上述所提及的复杂因素中提取出证据法改革者们必须要考虑的普遍因素。证据法改革者们需要考虑五个基本问题。

*架构问题：*证据法是规范法律体系中各方参与者——审判法官、陪审员和其他外行评审员、律师、当事人和证人（包括外行和专家）——之间互动的关键机制。证据法构建了审判的框架。它给每个角色成员分配了权力和裁量权。然而，审理的总体框架和个体在该框架内所扮演的角色可能需要视社会具体情况而定。于是乎，证据法的革新必须不仅需要追求在概念上有意义，而且同等重要的是，需要了解社会对于各类审判参与者们的期望值。当然，这两个变量是相互影响的。改革者们有时应当遵从社会期望值，而有时候又不需要这样做。一个很好的例子是，你们越来越多地在各种证据立法和提案中使用我们在美国称之为“证据开示”的程序。我相信完善的证据开示制度对于中国来说是个新概念，通过推动这些提案，你们的改革者们正慢慢影响人们接受这一概念。然而，这一点应该泛化，证据法从始至终都包含有最佳分析结构与社会期待或可行性并存的问题。

*认识论问题：*一个国家如何构造审判，以及如何塑造以便于审判的证据规则，受有关人类思维基本问题（了解某事意味着什么?）之信念的影响。审判是一项认识论活动，在其中有关认知的主张被提出、考量、拒绝或接受。我们所刚讨论的认知问题又引出了另一个基本问题：审判的单一目标或多重目标是

什么？典型的回答总是关乎于准确的事实认定。正如我们所试着表明的，这种代表性回答本身有着重大意义。不过，在追求事实真相的问题上审判同科学一样么？且更重要的是，其应当同科学一样么？科学性决策和法律性决定相比有何不同之处？不同于科学追求的是，法律决定不能够无限期的拖延以便收集到更多的信息。要作出的判决亦是实际上发生了什么，而非在探究深层次的普遍规律。也许最能够说明问题的是，法律领域不像在科学领域那样存在着可应用于典型案件的知识体系。反之，事实认定者在作出决定之前必须要导入必要的背景知识。如果细想起来审判与科学（至少是某些科学门类）并不雷同，其是否与历史相似呢？历史的焦点在事实上，但其常常是作为一种增进理解的手段。在审判中，理解基本上是无关的（除非是作为说理）。或者说这并不准确？审判是否应成为恢复和维持社会安宁的手段，而不用考虑任何“实际”发生情况？一个人是否以及在何种程度上认为一个科学性真理或某种对历史事实的深刻理解是可获得的，将影响到其对于特定证据规则的看法。

在我看来，关注上述认识论问题对于中国的改革者们来说极为重要。你们倾向于推崇“证据科学”概念。无疑，关于证据、证据法和二者的重要性有许多知识。但构建法律体系及其组成部分，如证据法，需要不同于纯科学精髓的知识类型。它要求在繁杂问题之间进行权衡和平衡，并安置不同类型的人所具有的多样化实用功能。法律领域几乎不受作为纯科学标志的控制性实验制约，而且人们不应将不同类型知识的追求混为一谈。此外，法律能够并确实在随着新社会问题的出现而进行相应调整。许多情况下，推动改革者向前进的内在动力来源于对变化情况的理性妥协与回应，而非绝对真理。

恐怕上文中我已经触及了最为重要的问题，即有关社会争议的认知可以通过多种渠道获得。我们可以将责任置于诉讼当事人或交由某个政府机构，并且任何社会中的关键问题都在于究竟何种模式更能促进有效的事实真相发现？庭审应当在何种程度上效仿自由市场；政府应该在何种程度上对其进行规范？在一定程度上，此类问题的答案来源于自然和人性的普遍规律，但同时其也受社会实践和期望值的影响。由此可以引申出下一个我所要讨论的“问题”。

*社会问题：*除了准确事实认定，审判还可以服务于许多其他目的。它们服务于非常重要的经济利益，这完全不同于其对当事人的影响。除了当事人之外，律师、法官、法庭书记员以及所有法庭工作人员都在审判中有着既定的经济利益。此外，审判还有潜在的象征性和政治性目的。机构和个人二者都通过审判方式来作出声明并在事实上传播着各式各样的经验教训。总之，有一系列十分复杂的问题昭示着审判的性质，改革者们必须至少要问问这些问题中是否

有任何一个会影响到证据法。

此处还有另一个深层次问题，即审判究竟是一种理想模式，还是种负面做法？法律体系的设计到底是为了鼓励审判，还是鼓励和解？其应当为什么而设计？各国社会在容忍争议的意愿之上是有区别的，审判的架构与鼓励私下解决争议之间存在着直接的相互关系。改革者们应当审慎地考虑这种平衡该如何建立。其与证据法直接交叉的一个好例子是特免权规则。健全的特免权规则能够保护人际关系和隐私，但也相应提高了诉讼成本，降低了诉讼作为解决争议选项的吸引力。

管理问题：证据法不止于构建事实认定；其还创造多种激励机制。我刚才提到了一个非常普遍的激励机制——个人在多大程度上会被鼓励来进行诉讼。但在绝大多数国家中，证据法能够为各种主流行为创设激励机制。我刚才提及的特免权就是一个例子，此外还有许多其他例子。从为鼓励对性侵害案件提起诉讼而设计的强奸相关性规则，到为鼓励个人通过排除危险情况来降低损害风险而设计的修复规则，证据法中的激励机制不胜枚举。准确的事实认定固然重要，但这里的深层次问题是当各种价值形成竞争关系时，该如何权衡准确的事实认定与其他社会价值之间的关系。

执行问题：在过去多次造访中国的经历中，我已经提醒了你们书本上的法律和实践中的法律两者的区别。编写法律和规则是一回事；以那些条款的起草者们所期望的方式执行法律又是另一回事。一部证据法典的起草者也许会有理有据地考虑将裁量权授予某种人——无论是审判法官还是律师，但其脑海中行使该裁量权的方法可能并不为该规定所规制的对象认同。更普遍地说，在如审判这样的社会活动中执行复杂的法典是很困难的。社会活动本身，比如审判，往往是易变且难以预知的，而且将审判所做的每一个判决交由其他权力方来进行复议是不可能的。

这里还潜藏着另一个深层次问题，这个问题首先涉及证据法和诉讼法之间的关系，还包括了这二者与实体法之间的关系。证据法所给予的，程序法可以夺走。并且，一方面证据法与诉讼法之间，另一方面这二者与实体法之间，确实有着类似的复杂相互作用。一国可以将诉讼程序设置得便于起诉，但这样一来，诉因的实质性定义就几乎不可能被证明。反之亦然：可以对权利进行宽泛的定义，但是这样一来，诉讼程序就几乎无法操作。

如此，作为总结，证据法的改革者需要考虑以下问题的影响：

架构问题

认识论问题

社会问题

管理问题，以及

执行问题

你们已经非常耐心地聆听我讲了这么长时间，因此我将会为本次演讲画上句点。我将回到演讲开始之处来结束本次演讲。在这个会议大厅里的你们以及全中国范围内正在沿着正确学习方法刻苦钻研证据法和诉讼法的人们，很大程度上已将中国法治和社会进步的希望扛在了肩上。若失去你们的不懈努力，中国的法治和社会进步都将不会发生。与此同时，这些努力都将涉及所有今天我仅仅简略提及的难题。与中国接触的这十年间，我已经开始熟识你们中的许多人，我也已经看到你们正在开始巧妙地着手解决这些困难任务。前路将是漫长而复杂的，但我坚信，今天中国已取得的巨大进步将会被未来更伟大的进步所超越。我充满希望地期待着伟大进步的到来，也期待着在这一过程之中继续发挥我微小的作用。

非常感谢。

The Framework for the Reform of Evidence *

Ronald J. Allen *

It is a great pleasure to be addressing you today, and a distinct honor. I have been working with the faculty of CUPL and other Chinese Universities for over a decade now, and this is my fifteenth trip to China to do lectures and meet with colleagues concerning matters of mutual interest. What began for me as a somewhat exotic excursion into the law of another nation has now become a part of the fabric of my life. And as a teacher and scholar, it is particularly gratifying to see the great progress that has been made in China through the contributions of the many Chinese scholars I have been privileged to have study with me at Northwestern University, and with whom I have interacted over the years in China and the United States.

The general title of this conference may appear a bit audacious. It is not often that a field of study implies through the title of its conferences that the scholars of that field believe that their efforts have contributed to the rule of law and the progression of civilization. Lest anyone think that the Chinese scholars who have organized this conference have belied their normal humility, I should hasten to point out that I was the one who suggested the title. The reason I suggested it is that it hints at a great and significant truth, two truths really. First, that the field of evidence is critical to the rule of law, and second that the rule of law is critical to the progression of society. I would go further and say that the single most important field of study to the rule of law is evidence, and that society can only progress within the rule of law.

* I am indebted to Jiang Yujia, a second year law student at Northwestern University, for her research assistance.

You in China have confirmed these truths with a natural and in my opinion regrettable experiment that we in the West call the Cultural Revolution. Among the many things that occurred during that lamentable time was the essential shutting down of the legal system, and the shutting of all but one of the law schools, I believe. This had the predictable effect of devastating the economy and causing a horrific drop in the gross domestic product of China. This natural experiment, though, continued after the end of the Cultural Revolution when your government liberalized the economy. At first there was a great burst of productivity, but it quickly began to subside, and the reason is precisely that a functioning legal system is an absolute requirement of a productive society. The creation of wealth depends on trade, but trade will not occur except through barter without a functioning legal system. It was the recognition of this fact that led your government to begin the long process of reestablishing a functioning legal system, a process that continues to this day.

As I will talk about in a few minutes, at the heart of that process is indeed the law of evidence, and thus I will say again what I have said before in China: Those of you in this room who are studying and furthering knowledge about the field of evidence, and its handmaiden procedural fields, are the single most important part of your country's continuing progress. Without you and your efforts, and without the continuing improvement of evidence and procedure, the economy will be retarded in its growth and rights will be meaningless; without the production of wealth, the aspirations of modern societies cannot be realized. More importantly, without accurate fact finding rights essentially have no significance whether those are economic, human, or political rights. These are the things that I want to talk with you about today, and I will begin with the rule of law.

There is great interest today in China and the world at large in the rule of law. The phrase "the rule of law" can mean many different things, however. What I mean by the phrase, and what all countries interested in the twin aims of stability and progress should mean by the phrase is, first, that there are generally agreed upon determinants of what makes a demand, command or order binding upon a certain set of people. H. L. A. Hart referred to this as the "rule of recognition," by reference to which a person can determine what is authoritative within a society. [1]As Hart pointed out, more is needed, including rules that allow a society to change its authoritative commands, its "law," in light of changed circumstances that the evolution of society invariably brings. These are often located in modern times in constitutions, such as that of China and the United States, that create certain institutions with such power. Yet, as Hart further pointed out, more is needed still, including a means of enforcing authoritative commands and resolving disputes about them. This again in modern times typically falls to courts and forms of adjudication. There is much more to be said about the philosophical basis of "the rule of law," of course, including the mechanisms for enforcement of commands emphasized by John Austin[2], the hierarchical nature of law emphasized by Hans Kelsen[3], and the relationship between law and morality that has driven the Har-Dworkin debate that as occupied a good deal of modern western jurisprudence for the last forty years, but I will put aside for today's purposes these deep and interesting questions and simply focus on the prerequisites for the rule of law identified by Hart, for they capture the conventional meaning of "the rule of law" as it is being used in conventional discourse, I believe.

The attractions of the Hartian view, and why so many people around the world are calling for reform that takes societies in that direction, are as profound as they are obvious. Law in the Hartian sense is part of the glue that holds society together peacefully. It provides the means by which rights and obligations can be known in advance, and negotiated around. I own something. You want it. You need to negotiate with me over its price rather than just seize it arbitrarily. There is thus a critical sense in which the law, rather than being restraining, is liberating. It channels the ways in which people can construct their lives and pursue their livelihoods and removes the risk of arbitrary and unpredictable intrusions into their personal spheres, whether from governments or other individuals.

① H. L. A. Hart, *The Concept of Law*.

② John Austin, *Lectures on Jurisprudence, or The Philosophy of Positive Law*, two vols., R. Campbell (ed.), 4th edition, rev., London: John Murray; reprint, Bristol: Thoemmes Press, 2002.

③ Hans Kelsen, *The Pure Theory of Law* (1934).

In this social dynamic, it is conventional to attribute the values of the rule of law primarily to the articulation of rights and their reciprocal obligations. There is some important truth to this view, but it obscures something equally profound, which is that without accurate resolution of disputes—without accurate fact finding, in other words—rights and obligations are meaningless. I have made this point to you many times in my lectures in China, but let me remind you once again, for the point cannot be emphasized enough, that facts are prior to and determinative of rights and obligations. Without accurate fact finding, rights and obligations are meaningless. Consider the simple case of ownership of the clothes you are wearing. Your ownership of those clothes allows you the "right" to possess, consume, and dispose of those assets, but suppose I demand that you return "my" clothes. That is, I insist that the clothes that you are wearing actually belong to me. What will you do? You will search for a decision-maker to whom you will present evidence that you bought, made, found, or were given the clothes in question, and, if successful in this effort, the decision-maker will indeed grant you those rights and impose upon me reciprocal obligations. The critical point is that those rights and obligations are dependent upon what facts are found and are derivative of them. The significance of this point cannot be overstated. Tying rights and obligations to true states of the real world anchors rights and obligations in things that can be known and are independent of whim and caprice. This is why the ideas of relevance and materiality are so fundamentally important to the construction of a legal system. They tie the legal system to the bedrock of factual accuracy. This point is truly universal. On the one hand, neither rights nor obligations nor policy choices can be pursued in the absence of knowledge of the actual, relevant states of affairs. On the other hand, tying rights to facts gives them solidity and stability so that they cannot be removed arbitrarily.

As many of you know, often when I emphasize the importance of facts, I use property rights as the example. Let me give another example, this time of a human right. At this point in events like this, most people normally expect an American to be critical of the Chinese record on human rights, but that is not the example I wish to discuss. Instead, it is the spying by the American government on both its own citizens, foreigners, and even foreign sovereigns that has been disclosed by Edward Snowden. I am not sure whether I think Mr. Snowden should be treated as a hero or a traitor, but I am confident that without his disclosures I and my countrymen would have been completely oblivious to the massive violations of our rights that have taken place during the Obama administration. Without that knowledge, there is simply no way I or anyone else could have vindicated our rights. Without the facts, one can almost say that no violations occurred.

Thus, it is not just adjudication in the Hartian triumvirate that matters, but accurate adjudication. Again as I've said many times in China, that is why those of you who are studying and advancing knowledge about evidence, procedure, and the structure of legal systems, and bringing that knowledge to bear to reform your law are absolutely fundamental to the continuing progression of your country. As you have moved from a less arbitrary to more predictable legal system, your prosperity and ability to flourish have improved commensurately. I commend you for your astonishing achievements, am humbled to have played a small role in them, and charge you to continue in these efforts.

There are thus aspects of the law structuring dispute resolution—evidence and procedure—that have universal aspects. And of course accurate dispute resolution involves rational people deliberating upon reliable evidence, which introduces more universal attributes into the mix. However, structuring dispute resolution is not just a matter of optimizing these universal aspects of the enforcement of rights and the meaning of rationality. It also has a heavily contextualized component. Here there are three critically important points to comprehend. First, all rules that structure the process of proof, are derived from and implement a theory of dispute resolution. The dominant theory of dispute resolution in the United States is the adversarial process, but this is not universal. The second and related point is that theories of dispute resolution, such as the adversarial system or continental (sometimes called the inquisitorial) system, are themselves derived from underlying conceptions of the appropriate role of government in the resolution of disputes between private individuals in civil cases and in the prosecution of criminal cases. In the Anglo American tradition, the role of the government in private dispute resolution has been largely facilitative. The government provides a fair and disinterested forum for the impartial resolution of private disputes, and that is essentially all the government has an obligation, or even a right, to do. In an extraordinary way, this conception of dispute resolution affects criminal cases as well. The government prosecutes cases, but the government is conceived of as analogous to a private party that stands on equal footing with the other private party, the defendant, before the courts. The courts are neutral, in other words, and are not part of the organs of government structured to further the government's specific policy interests in the particular trial; indeed, as is well known, the courts in the United States are famous for obstructing the policy objectives of the government through such things as exclusionary rules. Again, this is not a universal characteristic of legal systems.

The third preliminary point is at a deeper conceptual level. The judiciary and the other branches of government are all designed to further the political aspirations reflected in the founding documents and traditions of the country, such as the United States Constitution of the Chinese Constitution. This injects another contingency into the analysis, because not all countries have commensurate political theories. For example, the central political problem of governing in the United States is a principal-agent problem: The Government is the agent of the people, and the primary problem is how the principal—the people—can control its agent—the Government. This concern about controlling and limiting the central government out of fear of its tendency to concentrate power in itself is what explains the two defining features of the political structure of the United States, federalism and separation of powers. This stands in stark contrast with numerous eastern sovereigns in particular. For example, you have long had a theory of unitary political power located in the Communist Party, and thus the central political problem is the efficient implementation of the policy objectives of Government. These differences plainly affect the legal systems that are constructed in their reflection. One would predict that the Chinese government will tend to exercise more power and control in the dispute resolution process in order to efficiently implement its policy goals. In contrast, in the United States the government has more limited power and the courts are primarily a disinterested forum.

These two distinctions between types of legal systems and theories of government do not necessarily involve stark contrasts but come in many different shades. For example, the conception of the role of the government in the resolution of disputes is not uniform even in representative democracies that otherwise share many traits. In many Western European countries, for example, disputes are not "private" matters to the extent that they are in the United States, and the government plays a much more active role in virtually all phases of litigation. The government often is more actively involved in investigation, and the trial process is controlled more by the court than is true in the United States. This reflects the view that disputes between citizens have a public feature, and thus that the resolution of disputes is a matter of collective concern. In the United States, by contrast, private disputes are not understood to be matters of social concern for the most part, and the government plays a much less active role. The parties are responsible for investigating and preparing the case for trial, and in large measure controlling the presentation of evidence at trial. Similarly, appellate courts often purport to decide cases based only on the arguments presented to them by the parties, thus generating the possibility that cases with virtually identical facts will be decided differently due to the legal arguments advanced. The critical point to understand is that the obligation of the court extends to deciding the case correctly based on what the parties have put forth rather than to decide it "correctly" for all purposes.

The structure of legal systems is also affected by two additional variables. The first involves legal epistemology, which refers to beliefs concerning how effective different forms of dispute resolution are in producing accurate verdicts. In the United States, it is generally although not universally believed that adversarial investigation and presentation of evidence is more likely to yield a verdict consistent with the truth than is a process more dominated by a tribunal. The parties know their case better than anyone else and have the proper incentives to invest the optimal resources in dispute resolution. A government bureaucracy normally would be a poor substitute for the more thorough knowledge and more finely calibrated incentives of the parties. Those who favor more inquisitorial systems emphasize that control by a disinterested tribunal will lead to less abuse and manipulation of the evidence, which they believe may increase the chance that verdicts consistent with the truth will emerge.

The pursuit of truth is not the only social good, however, and there are disagreements about how that particular social good interacts with others, such as privacy. In the United States, the general view is that in civil cases the parties should have essentially unfettered access to all the pertinent information concerning a dispute before the trial begins. The process of obtaining that information is called discovery, and its robustness is one of the defining features of the American legal system. The idea is that trial should truly be an epistemological event and not full of either surprises or road blocks. However, all countries compromise the pursuit of truth by favoring from time to time other values, as I have discussed in various lectures here in China. What values outweigh truth again is quite socially contingent.

The last important preliminary point to mention is the effect that juries or lay assessors have on the structure of a legal system. In the United States, juries are at once revered and simultaneously treated as alien intruders into the otherwise professional world of the law who must be regulated and controlled. A considerable part of the law of evidence and procedure in the United States is driven by the judge-jury divide. It should be looked at to reform the structure of evidence law in other countries only with this point well in mind.

To sum up, as we think about the structure or reform of evidence law, we must keep in mind these five points:

1. Rules of evidence (and procedure) are part of a theory of litigation

2. Theories of litigation are themselves part of a theory of government

3. Theories of government vary dramatically

4. Dispute resolution involves fact finding, and there are disagreements about the most efficient and effective way to get to the truth, and relatedly the value of truth when it competes with other social goods

5. The presence of lay fact finders such as jurors may affect how the litigation process is otherwise structured.

The various issues that we have discussed above illuminate the depth and profundity of the conceptual foundations and implications of evidence, and together create the framework for the structure and reform of the law of evidence. What I have said so far may be conceptually useful, interesting, and perhaps even correct, but it is not very useful programmatically, is it? It situates the field of evidence in its larger context, but does not provide any sort of roadmap for the reformer of the law of evidence to follow. In what follows, I try to extract from the complex considerations referred to above the general considerations that must be attended to by the reformer of the law of evidence. The reformer of the law of evidence faces five general issues, or what I call "problems."

The Organizational Problem: The law of evidence is a critical mechanism to regulate the interactions of the various participants in the legal system: trial judge, jurors and other lay assessors, attorneys, parties, and witnesses (both lay and expert). The law of evidence constructs the framework for a trial. It allocates both power and discretion to each of the actors. However, the general framework for trials and the role individuals play within that framework can be highly socially contingent. Thus, the reform of the law of evidence must ask not just what makes most conceptual sense, but also and equally important, what are the social expectations of the various participants? These two variables interact, of course. Sometimes the reformer should defer to social expectations and sometimes not. A good example of this is the increasing use in your various evidence enactments and proposals of what we in the United States call discovery. Robust discovery is somewhat new to China, and by advancing these proposals your reformers are slowly conditioning people to accept them, I believe. This point should be generalized, however, and throughout the law of evidence is woven the issue of the best analytical structure and what is socially expected or feasible.

The Epistemological Problem: How one constructs trials, and thus the rules of evidence one fashions to facilitate trials, is a function of beliefs concerning one of the fundamental questions of human thought—what does it mean to know something? A trial is an epistemological event at which claims of knowledge are advanced, considered, rejected, or accepted. The question of knowledge just discussed leads to another fundamental question: what is the purpose or purposes of trials? The typical response has much to do with accurate fact finding, and as we have tried to make clear that typical response has enormous significance. But, are trials like science in its pursuit of truth, and more importantly should they be? How do scientific and legal decision making differ? Unlike scientific pursuits, legal decision-making cannot defer judgment until more information is collected. Also, the judgment to be made is what actually happened rather than what the underlying universal laws might be. Most tellingly, perhaps, there is no organized body of knowledge that is applicable to the typical case, as there is in science. To the contrary, the fact finder has to import the necessary background knowledge for a decision. If, on reflection, trials do not seem a lot like science (at least some types of science), are they like history? The focus of history is on facts, but as a means, generally, of greater understanding. At trials, understanding is largely irrelevant (except as a matter of persuasion) . Or is that not accurate? Should trials be the means by which social peace is restored and preserved regardless of any considerations of what "actually" happened? Whether, and to what extent, one thinks a scientific truth or a deep understanding of historical facts is obtainable will affect one's view of particular evidence rules.

In my opinion, the epistemological issue is critically important for Chinese reformers to concentrate on. You tend to refer to "evidence science." To be sure, there is much knowledge about evidence, the law of evidence, and the significance of both. But constructing legal systems and their constituent parts, such as the law of evidence, requires knowledge of a different sort than is the aspiration of the hard sciences. It requires the weighing and balancing of numerous issues, and the accommodation of very diverse utility functions of many different people. Very little within the field of law is subject to controlled experiments of the sort that are the hallmark of the hard sciences, and one should not conflate the different types of pursuit of knowledge. Moreover, the law can and does adjust as social issues unfold. Much of what the reformer does is driven by reasonable compromises and responses to changed conditions rather than absolute truth.

Perhaps the most important issue here is one I touched upon above, which is knowledge about social disputes can be obtained in different ways. One can put the burden on the litigants or on some governmental organ, and the critical question in any society is which model is more likely to foster efficient truth-seeking? To what extent should trials look like free markets; to what extent should the government regulate them? To some extent the answer to such questions comes from universal laws of nature and human nature, but at the same time will be informed by the contingencies of social practices and expectations. This leads to the next "problem."

The Social Problem: Trials may serve many other purposes in addition to accurate fact finding. They serve very important economic interests, quite apart from their effect on the parties. In addition to the parties, the lawyers, the judges, the court reporters, and all the court personnel have vested economic interests in trials. There are in addition potential symbolic and political purposes to trial. Both institutions and individuals make statements through the means of trials, and actually impart lessons of various kinds. There is, in short, an extraordinarily complex set of issues that inform the nature of trials, and the reformer must at least ask whether any of them should influence the law of evidence.

There is another deep question here, and that is whether trials are the ideal or instead are perverse. Is the legal system designed to encourage trials or settlement? What should it be designed for? Societies differ in their willingness to tolerate disputes, and there is a direct correlation between the structure of trials and the encouragement of private dispute resolution. How that balance is structure should be thought about carefully by the reformer. A good example of how this directly intersects evidence law is the law of privileges. Robust privileges can protect relationships and privacy, but they also increase the cost of litigating, making it a less attractive option for resolving disputes.

The Governance Problem: Evidence law does not just structure fact finding; it also create incentives of various kinds. I just mentioned a very general incentive—how much individuals will be encouraged to litigate. But the law of evidence can create, and in most countries does, incentives for various primary behaviors. Privileges, which I just mentioned, are one example, but there are many others. They range from rape relevancy rules that are designed to encourage the bringing of sexual assault cases to things like the repair rule that are designed to encourage individuals to reduce the risk of harm by eliminating dangerous situations. Accurate fact finding is important, but the deep question here is how accurate fact finding competes with other social values.

The Enforcement Problem : Many times in my trips to China, I have reminded you of the distinction between the law on the books and the law in action. It is one thing to write laws and rules; it is another to enforce them in the way anticipated by the drafter of those provisions. The drafter of an evidence code may think that allocating discretion to someone, whether trial judge or attorney, makes sense, but he will have in mind an approach to exercising that discretion that might not be shared by those being regulated by the rule. More generally, it is hard to enforce complex codes in social events such as trials. The event itself, the trial, is often fluid and unpredictable, and in any event it would be impossible to have every decision made at trial second guessed by some other authority.

Again, there is another deep question lurking here, which involves first the relationship between evidence law and procedural law, and in addition the relationship between both of them and substantive law. What evidence law gives, procedural law can take away. And there is a similarly complex interaction between evidence and procedure on the one hand, and substantive law on the other. One can have a procedural context that makes litigation easy to bring, but substantive definitions of causes of action that are essentially impossible to ever prove. And the opposite can be true: There can be broad definitions of rights, but procedural contexts that are essentially impossible to employ.

So, to sum up, the reformer of the law of evidence has to consider the implications of:

The Organizational Problem

The EpistemologicalProblem

The Social Problem

The Governance Problem, and

The Enforcement Problem

You have kindly listened to me for some considerable time, and thus I will bring these remarks to an end. I will do so by returning to where I began. You people in this room and across China who are so assiduously studying the law of evidence and procedure in good measure carry the hope for the rule of law and the progression of society on your shoulders. Neither will occur without your continuing efforts. At the same time, those efforts will involve all the complexities that I have just briefly alluded to today. I have come to know many of you well over the ten years or so I have been involved with your country, and I have seen how ably you have begun to discharge these difficult tasks. The road away will be long and complicated, but I am confident that the tremendous progress that has already occurred will be exceeded by even greater progress in the future. I look forward to seeing that happen hopefully continuing to play a small role in the process.

Thank you very much.

证据法的未来*

郑 飞 樊传明 译** 张保生 校

这个演讲题目多少有点艰巨，大概也不够谦逊。正如美国著名棒球手和经理等人常提醒我们的，预测特别是关于未来的预测是很困难的。值得庆幸的是，我的演讲范围可能比本届研讨会的范围还略窄一些。尽管这次会议及主要的主办方证据科学教育部重点实验室（中国政法大学）既关注证据法学又关注法庭科学，但我的论述将集中于证据法学。这并不意味着轻视法庭科学。恰恰相反，这实际上是一种赞许。说它是赞许，是因为世界上的法庭科学家们都非常清楚他们的未来是什么，并且他们在正确地追求它。他们的未来是去延续特别是在上个世纪以来发生的不可思议的科学知识大爆炸，是去掌握那种知识使其能被用来促进任何健全法律制度主要目标的实现，即促进纠纷的准确解决。

许多人起初会认为，我强调将纠纷的准确解决作为法律制度的主要目的，这令人难以理解。他们会反对说，主要目的应该是权利的保护和义务的履行。而我要再次提醒大家，因为这一点无论怎样强调都不过分，事实优先于权利和义务并且是它们的决定因素。没有准确的事实认定，权利义务便毫无意义。想想你对自己所穿衣服的所有权这样一个简单的例子。你对那些衣服的所有权，赋予你占有、消费和处分那些财产的“权利”。但假设我要求你归还“我的”衣服，即我坚持认为你穿的衣服实际上是属于我的，你会怎么办？你会寻求一位裁决者，并向其提出你购买、制作、发现或被赠予那些有争议的衣服的证据，如果这种努力成功了，该裁决者将实际上授予你那些权利，并对我强加相应的义务。关键点是，那些权利和义务取决于所认定的事实以及从中所衍生的东西。这一点的重要性怎样强调都不过分。设法使权利和义务与现实世界的真实状况相连，就将权利和义务锚定在可知的而非奇想和任性的事物之上了。这就是相关性和实质性的理念为什么对于法律制度的建构如此重要的原因。它们为法律制度奠定了事实准确性的基石。这一点确实具有普适性。在缺乏关于实际上的、相关的事情状态之知识的情况下，不可能实现权利或义务，或者从另

* 本文系艾伦教授在中国政法大学证据科学研究院 2011 年 7 月 16—17 日在北京主办的第三届证据理论与科学国际研讨会上的主题发言。本届会议的主题是“证据科学与司法公正”。

** 樊传明，中国政法大学博士研究生。

一个方面来说的政策选择。

法庭科学家对于他们所追求的东西没有疑问，那就是事实真相；因而对我来说，他们是工作在法律制度中的所有学者和执业者应当追随的典范。这并不是说你们法庭科学家的各种工作没有困难，没有提出任何艰难的概念性问题，我不是指这两种情况。尤其是当实验结果通过检验成为有很大争议的知识之时。同样的，检验结果应当如何在法庭上出示，充满了困难。当然，像其他人一样，法庭科学家偶尔可能为你们的检验结果提出比你们各种科学证成的真实情况更多的主张，而我们其余的人则必须防范这些主张。尽管如此，总体上看，你们对法学家来说是一种角色上的典范。

虽然在法庭科学任何特定子领域中所得出的具体结果，可能且应当引起基于认识论理由的激烈争议，但法庭科学的未来是清楚的，无须持续争论。但困惑出现了。如果法律制度的最深愿望是求真，为什么它不像在法庭科学中那样而成为证据法和证据法学的支配性原则呢？

正如我在中国各地演讲时所反复提到的，在相当大的程度上，求真是证据法学领域中一个重要的组织原则，这恰恰是因为准确性与权利和义务这两方面之间的关系。不过，法庭科学和证据法学之间、法庭科学家与法学家之间有一个关键性的区别。科学和科学家追求关于外部现实的知识，而法律和法学家是在创造作为一个更大社会组织及其治理结构之重要组成部分的人造制度。法庭科学完全被知识的追求所吸引；而法律和法律制度则被引向许多不同的方向。

你们也许记得两年前我在第二届证据理论与科学国际研讨会上的演讲中，我提到中国证据法未来的三项任务，它们是：

（1）第一，最重要的是，中国法律制度应使其证据规则与中国的需要和语境相一致。

（2）第二个任务是，在全国范围内讨论并就真正统一的证据规定达成一致。

（3）第三，中国证据法学要超越个别证据规则的离散性问题，阐明我所说的证据法“宏观”问题，或者对证据法影响更大、意义更深远的问题，例如：第一，司法证明的社会意义；第二，司法证明和与概率论的关系；第三，专家证言的运用；第四，程序与证据的关系。

贯穿这三项任务有一条共同主线，那就是仅仅关注零散的证据法律或规则是不够的。这反映了许多不同的方向，任何法律制度都被竞争性利益拽向这些方向。第一项任务，即根据中国自身需求将证据法特色化的需要，反映出你们的需求不同于其他国家的需求。第二项任务反映出，不同的人可能真诚地对证据法应当发挥什么作用持有不同意见，部分原因是在本国迫切的社会和政治需求是什么的问题上存在分歧。第三项任务概括了前面两点，并强调证据法影响着本国更大的社会和政治结构，同时证据法也受其影响。

总之，证据法并非只关心求真；它是一个同时追求许多不同利益的法律制度之不可分割的部分，这些利益常常具有竞争性。因而，预测它的未来是比预测法庭科学未来更困难的任务。这是一个重要观点，为了充分理解这一点，人们必须考虑创造一个法律制度的复杂性。法律制度的设计者面临大量政策选择。一些是与事实准确性的追求一致，但很多又与其相反。请注意，我用“政策问题”来描述社会可能追求的所有利益——从道德使命到非常实际和功利的需要。在这些问题中，必须安置的问题是：

对事实准确性的追求。人们可能合理地假定，基于固有认识论能力的自然推理过程运行良好，因而通常在追求事实准确性的过程中应得到遵从。这意味着，证据法可以相当简洁，并且基本上只由自然推理过程来决定案件结果。然而，导致人们犯错误的情形可能反复发生。在这种情况下，证据规则可尝试去纠正系统性错误。这解释了在可能被误导或造成不公正偏见的情况下要授予排除证据的权力。它也是其他规则的基础，如对品性和倾向证据的限制，以及要求证人以亲身知识出庭作证。然而，就当前目的而言，重要一点是，在哪些情况下人们会系统地犯错误，这很可能主要取决于文化。

准确性的价值。事实准确性确实是非常重要的愿景，但它绝非唯一愿景。它有成本，而且有时成本过高。一个法律制度过于专注事实的准确性，也许会破坏该法律制度正试图维护的社会环境。一个只值一美元的争端，却要花费一千美元的诉讼才得到一个事实准确的结论，那大概就不该对簿公堂了。这种诉讼可能只会减少整体社会福利，并阻碍纠纷的私人和解。当然，很难说界限在何处，这肯定取决于地方性的观点。

激励的价值。事实准确性不仅与成本有竞争关系，还与政府可合理追求的其他政策有竞争关系。这类政策有很多，而且取决于文化。特免权法律可培育和保护许多社会关系（配偶的、法律的、医疗的、心灵的和政府的关系等等）。有关事故的诉讼不应阻碍对风险的降低（事后补救措施规则）。纠纷和解可能比诉讼更好，这导致和解商谈中所作的陈述被排除。鼓励和解也是不能将诉讼费降得过低的理由之一。诉讼的公共补贴越多，诉讼就越多，私了谈判就会越少。还有其他可以追求的政策。在美国，为了规制警察的调查行为的需要，我们设置了庞大的排除规则体系。证据规则还能激励或阻碍提起特定类型的法律诉讼。同样是在美国，我们经历了这样一个时期，人们认为强奸受害者对侵害

她们的犯罪行为的举报受到了过分阻碍。作为回应，我们创立了一些减少这些行为在法庭上被滥用的证据规则，以避免这些个人可能被曝光而受到伤害。

对公正的总体考量，也可能对证据法产生影响，尽管这种变量的精确影响常常很难与更加明显的功利动机区分开来。一些人认为，对不公正的偏见证据的限制，不仅反映了对准确性的关注，更是对羞辱的担忧，这种情况同样适用于与强奸相关的规则。对先前行为和倾向证据的限制，在某种程度上反映了一种信念，即一个人不应当陷入过去的困境。传闻证据规则在某种程度上反映了与反对自己的证人进行对质的权利价值。

错误风险。一个不犯错误的法律制度是不可能的。最重要的是能识别可能犯的两种类型的错误：一种是对原告有利的错判（包括判无辜者有罪），我们称为Ⅰ型错误，或积极错误；二是对被告有利的错判（包括判有罪者无罪），我们称为Ⅱ型错误，或消极错误。资源配置和其他决定将影响这两种错误之间的关系。

理性人可能对这两种错误类型的意义存在分歧，但在法律制度的建构中，这两种错误类型都必须予以考虑。在美国，我们构建民事诉讼的目的，是要平衡对被告和原告的错误，以减少错误总量。相比之下，刑事司法程序在承认作出更多无罪释放错误代价的同时，旨在减少错误定罪的可能性。尽管情况是复杂的，这些观点在很大程度上解释了民事案件中的优势证据标准和刑事案件中的确信无疑标准。在民事案件中，无论哪种错误都会导致同样的资源错误分配。如果原告错赢一个标的500美元的裁决，一个公民（被告）就必须错舍500美元。如果被告错赢一个裁决——他（或她）不欠他人500美元，一个公民（原告）将被错误地剥夺他（或她）应当拥有的500美元。这两种情况可同样进行分析。相比之下，在美国刑事案件中，我们视一个错误定罪要比一个错误的无罪判决为更严重的伤害，因此通过要求确信无疑的证明而使定罪难以获得。即使可能（但绝不肯定）导致增加错判无罪的数量并在总体上增加错误总量的副作用，我们也在所不惜。

还要解释一下证据法运行的复杂环境，请注意，这种对错误的简单强调的做法可能是很不适当的，这有两个原因：首先涉及这样一种认识，即仅关注错误是不够的；一个法律制度还必须关注正确裁决。一个所有裁决都错但却平等对待控辩双方的法律制度，将满足均衡错误的要求。其次，一个对复杂案件拒绝裁判的法律制度能使该法律制度犯错误的总量最小化。尽管这两种方法都促进了错误管理的潜在目标，但它们都显得古怪而不可接受。原因在于，除了错误之外，正确裁决率也决定着法律制度的构建方式；换言之，优化问题有四个而非两个变量。[①]

除了对正确裁决的意义的忽视之外，对错误的简单专注也忽视了庭审情况与主要行为之间的关系。毋庸置疑，法律的存在是为了通过清晰地阐明行为标准、创造权利和激励符合法律要求的行为，来影响人们的主要行为。法律争端的正确裁判，对那些激励措施的运行是有益的，大概还是必要条件。如果一个人可以漠视法律权利而不受惩罚，这种漠视的几率很可能会大量增加。但这并非事情的全部。在美国，大多数案件包括民事和刑事案件，都以和解告终。因而，正确和错误裁决的真实比率不仅是庭审比率，也是纠纷解决的总体比率。那些比率反过来甚至影响着争端的出现。所有这些变量在对法律制度进行评估时都必须予以考虑。[②]

如上所述，考虑所有这些因素都意味着成本。无论法庭裁决自身之间，还是法庭裁决与主要行为之间的最佳关系可能如何，在一个无交易成本的制度中可能均非最佳，因为这里存在交易成本。某些正确裁决就其成本所取而言，可能并非物有所值，因而给法律市场外的某些争端定价不应感到遗憾，这是可能的。法律争端市场的运作与其他市场大概没有什么两样，成本下降将导致消费的增加。这就意味着，正式争端解决方式的选择，将被诸如谈判和妥协等非正式争端解决方式所代替。如果正式选项花费的成本太高，人们将寻求非正式解决方式，如妥协和谈判。在许多情形下，那也许更可取。

混杂政策问题。还有许多其他可能发生的问题，是法律制度的建筑师必须回答的。最重要的是为法律戏剧中的各色演员分配责任。包括这样一些问题：审判应该采用欧洲更流行的分段模式，还是美国那样一气呵成的模式？审判法官应该拥有多大的自由裁量权，当事人应该在多大程度上控制该进程？审判法官与上诉法官是什么关系？上诉法院应当对案件重新审理，还是仅限于对法律错误的审查？小型民事案件与大型商事案件被给予不同的对待是正当的吗？那么刑事案件呢？它们在构建方式上应当与民事案件有何区别？

从实质性措施上看，证据法的未来将取决于你们当中许多人对我刚才谈到的各种问题的研究。在大多数情况下，不同国家所从事的工作，将被其他国家学者和实务界充分理解。人类的推理和认知能力是相通的，尽管它们在不同语境中的含义可能有所不同。例如，你们在中国可能认为美国过于强调排除规则

① 罗纳德·J·艾伦和拉里·劳丹：《致命的困境》，载《得克萨斯州科技法律评论》，第41期，2008年，第65～92页。

② 同上；拉里·劳丹和罗纳德·J·艾伦：《致命的困境II：保释和犯罪》，载《芝加哥肯特法律评论》，第85期，2010年，第23页。

了，而我们在美国则会认为中国证据程序太松散和任意了。但我们用这些结论所表达的意思其实都是，某个国家对特定问题所采取的立场在不同背景下是次优的。这些分歧不是概念争议的结果，而是在特定社会背景下，对特定社会问题这样或那样的合理解决方法。

请注意，我已经超出了对证据法未来的预测，而进入到任何试图以精细方式来规制审判中运用推论的任务范围。这不是也不应当是证据法的任务。证据法以自然认知实践为己任，最多能在一个或另一个方向推进推论过程。的确，不论人们何时提议一个旨在防止法庭得出某个特定结果的规则，其实都该是值得怀疑的。这样一个规则的正当理由可能只是某种信念，即在某个特定领域存在高概率的不合理性。但该规则的制定者们为什么总要比那些裁判案件的人更理性呢？这就是为什么在我的国家，为了不使陪审团成员产生偏见而受到根本性误导，而强调让证据与陪审团保持距离，谢天谢地，这也是它实际上发生不多的原因。证据被更多地规制，以避免效率低下，以禁止富有的当事人用诉讼费来压制贫穷的当事人。

正如我们在美国所做的，你们将面对的一个重要问题是，证据规则的形式应该是什么样的。规则应该详尽到什么程度，并且一般准则应在自由裁量活动中实施到什么程度？③ 在这个问题和上述有关困难的观点之间也许存在某种张力，在审判中系统地构建推论过程的确是不可能的事。当然，那是一个须经检验的问题。然而，即使证据法规制范围十分狭窄，如何规制所及范围内的事情也会成为问题。以传闻为例子。人们可以表达一种限制传闻使用的偏好，并将这一问题留给审判法官来自由裁量决定；人们也可以提供详细的规则，就像《联邦证据规则》规则8规定的那样。

这些问题和议题并未穷尽证据法的未来问题；为了充分理解证据法的复杂性以及建构该法律制度的人们所面对的挑战，最后有一个问题必须加以考虑。正如我刚才的演讲所暗示，以及我先前多次在中国的证据法演讲所明示的，尽管对人类来说存在着普适性的东西，但人类组织方式本身是变化无穷的。法律制度是政府的关键组成部分，它们反映着深刻政治理论问题的解决方式。只需看一下中国和美国，这一点就很清楚了。由于美国的政治史，我们的国父们得出的结论是，政治权力应该被分散到政府的三个分支，每一支要发生效力都需要其他一支或两支。这旨在抵消西方观察者几乎普遍相信的倾向，即所有的权

③ 有关这一争论的精彩讨论，请参见埃利诺·斯威夫特：《证据法改革的一百年：塞耶的胜利》，载《加利福尼亚法律评论》，第88期，2000年，第24～37页。

力都有集权向心力并具有自身扩张的趋向性。总之，这就是我们有独立法院传统的原因，我们设想独立的法院对其他政府分支是一个潜在制动器。

有人将司法独立和法治联系在一起，但它们并非完全是同义词。想象一个社会以法治进行治理却没有西方式司法独立概念，这是可能的。然而，问题的关键在于，很难想象一个持续且充满活力的社会，它鼓励提高生产力和创新，却没有某种法治核心概念，使政府成为人民的代理人，而不是人民成为政府的雇佣，并限制掌权者反复无常的倾向。

我认为，这个会场里及全中国正如此勤奋学习和研究证据法的人，将是中国努力推进法治的先锋，而法治将使这个国家发挥其真正潜能。正如我来中国一次又一次说过的，我之所以这样说，是因为事实比权利更根本，而学过证据法的人知晓这一点，而且他们的工作赋予其意义。如果没有权利——无论其如何被定义，一个社会将处于贫弱状态。当你们和你们的学生弄懂了规制证据过程之潜在方式的复杂性时，你们就间接决定了你们的制度将促进还是阻碍法治，以及伴随而来的后果。我知道，法治在一些法律和政治话语中起着重要作用，但它由于太抽象而缺乏实质意义。相比之下，当你们从事一种维护权利所必要的工作时，你们就是在其最深刻的方面阐释着法治的含义。

所以，对于中国证据科学发展进程接下来的三个步骤，我现在想再增加第四步，这是为了明确你们所做工作的意义。证据法学者和法律执业者不仅仅是解决复杂规则的技师，而且是公平和正义社会的建筑师。但问题出现了，“公正”和“正义”这两个词意味着什么？要阐述这些问题，那是你们下一步的工作，你们可能注意到在美国也是如此。在美国证据法和程序法里正在进行的工作中，类似的问题变得比以往更明确了。

这些是困难而复杂的任务，但大量的概念性工作已经完成，尽管许多分歧仍然存在，例如，政府及其公民之间的关系究竟应当怎样。你们需要考察像约瑟夫·拉兹等人的工作，他们关注显性规则被中立裁决者遵从的情况④，罗纳德·德沃金等人的工作则关注作为整体的法律。⑤ 清晰性和确定性价值如何与追求公共利益的开明自由裁量权的价值进行权衡，你们对这些问题的想法如何体现在证据和程序规则中？在多大程度上，所有人都能随时造访一位现成的裁决者？对财富和社会稳定的追求如何相互增强或相克，纠纷解决方式如何与你

④ 约瑟夫·拉兹：《法治及其优点》，载《法律评论季刊》，第93期，1997年，第195页。

⑤ 特别参见罗纳德·德沃金：《哈特的后记以及政治哲学的品性》，载《牛津法律研究杂志》，第24期，2004年，第1页。

对这些问题的想法协调？是否应该有一条对不公正的法律提出质疑的林荫大道？

我想，这些问题将对中国证据法下一阶段的发展和未来起支配作用，其他国家也是如此。正如我先前说过和将要提到的一样，这些问题不仅对证据法，而且对作为整体的国家福祉都是至关重要的。更有趣的是，请注意，没有一个现代国家能在不对法治的某种版本作出承诺的情况下长久生存。的确，一个国家法律实施手段的缺乏，已成为现代国家衰败的主要原因之一。我想，你们致力于证据法和程序法的各位与其他任何群体一样，或者比他们更多地将国家的未来掌握在你们手里。如果你们继续努力工作，论证出在不发生社会分裂情况下的争端解决的合理方式，那是可能的；对争端解决能力的抑制会导致愤怒和不满的爆发，然而，如果你们国家继续在包容这些观念的方向上发展，未来将是极其光明的。

The Future of Evidence Law*

Ronald J. Allen

The title of this talk is somewhat daunting and perhaps lacking in humility. As the famous American baseball player and manager, and others, have often reminded us, predictions, especially about the future, are difficult. Thankfully, the scope of my talk can be somewhat narrower than the scope of this conference. The conference and the Key Laboratory of Evidence Science of the Ministry of Education (China University of Political Science and Law) which is its primary sponsor focus on both evidence law and forensic science, but my remarks will focus on evidence law. This is not meant as a slight to forensic science. Quite the contrary, it is in fact praise. It is praise because the forensic scientists of the world are quite clear what their future is, and they are right to pursue it. Their future is to continue the incredible explosion of scientific knowledge that has occurred in particular over the last century and to domesticate that knowledge so that it can be used to advance the primary objective of any sane legal system, which is to facilitate the accurate resolution of disputes.

Many would initially find my emphasis on accurate resolution of disputes as the primary objective of a legal system to be curious, and they would object that instead the primary objective should be the protection of rights and the enforcement of obligations. Let me remind you once again, for the point cannot be emphasized enough, that facts are prior to and determinative of rights and obligations. Without accurate fact finding, rights and obligations are meaningless. Consider the simple case of ownership of the clothes you are wear-

* Presented at: The Third International Conference on Evidence Law and Forensic Science, Beijing, China, July 16—17, 2011.

ing. Your ownership of those clothes allows you the "right" to possess, consume, and dispose of those assets, but suppose I demand that you return "my" clothes. That is, I insist that the clothes that you are wearing actually belong to me. What will you do? You will search for a decision-maker to whom you will present evidence that you bought, made, found, or were given the clothes in question, and, if successful in this effort, the decision-maker will indeed grant you those rights and impose upon me reciprocal obligations. The critical point is that those rights and obligations are dependent upon what facts are found and are derivative of them. The significance of this point cannot be overstated. Trying rights and obligations to true states of the real world anchors rights and obligations in things that can be known and are independent of whim and caprice. This is why the ideas of relevance and materiality are so fundamentally important to the construction of a legal system. They tie the legal system to the bedrock of factual accuracy. This point is truly universal. Neither rights or obligations, on the one hand, or policy choices on the other, can be pursued in the absence of knowledge of the actual, relevant states of affairs.

The forensic scientists have no doubts about what they pursue, and it is indeed truth; thus to me they are a model of what all scholars and practitioners working within the legal system should aspire to. This is not to say that your various tasks are not difficult, and do not pose any difficult conceptual problem, for both are false. In particular, when experimental results pass the test to become knowledge can be highly contested. Similarly, how results of testing should be presented in court is fraught with difficulty. And of course you forensic scientists, like everyone else, may on occasion claim more for your results than the true state of your various sciences justify, and the rest of us must be on guard against such claims. Still, in general you are a role model for legal scholars.

No, the future of forensic science is clear and needs no sustained debate, although the discrete results reached in any particular subfield of forensics can and should be hotly contested precisely on epistemological grounds. But a puzzle arises. If the deepest aspiration of a legal system is to the truth, why isn't that the governing principle of evidence and evidence scholarship, just as it is for forensic science?

To some considerable extent the pursuit of truth is an important organizing principle of the field of evidence, as I have lectured on repeatedly throughout China, precisely because of the relationship between accuracy on the one hand and rights and obligations on the other. Nonetheless, there is one critical difference between the forensic sciences and the law of evidence, and between forensic scientists and legal scholars. Science and scientists are pursuing knowledge about an external reality, whereas the law and legal scholars are creating a man-made system that is a very important part of the larger social fabric and its governing institutions. Forensic science is pulled purely by the pursuit of knowledge; the law and the legal system are pulled in many different directions.

You may recall that the last time I spoke to you, two years ago at the Second International Conference on Evidence Law and Forensic Science, I identified what I referred to as the next three tasks of Chinese Evidence law, and they were:

1. First, it is critically important that the Chinese legal system conform its rules of evidence to the needs and context of China.

2. The second task is to convene a national discussion and to come to agreement on truly uniform evidentiary provisions.

3. Third, evidence scholarship in China needs to advance beyond the discrete issues of individual rules of evidence and deal with what I call the "macro" or larger and more significant issues that evidence law effects, such as:

A. The social implications of juridical proof.

B. The relationship between juridical proof and probability theory

C. The use of expert testimony

D. The relationship between procedure and evidence

There is a common thread running through these three tasks, which is that it is inadequate to simply focus on discrete rules or laws of evidence. This reflects the many different directions in which any legal system is pulled by competing interests. The first, the need to particularize the law of evidence to your own needs in China, reflects that your needs will differ from those of other countries. The second reflects how different people can honestly disagree about what the law of evidence should do, in part because of disagreement about what the pressing social and political needs of the country are. The third generalizes these first two points and highlights that the law of evidence affects and is affected by the larger social and political structures of the country.

The law of evidence, in short, is not concerned exclusively with the pursuit of truth; it is an integral part of a legal system that pursues many different, and often competing, interests simultaneously. Thus, to predict its future is a more difficult task than predicting the future of forensic science. This is an important point, and to appreciate it fully one must consider the complexity of creating a legal system. An enormous number of policy choices face the designer of a legal system. Some are consistent with the pursuit of factual accuracy, but many are in opposition to it. Note that I use the phrase "policy issues" to accompany all interests that society may pursue ranging from moral imperatives to the quite practical and utilitarian. Among the issues that must be accommodated are:

Pursuit of Factual Accuracy. One might reasonably suppose that natural reasoning processes based on innate epistemological capacities work reasonably well, and thus typically should be deferred to in the pursuit of factual accuracy. This means that the law of evidence can be quite brief, and basically just let natural reasoning processes determine the outcome of cases. However, there may be recurring situations that lead people to error. In such a case, rules of evidence may attempt to correct for that systematic error. This explains the authorization to exclude evidence when it may be misleading or unfairly prejudicial. It also underlies other rules, such as limitations on character and propensity evidence, and the requirement that witnesses testify from firsthand knowledge. The important point for present purposes, though, is that the circumstances under which individuals systematically make errors probably is heavily dependent on culture.

The Value of Accuracy. Factual accuracy is surely a very significant desideratum, but it is by no means the only one. It has a cost, and the cost can sometimes be too high. A legal system overly preoccupied with factual accuracy may undermine the very social conditions that the legal system is trying to foster. A dispute worth only a dollar that would take a thousand dollars to litigate to a factually accurate conclusion perhaps should not be litigated. Such litigation may very well reduce overall social welfare and discourage private settlement of disputes. Where the limit is reached is difficult to say, of course, and surely depends on local views.

The Value of Incentives. Factual accuracy competes not just with cost but with other policies that a government reasonably may pursue. The list of such policies is long, and again culturally contingent. The law of privileges may foster and protect numerous relationships (spouses, legal, medical, spiritual, governmental, etc.) . Litigation of an accident should not discourage reduction of risk (the subsequent repair rule) . Perhaps settlement of disputes is preferred to their litigation, which leads to the exclusion of statements made during settlement talks. The encouragement of settlement is also a reason not to price litigation too low. The more the public subsidizes litigation, presumably the more of it there will be, and the less of private negotiation. There are still other policies that can be pursued. In the United States, we rest a vast body of exclusionary rules on the perceived need to regulate police investigative activities. Rules of evidence also can encourage or discourage certain kinds of law suits from being brought. Again in the United States, we went through a period in which we thought rape victims were being overly discouraged from reporting crimes against them, and one response was to create rules of evidence that reduced the abuse at trial that such individuals may have been exposed to.

General Considerations of Fairness may also influence the law of evidence, although the precise effect of this variable is often hard to sort out from more overtly utilitarian motivations. Some think that the limit on unfairly prejudicial evidence reflects not just the concern about accuracy but the concern about humiliation, as is also the case with rape relevancy rules. The limits on prior behavior and propensity evidence reflect in part a belief that an individual should not be trapped in the past. The hearsay rule to some extent reflects the values of the right to confront witnesses against you.

The Risk of Error. A mistake free legal system is not possible. It is critically important to recognize that two types of errors can be made-a wrongful verdict for a plaintiff (including a conviction of an innocent person), which we call a Type I or false positive error, and a wrongful verdict for a defendant (including an acquittal of a guilty person), which we call a Type II or false negative error-and resource allocation and other decisions will affect the relationship between these two types of errors.

Reasonable people can disagree as to the significance of these two types of errors, but both must be taken into account in the construction of the legal system. In the United States, we structure civil litigation to attempt to both equalize the errors made on behalf of plaintiffs and defendants and to reduce the total number of errors. The criminal justice process, by contrast, is designed to reduce the possibility of wrongful conviction at the admitted expense of making more mistakes of wrongful acquittals. Although the matter is complicated, these perspectives explain in large measure the preponderance standard in civil cases and the standard of proof beyond reasonable doubt in criminal cases. In civil cases, an error either way results in identical misallocation of resources. If the plaintiff wrongly wins a ＄500 verdict, a citizen (the defendant) wrongly must part with ＄500. If the defendant wrongly wins a verdict that he or she does not owe ＄500, a citizen (the plaintiff) wrongly will be deprived of ＄500 that rightfully he or she should possess. These two cases are identical analytically. In criminal cases, by contrast, in the United States we view a wrongful conviction as a more serious harm than a wrongful acquittal, and thus make convictions hard to obtain by requiring proof beyond reasonable doubt. We do so even though it is possible (but by no means certain) that a side effect will be increased numbers of false acquittals and an overall increase in the total number of errors.

Again to demonstrate the complex environment within which the law of evidence operates, note how this simple emphasis on errors can be radically inappropriate, for two reasons. The first involves the recognition that a focus on errors alone is inadequate; a legal system also has to be concerned with correct decisions. A legal system that got every decision wrong, but treated plaintiffs and defendants equally, would satisfy the requirement to equalize errors, and a refusal of a legal system to adjudicate difficult cases could very well minimize the total number of errors the legal system makes. Notwithstanding their operationalizing the underlying objectives of error management, both approaches seem quite odd and unacceptable. The reason is that, in addition to errors, the rates of correct decisions matters in deciding how to structure the legal system; the optimization problem, in other words, has four rather than two variables. ①

In addition to neglecting the implications of correct decisions, the simple concentration on errors neglects the relationship between what occurs at trial and primary behavior. No one doubts that law exists to affect primary behavior by articulating standards of conduct, creating rights, and providing incentives to conform conduct to legal requirements. Correct adjudication of legal disputes is a useful and perhaps necessary condition for those incentives to operate. If a person can disregard legal entitlements with impunity, the rate of such disregard is likely to go up substantially. But this is not the full story. Most cases, both civil and criminal, in the United States settle. Thus, the true rates of correct and erroneous decisions is not just the trial rates, but the overall rates of resolution. And those rates in turn effect whether disputes even arise. All of these variables must be taken into account in appraising the legal system. ②

As I suggested above, hovering over all of this is the implication of cost. Whatever might be the optimal relationship between trial verdicts themselves, and trial verdicts and primary behavior, in a system of no transaction costs might not be optimal where there are transactions costs. Some correct decisions may not be worth what they cost to achieve, and thus it is possible that pricing some disputes out of the legal market should not be regretted. The market for legal disputes probably operates like other markets, and a decline in cost would probably yield an increase in consumption. That means that the option of a formal dispute resolution will be substituted for an informal one, such as negotiation and compromise. If the formal option is too costly to pursue, people would pursue informal ones, such as compromise and negotiation. That may be preferable in many instances.

Miscellaneous Policy Questions. There are many other contingent questions that must be answered by the architect of a legal system. Most importantly are those allocating responsibility over the various actors in the legal dra-

① Ronald J. Allen & Larry Laudan, *Deadly Dilemmas*, 41 Texas Tech. L. Rev. 65-92 (2008).

② Id.; Larry Laudan & Ronald J. Allen, *Deadly Dilemmas II*: *Bail and Crime*, 85, Chi. Kent L. Rev. 23 (2010).

ma. These involve such questions as whether trials should be episodic events as is somewhat more prevalent in Europe or single shot events as in the United States, how much discretion should the trial judge have and how much should the parties control the process, what is the relationship between trial judges and appellate judges. Should there be trial de novo in the appellate court or is it limited to review of legal errors? Are small civil cases different from large commercial cases in ways that justify different treatment? What about criminal cases? How do they differ from civil cases in ways that reflect how they should be structured?

In substantial measure, the future of the law of evidence will be determined by the research many of you are doing into the kinds of issues that I have just identified. For the most part, the kind of work done in different countries will be perfectly understandable to scholars and practitioners from other countries. The attributes of human inference and cognition are universal, even though they may have differing implications in differing contexts. You in China, for example, may think that the United States emphasizes too strongly exclusionary rules, whereas we in the United States may think that China's evidentiary process is too lax and discretionary, but what we will both mean by such conclusions is that the position that some country has taken on a particular issue would be suboptimal in a different context. The disagreements will not be a result of conceptual disputes but over the plausibility of one approach or another to a particular social problem in a particular social context.

Note that I have out of my predictions for the future of evidence law and the list of tasks any attempt to regulate in a meticulous fashion the inferential process used at trial. This is not the task of the law of evidence, nor should it be. Evidence law takes natural cognitive practices as they exist, and can at best nudge the inferential process in one direction or another. Indeed, whenever a rule is proposed that is designed to protect the tribunal from reaching a particular result, one should be skeptical. The justification for such a rule can only be the belief that in some particular area there is a high probability of irrationality. But why would the rule makers be systematically more rational than the people who decide cases? This is why the emphasis in my country on keeping evidence from a jury in order not to prejudice the jurors is so fundamentally misguided, and also why, thankfully, in reality it does not occur very much. Evidence is regulated much more to avoid inefficiencies and to forbid a wealthier party from overwhelming a poorer one with legal costs.

One important question that you will face, as we do in the United States, is what the form of evidentiary regulation should be. To what extent should there be detailed rules, and to what extent should there be general guidelines enforced in a discretionary fashion?③ There may appear to be some tension between this question and the point made above about the difficulty, indeed impossibility, of systematically structuring the inferential process at trial. That, of course, is one of the issues that must be examined. Even if the regulatory reach of evidence law is quite narrow, however, the question of how to regulate what is within that reach remains. Take hearsay for example. One could express a preference for the limited use of hearsay and leave it the matter to a trial judge to make discretionary decisions, or one could provide a detailed rule such as those found in the Federal Rules of Evidence, Article 8.

These questions and issues do not exhaust the question of the future of the evidence law; there is one final issue that must be considered in order to fully understand the complexity of the law of evidence, and the challenge facing those who construct the legal system. Implicit in what I have just said, and as I have said explicitly in previous trips to China while lecturing on the law of evidence, although there is much that is common to humanity, the ways in which humans organize themselves varies almost infinitely. Legal systems are critical components of government, and they reflect the resolution of issues of deep political theory. One needs look no further than China and the United States to see this clearly. Because of the political history of the United States, our founders concluded that political power should be diffused over the three branches of government, with each needing one or both of the others in order to be effective. This was designed to counteract what western observers almost universally believe is the centripetal force of all power centers and their tendency to aggrandizement. In brief, this is why we have a tradition of independent

③ For an excellent discussion of this issue, see Eleanor Swift, *One Hundred Years of Evidence Law Reform: Thayer's Triumph*, 88 California Law Review 24-37 (2000).

courts that we conceive of as being a potential brake on other branches of government. China has no such political theory of separation of powers.

Some people associate an independent judiciary with the rule of law, but they are not quite synonymous. It is possible to imagine a society governed by the rule of law without a western conception of judicial independence. However, and this is the critical point, it is hard to imagine an ongoing and vibrant society that encourages productivity and innovation without some of the core concepts of the rule of law that make the government the agent of the people, rather than the people the agents of government, and that restrict the capricious tendencies of people in positions of authority.

In my opinion the people in this room and throughout China that are now so diligently studying and researching the law of evidence are the ones who will be in the vanguard of the effort to further in China a rule of law that allows this country to reach its true potential. I say this because, as I have said over and over again when I have come to China, facts are more fundamental than rights, and the people who study evidence know this, and their work gives it meaning. And without rights, however they are defined, a society will remain in an impoverished and vulnerable state. When you and your students are working out the intricacies of the potential ways to regulate the evidentiary process, you are indirectly determining whether your system will advance or retard the rule of law, with all its attendant consequences. I know that rule of law plays an important role in some jurisprudential and political discourse, but there it is so abstracted as to be essentially meaningless. By comparison, when you are working on what must happen to vindicate a right, you are dealing with the implications of the rule of law in its most profound aspect.

So, to the next three steps in the progression of evidence science in China, I now want to add a fourth, which is to make explicit what is implicit in the work that you do. Evidence scholars and practitioners are not just technicians working with complicated rules, but are instead the architects of a fair and just society. But the question arises, what do the words "fair" and "just" mean? That is your next task, to begin to address these questions, and you might be interested that this is so in the United States as well, where similar questions are now becoming ever more explicit in the work being done in evidence and procedure.

These are difficult and complicated tasks, but much conceptual work has already been done, although much disagreement remains as what precisely the relationship between a government and its citizens should be. You need to examine the work of people like Joseph Raz, who focuses on the following of explicit rules by neutral decision makers,④ and the work of people like Ronald Dworkin who focuses on law as integrity. ⑤How do the values of clarity and certainty weigh against the values of enlightened discretion pursuing the public interest, and how does whatever you think about such matters manifest itself in the rules of evidence and procedure? To what extent does access to a decision maker have to be made readily available to all? How do the pursuit of wealth and social stability reinforce or undercut each other, and how is dispute resolution to be structured to accommodate whatever you think of such questions? Should there be an avenue to contest an unjust law?

I think these questions will dominate the next phase of the progression and future of evidence law in China, as well as elsewhere. As I said earlier and will close on here, these questions are critical not just to evidence law but the well-being of the country as a whole. It is more than interesting to note that no modern state has long survived without a commitment to some version of the rule of law, and indeed the absence of the means of enforcing the law against the State has been one of the primary causes of the decline and fall of modern states. I think as much or more than any other group, those of you working on the law of evidence and procedure hold the future of the country in your hands. If your work continues, if are able to demonstrate that rational means of dispute resolution are possible without disrupting society and that the suppression of the ability to dispute leads to paroxysms of anger and discontent, and if your country continues to move in the direction of embracing those concepts, the future is extraordinarily bright.

④ Joseph Raz, *The Rule of Law and Its Virtues*, 93 The Law Quarterly Review 195 (1997).

⑤ See in particular, Ronald Dworkin, *Hart's Postscript and the Character of Political Philosophy*, 24 Oxford Journal of Legal Studies 1 (2004).

第四届证据理论与科学国际研讨会闭幕词*

张伟 译** 张保生 校

在这种场合，闭幕式的发言者们通常都会谈论，我们所有的与会者享受了一场多么美妙的知识盛宴。假若如此，我们就大大地低估了事实真相，这从过去两天会议讨论的情况就可以看出来，而真相是非常重要的。这次会议无疑是一场美妙的知识盛宴，但却远非如此，它还是来自世界各地、带着相当不同的观点的人士，在一个充满坦诚和友善的完满环境中，针对非常相似的问题各抒己见的美妙聚会。我们确实应该再一次感谢会议的东道主邀请我们与会，并感谢他们为筹划和举办这次会议所付出的辛勤努力！

当然，在任何奢华的盛宴上总有超出我们胃口太多的大餐可吃，这次盛会也不例外。我的注意力被证据、证明和事实认定等问题所吸引，我的发言将集中在这些问题上，但过去两天讨论的很多重要问题在我的发言中可能会被挂一漏万。同时，我希望法庭科学家们在会议的这个最后环节接受我的道歉。有两位法学教授完全忽略了法庭科学。我认为这实际上反映出有关法庭科学的一些有趣的事情，因为它可能是“可得性启发法”（availability heuristic）的一个例证。本次会议的整体筹划多少是由法学教授主导的，没错，就是这样。但请接受我的道歉，并请你们放心，下次我们不会重复这个错误。

我发现最有趣的大概是，众多的讨论反映出，证据问题研究在很大程度上实际上是人类境况的研究。因此，几乎在所有法律制度中都碰到了同样的问题，有时解决方案的构想、尝试、否决等也基本相同。关于这一点，龙宗智教授讲到自白问题的主题发言和姜小川的相关论文，就是一个很好的例子。当然，对自白的审查，也总是对自由意志、自愿性、强制性、滥用及一些要么确保可靠性要么至少可防范酷刑的潜在保障措施的审查。每一个国家都有同样的问题，每一个国家都创建了强迫嫌疑人招供的机制。

* 本译文原载于《证据科学》，第22卷，2014年第2期。

** 张伟，中国政法大学证据科学研究院博士研究生。

比如，即使声称没有辩诉交易制度强迫人们供认的欧洲国家，实际上也在这么做。最近，我与对美国辩诉交易实践感到悲哀的一位法国法官和其他学者进行了交谈。他们说，辩诉交易在法国是不必要的，可国家与刑事被告合作的比率仍然很高。我问："这怎么可能呢?"他们说："如果被告不供认的话，他的日子将不好过。"当然，这就是辩诉交易制度的核心所在，即激励被告进行合作。龙教授所讨论的躯体虐待等激励方式，在美国有漫长而肮脏的历史。现在，我们才刚刚步入一个新阶段，即要求对警察的讯问进行录像，来努力解决此类问题。通过那种方式，人们至少能看到发生了什么。但正如不少文章所指出的那样，所有可能的解决方案都有自身的缺陷。录像可以被警察操控，录像带可以由警察任意开关，可能使其与实际发生的情况不符。这是真的，但我并不认为这是绝望的理由；相反，这是我们要面对的一种挑战。法律运行的环境是复杂的、动态的。对这种环境进行干预，其结果往往不可预测。人们不能期望自己的改革成效完美无缺，相反，我们都必须认识到，在社会动力系统中有众多的力量在起作用，并对改革未完全朝着我们预期的方向前进做好应对的准备。

对于录像如何能被警察滥用的关注，以一种有趣的方式表明，只有警察想让人知道的东西才能被人知道。这直接促使我去思考，本次会议中最重要和意义深远的内容是，我们能在多大程度上知晓过去发生的事情，能在多大程度上获得事实真相。这是每一位大会主旨发言人所关注的，也是随后的每一位发言者以各种方式表示关切的。这些讨论再一次表明，我们所有人都面临类似的问题，这些问题也为今后的研究和改革的必经之路指明了方向。

所有论文面对的最深层的问题，是事实真相和知识的含义与蕴意。特别是对"事实真相"一词，我们听到许多关于它的不同色调的讨论，从绝对的到相对的事实真相，从法律真实到形式真实。我认为，这些都是贴在同一事情上的不同的标签，这样做尽管有意义，但随意使用这些标签的做法使本来简单的事情模糊化了。"事实真相"仅仅是一个命题是否准确地描述了它所指称的对象，或者用标准的哲学语言，它是否与其所描述的现实相符。"知识"仅仅是被确证的真实信念。法律中的真实和知识问题，并非由于这些理念可以进行选择，而是因为法律与科学的不同之处在于，法律问题不能拖延作出决定。如果我因你违反了合同并给我造成了 10 万元的损害而对你提起诉讼，而该法律制度却说"我们现在不能作出对你有利的决定，因为我们不能确定已获得了事实真相"。然后，因为法律制度不能确保获取了事实真相，你的诉讼赢了，我却输了。但那意味着，你得到了那些钱，而我却失去了它们。因此，我们都必须认识到，法律世界涉及求真和求知，而非获得事实真相和知识。那意味着，我们不得不面对我们将犯错误的可悲真理。总之，我们必须丢掉纯真的幻想，正视人类的现实。但正视可悲的现实一样可以使我们获得解放。放弃追求那些无法获取的东西，使我们把能够做好的事情做得最好。

我意识到，有人宣称，事实真相和知识是伪目标。我们听到一些哲学家，如海德格尔告诉我们：真理概念是没有意义的；理查德·罗蒂宣称：讨论真理问题只是浪费时间。坦率地说，哲学上始于19世纪后期、结束于20世纪中期的怀疑论转向，因其明显错误而几乎不值一提。伯特兰·罗素评论道：如果一个怀疑论者说的是真的，他是错误的；如果一个怀疑论者说的是假的，他也是错误的，因而他总是错误的，我们可以置之不理。这是什么意思呢？结合海德格尔所说的真理概念没有意义，他实际上是在说：真理没有意义，这是真的。如果他是正确的，他就是前后矛盾。真理没有意义与真理没有意义是真的，这两种说法不能同真。

是的，没有理由为真理或知识的存在问题而纠结。真正的难题是，在人类社会和我们法律制度受到种种局限的情况下，如何逼近真理和知识。在这里，问题可以简化为，我们通常思考为“证据”的东西——指被带到法庭上的无论是实物还是在庭上作证的人（或者庭审前提取的他们的陈述）与裁决者的自然推理过程之间的相互作用。我想对这个话题多说几句，但在此之前，我先要就推论过程赖以发生的法律制度的一般结构做一些说明。

不论是在这次会议上，还是在过去十年间，我们已经对彼此的法律制度有所了解。然而，就像学习一种语言非常困难（除非你生长的环境每天都要讲那种语言）一样，完全理解一种外国法律制度也是很困难的。在法律制度中发挥作用的东西，多数是公认的社会习俗，而不是规则。如果你不了解这些习俗，在许多情况下，你就不能理解以那些习俗为基础而采用的规则。因此，误解常常发生。人们听到其他法律制度中发生的一些事情时，好像觉得很愚蠢或荒谬，甚至是发疯的事情。人们匆忙地就认为“那种法律制度一定是愚蠢、荒谬和疯狂的”。但我要极力敦促你抑制住那种冲动。如果你听说另一个国家的一种法律制度是愚蠢、荒谬、疯狂或者是愚蠢到家了，它几乎肯定是错的。更好的尝试性解释是：你发生误解了，或者说是断章取义了，因而需要作更多的研究以发现事情的真相。

在这次会议期间，当讨论到不同法律制度的组织模式，特别是裁决的对抗式和纠问式模式时，我们已经接触了这一现象的生动例子。我们被告知，关于对抗制的最佳理解是，我引用的“法官是被动的裁判者……而且，赢者将是最强大、最精明的战士，不论其是对是错……有关美国对抗制的最一致的理论是：没人对寻求事实真相感兴趣，因而应当避免时间、金钱和各种司法活动的浪费。”这个观点来源于一位资深美国评论家罗斯科·庞德，他1964年去世，差不多有五十年了。仅这一点就足以引起研究者的注意，大概还有很多工作要做。

但是，如果一种现代法律制度不能保证高概率的准确结果，这种法律制度如何能够体现出其具有先进性？正如我昨天所说，没有准确的裁判，权利就毫无意义。如果诉讼的结果在很大程度上不是从事实的准确重建中得出的，而是由其他事情决定的，现代贸易将告终结。正是对准确诉讼的承诺，才阻止了人们破坏法律和背信弃义。如果合同的条款不能履行，我就不会签约。我知道，如果我违约，我将承担后果，因为如果我被起诉，此种法律制度通常能获得正确的事实。而且，在美国，我们有所谓公开的证据开示。诉讼的双方当事人必须向对方开示所有事情。这种制度甚至适用于刑事案件中的检察官，其必须向被告方开示可能有助于其辩护的所有事情。这显然旨在促进基于事实准确的裁决，而非支持有时所谓正义的理论。

因此，美国或英国某些孤陋寡闻的学者说了几十年的关于对抗制之最一致或最佳理由的观念，显然是错误的。然而，对抗制是否是一种值得采纳的好模式，这是一个有趣的问题。对于其潜在正当理由的真正答案，表明在我国出现的这些研究领域，在你们国家也应该有。对抗制的最佳正当理由，来自于运用微观经济学工具而进行的考察，对此，我欣慰地看到张卿撰写了一篇关于法律与经济学的文章。正如我昨天谈到的，诉讼不仅是一种认识论事件，或一种关于知识的事件，它还是一项制造或生产事件，在这个领域，问题涉及可靠证据的最有效的生产。

支持对抗制乃是高效和有效模式的理由，是基于双方当事人比其他任何人更了解自己的案件这样明显的事实。他们也知道争议的问题是什么，知道该案件为何值得诉讼——这自然也告诉人们那个案件值得投入多少资源。每一方都将自己的证据向对方开示，使双方当事人都拥有最多的知识和有效投资的最佳激励，进而能够决定去做他们认为最为适当的事情。这才是支持对抗制的真正正当理由，而不是像某些迂腐观念所强调的那样，它是一种看谁更强大或更精明的竞赛。

诚然，对抗制并不总是运行得完美无缺，但千万别让这种理想成为可能性的敌人。人们在明智地将一种制度与其他制度进行比较之前，需要分析这种制度何以良好运作及其局限性。仅仅其可能被滥用这一事实，涉及经济学家所称的交易成本。需要计算这些成本，但它们本身并不是决定性的。思考一下医院。人们不能因为有人死在医院或者有误诊发生，就将其关门。

再来思考一下纠问制。当政府方无论以何种方式来调查一起纠纷时，都不得不依赖当事人既有的知识。因此，不得不复制当事人已经对那些问题倾注的努力。此外，政府方并不像当事人那样了解纠纷或其来龙去脉。这可能导致双方成本增加：因为它不得不弥补知识的不足，确切说，是由于其劣质的知识增加了错误几率。此外，请注意当事人和法官激励机制上的关键区别。当事人有极大动力去追求自己的利益最大化。法官要最大化的利益却是他自己的个人利益，获得特定事实的正确认定很可能是为了获得晋升。确实，他若获得了正确的案件事实，就可以得到晋升，但他仍缺乏关于该案价值的知识。因此，法官在进行调查时，可能投入过少或过多的资源。

我已经说服你们了吗？希望还没有。我在这里阐述的观点，并不是在中国或任何别的地方应当采用对抗制，相反，要了解法律制度如何运作还有许多工作需要去做，只有到做好这些工作的时候，才能对如何构建它们作出明智的决策。

我想就本次会议的另一个主题即推论的性质，来表明类似的观点。我们每个人都为推论的性质而纠结，不知如何对其在法律制度中进行规制。让我告诉大家为什么这是一个难题。正如我前面提到的，这是因为通常所谓“证据”——证人证言、展示件等——以及由人脑对证据进行的评估，是相互作用的。在本次会议上，我们听到了只依证据来裁决事实的呼声，但那几乎是不可能的。它需要发挥智人头脑的能动性，借助人的常识和知识来处理和思考那些证据。问题在于，我们并非拥有同样的常识和知识，因为我们每个人都有独特的生活经历。这里，我们可以作出两种明确的选择。人们可以只依赖无私的事实认定者的良好判断，或者，人们可以证据规则、推定、推论等介入判断。陈瑞华教授在他的主旨发言中讨论了这个问题，我要说，我们确实存在他所提到的同样问题。立法机关和法官常常介入自然推理过程。通常这是因为他们认为，他们在一个案件中发现了一个或一些种类的错误，并通过一项法律或规则确保不再重复那些错误。正如陈教授明智指出的，问题是：那个规则或法律在下一个案件中将如何适用以及它是有利还是有害，这些是完全无法可预知的。每个案件都是独一无二的，通过编写规则来规制人类推论活动几乎是不可能的，因为，人类推论活动不可能准确预知一个法律制度中会出现的全部问题。

但这里至关重要的观点是，证据科学的核心恰恰是“证据”和裁决者的活跃头脑之间的相互作用。我很高兴看到，这个话题在中国引起了人们的兴趣，这是美国正在持续研究的一个基本问题。

该项研究很明确，针对的是人们如何进行自然推理，法律制度何时应当包含自然推理过程，何时应当以某种特定方式拒斥自然推理过程。我说得清楚一些，这再次成为证据法研究中的一个普遍问题。塔鲁夫教授在他的主题发言中谈到了这个问题，他对在美国已获得支配地位的相对似真模型作了所谓分析方法的比较。他确定了相对似真模型与他所谓的叙事连贯性（narrative coherence）的关系，并主张他偏爱分析方法。遗憾的是，除了裁决者应当考察案件的每一要素外，一种分析方法可能意味着什么则完全没有说清楚。

这里似乎还有一些误解。我简要讨论一下，只强调一点，即人们从事研究是必须仔细对待的问题。审判裁决的相对似真模型，是人们实际推理方式的经验描述。他们通过询问事件各种可能情况的解释而进行推理，然后判定哪种解释最似真。在审判中，多半是由当事人提供各种解释，然后设法提供证据来支持他们的故事。这种解释被用来填补审判中留下的漏洞，即人们不能通过概率推理来使其变得完全清楚的事情。实际上从来没有任何可靠的相对频度数据，出于我现在无法探究的复杂原因，主观概率也是无济于事的。此外，相对似真性理论直接图解了人类的一般推理方式，而不只是法官或陪审团成员在特定审判场合的推理方式。

在人的加工处理过程中，似然性判断的制作涉及所有认知工具，包括归纳推理、演绎推理、概率论、一致性、相容性、符合、效益等等。塔鲁夫教授把所有这些归结为叙事连贯性，这实则从根本上误解了美国正在从事的研究工作。叙事连贯性确实可能是一个变量，但它只是人们用于评价他们周围世界的众多工具之一。关于这一点，对于该理论的批评应当已经给出了提示，即最佳叙事解释可能包含着错误因素。这确实是真的，但这就是相对似真理论的特征描述明显错误的原因。如果事件解释的一个要素或成分是错误的，该解释就是错误的。事情就是这么简单。不错，在以自然方式思考诉讼事件时，人会犯错误，而且他们确实会犯错误，但当人们运用“分析方法”——无论这意味着什么——对事物进行推理时，他们同样会犯错误。

我还应当指出，相对似真论的知识背景是在哲学和科学领域均具有革命性的一种方法，即所谓对最佳解释的推论。这并不意味着，它是法律制度的最佳解释，但可以肯定的是，对其进行研究具有重要意义，这正是在美国证据法研究中发生的事情。

无论如何，你们看得出来，本届会议对我的思想有极大的触动，谁又会对此无动于衷呢？这是在我记忆中有幸出席的收获最大的一次学术盛会。我们都对这次会议的组织者感激不尽，我期待着在第五届证据理论与科学国际研讨会上与你们所有的人再次相见。唯一令我感到遗憾的是，这要再等两年。

Closing Speech at the 4th International Conference on Evidence Law and Forensic Science

Ronald J. Allen

The closing speakers at events such as this typically refer to what a wonderful intellectual feast had been served to the participants. In this case, though, that greatly underestimates the truth, and as you can tell from the discussions throughout these last two days, the truth is very important. It has been a fantastic intellectual feast, but it has been much more than that. It has also been a fantastic gathering of individuals from across the world bringing quite different perspectives to bear on quite similar problems in a perfect environment of candor and hospitality. We should really once more thank our various hosts for inviting us and for their efforts in planning and conducting this conference.

Of course, at any sumptuous feast, there are always too many things to eat than one's appetite allows, and that is no different here. My attention was drawn to the problems of evidence, proof, and fact finding, and my remarks will focus on those issues, but that leaves out much of importance that has been discussed over the last two days. And I hope the Forensic Science Community will accept my apologies for the makeup of this last panel. It has two law professors, and completely neglects Forensic Science. I think that reflects something interesting about Forensic Science, actually, for it is probably an example of the Availability Heuristic. Law professors are somewhat dominant in the overall planning of the conference, and well, there you are. But please accept my apologies and be assured that next time we will not repeat this error.

What I found most interesting, perhaps, was that much of the discussions reflected just how much the study of evidence is really the study of the human condition, and that as a result the same kinds of problems pop up in virtually all legal systems sometimes with analogous solutions being conceived, tried, rejected, and so on. A very good example of this was Prof. Long Zongzhi's keynote address on confessions and the related paper by Jiang Xiaochuan. Of course, an examination of confessions is also always an examination of free will, voluntariness, coercion, abuse, and potential safeguards either to ensure reliability or at least the absence of torture. Every single country has the same issue, and every single country creates mechanisms to put pressure on suspects to talk.

For example, even the European countries that claim they do not have plea-bargaining that pressures people to confess, in fact really do. I had a conversation with a French judge and academic recently who were lamenting the practice of plea bargaining in the U. S. They said that this was unnecessary in France, and still the State obtained a high rate of cooperation with criminal defendants. "How is this possible," I asked? "Because," they said, "it will go hard on the defendant if he does not confess." Of course that is a system of plea-bargaining, the critical aspect of which is giving defendants incentives to cooperate. The kinds of incentives that Prof. Long was discussing—physical abuse—have a long and sordid history in the U. S. We are only just now moving to a new phase in our efforts to deal with such matters through requiring police interrogations to be videotaped. That way, at least one can see what happened. But as a number of papers pointed out, every possible solution has its own pitfalls. Videotaping can be controlled by the police and the videotape turned on or off as they desire. That can lead to a skewed perspective on what actually happened. This is true, but I do not think it grounds for despair; it is instead a challenge to be met. The environment within which the law works is complex and dynamic. When an intervention is made into that environment, there will always be unanticipated consequences. One cannot expect one's reforms to work perfectly, but instead we all must recognize the multitude of forces at work in the social dynamic and be prepared to respond when reforms do not quite go the way they were intended.

In an interesting way, the concern about how videotaping can be abused by the police to show only what the police want to show leads directly to what I think has been the most important and profound aspect of this conference, which is the extent to which the past can be known and the truth can be obtained. This was a concern of each of the keynote speakers, and in one way or another the concern of each of the subsequent speakers. Once again, these discussions showed how we all face similar problems, and also they point to the direction in which both future research and reform must go.

The deepest problem that all of the papers faced was the meaning and implications of truth and knowledge. In particular with regard to the word "truth," we heard many different shades of its being discussed, from absolute truth to relative truth to the law's truth to formal truth. I think these are all different labels for the same thing, and to use these labels carelessly obscures what is simple although profound. "Truth" is simply whether a proposition accurately describes its referent, the thing to which it refers, or in the standard philosophical language, whether it corresponds with the reality it is describing. "Knowledge" is simply justified true belief. The problems in the law with truth and knowledge do not come from there being alternatives to these ideas but because the law, unlike science, cannot postpone decision. If I sue you for violating a contract with me that has caused me 100, 000 Yuan of damages, and if the legal system says "we cannot decide for you now because we are not certain that we have obtained the truth," then you win and I lose because the legal system will never be certain that it has obtained the truth. But that means you get to keep the money and I am deprived of it. We thus all have to recognize that the world of the law is one that involves striving for truth and knowledge rather than obtaining them. That means we have to face the tragic truth that we will make mistakes. We must, in short, lose our innocence and face directly the reality of the human condition. But that recognition is as much liberating as it is tragic. Freed from the demand of obtaining that which cannot be obtained allows us to go about the task of doing the best we can.

I realize that some people claim that truth and knowledge are false objectives. We heard for example that philosophers such as Heidegger informed us that the concept of truth has no meaning, and Richard Rorty claimed that discussing truth is just a waste of time. Frankly, what is called the skeptical turn in philosophy that began in the latter part of the 19th century and essentially ended in the middle of the 20th century should cause you literally no concern whatsoever because it is obviously false. As Bertrand Russell commented, if a skeptic is true in what he says, he is false and if he is false in what he says, he is false, therefore he is false and we can ignore him. What does this mean? Consider Heidegger claiming that the concept of truth has no meaning. What he is really saying is that it is TRUE that truth has no meaning. If he is correct then he is inconsistent. It cannot both be true that truth has no meaning and that it is true that truth has no meaning.

No, there is no reason to puzzle over the existence of truth or knowledge. The puzzle is how best to approximate them in the context of the limits of the human condition and our legal systems. Here the problem can be reduced to the interaction between what we normally think of as "evidence," which means the things brought to court whether objects or people who will testify (or their statements if taken before a hearing) and the natural reasoning processes of decision makers. I want to say a few words about that topic, but before I do so I want to begin with a few words about the general structure of legal systems, within which the inferential process occurs.

Both in this conference and over the last decade we have learned much about each other's legal systems. However, just as it is difficult to learn a language unless you grow up speaking that language everyday, it is difficult to fully understand a foreign legal system. Much of what goes on in legal systems is not structure by rules but by accepted social conventions; if you don't understand the conventions, you do not understand in many instances the rules that are being adopted in light of those conventions. Thus, misunderstandings happen quite frequently. One hears something about some other legal system, and it sounds silly or absurd, or even crazy, and you have the urge to think "That legal system must silly, absurd, and crazy." But I would very much urge you resist that impulse. If you hear something about a legal system in another country that sounds silly, absurd, crazy, or just plain stupid, it is almost surely false. The better tentative explanation is that you have misunderstood or taken something out of context, and you need to do more research to find out what the true state of affairs is.

We had a striking example of this phenomenon during this conference when different modes of organization of legal systems were discussed, in particular the adversary and inquisitorial modes of decision making. We were told that the best understanding of the adversarial system is, and I quote that "the judge is a passive umpire... and the winner will be the stronger and the smarter of the fighters no matter whether he was right or wrong... The most coherent theorization of the American adversarial system says that the search for truth is of no interest to anyone and therefore it should be avoided as a waste of time, of money and of judicial activities." The source for this view is an old American critic by the name of Roscoe Pound who died in 1964, almost 50 years ago. That alone should put the researcher on notice that perhaps a little more work is in order.

But how could a modern legal system in an advanced state function if the legal system did not guarantee a high probability of factually accurate outcomes? As I discussed yesterday, without accurate adjudication, rights are meaningless. If the results of litigation are for the most part driven by something other than an accurate reconstruction of the facts, modern commerce would come to an end. It is the promise of accurate litigation that stops people from breaking the law and from breaking their promises. I will not sign a contract unless I expect to adhere to its terms. I know that if I do not keep my promises I will bear the consequences because if I am sued the legal system typically gets the facts right. Moreover, we have in the United States what is called open discovery. The parties to litigation must turn over everything to the other side. This is even true of the Prosecutor in criminal cases, who must turn over to the defendant anything that might help the defense. This obviously is designed to facilitate decision based on factually accuracy rather than what is sometimes called the sporting theory of justice.

Thus, this idea that the most coherent or best justification for the adversary system is what some ill informed academics in the U. S. or Britain have said many decades in the past is obviously wrong. However, whether the adversary system is a good model to adopt is an interesting question, and the real answer to its potential justification points out areas of research that is occurring in my country and should occur in yours. The best justification for the adversarial system comes from looking at it with the tools of micro-economics, and I was very glad to see a paper on law and economics by Zhang Qing. Litigation is not only an epistemological event, an event about knowledge, as I discussed yesterday, it is also a manufacturing or production event where the issue is the most efficient production of reliable evidence.

The argument for the adversarial system as being efficient and effective starts from the obvious truth that the parties know their case better than anyone else. They also know what issues will be contested, and how much the case is worth—which of course tells you how much resources it is worth to invest in that case. You make each side turn over their evidence to the other side and then the two parties with the most knowledge and the best incentives to efficient investment then can decide to do what they think is most appropriate. This is the real justification for the adversary system, not some idiotic idea that it is competition to see who is the stronger or smarter.

To be sure, it does not always work perfectly, but do not let the ideal be the enemy of the possible. One needs to analyze how well a system works and its limitations before one can intelligently compare it to some other system. The mere fact that there can be abuses involves what the economists call transaction costs. They need to be accounted for but are not themselves determinative. Think of hospitals. You don't shut them down because people die there or mistakes are made.

Now consider the inquisitorial system. When the government in whatever guise investigates a dispute, it is has to replicate the pre-existing knowledge of the parties. It thus has to duplicate the effort already put into the problem by the parties. Moreover, it does not know the dispute or its context as well as the parties. This can lead to both increased cost, because it has to make up for its lack of knowledge, and to the increased chance of error, precisely because of its inferior knowledge. In addition, note the critical differences in the incentive structures of parties and judges. Parties have very good incentives to maximize their interests. The interest a judge will maximize is his own personal interest, which is as likely to be in getting a promotion as getting any particular factual finding correct. To be sure, he may get that promotion by getting the facts right in cases, but he still lacks knowledge as to the value of the case. Thus, he may invest way too little or way too much resources in the investigation.

Have I convinced you? I hope not. The point I am making here is not that the adversarial system should be adopted in China or anywhere else, but instead how much work needs to be done to understand how legal systems operate and only then can intelligent decisions be made as to how to structure them.

I want to make a similar point about another main theme of this conference, which is the nature of inference. Each of us is struggling with the nature of inference and how to regulate it in the legal system. Let me pinpoint why this is a problem. It is because of what I referred to earlier as the interaction of what is normally called "evidence" —testimony exhibits, etc. —and the evaluation of that evidence by a human mind. We heard calls at the conference for deciding facts based "only on the evidence," but that is literally impossible. It takes an active, intelligent human mind to process and think about the evidence by reference to that person's common sense and knowledge. The problem is that we do not all have the same common sense and knowledge because we each have had unique experiences in life. Here's where there are two stark choices that can be made. One can simply rely on the good judgment of a disinterested fact finder or one can intrude into that judgment with rules of evidence, presumptions, inferences and so on. Prof. Chen Ruihua in his keynote speech discussed this, and let me say that we have exactly the same issues he mentioned. Legislatures and judges are constantly interfering in the natural reasoning process. Usually this is because they think that they have observed an error or some sort in a case and to ensure against that error being repeated they pass a law or a rule. The problem, as Prof. Chen very intelligently pointed out, is that it is completely unpredictable how that rule or law will be applied in the next case and whether it will be helpful or harmful. Each case is unique and it is literally impossible to write rules to govern human inference that accurately anticipate all the possible problems that may emerge in a legal system.

But, the critical point here is that at the heart of evidence science is precisely this interaction between "evidence" and the active mind of a decision maker. I am glad to see the interest in that topic in China, and it is a fundamental part of the research that is ongoing in the United States.

Part of that research explicitly is directed towards how people reason naturally, when the legal system should embrace natural reasoning processes and when it should reject natural reasoning processes in some particular way. Let me be clear that this is again is a ubiquitous question in evidence research. Prof. Taruffo discussed this in his keynote speech where he compared what he called an analytical approach to the relative plausibility model that has gained ascendancy in the U. S. He identified the relative plausibility model with what he called narrative coherence, and argued that he preferred the analytical approach. Unfortunately, what an analytical approach might mean was completely unspecified except that a decision maker should look at each of the necessary elements of the case.

Again there seems to be some misunderstanding here. I will discuss it briefly simply to emphasize the point of how careful one must be in research. The relative plausibility model of decision making at trial is an empirical description of how people actually reason. They reason by asking what the various explanations of events might be and then deciding which is most plausible. At trial the parties provide the explanations for the most part and then try to produce evidence to support their stories. This explanation arose to fill the gap that was left when it became absolutely clear that people cannot reason probabilistically at trials. There is virtually never any reliable relative frequency data, and for complex reasons I cannot go into now subjective probabilities do not work either. Moreover, the relative plausibility theory maps directly on to how humans reason in general, and not just how judges or jurors reason in the peculiar setting of trials.

How the judgment of plausibility is made involves all the cognitive tools at a person's disposal, including induction, deduction, probability, coherence, consistency, consilience, efficiency and so on. Prof. Taruffo reduces all this to narrative coherence and by doing so fundamentally misconceives the work that is being done in the U. S. Narrative coherence certainly can be a variable, but it is only one among many that people use to appraise the world around them. A clue to this should have been given by the criticism made of the theory that the best narrative account may include a false element. True enough, but that's why this characterization of the relative plausibility theory is obviously false. If a necessary element or component of an explanation of events is false, the explanation is false. It is as simple as that. Again, humans can make mistakes and they certainly can when thinking in natural ways about litigated events, but so too can they makes mistakes when reasoning about things "analytically," whatever that might mean.

I should also point out that the intellectual background to the relativeplausibility theory is what is called inference to the best explanation, an approach which has revolutionized both science and philosophy. That does not mean it is the best explanation of the legal system, but it certainly justifies investigating its significance, as is how happening in evidence research in the U. S.

In any event, you can tell that I have been quite stimulated intellectually by this conference, and how could anyone not be stimulated by it? It was as rich a feast as I can remember ever having the honor of attending. We are all in the debt of the organizers, and I look forward to seeing all of you at the 5th International Conference on Evidence Law and Forensic Science. I only regret that that is two years away.

图书在版编目（CIP）数据

艾伦教授论证据法．上/［美］艾伦著；张保生，王进喜，汪诸豪等译．—北京：中国人民大学出版社，2014.9

（法学译丛·证据科学译丛）

ISBN 978-7-300-20082-8

Ⅰ.①艾…　Ⅱ.①艾…②张…③王…④汪…　Ⅲ.①证据-法学-研究　Ⅳ.①D915.130.1

中国版本图书馆 CIP 数据核字（2014）第 218874 号

"2011 计划"司法文明协同创新中心资助

"十二五"国家重点图书出版规划

法学译丛·证据科学译丛

丛书主编　张保生　王进喜

艾伦教授论证据法（上）

Prfessor Allen on Evidence (Volume I)

［美］罗纳德·J·艾伦　著

张保生　王进喜　汪诸豪　等 译

Ailun Jiaoshou Lun Zhengjufa

出版发行	中国人民大学出版社		
社　址	北京中关村大街 31 号	**邮政编码**	100080
电　话	010－62511242（总编室）		010－62511770（质管部）
	010－82501766（邮购部）		010－62514148（门市部）
	010－62515195（发行公司）		010－62515275（盗版举报）
网　址	http://www.crup.com.cn		
	http://www.ttrnet.com(人大教研网)		
经　销	新华书店		
印　刷	涿州市星河印刷有限公司		
规　格	170 mm×250 mm　16 开本	**版　次**	2014 年 9 月第 1 版
印　张	30.25 插页 2	**印　次**	2014 年 9 月第 1 次印刷
字　数	350 000	**定　价**	79.00 元